Revolutionizing Modern Education through Meaningful E-Learning Implementation

Badrul H. Khan
McWeadon Education, USA

A volume in the Advances in Educational Technologies and Instructional Design (AETID) Book Series

Information Science REFERENCE
An Imprint of IGI Global

Published in the United States of America by
Information Science Reference (an imprint of IGI Global)
701 E. Chocolate Avenue
Hershey PA, USA 17033
Tel: 717-533-8845
Fax: 717-533-8661
E-mail: cust@igi-global.com
Web site: http://www.igi-global.com

Library of Congress Cataloging-in-Publication Data

Names: Khan, Badrul H. (Badrul Huda), 1958- editor.
Title: Revolutionizing modern education through meaningful e-learning implementation / Badrul Khan, editor.
Description: Hershey PA : Information Science Reference, [2016] | Includes bibliographical references and index.
Identifiers: LCCN 2016011644| ISBN 9781522504665 (hardcover) | ISBN 9781522504672 (ebook)
Subjects: LCSH: MOOCs (Web-based instruction)
Classification: LCC LB1044.87 .R494 2016 | DDC 371.33/44678--dc23 LC record available at https://lccn.loc.gov/2016011644

This book is published in the IGI Global book series Advances in Educational Technologies and Instructional Design (AETID) (ISSN: 2326-8905; eISSN: 2326-8913)

British Cataloguing in Publication Data
A Cataloguing in Publication record for this book is available from the British Library.

For electronic access to this publication, please contact: eresources@igi-global.com.

Advances in Educational Technologies and Instructional Design (AETID) Book Series

Lawrence A. Tomei
Robert Morris University, USA

ISSN: 2326-8905
EISSN: 2326-8913

Mission

Education has undergone, and continues to undergo, immense changes in the way it is enacted and distributed to both child and adult learners. From distance education, Massive-Open-Online-Courses (MOOCs), and electronic tablets in the classroom, technology is now an integral part of the educational experience and is also affecting the way educators communicate information to students.

The **Advances in Educational Technologies & Instructional Design (AETID) Book Series** is a resource where researchers, students, administrators, and educators alike can find the most updated research and theories regarding technology's integration within education and its effect on teaching as a practice.

Coverage

- E-Learning
- Collaboration Tools
- Higher Education Technologies
- Online Media in Classrooms
- Curriculum Development
- Social Media Effects on Education
- Digital Divide in Education
- Adaptive Learning
- Virtual School Environments
- Game-Based Learning

IGI Global is currently accepting manuscripts for publication within this series. To submit a proposal for a volume in this series, please contact our Acquisition Editors at Acquisitions@igi-global.com or visit: http://www.igi-global.com/publish/.

The Advances in Educational Technologies and Instructional Design (AETID) Book Series (ISSN 2326-8905) is published by IGI Global, 701 E. Chocolate Avenue, Hershey, PA 17033-1240, USA, www.igi-global.com. This series is composed of titles available for purchase individually; each title is edited to be contextually exclusive from any other title within the series. For pricing and ordering information please visit http://www.igi-global.com/book-series/advances-educational-technologies-instructional-design/73678. Postmaster: Send all address changes to above address.

Titles in this Series

For a list of additional titles in this series, please visit: www.igi-global.com

Increasing Productivity and Efficiency in Online Teaching
Patricia Dickenson (National University, USA) and James J. Jaurez (National University, USA)
Information Science Reference • copyright 2016 • 327pp • H/C (ISBN: 9781522503477) • US $185.00 (our price)

Wearable Technology and Mobile Innovations for Next-Generation Education
Janet Holland (Emporia State University, USA)
Information Science Reference • copyright 2016 • 364pp • H/C (ISBN: 9781522500698) • US $195.00 (our price)

Creating Teacher Immediacy in Online Learning Environments
Steven D'Agustino (Fordham University, USA)
Information Science Reference • copyright 2016 • 356pp • H/C (ISBN: 9781466699953) • US $185.00 (our price)

Revolutionizing Education through Web-Based Instruction
Mahesh Raisinghani (Texas Woman's University, USA)
Information Science Reference • copyright 2016 • 391pp • H/C (ISBN: 9781466699328) • US $185.00 (our price)

Emerging Tools and Applications of Virtual Reality in Education
Dong Hwa Choi (Park University, USA) Amber Dailey-Hebert (Park University, USA) and Judi Simmons Estes (Park University, USA)
Information Science Reference • copyright 2016 • 360pp • H/C (ISBN: 9781466698376) • US $180.00 (our price)

Handbook of Research on Cloud-Based STEM Education for Improved Learning Outcomes
Lee Chao (University of Houston - Victoria, USA)
Information Science Reference • copyright 2016 • 481pp • H/C (ISBN: 9781466699243) • US $300.00 (our price)

User-Centered Design Strategies for Massive Open Online Courses (MOOCs)
Ricardo Mendoza-Gonzalez (Instituto Tecnologico de Aguascalientes, Mexico)
Information Science Reference • copyright 2016 • 323pp • H/C (ISBN: 9781466697430) • US $175.00 (our price)

Handbook of Research on Estimation and Control Techniques in E-Learning Systems
Vardan Mkrttchian (HHH University, Australia) Alexander Bershadsky (Penza State University, Russia) Alexander Bozhday (Penza State University, Russia) Mikhail Kataev (Tomsk State University of Control System and Radio Electronics, Russia & Yurga Institute of Technology (Branch) of National Research Tomsk Polytechnic University, Russia) and Sergey Kataev (Tomsk State Pedagogical University, Russia)
Information Science Reference • copyright 2016 • 679pp • H/C (ISBN: 9781466694897) • US $235.00 (our price)

IGI Global
DISSEMINATOR OF KNOWLEDGE
www.igi-global.com

701 E. Chocolate Ave., Hershey, PA 17033
Order online at www.igi-global.com or call 717-533-8845 x100
To place a standing order for titles released in this series, contact: cust@igi-global.com
Mon-Fri 8:00 am - 5:00 pm (est) or fax 24 hours a day 717-533-8661

Table of Contents

Preface xiv

Introduction 23

Chapter 1
Designing Meaningful Learning Environments in a Work-Integrated-Learning Course Using a DOCC Design 1
Kathy Jordan, RMIT University, Australia
Jennifer Elsden-Clifton, RMIT University, Australia

Chapter 2
Investigating Students' Interactions with Discussion Forums, Facebook, and Twitter in a MOOC and their Perceptions 18
Min Liu, The University of Texas at Austin, USA
Jina Kang, The University of Texas at Austin, USA
Emily McKelroy, The University of Texas at Austin, USA
Jason Harron, The University of Texas at Austin, USA
Sa Liu, The University of Texas at Austin, USA

Chapter 3
The Medium, the Content, and the Performance: An Overview on Media-Based Learning 42
Hans W. Giessen, Saarland University, Germany

Chapter 4
Teacher Conceptions and Approaches to Blended Learning Environments 56
Vicki Caravias, Swinburne University of Technology, Australia

Chapter 5
Evaluation of Mobile Learning with The Eight-Dimensional E-Learning Framework 80
Özlem Efiloğlu Kurt, Yalova University, Turkey
Esra İşgör Şimşek, Yalova University, Turkey

Chapter 6
Massive Open Program Evaluation: Crowdsourcing's Potential to Improve E-Learning Quality 109
Tonya B. Amankwatia, Regent University, USA

Chapter 7
To MOOC or Not to MOOC, That Is the Problem: A Learner's Perspective 131
Dilrukshi Gamage, University of Moratuwa, Sri Lanka
Shantha Fernando, University of Moratuwa, Sri Lanka
Indika Perera, University of Moratuwa, Sri Lanka

Chapter 8
Hispanic LEP, MOOCs, and Meetups 149
Ramón Talavera-Franco, Northeastern University, USA

Chapter 9
Guidelines for Design and Implementation of Mobile Learning 161
Mohamed Ally, Athabasca University, Canada
Mohammed Samaka, Qatar University, Qatar

Chapter 10
Learning without Boundaries MOOCs in Malaysia: Design and Implementation 177
Rachel Thomas Tharmabalan, University Science Malaysia, Malaysia

Chapter 11
Semantic Modelling for E-Learning Coordination 191
Atilla Elçi, Aksaray University, Turkey
Duygu Çelik Ertuğrul, Istanbul Aydin University, Turkey
Alev Elçi, Aksaray University, Turkey

Chapter 12
E-Learning and Faculty Development in Higher Education: A Comprehensive Project 226
Susan Gallagher-Lepak, University of Wisconsin, USA
Christine Vandenhouten, University of Wisconsin, USA

Chapter 13
E-Learning Readiness in Public Institutions 245
Fayiz Munsher Aldhaferri, Kuwait University, Kuwait

Chapter 14
Building Sustainable Capacity in Health Research through e-Learning in Resource Constrained Countries 266
Manu Gupta, IIHMR University, India

Chapter 15
Exploiting 3D Medical Equipment Simulations to Support Biomedical Engineering Academic Courses: Design Methodology and Implementation in a Small Scale National Project..................... 277
Adam Damianakis, Conceptum S.A., Greece
Pavlos Kallonis, Conceptum S.A., Greece
George Loudos, TEI of Athens, Greece
Dimitris Tsatsos, Conceptum S.A., Greece
Antonios Tsoukalis, TEI of Athens, Greece

Compilation of References 296

About the Contributors 332

Index.. 339

Detailed Table of Contents

Preface xiv

Introduction 23

Chapter 1
Designing Meaningful Learning Environments in a Work-Integrated-Learning Course Using a DOCC Design 1
Kathy Jordan, RMIT University, Australia
Jennifer Elsden-Clifton, RMIT University, Australia

As Higher Education increasingly moving towards a plethora of blended and fully online learning, questions are raised around the space and place of Work-Integrated Learning (WIL). This chapter reports on one institution's efforts to design and deliver a WIL course in a Teacher Education program adopting an open and distributed framework. The redesigned course, Orientation to Teaching, was a first year course in a Bachelor of Education (Primary) program at RMIT University, Melbourne, Australia. The redesign of the course was underpinned by a Distributed Open Collaborative Course (DOCC) design and as the workplace also became the site of learning, the theory of effective WIL curriculum (Orrell, 2011) also informed the design. This chapter examines the complexity of DOCC design in WIL contexts and uses Khan's 8 dimensions to frame the discussion.

Chapter 2
Investigating Students' Interactions with Discussion Forums, Facebook, and Twitter in a MOOC and their Perceptions 18
Min Liu, The University of Texas at Austin, USA
Jina Kang, The University of Texas at Austin, USA
Emily McKelroy, The University of Texas at Austin, USA
Jason Harron, The University of Texas at Austin, USA
Sa Liu, The University of Texas at Austin, USA

Given MOOCs being a relatively new format of online instruction, evidence-based research is needed to understand the role of MOOCs in changing the educational landscape, especially how students use the tools provided in MOOCs. This study investigated how students interacted with the discussion forum in a MOOC, and how they utilized Facebook and Twitter as an additional external space associated with this MOOC. Through both quantitative and qualitative data, the findings showed that MOOC participants found these tools to be helpful and can help create an active, collaborative, and participatory learning environment where they could share ideas and connect with other participants. The finding also indicated a poor interface design and low quality or low response to feedback can impact students' participation and perception of the usefulness of these tools. Results are discussed in the context.

Chapter 3
The Medium, the Content, and the Performance: An Overview on Media-Based Learning................ 42
Hans W. Giessen, Saarland University, Germany

This chapter focuses on aspects of the technological and interface dimensions of Badrul Khan's model, arguing that a correlation exists between the medium of instruction, students' performance, and the instructional content. Media-based learning is not necessarily more effective, simply because it uses a medium. Several variables exist that influence its success: the medium itself, its properties, production and consumption restraints; the content, and the way it can be presented in the context of a specific medium, and learners' cognitive styles. All these variables and more have to be taken into consideration, alone and interacting, in order to decide whether and where media-based learning is to be used, and where it might be counterproductive.

Chapter 4
Teacher Conceptions and Approaches to Blended Learning Environments.. 56
Vicki Caravias, Swinburne University of Technology, Australia

This chapter provides Australian perspectives on blended learning. An overview of the ways in which the concept of blended learning is interpreted in the Australian higher education is presented. This is followed by a discussion of the results of research carried out at one Australian University about teachers' conceptions on blended learning and their approaches to design and teaching in higher education. On the basis of twelve interviews with teachers, some important factors are analyzed pertaining to pedagogical, technological, interface, evaluation dimensions as well as resource support, management, ethical and institutional. Research results indicate that teachers consider their subject's learning objectives and apply the technologies and approaches that will work best for their students following the eight dimensions of blended learning environments.

Chapter 5
Evaluation of Mobile Learning with The Eight-Dimensional E-Learning Framework........................ 80
Özlem Efiloğlu Kurt, Yalova University, Turkey
Esra İşgör Şimşek, Yalova University, Turkey

Mobile learning has been a very popular topic in recent years as a result of the accelerating use of mobile devices. This learning type that offers education for everyone without any space and time limitation opens the doors for life-long learning. Even though mobile learning, which is employed to support the traditional education and ensure distant education, seems to have many advantages, it also possesses some disadvantages. Therefore, evaluating mobile learning in various dimensions will contribute to the literature through revealing the antecedents of these advantages and disadvantages. In this chapter, Khan's (2005) eight-dimensional e-learning framework is explained with its dimensions and adapted into mobile learning context. Subsequently, Coursera case which is among the MOOCs that are commonly used nowadays as a mobile interface is evaluated with reference to the framework.

Chapter 6
Massive Open Program Evaluation: Crowdsourcing's Potential to Improve E-Learning Quality 109
Tonya B. Amankwatia, Regent University, USA

Given the complexity of developing programs, services, policies, and support for e-learning, leaders may find it challenging to regularly evaluate programs to improve quality. Are there new opportunities to expand user and stakeholder input, or involve others in e-learning program evaluation? This chapter asks researchers and practitioners to rethink existing paradigms and methods for program evaluation. Crowdsourced input may help leaders and stakeholders address persistent evaluation challenges and improve e-learning quality, especially in Massive Open Online Courses (MOOCs). After reviewing selected evaluation paradigms, models, and methods, this chapter offers a possible role for crowdsourced input. This chapter examines the topics of crowd definition, affordances, and problems, to begin a taxonomical framework with possible applications for e-learning. The goal is to provide a reference for advancing the discussion and examination of crowdsourced input.

Chapter 7
To MOOC or Not to MOOC, That Is the Problem: A Learner's Perspective 131
Dilrukshi Gamage, University of Moratuwa, Sri Lanka
Shantha Fernando, University of Moratuwa, Sri Lanka
Indika Perera, University of Moratuwa, Sri Lanka

MOOCs are found to be next disruption for online education. It provides many avenues to students to who could not be access to world class education. xMOOCs have been experiencing by students since 2012 and courses keep adding every day in many MOOC platforms. However, it was found that not all the courses in MOOC platforms provide student satisfactions and quality. In other words, effectiveness of the courses in MOOCs varies significantly. Many MOOCs fail to meet the user goals. This concerns the MOOC consumers that there is no quality standard followed by the MOOC producers. In this chapter, authors evaluate 20 courses in MOOC platforms by actively participating and experiencing the behaviors. Evaluation is processed using 8 dimensional eLearning framework to explore the quality and readiness on the technology for future. Results expressed that MOOCs need thorough attention in designing so that it meets user goals and be effective to continue keeping the users interest.

Chapter 8
Hispanic LEP, MOOCs, and Meetups 149
Ramón Talavera-Franco, Northeastern University, USA

The 21st Century demands the transformation of education into a more collaborative system. School stakeholders should strengthen the sharing of educational resources to make them more attainable for students. Hispanic LEP Meetups as MOOC communities of practice hubs explores the challenges of one of the minority groups living in the United States that has been affected by school segregation practices: the Hispanic Limited English Proficient (HLEP) community—and proposes an alternative for them to continue their education by using Massive Open Online Courses (MOOCs) and by taking advantage of meetups to develop local communities of practice.

Chapter 9
Guidelines for Design and Implementation of Mobile Learning 161
Mohamed Ally, Athabasca University, Canada
Mohammed Samaka, Qatar University, Qatar

As technology evolves, there is a shift towards the use of mobile technology to deliver education both on-campus in a blended format and online delivery. This shift is moving at a very fast pace which is a major challenge for educational organizations which has to train staff and build the infrastructure for mobile delivery. Educators have to be trained on how to develop quality mobile learning materials, how to use the technology for the delivery, and how to provide quality support to students so that they are successful when using mobile technology to learn. This chapter provides guidelines for designing and implementing mobile learning.

Chapter 10
Learning without Boundaries MOOCs in Malaysia: Design and Implementation 177
Rachel Thomas Tharmabalan, University Science Malaysia, Malaysia

Massive Open Online Courses (MOOCs) have been the focus of mainstream media which promises to change the entire world education and create a meaningful impact for all. This book chapter reports on the design and implementation of Malaysian MOOC. Malaysia is the first country in the world to implement the MOOCs initiative for public universities. This new platform of learning is also in line with the National Higher Education Strategic Plan that includes life-long learning, e-Learning, internationalization, and knowledge transfer.

Chapter 11
Semantic Modelling for E-Learning Coordination 191
Atilla Elçi, Aksaray University, Turkey
Duygu Çelik Ertuğrul, Istanbul Aydin University, Turkey
Alev Elçi, Aksaray University, Turkey

This chapter reports a metadata model for e-learning coordination based on content semantics grounded on Semantic Web concepts. To start with, e-learning models are surveyed identifying process content, such as phases, activities, data schema, rules and relations, so on, as relevant for a coordination model. The study looks into the mechanism of e-learning environment and how e-learning processes can be classified for purposes of activity coordination. A metadata model for coordination of e-learning is being sought as expressed in Semantic Web concepts and transcribed using the related languages like OWL, RDF, SPARQL and others. A learner centric proposal is advanced which augments the IEEE Learning Technology Standards Committee's industry leader Learning Technology System Architecture. Examples are worked out and future research directions are identified. This is a continuing research project on application of Semantic Web initiative in e-learning; i.e., design and development of markup and annotation tools, relevant ontologies and intelligent agents in meeting learner needs.

Chapter 12
E-Learning and Faculty Development in Higher Education: A Comprehensive Project 226
Susan Gallagher-Lepak, University of Wisconsin, USA
Christine Vandenhouten, University of Wisconsin, USA

Growth of online higher education and advances in technology justify and encourage new models of faculty development related to e-learning. This chapter describes a multi-campus faculty development program using distance technology, a Community Of Practice (COP) model, and an e-learning framework. The Flexible Framework for E-Learning by Khan (2005) guided planning and implementation of the faculty development program. A variety of strategies were used to deliver the faculty development program including use of campus-based site leaders, participating scholars, monthly videoconferences, a faculty development handbook, hands-on use of new e-learning technologies, and a year-end conference. The program also included an evaluation of the interface design of courses used in a collaborative online nursing program with findings reported to faculty. Along with strategies used, barriers and evaluation of the multi-campus faculty development model are presented so that the faculty development model can be replicated across other universities and disciplines.

Chapter 13
E-Learning Readiness in Public Institutions... 245
Fayiz Munsher Aldhaferri, Kuwait University, Kuwait

This chapter reports on an e-Learning readiness study that was supported by Kuwait Foundation for Advancement of Sciences (KFAS) under project number (2013-11109-05) and carried out to assess the organizational and individual factors of the two major stakeholder groups (teachers and students) in the secondary education institutions to provide significant information to the policy makers and regulatory bodies for the development of successful e-Learning strategies. The chapter looks specifically at some factors at the initial stage of an e-Learning introduction that can have tremendous impact on the later stages of the process. Later on this chapter, discussion and suggestions are presented to be instrumental in implementing successful eLearning strategies for many countries, specifically Kuwait, and will also benefit e-Learning initiatives in similar institutions in other Gulf Cooperation Council (GCC) and beyond.

Chapter 14
Building Sustainable Capacity in Health Research through e-Learning in Resource Constrained Countries.. 266
Manu Gupta, IIHMR University, India

Social determinants like income level, nutrition, education, occupation, gender, and poverty influence the health status of individual, resulting in wide disparities in the health status of different socio-economic groups. Efforts to reduce health inequities can be strengthened by incorporating a Social Determinants of Health approach in creating Health Care policy. This will require an increase in the number of scientists in low and middle-income countries, with the necessary skills. This chapter focuses on a novel capacity building approach, adopted by a European Union funded project, entitled "Asian Regional Capacity Development for Research on Social Determinants of Health". The project uses innovative educational technologies to deliver education and training that would be helpful in building new research training capacity on social determinants of health, in low and middle-income countries. The capacity building approach adopted by the project, will reduce brain drain, is more climate friendly and also encourage gender equity within low and middle-income country-based training.

Chapter 15
Exploiting 3D Medical Equipment Simulations to Support Biomedical Engineering Academic Courses: Design Methodology and Implementation in a Small Scale National Project..................... 277

Adam Damianakis, Conceptum S.A., Greece
Pavlos Kallonis, Conceptum S.A., Greece
George Loudos, TEI of Athens, Greece
Dimitris Tsatsos, Conceptum S.A., Greece
Antonios Tsoukalis, TEI of Athens, Greece

Biomedical Imaging is a rapidly evolving area, where new versions of advanced medical equipment/new methodologies based on complex physical phenomena are developed. The cost for the effective training of both academic students/company employees in real training environments is high and in many cases impossible. Most of the times, it is not possible to effectively transfer knowledge due to the limitations of these environments, which has a strong effect both on the theoretical understanding and the practical skills of students. On the other hand, the exploitation of 3D simulations enables for better knowledge acquisition by learners, although not efficiently explored yet. Several studies support that this can be achieved by maximizing the interaction with simulations. To this end, interactive 3D Medical Equipment Simulations have been developed, by exploiting open source software and delivering them through the Web and eLearning Environments. The proposed chapter aims to present the need for such Environments, the development tools, challenges, solutions and possible applications.

Compilation of References 296

About the Contributors 332

Index 339

Preface

Dr. Badrul Khan's Framework for e-Learning is the organizing theme that runs through the chapters in this book. The Framework was developed in response to questions regarding the necessary conditions to create a meaningful e-learning environment and experience for all stakeholders. This preface will present an overview of the development of this influential framework and a short introduction to the chapters.

The code for the World Wide Web was released in 1992 and, very slowly, the Web came into being. Servers were set up and the Web, in its early years, was just used as an extension of early systems to deliver documents and files. One of the first web-supported university courses was a Distance Education course taught by Dr. Michael G. Moore at The Pennsylvania State University in Fall, 1994 to students in Finland, Estonia, Mexico, and the US. The first North American conference devoted to educational uses of the World Wide Web was NAWeb '95 in Fredericton, New Brunswick, Canada, followed by the NAUweb conferences at Northern Arizona University in 1996, 1997, and 1998. The first book published on *Web-based Instruction* appeared in 1997 and its editor, Dr. Badrul Huda Khan, made the keynote presentation at NAUweb '97.

After *Web-Based Instruction* was published in 1997, Dr. Khan received many inquiries about what exactly made for *meaningful web-based learning*, as this topic was still very new on the academic scene. Ever since then, Dr. Khan has been researching the answer to the question: "What does it take to provide meaningful online e-learning environments for learners, worldwide?"

It was obvious to Dr. Khan very early on that web-based instruction and learning doesn't exist in a vacuum; it is deeply embedded in a rich context that includes institutions, technology, teachers, trainers, and learners. After an extensive literature review and talking with hundreds of interested administrators, teachers, and learners, who contributed to his edited books, took his classes, and attended his workshops and conferences presentations, he developed *A Framework for Web-based Learning*. This was first presented at Utah State University in 1997. He and his students then refined the framework by using it as part of their coursework to review existing web-based instruction and training courses.

The Framework clustered the critical factors into eight dimensions and created an octagonal diagram that was initially called *A Framework for Web-Based Learning* and is now known as *A Framework for e-Learning* (as described in more detail in Chapter 1). The eight dimensions are:

- Pedagogical, Ethical, and Evaluation,
- Technological and Interface design,
- Institutional, management and resources support.

While the title of each dimension indicates a 'main theme,' the dimensions and their constituent factors are actually interrelated and interconnected, like a vast web to create the context in which e-learning exists. The factors are expressed as a set of interrelated questions to be asked to ensure full coverage of the dimension. Dr Khan determined that in the design, development, and evaluation of web-based teaching and learning, the dimensions and their factors must be thoroughly addressed and balanced in order for the whole of a web-based (then) and, now, any e-learning enterprise to function to the benefit of all stakeholders.

The Web-based Framework was first used by George Washington University graduate students (mostly professionals from government agencies, corporations and educational settings) in 2004. Students used the Framework in a ground-breaking review of institution-wide online programs at six higher education institutions in the U.S. and Canada, including; Regis University, Tallahassee Community College, University of Illinois-Springfield, University of Alaska, Illinois Online Network, British Columbia Open University.

The results of these program evaluations were shared with the contact persons in each institution. Participating institutions received reviews of pedagogical, technological, interface design, evaluation, management, resource support, ethical, and institutional aspects of their online programs. Institutions shared their views on using the Framework, noting they were better able to identify areas where they had strengths and weaknesses – helping them to better appropriate resources and develop future budgets. For example, one participating institution's online program did very well in the pedagogical issues, but poorly in ethical issues. By using the Framework, students advised: "Since the pedagogical design of e-learning is satisfactory, there is no need to either replace the existing instructional designer or hire new one. Since the plagiarism and intellectual property rights issues were not adequately addressed, assistance from individuals with expertise in legal and copyright issues should be considered in [the] future."

The web-based learning framework was published in 2001 as Chapter 8 in Dr. Khan's next edited book *Web-based Training* (Khan, 2001). Since that time, his framework has been expanded to address blended learning, e-learning, mobile learning, learning in virtual worlds, and, most recently, MOOCs (Corbeil, Corbeil, & Khan, 2016).

The framework is both versatile and comprehensive and has the potential to be useful for the following stakeholders:

1. Instructors can use the framework as a resource in their teaching and training.
2. Instructors and support staff can use the framework to plan, design, evaluate, and implement e-learning.
3. Administrators can use them to organize resources to support e-learning.
4. Interface designers for large fixed and small mobile screens.
5. Administrators at local, regional, and national levels to develop strategic plans for e-learning initiatives.
6. Virtual/corporate university designers planning distributed learning systems, corporate universities, virtual universities, and cyber-schools.
7. Providers of e-learning schools to understand the level of services the learners (or consumers) expect.
8. Accrediting agencies to review the quality of instruction and support services.
9. Evaluators at any level who want to be sure that their evaluations are comprehensive and complete.

In subsequent publications, the framework has been elaborated into checklists (Khan 2005a, 2005b) to ensure that each factor in each dimension is addressed, even if it is only to check it off with a (Does Not Apply). The framework does not provide a scoring rubric because that is not the point of its use. The framework constantly reminds its users that all dimensions of the e-learning enterprise are interrelated and interconnected and all must be addressed.

This current book seeks to provide readers with a broad understanding of the use of the e-learning framework in open and distributed learning environments and the many dimensions that directly influence their effectiveness as seen through the lens of the framework. The chapters explore the framework's dimensions: digital pedagogy, administrative models, technological advancements, user-interface design, and usability and many address the issues that have arisen around the use of MOOCs in their various flavors. Such courses are still in their infancy, and the body of research documenting their effectiveness is still small. In order to better approach the design, development, implementation, and evaluation of MOOCs, research using the e-learning framework for evaluation is presented to aid in the better utilization of the resources offered by this new era of digital learning technology.

This is an edited book with many internationally-based authors, so the insights presented reflect both richness and diversity. The contributors offer a variety of points of view, presented through the lens of different versions of the e-learning framework, and these opinions may differ from one another on the same issues. Some of the contributors have explicitly used various versions of the framework; some have not. This is not a cook-book; each reader must take what is here and adapt it to their own situations; the variety in the chapters gives some indication of the scope and flexibility possible.

The book begins with an introductory chapter by Dr. Khan and the subsequent chapters are arranged in the following order:

1. Chapters 1-8 address the Educational Dimensions: Pedagogical, Ethical, and Evaluation.
2. Chapters 9-11 address the Technology Dimensions: Technological and Interface design.
3. Chapters 12-15 address the Management Dimensions: Institutional, Management and Resources support.

INTRODUCTION: A GLOBAL FRAMEWORK FOR E-LEARNING

This chapter introduces and defines the concept of e-learning and open and distributed learning environments. The distinction between traditional instruction and e-learning is described, followed by a discussion of e-learning system features and the particular case of learner-focused e-learning systems, and what is involved in creating 'meaningful' e-learning. The Global Framework for e-learning is introduced, with its Dimensions: Institutional, Management, Technological, Pedagogical, Ethical, Interface Design, Resource support and Evaluation, its Factors and Issues. The Dimensions are described individually, then the factors are listed, followed by the issues/questions generated for those factors. The e-learning feature "ease of use" is reviewed using the eight dimensions for one of the stakeholder groups: "students". The Framework can also be used for evaluation and can be applied to other learning situations, including MOOCs and mobile learning.

CHAPTER 1: DESIGNING MEANINGFUL LEARNING ENVIRONMENTS IN A WORK-INTEGRATED LEARNING COURSE USING A DOOC DESIGN

As Higher Education increasingly moves towards a plethora of blended and fully online learning, questions are raised around the space and place of Work-Integrated Learning (WIL, also known as practicums, field placements, "pre-service teaching", etc.) This chapter reports on one Australian institution's efforts to design and deliver a WIL course in a Teacher Education program adopting an open and distributed framework. The redesigned course, Orientation to Teaching, was a first year course in a Bachelor of Education (Primary) program at RMIT University, Melbourne, Australia. The redesign of the course was underpinned by a Distributed Open Collaborative Course (DOCC) design – informed by MOOC principals and, as the workplace also became the site of learning, the theory of effective Work-Integrated Learning curriculum also informed the design. This chapter examines the complexity of DOCC design in Work-Integrated Learning contexts and uses Khan's eight dimensions to frame the discussion and to inform the design of the distributed course involving over 200 students at different school locations.

CHAPTER 2: INVESTIGATING STUDENTS' INTERACTIONS WITH DISCUSSION FORUMS, FACEBOOK, AND TWITTER IN A MOOC AND THEIR PERCEPTIONS OF THESE TOOLS

Given that MOOCs are a relatively new format for online instruction, evidence-based research is needed to understand the role of MOOCs in the changing educational landscape, especially how students use the communication tools provided in MOOCs. This study investigated how students interacted with the discussion forum in a MOOC, and how they utilized Facebook and Twitter as an additional external space associated with this MOOC. Less than half the students participated in any of the discussions. Khan's Framework dimensions of interface design, resource support, pedagogical and ethical were used in the data analysis as were Moore's (1989) Three Types of Interaction (student to student, student to instructor, student to content). Through both quantitative and qualitative data, the findings showed that MOOC participants found these tools to be helpful and can help create an active, collaborative, and participatory learning environment where they could share ideas and connect with other participants. Considerably more students participated by reading posts to the discussion forum, Facebook and Twitter than did posting themselves. The findings also indicated a poor interface design and low quality or low response to feedback from teachers and peers can impact students' participation and perception of the usefulness of these tools. The diversity of MOOC participants (i.e., diverse knowledge levels, language skills, and geographical locations) creates challenges to communication in MOOCs that should be taken into consideration in the design of MOOC activities.

CHAPTER 3: DIMENSIONS FROM THE POINT OF VIEW OF THE MEDIA AND THEIR PROPERTIES

This chapter focuses on aspects of the technological and interface dimensions of Badrul Khan's model, arguing that there is a correlation between the medium of instruction, students' performance, and the instructional content. Media-based learning is not necessarily more effective, simply because it uses a medium. Some students self-select online learning because they are successful; others with different learning styles just are not successful, for a variety of reasons. Several variables exist that influence student success: the medium itself, its properties; production and consumption restraints; the content and the way it can be presented in the context of a specific medium; and learners' cognitive styles. All these variables and more have to be taken into consideration, alone and interacting, in order to decide whether and where media-based learning is to be used, and where and with whom it might be counterproductive.

CHAPTER 4: TEACHER CONCEPTIONS AND APPROACHES TO BLENDED LEARNING ENVIRONMENTS

This chapter provides an Australian perspective on blended learning in the face of its becoming a requirement for all higher education teachers. An overview of the ways in which the concept of blended learning is interpreted in the Australian higher education establishment is presented. This is followed by a discussion of the results of research carried out at one Australian University about teachers' conceptions about blended learning and their approaches to course design and teaching in higher education. On the basis of twelve interviews with teachers using blended learning, some important factors are analyzed pertaining to Khan's (1997) model: pedagogical, technological, user interface, and evaluation dimensions as well as resource support, management, ethical, and institutional. Research findings indicate that teachers consider their subject's learning objectives and apply the dimensions and approaches that will work best for their students. The author suggests that the findings of this study can be used to inform these approaches, whether they are focused specifically on academic pathway programs or more broadly across all blended learning courses.

CHAPTER 5: EVALUATION OF MOBILE LEARNING SYSTEMS WITH THE EIGHT-DIMENSIONAL E-LEARNING FRAMEWORK

Mobile learning, using a variety of portable, small-screen devices, offers access to education for everyone free of space and time limitations. Even though mobile learning, when used to support traditional education and enhance distant education, seems to have many advantages, there are also some significant disadvantages. Therefore, evaluating mobile learning using the various dimensions of Khan's (2005) Framework will contribute to the literature and to practice through revealing the antecedents of these advantages and disadvantages. Khan's (2005) eight-dimensional e-learning framework is explained with its dimensions specifically adapted for use in mobile learning contexts. As an example of the application of the Framework for Mobile Learning, Coursera, which is among the MOOCs that has a dedicated interface for mobile devices, is evaluated.

CHAPTER 6: MASSIVE OPEN EVALUATION – THE POTENTIAL ROLE OF CROWDSOURCING FOR IMPROVING E-LEARNING QUALITY

Given the complexity of developing programs, services, policies, and support for e-learning, academic and training leaders may find it challenging to regularly evaluate programs to improve quality. Are there new opportunities to expand user and stakeholder input, or involve others in e-learning program evaluation? This chapter asks researchers and practitioners to rethink existing paradigms and methods for program evaluation. Crowdsourced input is defined and suggestions made to help leaders and stakeholders address persistent evaluation challenges and improve e-learning quality, especially in Massive Open Online Courses (MOOCs). After reviewing selected evaluation paradigms, models, and methods, this chapter offers a possible role for crowdsourced input and examines the topics of crowd definition, affordances, and problems, to begin a taxonomical framework with possible applications for e-learning. Crowd intelligence can potentially move e-learning stakeholders closer to realizing more innovative designs and learner support. As educators strive to make e-learning more global, inclusive, and learner-centered, program evaluators should do the same with e-learning evaluation.

CHAPTER 7: TO MOOC OR NOT TO MOOC? THAT IS THE PROBLEM – A LEARNER'S PERSPECTIVE

The authors of this chapter decided to investigate the perspective of MOOC participants and actively participated in and completed 20 MOOC courses on different platforms over a period of 2 years. They were aware that quality in MOOC courses is not consistent and students have little opportunity before enrolling to determine if a particular MOOC will meet their educational goals. The authors used Khan's Framework to evaluate their experiences, turning the factors in each dimension into Likert-scale questions and assigning a score to each course, which led to their discovering a wide gap in scores. The lowest scoring courses focused largely on information transmission though long videos with little interaction and little evidence of instructor presence. The highest scoring courses were highly interactive and engaging with discussion, instructor feedback and assignments to keep student interest high. Results expressed that MOOCs need thorough attention in designing so that they will meet user goals and be effective to continue keeping the users interest.

CHAPTER 8: HISPANIC LEP MOOCs + MEETUPS

The Hispanic LEP Coding MOOCs + MeetUp proposes a plan as an alternative for the Hispanic Limited English Proficient community to continue their education by using Massive Open Online Courses (MOOCs) around IT and Computer Coding topics and by developing communities of practice through Meetups. "Meetups" are face-to-face organized opportunities for MOOC members to meet regularly throughout the course of a MOOC to share in their learning. By focusing on the Hispanic student's needs, the study proposes a plan of action that involves a culturally relevant education perspective and the participation of different educational stakeholders interested in supporting the Hispanic community.

CHAPTER 9: GUIDELINES FOR THE DESIGN OF MOBILE LEARNING

This chapter provides guidelines for designing and implementing mobile learning from the perspective of many of the stakeholders. As technology evolves, there is a shift towards the use of mobile technology to deliver education both on-campus in a blended format, and online delivery. This shift is moving at a very fast pace, which creates a major challenge for educational organizations which have to train staff, organize resources, and build the infrastructure for mobile delivery. Educators have to be trained on how to develop quality mobile learning materials, how to use the technology for the delivery, and how to provide quality support to students so that they are successful when using mobile technology to learn.

CHAPTER 10: LEARNING WITHOUT BOUNDARIES – MOOCS IN MALAYSIA: DESIGN AND IMPLEMENTATION

Massive Open Online Courses (MOOCs) in Malaysia are a very recent development but just the latest step in a ten-year effort to provide quality online learning in Malaysian education. Higher Education institutions in Malaysia have consolidated their efforts since 2007 to share expertise and experience in developing and presenting online courses. The first Malaysian higher education institution announced its pilot MOOC offering in March 2013. In 2014, five more higher education institutions cooperated to begin offering MOOCs on two different platforms. At the moment, these initiatives represent a preliminary phase in MOOCs, where Malaysia's approach can be described as exploratory, focusing less on reaching the widest possible audience, making a significant mark globally or competing with established providers like Coursera, edX and Udacity, but more on learning to use web-based technology to complement current educational delivery systems at the higher education level and introducing MOOCs to the general Malaysian audience.

CHAPTER 11: SEMANTIC MODELING FOR E-LEARNING COORDINATION

This chapter discusses a continuing research project on Interface design and the application of a Semantic Web initiative in e-learning; i.e., the design and development of markup and annotation tools, relevant ontologies and intelligent agents in meeting learner needs. This will harness the possibilities of computers' artificial intelligence capabilities to individualize and personalize the learning experience, based on student input. This chapter presents a metadata model for e-learning coordination based on content semantics grounded on Semantic Web concepts. E-learning models are surveyed to identify process content, such as phases, activities, data schema, rules and relations, so on, as relevant for a coordination model. The study looks into the mechanism of the e-learning environment and how e-learning processes can be classified for purposes of activity coordination. A metadata model for coordination of e-learning is being sought as expressed in Semantic Web concepts and transcribed using the related languages like OWL, RDF, SPARQL and others. A learner centric proposal is advanced which augments the IEEE Learning Technology Standards Committee's industry leader Learning Technology System Architecture. Examples are worked out and future research directions are identified.

CHAPTER 12: A COMPREHENSIVE PROJECT – E-LEARNING AND FACULTY DEVELOPMENT IN HIGHER EDUCATION

The growth of online higher education and advances in technology justify and encourage new models of faculty development, related to e-learning. This chapter describes a multi-campus faculty development program in five Nursing programs using distance technology, a community of practice (COP) model, and an e-learning framework. Khan's (2005) Flexible Framework for E-Learning guided the planning and implementation of the multi-year, multi-campus, faculty development program. This chapter focuses particularly on the fifth year of the program that specifically addressed e-learning. A variety of strategies were used to deliver the faculty development program including use of campus-based site leaders, participating scholars, monthly videoconferences, a faculty development handbook, hands-on use of new e-learning technologies, and a year-end conference. The program also included an evaluation, using Khan's Framework, of the interface design of the courses used in a collaborative online nursing program with findings reported to faculty. Along with the strategies used, barriers and evaluation of the multi-campus faculty development model are presented so that the faculty development model can be replicated across other universities and disciplines.

CHAPTER 13: ELEARNING READINESS IN PUBLIC INSTITUTIONS

This chapter reports on an e-learning readiness study that was supported by the Kuwait Foundation for Advancement of Sciences (KFAS) under project number 2013-11109-05. The study was carried out to assess the organizational and individual "readiness for e-learning" factors and perspectives of two major stakeholder groups (teachers and students) in the secondary education institutions in Kuwait. The research questionnaires are included and responses analyzed in this chapter. Results provided significant information to the Kuwaiti policy makers and regulatory bodies for the development of successful e-learning strategies. The chapter looks specifically at some factors at the initial stage of an e-learning introduction that can have tremendous impact on the later stages of the process. Later on this chapter, discussion and suggestions are presented to be instrumental in implementing successful e-learning strategies for many countries, specifically Kuwait, and will also benefit eLearning initiatives in similar institutions in other Gulf Cooperation Council (GCC) and beyond.

CHAPTER 14: BUILDING SUSTAINABLE CAPACITY IN HEALTH RESEARCH THROUGH E-LEARNING IN RESOURCE CONSTRAINED COUNTRIES

This chapter focuses on a novel capacity building approach adopted by a European Union funded project, entitled "Asian Regional Capacity Development for Research on Social Determinants of Health", to increase the number of available health-care research scientists in Asian countries. Social determinants like income level, nutrition, education, occupation, gender, and poverty influence the health status of an individual, resulting in wide disparities in the health status of different socio-economic groups. Therefore, efforts to reduce health inequities can be strengthened by incorporating a Social Determinants of Health (SDH) approach in creating Health Care policy. However, this will require an increase in the number of health research scientists in low and middle-income countries, having the research and investigation skills to conduct the necessary research on existing conditions. The chapter describes the project's innovative use of educational technologies to deliver education and training that would be helpful in building new research training capacity on social determinants of health in low and middle-income countries. The capacity building approach adopted by the project will reduce brain drain, is more family and climate friendly, and will also encourage gender equity within low and middle-income country-based training.

CHAPTER 15: EXPLOITING 3-D MEDICAL EQUIPMENT SIMULATIONS TO SUPPORT BIOMEDICAL ENGINEERING ACADEMIC COURSES

This chapter discusses an innovative program to build 3-D training simulations for students and trainees in the field of Biomedical Imaging. Biomedical Imaging is a rapidly evolving area, where new versions of advanced medical equipment and new methodologies based on complex physical phenomena are constantly being developed. This makes constant pre-service and in-service training critical for medical technicians using imaging equipment. The cost for effective training of both academic students and company employees in real training environments is high and in many cases impossible, due to lack of access to the latest versions of imaging equipment. It is often not possible to effectively transfer knowledge due lack of access to equipment in the field, which has a strong effect both on the theoretical understanding and the practical skills of students. On the other hand, the exploitation of 3-D simulations enables for better knowledge acquisition by learners and the opportunities for unlimited virtual practice. To this end, interactive 3-D medical equipment simulations have been developed by exploiting open source software and delivering them through the Web and e-Learning environments. This chapter presents the need for such environments, the development tools used, the challenges, solutions and possible applications.

REFERENCES

Corbeil, J. R., Corbeil, M. E., & Khan, B. H. (2016). *The MOOC case book: Case studies in MOOC design, development and implementation*. Ronkonkoma, NY: Linus Learning.

Khan, B. H. (Ed.). (1997). *Web-based instruction*. Englewood Cliffs, NJ: Educational Technology Publications.

Khan, B. H. (Ed.). (2001a). *Web-based training*. Englewood Cliffs, NJ: Educational Technology Publications.

Khan, B. H. (2001b). A framework for web-based learning. In B. H. Khan (Ed.), *Web-based training* (pp. 75–98). Englewood Cliffs, NJ: Educational Technology Publications.

Khan, B. H. (2005a). *Managing e-learning design, delivery, implementation and evaluation*. Hershey, PA: Idea Group Inc. doi:10.4018/978-1-59140-634-1

Khan, B. H. (2005b). *E-learning quick checklist*. Hershey, PA: Idea Group Inc. doi:10.4018/978-1-59140-812-3

Moore, M. G. (1989). Editorial: Three types of interaction. *American Journal of Distance Education*, *3*(2), 1–7. doi:10.1080/08923648909526659

Introduction

A GLOBAL FRAMEWORK FOR E-LEARNING

With the rapid growth of the Internet and digital technologies, the Web has become a powerful, global, interactive, dynamic, economic, and democratic medium of learning and teaching at a distance (Khan, 1997a, Taylor, 2014). The Internet provides an opportunity to develop learning-on-demand as well as learner-centered instruction and training. There are numerous names for the wide variety of online learning activities, including Web-Based Learning (WBL), Web-Based Instruction (WBI), Web-Based Training (WBT), Internet-Based Training (IBT), Distributed Learning (DL), Advanced Distributed Learning (ADL), Distance Learning, Online Learning (OL), Mobile Learning (or m-Learning) or Nomadic Learning, Remote Learning, Offsite Learning, a-Learning (anytime, anyplace, anywhere learning), Massive Open Online Course (MOOC), etc. In this book, the term *e-learning* is used to represent all open and distributed learning activities.

Designing and delivering instruction and training on the Internet requires thoughtful analysis and investigation, combined with an understanding of both the Internet's capabilities and resources and the ways in which instructional design principles can be applied to tap the Internet's potential (Ritchie & Hoffman, 1997). Designing e-learning for open and distributed learning environments is new to many of us. After reflecting on the factors that must be weighed in creating effective open and distributed learning environments for learners worldwide, the following definition of e-learning is used in this book.

E-learning can be viewed as an innovative approach for delivering well-designed, learner-centered, interactive, and facilitated learning environments to anyone, any place, any time by utilizing the attributes and resources of various digital technologies along with other forms of learning materials suited for the open and distributed learning environment.

The above definition of e-learning raises the question of how various attributes of e-learning methods and technologies can be utilized to create learning features appropriate for diverse learners in an open and distributed environment.

Open and Distributed Learning Environment

What is an open and distributed learning environment? A clear understanding of the *open* and *distributed* nature of the online learning environment will help us create meaningful flexible e-learning (Khan, 2012). According to Calder & McCollum (1998) "The common definition of open learning is learning at your own time, pace and place" (p. 13). Ellington (1997) notes that open and flexible learning allows learners to have some say in how, where, and when learning takes place. Saltzberg & Polyson (1995) noted that distributed learning is not synonymous with distance learning (which also encompasses correspondence education, radio and television), but, they stress its close relationship with the idea of distributed resources:

Distributed learning is an instructional model that allows instructor, students, and content to be located in different, non-centralized locations so that instruction and learning occur independent of time and place... The distributed learning model can be used in combination with traditional classroom-based courses, with traditional distance learning courses, or it can be used to create wholly virtual classrooms. (p. 10)

Janis Taylor (2004) of Clarke College in Iowa, who teaches students coming from different places in the Midwest, commented on open and distributed learning:

Consider a student user who described her online education as open because she can sit out on her back deck supervising her children in the swimming pool while doing her homework. Now that's open-air and open learning. One of my pre-service teachers works in a chemical lab in Cleveland, another is a court reporter three hours drive from me and another is a nurse in rural western Iowa. I, their teacher, am sitting in a small liberal arts college in eastern Iowa, a state badly needing to tap new people to come into the teaching profession. How could I get them all here to my campus if e-learning weren't distributed? This open and distributed learning environment made learning flexible for a young traveling business woman who says "I take my college course, my instructor, and all of my fellow students with me on every business trip. With my laptop in my hotel room, I can view my teacher's demonstration, discuss it with my classmates in the Chat Room, and turn in my assignment by email." Now that's a flexible college program (personal communication, June 22, 2004).

Flexibility in learning is, therefore, dependent on the openness of the system and the availability of learning resources distributed in various locations. A clear understanding of the *open and distributed* nature of learning environments will help us create meaningful learning environments with increased flexibility. Figure 1 graphically shows how an open philosophy of education, when combined with distributed educational systems and technology, results in flexibility for student learning.

Figure 1. Open and distributed learning provides flexibility

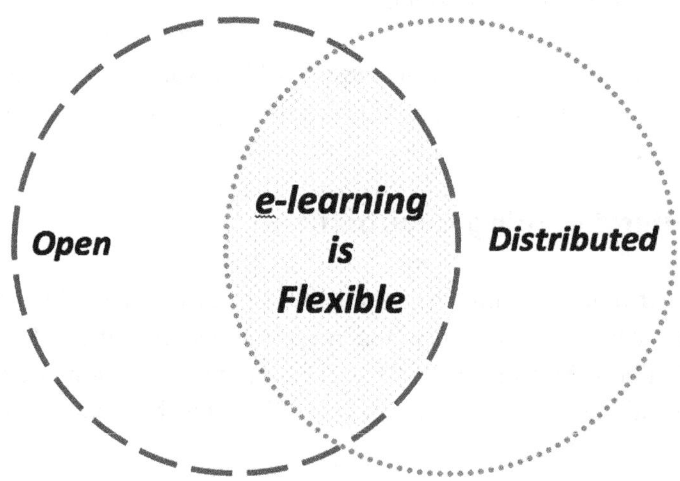

Traditional Instruction and e-learning

The design and format of open and distributed e-learning can be quite different from traditional classroom instruction. Traditional classrooms are space bound. Traditional instruction treats learning pretty much as a *closed system*, taking place within the confines of a given classroom, school, textbook, field trip, etc. (Greg Kearsley, personal communication, January 27, 2000). The traditional classroom-taught courses are not necessarily closed systems; many teachers assign students to do library based research papers, interview members of a professional community, engage in service-learning activities, and extend their learning initiatives far beyond the classroom itself. Unfortunately, many classes are bound by their four walls and involve only the thoughts of the instructor, the textbook writer, and occasional student comments. Classroom courses are also closed in the sense that they are limited to only those students who can physically come to the location (Janis Taylor, personal communication, May 24, 2004)

On the other hand, e-learning extends the boundaries of learning, so that learning can occur in the classroom, from the home, and in the work place (Relan & Gillani, 1997). It is a flexible form of education because it creates options for learners in terms of where and when they can learn (Krauth, 1998). A well-designed e-learning course allows learners to become actively involved in their learning processes. However, a poorly designed e-learning course can be just as rigid, dogmatic, and non-interactive as a poorly taught face-to-face course. The scope of openness and flexibility in e-learning is dependent on how it is designed. "While having an open system has its appeal, it can make designing for it extremely difficult, because in an open system, the designer agrees to give up a certain amount of control to the user" (Jones & Farquhar, 1997, p. 240). The more open the learning environment, the more complex is the planning, management, and evaluation of it (Land & Hannafin, 1997). For example, the instructor cannot monitor who helps the student on tests unless they are proctored.

E-Learning System Features

We all know that a well-designed e-learning program can provide numerous features that are conducive to learning. However, these features should be meaningfully integrated into an e-learning program to achieve its learning goals.

The following are examples of some e-learning features:

Interactivity, authenticity, learner-control, convenience, self-containment, ease of use, online support, course security, cost effectiveness, collaborative learning, formal and informal environments, multiple expertise, online evaluation, online search, global accessibility, cross-cultural interaction, non-discriminatory, etc.

The more features conducive to learning that are integrated meaningfully into an e-learning course, the richer the learning environment becomes. The challenge is to make sure each of these learning features is created by addressing (1) issues critical for all stakeholder groups, including learners, facilitators, and support stuff, (2) types of learning contents and (3) capabilities of digital technologies to support learning (Romiszowski, 2004).

Learner-Focused E-Learning Systems

A leading theorist of educational systems, B.H. Banathy (1991), makes a strong case for learning-focused educational and training systems where "the learner is the key entity and occupies the nucleus of the systems complex of education" (p. 96). For Banathy (1991) "*when learning is in focus*, arrangements are made in the environment of the learner that communicate the learning task, and learning resources are made available to learners so that they can explore and master learning tasks" (p. 101). A distributed learning environment that can effectively support learning-on-demand must be designed by placing the learners at the center of the focus. In support of learner-centered approach, Moore (1998) states:

Our aim as faculty should be to focus our attention on making courses and other learning experiences that will best empower our students to learn, to learn fully, effectively, efficiently, and with rewarding satisfaction. It is the responsibility of our profession to study ways of maximizing the potential of our environments to support their learning and to minimize those elements in their environments that may impede it. (p. 4).

Success in an e-learning system involves a systematic process of planning, designing, evaluating, and implementing online learning environments where learning is actively fostered and supported. An e-learning system should not only be meaningful to learners, but it should also be meaningful to all stakeholder groups including instructors, support services staff, and the institution. For example, an e-learning system is more likely to be meaningful to *learners* when it is easily accessible, clearly organized, concise and well written, authoritatively presented, learner-centered, affordable, efficient, flexible, and has a facilitated learning environment. When learners display a high level of participation and success in meeting a course's goals and objectives, this can make e-learning meaningful to *instructors*. In turn, when learners enjoy all available support services provided in the course without any interruptions, it makes *support services staff* happy as they strive to provide easy-to-use, reliable services. Finally, an e-learning system is meaningful to *institutions* when it has a sound return-on-investment (ROI), a moderate to high level of learners' satisfaction with both the quality of instruction and all support services, and a low drop-out rate (Morrison & Khan, 2003).

A GLOBAL FRAMEWORK FOR E-LEARNING

The design of open and distributed e-learning environments requires a comprehensive understanding of "*What does it take to provide successful virtual learning environments for learners worldwide?* Since 1997, I have communicated with learners, instructors, administrators, technical and other support services staff involved in virtual learning in both academic and corporate settings all over the world. I have researched virtual learning issues discussed in professional discussion forums, and I have designed and taught online and blended learning courses. I have surveyed online educators and students (Khan & Vega, 1997; Smith & Khan, 2007 and Khan, Cataldo & Bennett, 2007). Also, as the editor of *Web-Based Instruction (1997), Web-Based Training (2001), E-learning Quick Checklist (2005), Flexible Learning in an Information Society (2007), Learning on Demand: ADL and the Future of E-learning (2010), User Interface Design for Virtual Environments: Challenges and Advances (2012), International Handbook of E-Learning* (2015), *The MOOC Case Book: Case Studies in MOOC Design, Development and Implementation* (2016), and *Khan's E-Learning Tips* (2016). I have had the opportunity to work closely on critical virtual learning issues with more than 500 authors worldwide, who have contributed chapters to these books.

Figure 2. Global (octagon) framework for e-learning

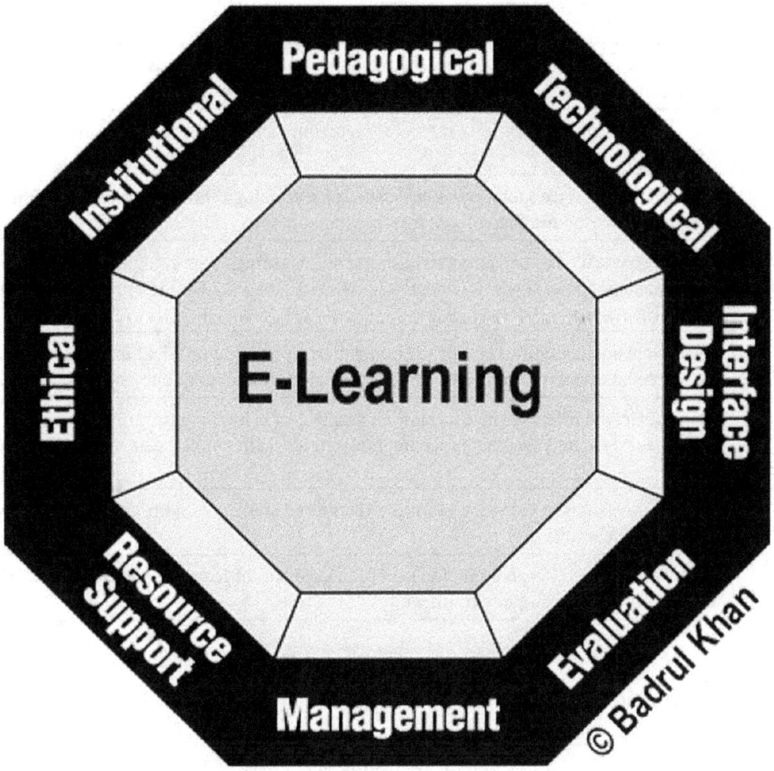

Through these activities, I have learned that e-learning represents a paradigm shift, not only for learners, but also for instructors, administrators, technical, and other support services staff, and the institution. Just as we are accustomed to teaching and learning in a closed system like a physical classroom, the openness of virtual learning is new to us. To create effective virtual learning environments for diverse learners, we need to jump out of our closed system mentality and change our mindset. We need to be more attentive to a variety of new and emerging issues of e-learning, and address them in the design stages of learning environments. That's the paradigm shift! In order to facilitate such a shift, and in response to the range of issues I saw in my research, I created a *Framework for E-learning* (see Figure 2).

Through my research I found that numerous factors help to create a meaningful virtual learning environment, and many of these factors are systemically interrelated and interdependent. A systemic understanding of these factors can help us create meaningful virtual learning environments. I have clustered these factors into eight dimensions: *institutional, management, technological, pedagogical, ethical, interface design, resource support*, and *evaluation* (see Figure 2).

Each of the eight dimensions has sub-dimensions or factors, and each factor can generate one or more issues or checklist questions.

Dimensions (Table 1) e.g., *1. Institutional*
Factors (Table 2) e.g., *1.3.2. Orientation*
Issues (Table 3) e.g., a checklist item or a Quality Assurance Criteria (QAC) item such as *Are instructor / tutor / technical staff available during online orientation?*

Table 1. Eight dimensions of e-learning environments

Dimensions	Descriptions
Institutional	The institutional category is concerned with issues of administrative affairs, academic affairs, faculty development and support, and student services related to e-learning.
Management	The management of e-learning refers to the maintenance of the learning environment and distribution of information.
Technological	The technological category examines issues of technology infrastructure in e-learning environments. This includes infrastructure planning, hardware and software.
Pedagogical	The pedagogical category refers to teaching and learning. This category addresses issues concerning content analysis, audience analysis, goal analysis, medium analysis, design approach, organization, and learning strategies.
Ethical	The ethical considerations of e-learning relate to social and political influences, cultural diversity, bias, geographical diversity, learner diversity, the digital divide, etiquette, and legal issues.
Interface design	Interface design refers to the overall look and feel of e-learning programs. Interface design categories encompass page and site design, content design for different devices, navigation, accessibility and usability testing.
Resource support	The resource support category examines the online student support and resources required to foster meaningful learning.
Evaluation	The evaluation of e-learning includes both assessment of learning and evaluation of the instructor, instruction and learning environment.

Table 2. Dimensions and factors of e-learning environments

	1. Institutional
1.1 Administrative Affairs	1.1.15. Needs Assessment
	1.1.16. Readiness Assessment (Financial, Infrastructure, Cultural and Content readiness)
	1.1.17. Organization and Change (Diffusion, Adoption and Implementation of Innovation)
	1.1.18. Implementation
	1.1.19. Budgeting and Return on Investment
	1.1.20. Partnerships with Other Institutions and Stakeholders
	1.1.21. Program and Course information Catalog (Academic Calendar, Course Schedule, Tuition, Fees, & Graduation)
	1.1.22. Marketing and Recruitment
	1.1.23. Admissions 1.1.24. Financial Aid
	1.1.25. Registration and Payment
	1.1.26. Information Technology Services
	1.1.27. Instructional Design and Media Services
	1.1.28. Graduation Transcripts and Grades
1.2 Academic Affairs	1.2.1 Accreditation 1.2.2 Policy 1.2.3 Instructional Quality 1.2.4 Faculty and Staff Support 1.2.5 Class Size, Workload and Compensation and Intellectual Property Rights

continued on following page

Table 2. Continued

1.3 Student Services	1.3.1 Pre-enrollment Services 1.3.2 Orientation 1.3.3 Faculty and Staff directories 1.3.4 Advising 1.3.5 Counseling 1.3.6 Learning Skills Development 1.3.7 Services for Students with Disabilities 1.3.8 Library Support 1.3.9 Bookstore 1.3.10 Tutorial Services 1.3.11 Mediation and Conflict Resolution 1.3.12 Social Support Network 1.3.13 Students Newsletter 1.3.14 Internship and Employment Services 1.3.15 Alumni Affairs 1.3.16 Other Services
2. Pedagogical	
2.1 Content Analysis	
2.3 Goal Analysis	
2.2 Audience Analysis	
2.4 Medium Analysis	
2.5 Design Approach	
2.6 Organization	
2.7 Learning Strategies	2.7.01 Presentation 2.7.02 Exhibits 2.7.03 Demonstration 2.7.04 Drill and Practice 2.7.05 Tutorials 2.7.06 Games 2.7.07 Story Telling 2.7.08 Simulations 2.7.09 Role-playing 2.7.10 Discussion 2.7.11 Interaction 2.7.12 Modeling 2.7.13 Facilitation 2.7.14 Collaboration 2.7.15 Debate 2.7.16 Field Trips 2.7.17 Apprenticeship 2.7.18 Case Studies 2.7.19 Generative Development 2.7.20 Motivation
3. Technological	
3.1 Infrastructure Planning (Technology Plan, Standards, Metadata, Learning Objects)	
3.2 Hardware	
3.3 Software (LMS, LCMS, Enterprise Application)	
4. Interface Design	
4.1 Page and Site Design	
4.2 Content Design	
4.3 Navigation	

continued on following page

Table 2. Continued

4.4 Accessibility	
4.5 Usability Testing	
5. Evaluation	
5.1 Assessment of Learners	
5.2 Evaluation of Instruction & Learning Environment	
5.3 Evaluation of the Program	
6. Management	
6.1 Maintenance of Learning Environment	
6.2 Distribution of Information	
7. Resource Support	
7.1 Online Support	7.1.1 Instructional/Counseling Support 7.1.2 Technical Support 7.1.3 Career Counseling Services 7.1.4 Other Online Support Services
7.2 Resources	7.2.1 Online Resources 7.2.2 Offline Resources
8. Ethical Considerations	
8.1 Social and Political Influence	
8.2 Cultural Diversity	
8.3 Bias	
8.4 Geographical Diversity	
8.5 Learner Diversity	
8.6 Digital Divide	
8.7 Etiquette	
8.8 Legal Issues	8.8.1 Privacy 8.8.2 Plagiarism 8.8.3 Copyright

The purpose of this Framework is to help us think through every aspect of what we are doing during the steps of the e-learning design process. Therefore, we should look at each of the eight dimensions or categories of this Framework (see Table 2 and Table 3), and show what questions (see checklist section) we should ask about each dimension as we design a flexible learning segment, which can be a lesson, a course or an entire program.

Eight Dimensions of E-Learning Environment

Each dimension of the framework is composed of a number of factors. Table 2 lists several factors under each dimension. It is important to note that the factors identified here by no means exhaustive. As we learn more about e-learning environments, more and more factors may be added to the list.

Table 3. E-learning feature review

E-Learning Feature	E-Learning Dimension	Quality Assurance Criteria (QACs)	Assessment Rating (Score Card)		
			Excellent	Sufficient	Deficient
Ease of Use	Institutional	Are instructor/tutor and technical staff available during online orientation?			
	Management	Does the course notify students about any changes in due dates or other course relevant matters such as server down?			
	Technological	Are students taught how to join, participate in, and leave a mailing list?			
	Pedagogical	Does the course provide a clear description what learners should do at every stage of the course?			
	Ethical	Does the course provide any guidance to learners on how to behave and post messages in online discussions so that their postings do not hurt others' feelings?			
	Interface design	How quickly can users find answers to the most frequently asked questions on the course site?			
	Resource support	Does the course provide clear guidelines to the learners on what support can and cannot be expected from a help line?			
	Evaluation	If learners are disconnected during an online test, can they log back and start from where they left off?			

There are questions similar to those in Table 3 that can be used to review how a feature such as *ease of use* can be made a part of an e-learning program. All these questions in Table 3 covering the eight e-learning dimensions point to one critical element, *is it really easy to use*? Therefore, for each feature we should explore as many issues as possible within the eight dimensions of the e-learning environment with that question in mind.

Issues/Questions used for E-Learning Environments

Each factor in Table 2 focuses on a specific aspect of an e-learning environment. One could ask, "What are the critical issues associated with many of these factors that can help in the design of meaningful e-learning environments?"

There may be numerous issues within each factor of each e-learning environment. These issues can be explored as *questions* that designers should ask themselves when planning an e-learning environment. Each e-learning project is unique. It is important to identify as many issues – in the form of questions – as possible for your own project by using the octagon framework. One way to identify critical issues is by putting each stakeholder group – such as learner, instructor, support staff, etc. – at the center of the framework and raising issues along the eight dimensions of e-learning from that group's perspective. This is important because the perspective on institutional issues, for instance, can change radically between the administrators' point of view and that of students. This way you can identify many critical issues and formulate questions that must be addressed in order to create a meaningful e-learning experience for your particular group. By repeating the same process for other stakeholder groups, you can generate a comprehensive list of issues/questions for your project.

As indicated previously, the purpose of this Framework is to help us think through every aspect of what we are doing during the steps of the e-learning design process when change and revision are far less costly. Therefore, it is important to review each of the eight dimensions of this Framework, and explore what questions we should ask about each dimension as we design an e-learning environment segment, which can be a *learning feature, a lesson, a course,* or an *entire program.*

USING THE FRAMEWORK FOR EVALUATION

The Framework can also serve as a diagnostic tool for a holistic evaluation of an e-learning environment. In this section, an e-learning *feature* is reviewed from the perspectives of quality assurance criteria and assessment rating.

Quality Assurance Criteria and Assessment Rating

Quality Assurance Criteria items (QACs) are specific questions assessing the quality and utility of e-learning features and products. QAC items represent the key issues within each dimension of the e-learning environment (i.e., pedagogical checklist items, technological checklist items, etc.). It may be challenging to come up with questions for some dimensions of the Framework for some specific stages of the e-learning design process, given the interrelationship among the characteristics of the eight dimensions. In such situations, I recommend you continue with other dimensions and return to the problematic ones later. Some questions may appear to be a good fit for more than one dimension. You may come up with or find some QAC questions not fitting into any of the eight dimensions of the framework—that's ok—we can use them as long they are critical and relevant for evaluating e-learning.

In addition to structured questions (i.e., quantitative or hard data) in the QAC, for a comprehensive program evaluation of e-learning, it is necessary to gather qualitative or "soft data," such as constructive comments and feedback from stakeholders, reviews of documents, and site visits.

The *Assessment Rating* is used as a Score Card for the evaluation of e-learning features and products. The QAC questions support the assessment of a program's progress in completing the critical e-learning activities and an *Excellent-Sufficient-Deficient* rating is used as Assessment Rating (Score Card).

- **Excellent:** Yes, the issue(s) discussed in the question are well-addressed.
- **Sufficient:** Yes, the issue(s) discussed in the question are partially-addressed.
- **Deficient:** No, the issue(s) discussed in the question are not-addressed.

How do you go about selecting a rating of *excellent, sufficient* or *deficient*? Is there an established benchmark to use? In some instances, there is. If there is an existing benchmark used by the institution or program being reviewed, I suggest that you should use it. The ultimate intention is to judge the status of a product in the context in which it is being used, using the best possible information available. Some benchmark criteria may not always be fully applicable to some institutional contexts. Even so, judgment will always be subjective. The Framework-guided review encourages the most transparent, unbiased, and reasonable judgment in the review of a product.

REVIEW OF E-LEARNING FEATURES WITH THE FRAMEWORK

As indicated earlier, all e-learning features must be designed to help students achieve their learning goals. An e-learning program consisting of well-designed instructional features can lead to its success. The eight dimensions of the e-learning framework can identify the critical issues to be dealt with in a particular e-learning environment, and provide guidance on addressing them.

We can improve the effectiveness of an e-learning feature by answering the questions raised in the framework. For example, *ease of use* is one of most important features in an e-learning environment. To demonstrate, in Table 3, only one e-learning feature (i.e., *ease of use*) is reviewed for its effectiveness in a course from the perspective of each of the eight dimensions for one of the stakeholder groups (i.e., students). Similar reviews can be conducted for other stakeholder groups (i.e., instructors, technical staff, etc.).

Framework Applicable to Massive Open Online Courses (MOOCs)

With the emergence of new communication and computing technologies, we are becoming increasingly accustomed to new buzzwords to describe different forms of technology-based learning. One of the latest buzzwords is "MOOC," short for "Massive Open Online Course" (Corbeil, Corbeil & Khan, 2016).

With the introduction of a new wave of online delivery methods, you may wonder, whatever happened to the term "e-learning?" To assure you, e-learning is still alive and will be with us, in one form or another, for all time. If the "e" in e-learning is short for "electronic," then, as long as media is delivered electronically, e-learning will continue to exist in technology-based education. Just as the term *Electronic Performance Support Systems* (EPSS), first coined in 1991, is still in active use today, e-learning is also alive and well, but with extended capabilities and identities. One of its most recent manifestations is the MOOC, the massive open online course designed to offer large-scale, free education courses to the masses (Milheim, 2013).

While there are benefits to this form of delivery, MOOCs currently face several challenges. Milheim (2013) cites four major problems associated with MOOCs: (1) high dropout rates; (2) lack of a viable financial model; (3) credentialing; and (4) academic integrity. However, failure in e-learning courses is more often associated with poor execution of some aspects of the initial project design and dissemination/implementation (Romizowski, 2004).

Figure 3. E-learning framework applicable to MOOCs

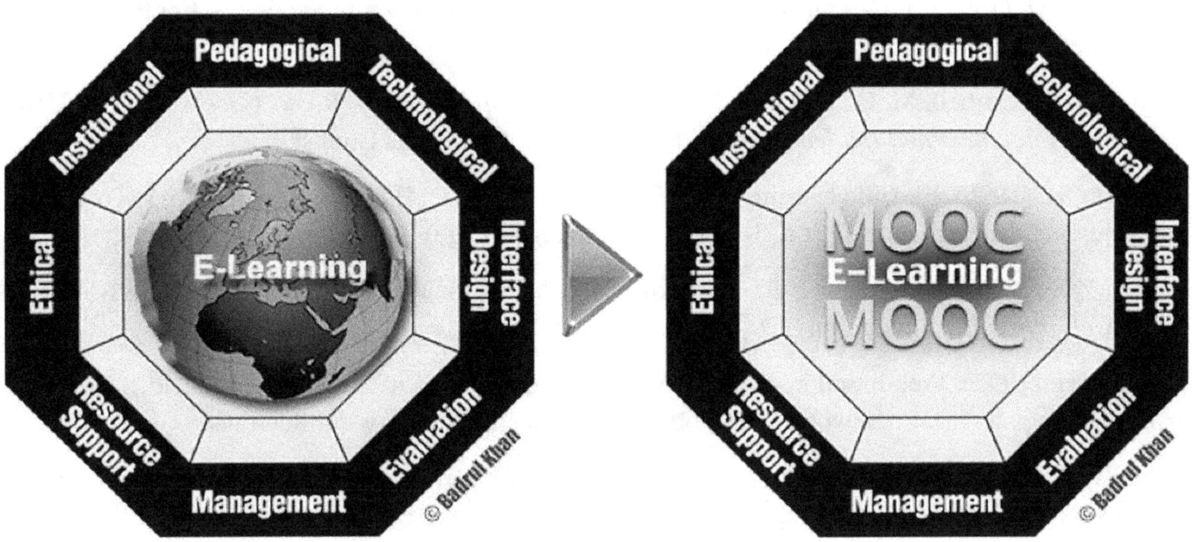

By their definition, MOOCs are delivered through an open and distributed e-learning environment. The design, development, implementation, and evaluation of open and distributed learning systems, such as MOOCs, requires a thoughtful analysis and investigation of how to use the attributes and resources of the Internet and digital technologies in concert with instructional design principles and issues important to various dimensions of online learning environments (Khan, 2012). The e-learning framework (http://BadrulKhan.com/framework) which was developed in 1997 for the book *Web-Based Instruction* (Khan, 2005) is applicable to MOOCs, as a form of WBI. Various factors discussed in the eight dimensions of the framework can provide guidance in the design, development, delivery, and evaluation of open and distributed learning environments such as MOOCs (see Figure 3).

CONCLUSION

Designing open and distributed learning systems for globally diverse learners is challenging; however, as more and more institutions offer flexible learning to students worldwide, we will become more knowledgeable about what works and what does not work. We should try to accommodate the needs of diverse learners by asking critical questions along the eight dimensions of the Framework. The questions may vary based on the different features of each flexible learning system. The more issues – in the form of checklist questions – within the eight categories of the Framework we explore, the more meaningful and supportive is the learning environment we can create. Given our specific contexts, we may not be able to address all issues within the eight categories of the Framework, but we should address as many as we can in order to provide increased flexibility for learners.

Badrul H. Khan
McWeadon Education, USA

REFERENCES

Banathy, B. H. (1991). *Systems designs of education: A journey to create the future*. Englewood Cliffs, NJ: Educational Technology Publications.

Corbeil, J. R., Corbeil, M. E., & Khan, B. H. (2016). *The MOOC Case Book: Case Studies in MOOC Design, Development and Implementation*. Ronkonkoma, NY: Linus Books.

Ellington, H. (1995). Flexible learning, your flexible friend. In C. Bell, M. Bowden, & A. Trott (Eds.), *Implementing flexible learning* (pp. 3–13). London: Kogan Page.

Jones, M. G., & Farquhar, J. D. (1997). User interface design for Web-based instruction. In B. H. Khan (Ed.), *Web-based instruction* (pp. 239–244). Academic Press.

Khan, B. H. (1997). Web-based instruction: What is it and why is it? In B. H. Khan (Ed.), *Web-based instruction* (pp. 5–18). Englewood Cliffs, NJ: Educational Technology Publications.

Khan, B. H. (Ed.). (2012). *User Interface Design for Virtual Environments: Challenges and Advances*. Hershey, PA: IGI Global Publishing. doi:10.4018/978-1-61350-516-8

Khan, B. H., Cataldo, L., Bennett, R., & Paratore, S. (2007). Obstacles encountered during e-learning. In B. H. Khan (Ed.), *Flexible learning in an informaiton society* (pp. 307–320). Hershey, PA: Information Science Publishing. doi:10.4018/978-1-59904-325-8

Khan, B. H., & Vega, R. (1997). Factors to consider when evaluating a Web-based instruction course: A survey. In B. H. Khan (Ed.), *Web-based instruction* (pp. 375–380). Englewood Cliffs, NJ: Educational Technology Publications.

Krauth, B. (1998). Distance learning: The instructional strategy of the decade. In G. P. Connick (Ed.), *The distance learner's guide*. Upper Saddle River, NJ: Prentice Hall.

Land, S. M., & Hannafin, M. J. (1997). Patterns of understanding with open-ended learning environments: A qualitative study. *Educational Technology Research and Development*, *45*(2), 47–73. doi:10.1007/BF02299524

Milheim, W. D. (2013, May-June). Massive Open Online Courses (MOOCs): Current applications and future potential. *Educational Technology*, 38–42.

Moore, M. G. (1998). Introduction. In C. C. Gibson (Ed.), *Distance learners in higher education*. Madison, WI: Atwood Publishing.

Morrison, J. L., & Khan, B. H. (2003). The global e-learning framework: An interview with Badrul Khan. *The Technology Source*. A Publication of the Michigan Virtual University. Retrieved from http://technologysource.org/article/global_elearning_framework/

Relan, A., & Gillani, B. B. (1997). Web-based instruction and traditional classroom: Similarities and differences. In B. H. Khan (Ed.), *Web-based instruction* (pp. 41–46). Englewood Cliffs, NJ: Educational Technology Publications.

Ritchie, D. C., & Hoffman, B. (1997). Incorporating instructional design principles with the World Wide Web. In B. H. Khan (Ed.), *Web-based instruction* (pp. 135–138). Englewood Cliffs, NJ: Educational Technology Publications.

Romiszowski, A. J. (2004). How's the e-learning, baby? Factors leading to success or failure of an educational technology innovation. *Educational Technology*, *44*(1), 5–27.

Saltzbert, S., & Polyson, S. (1995, September). Distributed learning on the World Wide Web. *Syllabus*, *9*(1), 10–12.

Smith, H. L., & Khan, B. H. (2007). Program Satisfaction survey instrument for online students. In B. H. Khan (Ed.), *Flexible learning*. Englewood Cliffs, NJ: Educational Technology Publications.

Taylor, A. (2014). A look at web-based instruction today: An interview with Badrul Khan, Part 1. *eLearn Magazine*. Retrieved from http://elearnmag.acm.org/archive.cfm?aid=2590180

Chapter 1
Designing Meaningful Learning Environments in a Work-Integrated-Learning Course Using a DOCC Design

Kathy Jordan
RMIT University, Australia

Jennifer Elsden-Clifton
RMIT University, Australia

ABSTRACT

As Higher Education increasingly moving towards a plethora of blended and fully online learning, questions are raised around the space and place of Work-Integrated Learning (WIL). This chapter reports on one institution's efforts to design and deliver a WIL course in a Teacher Education program adopting an open and distributed framework. The redesigned course, Orientation to Teaching, was a first year course in a Bachelor of Education (Primary) program at RMIT University, Melbourne, Australia. The redesign of the course was underpinned by a Distributed Open Collaborative Course (DOCC) design and as the workplace also became the site of learning, the theory of effective WIL curriculum (Orrell, 2011) also informed the design. This chapter examines the complexity of DOCC design in WIL contexts and uses Khan's 8 dimensions to frame the discussion.

INTRODUCTION

Where once online learning was the exception and the domain of distance education and open learning, it is fast becoming the norm within higher education as institutions seek to design and deliver courses that meet the needs of their learners. This rapid growth has been aided by the development of educational technologies that enable courses to be more readily delivered through Learning Management Systems (LMS) and an accompanying suite of computer applications. There has also been a proliferation of online

DOI: 10.4018/978-1-5225-0466-5.ch001

learning environments including fully online courses, blended courses that provide "the best of both" (Young, 2002), and variations of open and distributed courses such as Massive Open Online Courses (MOOCs).

The history of MOOCs stems from the Open Education Resources (OER) movement of the late 1990s, the term MOOC being coined by Dave Cormier in 2008 (Reilly, 2013). More recently, the New York Times declared 2012 'The Year of the MOOC' (Reilly, 2013). Since their beginnings, MOOCs have continued to evolve, and De Coutere (2014) laments that there is now an "alphabet soup of acronyms" including "mini-MOOC, BOOC (big open online course), MOOD (massive open online discussion), SMOC (synchronous massive online course), SPOC (small private online courses), and ROOC (regional open online course)" (p. 22). Large, commercially developed courses, delivered through companies such as Coursera, are now often referred to as xMOOCs, while those that involve more student-generated content using connectivist pedagogy are referred to as cMOOCs (the 'c' standing for connectivist). Another recent development has been the Distributed Open Collaborative Course (DOCC) in which expertise is distributed across the membership of the community and content is appropriated and adapted by the users (students and teachers) to suit their own learning context (Juhasz & Balsamo, 2012).

One of the main reasons MOOCs have gained such attention is due to their capacity to seemingly provide open access to "all", including those that traditionally do not attend tertiary education institutions or those who would otherwise not have the opportunity. MOOCs are also perceived as simple, without large outlay and are designed to teach an infinite number of learners (Baggaley, 2013; Khalil & Ebner, 2013). The research around MOOCs has raised a number of issues, as Reilly (2013) suggests, "the MOOC learning environment presents unique challenges to course design, delivery and pedagogy" (p. 1309). While having large enrolments, MOOCs have very low completion rates, as well as low learner engagement and low levels of interaction between the learner and instructor (Khalil & Ebner, 2013). Many of these issues arise because MOOCs are underpinned by the assumption that learners are autonomous and self-motivated and there is little capacity in the MOOC platforms for teacher feedback. There has also been concerns around the assumption of access for "all" as MOOCs still require internet access and English language proficiency. There are also significant concerns around accreditation (intellectual property, cheating, licensing and credentialing) that have yet to be resolved.

As Higher Education continues to develop online learning environments, and favours the open and distributed design and delivery of courses such as MOOCs, cMOOCs and DOCCs, the question of where this leaves Work-Integrated Learning (WIL) courses becomes pertinent. WIL courses are those in which the workplace becomes a site of learning, and which aim to improve employability and assist in the transition from university to work (Brimble & Freudenberg, 2010). In countries such as Australia, WIL is becoming increasingly important in universities as governments see it as a means to prepare a future workforce for a changing economy. Therefore, this research seeks to explore the questions "How can we design and deliver an effective WIL learning environment?" What principles should frame our decision-making? What might a WIL course look like within an online, open, and distributed model? What can we learn from such a redesign?

This chapter provides a case study of one institution's efforts to design and deliver a WIL course in a Teacher Education context that adopts an open and distributed framework. The course, *Orientation to Teaching*, is a first year course in a four year Bachelor of Education Program, at RMIT University, Melbourne, Australia. The course redesign was informed by the design features of a DOCC alongside effective WIL principles and Khan's 8 dimensional e-learning framework.

BACKGROUND

To inform this case study, a literature review will examine the interplay between the three broad conceptual fields: DOCC pedagogical design, effective WIL principles and Khan's 8 dimensions. Each of these fields informed the design and delivery of the course *Orientation to Teaching* and are discussed in turn, with Khan's 8 dimensions used to structure the discussion of the case study.

Work-Integrated-Learning in Higher Education Contexts

The term Work-Integrated-Learning (WIL) emerged in the 1990s. This term is problematic as different disciplines traditionally use different terms to describe a similar process such as clinical placement, practicum, work engagement etc. (Orrell, 2011). Commonly WIL is used to describe programs in which students "engage with workplaces and communities as a formal part of their studies" (Orrell, 2011, p. 1). The broad purposes of WIL is to foster work readiness, employability and to encourage life-long learning (Billet, 2009; Orrell, 2011). While being employable does refer to having capabilities required by employers, WIL is more than just developing the knowledge and skills to readily transition to the workplace. WIL is also about engaging in and reflecting on practice (Billet, 2009) as well as generating new ways of knowing within and through practice. One of the underlying assumptions of WIL is that students will gain knowledge and skills particular to the workplace that they cannot readily achieve in formal classrooms that could be vital for developing professional identities.

WIL programs were once somewhat invisible in higher education, but have expanded in Australia, supported by government interest in students gaining work-related experiences in order to be more employable and work-ready. Australia has a national body, the Australian Collaborative Education Network (ACEN) that shares knowledge around WIL. Under this guidance, universities in Australia have a set of national attributes around WIL. There is now a significant body of research and scholarship involving WIL, and a new epistemology is emerging.

Partnerships, and having respect for stakeholders' needs, their perspectives and understandings, are seen as important to WIL. This has become more apparent as the challenge of finding workplace placements for students is becoming increasingly difficult (especially when accrediting bodies mandate it, as is the case with Teacher Education). Another major challenge is how to integrate WIL practice settings and university teaching. There is concern that WIL can be ad hoc and that WIL needs to be embedded throughout a program. Rather than just experiencing the workplace, students need to be able to apply what has been learnt in university in the workplace setting. This involves the intentional integration of theory and practice knowledge. To do so, students need to be agents; they need to have a set of personal capacities that enable them to judge, to reflect, and to make improvements or transform their practice (Billett, 2009).

Orrell (2011) was commissioned by the Office of Learning and Teaching (an Australian Government initiative) to identify good practices in WIL in Australia. Following her review of 28 funded studies and final reports, she suggested that there are a number of key principles to successful WIL programs including institutional, educational and partnership elements. These have informed the redesign of the *Orientation to Teaching* course and are outlined in Table 1.

Table 1. Essential principles for successful WIL

Institutional	• Shared vision of WIL in university • Recognition of WIL in university including adequate resourcing • Recognition that university and workplace both have roles in learning • Use existing services
Educational	• Induct and prepare students for workplace • Provide structured, reflective, self/peer learning experiences • Provide elements of risk to learning experiences • Use technology to support WIL learning
Partnerships	• Ensure workplace site familiar with prior university learning • Include all stakeholders in WIL development • Provide professional learning for workplace and university staff • Build mature relationships with workplace (mutual benefit)

WIL in Teacher Education

Australia has a large number of Teacher Education programs. In 2014 there were 450 programs delivered across 48 providers, including 43 universities (TEMAG, 2014). In 2013 79,623 students were enrolled in teacher education in 2013 (TEMAG, 2014). In 2011, the Australian Government introduced a national approach to accreditation for Teacher Education regulated by the Australian Institute for Teaching and School Leadership (AITSL). Teacher Education providers are required to meet a set of program standards around development, structure and delivery, as well as student selection. They also need to document the practicum or WIL component of their programs, including; partnership relationship with schools, the nature and length of practicum, as well as the learning activities and assessment undertaken, measured against a set of graduate level standards. Practicum needs to consist of at least 80 days for undergraduate programs and 60 days for graduate entry and must involve "well-structured, supervised and assessed teaching practice in schools" (AITSL, 2011, p. 15). Practicum takes multiple forms across universities from block type placements in which students are sent to schools for a set number of weeks at a time, to others where students are placed one day a week over a period of time and some offer internships and more extended placements. There are also examples of virtual placements, overseas placements and practicum in alternative educational settings.

There is a wealth of research that acknowledges the benefits of placement and the qualities that contribute to effective WIL. For instance, the *Top of the Class* report (Australian Parliament House of Representatives Standing Committee on Education and Vocational Training, 2007) argues that a quality practicum in Teacher Education includes: integrating theory and professional practice across a program, involves partnerships, has clear and progressive stages for skill, knowledge, and disposition development, provides diverse school experiences, assesses pre-service teacher activity and performance, involves resource needs analysis, is flexible and fosters ongoing evaluation.

Although WIL or the practicum is seen as an essential part of becoming a teacher, vital for the development of practical skills in teaching and the foundation of quality teacher education (Ure, Gough & Newton, 2009), it is a site of contestation between pre-service teachers, teacher mentors, schools, governments and universities. Often underpinning these debates is criticism around how universities conceive of practicum. There are numerous national reports into Teacher Education that have focused attention on the perceived variability and questionable quality of WIL programs in Australia. In 2007, the Australian Parliament House of Representatives Standing Committee on Education and Vocational

Training tabled the *Top of the Class* report on the inquiry into Teacher Education. In this report, it iterated that "high quality placements for school-based professional experience are a critical component of teacher education courses" (p. 67) but that there was little consensus around "how much practicum there should be, when practicum should begin and the best structure for practicum" (p. 67). Furthermore, it commented that, "the persistence of the problems with practicum can largely be attributed to the current division of responsibilities for delivering teacher education and the lack of a sense of shared responsibility between the major parties" (p. 75). The report raised a number of concerns around practicum. These included: difficulty in finding placements (as there is no obligation for schools to offer places); difficulty in finding Teacher Mentors who will supervise students while on practicum (teachers receive little payment and have many other obligations); issues about the quality of Teacher Mentors (as universities have little choice); concerns about the lack of connection between practicum and theoretical components; issues around communication between university and schools; lack of support of students by the university while on practicum; and a lack of clear expectations by the university to practicum sites of what the practicum should involve.

More recently, the Teacher Education Ministerial Advisory Group (TEMAG) Report *Action Now: Classroom Ready Teachers* was released which identified a number of key directions, key proposals and recommendations similar to that of the earlier report (2014). Again, the importance of forming partnerships between providers and schools was a key finding, so too the need to integrate theory and practice. One of its 38 recommendations was that universities form partnerships with schools to deliver practicum, a shift in policy direction.

Similar concerns from a US perspective were raised by Zeichner (2010), who suggested that universities tend to conceive of practicum as an administrative task rather than one around the learning needs of the pre-service teacher. He suggests that universities often have very little involvement in the details of the practicum and leave these to be worked out between pre-service teachers and Teacher Mentors. He suggests that sessional or part-time university staff are more often than not directly involved in the practicum. It is important to note however that Zeichner (2010) also criticises schools for having little knowledge about what happens at the university, and raises a number of other concerns including the role of Teacher Mentors in the practicum, arguing that they receive little acknowledgement and monetary reward for their efforts.

Given this breadth of research, Teacher Education has long been challenged to reconceptualise the connection between university-based coursework and the school-based practicum (Grossman, Hammerness & McDonald, 2009). Yet, Teacher Education has thus far struggled to tackle the redesign of courses to better build this connection (Grossman et al, 2009; Darling-Hammond, 2006). The case study in this chapter will argue that the DOCC model has potential to move towards a stronger theory/practicum design and address many of the issues identified by the research, while also meeting new policy directions.

Distributed Open Collaborate Courses (DOCCs)

Distributed Open Collaborate Courses (DOCCs) are a remodelling of the Massive Open Online Courses (MOOCs). The term DOCC was first used by FemTechNet (a network of scholars, artists, students who work in and around the borders of technology, science and feminism) to describe an alternative model to the MOOC. Currently the DOCC has only been associated with FemTechNet and is underpinned by feminist theory. Their design focussed on processes of collaboration, power sharing and diversity of opinion and experience (Juhasz & Balsamo, 2012). As opposed to a MOOC, Juhasz and Balsamo argue

Table 2. Representation of the principles utilised in a DOCC design

Principles	DOCC Design
Commitment to shared power	Created collaboratively by staff from multiple institutions – notion of distributed expertise
Commitment to diverse opinion and experience	Shared content production – each nodal course produced by one institution, who knows the students, institution, location and discipline, but courses would have credit
Understanding that technology can enable interaction	Use of technology to enable collaboration and course delivery
Commitment to collaboration	Connected collaborative learning via nodal or connected courses

that "the fundamental difference is that a DOCC recognises and is built on the understanding that expertise is distributed throughout a network, among participants situated in diverse institutional contexts, within diverse material, geographic, and national settings" (2012, p. 9).

Whereas a MOOC is generally structured around a single course associated with one institution and led by one or two leaders with a large ratio of teacher to student, the DOCC model centres on connected collaborative learning. It is similar to a cMOOC; however, the DOCC involves a number of institutions that collaborate to deliver a series of connected courses around a shared theme. Open learning resources are created collaboratively and underpinned by an understanding of distributed expertise, not that of just teacher to student but student to teacher and student to student.

The first DOCC in 2013, *Feminist Dialogues on Technology,* involved instructors at 15 universities and colleges. Its structure had each participating institution teaching a 'nodal course' designed to suit their particular students, institution, location and discipline (Juhasz & Balsamo, 2012). All learning materials were also made available to self-directed learners (those not associated with one of participating institutions) through the website. According to Losh (2014), despite its grounding in critical pedagogy or radical pedagogy, the course "placed value on adopting relatively conservative approaches in some fundamental areas" (p. 147). For example the course wanted all those involved to work together, to engage, and to have shared experiences such as those associated with conventional classrooms, because of the belief that a shared physical space and place enables a community to develop, and where ideas could be built and recorded (Losh, 2014). Some of the key design principles are outlined in Table 2:

Alongside the rise of online, blended learning and models such as MOOCs and DOCCS, there have also been a number of planning, implementation and evaluation frameworks developed to critique the quality of these learning environments. In this chapter's case study Khan's (2005) eight dimensional e-learning framework was used to plan, evaluate and critically analyse the DOCC online environment that was designed to facilitate the WIL context of the course.

Khan's E-Learning Framework

There have been several attempts to create models, frameworks and/or criteria to evaluate the quality of online learning environments. Although each has merits, this case study draws upon the framework developed by Khan to establish a "comprehensive review system to get a real picture of what works, what doesn't and where needs improvement" (2008, p.10). The eight dimensions of this framework include:

1. **Pedagogical:** Refers to teaching and learning. This dimension addresses issues concerning *content, audiences, goal* and *media analysis; design approach; organization and methods and strategies* of e-learning environments.
2. **Technological:** Examines issues of technology infrastructure in e-learning environments. This includes *infrastructure planning, hardware* and *software.*
3. **Interface Design:** Refers to the overall look and feel of e-learning programs. The interface design dimension encompasses *page and site design, content design, navigation,* and *usability testing.*
4. **Evaluation:** Includes both *assessment of learners, and evaluation of the instruction* and *learning environment.*
5. **Management:** Refers to *maintenance of* the *learning environment* and *distribution of information.*
6. **Resource Support:** Examines the *online support* and *resources* required to foster meaningful learning environments.
7. **Ethical:** Relates to *social and political influence, cultural diversity, bias, geographical diversity, learner diversity, information accessibility, etiquette,* and *the legal issues.*
8. **Institutional:** Issues of *administrative affairs, academic affairs* and *student services* related to e-learning (Khan, 2008, p, 2).

RESEARCH DESIGN

This chapter presents a case study of one university's endeavour to design and delivery a WIL course framed by Khan's dimensions and informed by WIL and DOCC principles. Case study is an approach or research method that focuses on an in-depth, up-close, detailed examination of a particular entity or event at a particular time. This chapter presents a case study of a new WIL course being implemented into the first year of the Bachelor of Education primary program, in the School of Education at RMIT University, Melbourne Australia. The School of Education is one of a number of initial Teacher Education providers in Victoria, Australia. Each year the School organises over 2,000 practicum placements in approximately 450 primary schools, 100 secondary schools and 450 early childhood settings. In 2014, the School introduced a new model of practicum to the Bachelor of Education (Primary) program as part of the reaccreditation process. One of the first year courses, *Orientation to Teaching,* serves as the case study for this chapter. This course was delivered in Semester 1, 2014 to 210 pre-service teachers who were predominantly preparing to be generalist primary school teachers; the majority of whom were female, aged between 18 to 39 years, Australian-born and had English as their language spoken at home (81.3%).

Data for this case study was collected from a range of sources. It draws upon pre-service teacher survey data of their perceptions of the course, with particular attention on the design and delivery of the course. The instrument asked the pre-service teachers to indicate to what extent a listed set of design features mattered to them using a four-point scale (a lot, some, a little, not at all). Findings were then analysed and key trends identified. Focus group data was also drawn upon, which used open-ended questions to explore pre-service perceptions of the course design and delivery. Multiple focus groups were organised and coordinated by an independent facilitator who audiotaped discussions, later transcribing and then coding the findings. Some 42 pre-service teachers (approximately 18%) who had completed the course *Orientation to Teaching* completed the survey and 68 (approximately 32%) pre-service teachers participated in focus group discussions. Detailed findings from both the survey and the focus groups have been reported elsewhere (Authors, 2015). Artifacts from the course itself, including the course description and learning activities were also collected to provide depth to this case study. The rest of the chapter reports on the case study.

COURSE DESIGN AND DEVELOPMENT

Khan's (2008) eight dimensions generates a number of questions for planning, implementing and evaluating an online environment that can be used by course designers and were used as a guiding framework for this case study. To begin with, each of the dimensions were used as a springboard to tease out and identify issues; these issues were then presented in the form of questions relevant to the WIL course. These are shown in Table 3. Then each of the dimensions was used to frame the case study presented in the ensuing discussion.

These key questions were then used to frame the course redesign. Each dimension will be discussed in turn below. For each dimension there will be discussion around two foci, firstly, the discussion of how the course *Orientation to Teaching* addressed the dimension, and secondly, data from the pre-service teachers' survey and focus group will be used to support this discussion.

Institutional Dimension

To align with the instructionally effective WIL principles outlined in Table 1, a decision to adopt a new approach to WIL in the School was taken. Concerns about WIL were not new in the School; they often featured in staff conversations especially around practicum time when a number of issues resurfaced. These included: issues around difficulty and time investment in finding placements; anxiety of pre-service teachers; cost and workload issues around visiting students on practicum; how to support pre-service teachers when on practicum; assessment in WIL courses; and the value assigned to placement courses given they were previously zero credit point courses (ungraded). The need to accredit programs in line with new national requirements became the impetus, as well as the appointment of a staff member to oversee the review of WIL courses.

A new model was then drafted. The new model was influenced by a number of factors including the concerns with practicum previously discussed, the accreditation requirements that required providers to form partnerships with schools, and that graduates need to meet a set of professional standards (knowledge, skills and dispositions). Also influencing the new model was the WIL literature that proposed that WIL courses should provide authentic experiences and involve active, reflective and challenging learning experiences (Orrell, 2011). So too, government reports such as TEMAG (2014) that advocate a more practical focus. The working party that developed the model also consulted with schools and pre-service teachers, conducting a survey of their expectations of WIL.

The new model proposed that WIL courses be embedded within programs and become assessable (graded). Courses in the first and second year of the Bachelor of Education program would be site-based in schools so as to interconnect theory and practice, and would be taught by practising teachers. These features were a significant departure from previous practice and raised the most discussion. The model was then opened for staff discussion for six months to give voice to diversity in opinion, a principle highly valued in feminist pedagogy. Various aspects of the model were redefined in response to feedback, although the core elements of shared responsibility, site-based course work and learning experiences that connected theory and practice remained.

Table 3. Planning considerations using Khan's eight principles

Dimensions	Some Questions to Consider, Drawing on WIL and Feminist Principles
Institutional (administrative, academic and student)	• Is the School of Education ready for such a change in the way it designs and delivers WIL courses? • Have we built a financial and pedagogical case for change to the Head of School? To staff? To pre-service teachers? To our wider partners? • How do we establish (and then sustain) real partnerships with schools needed to make this redesign work? Given feminist principles, how will power be distributed among the partnership? Will there be a hierarchy? • How will we foster collaboration and shared responsibility with our partners? What professional learning will our partners need in the first instance? Later? • What does AITSL, our accrediting body, require in terms of WIL? In terms of partnerships? Do we meet their requirements? • How will we orientate our pre-service teachers to this new WIL course? How will our pre-practicum briefings prepare pre-service teachers for their roles and responsibilities when undertaking this WIL course? • Have we got WIL processes and policies in place?
Pedagogical (teaching and learning)	• What are the course requirements for a WIL course? In relation to RMIT? Best practice? Our accrediting body? • What are the course objectives and outcomes? What assessment strategies will we use to target these objectives and assessment? And assess against which Professional Standards? • Given that a WIL course should prepare students for the workplace, what knowledge, skills and dispositions will this course focus on? How will this course facilitate work readiness? How will we know if it has been achieved? • What specific teaching strategies will we employ in this course? For example, flipped classroom, podcasts, scenarios, text-based instruction? Why or why not? • What learning devices will be use? Why these and not others? Given the literature says that learning should be active, structured, authentic, reflective/ self and peer, how can we in-build these into the course? For example, what audits? What evaluations? What reflections? What real observations in classrooms, discussions with Teacher Mentors, school principals, other staff? • How will we build on prior learning from previous WIL courses? Will we use goal setting, if so, what form? • How will we build risk-taking rather than comfort? • How can we 'best' deliver this course? Is the university site appropriate? What about a school site? What are the advantages? The logistics? • How can we involve practising teachers in the design, implementation and evaluation of this course? • How will the content foster diversity in opinion as well as experience?
Technological (infrastructure, hardware and software)	• What LMS will we use to deliver this course? What are the relative advantages of Blackboard and Google Sites? Will they provide access to pre-service teachers and schools? Are they both easy to use by multiple stakeholders? Can a range of educational tools be embedded? • What technologies will we use to support effective learning? • What educational-specific applications will we use? How will we choose them? To what extent will decision-making be influenced by pedagogical objectives? Cost? Accessibility? • What general-type applications will we use? Are there other purposes at play here? What about length of learning experience and quality of learning experience? • What technologies will students use in this course? Why?
Interface design (look and feel)	• What broad approaches will we adopt to course design, site and page layout? • Who will support user testing of the site? • How will users interact with the Google Site?
Evaluation (learners and learning environment)	• How will we assess the effectiveness of this course? • What data collection will we collect? How? • What feedback do we want to receive from pre-service teachers? From Teacher Mentors in schools?
Management (learning environment and information)	• Who will design the course? Produce course content? Who will distribute? • Who will teach this course? Why or why not? • To what extent is staffing influenced by practical skills? • How do students upload course assessments securely? • Given there are over 200 students in this course, what scheduling requirements do we need to consider and which are more important? • What will this course cost, to design, implement and evaluate? • Who manages the content once it is uploaded and live? Who provides additional feedback, resources, hints, models if needed to be pedagogical effective?
Resource support	• Where will we avail ourselves of technical support? Students? • What online resources can we utilise in this course e.g. government agencies? • How can we encourage our partners to be involved in resource development?
Ethical (recognition of diversity)	• How will we design and deliver this course to recognise and validate that schools/ sites are diverse? • How will we ensure that this course caters for all students including the mature aged and international students? • Have we ensured that the course acknowledges its origins – its bias and prejudices? • Does the course enable ease of access to students with different levels of access and internet speeds? • How will we encourage pre-service teachers to adopt a professional relationship with their Teacher Mentor and their peers?

Partnerships were key to the new approach to WIL, alongside the desire to build a culture of shared responsibility for Teacher Education (Orrell, 2011). This was a departure from previous placement partnerships which had been similar to that described by Zeichner (2010) as, a relationship of administrative convenience. Forming authentic partnerships where they had not previously been present was approached as a long-term objective. Numerous meetings were held with school principals and Teacher Mentors to explore the proposed new model and to resolve any practical issues. Schools were overwhelmingly supportive of the approach, with some principals commenting that they thought the new model would better prepare graduates for the workplace. Forming and sustaining partnerships is an ongoing commitment by the School, and one that is recognised to have its challenges.

A number of processes were then developed and put into place to support the new WIL model and its DOCC approach to course design and delivery. For example, processes were developed to inform pre-service teachers about the new model and their roles and responsibilities on practicum. Key processes were also developed to create more open communication channels with partner schools, previously seen as a concern (Zeichner, 2010). This communication included summaries of programs and courses, snapshots of graduate professional standards, and prepared handbooks.

Pedagogical Dimension

When designing and delivering any new course, a large number of pedagogical decisions need to be made. For ease of discussion, these have been grouped into several categories:

Objectives and Outcomes

One of the initial decisions was determining the pedagogical priorities, learning objectives and the learning outcomes and how these aligned with the graduate professional standards and progression of learning skills. Influencing this decision was the principles of effective WIL curriculum, which emphasised the need for WIL courses to prepare work-ready graduates (Orrell, 2011). Therefore, this course focused on introducing students to schools and foundational skills of teaching.

Learning Framework

The pedagogical approach of flipped learning was chosen. The concept of a flipped-classroom, in its simplest form, involves moving key content and concepts outside the tutorials/lecture time, to allow for more classroom time for "active learning, including application of content in the form of case studies, discussions, or simulation experiences" (See & Conry, 2014, p. 585). Students were going to be required to engage with core content, including viewing and analysing YouTube videos, viewing podcasts and simulations and completing 'audits of practice', prior to attending the workshop. While this decision was made on pedagogical grounds, it was also influenced by pragmatic considerations. As around 200 pre-service teachers would be placed in 14 primary schools, they needed to be fully prepared for these experiences and as well having acquired the necessary knowledge and skills to learn through this experience. A flipped approach seemed to offer the most suitable framework for these learning opportunities. For instance, pre-service teachers complete a classroom-based audit: *What does your classroom say?* where they are required to compare and contrast images of classrooms with the actual classroom they are placed in. This data was then used as the basis of the on-site tutorial.

Another key decision was to pair (buddy) pre-service teachers together, and require them to undertake some peer learning activities. Doing so would not only provide collaborative learning experiences (valued by both WIL and feminist theory) but would also provide a supportive learning environment, and therefore support their transition to university and to schools. Feedback from pre-service students in focus group discussion suggests this feature was very important to them.

Teaching Framework and Strategies

One of the key pedagogical decisions was that the course would be co-designed collaboratively by both practising teachers and university educators as a deliberate attempt to address the apparent divide between theory and practice often reported in the literature and government reports. Fostering a shared responsibility was one of the central tenants of the course design and delivery within a DOCC model. As explored earlier in this chapter, universities are often positioned as the experts to teach the theory, with schools being responsible for the development and teaching of the practice (Australia Parliament House of Representatives Standing Committee on Education and Vocational Training, 2007). One of the key pedagogical objectives of this course was to better interconnect theory and practice. This objective was enacted through a series of Think Tank Days, where practicing teachers and teacher educators broadly discussed practicum, and specifically the WIL course *Orientation to Teaching,* including; focus areas, content, and pedagogical approaches (such as observations, audits and links to textbook). In this way power was distributed among the participants, although a hierarchy was required to make final decisions, and these rested with the academic leader. The course was deliberately designed so that pre-service teachers had to apply knowledge from the course in their Teacher Mentor's classroom, or conversely, use materials, texts and experiences from this classroom as the basis for site-based tutorials.

Another key decision involved the appointment of practising teachers who would teach the course on-site in the partner school. This decision was based on the broad belief that these teachers would know the particularities of that school context, would be aware of its priorities and programs, and so be able to localise course content to that particular context. This notion of distributing content amongst the community is an important feature of a DOCC. Practising teachers, would be able to draw upon their recent experience (as well as their knowledge of current pedagogical strategies) and thereby connect theory and practice more readily for the pre-service teachers. Focus group discussion revealed that the majority of pre-service teachers appreciated this explicit bridge of theory and practice provided by the teacher. As one pre-service teacher commented in a focus group, "I found [being on site] really cemented a lot of things that we've been learning about." And this comment: "I enjoyed seeing how the theory we were taught was instantly reflected in teaching practices. It allowed me to be critically aware of how other teachers incorporated or rejected the theories and set my own opinions accordingly."

Teaching strategies were purposefully selected to encourage the type of learning advocated by Orrell (2008) such as structured, reflective, self and peer learning experiences and using workplace specific examples. There was an emphasis on engaging with key ideas (via a flipped learning approach), audits and observations of practice, as well as reflection on observation, experience and learning, and self and peer learning. Strategies were also selected to foster diversity in opinion and to challenge thinking. Being empowered to be an active partner in their learning was reflected in a number of comments made by pre-service teachers in the focus groups. For instance: "we were treated like teachers… it was a teacher-to-teacher relationship whereas here [university] I always feel like a student".

Table 4. Preparation for the teaching profession

Q. To what extent (a lot, some, a little, not at all) did this course introduce you to each of the following aspects of teaching as a profession?				
This course introduced students to:	**A lot %**	**Some %**	**A Little %**	**Not at All %**
Ethical conduct required of teachers	43	47	10	0
Routine duties of teachers	50	38	12	0
Using teaching strategies (questioning and feedback)	84	16	0	0
Professional behaviour required of teachers	68	27	5	0
Having professional conversations	41	36	23	0
Being a member of a school community	45	34	21	0
Learning from teachers	68	22	10	0
Having respectful relationships with colleagues	61	30	9	0
Being part of a professional team	68	22	10	0

Sections of the survey focused on examining whether pre-service teachers felt the course introduced them to teaching as a profession and whether it supported specific work-skills. These are reported in Table 4. Aligned with the principles of effective WIL curriculum, the pre-service teachers thought that they had been introduced to all the listed aspects of the profession. They thought they had been most introduced to 'using teaching strategies', followed equally by 'professional behaviour required of a teacher', 'learning from teachers' and 'being part of a professional team'. They also thought that the course introduced them to the listed work skills in Table 5. In particular, they thought it introduced them to 'questioning' and 'feedback'.

Technological Dimension

Aligned with the DOCC principle of the use of technology to enable collaboration and course delivery, the infrastructure decisions made to support the design and delivery of the course were complex. RMIT University uses Blackboard as its LMS, however one of the limitations of this LMS is that it only enables access to those with an RMIT account, guest access is not activated. Therefore, using Blackboard would

Table 5. Preparation and development of work-related skills

Q. To what extent (a lot, some, a little, not at all) did this course introduce you to each of the following practical teaching skills?				
This course introduced students to:	**A lot %**	**Some %**	**A Little %**	**Not at All %**
Beginning lesson planning	49	36	15	0
Questioning	87	13	6	0
Feedback	79	11	5	0
Reflecting on own practice	58	39	3	0
Positive behaviour management (positive framing)	45	50	5	0

have denied access to the school-based tutors who were to teach the course, and to Teacher Mentors, who were supporting the learning of pre-service teachers. An alternative platform was sought that would enable the partner schools greater access in order to encourage connections and shared understanding of course content and expectations. Aligned with WIL principles, ensuring that the course content was accessible to all parties (practising teachers in partner schools, the university faculty and pre-service teachers) became a key challenge. After some deliberation and experimentation (such as impact of firewalls in schools etc.), the Google Sites platform was adopted as it enabled open access (all course materials could be shared) and anywhere/anytime access across different operating systems. Google Sites became the principle means for practicing teachers and university staff to communicate with one another about course requirements to share information about their own practices and specific course materials.

From the outset the decision was made that the course would involve multimodal content and employ a range of technological tools to support learning and to expose pre-service teachers to technologies in order to increase their knowledge and application in practice. Thus, course content took the form of short podcasts of key knowledge and support around assessment tasks. Tools such as Padlet were used to foster greater collaborative and peer learning deemed important in the WIL literature (Orrell, 2011). A Facebook Group (closed site), for pre-service teachers to discuss what mattered to them was also created. As the tutors were based in primary schools Google Hangout became the main communication tool, this avoided complications of scheduling. Moderation podcasts were also used to support consistency in marking by school-based tutors.

In analysing the data from the focus group, there were only a few comments about the online design features of the course. This issue was not as dominant as the other themes that emerged. For example, one student stated that the online material enabled “quick and easy access to material that I needed”. For others it aided their study: “the Google Site had everything on it, it’s convenient and every time they say go and find this, we knew exactly where to get it and there was no confusion, it was just straight forward and helpful”.

It was interesting that in the focus group the pre-service teachers did not focus to any great extent on the multi-model content of the course, rather other things, such as relationships with their Teacher Mentor, preoccupied their thinking. Arguably, using online tools and content was not new or confronting, whereas, being on-site in schools for the first time may have been.

Interface Dimension

Decisions around the interface to use for this course were less complicated, as the decision to use a Google Site as the LMS. Specific decisions about ‘look and feel’ were relatively straightforward, with a basic design being used and navigation via a menu bar. Each week/theme was structured in the same way. For example, each week outlined the following elements: workshop focus, learning intentions, pre-workshop tasks, workshop resources such as activities and podcasts and success checklists to enable users to easily navigate and provide structure which is important principle for WIL courses.

As this was the first time a DOCC approach had been used, the team were mindful that numerous changes were likely to be made not only to the site, but also to content and pedagogy in future iterations. As content was uploaded advice was sought on its user-friendliness from colleagues in the School of Education and a small group of current pre-service teachers. A few issues around ensuring students could undertake the learning activities, including those with very low technical skills, were raised and these were addressed by giving options in these circumstances.

Evaluation Dimension

Multiple sources of evaluation were built into the course. These included:

- **Formative Feedback:** An important feature of learning activities e.g. traffic light reflections and padlet exit slips.
- **Orientation to University Survey:** An informal survey, completed by first year students within the initial weeks of starting the program.
- **Orientation to Teaching Evaluation Survey:** Survey data, completed by volunteer first year students after completing this course to evaluate its design features, strengths and limitations, as part of a larger research project being undertaken by the applicants.
- **Orientation to Teaching Focus Groups:** Focus group data, collected from four groups of students (buddied group, non-buddied group, international group and open group) about their experiences of this course, as part of the larger research project.
- **Statistical Data from Course Experience Survey:** Data was collected via standard RMIT course evaluation processes.
- **Student Staff Consultative Committee Data:** Minutes from the committee meetings.
- **Feedback from Industry:** Data survey of key personnel from our partnership schools.

Some of this data informs this case study and other data informed future iterations of this course.

Management (Learning Environment and Information)

Many of the decisions around the management of this course have been included in previous discussions. The course employed a range of online tools and multimodal content geared towards specific learning objectives and pedagogical engagement. This content was then taught on-site in 14 primary schools in the Northern suburbs of Melbourne by a school-based tutor who was a practising teacher, employed by the university. This school-based tutor localised the content to suit the specific school context. Some 200 first year pre-service teachers, organised into groups of 12 to 16, undertook this course on-site. As they undertook the course they practically applied their knowledge and skills in a Teacher Mentor's classroom through activities such as audits and observations. The pre-service teachers were required to complete a number of assessment tasks which were assessed by the school-based tutor.

Resource Support Dimension

Based on the partnership considerations for WIL (Table 1), one of the key decisions made regarding resourcing the course was to involve both practising teachers and university teachers in its production. As a result, there was access to expert knowledge about resources (practical and theoretical). An underlying aim of the course was to model best practise so appropriating online resources that had high educational value to pre-service teachers was essential. Specific podcasts were designed and developed that drew upon teachers from the partnership schools. A number of other resources were accessed or developed with assistance from a range of professional repositories and sites, including the Department of Education and Training, Victorian Curriculum and Assessment Authority.

Ethical Dimension

The first year student cohort comprises students from diverse cultural and socio-economic backgrounds including international students and students with learning disabilities and impairments. The combination of peer learning, small groups, and online-guided learning, outlined previously in this chapter, catered for the needs of multiple and diverse students.

International students, particularly those from non-Western backgrounds, face significant challenges that can impede their successful transition to their new university environment, including communication issues, cultural differences, and developing relationships. The design of the course was mindful in addressing these needs. For instance, international students are part of a larger group of students who are familiar with the culture of Australian classrooms and, through group discussions, both formally and informally, they support international students to understand and interpret that culture: "at our school [on-site], all of us, all 16 of us sit down together and talk about how the day was going, what we didn't understand, what we liked, what we didn't like, what we learned today".

International students, as well as students with learning difficulties and disabilities, also benefited greatly from being able to review key concepts covered in the workshops, both on-site and on-campus, and in the online podcasts. The ability to replay the lecture-in-review and assessment support podcasts and to pause and reflect or clarify terms, was beneficial to students with language and learning difficulties. International students particularly commented favourably on the importance of podcasts in clarifying expectations about assessment tasks:

I really liked the podcast about the assignment. It was easy to understand and go step by step. I know that is the correct one.... everyone gives me different ideas, information about what we are supposed to do, but the podcast tells me exactly what I have to do, clearly.

First year students also benefited from undertaking their placement in diverse primary school settings. The schools, while in the Northern Region (Melbourne's northern suburbs), were quite different from one another. For instance:

School A: A school committed to providing the highest quality education for 104 students who have intellectual disabilities.

School B: Located in the rapidly expanding growth corridor and in 2014 has an enrolment of 970 students operating across 42 grades. Sixty-eight per cent of the school population has a language background other than English.

School C: A large school with 1010 students and 96 staff. It has 53 different nationalities and Educational Maintenance Allowance goes to 37% of families, indicating a low-SES student cohort.

These partnerships with diverse schools provide future teachers with meaningful opportunities to work with young people with diverse linguistic, cultural, religious and socioeconomic backgrounds.

CONCLUSION

This chapter provides a case study of the conception of a WIL course within the higher education sector, a sector which is increasing adopting open and distributed learning frameworks. In particular, this chapter documents a model of curricula design for Teacher Education, one based on a partnership between practicing teachers and university staff, where they share responsibility for the development of a DOCC. The discussion of the case study was framed around Khan's 8 dimensional e-learning framework: pedagogical, technological, interface, evaluation, management, resource support, ethical and institutional. This chapter began by outlining the three fields of the literature including effective WIL principles, DOCC framework and Khan's 8 dimensions. Each of these 8 dimensions were discussed in relation to the planning and implementation of the redesigned WIL course *Orientation to Teaching,* drawing upon data from surveys and focus groups. It focused on the pedagogical dimensions in relation to the DOCC design features such as shared responsibility, co-constructed curriculum design, scope for localised content and use of practicing teachers to distribute learning. The online learning decisions such as interface and design, managerial dimensions and the institutional dimensions were also outlined to demonstrate the wider considerations of course design. Initial data showed that there is a space and place for WIL within the new open and distributed learning environment. As this chapter demonstrated, the DOCC design, effective WIL principles and Khan's 8 dimensions proved productive in navigating the complexity of a WIL course within open and distributed learning contexts.

REFERENCES

Australia Parliament House of Representatives Standing Committee on Education and Vocational Training, & Hartsuyker, L. (2007). *Top of the class: Report on the inquiry into teacher education.* Canberra: House of Representatives Publishing Unit.

Australian Institute for Teaching and School Leadership (AITSL). (2011). *Accreditation of initial teacher education programs in Australia: Standards and procedures.* Retrieved from: www.aitsl.edu.au/docs/default-source/default-document-library/accreditation-of-initial-teacher-education

Baggaley, J. (2013). MOOC rampant. *Distance Education, 34*(3), 368–378. doi:10.1080/01587919.2013.835768

Balsamo, A., Boyer, P., Cole, C. L., Fernandes, M., Gajjala, R., Irish, S., …Wexler, L. (2013). *Transforming higher education with distributed open collaborative courses (DOCCs): Feminist pedagogies and networked learning.* FemTechNet Whitepaper. Retrieved from: http://femtechnet.org/wp-content/uploads/2014/10/FemTechNetWhitePaperSept30_2013.pdf

Billett, S. (2011). *Vocational education: Purposes, traditions and prospects.* Dordrecht, Netherlands: Springer. doi:10.1007/978-94-007-1954-5

Brimble, M., & Freudenberg, B. (2010). Will WIL'ing work? *B-Hert News, 28,* 2–4.

Darling-Hammond, L. (2010). Teacher education and the American future. *Journal of Teacher Education, 61*(1-2), 35–47. doi:10.1177/0022487109348024

De Coutere, B. (2014). To MOOC, or not to MOOC. *Training Journal*, 18-22.

Grossman, P., Hammerness, K., & McDonald, M. (2009). Redefining teacher: Re-imagining teacher education. *Teachers and teaching. Theory into Practice*, *15*(2), 273–290.

Juhasz, A., & Balsamo, A. (2012). An idea whose time is here: FemTechNet – A distributed online collaborative course (DOCC). *Ada: A Journal of Gender, New Media, and Technology*, (1). doi:10.7264/N3MW2F2J

Khalil, H., & Ebner, M. (2013). How satisfied are you with your MOOC? - A Research study on interaction in huge online courses. In J. Herrington et al. (Eds.), *Proceedings of World Conference on Educational Media and Technology 2013* (pp.830–839). Victoria, British Columbia: Association for the Advancement of Computing in Education (AACE).

Khan, B. H. (Ed.). (2005). *Managing e-learning: Design, delivery, implementation, and evaluation.* Hershey, PA: IGI Global. doi:10.4018/978-1-59140-634-1

Khan, B. H., & Granato, L. A. (2008). *Program evaluation in e-learning*. Retrieved from http://asianvu.com/bk/elearning_evaluation_article.pdf

Losh, E. (2014). *The war on learning: Gaining ground in the digital university*. Cambridge, MA: The MIT Press.

Merriam, S. (1998). *Qualitative research and case study applications in education* (Rev. ed.). San Francisco, CA: Jossey-Bass.

Orrell, J. (2011). *ALTC good practice report: Work-integrated learning*. Sydney, Australia: Australian Learning and Teaching Council.

Reilly, C. (2013). MOOCs deconstructed: Variables that affect MOOC success rates. In J. Herrington et al. (Eds.), *Proceedings of World Conference on Educational Media and Technology 2013* (pp. 1308–1338). Victoria, British Columbia: Association for the Advancement of Computing in Education (AACE).

See, S., & Conry, J. M. (2014). Flip my class! A faculty development demonstration of a flipped-classroom. *Currents in Pharmacy Teaching and Learning*, *6*(4), 585–588. doi:10.1016/j.cptl.2014.03.003

Stake, R. E. (1995). *The art of case study*. Thousand Oaks, CA: Sage Publications.

Teacher Education Ministerial Advisory Group (TEMAG). (2014). *Action now: Classroom ready teachers*. Retrieved from: http://docs.education.gov.au/node/36783

Ure, C., Gough, N., & Newton, R. (2009). *Practicum partnerships: Exploring models of practicum organisation in teacher education for a standards-based profession (final report)*. Retrieved from: http://www.vit.vic.edu.au/SiteCollectionDocuments/PDF/practicum%20partnerships.pdf

Young, J. R. (2002). 'Hybrid' teaching seeks to end the divide between traditional and online instruction. *The Chronicle of Higher Education*, *48*(28), A33.

Chapter 2
Investigating Students' Interactions with Discussion Forums, Facebook, and Twitter in a MOOC and their Perceptions

Min Liu
The University of Texas at Austin, USA

Emily McKelroy
The University of Texas at Austin, USA

Jina Kang
The University of Texas at Austin, USA

Jason Harron
The University of Texas at Austin, USA

Sa Liu
The University of Texas at Austin, USA

ABSTRACT

Given MOOCs being a relatively new format of online instruction, evidence-based research is needed to understand the role of MOOCs in changing the educational landscape, especially how students use the tools provided in MOOCs. This study investigated how students interacted with the discussion forum in a MOOC, and how they utilized Facebook and Twitter as an additional external space associated with this MOOC. Through both quantitative and qualitative data, the findings showed that MOOC participants found these tools to be helpful and can help create an active, collaborative, and participatory learning environment where they could share ideas and connect with other participants. The finding also indicated a poor interface design and low quality or low response to feedback can impact students' participation and perception of the usefulness of these tools. Results are discussed in the context.

DOI: 10.4018/978-1-5225-0466-5.ch002

INTRODUCTION

As indicated in the call for this book (Khan, January 26, 2015), "Massive Open Online Courses (MOOCs) are reshaping the educational landscape, offering a new mode of open and distributed e-learning that has the potential to provide quality education for millions of students all over the world." A MOOC, as defined by the Oxford Dictionary (2011), is a course of study that is made available via the Internet without charge to a rather large number of people. While there is significant interest in this relatively new format of online instruction, evidence-based research is still emerging as to its role in changing the educational landscape. Currently, most MOOCs are xMOOCs in which the course typically includes discussion forums. Sometimes these MOOCs include social media tools as a critical way to engage a large number of students, in addition to video lectures, assignments, and quizzes. One of the main criticisms of xMOOCs is the lack of participation and interaction between students and instructors and among other students due to their massive size (Daniel, 2012; Miyazoe & Anderson, 2013). There is insufficient research documenting how students interact with the tools provided. This study aimed to investigate how students interacted with discussion forums and social media tools, such as Facebook and Twitter, in a MOOC; and how useful these tools were to support the students' learning.

BACKGROUND

Khan (2009) indicated that e-learning taking place in a distributed, open system extends beyond the confines of a traditional classroom or textbook to provide a space that is flexible and allows individuals to decide where and when they want to learn. Therefore, for e-learning to be successful, learners in these environments need immediate attention and feedback to continue their learning and not feel isolated, or they will drop out. Khan's (2005) eight-dimensional e-learning framework provides a systematic way to review and assess the impact of technology-based initiatives, and offers a way to examine new online instructional formats such as MOOCs to create a meaningful learning environment. Four factors of this framework — interface design, resource support, pedagogical, and ethical — are particularly relevant to this study. According to the framework, the interface design refers to the overall look and feel of the Learning Management Systems (LMS), including content design, navigation, and usability. The resource dimension examines both the technical and human resources support needed to create meaningful and successful online learning environments, including digital libraries, online tutorials, newsletters, journals, podcasts, and FAQs. The pedagogical dimension includes issues related to teaching and learning such as the design approach and instructional strategies. Creating a student-centered environment that allows individuals to take control of their learning can help students achieve their own learning goals. Additionally, the use of multiple tools and instructional activities can also help facilitate learning for these individuals. One example of this is the use of a discussion forum in online instruction. According to Khan (2005), "A well-designed discussion forum in an e-learning course can create an active, interactive, and participatory learning environment" (p. 192). Khan also suggested that creating an online space that encourages meaningful engagement and interaction with peers, instructors, or online resources further supports students' learning. The ethical dimension addresses the geographical and diversity of the students (Khan, 2005).

When students engage in an e-learning setting, such as a MOOC, they are not only interacting with the technology infrastructure (e.g., LMS) through its interface, but also other factors. According to Moore (1989), there are three types of interaction in distance education: the learner-content interaction between "the learner and the content or subject of study," the learner-instructor interaction between "the learner and the expert who prepared the subject material," and the learner-learner interaction "between one learner and other learners, alone or in group settings, with or without the real-time presence of an instructor" (p. 4). Siemens, Gaševića, and Dawson (2015) also argued the learning experience is primarily shaped by the interaction of learners with the content, other learners, and the instructors. Numerous studies have been conducted based on Moore's three types of interaction theory (Bernard et al., 2009; Onah, Sinclair, & Boyatt, 2014; Swan, 2002). For example, Swan (2002) discussed all three types interaction in an empirical investigation by using the data collected from 73 online courses. Their findings suggested a significant relationship between students' perceived learning, perceived interaction with the instructor, perceived interaction with peers and their satisfaction with the courses. Bernard et al. (2009) conducted a meta-analysis and found that all three forms of interaction produced positive effect sizes on academic performance. In other words, interaction is important for online teaching and learning.

In xMOOCs, one of the most common ways to interact with the content, instructor, and particularly other learners is through discussion forums built in a LMS. Bali (2014) found through personal experiences that these forums were a highlight of MOOCs, since they "provided space to discuss areas not covered in the course" (p. 47). While some users may find these forums helpful, not all students participated in discussion forums. Breslow et al. (2013) found that only 3% of the students posted to the forum of MIT's first MOOC and that 90% of forum activities came from students who did not post or reply to any of the discussions. In examining learners' perspectives of taking an xMOOC, Liu et al. (2014) found that students had an overall positive experience and learned new knowledge and skills, but indicated the discussion forum was the least liked aspect of the course. Given the massive size in a typical MOOC, it is difficult, if not impossible, for MOOC instructors to interact directly with all of the enrolled students (Khalil & Ebner, 2013); and MOOC instructors and providers often leverage the distributive expertise of the participants (Stewart, 2013). This usage of participants can also present challenges as learners often differ in their prior knowledge of the MOOC content, language skills, confidence and motivation levels (Breslow et al., 2013; DeBoer, Ho, Stump, & Breslow, 2014; Kop, Fournier, & Mak, 2011). Mak, Williams, and Mackness (2010) found that if the forums have minimal interaction with the instructor, conversations can degenerate causing users to leave the forum and seek out other forms of social media. Purser, Towndrow, and Aranguiz (2013) also found that the instructor's 'lay-low' decision to let students engage in their own discussions was mistakenly taken by some students as being absent. Additional research by Tomkin and Charlevoix (2014) found that the involvement of the instructor has no statistically significant impact on the completion of the course, but may lead to a slightly higher participation rate in the forums.

Given the challenges of using discussion forums in xMOOCs, increasingly, social media is being included to compliment the existing discussion forums in xMOOCs. This trend toward increased use of social media is supported by the NMC Horizon Report (Johnson, Adams Becker, Estrada, & Freeman, 2014) which identified social media as a fast trend that is driving changes in higher education over the next one-to-two years. Social media allows instructors and students an additional communication platform outside of the MOOC discussion forums. Research has found that social media, such as Facebook and Twitter, can establish a sense of community in MOOCs (Purser et al., 2013) and allow students to engage in public discourse (Shen & Kuo, in press). Studies have shown that people use social media tools to share their personal interests and resources, express individuality and creativity, discuss topics of interest, and communicate with classmates about course-related topics (Alario-Hoyos, Pérez-Sanagustín, Delgado-Kloos, Muñoz-Organero, & Rodríguez-de-las-Heras, 2013; Hung & Yuen, 2010; Lin, Hoffman, & Borengasser, 2013).

Due to the asynchronous nature of social media, Facebook has been shown to allow students to participate at their own level of engagement, setting, and time while providing an enriched learning environment in a blended classroom (Churcher, Downs, & Tewksbury, 2014). Kop et al. (2011) found that in a study of two MOOCs, the participants organized Facebook groups as a means of sharing experiences and providing peer support. While many native English speakers may find similar affordances in the discussion forum, non-native English speakers participating in a MOOC formed their own Facebook group as a refuge (Breslow et al., 2013).

In addition to Facebook, Twitter has also been used as another communication platform with MOOCs. Levy (2011) found that students who were actively engaged in the MOOC voluntarily connected to others through the use of a shared hashtag. Twitter has also been found to establish a sense of community. Purser et al. (2013) sent welcoming e-mails before the launch of a MOOC that encouraged students to use a shared Twitter hashtag, Google Plus, and personal blogs. Even though the course had a discussion forum, students continued to use the established social media as a means of communication. Twitter also serves as a space where people around the world can engage in public discourse about MOOCs. Based on one year of monitoring Twitter activity about MOOCs, Shen and Kuo (in press) found that generally comments were slightly more positive than negative. Although a large number of participants from around the world tweeted about MOOCs, there emerged a small group (5-10%) of influencers who accounted for 50% of retweets.

Although discussion forums and social media have been shown to work in tandem as a means of connecting students and instructors, they do present challenges. For example, Onah, Sinclair, and Boyatt (2014) examined learners and instructors interaction in a MOOC in that students were allowed to join either peer-supported or tutor-supported forums. While the peer-supported forum was mainly used by students to discuss ideas and answer each other's questions, the tutor-support forum was monitored by tutors who provided support to students as needed that included quick and definitive answers to questions. The researchers found that among the drawbacks of both forums was the overall low usage, and postulated this may have been due in part to the inadequate support provided in the peer-supported forums. Too much support can also limit participation. The researchers observed this in the tutor-supported forums when tutors provided a definitive answer, which resulted in no further discussion. Sinha (2014) found that students who engaged in active discussions were from a small group of students, and interestingly, at the beginning of the course communicated with new students. However, as the course moved on, these students only talked among themselves, failing to engage the other students in their discussions. Therefore, understanding how students interact with the content, instructor, and their peers using a variety of common tools such as discussion forums and social media in xMOOCs is the goal of this study.

STUDENTS' INTERACTIONS WITH DISCUSSION FORUMS, FACEBOOK, AND TWITTER AND THEIR PERCEPTIONS

Purpose of the Study and Research Questions

The goal of this study was to investigate how students interacted with discussion forums and social media tools such as Facebook and Twitter from two aspects: the usage of the tools and students' perceptions of these tools. Discussion forums were used as part of formal instruction in this xMOOC. Facebook and Twitter were used as additional external spaces associated with this MOOC. Our research questions were:

- How did students use discussion forums in the MOOC?
- How did the students use the Facebook group and Twitter feed associated with the MOOC?
- How useful were the discussion forums, and how useful was it to get feedback from peers in discussion forums?
- How useful were the Facebook group page and the Twitter feed?

Participants and Research Context

Participants in this study were the students enrolled in a five-week MOOC titled, *Introduction to Infographics and Data Visualization*, offered through the Knight Center for Journalism in the Americas in the College of Communications at the University of Texas at Austin, from Oct. 6 - Nov. 9, 2013. A total of 4078 individuals were enrolled in the MOOC, representing 148 countries. Thirty percent of the enrollees were from the United States. One instructor using the Moodle LMS taught this MOOC. While all students were invited to participate in a survey given after the MOOC ended, 320 participants (46% of males [n=148], 54% of females [n=172]) who completed the survey made up the sample for this study. Eighty-three percent of the participants (n=267) were working professionals.

This MOOC consisted of reading materials, video lectures, and tutorials for learning technical tools. There were quizzes and weekly discussion forums used to engage and evaluate participants' performance. The weekly discussion forums included exercises for the participants to engage with the content and interact other peers. The activities progressed each week with weeks one and two primarily consisting of textual discourse. For weeks three to five, the activities were project-based where the participants were asked to create and post an infographic design they created. The students were asked to engage with other students and provide feedback on each other's design to increase learning and understanding of the design process. Based on the peer feedback and new information received in the course, the students posted their revised infographic the following week. The MOOC also utilized a Facebook group page and Twitter feed with a dedicated hashtag associated with it. This MOOC was not graded, but a certificate of completion was provided if a participant met all of the specified requirements. The requirements for obtaining a certificate included scoring 80% or higher on the quiz, completing two or more exercises, participating in the discussion forum at least twice, completing the online certificate form, and paying a $30 fee.

Data Sources and Analysis

Two types of data sources, consisting of both quantitative and qualitative data, were included in this study:

1. The usage data of discussion forums, Facebook page, and Twitter feed; and
2. The survey responses regarding the usefulness of the discussion forums, the course Facebook page, and the course Twitter feed.

A survey used in prior research on MOOCs (Liu et al., 2014) was refined for this study. The survey consisted of questions on demographics and those related to the research questions of this study:

- Are you in the field of journalism?
- Is this your first time taking a MOOC?
- How many exercises and assignments have you completed?
- How useful were discussion forums?
- How useful was it to get feedback from your peers [in discussion forums] for this MOOC?
- How useful was the Facebook group page? Why?
- How useful were the Twitter feeds? Why?

Each participant's usage data from the discussion forums was extracted from the Moodle LMS. This data provided information about the participant's interactions within the forum and consisted of the participant's username, the date and time, the action that occurred, the page URL, and the page title. The usage data of the instructor, teaching assistant, and course administrator were removed, and only the students' usage data was kept for analysis. The frequency of students' participation in weekly discussions, including both viewings and postings, was tallied. A student *posting* includes each time the participant entered a comment to the discussion forum. A student *viewing* includes each time that the participant viewed a post to the discussion forum.

A Facebook page and Twitter feed were included with the MOOC to extend the learning space in the course. The usage of these two social media tools was extracted separately. The Facebook raw data consisted of all the time-stamped posts, comments, and likes during the five-week course period. This data was cleaned and organized into quantitative data (i.e., the number of posts, comments, and likes) and qualitative data (i.e., the content of the posts and comments). Information such as username, role, date of posting/commenting was retained for examining the relationship among the posting and commenting actions. The Twitter raw data was gathered from the Twitter search page because Twitter limits third-party searching using their API (application program interface) to only seven days of data. The time-stamped data (i.e., username, account name, date, time, text of tweet, number of replies, number of retweets, and number of favorites) was extracted and organized. Qualitative data such as the text of tweets was separated from the quantitative data. Special attention was paid to any conversations for any possible interactions among the students.

For the quantitative data, descriptive analyses were performed on the survey, Facebook, and Twitter data (e.g., Likert scale questions, number of posting/comments/tweets). The qualitative data included the open-ended responses from the survey and text from the Facebook postings/comments and Twitter tweets, and was analyzed following the guidelines by Miles, Huberman, and Saldaña (2014). Two re-

Table 1. Sample top posts by code to the Facebook page

Code	% of Total Codes	Sample Posts
Resources	41.6%	This is a very nice issue of the brazilian design magazine Zupi, it's all about infographics with interviews and more: [URL] some another issues are free on Issuu; Tools you can use [URL] is a collection of some of the most important, effective, useful and practical data visualisation tools. The content covers the many different resources used to create and publish visualisations, tools for working with colour, packages for handling data, places to obtain data.
Examples	26.2%	25 Amazing Food Infographics, Drawn From 49,733 Recipes [URL] WIRED; Good infographic published today in Folha de São Paulo. It's in portuguese, sorry for those who can't undestand it. It shows the difference between left and right wing beliefs in Brazil. It concludes most people in Brazil have a right wing ideology (eg: 85% think that believing in God makes someone a better person).[URL]
Advertisement	8.4%	For those of you who have watched the first video for Week 3, Donald Norman is going to be teaching design a MOOC [URL] If you interested in other free Design/Storytelling related MOOCs, here's one I came across, also learning by doing. They look very interesting. [URL] This autumn everyone can be a student. We make online learning interactive, scalable and social. Join the MOOC revolution! [URL]
Course Reminders	5.9%	Dear students of the 3rd MOOC, I've posted the summary message about Week 1 [URL]. Don't read it if you have not participated in the Week 1 discussion yet All, We have added hashtag # vizmooc for sharing about our mooc. This hashtag is more specific to the course and will make it easier for students to share via twitter. I've also added a How to Get Started Guide in the main page area of the course. This is a detailed guide with screen caps and has info about the quiz in week 2. I hope it will prove helpful to all.

searchers independently coded each data source, and a second researcher checked the coded responses for verification. Throughout the coding process, the codes were continuously checked against the raw data and refined. Any disagreements between the two researchers were resolved among the research team when all team members discussed the coding and made necessary modifications until the inter-rater reliability reached 100%. In presenting the quotes in Tables 1 and 2, we used the original statements by the participants (not the edited ones).

Table 2. Sample top posts by code to the Twitter

Code	% of Total Codes	Sample Posts
Examples	47.2%	Fellow #vizmooc participants: Check out this realtime #dataviz of global DDoS attacks [URL]; Infographic: Rubik's Cube Solved in 20 Moves (or Less) [URL] #infographic #dataviz #vizmooc
Resources	20.8%	2 part video series: Ethics in data collection & sharing, from [URL] #dataviz #vizmooc; Big data, little newsroom: Resources for #ddj anybody can use [URL] via @[USER] #dataviz #infographic #vizmooc
Personal Feeling	9.4%	Finished @utknightcenter #vizmooc. Thx @[instructor]! You taught me a lot. 'Really need to learn @Illustrator now. "Vamos fazer uma arte!" ("Let's make a piece of art!") is not an ideal message to create infographics #vizmooc

Study Findings

Findings from the Usage Data: Discussion Forum Usage

The participants' overall usage data from the MOOC showed that among the four course activities, postings to the discussion forum had a lower frequency compared to the participants' viewing of the course readings and videos. However, participants' viewings of the discussion forum posts had the highest frequency (see Figure 1). There was an increase in discussion forum postings from weeks two (n=241) to four (n=859). This upward trend in posting could possibly be explained by the fact that the students had to complete two exercises and post their infographic design during these last three weeks to pass the course and be eligible to receive a certificate. Additionally, during weeks four and five students were asked to post the final versions of their infographic design to the forum, which can also explain the increase in the viewings of the discussion forum posts for these weeks.

We further examined the usage data from the participants who rated in the survey the discussion forum as (un)useful or indicated that peer learning in the discussion forums was (un)useful. While the groups that rated the discussion forums as helpful (n=47) or unhelpful (n=58) showed similar usage patterns (see Figure 2), the groups that rated peer learning helpful (n=41) or unhelpful (n=57) showed quite different usage patterns (see Figure 3). During the five weeks of the course, participants who rated

Figure 1. Overall discussion forum usage

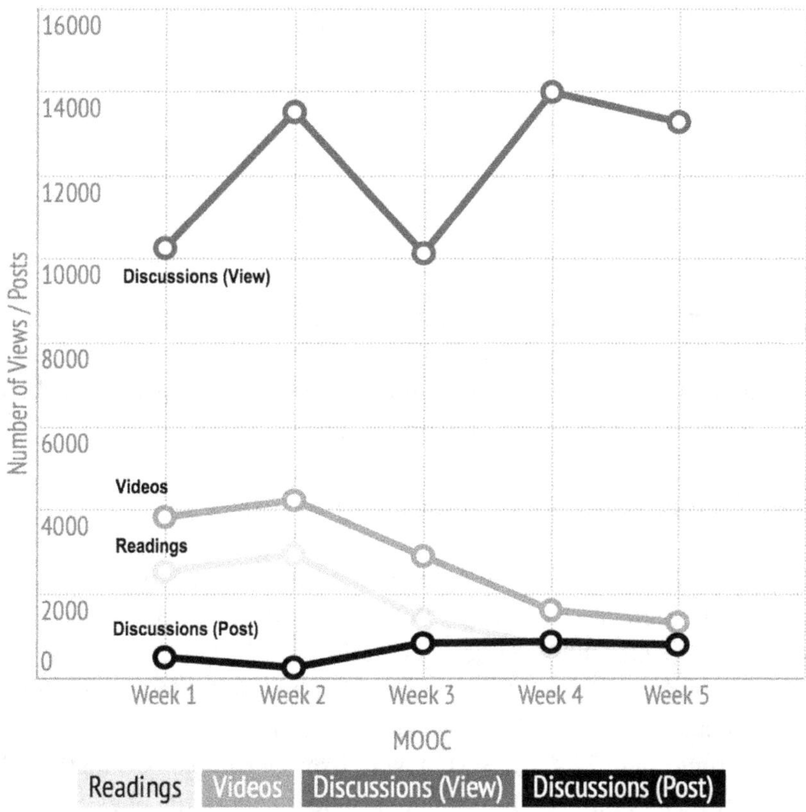

Figure 2. Comparing participation in discussion forums between discussion forum helpful vs. unhelpful groups: viewing (top) and posting (bottom)

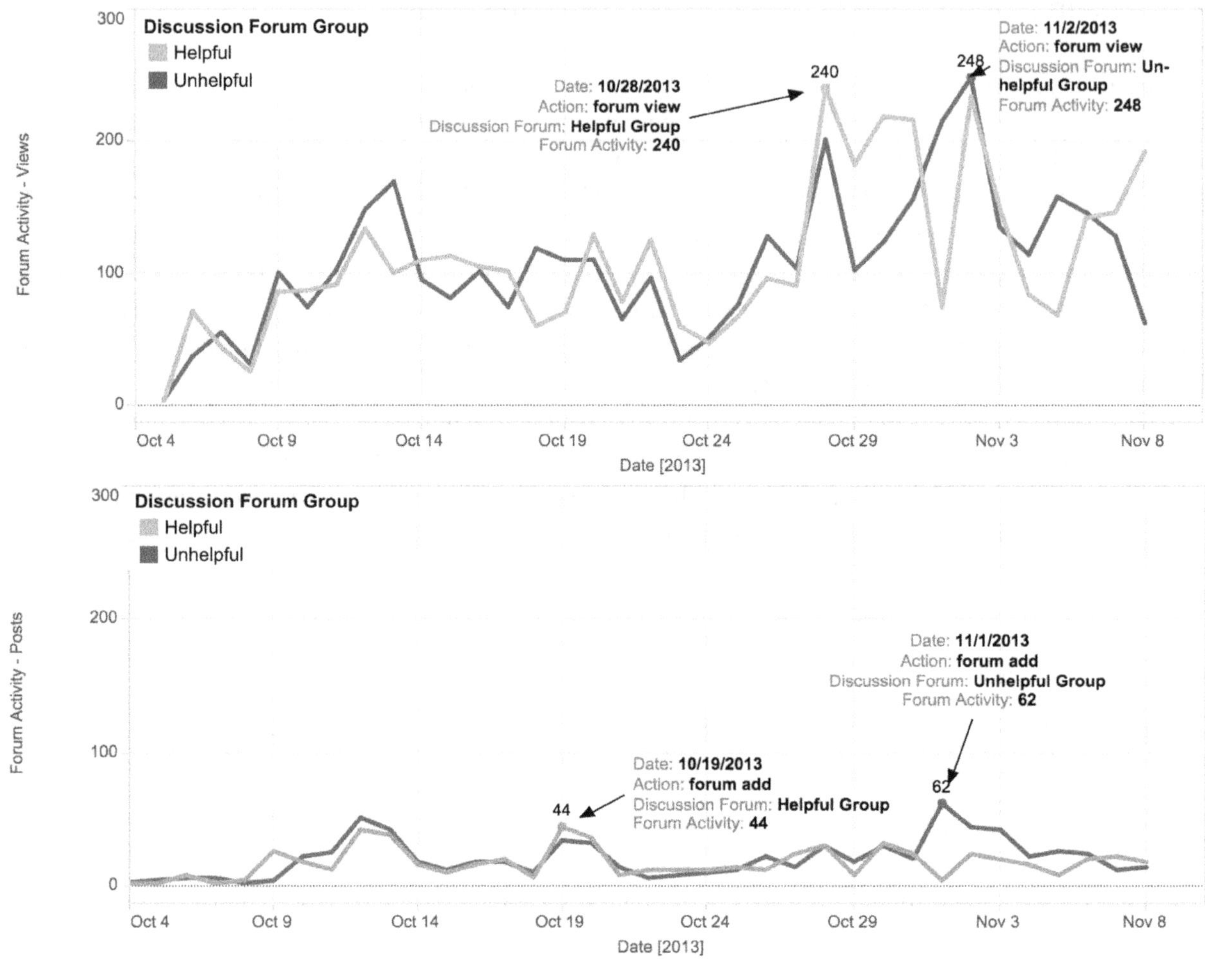

peer learning helpful posted more in the discussion forums than those who rated peer learning as unhelpful. This difference between the two groups was observed in the number of views the participants made to the discussion forum pages. Specifically, the number of viewings (n=411) by the helpful group was more than two times as many as that (n=181) by the unhelpful group.

Findings from the Usage Data: Facebook Usage

The Facebook group had 4054 members (99% of the total MOOC participants, in which there might be people who were not the participants of this MOOC). During the five-week course period, there were a total of 236 posts, 241 comments, and 975 likes (see Figure 4). Of these, 52.1% (n=123) of the postings were from the instructor and 47.9% (n=113) were from participants, 45.2% (n=109) of the comments were from the instructor and 54.8% (n=132) were from participants, and 67.6% (n=659) of the posting likes were from the instructor and 32.4% (n=316) were from participants. The top 10 participants contributed about 31% of the posts, 58.3% of the comments, and 43.7% of the likes out of all the participants.

Figure 3. Comparing participation in discussion forums between peer learning helpful vs. unhelpful groups: viewing (top) and posting (bottom)

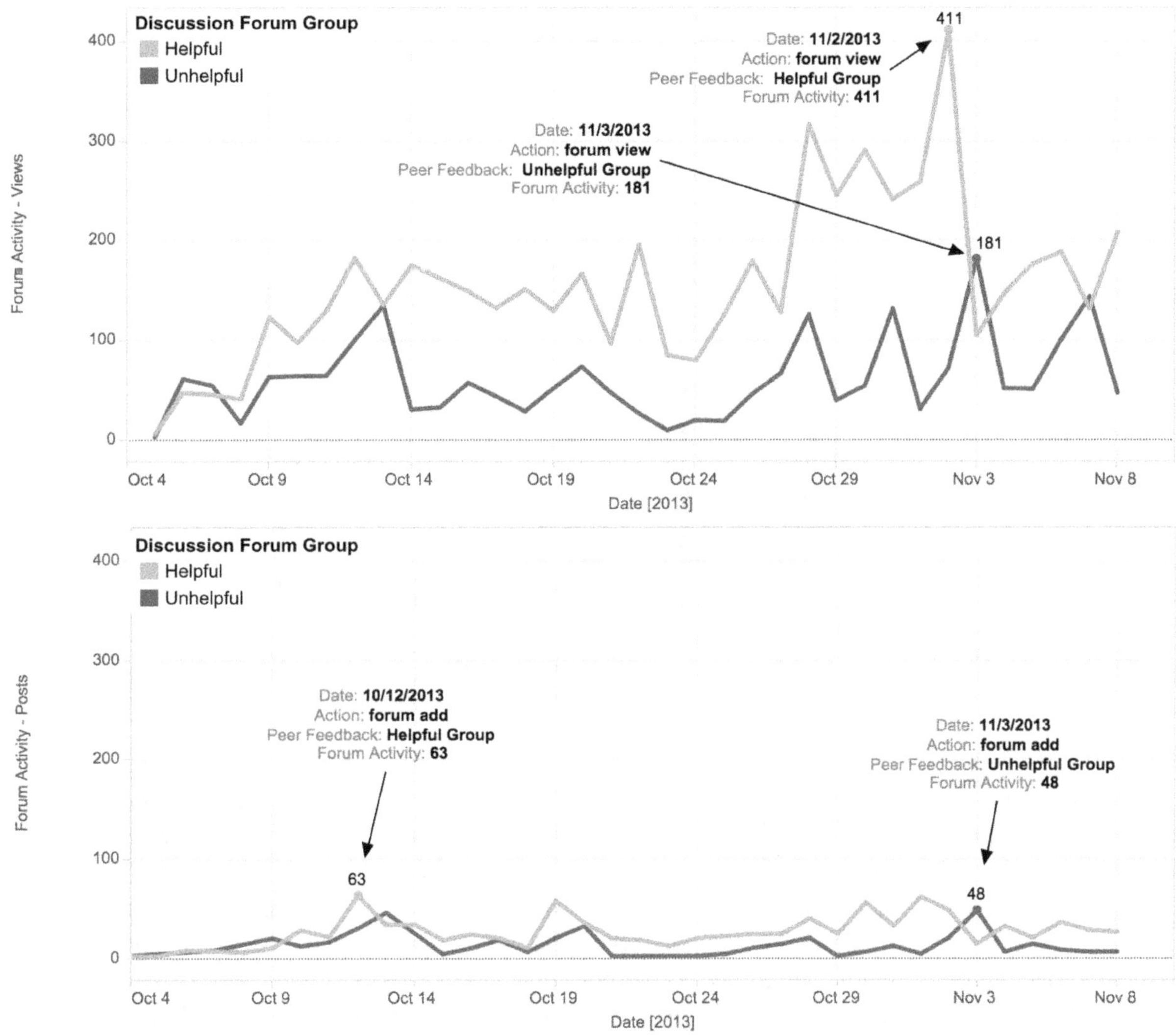

It is interesting to point out the same three participants were among the top 10 contributors for all three categories and another three participants were among the top 10 contributors for two categories. An indication that these participants were active Facebook users at least for this MOOC.

Analysis of the content of the Facebook postings showed the top types of the post were 1) resources (41.6%, *n*=84), 2) examples (26.2%, *n*=53) of infographics or data visualizations, 3) advertisements (8.4%, *n*=17) for networking opportunities, and 4) course reminders (5.9%, *n*=12) (see sample posts in Table 1). Of these total numbers of the posts, the top type of posts made by the instructor included 1) resources (68.3%, *n*=71) 2) advertisements (12.5%, *n*=13), and 3) course reminders (11.5%, *n*=12); and the top type of posts by the participants included 1) examples (50.0%, *n*=49), 2) resources (13.3%, *n*=13), 3) help with the course (6.1%, *n*=6), and 4) tools (6.1%, *n*=6). It is worth noting that participation in the Facebook group continued after the course was officially over. The posts that occurred after the end date of the course were primarily to share additional resources.

Figure 4. Facebook usage over five weeks

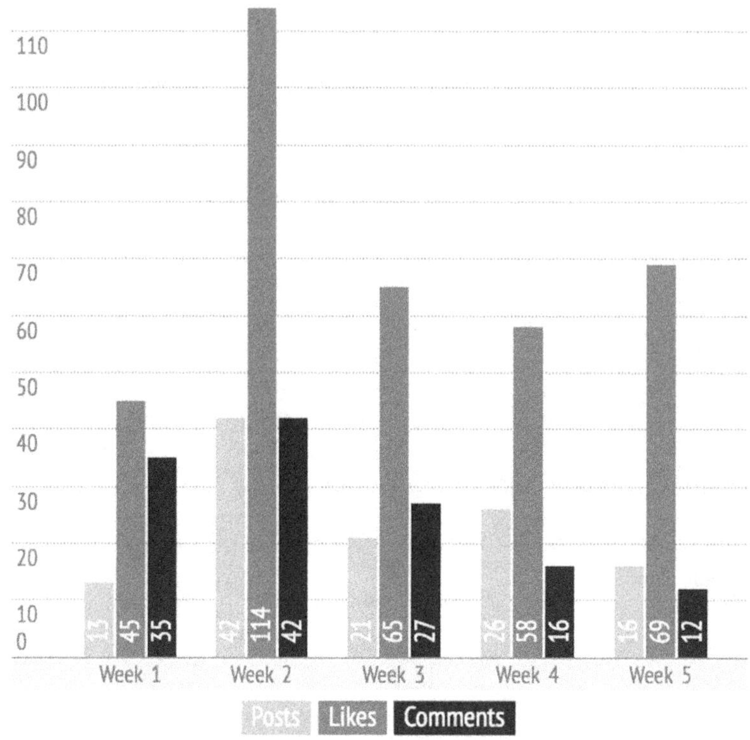

Further analysis of the types of the posts showed the posts for different purposes appeared to have a different life span. For example, Figures 5 and 6 showed a comparison of different lifespans between the "Examples" and "Help" posts. For the "Examples" posts, there was a total of ten conversations, and for the "Help" posts, there was a total of four conversations. In these two figures, the x-axis is the time in minutes when the post received a comment while the y-axis represents the comments for each post. As shown in Figure 5, the lifespan of an "Examples" post (i.e., from the time it was first posted to the last comment received) is not as long as that of a "Help" post. The longest lifespan of the "Examples" post is within 30 hours (1,751 minutes), and the shortest is 2 hours (120 minutes). On the other hand, the "Help" posts are fewer, but longer. For example, one of them stayed alive for 265 hours (15,922 minutes, see Figure 6).

Figure 5. Lifespan for "examples" posts

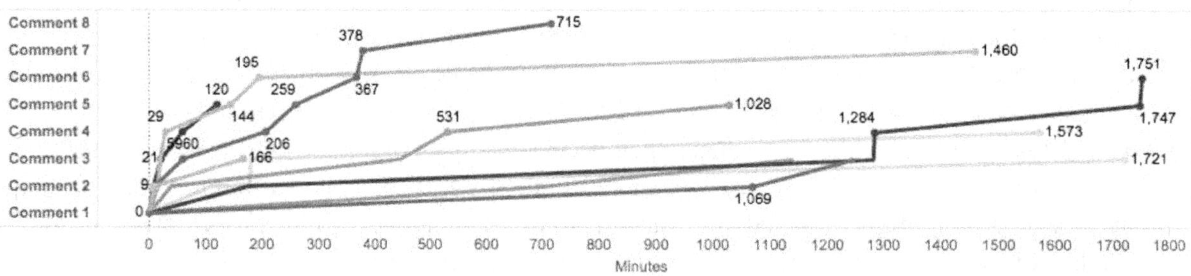

Figure 6. Lifespan for "help" posts

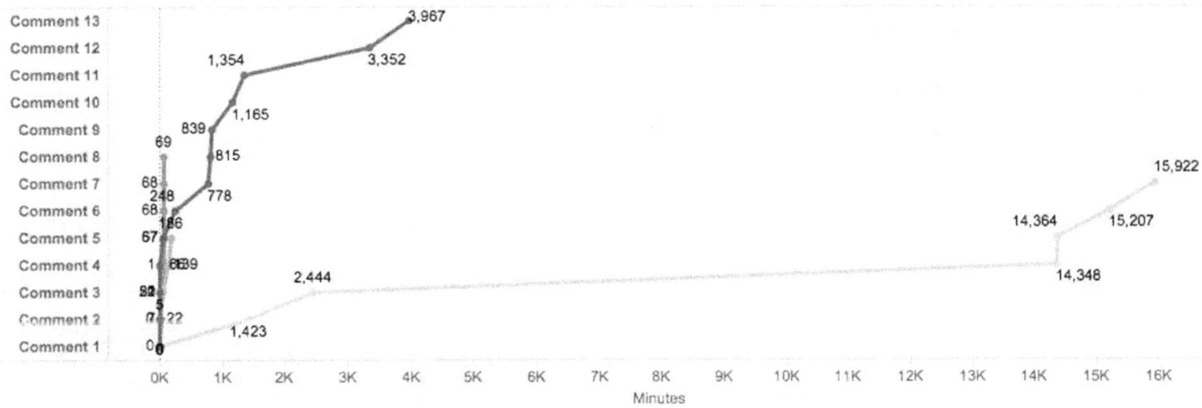

Findings from the Usage Data: Twitter Usage

Tweets with the #vizmooc hashtag did not begin until the end of the second week of the course. This delay is due to the original hashtag being too generic and used by other people outside of the course. As a result, at the end of the second week, the instructor changed to a distinct hashtag exclusively for this course. During the five weeks of the course, there were a total of 38 tweets (5.3%, n=2 from the instructor; 94.7%, n=36 from the participants) and 25 replies (40%, n=10 from the instructor; 60%, n=15 from the participants). That is, most of the original tweets were from the participants, but about 40% of the replies were from the instructor. Figure 7 showed the days and times when the tweets happened. It appears tweets occurred the most on Sunday and least on Saturday and occurred the most during 9:00 a.m. to 11:59 a.m. Four participants tweeted the most with a range of four to six tweets each, one participant tweeted twice, and the remaining 14 participants tweeted only once. Two participants made the most replies, ranging from four to five. One participant replied twice, and the remaining four participants only replied once. The participant who tweeted the most frequently was also the one who replied most often while the participant who had made the second largest number of replies only tweeted once.

Analysis of the Twitter feeds showed that the top types of posts were 1) examples (47.2%, n=25), 2) resources (20.8%, n=11), and 3) personal feelings (9.4%, n=5) (see Table 2). It is interesting to point out there were only two posts by the instructor, which included a post for the promotion to follow the course hashtag and a resource for further assistance with the course topic. The top types of tweets made by the participants included:

1. Examples (49.0%, n=25),
2. Resources (19.6%, n=10), and
3. Personal feelings (9.8%, n=5).

It is worth noting that Twitter participation continued on a regular basis after the course was officially over. The tweets that occurred after the end date of the course were to share additional resources or to let other people know they had completed the course.

Figure 7. Twitter usage over five weeks

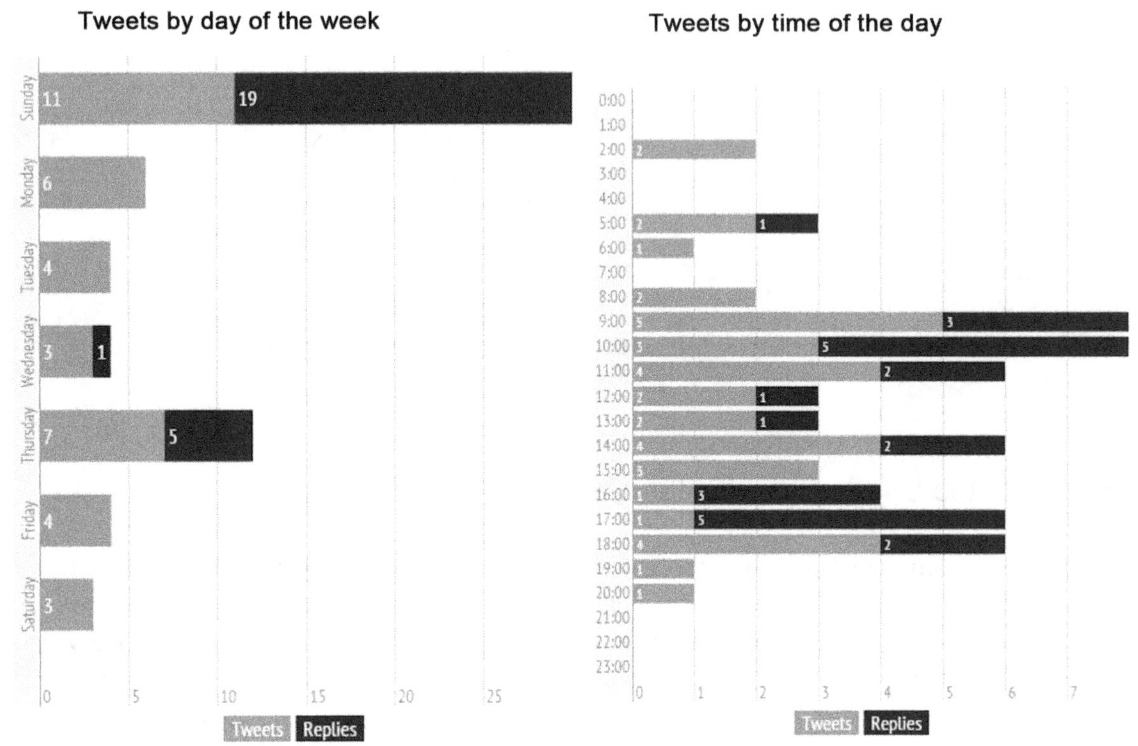

In addition, there were a total of seven conversations that took place on Twitter. These conversations ranged from one reply to eight replies, with an average of 3.4 replies (see Figure 8). The shortest length of time for a conversation consisted of one reply within the same minute as the posting, while the longest length of time also was one reply, which occurred 2011 minutes (1.4 days) after the original post. The average length of conversation was 416 minutes (6.9 hrs), but it is important to note this number may be skewed high due to an outlier. With the outlier removed the average Twitter conversation lasted two and a half hours (150.7 minutes).

Figure 8. Length of Twitter conversations

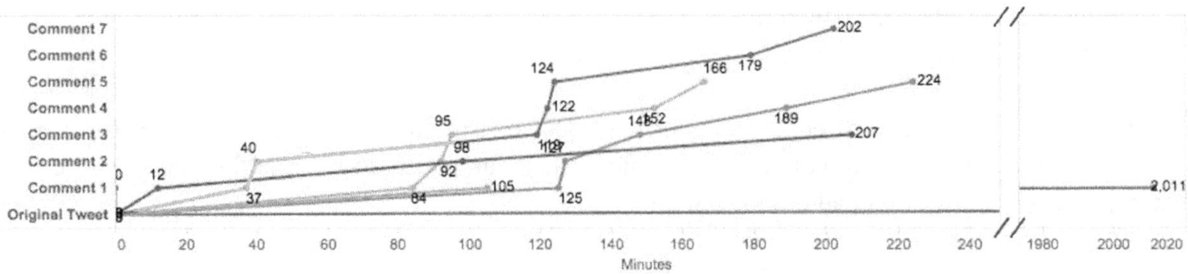

Figure 9. Participants' perception of discussion forum (left) and peer feedback (right)

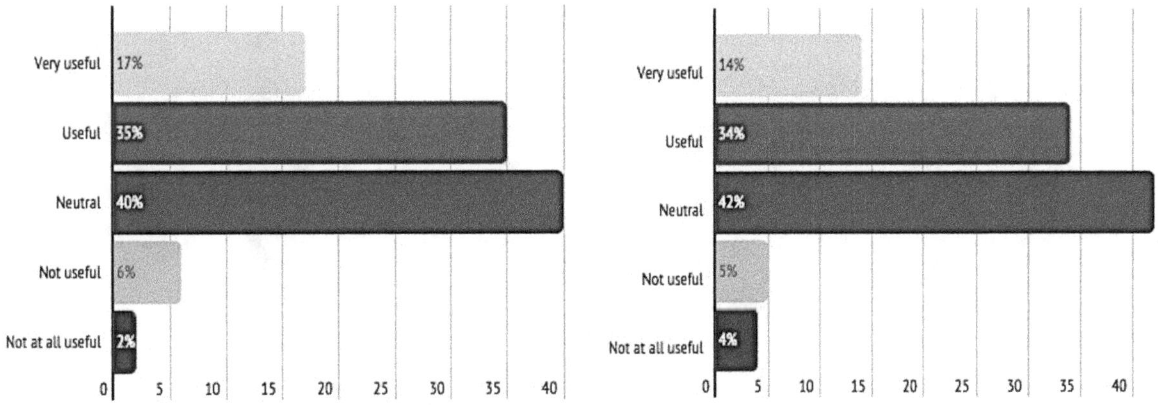

Findings on Students' Perceptions: Survey Quantitative Results

The descriptive analysis showed that when participants were asked, "How helpful was the discussion forums provided in this MOOC?" 52.5% were positive (35%, *n*=113 "Helpful" and 17%, *n*=54 "Very Helpful"), 7.5% were negative (6%, *n*=18 "Unhelpful" and 2%, *n*=6 "Very Unhelpful"), and 40% (*n*=128) were neutral about the usefulness of the discussion forums. In response to "How useful was it to get feedback from your peers for this MOOC?" 48% (*n*=153) responded positively (14%, "Very Useful" and 34%, "Useful"), 42% (*n*=135) indicated 'neutral,' and 9% (*n*=31) responded negatively (5%, "Not useful" and 4%, "Not at All Useful") (see Figure 9). Of the participants that reported they completed most or all of the assignments and activities (*n*=175), 64.6% (*n*=113) found the feedback received from their peers was useful as compared to 26.3% (*n*=46) that were neutral and 9.2% (*n*=16) that did not find it beneficial to their learning.

In response to "How useful was the course Facebook group page?" 28% (*n*=86) responded positively (9%, "Very Useful" and 19%, "Useful"), 24% (*n*=75) indicated "Neutral," 15% (*n*=47) responded negatively (9%, "Not Useful" and 6%, "Not at All Useful") and 32% (*n*=110) did not use it (see Figure 10). In response to "How useful was the course Twitter feed?," 13% (*n*=42) responded positively (5%, "Very Useful" and 8%, "Useful"), 31% (*n*=96) indicated "Neutral," 15% (*n*=46) responded negatively (8%, "Not Useful" and 7%, "Not at All Useful") and 40% (*n*=125) did not use it (see Figure 10). That is, for using Facebook, there were more positive than negative responses, about one-quarter indicated "Neutral," and about one-third did not use it. For using Twitter, on the other hand, there were about the same number of positive and negative responses, about one-third indicated "Neutral," and over one-third did not use it.

Survey Qualitative Results

The qualitative open-ended responses from the survey provided reasons for students' responses as discussed above using the quantitative data.

Figure 10. Participants' perception of Facebook and Twitter associated with the MOOC

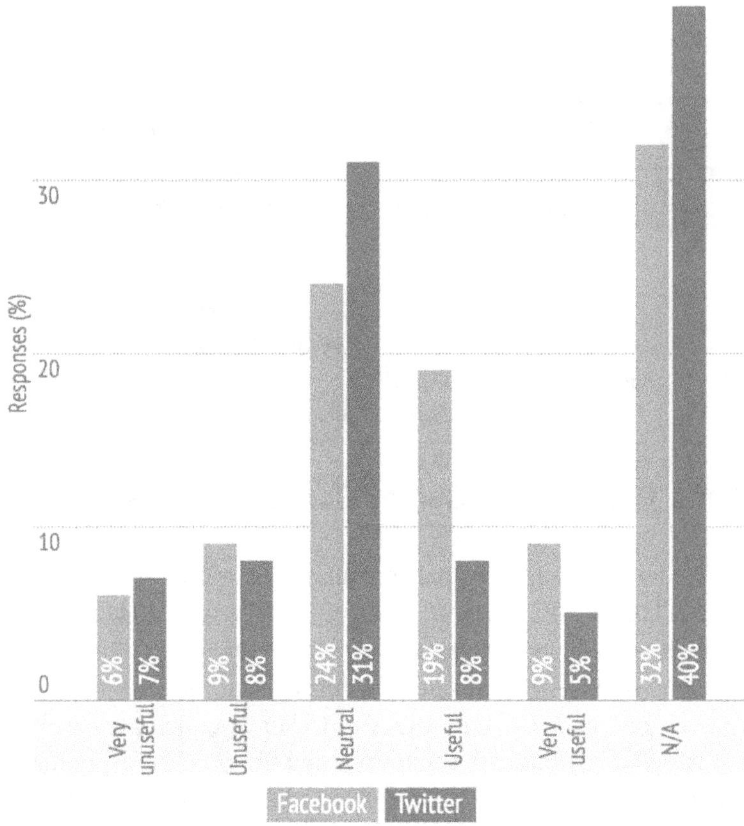

Perception about Discussion Forums

Discussion forums were used by the participants to discuss course content and to evaluate and provide feedback on peer's assignments. Analysis of the open-ended responses revealed that 57.9% of responses (n=217) were positive about the discussion forums, 28.3% (n=106) were negative, and 13.9% (n=52) indicated they did not participate. The positive responses revealed that the peer review process was helpful and allowed for sharing of ideas. Participants felt that the active interaction with the instructor and peers supported their learning experience as demonstrated by the following comment: "The best way to improve at data visualization is to practice. Feedback from peers will allow me to improve my data visualization in the future, and also provided me with useful pointers." Additionally, participants saw value in sharing with others that worked in the same industry or had similar interests. One participant commented on this: "You get a sense of what other people think of your work, especially if you work in [a] publishing company."

The use of discussion forums provided students an opportunity to learn how to critique infographics and data visualizations and further their understanding of the MOOC topic. Participants stated, "The exercises to critique and redesign infographics…were thought-provoking, and the hands on design experience was a great tool for really getting into the techniques that we were learning about: storytelling, design choices (layout, color, font, etc.), and designing interactivity in graphics." and "In providing feedback to others I felt I learnt a lot by having to look at a wide variety of aspects to identify those where the author was strong and possible extensions."

Of the participants that did not find the discussion forums useful, the reasons included lack of quality of feedback (6.9%, *n*=26), not receiving feedback from peers (6.1%, *n*=23), not receiving enough feedback to be meaningful (5.9%, *n*=22), feedback unorganized leading to confusion (3.2%, *n*=12), or the participants felt there were too many people for the activities (2.7%, *n*=10). One participant stated, "The feedback seemed a little inconsistent, but is generally helpful." Another stated, "Some people had useful comments or offered to help. Some seemed to be engaging only to tick the boxes of the course. I had only two people rate my work, and one of those was clearly not very interested." Some responses indicated that some feedback "didn't have depth" and were "short and superficial." A possible reason for this mixed finding could be due to participants' different levels of expertise on the topic, and/or the diversity of participants from around the world for which language could be an issue. For example, one student stated, "It is difficult to interpret feedback from peers around the globe because standards…are different in different countries and this is reflected in the sensibilities and feedback provided." Another participant stated, "I believe that people were at different levels. So the feedback was not uniform."

Perception about Facebook Group

Analysis of the open-ended survey responses revealed that 53.1% (*n*=137) found the Facebook group useful, 10.1% (*n*=26) did not find it useful, and 36.8% (*n*=95) did not use the Facebook group. The most useful aspects included: connecting with people in the field all over the world (19%, *n*=49), sharing of resources (16.3%, *n*=42), getting course updates or reminders (4.7%, *n*=12), and learning from peers (2.3%, *n*=6).

Some participants indicated that the Facebook group provided more opportunities to connect with others who were truly interested in the course topic, "instead of the forums where a lot of people seemed less interested." Sharing resources was also considered to be a highlight of using the Facebook, because "[The Facebook group] describe other paths for learning, workshops, seminars; as well as providing a continuous stream of inspirational examples." The shared resources can be used after the MOOC course ended, as one participant commented, "I was almost overwhelmed with course tasks, so didn't have any time to browse lots in the Facebook during the course. But I will visit it later to see what have been discussed." Additionally, some participants felt the Facebook group allowed them to receive a direct notification when others responded to their postings or updated new postings while the discussion forums did not. The instructor regularly posted course updates and reminders of important notifications such as the due date of course assignments, which was found to be useful to the participants. Some commented, "When the Professor would post something and it showed up in my feed, that was great" and "[I] learnt more about ongoing projects, researches, groups apart from the ones in the course." Furthermore, learning from peers through postings on the Facebook group was another aspect indicated as helpful by the participants. One participant mentioned, "[The Facebook group is] interesting for debating different examples of graphics."

Perception about Twitter Feed

Regarding Twitter, while over one-third of the participants (42.3%, *n*=22) found it useful, 17.3% (*n*=9) found it not useful, and 40.4% (*n*=21) indicated they did not use Twitter or any social media tools or indicated that they did not have time to use the tool. Some participants did not follow the Twitter feeds because they felt "they [the feeds] weren't really part of the course." Many participants indicated negative experiences of using Twitter because it included too much information (3.8%, *n*=2) and lacked meaningful information (5.8%, *n*=3). One participant mentioned, "I saw a few of these postings and thought they were useful to demonstrate the ongoing dynamic nature of the profession. However, I have difficulty dealing with my existing email so don't want more information flowing in." Compared to the Facebook page, the participants found Twitter had less interaction, as shown in this sample comment: "I wish tweets had taken more advantage of the hashtags. There was little interaction, less than on Facebook."

On the other hand, some participants commented on the positive aspects of using Twitter that included connectivity with peers (11.5%, *n*=6), resources (9.6%, *n*=5), course updates or reminders (5.8%, *n*=3), and active interaction with others (5.8%, *n*=3). They found Twitter as an easy and practical way "to find what participants in the course are talking about in the web" and "to keep track of important aspects of the MOOC." In addition, the participants could easily connect with other MOOC participants via Twitter. One participant commented, "Because I used twitter and I guess somehow people from the course found me via # and connected."

SOLUTIONS AND RECOMMENDATIONS

In this study, we investigated how MOOC participants interacted in the course discussion forum, and how they utilized Facebook and Twitter as an additional external space associated with this MOOC. The study also examined the students' perception of these tools, and if they found the tools to be useful to support their learning. We will address our findings by using four dimensions of Khan's (2005) e-learning framework (i.e., interface design, resource support, pedagogical, and ethical), Moore's (1989) three types of interaction (i.e., learner-content interaction, learner-instructor interaction, and learner-learner interaction), and related aforementioned literature. The aim of the study was to understand if the use of the multiple interactive spaces were helpful for the xMOOC participants by creating an active, collaborative, and participatory learning environment.

Use of Discussion Forums as a Way to Support Peer Learning

Khan (2005) indicated in the pedagogical dimension of the e-learning framework that the use of instructional strategies to support interaction could allow participants to explore ideas and share feelings with peers and the instructor. In this study, the overall use of the discussion forums by the participants to interact with peers was not high. The overall usage patterns showed that although the participants did not post many comments, they were more engaged in visiting the forums to review peer's discussions (e.g., 62 maximum number of postings vs. 248 maximum number of views as shown in Figure 2). This finding supports the literature that suggests active and passive learners exhibit different types of learning patterns and different levels of engagement exist within the same MOOC (Fini, 2009; Kop, 2011; Milligan, Littlejohn, & Margaryan, 2013). The findings showed similar usage patterns in terms of number of views and postings regardless of how helpful the participants felt about the discussion forums. The participants who rated peer learning helpful, on the other hand, posted both more comments and had more views in the forums over the entire course period than those who rated peer learning to be unhelpful. It is possible those who did not receive useful feedback from peers rated the peer learning in the forums as not helpful.

The findings regarding the students' perception toward the discussion forums showed the participants found sharing ideas and working with others with similar interests or in the same field were the most valuable aspects of the MOOC experience (Khan, 2005). Peer learning through using the discussion forums also provided the participants with learning opportunities to gain a deeper understanding of the topic by evaluating others' work and getting feedback from the instructor on their assignments. Such findings are examples of Moore's (1989) three types of interaction and highlight the importance of peer-to-peer or instructor feedback in distributed learning (Anderson & Dron, 2010).

However, some participants indicated a less positive learning experience in using the discussion forums and considered peer learning in the forums not useful due to low quality of feedback, not receiving any peer feedback, or the feedback was unorganized and lead to confusion. In the interface dimension of the e-learning framework, Khan (2005) emphasized "the design of an e-learning interface is critical because it determines how learners interact with the presented information" (p. 325). Further, having organized page and site design and easy navigation are important considerations for the success in an e-learning environment. Poor interface design could explain why the participants indicated feedback was unorganized or confusing, thus resulting in low interactions and inadequate feedback in the discussion forum. In a previous research study, we highlighted the importance of the MOOC design to enhance the learning experience for participants (Liu, Kang, & McKelroy, 2015). We found that having an unorganized interface deterred participants from interacting to their full potential, thus resulted in a lack of interaction and peer feedback.

Khan's (2005) ethical dimension of the e-learning framework addressed the geographical and diverse background of the students. Participants indicated that the feedback received in the discussion forum lacked depth and quality. One possible explanation for this finding could be explained by the diversity of the learners (Breslow et al., 2013; DeBoer et al., 2014; Kop et al., 2011; Selingo, 2014). In this MOOC, the participant's level of expertise varied on the topic (i.e., journalism professionals compared with individuals with no prior experience with the topic). Secondly, differing language abilities (i.e., geographically separated participants) could have presented communication barriers. Khan (2005) stated, "a non-native speaker of the discussion forum may encounter difficulty in expressing clearly in his/her writings which may present him/her as different to other participants" (p. 299). The geographical diversity of the participants in this study (i.e., 148 countries represented) may have created challenges for participants to engage meaningfully. Therefore, these indications could explain the low level of interactions, lack of depth, and poor quality that the participants experienced. While having a diverse learner population is probably expected in a MOOC, MOOC course designers and instructors should be especially sensitive to these issues and implementing instructional strategies to minimize any possible negative effects.

Use of Facebook and Twitter as an Additional Social and Learning Space

Khan's (2005) pedagogical dimension of the e-learning framework and Moore's (1989) interaction theory also suggested that creating an online space that encourages meaningful engagement and interaction with peers, instructors, or online resources further supports students learning. The use of a Facebook group and Twitter hashtag in this study provided an additional social space for the MOOC participants to engage and interact with the course content. At the time of this paper, there were a total 4054 members in the Facebook group page. Of all the student postings during the time period of the MOOC, 10 contributors were the most active (e.g., making 31% of 236 posts, 58.3% of 241 comments, 43.7% of 975 likes). Previous research has shown that when social media was used in association with a MOOC, often a small group of individuals were actively engaged in using the tools while the majority did not participate, and only viewed postings by their peers (Liu, McKelroy, Kang, Harron, & Liu, in press; Shen & Kuo, in press).

Usage of Facebook or Twitter as an additional social space may require the support of the instructors as to how they conceive the tool to be used and to increase engagement among participants (Churcher et al., 2014; Khan, 2005; Liu et al., in press). Compared to the usage of the Facebook group in this MOOC, the overall Twitter usage was lower, only 38 tweets and 25 replies. It is possible when two similar social media tools were available simultaneously, the participants used one more than the other. In this study, there was minimal activity by the instructor with Twitter. This lack of activity was mirrored by the students who were less active with Twitter compared to Facebook where the instructor was more active. The tweeting patterns showed the participants mainly tweeted during the weekends and during the mornings. The fact that most participants (83%, n=267) were working professionals could explain why the tweets mostly occurred during the weekends; that is, to avoid busy working days.

The analysis of the content of both the Facebook posts and Twitter feeds showed that the main types of posts were resources and examples that related to the course topic. Interestingly, the longest length of time for a conversation was 1.4 days with only one reply after the original post on Twitter, while the one on Facebook was 2.7 days with several following replies. This finding could possibly be due a different number of participants and also the nature of each social media. On Facebook, it is easier for a member to track posts since it has a static group page, which provides the members a notification function of a new post or new reply. However, there is no membership on Twitter; that is, anyone can use a hashtag. Therefore, people need to use certain hashtags to organize conversations around subjects (Hiscott, 2013).

It is noted that almost half of the participants did not use the Facebook group page or Twitter during the MOOC. However, among the ones who used these social media tools, the participants found these additional social spaces helpful. Participants cited the following as the top useful aspects of using these tools: connectivity with peers, external resources, and course updates or reminders. These reasons were the same top reasons found in our previous study (Liu et al., in press). The resource support dimension of Khan's (2005) e-learning framework indicated that students should have access to instructional supports and additional resources to aid in their learning and engagement in the course. Through the use of these social media tools, students were able to stay current with course reminders and updates as well as share online resources that would not have been possible in the discussion forums. Compared to the discussion forums, these social media tools allowed the participants to connect continuously with people who are truly interested in the topic. For example, after the course ended, some participants tweeted and posted to the Facebook group additional resources to share with others and also let others know they successfully completed the course, which is consistent with the findings by others (Purser et al., 2013). Our findings in this study support the roles of social media tools as discussed in the literature such as exchanging information, communicating with others, and staying connected with the MOOC participants from around the world (Halpern & Gibbs, 2013; Hung & Yuen, 2010).

FUTURE RESEARCH DIRECTIONS

Based on the findings of this study, a few areas need further research. The findings showed that over 60% of the participants that reported they completed most or all of the assignments and activities found the feedback received from their peers in the discussion forum to be useful. It is possible those who did not receive useful feedback from peers rated the peer learning in the forums as not helpful, and those who did not consider peer feedback helpful did not complete all of the assignments. Therefore, there seems to be a connection between the completion of assignments and students' perception, which warrants further research.

Additionally, the MOOC in this study utilized both Facebook and Twitter as social media tools to further support peer interaction about the course content. The results indicated that the instructor utilized Facebook more than Twitter, and there was a higher Facebook usage as compared to the Twitter usage from students. Research is needed to examine the role of instructors in using social media and discussion tools and how that might influence students' use of these tools. Further research is needed to examine the extent of a variety of tools associated with a MOOC, if it is necessary to have more than one similar tools in a MOOC and if so, how these similar tools are used.

CONCLUSION

In summary, this study examined how the MOOC participants interacted with the course discussion forum and social media tools to support their experience by investigating the students' usage patterns and perception of these tools. Through both quantitative and qualitative data, the findings of this study provided evidence of how the participants used discussion forums and Facebook and Twitter to interact with the content, instructor and peers. The findings showed that the MOOC participants found the tools to be helpful and can help create an active, collaborative, and participatory learning environment where they could share ideas and connect with other participants. This snapshot of what happened in this MOOC provided some insights of understanding students' perspective in taking MOOCs, which is needed to understand how to improve the learning experience for participants (Milligan et al., 2013; Saadatmand & Kumpulainen, 2014).

However, a poor interface design was found to impact students' participation and perception of usefulness. Some participants indicated a less optimistic learning experience in using the discussion forums. These participants considered peer learning in the forums not useful due to the low quality or low response of feedback. The discussion forums were found to be less organized and confusing. The diversity of MOOC participants (i.e., diverse knowledge levels, language skills, and geographical locations) creates challenges in MOOCs that should be taken into consideration in the design of MOOC activities.

REFERENCES

Alario-Hoyos, C., Pérez-Sanagustín, M., Delgado-Kloos, C., Muñoz-Organero, M., & Rodríguez-de-las-Heras, A. (2013). Analyzing the impact of built-in and external social tools in a MOOC on educational technologies. In D. Hernández-Leo, T. Ley, R. Klamma, & A. Harrer (Eds.), *Scaling up learning for sustained impact* (pp. 5–18). Berlin: Springer. doi:10.1007/978-3-642-40814-4_2

Anderson, T., & Dron, J. (2010). Three generations of distance education pedagogy. *The International Review Of Research In Open And Distributed Learning, 12*(3), 80-97. Retrieved from http://www.irrodl.org/index.php/irrodl/article/view/890/1663

Bali, M. (2014). MOOC pedagogy: Gleaning good practice from existing MOOCs. *MERLOT. Journal of Online Learning and Teaching, 10*(1), 44–56.

Bernard, R. M., Abrami, P. C., Borokhovski, E., Wade, C. A., Tamim, R. M., Surkes, M. A., & Bethel, E. C. (2009). A meta-analysis of three types of interaction treatments in distance education. *Review of Educational Research, 79*(3), 1243–1289. doi:10.3102/0034654309333844

Breslow, L., Pritchard, D. E., DeBoer, J., Stump, G. S., Ho, A. D., & Seaton, D. T. (2013). Studying learning in the worldwide classroom: Research into edX's first MOOC. *Research & Practice in Assessment, 8*(1), 13–25.

Churcher, K. M. A., Downs, E., & Tewksbury, D. (2014). "Friending" Vygotsky: A social constructivist pedagogy of knowledge building through classroom social media use. *The Journal of Effective Teaching, 14*(1), 33–50.

Daniel, J. (2012). Making sense of MOOCs: Musings in a maze of myth, paradox and possibility. *Journal of Interactive Media in Education, 3*(18), 1–20. doi:10.5334/2012-18

DeBoer, J., Ho, A. D., Stump, G. S., & Breslow, L. (2014). Changing ''course'': Reconceptualizing educational variables for massive open online courses. *Educational Researcher, 43*(2), 74–84. doi:10.3102/0013189X14523038

Fini, A. (2009). The technological dimension of a Massive Open Online Course: The case of the CCK08 course tools. *International Review of Research in Open and Distance Learning, 10*(5). Retrieved from http://www.irrodl.org/index.php/irrodl/article/view/643/1402

Halpern, D., & Gibbs, J. (2013). Social media as a catalyst for online deliberation? Exploring the affordances of Facebook and YouTube for political expression. *Computers in Human Behavior, 29*(3), 159–1168. doi:10.1016/j.chb.2012.10.008

Hiscott, R. (2013, Oct. 8). *The Beginner's Guide to the Hashtag* [Web log post]. Retrieved from http://mashable.com/2013/10/08/what-is-hashtag/

Hung, H., & Yuen, S. C. (2010). Educational use of social networking technology in higher education. *Teaching in Higher Education, 15*(6), 703–714. doi:10.1080/13562517.2010.507307

Johnson, L., Adams Becker, S., Estrada, V., & Freeman, A. (2014). *NMC Horizon Report: 2014 Higher Education Edition.* Austin, Texas: The New Media Consortium.

Khalil, H., & Ebner, M. (2013). "How satisfied are you with your MOOC?" - A Research Study on Interaction in Huge Online Courses. In J. Herrington et al. (Eds.), *Proceedings of World Conference on Educational Multimedia, Hypermedia and Telecommunications 2013* (pp. 830-839). Chesapeake, VA: Association for the Advancement of Computing in Education (AACE).

Khan, B. H. (2005). *Managing e-learning: Design, delivery, implementation and evaluation.* Hershey, PA: Information Science Pub. doi:10.4018/978-1-59140-634-1

Khan, B. H. (2009). The global e-Learning framework. In S. Mishra (Ed.), STRIDE handbook 8 (pp. 42-51). New Delhi, India: The Indira Gandhi National Open University (IGNOU).

Kop, R. (2011). The challenges to connectivist learning on open online networks: Learning experiences during a massive open online course. *International Review of Research in Open and Distance Learning, 12*(3), 19–38.

Kop, R., Fournier, H., & Mak, J. (2011). A pedagogy of abundance or a pedagogy to support human beings? Participant support on massive open online courses. *International Review of Research in Open and Distance Learning, 12*(7), 74–93. Retrieved from http://www.irrodl.org/index.php/irrodl/article/view/1041/2025

Levy, D. (2011). *Lessons learned from participating in a connectivist massive online open course (MOOC)*. Paper presented at the Chais Conference on Instructional Technologies Research 2011: Learning in the technological era, Raanana, Israel.

Lin, M. G., Hoffman, E. S., & Borengasser, C. (2013). Is social media too social for class? A case study of Twitter use. *TechTrends, 57*(2), 39–45. doi:10.1007/s11528-013-0644-2

Liu, M., Kang, J., Cao, M. W., Lim, M. H., Ko, Y. J., Myers, R., & Schmitz Weiss, A. S. (2014). Understanding MOOCs as an emerging online learning tool: Perspectives from the students. *American Journal of Distance Education, 28*(3), 147–159. doi:10.1080/08923647.2014.926145

Liu, M., Kang, J., & McKelroy, E. (2015). Examining learners' perspective on taking a MOOC: Reasons, excitement, and perception of usefulness. *Educational Media International, 52*(2), 129–146. doi:10.1080/09523987.2015.1053289

Liu, M., McKelroy, E., Kang, J., Harron, J., & Liu, S. (2016). Examining the use of Facebook and Twitter as an additional social space in a MOOC. American Journal of Distance Education, 30(1), 14-26.

Mak, S., Williams, R., & Mackness, J. (2010). *Blogs and forums as communication and learning tools in a MOOC*. Paper presented at the 7th International Conference on Networked Learning 2010, Lancaster.

Miles, M. B., Huberman, A. M., & Saldaña, J. (2014). *Qualitative Data Analysis: A Methods Sourcebook*. SAGE Publications, Inc.

Milligan, C., Littlejohn, A., & Margaryan, A. (2013). Patterns of engagement in connectivist MOOCs. *MERLOT Journal of Online Learning and Teaching, 9*(2), 149-159. Retrieved from http://jolt.merlot.org/vol9no2/milligan_0613.pdf

Miyazoe, T., & Anderson, T. (2013). Interaction equivalency in an OER, MOOCS and informal learning era. *Journal of Interactive Media in Education, 2*, 1–15. doi:10.5334/2013-09

Moore, M. G. (1989). Editorial: Three types of interaction. *American Journal of Distance Education, 3*(2), 1–7. doi:10.1080/08923648909526659

Onah, D. F., Sinclair, J., & Boyatt, R. (2014). Exploring the use of MOOC discussion forums. In *Proceedings of London International Conference on Education*. LICE.

Oxford Dictionary. (2011). Concise Oxford English Dictionary (A. Stevenson & M. Waite Eds.; 12th ed.). Oxford, UK: Oxford University Press.

Purser, E. R., Towndrow, A., & Aranguiz, A. (2013). Realizing the potential of peer-to-peer learning: Taming a MOOC with social media. *e-Learning Papers, 33*, 1-5.

Saadatmand, M., & Kumpulainen, K. (2014). Participants' perceptions of learning and networking in connectivist MOOCs. *MERLOT Journal of Online Learning and Teaching, 10*(1), 16–30.

Selingo, J. J. (2014). *MOOC U: Who is getting the most out of online education and why*. New York: Simon and Schuster.

Shen, C. W., & Kuo, C. J. (in press). Learning in massive open online courses: Evidence from social media mining. *Computers in Human Behavior*. doi:10.1016/j.chb.2015.03.013

Siemens, G., Gaševića, D., & Dawson, S. (2015). *Preparing for the digital university: A review of the history and current state of distance, blended, and online learning*: Athabasca University. Retrieved from http://linkresearchlab.org/PreparingDigitalUniversity.pdf

Sinha, T. (2014). *Supporting MOOC instruction with social network analysis.* arXiv preprint arXiv:1401.5175

Stewart, B. (2013). Massiveness + openness = new literacies of participation? *MERLOT Journal of Online Learning and Teaching, 9*(2), 228-238. Retrieved from http://jolt.merlot.org/vol9no2/stewart_bonnie_0613.htm

Swan, K. (2002). Building learning communities in online courses: The importance of interaction. *Education Communication and Information*, *2*(1), 23–49. doi:10.1080/1463631022000005016

Tomkin, J. H., & Charlevoix, D. (2014). Do professors matter? Using an a/b test to evaluate the impact of instructor involvement on MOOC student outcomes. In *Proceedings of the first ACM conference on Learning@ Scale Conference* (pp. 71-78). ACM.

ADDITIONAL READING

Allen, I. E., & Seaman, J. (2014). *Grade change: Tracking online education in the United States*. Babson Survey Research Group and Quahog Research Group, LLC.

Liyanagunawardena, T. R., Adams, A. A., & Williams, S. A. (2013). MOOCs: A systematic study of the published literature 2008-2012. *International Review of Research in Open and Distance Learning, 14*(3), 202–227. Retrieved from http://www.irrodl.org/index.php/irrodl/article/view/1455/2531

McAuley, A., Stewart, B., Siemens, G., & Cormier, D. (2010). *The MOOC Model For Digital Practice*. Retrieved from http://www.elearnspace.org/Articles/MOOC_Final.pdf

Siemens, G. (2012). *MOOCs are really a platform*. Retrieved from http://www.elearnspace.org/blog/2012/07/25/moocs-are-really-a-platform/

Yuan, L., & Powell, S. (2013). *MOOCs and open education: Implications for higher education - A white paper. JISC CETIS*. Retrieved from http://publications.cetis.ac.uk/2013/667

KEY TERMS AND DEFINITIONS

Advertisement: A code used in this study to categorize instances where the participant or instructor posted, via the Facebook group or in a Twitter feed, an announcement for a networking opportunity related to the course topic (e.g., an event, activity, future conference, other MOOC, etc.)

Course Reminders: A code used in this study to categorize instances where the instructor posted to the Facebook group or in Twitter feed reminders for course activities and assignments.

Data Visualizations: A presentation of data in a graphical or pictorial layout that allows individuals to understand information more easily and quickly.

Discussion Forum: An online method of sharing ideas, opinions, or responding to others comments. Typically requires a host site or LMS to facilitate the online discussion.

Examples: A code used in this study to categorize instances where a participant or instructor posted examples of artifacts that related to the course content (e.g., infographic from a website) via the Facebook group or Twitter feed.

Facebook Group: A page from Facebook that is created specifically for an organization or unit to connect members. Individuals can join the group and post their thoughts to interact with other members through discussion threads.

Infographic: A visual representation, such as a chart or diagram, used to simplify large amounts of data so that it is easy to understand.

Learning Management System (LMS): A web-based software application or technology that is used to implement and assess specific learning content by allowing for the creation, delivery, and tracking of course modules.

Peer Learning: Learning that occurs through peer-to-peer interaction or through the sharing of ideas with a group of learners.

Personal Feeling: A code used in this study to categorize instances where a participant or instructor posts comments to the Facebook group or in a Twitter feed that express personal feelings about their experience in the MOOC.

Resources: A code used in this study to categorize instances that a participant or the instructor provided resources (e.g., links to web articles, books for further reading, or online videos regarding the topic) to others via the Facebook group or in a Twitter feed.

Social Media: The collective of communal based online communication channels that are dedicated to creating interaction, modes to share content, and to create collaboration among members.

Twitter: Twitter is a free social media tool that allows registered users to broadcast short posts or *tweets* that are limited to 140 characters. An individual can add a hashtag to their post to connect *tweets* into a conversation thread or topic. A hashtag (appears as #reference) acts as a label to identify related discussions.

Usage Data: Each participant's usage data from the discussion forums, extracted from the Moodle LMS, which represents the participant's interactions within the forum including the participant's username, the date, time, the action that occurred, the page URL, and the page title.

Chapter 3
The Medium, the Content, and the Performance:
An Overview on Media-Based Learning

Hans W. Giessen
Saarland University, Germany

ABSTRACT

This chapter focuses on aspects of the technological and interface dimensions of Badrul Khan's model, arguing that a correlation exists between the medium of instruction, students' performance, and the instructional content. Media-based learning is not necessarily more effective, simply because it uses a medium. Several variables exist that influence its success: the medium itself, its properties, production and consumption restraints; the content, and the way it can be presented in the context of a specific medium, and learners' cognitive styles. All these variables and more have to be taken into consideration, alone and interacting, in order to decide whether and where media-based learning is to be used, and where it might be counterproductive.

INTRODUCTION

Does Media-Based Learning Make Sense?

In the early stages of media-based learning, Clark (1983), implied in a frequently mentioned article, that the instructional media probably does not have a decisive influence on the learning process.

BACKGROUND

The "Language Networks "project within the program "Lifelong Learning" of the German Federal-Länder-Commission for Educational Planning and Promotion Research was under the author's direction, and it investigated the advantages and problems of media-based language training. It soon became clear

DOI: 10.4018/978-1-5225-0466-5.ch003

during the early stages of the literature review, that a final conception about media-based learning is more complex, including its verifiability, than generally assumed (Giessen, 2004).

Initially–and very broadly–the majority of the studies reviewed confirmed a performance imbalance between traditional and media-based learning. The studies involved were of a quantitative nature, and usually school classes or groups of learners were compared. Here the socio-graphic composition of the groups, and the learning content were kept as identical as possible, so that the only altered variable was related to media-based instruction. In the context of these experimental studies, media-based instruction proved to be, in direct comparison with traditional classroom instruction, on average not worse than the conventional instruction methods – however, in general, not significantly better.

There were observations indicating that individual pupils can do better with media-based learning than with traditional instruction, while on the contrary, other learners had greater difficulties, got along not so well and even produced worse results with media-based learning than with traditional instruction. Accordingly, the experimental studies mentioned above (and being described in the next paragraphs with more detail) might hide a division of the pupils into those who profit from learning with the computer and others who did not get along so well with media-based instruction.

THE IMPACT OF TIME ON TASK

Which other variables could play a role in this context? Wallace and Mutooni had already pointed out in 1997 that users of computer-based programs indicated, in contrast to the participants in classroom-based events, the tendency to adhere to individual learning topics until a high level of content understanding had been reached. They also had a more flexible approach to learning than their fellow students, and spread this process throughout the day. It became apparent that media-based learning requires more time than traditional learning. Learners, who were not able, or did not want to devote sufficient time to computer based learning, did not benefit from media-based instruction. The opposite was the case for those who chose to invest the necessary time.

On the contrary, Pitman, Gosper, and Rich (1999) analyzed the grades and the learning behavior of 348 students. Here it became clear that the students with higher grades had more frequently and regularly requested and used the computer-based additional options than the students with lower grades. Schulman and Sims (1999) confirmed this assumption – they also noticed that the better learners preferred to learn using media-based resources and used this alternative more often, while the less successful learners normally chose traditional forms of learning.

Different time lengths would thus be a criterion that may be important for the success of media-based instruction. Apparently, sufficient periods of time are required to learn efficiently with a computer – and that is clearly more time than with traditional, classroom learning methods. Anyone who devotes, or is willing to devote the necessary time seems to have a greater learning success. This is also confirmed by additional surveys, qualitative studies and evaluations, for instance by Scott, Durnell, Cramton, Gauvin, Steinke and Patterson (1997), who interviewed 123 distance learners for their perceptions in connection with a multinational e-learning project. The respondents stated that longer time lengths and adequate time coordination were of utmost importance. Ward and Newlands (1998) also reached a similar conclusion. The respondents stated that the main advantage achieved was their autonomy when determining the time and pace of their own learning process. This also had the effect that the learners involved invested longer periods of time in the learning contents, until they had processed all the information. Therefore, the main conclusion of Ward and Newlands (1998) was that through media-based learning more content can be acquired, but also that more time is needed to achieve this. This was also confirmed by Usip and Bee (1998), who stressed the importance of the *time* factor in media-based learning. They analyzed the differences in the attributes of the users of online offerings and attendance at lecture hours. Their main finding was that the users of computer-based options appeared to be, on average, not worse, but better than their fellow learners. One decisive argument was that, in this case also, more time was needed to acquire the learning contents, but generally in a more concentrated manner, for instance, when working through tests and performance assessments. The group of participants that was ultimately successful was the one that had a large amount of time available for learning activities.

Nevertheless, during the "Language Networks" project within the program "Lifelong Learning" of the German Federal-Länder-Commission for Educational Planning and Promotion Research, it became evident that an additional explanatory perspective behind these facts was needed. Apparently, the objective amount of time available does not play the attributed decisive role – as many pupils were unwilling to invest a sufficient amount of time because they did not particularly appreciate media-based learning. The surveys indicated that this was mainly due to two factors: the *learning contents* and the *learner type*.

Of course, there are forms of media-based learning in which, similar to traditional instruction, individual learners and their specific preferences and difficulties can be taken into consideration, such as with videoconferences (Bufe & Giessen, 2005; Bufe & Giessen, 2011). Partly, this also applies for so-called "social media", at least, again, in connection with its particular type of application.

The situation is quite different in the case of media-based learning units, tutorials, and practices, etc., which are usually standardized and where the media plays a dominant role. In many cases, acceptance or refusal to use media-based learning units are the only choices for the learner. Media-based learning is precisely developed to make the learning contents available with a certain effectiveness for large numbers of learners. Nevertheless, the result is that the learners who might be more suited for other forms of learning are forced to subject themselves to media-based methods of content delivery.

There are, of course, also options that are not imposed by schools or school teachers – for instance CDs used with language courses or similar online offerings. Nevertheless, a direct empirical comparison between two learning groups cannot be made in this context. In principle, such options seem to meet a certain demand that can be interpreted as an indicator for their efficiency. It could be the case that an early self-selection of potential learners takes place – this means that these offerings are only taken up by those who can handle media-based learning materials in an effective and targeted manner. Others probably would not want to take such offerings in the first place.

Moreover, it became apparent very early that the motivation to use media-based learning options must be seen in a more differentiated light. The quality of learning or its practical results is only one, and, sometimes, not even the most important category for deciding in favor of such an option – other categories that are as relevant or, sometimes, even more relevant are, for instance, the flexibility of time and space in the learning process and their achievable added values. The expectations in terms of educational quality and the relationship of effort invested to results achieved were, in this case, less important (Kariya, 2003). The existence of a robust market for educational media is, therefore not an argument that contradicts the assumption that there are different learner types, some of whom have difficulties with media-based learning.

LEARNER TYPES

The fact that there are different learner types has been known for a long time. Reference is made to the historical research of Kurt Lewin from 1942. Likewise, the fact that there are different learner types among computer users is not a new finding. This insight was made popular by Sherry Turkle's book in 1984. Although the existence of different learner types, also in the context of media-based learning, should not be a surprise, and can definitely be seen as a part of Badrul Khan's (2005) e-learning model, it is noticeable that this is rarely taken into account when producing e-learning material.

As already mentioned, evaluation of the success of media-based learning is usually determined at a group level. When the evaluation leads to average results, that are not worse than the ones attained with traditional instruction methods, the lack of consideration of different learner types is hardly noticeable, at least in the context of the evaluation. It may then occur that indeed, some learners profit from media-based learning options (but perhaps at the price of an increased time input), while other learners with greater difficulties 'get lost' in the evaluations. The perspective of the learner has so far played only a subordinate role, since this is an individual category which cannot be easily depicted on a quantitative level, for instance for the granting of funds for the production of learning contents or for feedback from supervisory authorities.

For this reason, it took some time until studies that deal with the issue of learner types in the context of media-based learning were proposed. The insight that the "learner's perspective" (Ehlers 2004) or individual, cognitive learning styles are of importance for media-based learning first appeared in studies at the middle of the last decade.

In any case, it is clear that the concept which states that media-based learning and traditional learning are of equal value, ignores important aspects – that, by the way, are related to both learning forms: some learners profit significantly more from media-based learning than from traditional learning (Giessen 2004, pp.44-47). What therefore are the variables that make media-based learning more successful – and when is it perhaps better to abstain from it? Surely, there are also situational and individual aspects that have an effect in individual cases; on a supra-individual level, the medium or also the type of media-based learning materials and the learner type seem to play the major role. Therefore, this author will concentrate hereinafter on these variables: Contents, media, and learner types.

CONTENTS

In principle – and apart from media-based learning – it is a commonplace that not all contents can be transmitted equally well with every media form. The following example illustrates this: Why are newspapers and magazines, in most cases, the sources of investigative reporting that can even provoke a crisis in a political system, like the *Washington Post* and the *Watergate Affair* in the USA in the 1970s or the *Boston Globe's* investigation of abuses in the Catholic Archdiocese of Boston in 2002? Why can this level of investigative journalism be achieved by daily newspapers, which are read by comparatively few, but certainly influential and opinion forming people, and not by television journalists, who have bigger audiences? A look at television reports clarifies quickly why this was the case. The television reporters could film the buildings related to both cases from outside and, of course, they did not have pictures of break-in at the *Watergate Hotel* nor the conduct of the Roman Catholic priests of the Boston archdiocese. Investigative journalism concerning individual scandals is, in this case, barely possible on television, because everything there has to be illustrated with video and sound bytes. This is, of course, not the case in investigative journalism. For instance, when a television camera team detects moldy food in a supermarket, it can produce impressive images that have a strong effect on the public. But in an environment where acts are no longer observable because they were carried out in the past by persons who operated secretly, there are no associated images and not even the chance to film them. Since it is almost impossible to produce investigative reports without authentic images about the behavior of the persons involved, generally this is not even attempted in television programs. This abstinence from dealing with such issues is a consequence of the requirements of this medium. Newspapers, on the other hand, can easily provide such reports and describe how the information was researched from many different sources. Such scandals have nearly always been made public by press reports in the print media. The medium is certainly decisive – as shown in this example – when determining which contents should be presented, and what public impact they might have. This insight evidently also applies for other forms of learning materials.

MEDIA

The following is a discussion of an example from a research project on the subject of 'Language Learning and Media' conducted by the author that involved the use of video clips that were produced for a multimedia offering where native speakers could be seen and heard (Giessen, 2006). The integration of authentic speech samples seemed to be a clear added value of this medium; in particular the comprehension of language could be facilitated using a synchronous input of mouth movements and phonetic production. Its integration into a multimedia offering involved the video material being shown by default in a small window - not full screen - like a small television image. The viewing window did fill more than one fourth of the screen area, but was big enough to make the mouth movements easily visible. The learners could also switch over to a full-screen representation, but this demanded an active intervention from the learner. In the standard screen representation, the *frame* alternative is a part of the multimedia options that was seen as an additional alternative. For instance, the navigation bar, and the additional information is always available, as it was for the video clips.

The test users did not use the video segments in the manner that the researchers had expected. They stopped using the application before it was finished playing. Why did this unexpected behavior occur? The researchers observed the users, and also conducted several interviews with them. They discovered that this behavior was not due in principle to the video-based contents. The test users found the video productions in full-screen representation appealing, interesting, and didactically helpful. The unexpected user behavior was caused rather by very specific media characteristics. The students found that the primary problem when viewing video clips in computer-based multimedia products seemed to be the short distance between the watcher and the computer monitor. The learners sat very close to the monitor in order to click exactly on *icons* or *hyperlinks* with the mouse. As a rule, they focused on only a sector of the monitor screen, and sometimes only a single spot on the screen. This, of course, lead to a narrowing of focus and attention. Furthermore, the character resolution of their computer monitors was relatively low, which rapidly caused eye fatigue. Also the body posture had to be static for long periods of time. The computer monitor could not be shifted easily when their sitting position became uncomfortable and precisely when learners focused over a long period on a single spot of the monitor, their body posture was particularly tense; and this of course, reinforced fatigue effects. All the interviewed learners felt that focusing over a long period on a restricted area of the monitor in order to follow information was 'arduous'. This can lead to the learners taking different courses of action when viewing video clips in computer-based multimedia. The users tended not to focus for very long at the rather small video frame, but instead allowed their eyes – and attention - to roam. This was enticing because there were additional frames and information next to the video image, which drew the user's attention, caused by embedding the video frame in a visual surrounding which was also, at the same time, a rich information environment. Many learners in this "Language Learning and Media" research project actually confirmed that they may play, but did not watch a video clip for very long. Many learners had the subjective impression that they could still follow the contents, because they could hear the acoustic information and therefore would not miss any information. But they were inevitably less focused – and naturally, missed complctcly the additional visual information.

Apparently an additional course of action was required regarding the testing of the possibilities of interactivity, which now could be used with moving pictures with *time based media*. Many users viewed the beginning of a video and then moved forward with the slide bar over the course of the film to determine if it was worth viewing the whole clip. When they gained the impression that it was worth viewing the whole video, they would usually look back for the position where they had 'exited'. They did not start again from the beginning, because viewing a known passage again was perceived as *boring*. It was relatively difficult to find the exact position where a video was exited. With the navigation bar, it was only possible to head approximately for a certain position, and hardly anyone keeps in mind the time code data when moving back and forth using the navigation bar. As a rule, the users could not find the exact position in the film where they had exited, so that they might see a passage twice, or miss a part of it. Often, learners left the video sequence because they were not able to reconstruct the content. Similar behavior also occurred when learners used tablets and smartphones (see also Giessen, 2013).

It is worth stating again that, in general, these alternative courses of action only occurred with videos that were embedded in multi-media, distracting environments, where the video image was relatively small and next to the navigation bar or an additional window, which distracted the user's attention. This naturally does not apply where a computer monitor with 'full-screen display' 'is used exclusively as a 'flat TV screen substitute', which modifies many of the external conditions. The sitting posture changes – here the computer is only the channel for a television production, and will be only used as such. The behavior described also does not apply when the learning process takes place in a class or a training course, and the learners are instructed to view the information simultaneously. This description already illustrates the inadequacy of such situation. Still, the social pressure that derives from the instructors or their classmates, who observe each other during this process, is apparently sufficient that the users tend to view video applications from beginning to end without searching or skipping portions. Multimedia options are, on the other hand, part of traditional self-learning media, and in such circumstances, the observed difficulties occur almost without exception when using authentic video material.

The researchers determined that the seemingly obvious idea of producing 'authentic language material' as multimedia self-learning media for computers, to facilitate for the learners an easier access to the target language, seems based on a misunderstanding. Basically, 'authentic language material' appears to be more suitable for streaming media or DVDs. Here, however, other advantages of a computer-based multimedia product like media changes, so that direct exercises cannot be integrated into the media, so cannot be used. In the context of computer-based multimedia techniques, however, video clips with authentic language samples appear to be rather ineffective, although its use may initially seem obvious and appropriate.

Different user behaviors were observed by the researchers when learners were viewing video clips, depending on whether they were used alone or in a group, and this suggests that media-based self-learning demands a particularly high level of self-discipline. In turn, the degree of self-discipline exerted is mostly determined by individual learners. The example of media-based learning using authentic language samples on video clearly shows the close link that exists between media production and their constraints and possibilities on the one hand, and the individual learner-type on the other hand.

SERIOUS GAMES

Similar observations can be found in regard of *Serious Games*, a genre in its own right in computer-based ludative teaching and learning (for an overview see: Ritterfeld et al., 2009; Fromme & Unger 2012; Bredl & Bösche 2013; Giessen, 2015a). For example, many learners try to avoid 'learning modes' in order to return to a 'gaming mode' as fast as possible (Kerres et al., 2009). In consequence, all meta-analyses found by the author (Squirre, 2003, Kirriemuir & McFarlane, 2004; Heers, 2005; Vogel et al., 2006; Arnseth, 2006; O'Neil et al., 2005; Ritterfeld et al., 2009; Wouters et al., 2009) state that, until now, meager findings have existed in regard to the teaching and learning effects of *Serious Games.* Ke (2005) insisted that all empirical results regarding *Serious Games* depend on the technical development and the tools used; thus the current state-of-the-art should not primarily lead to the question of *whether or not* games should be integrated in a learning environment, but *how* this could be done best, with what topic, at what opportunity, in what embedment – thus, with what kind of "instructional game design" – and with what kind of learners.

LEARNER TYPES

The interaction between media-based learning material and learner types has appeared in different contexts. Bufe and Giessen (2005, 2011) (and analogously, for instance Bailey and Iqbal, 2007) emphasized that interactive online communication, which seems to be a clear, added value of the media-based language learning, as they can be produced with native speakers, suffers from the surprising fact that spontaneity is hardly possible in this context. Also, in the case of synchronous communication scenarios, for instance in video-conferences, disturbing delays of greater or lesser duration occur. Principally, there is also a lack of several items of additional communicative information, so that irony, annoyance, or boredom cannot be detected. This can negatively impact communication.

Besides the media effects, there are also other individual aspects, starting with students' widely differing perceptive abilities (Montgomery, 1999). Visual learners are better off when presented with graphical displays; whilst auditory learners are more successful when presented with information acoustically (Ferrari & Sternberg, 1998). The use of media-based learning materials by students will therefore never be the same; certain media may be adequate for some learners, but not for other learners. Therefore, it is difficult to develop general rules for the application of media.

Workman (2004) was able to demonstrate that there are qualitative differences between the World Wide Web and CD-ROMs when working on learning tasks. In this context, learning on the world-wide web had a stronger social involvement and required and induced more interactions. It should be added that being connected to the Internet and thus having the chance to switch to other web pages (or the mail program, for that matter) causes more distractions, whether this is obvious to the user or not. In any case, media-based learning on the world-wide web was less structured. However, this media has proved to be a positive experience for social learners. In contrast, learning using a CD-ROM was perceived as rather monotonous, but significantly more structured, which was positive for learners, who learn introspectively. It could even be demonstrated that learners who can better handle abstract content are more efficient web-based learners. In contrast, learners who favor specific information and wish to acquire this step-by-step, preferred learning with a CD-ROM. This research indicated that the decision whether the computer-based learning materials should be developed for the web or for a home computer is of importance, because of the specific advantages and disadvantages for the different learner types. Similar findings exist in regard of learning from paper or in the context of animated applications (Brandl, 2002; Stepp-Greany, 2002; Wästlund et al., 2005; Ackerman & Lauterman, 2012; Giessen, 2014; Mueller & Oppenheimer, 2014; Park et al., 2014, Marcinkonienė & Zdanytė, 2015).

Empirical findings regarding the importance of media and learner type date back to the 1990s (Fussell & Benimoff, 1995), and in research since there have been many similar observations (see, for instance, Tamim et. al., 2011), so that the assumption of Clark (1983) mentioned at the beginning of this chapter, which claims that a specific media is irrelevant for the learning process, can no longer be accepted. Altogether, it can be stated that when developing media-based learning materials, a one-and-only, true method does not exist. Evidently, many results are individual, situational, and context specific (Bangert, 2008; Giessen, 2015b), nevertheless, it is possible to make statements about the context where media-based learning - in a specific media - can be used purposefully and effectively. Many attempts have been made to theoretically explain the different responses observed from students.

THEORETICAL ANNOTATIONS

Meantime, there are different theories regarding, in particular, the use of media. The approaches of Herbert Marshall McLuhan (1962) are already well known, as is the related 'media richness theory' of Richard Daft and Robert Lengel (1984). Depending on how much the learners (or generally speaking: the users) are absorbed in the learning medium, Daft and Lengel (1984) speak about different degrees of "media richness": Less 'rich' media is not intensive enough to achieve an overall focusing of students' attention; for instance: discussions forums, chats, e-mail, or other forms of text communications. Another media deficit, which may cause a media platform to look *weak* includes the lack of direct feedback to the learner within the medium used. The result is almost unavoidably attention deficits and uncertainty regarding the tasks to be completed. Subsequently, using *weak* media means that the process of self and, even more so, collaborative learning (see also Mason, 2004) demands greater cognitive efforts from students, who quickly start to determine what is actually intended by the instructor and to what extent this serves what the student wants. This is perhaps the reason why more self-discipline is required in the context of media-based learning than in traditional learning situations.

Relatively new, though, are scholars' attempts to link media theory with studies on learner types. For a long time these considerations did not play a role in scholarly consideration (Flavell, 1992; Sternberg & Grigorenko, different cognitive learner types (Grigorenko & Sternberg, 1995). These studies, however, were usually related to traditional instruction, but it should be noted that there are marked differences between information processing and learning (Rehder & Hoffmann, 2005). Its connection with media implementation was first mentioned in the 1990s (see Pillay, 1998). It is crucial to note here how learners collect and process information (Hayes & Allinson, 1998) and subsequently address the problems and make pertinent decisions (Gardner, 2009). A decisive theoretical approach in this context is the *cognitive load theory* of Hazeltine, Ruthruff and Remington (2006). Related ideas come from Robert J. Sternberg (1997) with his quite complex and not always easy to apply *theory of mental self-government.* This theory assumes that learners, when under ideal and free conditions, organize their learning process in accordance with their cognitive abilities. This leads to various forms of mental representation or diverse codings.

Learners with different learning styles therefore need different learning situations and strategies. Some can learn better in the context of interactive group processes; others need quietness in order to be able to concentrate. This example has been chosen because it enables, at first theoretically, a link to the above mentioned media theories. The *interactive learner* group mentioned first will probably profit clearly from diverse media learning forms, for instance from discussion forums. For introspective learners discussion forums are, on the contrary, an impediment in the learning process.

Another example refers a well-known observation concerning the fact that a different group of learners can learn best when observing processes (Bandura, 1978). Apparently, mirror neurons are activated when students can observe the efforts of other learners. This increases their self-motivation and, ultimately, their learning achievements. Here, it can be assumed that media samples can have a positive effect e.g., observing and learning from television programs. On the other hand, yet another group of learners must make their own experiences that they can record and process successfully. Thus, mediated communication constitutes a limitation for them. Nevertheless, it may be that learners, who need individual experiences when learning, have an advantage through, and in online-learning environments – at least in comparison with the *observing learner type*. So we have here – at least theoretically – a specific allocation of learner type and diverse scenarios of mediated learning.

Different learner types require information of varying density and extent in order to be able to profit from instructional and learning efforts. Knowing the students' preference for density and extent in information is necessary to assess the efforts, the problems, and the effectiveness of the respective learning process within metacognitive processes (Hayes & Allinson, 1998). Maybe this can be explained with the findings of Baruch and Nicholson (1997), who determined that learners with a strong tendency to uncertainty avoidance – who also have a very limited willingness to take risks and to get along without explicit certainty – feel rather uncomfortable with self-learning media. Additionally, there are parallels to other findings mentioned above: Since online media increases the level of ambiguity with regard to both the tasks and the expectations placed on the respective learner - and placed by the learners on themselves - learners with a low level of tolerance for uncertainty and a high level of uncertainty avoidance are at a disadvantage here, while for learners with a high level of uncertainty tolerance and low uncertainty avoidance, mediated learning can even generate additional advantages.

RECOMMENDATIONS

Obviously, it is desirable for instructors and instructional designers to know if and how media-based learning materials can be used appropriately and efficiently. In assessing whether its use is, in fact, appropriate, the findings described above, that media-based learning is basically more time-consuming than traditional learning seems at this point particularly relevant. According to this, it is important both for the instructors and the learners to use media-based learning materials in such a way that the increase in value of the content rises accordingly and the majority of learners benefit from it.

FUTURE RESEARCH DIECTIONS

A systematic approach to media choices must take into account at least the following aspects:

1. **What Is the Effect of the Medium?** Book, video on computers, television sets, smart phones, CD-ROM or DVD, VoIP (e.g. Skype), learning platforms, apps?
2. **What Are the Content Characteristics?** e.g. Which language is to be used? Is the object to study grammar, regional studies, or pronunciation practice? Is grammar for native speakers, acquisition of the first foreign language, pluri-lingual instruction?
3. **Who Are the Learners?** Are they visual, auditory or kinesthetic learner types? A child or an adult learner? Monolingual, bilingual or maybe multilingual learner? Does gender eventually play a role? Or possibly also cultural characteristics?

CONCLUSION

As Khan (2005) e-learning model, described in detail elsewhere in this volume, already demonstrates, media-based learning is very complex and a lot of aspects have to be taking into reconsideration. This chapter focused on two aspects that were rarely seen in relation: the very medium and the learning type. It could be shown that success very much depends on accepting these factors.

As seen from the discussion above, it is questionable whether a systematic approach that can link together contents, user type, and medium can be developed. As stated above, for this author, this seems be hardly possible since the above-mentioned variables and their interactions give rise to too many differing conditions. New variables are constantly being added to the manifold and, as yet, largely uninvestigated interactions between three main variables. This includes the technical developments that continuously change the media itself, setting off new conditions.

One possible instructional reaction is to always have an insight into the effects of the different variables. This is not so 'new' and less difficult to implement than it sounds, because every form of instruction needs an adaptation process between instructor and learner. It is therefore important to trust the intuition of the instructors and the learners and not to promote media-based learning where its use may be counterproductive or problematic regarding the effort-benefit relation, when using media only because it is still *stylish* and *fashionable*.

REFERENCES

Ackerman, R., & Lauterman, T. (2012). Taking reading comprehension exams on screen or on paper? A metacognitive analysis of learning texts under pressure. *Computers in Human Behavior*, *28*(5), 1816–1828. doi:10.1016/j.chb.2012.04.023

Arnseht, H. C. (2006). Learning to play or playing to learn. A critical account of the models of communication informing educational research in computer gameplay. *The International Journal of Computer Game Research*, *6*(1). Retrieved from http://gamestudies.org/0601/articles/arnseth

Bailey, B. P., & Iqbal, S. T. (2007). Understanding changes in mental workload during execution of goal-directed tasks and its application for interruption management. *ACM Transactions on Computer-Human Interaction, 14*(21), 1-21.

Bandura, A. (1978). The self-system in reciprocal determinism. *The American Psychologist, 33*(4), 344–358. doi:10.1037/0003-066X.33.4.344

Bangert, A. W. (2008). The influence of social presence and teaching presence on the quality of online critical inquiry. *Journal of Computing in Higher Education, 20*(1), 34–61. doi:10.1007/BF03033431

Baruch, Y., & Nicholson, N. (1997). Home, sweet work: Requirements for effective home-working. *Journal of General Management, 23*(2), 15–30.

Brandl, K. (2002). Integrating internet-based reading materials into the foreign language curriculum: From teacher-to student-centered approaches. *Language Learning & Technology, 6*(3), 87–107.

Bredl, K., & Bösche, W. (Eds.). (2013). *Serious games and virtual worlds in education, Professional development, and healthcare*. Hershey, PA: IGI Global. doi:10.4018/978-1-4666-3673-6

Bufe, W., & Giessen, H. W. (Eds.). (2005). Videoconferencing grenzübergreifend - La visioconference transfrontaliere. Paris: L'Harmattan.

Bufe, W., & Giessen, H. W. (2011). Videokonferenz als medium der grenzdidaktik. In Wider den einheitsunterricht. Deutschlernen an der grenze (pp 23-35). Liberec: Technical University of Liberec Press.

Clark, R. E. (1983). Reconsidering research on learning from media. *Review of Educational Research, 53*(4), 445–459. doi:10.3102/00346543053004445

Daft, R. L., & Lengel, R. H. (1984). Information richness: A new approach to managerial behavior and organizational design. In Research in organizational behavior (vol. 6, pp. 191-233). Homewood, IL: JAI Press.

Ehlers, U. (2004). *Qualität im e-learning aus lernersicht. Grandlagen, empirie and modellkonzeption subjektiver qualität*. Wiesbaden: VS-Verlag. doi:10.1007/978-3-663-11211-2

Ferrari, M., & Sternberg, R. J. (1998). *The development of mental abilities and styles*. In W. Damon, D. Kuhn, & R. S. Siegler (Eds.), Handbook of child psychology (Vol. 2, pp. 899–946). New York: Wiley.

Flavell, J. H. (1992). Cognitive development: Past, present, and future. *Developmental Psychology, 28*(6), 998–1005. doi:10.1037/0012-1649.28.6.998

Fromme, J., & Unger, A. (Eds.). (2012). *Computer games and new media cultures. A handbook of digital games studies*. Heidelberg, Germany: Springer. doi:10.1007/978-94-007-2777-9

Fussell, S. R., & Benimoff, N. I. (1995). Social and cognitive processes in interpersonal communication: Implications for advanced telecommunications technologies. *Human Factors, 37*(2), 228–250. doi:10.1518/001872095779064546 PMID:7642182

Gardner, H. (2009). Fünf kompetenzen für die zukunft. In Medienpädagogik: Emotionale Intelligenz in der Schule. Unterrichten mit Geschichten (pp. 138-149). Weinheim: Beltz-Verlag.

Giessen, H. W. (2004). *Sprachnetzwerke in grenzräumen*. Saarbrücken: LPM.

Giessen, H. W. (2006). *Videosegmente als authentische lehrmaterialien für den sprachunterricht in computergestützten multimedia-produktionen?* Retrieved from http://www.vep-landau.de/bzf/2006_45/07_Giessen_091-096.pdf

Giessen, H. W. (2013). Formale aspekte bei der videoproduktion für handys. *Journal of Serial Narration on Television*, *4*(Winter), 33–52. Retrieved from http://www.uni-saarland.de/fileadmin/user_upload/Professoren/fr41_ProfSolteGresser/serial-narration/PDFs/Journal_04-2013/033-052_a23dnd7.pdf

Giessen, H. W. (2014). Über den Einsatz medienadäquater Präsentationsformen im Fremdsprachenunterricht: Darstellung der Methode und Anmerkungen zum thematisierten Inhalt. In Fremdsprachenunterricht im Spannungsfeld zwischen Sprachwissen und Sprachkönnen. Saarbrücken: htw.

Giessen, H. W. (2015a). Serious games effects: An overview. *Procedia: Social and Behavioral Sciences*, *174*, 2240–2244. doi:10.1016/j.sbspro.2015.01.881

Giessen, H. W. (2015b). Media-based learning methodology: Stories, games, and emotions. In *The international handbook of e-learning* (Vol. 2, pp. 43–54). London: Routledge.

Grigorenko, E. L., & Sternberg, R. J. (1995). Thinking styles. In International handbook of personality and intelligence (pp. 205-229). London: Plenum Press doi:doi:10.1007/978-1-4757-5571-8_11 doi:10.1007/978-1-4757-5571-8_11

Hayes, J., & Allinson, C. W. (1998). Cognitive style and the theory and practice of individual and collective learning in organizations. *Human Relations*, *51*(7), 847–871. doi:10.1177/001872679805100701

Hazeltine, E., Ruthruff, E., & Remington, R. W. (2006). The role of input and output modality pairings in dual-task performance: Evidence for content-dependent central interference. *Cognitive Psychology*, *52*(4), 291–345. doi:10.1016/j.cogpsych.2005.11.001 PMID:16581054

Heers, R. (2005). *Being there: Untersuchungen zum Wissenserwerb in virtuellen Umgebungen*. Tübingen: Eberhard-Karls-Universität, Diss. Informations-und Kognitionswissenschaften.

Kariya, S. (2003). Online education expands and evolves. *IEEE Spectrum*, *40*(5), 49–51. doi:10.1109/MSPEC.2003.1200179

Ke, F. (2009). A qualitative meta-analysis of computer games as learning tools. In R. E. Ferdig (Ed.), *Handbook of research on effective electronic gaming in education* (pp. 1–32). Hershey, PA: IGI-Global. doi:10.4018/978-1-59904-808-6.ch001

Kerres, M., Bormann, M., & Vervenne, M. (2009). Didaktische konzeption von serious games: Zur verknüpfung von spiel- und lernangeboten. *Medienpädagogik* Retrieved from http://mediendidaktik.uni-due.de/sites/default/files/kerres0908_0.pdf

Khan, B. H. (2005). *Managing e-learning: design, delivery, implementation, and evaluation*. Hershey, PA: Information Science Publishing. doi:10.4018/978-1-59140-634-1

Kirriemuir, J., & McFarlane, A. (2004). *Literature review in games and learning*. Bristol: Futurelab. Retrieved from http://hal.archivesouvertes.fr/docs/00/19/04/53/PDF/kirriemuir-j-2004-r8.pdf

Lewin, K. (1942). Field theory of learning. In Yearbook of the national society for the study of education (pp. 215-242). doi:doi:10.1037/11335-006 doi:10.1037/11335-006

Marcinkonienė, R., & Zdanytė, J. (2015). Conventional and digital media in language learning. *Proceedings ICoN, 2015*, 101–111.

Mason, R. (2004). Online education using learning objects. *British Journal of Educational Technology, 35*(6), 752–754. doi:10.1111/j.1467-8535.2004.00432_9.x

McLuhan, H. M. (1962). *The gutenberg galaxy: The making of typographic man*. Toronto: University of Toronto Press.

Montgomery, D. A. (1999). Human sensitivity to variability information in detection decisions. *Human Factors, 41*(1), 90–105. doi:10.1518/001872099779577246

Mueller, P. A., & Oppenheimer, D. M. (2014, June). The pen is mightier than the keyboard: Advantages of longhand over laptop note taking. *Psychological Science, 25*(6), 1–10. doi:10.1177/0956797614524581 PMID:24760141

O'Neil, H. F., Wainess, R., & Baker, E. L. (2005). Classification of learning outcomes: Evidence from the computer games literature. *Curriculum Journal, 16*(4), 455–474. doi:10.1080/09585170500384529

Park, J., Yang, J., & Hsieh, Y. C. (2014). University level second language readers' online reading and comprehension strategies. *Language Learning & Technology, 18*(3), 148–172.

Pillay, H. (1998). An investigation of the effect of individual cognitive preferences on learning through computer-based instruction. *Educational Psychology, 18*(2), 171–182. doi:10.1080/0144341980180203

Pitman, A. J., Gosper, M., & Rich, D. C. (1999). Internet-based teaching in geography at Macquarie University: An analysis of student use. *Australasian Journal of Educational Technology, 15*(2), 167–187. doi:10.14742/ajet.1855

Rehder, B., & Hoffman, A. B. (2005). Eye tracking and selective attention in category learning. *Cognitive Psychology, 51*(1), 1–41. doi:10.1016/j.cogpsych.2004.11.001 PMID:16039934

Ritterfeld, U. (2011). Beim spielen lernen? Ein differenzierter blick auf die möglichkeiten und grenzen von serious games. *Computer + Unterricht, 84*, 54-57.

Ritterfeld, U., Cody, M. J., & Vorderer, P. (2009). *Serious games: Mechanisms and effects*. New York: Routledge.

Schulman, A. H., & Sims, R. L. (1999). Learning in an online format versus an in-class format: An experimental study. *T.H.E. Journal, 26*(11), 59–65.

Scott, D., Durnell Cramton, C., Gauvin, S., Steinke, G., & Patterson, K. (1997). Internet-based collaborative learning. An empirical evaluation. *Proceedings of the 3rd Ausweb Conference*. Retrieved from http://ausweb.scu.edu.au/proceedings/donscott/index.html

Squire, K. D. (2003). Video games in education. *International Journal of Intelligent Simulations and Gaming, 2*(1). Retrieved from http://website.education.wisc.edu/~kdsquire/tenure-files/39-squire-IJIS

Stepp-Greany, J. (2002). Student perceptions on language learning in a technological environment: Implications for the new millennium. *Language Learning & Technology*, *6*(1), 165–180.

Sternberg, R. J. (1997). *Thinking styles*. New York: Cambridge University Press. doi:10.1017/CBO9780511584152

Sternberg, R. J., & Grigorenko, E. L. (1997). Are cognitive styles still in style? *The American Psychologist*, *52*(7), 700–712. doi:10.1037/0003-066X.52.7.700

Tamim, R. M., Bernard, R. M., Borokhovski, E., Abrami, P. C., & Schmid, R. F. (2011, March). What forty years of research says about the impact of technology on learning: A second-order meta-analysis and validation study. *Review of Educational Research*, *81*(1), 4–28. doi:10.3102/0034654310393361

Turkle, S. (1984). *The second self: Computers and the human spirit*. Cambridge, MA: MIT Press.

Usip, E. E., & Bee, R. H. (1998). Economics: A discriminant analysis of students' perceptions of web-based learning. *Social Science Computer Review*, *16*(1), 16–29. doi:10.1177/089443939801600104

Vogel, J. J., Vogel, D. S., Cannon-Bowers, J., Bowers, C. A., Muse, K., & Wright, M. (2006). Computer gaming and interactive simulations for learning: A meta analysis. *Journal of Educational Computing Research*, *34*(3), 229–243. doi:10.2190/FLHV-K4WA-WPVQ-H0YM

Wallace, D. R., & Mutooni, P. (1997). A comparative evaluation of world wide web-based and classroom teaching. *The Journal of Engineering Education*, *86*(3), 211–219. doi:10.1002/j.2168-9830.1997.tb00287.x

Ward, M., & Newlands, D. (1998). Use of the web in undergraduate teaching. *Computers & Education*, *31*(2), 171–184. doi:10.1016/S0360-1315(98)00024-4

Wästlund, E., Reinikka, H., Norlander, T., & Archer, T. (2005). Effects of VDT and paper presentation on consumption and production of information: Psychological and physiological factors. *Computers in Human Behavior*, *21*(2), 377–394. doi:10.1016/j.chb.2004.02.007

Workman, M. (2004). Performance in Computer-based and Computer-aided Education: Do Cognitive Styles Make a Difference? *Journal of Computers in Human Behavior*, *20*, 517–534. doi:10.1016/j.chb.2003.10.003

Wouters, P., van der Spek, E. D., & van Oostendorp, H. (2009). Current practices in serious game research: A review from a learning outcomes perspective. In T. Connolly, M. Stansfield, & L. Boyle (Eds.), *Games-based learning advancements for multi-sensory human computer interfaces: Techniques and effective practices* (pp. 232–250). Hershey, PA: IGI-Global. doi:10.4018/978-1-60566-360-9.ch014

Chapter 4
Teacher Conceptions and Approaches to Blended Learning Environments

Vicki Caravias
Swinburne University of Technology, Australia

ABSTRACT

This chapter provides Australian perspectives on blended learning. An overview of the ways in which the concept of blended learning is interpreted in the Australian higher education is presented. This is followed by a discussion of the results of research carried out at one Australian University about teachers' conceptions on blended learning and their approaches to design and teaching in higher education. On the basis of twelve interviews with teachers, some important factors are analyzed pertaining to pedagogical, technological, interface, evaluation dimensions as well as resource support, management, ethical and institutional. Research results indicate that teachers consider their subject's learning objectives and apply the technologies and approaches that will work best for their students following the eight dimensions of blended learning environments.

INTRODUCTION

Learning Management Systems (LMS) provide the opportunity to deliver blended learning approaches that combine a mix of Information and Communications Technology (ICT) with various learning resources and delivery methods. Blended learning is seen as a link between teachers, students and classrooms located in different places to enhance learning. It has been widely argued in the literature that there are four main advantages while incorporating the blended learning approach into teaching practice: greater flexibility of time; lack of dependence on the time constraints of the teacher; time for reflection; and meeting different needs and learning styles. The younger generations according to Prensky's (2010) "digital natives" use online technologies for their social and informational activities whilst older generations use these technologies less so. Furthermore, students engage in ways they prefer according to their preferences, interests or abilities. This chapter provides Australian perspectives that examine

DOI: 10.4018/978-1-5225-0466-5.ch004

blended learning issues for teachers and students. Research findings from twelve interviews carried out with teachers from an Australian university, who have had a recent experience using the blended learning approach in their subject design and teaching in Engineering, Design, Business and Information and Communications Technology disciplines in academic pathways programs at the undergraduate level. An academic pathways program is a program of study that allows students to progress from one qualification to another where the first course is recognised as an entry requirement and provides advanced standing to the second. For example, Diploma of Information Technology (Unilink) provides a direct pathway to second-year university. The aim of the study was to advance the body of knowledge in two aspects. Firstly, by applying previous theoretical frameworks developed to understand conceptions and approaches to teaching (Kember & Kwan, 2000); and using the web (Roberts, 2003) and blended learning (Gonzalez, 2009; McConnell & Zhao, 2006). Secondly, how components from Khan's E-Learning framework affect teachers' approaches to integrating pedagogy and content knowledge using blended learning environments.

BACKGROUND

Over the past twenty years the introduction of the Internet and the use of Information and Communication Technology (ICT) that enhance knowledge and performance have been integrated into many university courses (S. Jones, Johnson-Yale, Millermaier, & Pérez, 2008). Within higher education, Kanuka and Kelland (2008) reflect that:

Higher education literature on e-learning technology is replete with research that tinkers with, and then tests the effects if, instrumental practices. The ultimate aim is to determine once and for all, what works and what does not – passing by the questions of why (p.61).

In Australia most universities have incorporated learning management systems such as Blackboard into their teaching practices (Ellis, Goodyear, Prosser, & O'Hara, 2006; Ellis, Steed, & Applebee, 2006) to support teachers in delivering material to students.

As Prendergast (2004) argues:

Too often considerations about information technology have become the dominant factors in many strategies adopted by academic institutions. This has resulted in a rich information technological environment that fails to capture, motivate or retain learners (Prendergast, 2004, p.2).

Brabazon (2002) supports this view, by stating that: Teachers and teaching are being challenged and undermined through the Internet. Learning is not technologically dependent. It is reliant on commitment, interest and passion (p.17).

For the purposes of this book chapter, blended learning is defined as learning activities that involve a combination of face-to-face interactions and technologically mediated interactions between students, teachers and learning resources (Bliuc, Goodyear, & Ellis, 2007). In blended learning teachers who use a learning management system can share course materials, syllabus, opinions and online assessments as well as use e-mail, discussion boards, calendars, blogs, journals, along with traditional face-to-face activities such as lectures and tutorials.

There are several reasons behind the drive to incorporate ICT into the educational process. First, pressure to utilise ICT at a university level comes from changes in the student demography. According to Concannon, Flynn and Campbell (2005) the surge in "full time part time students is a phenomenon of recent years, where school leavers take part-time jobs whilst attending university" (p. 502). For students who work full time, the flexible design accommodates their busy schedules. Without this flexibility, students may not be able to pursue their degrees. Blended learning environments suit both students who learn more efficiently in face-to-face interaction and students who prefer online learning.

Second, blended learning has the potential to promote lifelong learning in higher education (Dzakiria, Wahab, & Rahman, 2012). In their qualitative study, Dzakiria, Wahab and Rahman (2012) investigated the learning experiences of students undertaking studies at University Utara Malaysia. They found that blended learning's "flexibility nature can promote lifelong learning anywhere, and anytime" (p. 299). This is supported by research carried out by Masalela, (2009) whose qualitative study examined factors that influenced fifteen faculty members' decision to use blended learning and found that learners become self-directed, develop critical thinking skills and become independent thinkers through blended courses. In addition, develop lifelong skills to use when they leave the university.

Third, changes in the market for delivery of education comes from innovation in new technologies. In the case of University of Central Florida (Dziuban & Moskal, 2001), a course that met in a classroom three times a week was reduced to a single classroom session with the other two sessions replaced by two hours of online instruction. The university was able to operate multiple classes in one physical classroom using the technological infrastructure of the university. In addition, blended learning enables multi-university offerings (Jefferies, Grodzinsky, & Griffin, 2003) and facilitates elective courses (Verkroost, Meijerink, Lintsen, & Veen, 2008). Lastly, there is pressure from the government in Australia for universities to increase participation and widen access to higher education (Jones & Lau, 2010).

It has been widely argued in the literature that there are four main advantages while incorporating the blended learning approach into teaching practice:

1. Greater flexibility of time. Freedom for students to decide when each online lesson will be learned (Bouhnik & Marcus, 2006; Demetriadis & Pombortsis, 2007).
2. Lack of dependence on the time constraints of the teacher (Edginton & Holbrook, 2010; Lock, 2006).
3. Time for reflection. Freedom for students to express thoughts, and ask questions, without limitations (Chamberlin & Moon, 2005; Liaw, Huang, & Chen, 2007).
4. Meeting different needs and learning styles (Ho, Lu, & Thurmaier, 2006).

Research literature elsewhere indicates that blended learning can bring teachers and students closer together (Aspden & Helm, 2004; Graetz & Goliber, 2002). Aspden and Helm (2004) explored student engagement and interaction with students in the context of a blended learning situation and argue that the blended learning approach can help bring teachers and students together. By making appropriate use of a mix of technologies students can feel increased connectivity with both their fellow students and university staff. Furthermore, Garrison and Anderson (2003) argue while access to information is an important part of learning, student's learning is largely achieved through engagement and interaction with other students. Chen and Looi (2007) also indicated that online discussion contains more opportunities for the practice of in depth clarification and inference skills.

To increase the likelihood of positive student learning outcomes while using the blended learning approach teachers must adopt new technologies (Piccoli, Ahmad, & Ives, 2001). Simply placing existing material (e.g. class handouts and Powerpoints) online does not serve the students. Gerbic (2011) refers to placing existing materials online as the "juxtaposition of two pedagogical settings" (p. 222). Instead, the focus should be on recognising the potential of the blended learning approach to enhance student's learning outcomes. Garrison and Vaughan (2008) state that effective blended courses require these elements:

1. In-class activities that link to the online assignments to reinforce the intent of activities outside the classroom;
2. A shift from teacher-centred to learner-centred activities in the classroom as well as online;
3. Focus on student responsibility for navigating online resources and conducting online research; and
4. Evaluation instruments that provide frequent feedback.

Teachers publish their learning resources on the learning management website and students access those resources through computer networks. A positive attitude towards computers and the Internet, for example, where teaching staff are not afraid of the complexity of using computers, will result in effective learning materials in a blended learning environment (Piccoli et. al., 2001). Research results suggested that applying online technology in the classroom enhances students' achievement (Masalela, 2009). Those tasks such as capturing student's accomplishment through an electronic grade book, reviewing course materials and communicating with teachers can be carried out more efficiently. In their quantitative study Amrein-Beardsley, Foulger and Toth (2007) investigated nine instructors' perceptions of their students' and their own experiences with hybrid courses. From the questionnaires they concluded that students found the online grade book and announcements most useful. Students appreciated instructors who graded assignments and posted them in the grade book in a timely and efficient manner. Students found the course document downloads, Internet sites and links sent to them from the instructors equally useful in terms of technology tools that enhanced their learning.

Despite these advantages for blended learning, simply infusing technology into classrooms will have little impact on student learning if teachers are not supported in learning how to use the technology. Salmon (2005) stated that uploading PowerPoint slides into the learning management system is not enough to create good quality online learning materials. This view is supported by Heinze and Proctor's action research study that examined staff opinions regarding the delivery of a program at the University of Salford using blended learning. Heinze and Proctor (2004) found that simply using a learning management system instead of web pages to deliver handouts and presentations and combining it with discussion boards resulted in staff stating that they were not really doing any e-learning on the course.

Khan's (2008) E-Learning framework was chosen to frame this discussion of blending learning environments because the framework can be used as a guide to plan, develop, deliver, manage, and evaluate blended learning programs. The framework's pedagogical dimension proposes that teachers consider their subject's learning objectives and understand how to apply the technologies and approaches that will work best for their students. The framework comprises 8 dimensions, each containing sub-dimensions, and under each sub-dimension are lists of questions that can help teachers to cover important aspects of integrating pedagogical and content knowledge using blended learning environments to develop high quality e-Learning.

Figure 1. The e-learning framework

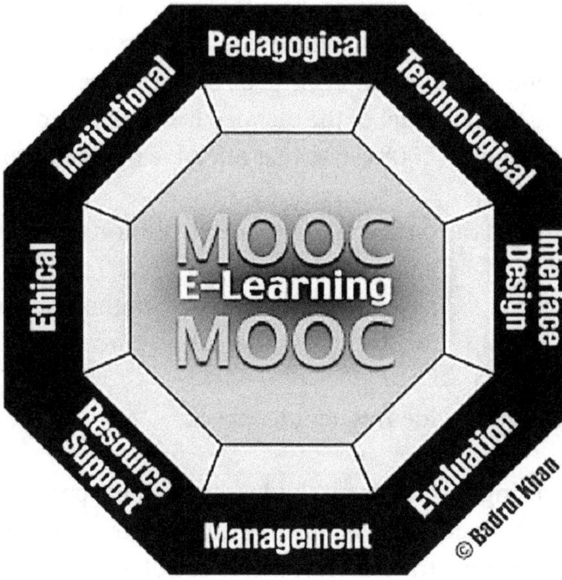

KHAN'S E-LEARNING FRAMEWORK

The organization of this chapter is based on E-Learning framework (see Figure 1).

Khan's E-Learning framework recognizes that a success in any institutional implementation of blended learning must involve a systematic process of planning, designing, evaluating, and implementing a blended learning environment where students' learning is encouraged and supported. For instance, a learning management system, such as Blackboard, should not only be purposeful to students, but it should also be useful to teachers and the educational institutions.

In blended learning teachers who use a learning management system can share course materials, syllabus, opinions and online assessments as well as use e-mail, discussion boards, calendars, blogs, journals, along with traditional face-to-face activities such as lectures and tutorials. Several researchers support blended learning (Concannon et al., 2005; Sharpe, 2006). Blended learning environments can provide access to online learning materials for students with different learning styles and engage learners interactively (Concannon et al., 2005; Sharpe, 2006). In two studies, one in the UK and one in Australia, the use of blended learning environments together with access to online learning materials were found to be determining factors behind increased student engagement and motivation (Concannon et al., 2005; De Lange, Suwardy, & Mavondo, 2003). Rodriguez and Anicete (2010) state that learning management systems, such as Modular Object Oriented Dynamic Learning Environment (MOODLE), can support students to develop more responsibility for their learning. This view is supported by Masalela (2009). In keeping with Motteram's observations, (2006), Rodriguez and Anicete (2010) found that the blended learning approach enhanced the learning experience as the course structure enabled students to deal with topics in their own time and to organise themselves better around the tasks in their own time. However, other authors found that blended learning environments had both positive and negative outcomes, and there was the possibility of negative effects such as innovation fatigue amongst staff and students (Oliver & Trigwell, 2005).

In addition, blended learning courses can support students and prove to be very useful in improving teachers' abilities to respond a wide range of students' needs. Ho (2006) states that blended learning courses result in lower dropout rates compared to fully online courses. This view is supported by Dziuban and Moskal (2001) who reported that students' withdrawal rates were reduced in blended learning courses.

There are eight dimensions used in Khan's eLearning framework: pedagogical, technological, interface design, evaluation, management, resource support, ethical and institutional. Please see the comprehensive discussion of Khan's (2008) e-learning framework in the Introduction chapter of this book.

TEACHERS' PRIOR CONCEPTIONS AND APPROACHES TO BLENDED LEARNING

Teachers' conceptions of blended learning have been investigated with previous studies reporting research into teaching with e-learning and teachers' experiences of working with blended learning environments (Dziuban & Moskal, 2001; Edginton & Holbrook, 2010; Ellis, Steed, et al., 2006; Gedik, Kiraz, & Ozden, 2013; Gonzalez, 2009; Jokinen & Mikkonen, 2013; King & Arnold, 2012; Lameras, Paraskakis, & Levy, 2008; McConnell & Zhao, 2006; McShane, 2004; Napier, Dekhane, & Smith, 2011; Ocak, 2011; Roberts, 2003; Steel, 2009).

Firstly, previous research results suggest that teachers' conceptions of the meaning of blended learning as a way to provide information to their students by way of lecture notes, online learning resources and links to external websites (Gonzalez, 2009; Lameras, Levy, Paraskakis, & Webber, 2012; McConnell & Zhao, 2006; Oh & Park, 2009; Roberts, 2003). Blended learning allows teachers an ongoing opportunity to experiment with new approaches to learning and new types of educational technology such as the Web and learning management systems. Learning management systems enable the delivery of a variety of media including text, video and audio.

McConnell and Zhao's (2006) research findings suggest that face-to-face instruction using lectures were the preferred method of teaching with each teacher acknowledging the "sheer power of the lecture in the Chinese higher education system" (2006, p. 519). These results are supported by Oh and Park's (2009) who reported that the most commonly selected instructional delivery format used by faculty was "face-to-face instruction with supplementary online instructional components" (2009, p. 333). These results suggest that some teachers conceive e learning as not a good way to deliver course content to students with teachers preferring face-to-face methods.

Conversely, Robert's (2003) phenomenographic study discovered three conceptions of teaching using the Web:

1. The web as a source of subject information (2003, p. 145): in this conception the Web is the medium used to distribute information to students. Teachers upload learning materials such as lecture notes and direct students to websites to retrieve information.
2. The web is used for individual and independent self-paced learning (2003, p. 146): students use the Web to complete subject activities.
3. The web is used for group analysis, decision making and dialogue (2003, p. 147): The Web is used for students to interact with one another and create communities of inquiry (Garrison & Arbaugh, 2007).

The research results above are consistent with previous research outcomes from Kember and Khan (2000) who suggested that teachers rely on 'content-centered' approaches to transmit information to students. Like Roberts, McConnell and Zhao, Gonzalez also found teachers' conceptions focused on access to learning materials and information transfer. Gonzalez's (2009) phenomenographic study identified three conceptions of what eLearning should be used for:

1. For individual access to learning materials and information, and for individual assessment (2009, p. 312);
2. For learning-related communication (2009, p. 312); and
3. For networked learning (Gonzalez, 2009, p. 312).

Gonzalez (2009) found that university teachers "having a 'content-centered' approach to teaching can be defined as 'informative-individual learning focused'; while those university teachers having a 'transitional or learner-centered' approach can be defined as 'communicative-networked learning focused'" (2009, p. 311).

Similar to the 'content-centered' conceptions found in the above studies, outcomes from Lameras, Paraskakis and Levy (2012) showed that teachers conceived eLearning as a way to transfer information to students where learning resources were uploaded for students to use on their own. This enables students to learn at their own pace. Lameras, Paraskasis and Levy's (2012) qualitative study identified four categories that describe the use of virtual learning environments as a means of supporting:

1. Information transfer (p.145);
2. Application and clarification of concepts (p.145);
3. Exchange and development of ideas, and resource exploration and sharing (p.145); and
4. Collaborative knowledge-creation, and development of process awareness and skills (p.145).

Secondly, previous research results indicate teachers' conceptions of 'eLearning as a way to engage in communication-collaboration-knowledge building' (Gonzalez, 2010, p. 64) and seen to engage students in discussion, developing understanding and building knowledge (Ellis, Steed, et al., 2006). In their qualitative study, Ellis et al. (2006) identified four conceptions of blended teaching:

1. Blended teaching as helping students develop and apply new concepts (2006, p. 324)
2. Blended teaching as developing student understanding through aligning media to intended learning outcomes (2006, p. 324);
3. Blended teaching as providing students with information (2006, p. 325); and
4. Blended teaching as replacing part of the responsibility of being a teacher (2006, p. 326).

Thirdly, blended learning is conceived as a way of engaging students in learning activities that may lead to higher-level learning experiences (Garrison & Kanuka, 2004). This is consistent with Kember and Kwan's (2000) learner-centered approach where teachers focus on the learning process. These conceptions are also consistent with McConnell and Zhao's, (2006) definition of networked learning where teachers place material online and students are expected to learn at their own pace. The fundamental principles underlying networked learning are learner-centered where the learning is outcome-focused and requires engagement, group collaboration and the creation of communities of inquiry (Garrison & Arbaugh, 2007).

McConnell and Zhao (2006) found that teachers recognized a connection between students achieving their learning outcomes and the role of technology in blended settings helping students develop higher order thinking. These results are supported by Garrison and Kanuka (2004) who argued that blended environments can support and transform universities by building a Community of Inquiry (Garrison & Arbaugh, 2007) and develop higher order thinking. Research results indicate that teachers should take deliberate action once courses begin towards creating a community of inquiry (Garrison & Arbaugh, 2007) such as monitoring and responding to online discussion board postings (Conrad, 2005).

In another qualitative study, King and Arnold (2012) identified four factors that contribute to the success of blended learning courses:

1. **Course Preparation (2012, p. 51):** The professors prepared their blended courses in various ways and used technology, such as Skype, wikis and blogs in addition to the learning management system.
2. **Course Design (2012, p. 52):** The professors used the content feature of the learning management system to post course documents and assignments which support the content-centered approach of teaching (Kember & Kwan, 2000).
3. **Communication (2012, p. 53):** The importance of communicating with students in a timely manner is consistent with research findings in blended learning (Ho et al., 2006). The professors used the discussion board in various ways. One professor required the students to complete weekly journals that were viewed by student and professor only enabling a confidential dialogue and giving the student time to reflect on what they had learnt.
4. **Motivation (2012, p. 54):** These results are supported by research carried out by (Aycock, Garnham, & Kaleta, 2002).

Jokinen and Mikkonen's (2013) qualitative study described teachers' experiences of planning and implementing teaching and learning in a blended learning based nursing programme. These researchers found that teachers experienced the blended learning approach positively despite challenges from the viewpoint of planning and design. According to the study careful planning is required by teachers to ensure the combination of face-to-face learning and learning in practice with technology-mediated learning activities. These findings are supported by previous studies of Salmon (2005) and Heinze and Proctor (2004). Ocak's (2011) qualitative study examined problems and challenges faculty members encountered in blended learning environments. They found that class discussions that take place on discussion boards or blogs provide teachers with an electronic record that can be reviewed over and over again to examine how students have participated and progressed over time.

These predominantly qualitatively studies draw attention to the importance of teachers' conceptions and beliefs about teaching in face-to-face and online settings. Although extensive research has been done on blended learning, empirical studies on teaching and teachers' perspectives of the blended learning approach have not been well documented. Teachers' concerns regarding the integration of the blended learning approach with pedagogical and content knowledge has alsonnot been well represented in the literature (Stacey & Gerbic, 2008). The lack of clarity on problems integrating the blended learning approach into teaching makes it necessary to investigate what the perceptions of teachers are and how teachers can improve the teaching and learning outcomes of their students using the blended learning approach.

THE RESEARCH

This study was an enquiry into the background, functions and concerns of teachers focusing on their perspectives regarding the integration of the blended learning approach with pedagogical and content knowledge. This required a method of investigation that allows for the interpretation of social phenomena. Cronbach (1975, p. 123) calls this "interpretation" by context". By concentrating on a single phenomenon or entity ("the case") this method aims to uncover the interaction of significant factors characteristic to the phenomenon.

The qualitative approach allows the researcher to focus deeply on ideas, expand them, give interpretative richness and contextualize the phenomenon under study. Qualitative case study is an ideal design for understanding and interpreting observations of educational phenomena. As a researcher, exploring teachers' conceptions regarding blended learning environments, it seemed best to take a qualitative, phenomenographic approach and discover what mattered most to teachers by asking them personally, without any presumption on the part of the researcher. The central question, which is the basis for the study is:

What do teachers believe are the key aspects of integrating pedagogical and content knowledge using blended learning environments?

Phenomenography has also been used to explore approaches to teaching (Trigwell, Prosser, & Waterhouse, 1999) allowing for the interpretation of social phenomena, in this case the way in which Australian university teachers understand how to integrate pedagogy and content knowledge using blended learning environments. Phenomenographic research findings illuminate differences in ways of understanding, and how these different ways of understanding are related to one another.

The sample included twelve teachers from an Australian University who were teaching in Engineering, Design, Business and Information and Communications Technology disciplines in academic pathways programs at the undergraduate level. The sample was purposive to include teachers who had previously been teaching face-to-face but now using the blended learning approach in their subject design (Merriam, 1988). Purposive sampling is used primarily when there are a limited number of people that have expertise in the area being researched. There is a pool of over forty teachers teaching in academic pathways programs at the University where the study was conducted. For inclusion in the study, participants had to be subject convenors and to have been teaching using a blended learning approach within the last year.

An investigation into the background, functions and concerns of teachers requires understanding the meaning teachers give to certain phenomena. Interview is the most commonly method for collecting data on conceptions, experiences and beliefs and is the primary method for phenomenographic data collection. Interview questions were semi-structured in order to let the participant choose the dimensions of the question they wanted to respond to (Marton, 1988). The dimensions they choose are an "important source of data because they reveal an aspect of the individual's relevance structure" (Marton, 1986, p. 42). The individual questions focus on and illuminate the central experience while attempting to frame the variation within the experience. The emphasis during each interview was to stimulate the participant's reflection upon their experience. This conforms to Marton's view that the phenomenographic interview provokes a change from unreflected to reflected awareness (Marton, 1994). During the interview, the aim is to "make things which are unthematised and implicit into objects reflection, and hence thematised and explicit" (Marton, 1994, p. 4427).

Participants were interviewed individually for 45-60 minutes. After a brief conversation about their contexts of teaching, the following opening question was used to ensure that participants had some idea about the meaning of blended learning: 'What do you mean by blended learning?' The opening question was followed by questions about teachers' conceptions of blended learning in order to deepen the interview. This was followed by questions regarding how teachers approach integrating pedagogy and content knowledge using blended learning environments such as 'How do you approach blended learning in your teaching of this subject?'

In terms of teacher experiences, the study focused on the perceptions and problems that these teachers faced when integrating pedagogy and content knowledge into a blended learning environment, the strategies they employed to address these problems, and how they used the blended learning tools (e.g., learning management system, chat rooms, conference/video conferencing and emails) to overcome these challenges. The interview continued with a request for the participant to explain the subject that they have been teaching using the blended learning approach. Participants were encouraged to use prompts such as subject documentation and online access to their Blackboard learning management website during the interview. The semi-structured interview had specific topic areas that aligned with critical dimensions from Khan's eLearning framework that needed to be discussed during the course of the interview, however the ordering of the questions was left to the interviewer (Bryman & Teevan, 2004). This accorded the interviewer the flexibility to respond to issues raised by participants (Bryman & Teevan, 2004). The interview process allowed probing of the participant's responses through follow-up questions. Dependability was enhanced as the interviews were conducted by the same interviewer using an interview guide (Widäng & Fridlund, 2003).

Each interview was recorded, transcribed verbatim and then analyzed. In phenomenography, the accepted procedure is to use an iterative process to investigate the relation between meaning (how the phenomenon is experienced) and structure (different ways of experiencing). To identify this relationship in the study, a four phase analysis procedure was used based on Marton and Booth's (1997) and Bruce (1997, pp. 104-106) processes of analysis: These phases are:

- **Becoming Familiar with the Transcripts:** All teachers' responses from the interviews were read and re-read several times by the researcher before any attempt to begin the formal analysis. This process provided an insight into what the teachers were saying, and the common issues and differences among them. Key themes and variations were identified from these initial extracts.
- **Identifying Meanings:** In addition to the work already done in highlighting key themes and potential variations, the transcripts were imported into nVIVO qualitative research software for textual coding and analysis.
- **Structuring Experiences:** The outcome of this phase was the identification of similarities and differences that help with the classification of "categories of description" in terms of their associations with the conceptions of teachers.
- **Establishing the Outcome Space:** This phase involved arranging the categories of description into a logical structure, representing both the meaning and structural aspects.

This research study adds to and extends previous research by investigating the teachers' conceptions and approaches to integrating pedagogy and content knowledge using blended learning environments using Khan's E-Learning framework. The lack of clarity on problems integrating the blended learning approach into teaching makes it necessary to investigate what the perceptions of the teachers are and how teachers can improve the teaching and learning outcomes of their students using the blended learning approach.

FINDINGS

Teachers are familiar with the structure of a traditional educational system where teacher-led, face-to-face classes are the learning environments. Blended learning environments are a mix of online learning and face-to-face classes. On the basis of twelve interviews with teachers some important factors were determined pertaining to pedagogical, technological, interface, evaluation dimensions as well as resource support, management, ethical and institutional. Khan's eLearning framework was used to structure the interview questions and then the researcher used those dimensions in the analysis phase of the study. Each dimension in the framework represents a category of conception that need to be addressed by teachers to create meaningful learning experiences for their students.

The Pedagogical Dimension

The pedagogical dimension of e-learning refers to teaching and learning. This dimension suggests that pedagogy is one of the main drivers of teaching and learning and there are many issues such concerning content, target audience analysis, learning outcomes, goals, medium analysis, design approach, organization and learning strategies for teachers to consider. Responses in this category of conception related to teachers' conceptions of blended learning and how teachers decide what topics to cover online and what topics to cover face-to-face. In response to the question 'What do you mean by blended learning?' Five teachers reported thinking that the online elements of blended learning environments are primarily used as a mechanism to store and deliver subject content. This category of conception focuses on providing learning resources and assessments through blended learning environments to students and students accessing those resources.

All my lecture notes and theory notes are available on Blackboard, so it mirrors what I do (Teacher MED).

It's basically a repository for students. Number one place for information (Teacher MEB).

These five teachers believed that the "real" teaching happened in the classroom and that the learning management system was just a place to store content. One teacher emphasized the importance of face-to-face teaching.

... I don't want the technology to become a replacement for the learning process ... I want to make it easy for students to learn how to solve the problems that are presented to them in the subject (Teacher MBD2).

In response to the question "What are your thoughts about using the learning management system in your teaching? Four teachers reported that the learning management system is a repository to store content.

It's basically a storage area for me (Teacher MED).

Blended learning environments suit students who prefer face-to-face interaction in addition to students who prefer online learning. In response to the question "What is your rationale for deciding what topics to cover online and what topics you are going to cover face-to-face?" Five teachers reported that there should be no difference between the student experience of accessing the information face-to-face or online.

... the materials covered face-to-face should also be supported online (Teacher MBD2).

One teacher reported that they decide what to topics to cover face-to-face or online based on their experience and their cohort of students.

I change my strategy depending on the students (Teacher MDC).

Another teacher reported that subjects from the Information Technology discipline should be available for students online.

... all the resources go up there but when it comes to the assessments tasks, obviously if you're teaching a Information Technology subject ... you should be using a business information system for demonstration purposes (Teacher FIE).

Blended learning allows teachers an ongoing opportunity to experiment with new approaches to the delivery of teaching and learning and new types of educational technology. Learning management systems enable the delivery of a variety of media including text, links, video and audio. Teachers' responses in this category of conception emphasized one aspect of blended learning environments: as a tool for information delivery. Four teachers identified the importance of providing students with supplementary resources, such as giving students access to links to websites and articles.

So I want them to be able to access their notes ... I have found that I can give them access to so many different links, so many articles. Not all of them are compulsory to read, but they are good to know, and I've found that students actually look at them (Teacher FIB).

One teacher believes that classroom time should still used for lectures.

... the flipped classroom that's becoming the latest sort of rage. Its not exactly a flipped classroom that I want. I still want to keep the lectures, but I want to have the extra resources ... podcasts, short videos, clips (Teacher FIE).

Alternatively, one teacher reported that class time should be devoted to answering student questions and clarifying concepts.

I want the students to learn something before they come to the labs. So, I put some of the stuff online before coming to class. I want them to emphasize a bit more on that, to focus more on that, and then come to class (Teacher MED2).

Several teachers reported that they transfer all their "hard copy" content into "online" content and then add links to websites.

I always begin when I'm starting that transfer into lessons .... upload Word documents. and then add links to websites ... free online activities that students can work on (Teacher FIC).

The pedagogical dimension is also related to how teachers support and communicate with students using blended learning environments. Eight teachers reported using the learning management system to engage students.

… discussion boards in Blackboard are particularly useful for student communication (Teacher MBD).

… I'll post content to that class group, and with that little announcement saying, "Hey, a lot of you weren't here today. This is what we did. Have a look at it. And if you've got questions, you can ask me about it in the next class." So it's really good support that way (Teacher FIC).

Teachers' responses in this category focused on one of the key features of learning management systems: synchronous and synchronous communication between teacher-student and student-student using discussion boards and announcements. Three teachers reported that they use discussion forms for students to talk amongst themselves.

In response to the question ' Do you use the learning management system in your teaching? Four teachers reported that their subject material was not suitable for blended learning environments.

… because my subjects don't do assignments and so on … doing pracs online didn't work very well for me because they were hand written and then they had to scan them (Teacher MED).

The subject does not lend itself to discussion boards (Teacher MEB).

Six teachers use a mix of technologies to increase connectivity between both their students and fellow teachers. This category of conception focuses on blended learning environments being used to bring teachers and students together.

What we'll do is I'll go in as the demo student, and we'll do them as a group together and answer A, B or C together (Teacher FIC).

In response to the question 'Do you consider any factors when you're deciding to develop online materials or activities?

One teacher pointed out the high level of computing knowledge required by students enrolled in academic pathways programs at the University.

… on-line content … requires fairly high level navigational skills and literacy skills to work their way around the learning management system … it's not obvious I think when you're sitting in front of a computer screen which button to press, where to go, what to do next… so I'm very conscious of the demands on our international students (Teacher FIC).

The high level of computing knowledge required by students enrolled in academic pathways programs is a concern to teachers teaching at the University. It is not known whether international students are able to manage their own learning using online learning environments.

Research results indicate that teachers' conceptions of teaching using blended learning environments relate mostly to teachers utilizing learning management systems and face-to-face classes to provide content (lecture notes, readings, practical activities) to students. Teachers rely on the 'pedagogical' dimension to transmit information to students and this is consistent with previous research outcomes from Kember and Kwan (2000) and is supported by research carried out by McConnell and Zhao as well as Roberts and Gonzalez (Gonzalez, 2009; McConnell & Zhao, 2006; Roberts, 2003).

The Technological Dimension

The technological dimension of e-learning examines issues of technology infrastructure in e-learning environments. This includes infrastructure planning, hardware and software. Responses in this category of conception related to teachers' difficulty learning how to use the learning management system and whether teachers have access to hardware and software required to develop online learning resources.

In response to the question 'Did you receive technical assistance developing the subject for blended learning'? Seven teachers reported that they did not receive any technical support or assistance to develop their Blackboard learning management website. These teachers reported difficulties in learning how to use the learning management system.

I had to work it out myself (Teacher MDC).

Five teachers reported attending a professional development workshop organised by the University. Despite this, teachers still reported feeling less confident with their performance online.

... I'm still getting help with ... and discussion boards I did get a little bit of help with, but not much (Teacher MED).

In response to the question 'Do you have the resources required to develop the subject for blended learning? All teachers reported that they have the necessary hardware and software required to develop their subjects for blended learning. All hardware and software is provided by the University and available to all teachers.

The Interface Design Dimension

The interface design refers to the overall look and feel of e-learning programs. Interface design dimension encompasses page and site design, content design, navigation, accessibility and usability testing.

Teachers at the University are not able to make changes to the interface of the learning management system Blackboard. The University has a "standardized" template whereby all teachers subject learning management system websites must "look and feel" the same way with respect to fonts, colors and menu options.

Teachers should ensure that each Blackboard learning management websites stores information in the same place and in the same order for each subject. A consistent approach is required across courses so students do not have to search for materials in different places within their Blackboard learning management websites. Teachers rely on the interface dimension to design the look and feel of blended learning courses.

The Evaluation Dimension

The evaluation for e-learning includes both assessment of learners and evaluation of the instruction and learning environment. Responses in this category of conception related to how blended learning environments can be used to assess students using online tests and exams.

Practice tests and practice test solutions, tests, exams and exam solutions all available on Blackboard (Teacher MED).

In this category of conception, teachers developed quizzes in the form of multiple-choice questions and made them available online for students to self-test their progress and learning. The teachers relied on Bloom's taxonomy to design the assessments. Students receive immediate feedback on whether their answers are correct, and what the correct response should be for that question.

One teacher reported developing quizzes that the students can complete during in the classroom.

I've setup a few Respondus quizzes that students can do in the classroom. So, we'll do them together in the classroom (Teacher FIC).

Classroom time is still devoted to answering student questions and clarifying concepts and giving students the opportunity to answering questions and giving students immediate feedback.

Another teacher reported that the immediate feedback provided to students regarding online assessments was very useful.

... particularly with Blackboard, you can see their progress on the performance dashboard and you can see who's actually participating and who isn't (Teacher FIE).

Most teachers welcomed the opportunity to take advantage of other forms of assessment made possible by having an online component to their subjects. However, one teacher reported that the technology should not be the main driver of online assessments.

... I think it's just another tool ...to give the computer so much control over pedagogical decisions ... does that even make the exam valid? (Teacher FDC).

The Management Dimension

The management of e-learning refers to the maintenance of learning environment and distribution of information. At the beginning of every teaching period, Blackboard leaning management websites are created for each subject by the staff from the Information Technology Support (ITS) department at the University. Teaching staff have access to their subject's website a few weeks in advance of a new teaching semester. These subject websites are consistently "rolled-over" from one teaching period to another. Teachers need to mostly update the learning resources within each subject website from semester to semester. The management of each subject website is the responsibility of the subject convenor.

The Resource Support Dimension

The resource support dimension of the e-learning examines the online support and resources required to foster purposeful learning. The University has a dedicated Information Technology Support (ITS) department providing support to all teaching staff and students with all systems including the learning management system Blackboard. The ITS department ensure that the Internet is up and running and available to all teaching staff and students.

The Ethical Dimension

The ethical considerations of e-learning relate to social and political influence, cultural diversity, bias, geographical diversity, learner diversity, digital divide, etiquette and the legal issues. Teachers reported that changes in the student demography prompted them to utilise the blended learning format at the university level. For students who work full time, the flexible design accommodates their busy schedules. Without this flexibility, the students may not be able to pursue their studies.

I can see advantages for people who are working part-time (Teacher FIC).

Three teachers reported that chat discussions are scheduled at reasonable times to accommodate students in different time zones.

I schedule multiple chat discussions to include our students in Australia, China and Sri Lanka (Teacher FIC).

In response to the question 'What factors influence how you incorporate and use the blended learning approach in your teaching'?

One teacher reported that they incorporated the blended learning approach into their teaching as their students use online technologies for their social and informational activities.

Because I want to be teaching the modern way (MED2).

One teacher raised their concern for students who do not have access to the internet at home. These students need to come on-campus to complete the online portion (submit their assessments via Blackboard).

Another teacher highlighted that students having problems with English are disadvantaged with online assessments tasks.

.... aware of the English as a second language .... I tend to watch out for the language very much (Teacher FIE).

Research results indicate that teachers are sensitive to diversity in geographical time zones scheduling chat discussions where students can reasonably be expected to live in different zones. Teachers rely on the 'ethical' dimension to schedule chat discussions and this is consistent with previous research outcomes from Garrison and Anderson (2003) who argue that access to information is an important part of learning however student's learning is largely achieved through engagement and interaction with other students.

The Institutional Dimension

The institutional dimension is concerned with issues of administrative affairs, academic affairs and student services related to e-learning. Blended learning is implemented as part of a strategy whereby all units of study are supported by Blackboard learning management system websites. Teachers are required to incorporate the blended learning approach into their work practices. One of University's targets is that all stakeholders will become engaged with the new Internet technologies. To underpin this it is necessary to develop a strong expertise platform within faculties and departments in the University.

Training and professional development programs were offered by faculty-based e-learning coordinators, supported by each faculty's budget, that provide induction programs for staff new to teaching and a wide-range of informal staff development activities. The University has placed blended learning at the core of its strategic plan. In response to the question 'What motivated you to try the blended learning approach at the University?'

Several teachers reported that it was a directive of the university.

There was a minimum requirement. So we had to have all of our grades (Teacher FIC).

The researcher sensed some resentment on the part of teachers towards blended learning and thus the adoption of online teaching and learning because the decision to try the blended learning approach had been mandated by the institution.

Three teachers reported that changes in the market for delivery of education motivated them to use these new technologies.

... to support the students who've missed classes with the material that is uploaded into Blackboard (Teacher MEB).

... students can actually access the materials anytime, anywhere, any place which is what they want (Teacher FIC).

One teacher reported that the blended learning approach was suitable students with special needs.

... students who are physically impaired or who aren't as mobile as others, so they can study from home in way that's comfortable and meaningful for them (Teacher FIC).

In response to the question 'How much time and effort do you put into preparing your subject for blended learning?

All teachers reported that they spend a lot more time developing resources for blended learning compared to face-to-face subjects.

I feel a lot more ... and that might be just because my experience is on lesson planning for face-to-face classrooms and I've been doing that for more than 10 years (Teacher FIC).

RECOMMENDATIONS

Based on the findings discussed above, teachers' conceptions and approaches to blended learning environments reflect all eight dimensions of the E-Learning framework. Teachers focus more on the learning strategies section of the pedagogical dimension than institutional and management dimensions. Findings in this study are consistent with those of the other phenomenographic studies that have examined teachers' conceptions and approaches to blended learning. Findings in this study also correspond with the descriptive categories identified in qualitative studies of content-centered and learned-centered approaches of teaching in higher education (Kember & Kwan, 2000). This study highlights a number of factors that have impacted on teachers' conceptions and approaches to using blended learning environments. From this research, these are the practical recommendations this author would like to make to in some way change teacher conceptions and approaches towards blended learning environments.

A foremost recommendation is that teachers need to follow instructional design guidelines which will help teachers integrate pedagogy and content knowledge for both designing classroom activities (face-face teaching) and those designed for online interaction (discussion boards, group work etc.). For example, classroom activities should help prepare students for the online components of the subject. Teachers develop pedagogical activities that require students to reflect on what they are learning and to share their reflection with their teachers and fellow students.

A second recommendation to enhance the use of blended learning environments involves arranging professional development for teachers on the principles of instructional design (Kearsley & Blomeyer, 2004). Research findings indicate that despite teachers attending professional development workshops organized by the University they are unfamiliar with instructional design principles. Some teachers are new to blended learning environments and require assistance not only on how to incorporate the learning management system into their teaching practice but more importantly acquire an understanding of the underpinning concepts of instructional design.

A third recommendation is that all students enrolled in academic pathway programs undertake an induction session on how to navigate and use the learning management system Blackboard at the beginning of their studies at the University. Research findings highlight teachers concerns regarding international students and their ability to manage their own learning using online environments.

A fourth recommendation is that teachers engage with their students at the beginning of their course by creating a community of inquiry. Research findings indicate that teachers are advised to take deliberate action once courses begin towards creating a community of inquiry (Garrison & Arbaugh, 2007) such as monitoring and responding to online discussion board postings (Conrad, 2005). Teachers can use discussion boards to present a topic or issue and have students respond to questions, provide their own perspectives while also evaluating and responding to the opinions of others.

This research study concludes that subjects from the Business, Design, Information and Communication Technology disciplines were more suitable for teachers to use blended learning environments. In this regard, a further recommendation is that there may be a relationship between the subject taught and different teachers' conceptions and approaches to using blended learning environments. Some teachers reported that their subject material was not suitable for blended learning environments.

CONCLUSION

There are 43 universities (40 public universities, two international universities, and one private specialty university) in the country of Australia (Australian Government, 2015). Most universities in Australia have incorporated learning management systems into their teaching practices (Ellis, Goodyear, et al., 2006; Ellis, Steed, et al., 2006) to support teachers in delivering material to students.

This chapter highlights the importance of teachers' conceptions, beliefs and experiences and their approaches to both designing and teaching in blended learning environments. Blended learning environments imply combining a number of dimensions based on pedagogy, technology, interface design, evaluation, management, resource support, ethical and institutional. Blended learning environments require finding the "right mix" among online and face-face teaching. Research findings indicate that teachers consider their subject's learning objectives and apply the dimensions and approaches that will work best for their students. The author suggests that the findings of this study can be used to inform these approaches, whether they are focused specifically on academic pathway programs or more broadly across all blended learning courses.

From the thoughts presented in this chapter, one can conclude that future research on blended learning will focus on empirical studies on teaching and teachers' perspectives of the blended learning approach. Teachers' concerns regarding the integration of the blended learning approach with pedagogical and content knowledge has not been well represented in the literature (Stacey & Gerbic, 2008). The lack of clarity on problems integrating the blended learning approach into teaching makes it necessary to investigate what are the perceptions of the teachers and how teachers can improve the teaching and learning outcomes of their students using the blended learning approach

REFERENCES

Amrein-Beardsley, A., Foulger, T. S., & Toth, M. (2007). Examining the Development of a Hybrid Degree Program: Using Student and Instructor Data to Inform Decision-Making. *Journal of Research on Technology in Education*, *39*(4), 27.

Aspden, L., & Helm, P. (2004). Making the Connection in a Blended Learning Environment. *Educational Media International*, *41*(3), 245–252. http://www.doi.org/10.1080/09523980410001680851

Australian Government. (2015). *Study in Australia*. Retrieved from https://http://www.studyinaustralia.gov.au/global/australian-education/universities-and-higher-education

Aycock, A., Garnham, C., & Kaleta, R. (2002). Lessons learned from the hybrid course project. *Teaching with Technology Today, 8*(6), 9-21.

Bliuc, A.-M., Goodyear, P., & Ellis, R. A. (2007). Research focus and methodological choices in studies into students' experiences of blended learning in higher education. *The Internet and Higher Education*, *10*(4), 231–244. Retrieved from http://www.doi.org/10.1016/j.iheduc.2007.08.001

Bouhnik, D., & Marcus, T. (2006). Interaction in distance,Äêlearning courses. *Journal of the American Society for Information Science and Technology*, *57*(3), 299–305. http://www.doi.org/10.1002/asi.20277

Brabazon, T. (2002). *Digital hemlock: Internet education and the poisoning of teaching*. Sydney: UNSW Press.

Bruce, C. (1997). *The Seven Faces of Information Literacy*. Adelaide: Auslib Press.

Bryman, A., & Teevan, J. J. (2004). *Social research methods* (Vol. 2). Oxford University Press.

Chamberlin, S., & Moon, S. (2005). Model-eliciting activities: An introduction to gifted education. *Journal of Secondary Gifted Education*, *17*(1), 37–47.

Chen, W., & Looi, C.-K. (2007). Incorporating Online Discussion in Face to Face Classroom Learning: A New Blended Learning Approach. *Australasian Journal of Educational Technology*, *23*(3), 307–326.

Concannon, F., Flynn, A., & Campbell, M. (2005). What campus-based students think about the quality and benefits of e-learning. *British Journal of Educational Technology*, *36*(3), 501–512.

Conrad, D. (2005). Building and maintaining community in cohort-based online learning. *Journal of Distance Education*, *20*(1), 1.

Cronbach, L. J. (1975). Beyond the two disciplines of scientific psychology. *The American Psychologist*, *30*(2), 116–127.

De Lange, P., Suwardy, T., & Mavondo, F. (2003). Integrating a virtual learning environment into an introductory accounting course: Determinants of student motivation. *Accounting Education*, *12*(1), 1–14.

Demetriadis, S., & Pombortsis, A. (2007). E-lectures for flexible learning: A study on their learning efficiency. *Journal of Educational Technology & Society*, *10*(2), 147.

Dzakiria, H., Wahab, M. S. D. A., & Rahman, H. D. A. (2012). Blended Learning (BL) as Pedagogical Alternative to Teach Business Communication Course: Case Study of UUM Executive Diploma Program. *Turkish Online Journal of Distance Education, 13*(3).

Dziuban, C., & Moskal, P. (2001). Evaluating distributed learning at metropolitan universities. *EDUCAUSE Quarterly*, *24*(4), 60–61.

Edginton, A., & Holbrook, J. (2010). A blended learning approach to teaching basic pharmacokinetics and the significance of face-to-face interaction. *American Journal of Pharmaceutical Education*, *74*(5). PMID:20798797

Ellis, R. A., Goodyear, P., Prosser, M., & O'Hara, A. (2006). How and what university students learn through online and face-to-face discussion: Conceptions, intentions and approaches. *Journal of Computer Assisted Learning*, *22*(4), 244–256.

Ellis, R. A., Steed, A. F., & Applebee, A. C. (2006). Teacher conceptions of blended learning, blended teaching and associations with approaches to design. *Australasian Journal of Educational Technology*, *22*(3), 312.

Garrison, D. R., & Anderson, T. (2003). *E-learning in the 21st century: A framework for research and practice*. New York: Routledge.

Garrison, D. R., & Arbaugh, J. B. (2007). Researching the community of inquiry framework: Review, issues, and future directions. *The Internet and Higher Education*, *10*(3), 157–172.

Garrison, D. R., & Kanuka, H. (2004). Blended learning: Uncovering its transformative potential in higher education. *The Internet and Higher Education*, *7*(2), 95–105. http://www.doi.org/10.1016/j.iheduc.2004.02.001

Garrison, D. R., & Vaughan, N. (2008). *Blended learning in higher education; framework, principles, and guidelines* (Vol. 23). Academic Press.

Gedik, N., Kiraz, E., & Ozden, M. Y. (2013). Design of a blended learning environment: Considerations and implementation issues. *Australasian Journal of Educational Technology*, *29*(1).

Gerbic, P. (2011). Teaching using a blended approach - what does the literature tell us? *Educational Media International*, *48*(3), 221.

Gonzalez, C. (2009). Conceptions of, and approaches to, teaching online: A study of lecturers teaching postgraduate distance courses. *Higher Education*, *57*(3), 299–314.

Gonzalez, C. (2010). What do university teachers think eLearning is good for in their teaching? *Studies in Higher Education*, *35*(1), 61–78.

Graetz, K. A., & Goliber, M. J. (2002). Designing collaborative learning places: Psychological foundations and new frontiers. *New Directions for Teaching and Learning*, (92): 13–22. http://www.doi.org/10.1002/tl.75

Heinze, A., & Procter, C. (2004). *Reflections on the use of blended learning*. Academic Press.

Ho, A., Lu, L., & Thurmaier, K. (2006). Testing the reluctant professor's hypothesis: evaluating a blended-learning approach to distance education. *Journal of Public Affairs Education*, 81-102.

Jefferies, P., Grodzinsky, F., & Griffin, J. (2003). Advantages and problems in using information communication technologies to support the teaching of a multi-institutional computer ethics course. *Journal of Educational Media*, *28*(2-3), 191–202.

Jokinen, P., & Mikkonen, I. (2013). Teachers' experiences of teaching in a blended learning environment. *Nurse Education in Practice*. PMID:23608218

Jones, S., Johnson-Yale, C., Millermaier, S., & Pérez, F. S. (2008). Academic work, the Internet and US college students. *The Internet and Higher Education*, *11*(3-4), 165–177.

Jones, & Lau, A. M. S. (2010). Blending learning: widening participation in higher education. *Innovations In Education And Teaching International*, *47*(4), 405-416.

Kanuka, H., & Kelland, J. (2008). Has e-learning delivered on its promises? Expert opinion on the impact of e-learning in higher education. *Canadian Journal of Higher Education*, *38*(1), 45–65.

Kearsley, G., & Blomeyer, R. (2004). Preparing K-12 teachers to teach online. *Educational Technology: The Magazine for Managers of Change in Education,* (1), 49-52.

Kember, D., & Kwan, K.-P. (2000). Lecturers' approaches to teaching and their relationship to conceptions of good teaching. *Instructional Science*, *28*(5), 469–490.

Khan, B. H., & Granato, L. A. (2008). *Program evaluation in e-learning*. Retrieved from http://citeseerx.ist.psu.edu/viewdoc/download?doi=10.1.1.456.3097&rep=rep1&type=pdf

King, S. E., & Arnold, K. C. (2012). Blended Learning Environments in Higher Education: A Case Study of How Professors Make It Happen. *Mid-Western Educational Researcher*, *25*(1), 44–59.

Lameras, P., Levy, P., Paraskakis, I., & Webber, S. (2012). Blended university teaching using virtual learning environments: Conceptions and approaches. *Instructional Science*, *40*(1), 141–157. http://www.doi.org/10.1007/s11251-011-9170-9

Lameras, P., Paraskakis, I., & Levy, P. (2008). *Conceptions of teaching using virtual learning environments: preliminary findings from a phenomenographic inquiry*. Paper presented at the 6th International Conference on Networked Learning.

Liaw, S.-S., Huang, H.-M., & Chen, G.-D. (2007). An activity-theoretical approach to investigate learners' factors toward e-learning systems. *Computers in Human Behavior*, *23*(4), 1906–1920. Retrieved from http://www.doi.org/10.1016/j.chb.2006.02.002

Lock, J. V. (2006). A new image: Online communities to facilitate teacher professional development. *Journal of Technology and Teacher Education*, *14*(4), 663–678.

Marton, F. (1986). Phenomenography - A research approach to investigating different understandings of reality. *Journal of Thought*, *21*, 28–94.

Marton, F. (1988). Phenomenography: A research approach to investigating different understandings of reality. *Qualitative Research in Education: Focus and Methods, 21*, 143-161.

Marton, F. (1994). Phenomenography. In T. Husen & T. N. Postlethwaite (Eds.), The International Encyclopedia of Education (2nd ed.; pp. 4424-4429). Pergamon.

Marton, F., & Booth, S. (1997). *Learning and awareness*. Mahwah, NJ: L. Erlbaum Associates.

Masalela, R. K. (2009). Potential benefits and complexities of blended learning in higher education: The case of the University of Botswana. *Turkish Online Journal of Distance Education*, *10*(1), 66–82.

McConnell, D., & Zhao, J. (2006). Chinese higher education teachers' conceptions of e-Learning: Preliminary outcomes. Paper presented at the 23rd Annual Ascilite Conference: Who's Learning? Whose technology?

McShane, K. (2004). Integrating face-to-face and online teaching: Academics' role concept and teaching choices. *Teaching in Higher Education*, *9*(1), 3–16.

Merriam, S. B. (1988). *Case study research in education: A qualitative approach*. Jossey-Bass.

Motteram, G. (2006). Blended education and the transformation of teachers: A long term case study in postgraduate UK Higher Education. *British Journal of Educational Technology*, *37*(1), 17–30. Retrieved from http://www.doi.org/10.1111/j.1467-8535.2005.00511.x

Napier, N. P., Dekhane, S., & Smith, S. (2011). Transitioning to Blended Learning: Understanding Student and Faculty Perceptions. *Journal of Asynchronous Learning Networks*, *15*(1), 20–32.

Ocak, M. A. (2011). Why are faculty members not teaching blended courses? Insights from faculty members. *Computers & Education*, *56*(3), 689–699. Retrieved from http://www.doi.org/10.1016/j.compedu.2010.10.011

Oh, E., & Park, S. (2009). How are universities involved in blended instruction? *Journal of Educational Technology & Society*, *12*(3), 327–342.

Oliver, M., & Trigwell, K. (2005). Can'Blended Learning'Be Redeemed? *E-Learning and Digital Media*, *2*(1), 17–26.

Piccoli, G., Ahmad, R., & Ives, B. (2001). Web-Based Virtual Learning Environments: A Research Framework and a Preliminary Assessment of Effectiveness in Basic IT Skills Training. *Management Information Systems Quarterly*, *25*(4), 401–426.

Prendergast, G. (2004). *Blended collaborative learning: online teaching of online educators*. Global Educator.

Prensky, M. (2010). *Teaching Digital Natives*. London: SAGE Ltd.

Roberts, G. (2003). Teaching using the web: Conceptions and approaches from a phenomenographic perspective. *Instructional Science*, *31*(1-2), 127–150.

Rodriguez, M. A., & Anicete, R. C. R. (2010). Students' Views of a Mixed Hybrid Ecology Course. *MERLOT Journal of Online Learning and Teaching*, *6*, 791–798.

Salmon, G. (2005). Flying not flapping: A strategic framework for e-learning and pedagogical innovation in higher education institutions. *ALT-J*, *13*(3), 201–218.

Sharpe, R. (2006). *The undergraduate experience of blended e-learning: a review of UK literature and practice*. The Higher Education Academy York.

Stacey, E., & Gerbic, P. (2008). *Success factors for blended learning*. Paper presented at the Australian Society for Computers in Learning in Tertiary Education 2008, Melbourne.

Steel, C. (2009). Reconciling university teacher beliefs to create learning designs for LMS environments. *Australasian Journal of Educational Technology*, *25*(3), 399–420.

Trigwell, K., Prosser, M., & Waterhouse, F. (1999). Relations between teachers' approaches to teaching and students' approaches to learning. *Higher Education*, *37*(1), 57–70.

Verkroost, M. J., Meijerink, L., Lintsen, H., & Veen, W. (2008). Finding a balance in dimensions of blended learning. *International Journal on E-Learning*, *7*(3), 499–522.

Widäng, I., & Fridlund, B. (2003). Self-respect, dignity and confidence: Conceptions of integrity among male patients. *Journal of Advanced Nursing*, *42*(1), 47–56. PMID:12641811

KEY TERMS AND DEFINITIONS

Academic Pathways Program: Program of study that allows students to progress from one qualification to another where the first course is recognised as an entry requirement and provides advanced standing to the second qualification.

Blended Learning Environments: A learning environment that combines both online learning and face-face teaching.

Blended Learning: Learning activities that involve a combination of face-to-face interactions and technologically mediated interactions between students, teachers and learning resources.

Content-Centered Approaches: A learning approach where teachers focus on student's access to learning materials and information transfer.

Learned-Centered Approaches: A learning approach where teachers focus on the learning process.

Learning Management Systems: A software application that combines Information and Communications Technology (ICT) with various learning resources and delivery methods.

Phenomenography: Qualitative research methodology that investigates the different ways of understanding and how these different ways of understanding are related to one another.

Chapter 5
Evaluation of Mobile Learning with The Eight-Dimensional E-Learning Framework

Özlem Efiloğlu Kurt
Yalova University, Turkey

Esra İşgör Şimşek
Yalova University, Turkey

ABSTRACT

Mobile learning has been a very popular topic in recent years as a result of the accelerating use of mobile devices. This learning type that offers education for everyone without any space and time limitation opens the doors for life-long learning. Even though mobile learning, which is employed to support the traditional education and ensure distant education, seems to have many advantages, it also possesses some disadvantages. Therefore, evaluating mobile learning in various dimensions will contribute to the literature through revealing the antecedents of these advantages and disadvantages. In this chapter, Khan's (2005) eight-dimensional e-learning framework is explained with its dimensions and adapted into mobile learning context. Subsequently, Coursera case which is among the MOOCs that are commonly used nowadays as a mobile interface is evaluated with reference to the framework.

INTRODUCTION

Small mobile communications devices are currently used for a variety of purposes in our daily lives and play a significant role in accessing information, for interaction, and even conducting learning activities. Sharples (2000) reported that the use of these mobile devices in learning activities has led to e-Learning (that typically uses desktop computers or portable laptops with large screens) developing into truly mobile learning. Similarly, Quinn (2000) named e-Learning, which can be achieved through movable operational tools, as mobile learning. According to Gulbahar's (2012) definition, mobile learning refers to ensuring education and teaching through small mobile devices such as PDAs, smart phones, movable media players, tablets, and mobile phones.

DOI: 10.4018/978-1-5225-0466-5.ch005

Mobile learning allows access to educational information and activities using small, mobile devices at any place and time (Roger, 2011) and brings many advantages to users. Attewell (2005) summarized these advantages as follows: They help students to develop their reading, writing, and computational skills; realize their own abilities; determine the areas requiring help and support; improve their self-confidence and self-respect; and acquire independent and collaborative learning experiences. In addition, Woodill (2011) emphasized that mobile learning has some benefits such as ensuring the long-time focus of learner, being both efficient and effective, saving time and costs, allowing the opportunity to update information dynamically, being personal, and permitting the access to information through various resources.

By means of these advantages provided by mobile technology, learning will acquire a new dimension in the future. Ally (2014) argues that there are some trends that educators and policy makers should be aware of. These trends are as follows:

- The role of instructor turns into that of a facilitator of learning from a presenter of information.
- Learning takes place at any time of the day and in any place.
- Students can reach learning materials at any time and from any place through electronic repositories.
- There will be no geographic barriers which can prevent access to learning materials through the Internet.
- Students and teachers will be able to access learning materials as open educational resources under Creative Commons licences.
- Learning will not be teacher-centered, but rather learner-centered.
- More multimedia materials will be used to meet the needs of current and upcoming generations of learners.
- Learning systems will be intelligent and will be able to follow the learners' development.

Nowadays, most people carry their mobile devices, such as smart phones, laptop computers or tablets, with them constantly for entertainment, communication, work, and education related purposes. These devices that we encounter at almost every moment in our lives, have undoubtedly a significant role in an educational sense and there are some important points about these devices in the learning materials' development process. Sharples (2000) summarized these points as follows:

- **Portable:** It should be accessible at any moment and in any place when and where the user needs.
- **Personal:** It should be suitable for the skills and learning styles of learners and should support personal learning.
- **Unobtrusive:** The design of mobile learning screens should be clear and simple rather than ornate and complex.
- **Accessible:** The communication between learners, experts, and students should be facilitated.
- **Adaptable:** It should be adaptable for individual skills and the development of information.
- **Permanent:** It should be both permanent and continuous against the potential changes in technology.
- **Practical:** It should be suitable for daily activities such as communication, work, and learning.

There are some rules to be considered while designing applications to be used in mobile devices. These rules were highlighted by Madeira et al., (2009) as follows:

- If its aim is to make developed courses flexible in time and space, these courses should be developed to be usable everywhere.
- Language used in the presentation of materials should be simple, plain, clear, and the type should be easy to read.
- Pictures and animations should be used to show how to use theoretical concepts.
- An automatic assessment system should be created for the self-assessment of each student in exercises and tests.
- Games and fun activities should be available to encourage and motivate students.
- Applications should be designed to let students see what they have studied, in which applications they encountered challenges, how much time they spent and their evaluation results.
- The system should be designed in such a way as to collect students' demographic information, number of accesses to the platform, content views, exam results, and to keep the information in a secure database.

Elias (2011) adapted the principles of Universal Instructional Design (UID) to mobile learning. These principles are given as: equitable use; flexible use; be simple and intuitive, perceptible information, tolerance for error, low physical and technical effort, the presences of a community of learners and support, and instructional climate, as explained in detail below:

- **Equitable Use:** In mobile learning, course content should be accessible via various tools for people in different locations and of varying skills. Access to content should be provided in its simplest form. Short Messaging Systems (SMS) or texting technology is preferred, due to high levels of penetration in the communication world. In addition, using cloud computing file-storage and sharing sites for access to content enables students to store and access more information and develop more complex projects; in this way students will be more fully engaged in the process of learning.
- **Flexible Use:** Course content should be suitable for the skills, characteristics, working hours, connection levels and usage method preferences of the maximum number of learners. The content of learning packages should be fashioned into small chunks. Different from traditional learning, the course context should be open to unconventional assignment options and enable students to be able to animate and illustrate the courses.
- **Simple and Intuitive:** Unnecessary complexity should be eliminated and the course design should be simple and intuitive. User interfaces should be as simple and clean as possible; the content should fit comfortably into even the smallest screen. Coding should be simple as this minimizes file sizes, increases download rates and supports advanced programming functions, even in mobile devices that do not normally support it. Using open sites and software can reduce costs of access to online resources.
- **Perceptible Information:** Descriptive information such as titles, descriptions, alternative text etc. can be added to the material to be used.
- **Tolerance for Error:** UID principles attempts to minimize the dangers and possible adverse results that might occur during the design of learning environments. Learning aids can be included in learning packages help guard against the potential errors that can be encountered by learners while accessing a task or learning materials via a mobile device, and will help learners obtain "just in time" support without any further delay.

- **Low Physical and Technical Effort:** Mobile learning should be developed using low physical and technical effort. To this end, support tools developed in accordance with mobile learning designs can be used.
- **Community of Learners and Support:** Just as in online learning, learners should also be supported to use multiple communication methods in mobile learning.
- **Instructional Climate:** This UID principle focuses on the effect of the instructor in course delivery. Mobile learning instructors can send messages to learners in order to keep in touch via many different channels. For example, instructors may send regular reminders, requests, quizzes, and questions to students. In addition, they can receive feedback through various methods and can create spaces to house student-generated learning content.

KHAN'S FRAMEWORK FOR MOBILE LEARNING

Khan (2007) assessed e-Learning in general under eight dimensions: pedagogical, technological, interface design, evaluation, management, resource support, ethical and institutional. In this section, elearning will be reviewed based on Khan's (2007) framework and then those dimensions will be specifically adapted to mobile learning systems (Figure 1).

Pedagogical

It is important to have knowledge about some fundamental pedagogic principles, aside from being able to use technology, in order to ensure the maximum level of learning through mobile devices. Educators should develop strategies that will improve user interaction with learning activities using mobile devices, besides being able to develop learning materials that can be accessed and displayed through

Figure 1. Badrul Khan's framework for mobile learning
(Ally, 2014)

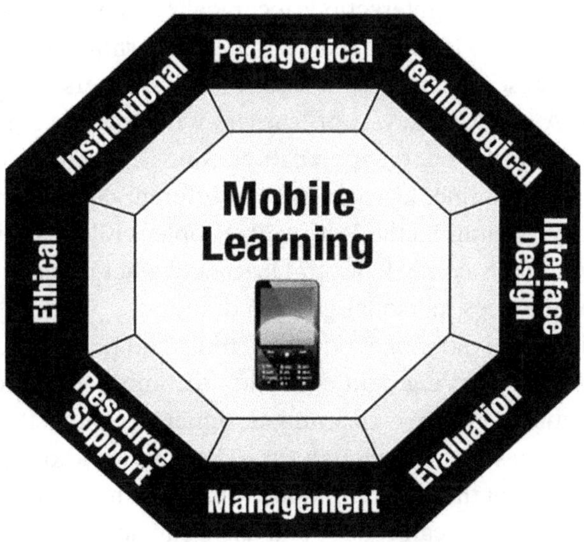

these devices' small screens. At the same time, those who design learning materials for these mobile devices are expected to use the necessary strategies for reducing the work load of the user while using the device and supporting learning by offering the highest quality learning materials. According to O'Malley et al. (2003), efficient access methods and the mobile learning pedagogy required to present information through mobile devices have not yet been satisfactorily developed. However, the Khan framework (2005) brings a significant contribution to the pedagogy of mobile learning in this sense. According to the framework, the pedagogic dimension of e-Learning comprises varying issues related to learning and teaching. These are content analysis, audience analysis, goal analysis, media analysis, design approach, and organization, and method and strategies that assess the principles and methods of teaching and learning (Khan, 2012; Ally, 2014):

- **Content Analysis:** Is generally made by subject matter experts and determined according to content learning goals. The kind of content can be successfully delivered online is a question that can be answered by designers by analyzing case studies and considering successful and unsuccessful online learning experiences. Not all forms of content presentation are suitable for the electronic environment. The content is determined in accordance with the goals of learning content course. In the design of e-Learning, the stability of course content should be taken into account as well. While content that does not require any update is categorized as 'static' (e.g. historical events, grammar rules, etc.), content that may potentially change over time, or require frequent updating, is categorized as dynamic (e.g. laws, policies, assignments etc.). As dynamic content should be changed from time to time, course content should be designated in programming as *static* or *dynamic*. Content that is not updated in a timely manner might be a disappointment for learners (Khan, 2005). These points that should be considered concerning all course content, are also valid for mobile learning. It is not appropriate to just import old content and drop it into mobile learning without redesign to fit the new context. Improved productivity and knowledge retention, increased compliance or risk reductions through expedient content are necessary to get a return for the investment. According to Castle (2013), dividing content into two-minute segments has been suggested as a rapid and inexpensive way to send content over mobile phone networks. Castle (2013) reported that users starts to lose concentration approximately 90 seconds later during mobile phone and learning content interaction; technical consideration reductions and two-minute segments can make it easier to learn by sharpening key learning points.
- **Audience Analysis:** Focuses on the characteristics of e-learners expected to use a particular set of learning materials. A careful analysis of learners will generate significant information for the design of learning activities for a target population. Since e-Learning can be accessed by any student in any place and at any time, learners having different cultures and backgrounds may differ in terms of appropriate learning methods as well. People with disabilities are another group that should be assessed within this context. Several learner characteristics such as age, education level, learners' interests, experiences, personal goals and attitudes, learning preferences, writing/reading/mathematical skills, motivation, keyboarding skills and previous experience with e-Learning can be determined through varying data collection techniques like survey, interviews, observations, and this information can help e-Learning designers to understand their target audience better (Khan, 2005). In the past, it was enough for a designer to know generalities about the target audience; however, this is not the case for mobile learning. The target audience is more complex in mobile learning, mobile devices can change and users can have very different mobile experiences. This is among the important challenges of mobile learning (de Waard, 2014).

- **Goal Analysis:** Process helps to determine and explain aims in an e-Learning project. Having clear goals and objectives is as important as achieving them for a learner in e-Learning (Khan, 2005). Defining clear goals in mobile learning is one of the most important factors that help learners to complete their tasks (Laurillard, 2007).
- **Media Analysis:** Relates to analyzing different media such as books and printed materials, the internet, or other technologies to determine their suitability for use in e-Learning. E-Learning designers should have a knowledge of the capacities of multimedia components such as text, graphics, animation, audio, video, and so on to determine which would support their learning goals (Khan, 1997). Mobile learning supports the transmission and delivery of rich, multi-media content. At the same time, it also supports discussion and discourse, in real-time, synchronous and asynchronous, using voice, text and multi-media. Varying disciplines, for example sociology or literature or, alternatively, engineering may require different forms of information presentation (Traxler, 2007).
- **Design Approach:** For e-Learning activities depends on the type of domain of knowledge of the e-Learning content. The pedagogic philosophy of the whole design is affected by the content. Another important theoretical consideration in the design of World Wide Web courses is the control of learning activities. This is achieved by student-centered and program-centered learning activities. Student-centered learning refers to students' creation of self-learning opportunities to meet their own learning needs by choosing their own educational activities. The opposite of this learning includes highly structured courses, the learning content of which is designed and organized by course designers. Students are frequently rendered passive information consumers by the instructor. Each of these frameworks significantly affects the results of education methods (Bannan & Milheim, 1997; Khan, 2005). These factors are important in mobile learning as well. Old versions of learning designs end with a summary by the instructor while the contributions of students can be seen at the end of the course in mobile learning design (Laurillard, 2007). The effective use of mobile technologies ensures an uninterrupted access to a wide range of activities between the student and instructors (Hedberg, 2014).
- **Organization:** Refers to the regulation of content in ways consistent with the purpose of enabling learners to achieve their goals and objectives (Khan, 2005). Educators can transmit and manage courses in mobile devices by means of mobile technologies. Flexible and affordable learning can be offered to everyone in mobile environments by means of Open Education Resources (OER) (Ally & Samaka, 2013).
- **Method and Strategies:** Is another important factor of the pedagogic dimension concerning learning and instruction (Khan 2005, Ally 2014). This dimension also investigates the delivery method of course activities, suitability of learning environments that are necessary factors for an intended audience to achieve their learning goals (Ally, 2014). Interactive learning strategies in mobile learning motivate and engage learners and encourage them to complete their education instead of dropping-out of school (Ally, 2014).

Technological

Another significant dimension in the systems used in mobile learning is technology. In this dimension, Khan (2001) emphasized the importance of infrastructure planning, hardware, and software. Sufficient infrastructure support should be provided for those who will receive learning content from mobile devices; required hardware for the content should be defined clearly and required software for the content should be provided. Unless these conditions are met, mismatched or inadequate technology can makes learning difficult. Mcconatha, Praul & Lynch (2008) argue that students fail in practice due to equipment limitations and software problems of the tools used in mobile learning. Similarly, Riva and Villani (2005) reported that infrastructural, hardware, and software problems such as the limited memory of mobile tools, small size of screens, disconnections from time to time, limited battery life, small keyboards, the need for different operating systems for different devices, hardship of publication in different scanners and platforms, security problems etc. may occur. In order not to experience such problems, mobile devices should be assessed and selected in accordance with the technology dimensions of Khan (2005)'s framework:

- **Infrastructure Planning:** Is one of the important dimensions in mobile learning environments since each e-Learning environment is built upon a digital infrastructure (Khan, 2005). This digital infrastructure should be designed, planned, built, maintained, and staffed in the same manner as the physical infrastructure (Boettcher & Kumar, 2000). Boettcher and Kumar (2000) emphasized that an e-Learning infrastructure should be scalable, sustainable, reliable, and consistently available. These features also should be integrated into mobile learning as mobile learning environments are built in similar ways to those of e-Learning environments. However, the limitations of mobile learning should be taken into consideration during this building process.
- **Hardware:** For e-Learning consists of computers, servers, modems, networking devices, wireless devices, printers, scanners, cameras, microphones, storage devices (e.g., hard drives, CD-ROM, DVD, etc.), and other equipment (Khan, 2005). The hardware for mobile learning does not have such a wide spectrum and the hardware limitations of mobile devices cause problems for designers and users. For example, extra random access memory (RAM) can be added from external memory cards to many electronic tools but this feature is not included in all mobile devices. In addition, virtual and on-screen keyboards, through which data input is made in current mobile devices, are not user-friendly and lead to slow and challenging data input. Small screen sizes with poor resolution, color, and contrast are other hardware problems for mobile learning (Elias, 2011).
- **Software used in E-Learning:** Consists of word processors, e-mail packages, presentation programs, graphic software, reader software, browsers and plug-ins, spreadsheets, databases, learning management systems (LMS), learning content management systems (LCMS), authoring tools and enterprise software, and so on (Khan, 2005). Assessing the software available for mobile learning, we can say that it comprises apps and programs different from those used for e-Learning. Today, mobile devices are multifunctional tools that offer a lot of features to users, both in the business world and in the user's social life. These tools enable users to reach their e-mails, use instant messaging software, surf the Internet, use common office tools etc.; and more applications are being developed day by day. Mobile device operating systems, their different 'flavors' (iOS, Android, Windows, Chrome, etc.), application development languages and application supports should be taken into consideration when mobile learning applications are being developed.

Interface Design

Mobile devices such as smart phones, tablets, and pocket computers have become widespread, hence an important part of our daily lives. In order to enable people to more efficiently use these devices in their business and social life, their interface should be designed properly. In this design, the purpose should be to explore the most efficient way to give comprehensible electronic messages to users (Skaalid, 1999). A well-designed interface for small, low resolutions screens has many significant advantages, such as improving the quality of work, improving the satisfaction level of the user, increasing labor productivity, and providing security for the system controlled by the software (Liu, 1997). Page and website design, content design, navigation, accessibility, and usability testing are crucial for designing a good interface (Khan, 2005).

- **Webpage and Website Design:** Are about appearance and functionality. Web pages should be well organized; browsing and access should be easy; and it should provide ease of use for user (Khan, 2005). Page design in mobile tools should include the same features. In the video assets used for mobile design, file size should be minimized as much as possible because many users have limited connectivity and must pay for each data or image download, by size. In order to eliminate the perception problems that may occur, due to the limited screen size of mobile devices sufficient white space should be included, which will allow elements such as image, typography, and animation to be easily seen should be taken into consideration (Alican, 2011).
- **Content Design:** For e-Learning is one of the important determinants for web usability and Nielsen (1997) has prepared guidelines for quality content designs. According to the research conducted to determine how people read websites, 79% of test users scanned a new page while only 16% read the page word by word. For this reason, web pages should be scannable and should include meaningful subtitles, bulleted lists, the inverted pyramid style, starting with the conclusion and using half the words (or less) than conventional writing (Nielsen, 1997). Content should always be clear in style and readable. To this end, standard writing formats such as grammar, capitalization, punctuation, usage, spelling, and paragraphing should be used. Graphics related to the content (icons, buttons, images etc.) and other multimedia components (audio, video etc.) should be used to complement the text content. Writing content should be basic, clear and direct. In addition, its reading level should be appropriate for readers from every level (Khan, 2005). Considering these features for mobile devices, we can emphasize similar features. Mobile site content should be more simplified than typical websites; and should be eliminated from the sections that may cause extra time and money for users (Alican, 2011).
- **Navigation:** Is another important issue for interface design. The site should guide the user around the information to be accessed and should also help the user not to get lost among the pages. The user should be able to easily go a few steps back or to the homepage whilst moving to sub-sections in a very short space of time. This can only be ensured by a plain design, a structured site tree, proper sectioning of the site, and consistency of interface and the exclusion of unnecessary effects (Khan, 2005). In mobile learning, browsing through sites using keys and menus leads to problems due to the small screen sizes of mobile devices. Studies show that keys are not practically usable in mobile devices and it is hard to find direction between images in these devices (Schwabe & Göth, 2005). In order to prevent such problems, main and sub categories should be accurately defined, transitions should be shaped, and buttons for the main category should always be positioned on screen to ensure user's ease of access to them while a flow chart is being formed (Alican, 2011).
- **Accessibility:** Is about the fact that open, flexible, and distributed e-Learning environments designs should be suitable for all potential students. While designing an e-Learning site, there are two barriers that prevent accessibility of contents for all users. These are technical issues (such as bandwidth) and design issues (such as images and videos without text alternatives) (Khan, 2005).

Accessibility involves similar problems for mobile learning as well. Users encounter problems such as device variability, slow download speed, and limited Internet access, small screen sizes with poor resolution, color, and contrast, awkward text input, limited memory, etc. in their mobile devices (Elias, 2011). Such problems cannot be resolved technically by users, short of buying different mobile technologies. Therefore, such problems should be considered in design and content developing for mobile learning. For example, designers should always keep in mind that a user does not always have access to the Internet and thus, content should be designed and sized to be suitable for download to a mobile device. Media elements should have small sizes and all unnecessary components should be removed from the design.

- **Usability Testing:** Is a tool used to developed interface design (Khan, 2005). Usability is the combination of factors that affect the interaction between a user and a product or system (Nielsen, 1993). Usability in mobile learning causes problems due to the limitations of mobile devices and these problems have been summarized by Zhou and Xia (2010) as follows:
    - **Small Screen:** A tool should be portable and small to be mobile. However, it is challenging for users to operate with small screens.
    - **Value Inputs:** Value inputs with touch-operated screens are slower than inputs with keyboard and access to menus with touch-operated screens increases error rate.
    - **Download Delays:** Download delays occur even when 3G or 4G services are the fastest download service.
    - **Ignorance of Mobile Users:** Most of websites are designed using desktop computers, and designed to be accessed using full sized screens. Access by mobile users is ignored and when asked to access these sites via mobile devices, users encounter designs that do not comply with mobile devices.

Evaluation

Assessment and evaluation fulfills the duty of determining missing and insufficient aspects of an applied program, improving teaching and data collection, and providing direction during program development (Baykul, 2000). As in all other systems, the assessment and evaluation process is crucial in e-Learning systems as well. Within the scope of this idea, Khan (2005) emphasized the necessity of both the assessment of learners and evaluation of instruction and the learning environment. The assessment of learners is important for students to see their own insufficiencies. The evaluation of instruction and the learning environment is important to determine the healthy mechanism of a system. In the systems of mobile learning, being the intersection of mobile devices and e-Learning (Jones & Jo, 2004), the same evaluation is just as necessary. Ally (2014) emphasized that an evaluation is made with the purpose of defining the effectiveness of the development process and mobile learning delivery:

- **Assessment of Learners:** Is made to assess the development of students through methods such as individual testing, participation in group discussions, questions, and portfolio development in e-Learning (Khan, 2005). Similarly, it is important for students to be able to test and assess themselves and to see their insufficiencies in mobile learning. While structuring the system of mobile learning, the presence of such an assessment system should be ensured.

- **Evaluation of Instruction and the Learning Environment:** Is another important title under the evaluation dimension. The evaluation of instruction and learning environment in the online learning environment is different from the traditional face-to-face classroom-based environment. In a traditional place-based environment, students generally evaluate the instructor through their own course materials. However, in online learning environments, courses are usually designed, developed, delivered, and supported by various individuals and support units within an institution. The instructor is just one element in the learning environment and evaluation of an instructor should not be mixed in with the evaluation of the learning environment. The evaluation of the learning environment can be made in different dimensions such as the quality of the course design, support services, efficiency of technology infrastructure (Khan, 2005). As a matter of fact, mobile learning is a new approach for many institutions and, therefore, it is important to evaluate the results of the educational design process in mobile learning. This evaluation is generally carried out through determining whether educational design is appropriate or not with a group of students following the development of the first course. The instructor may continue giving courses in the same way in accordance with the feedback given by students or prefer a redevelopment process by revising the educational design (Ally, 2014).

Management

It is important to have clear information about the people, processes, and products involved in e- Learning in order to be able to manage e-Learning projects. The people-process-product – the elements referred to as the 'P3 continuum' by Khan (2014) – can be used in the comprehensive planning of e-Learning. People included in the process take the role of preparing e-Learning materials and making them suitable for the target audience. Depending on the scope and aim of the project, participant numbers may differ during the various stages. In a small or medium-scaled e-Learning project, a participant may undertake multiple duties, while they may have a more comprehensive but only one specific duty in a large-scaled project.

The process of creating quality e-Learning products starts with a comprehensive analysis of the content and context and ends with a quality check. The final product is now ready to be sent to the client. According to Khan (2005), a typical e-Learning process consists of analysis, planning, design, development, delivery and evaluation stages as presented in Figure 2.

Figure 2. E-learning process model

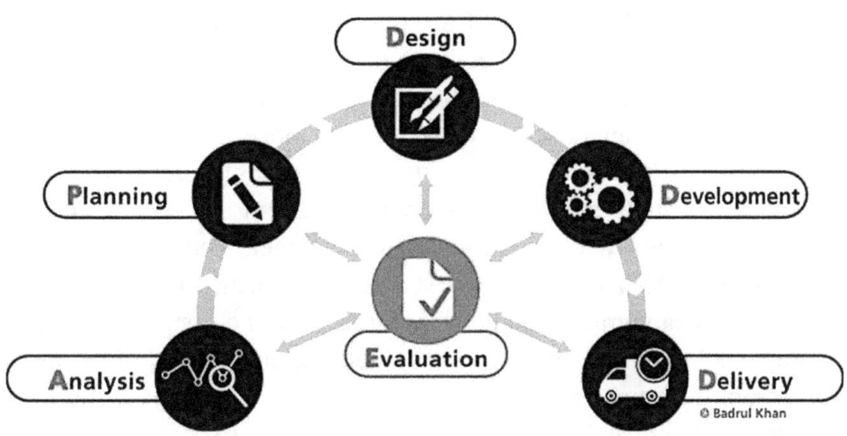

As can be seen in Figure 2, this is a reiterative process that receives constant corrective feedbacks. Afterwards, these feedbacks are included into various stages. Individuals in the e-Learning process should be in contact with each other and should work together to revise materials where necessary. It should be remembered that different terms (i.e., planning, analysis, etc.) can be used for e-Learning stages by different people; regardless of what it is called, each stage of this process should be completed.

Apart from all these stages, management of e-Learning projects requires a systematic and integrated approach. It is critical to consider all these processes during the transfer into a mobile learning environment. Proper project management and quality control techniques should be used to complete mobile learning projects in a timely manner and project team members should have the required skills to develop quality learning materials. Mobile learning materials are generally developed by experts from different fields like instructional design, multimedia, user interface design, mobile devices applications, and software. Another important task of the project manager is to ensure that team members work together to develop quality learning materials (Ally, 2014). Considering all these processes, we can say that the management dimension is crucial and necessary for the functioning of the system. Khan (2005) divided this dimension into two categories: the maintenance of the learning environment; and distribution of information:

- **Maintenance of the Learning Environment:** Includes staffing, budgeting, and management of the course content and learning resources, mechanisms for evaluation, security measures, etc. For example, decisions about which course content should be created, copyright issues surrounding course materials, student submissions, whether there is a system available to keep information such as online quizzes secure etc. are the issues covered under this dimension (Khan, 2005). In this category, for mobile learning, security risks and vulnerability attack issues are among some of the most important concerns related to mobile learning environments. Smart phones and tablets, having particularly high usage rates, have become targets as they are especially vulnerable to physical and digital attacks (Howell, Love & Turner, 2008). 'Physical attacks' includes theft of mobile devices – a distressingly common occurrence. In this respect, learner records, e-portfolio data, assessment grades, and feedback are among some of the sensitive information that should be protected (Kambourakis, 2013). In order to protect this information, the institution should take the necessary precautions and students should similarly take great care as well. Likewise, connecting to reliable and tested networks to protect data, and refraining from downloading mobile learning content from unreliable websites are among some basic precautions (Shonola & Joy, 2014).
- **Distribution of Information:** Comprises the delivery of online and offline learning materials such as schedules, syllabuses, announcements, course relevant contact information, learning and testing materials, and students' grades from quizzes, assignments, exams, and projects. This dimension indicates that students need consistent and safe access their testing materials and their grades. The course software should warn students about any changes through communication channels such as e-mail, announcement pages, alert boxes, a running footer added to a pages, phone calls etc. (Khan, 2005). That is also the case for mobile learning. The system should warn students about any changes related to the course or about any other important issues unrelated to the course through a suitable communication channel. The syllabus and curriculum should be previously announced; announcements should be published regularly; student grades, assignments, projects and exam grades should be recorded into the system in a timely manner. Through informing students in this way, it ensures that students can easily follow the course, they are not unconnected from the course and, in this way, students are engaged, and hence learning can be achieved more effectively and students are more motivated to complete courses.

Resource Support

Resource support plays an important role in creating a meaningful learning environment in e-Learning systems. Khan (2005) believes that this support should be given as available online support and resources. Online support should address student needs for help both with course content and technical support. Whenever learners need this support, they should be able to access it without any space or time limitation at any time, day or night. Apart from this support, the system should offer the resources of previous studies to learners. Resource support is not only valid for e-Learning systems, but for learning using mobile devices. Ally (2014) emphasized that the resource support dimension should include technical support and human resources support in order to create a meaningful and successful mobile learning environment:

- **Support:** Refers to supporting e-Learning courses in two dimensional ways, being both instructional and counseling support; and technical support. Instructional and counseling support refers to the support given to students when organizing for online learning. Online technical support is one of the most important support services in these learning environments and helps students so they can carry out technical transactions such as logging on, uploading and downloading files, for troubleshooting, and so on (Khan, 2005). This is also the case for mobile learning. Learners need a range of services and these services are counseling and guidance, mentoring, pastoral care, career advice, and presentation within their institution and so on (Kukulska-Hulme & Traxler, 2008). For example, instructors should help learners in understanding and learning about the course content and should give all required and necessary instructional support. The role of instructor should be that of a guide in facilitating the learning, not solely as a presenter of information (Ally, 2014).
- **Resources:** Are original documents, public domain books, summaries of or discussions about books in print, reference works, scholarly papers, new concepts, notification of both face-to-face and online conferences, job information, and so on in e-Learning. These resources are divided into online and offline resources. Online resources consist of multimedia archives, mailing lists and their archives, Frequently Asked Questions (FAQs), glossaries, e-books, dictionaries, calculators, digital libraries, computer tutorials, online experts, journals, magazines, newsletters, newspapers, and digital documents; while offline resources include hard-copy books, journals, magazines, newsletters, newspapers, documents, reference works, access to experts, etc. (Khan, 2005). These resources listed for e-Learning are valid for mobile learning as well. Learners can gain access to help mechanisms without any time/space limitation whenever they need, can support their learning and progress in their education with comfortable and safe steps thanks to the support of these resources.

Ethical

In Khan's learning model, the ethical dimension is comprehensively analyzed. Ethics is discussed using the subtitles of social and cultural diversity, bias and political issues, geographical diversity, learner diversity, digital divide, etiquette, and legal issues (Khan, 2005):

- **Social and Cultural Diversity:** Should be taken into consideration by e-Learning designers during the design process. Similarly, cultural details used in course material should be carefully chosen. In the designing stage, users from different cultures might be asked to visit the website of the related course or view proposed materials and provide feedback. Different symbols can have different meanings in different cultures. For example, while red symbolizes good luck in China, it is used for warning signs in the USA. In most countries, a beer and a pork sandwich might represent a good lunch, however, these symbols may not be so welcome in a Muslim country or among Jewish populations (Khan, 2005). Social and cultural diversity should be considered during the transfer of e-Learning designs into mobile environments. In the literature, there is a limited number of studies that focus directly on mobile learning and cultural diversity relations; yet studies about access to different learning resources through mobile devices (library resources and references services, information seeking etc.) revealed that addressing cultural diversity is effective (Hudson, 2010; Barnhart & Pierce, 2011).
- **Bias and Political Issues:** Are among the important issues for an e-Learning content designer. A tendency towards presenting course materials that emphasize a certain point of view – or totally ignore competing views - may constitute bias. E-Learning designers should cooperate with content experts in order to eliminate obvious bias in content. In some societies, political and religious organizations may negatively affect the inclusion of that society into e-Learning activities on the grounds that the society may differ from themselves in terms of political or religious beliefs. Changes in governments of some countries may also affect e-Learning initiatives. Similarly, an e-Learning course or content can be affected by political ideologies and religious beliefs in some societies (Khan, 2005). These concerns are also valid for mobile learning and mobile learning implementation can be successful if bias and political issues are considered at the design stage (Hartnell-Young, 2008; Passey, 2010).
- **Geographical Diversity:** Is another issue that should be considered carefully in online education. As e-Learning is open to the participation of students in varying geographic locations in the world, the locations of participants, different time zones, various levels of Internet access and seasonal vacation times should be taken into consideration. These considerations are also valid for mobile learning. Students may not feel comfortable taking part in online activities or submitting their assignments on national and religious holidays. For example, scheduled chat discussions in a group work activity may not work for students coming from different time zones or students may find it hard to take part in group activities during their vacations. In addition, designers should pay attention to regional and international economic and technical limitations (Khan, 2005; Traxler, 2010).
- **Learner Diversity:** Is another important subtitle among the ethical dimensions. Each learner has a unique learning style. In online courses, the diversity of the student population is a significant challenge for an instructor to develop a lecture or other learning materials to meet the needs of a wide range of students from various different backgrounds, experience and expertise in e-Learning. Khan (2005) suggests instructors ask students to send their brief biography before starting a course and encourage students to communicate with each other. These suggestions for accommodating learner diversity are also valid for mobile learning.
- **Digital Divide:** Refers to the gap between those having access to the Internet and other information technologies and others who do not have this access. It would be wrong to assume that students are always those on the down side of the divide from their instructors; frequently students are more computer literate, own newer and more powerful devices and have faster Internet access

than their instructors. A lack of internet access at home; difficulty in understanding e-Learning content; not being able to see e-Learning content as culturally or geographically relevant; and varying internet access rates in different geographic locations are some of the factors creating the digital divide. In addition, people with disabilities frequently encounter more obstacles, especially with access and input, when compared to others in the e-Learning environment (Khan, 2005; Peng et al. 2009). Even though the digital divide cannot be completely eliminated, common policies, that can be developed by communities and governments, should be followed by providers of technology infrastructure, software, hardware, internet services and e-Learning contents to minimize the gap. In the designing stage of mobile learning activities, the digital divide should be taken into consideration. These policies should focus on how equal access to mobile learning resources can be ensured for a wider population (Laouris & Eteokleous, 2005; Low &O'Connell, 2006).

- **Etiquette:** Consists of rules for common, respectful behavior in an online learning community. In an e-Learning environment, students should be given guidelines for netiquette (network or Internet etiquette) while messaging in discussion forums, newsgroups or communicating through e-mail or instant messaging in the course. With highly diverse student groups, these guidelines should be developed by the students themselves, with instructor guidance. These guidelines should always state that participants should not make personal attacks on each other in synchronous or asynchronous communication. These personal attacks do not only disturb the learning process but also disturb the interaction between participants. Khan (2005) suggests organizing orientation sessions that include a discussion of netiquette of e-Learning courses in order to prevent possible problems during online discussions. Based on these points, mobile learning will create its own culture (Traxler & Bridges, 2004; Kukulska-Hulme & Traxler, 2005).
- **Legal Issues Such as Privacy, Plagiarism, and Copyright Issues:** are other issues that require attention (Khan, 2005). Institutions should develop e-Learning policies and guidelines at the very beginning of the e-Learning initiative. Institutions should have a privacy policy and inform students about how their personal information will be protected and the extent to which they should share with other participants. At the beginning of the course, students should be informed about the openness of the Web and appropriate privacy guidelines, e.g. discussions within courses are private to the members of the course and should not be shared with non-members. Content authors, instructors, tutors, facilitators, guest speakers and students should be informed about the need to avoid plagiarism and to address copyright issues in e-Learning (Khan, 2005). These legal issues are also relative to mobile learning content as well. A mobile learning instructor should pay attention to ethical guidelines such as fair treatment to learners and creating a constructive criticism environment while tutoring. Learners should also pay attention to ethical guidelines while using technology in order to complete their courses. For example, learners should show respect to each other in their interactions and avoid plagiarism in their course contributions. Mobile learning material developers should consider copyright arrangements and privacy guidelines; the personal and sensitive data of learners should be protected (Ally, 2014).

Institutional

Institutions should develop comprehensive strategic and business plans for successful e-Learning initiatives. In addition, e-Learning strategies should comply with the missions and strategic plans of institutions. As the number of the institutions offering e-Learning services increases, learners have greater opportunities to compare the suitability of quality, service, cost, and education providers. Distance learners will demand the same services offered to traditional campus-based students as well. Therefore, institutions should be prepared to provide a high-quality education along with the best online learning resources and support. According to Khan (2005) the institutional dimension of e-Learning includes administrative affairs, academic affairs and student services related to e-Learning:

- **Administrative Affairs:** Encompass issues related to needs assessment, readiness assessment, organization and change (diffusion, adoption, and implementation of innovation), budgeting and returns on investment, partnerships with other institutions, program and course information catalogs, marketing and recruitment, admissions, financial aid, academic calendar and course schedules, tuition and fees, registration and payment, information technology services instructional design and media services, graduation, transcripts, and grades (Khan, 2005). In this scope, institutions should provide the required infrastructure and support during the preparation of mobile learning environments. For example, the website of an institution should be designed to be mobile-friendly to enable learners to access information and services via their mobile devices. An institution should provide services and infrastructure that will support learners from the time of enrollment in courses or programs up until they complete the course (Ally, 2014).

At this point, we can also say that the cost of mobile content development is high. However, this cost decreases day by day. Content, once produced, can be used and repurposed for many times with not additional costs with the exception of the update costs. However, institutions should consider the differences among mobile devices while developing mobile content and should make improvements within this consideration. They should redesign their content to fit within small screens and should use the mobile experience as a new way to communicate with users (Griggs, 2009).

- **Academic Affairs:** Can encompass accreditation, policies, instructional quality, faculty and staff support, workload, class size compensation, intellectual property rights and so on (Khan, 2005). The salient aspects for mobile learning in this dimension are the impact that limitations such as the way small screen sizes, limited screen resolution and input mechanisms that are hard to use adversely affect the mobile learning environment and thus can impede learning and degrade instructional quality. Faculty and staff, especially mobile learning developers, may require additional training and support as they adapt to those limitations. Class sizes should be kept small to avoid overloading instructors as everything takes more time in online learning environments.
- **Student Services:** Should be comprehensive and efficient for all online students. E-Learning and mobile learning students should be able to access online the appropriate academic and support services already provided for face-to-face course students. These support services may differ by the unique needs of distance learners. These services include pre-enrollment services, orientation, advising, counseling, learning skills development services, services for students with disabilities, library support, bookstore, tutorial services, mediation and conflict resolution, social support network, student's newsletter, internship and employment services, alumni affairs, and other services. Institutions should not ignore providing toll-free numbers for the service access of distance learners (Khan, 2005). Those who use mobile technology from a distance to complete their courses should be able to access institution services virtually. For example, virtual library support should be available and learners should be able to access library resources, like interlibrary loans, at any

time and from any place. An institution should also give tutorial support to learners within their previously determined standards. For example, there should be available guidelines that explain the timelines within which a tutor should respond to the questions posted by learners or how rapidly feedbacks should be provided for learners' assignments (Ally, 2014).

COURSERA AS AN EXAMPLE OF A MOBILE MOOC, ANALYSED USING KHAN'S E-LEARNING FRAMEWORK

A recent innovation in online learning has rapidly become widespread - the Massive Open Online Course (MOOC) – and, being a part of a new application of online education have now been offered to users by many institutions, organizations and educators. These systems are distance education environments that enable any person in any place in the world to enroll in the course without having to pay any entrance fees, and take lectures and use open content (Esposito, 2012). MOOCs consist of online tools such as video courses, discussion forums, peer assessment and give people the opportunity to choose courses from reputable universities like Stanford, MIT, Edinburgh, etc. (Harding, 2012). In these systems, instructors lead the course via videos and students follow the course at their own learning pace (Mangelsdorf, 2012). In short, 'MOOC' refers to courses that are being made openly available to masses of people (sometimes in the thousands in a single course) with no entry criteria besides the student's desire to take the course. They are offered free or charged through tools like videos, presentations, audio etc. in an online environment.

The aim of MOOCs is to popularize access and usage; to ensure sustainability by creating a brand; to empower economy by reducing expenses and increasing income; to improve educational outputs; to create innovation and to conduct research in learning and teaching (Hollands & Tirthali, 2014). MOOCs generally consist of lectures, videos, tests, assignments, discussion platforms and blogs, but they differ by university or the people that prepare the content (Glance, Forsey & Riley, 2013).

The term 'MOOC' was first suggested by two entrepreneurs David Cormier and Bryan Alexandar in 2008. Stephen Downes and George Siemens made MOOCs an online service and a free-of-charge tool in 2008 (Downes, 2013). At Manitoba University in Canada, a course titled "Connectivism and Connected Knowledge" was opened. It was different to other online distant education courses, since it involved varying design purposes such as open access to all students, it was scalable, had determined start and finish times, and was based on based on connectivist principles etc. First of all, the course was opened for 24 students on a credit basis; however, when it was turned into an open online course, 2200 more students took places in the course for free (Siemens, 2013). In 2011, Sebastian Thrun and Peter Norvig from Stanford University opened the course "Artificial Intelligence". Registration was free and open to anyone who wanted to sign up so 160.000 students from 190 countries enrolled in this course (Pappano, 2012; Waldrop 2013).

Hill (2012) summarizes the history of MOOCs from their emergence in 2008 through their rapid rise in 2012 as presented in Figure 3.

Publicly well-known MOOC platforms such as Coursera, EdX, and Udacity, have become popular because their courses offer free-of-charge content created by elite universities within the last 2 years (Daniel, 2012). The year 2012 was named "The Year of MOOCs" (Pappano, 2012). The most commonly known MOOC platforms are Coursera, EdX, Udacity, Khan Akademy, Udemy, and FutureLearn. The distribution of the courses within these systems is presented in Figure 4.

Figure 3. History of MOOCs
(Hill, 2012)

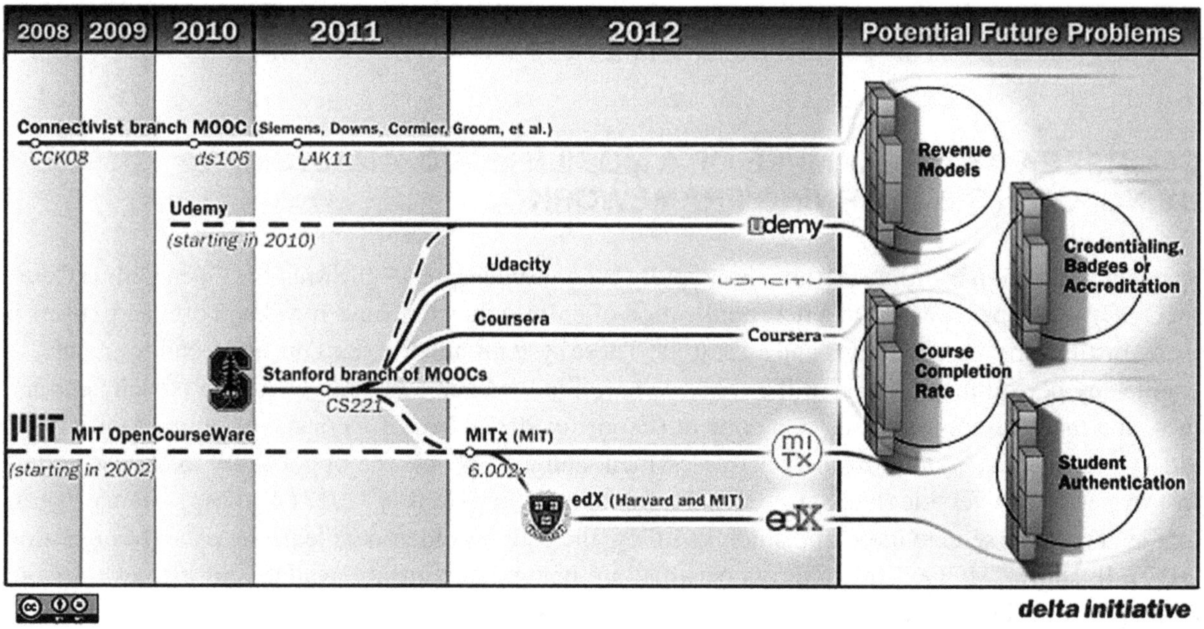

Coursera is one of the MOOC platforms that has a mobile interface and has a 38% market share as can be seen in Figure 4. It was built by Daphne Koller and Andrew Ng, who were professors at Stanford University in 2012. The company created a learning platform and cooperation was established with more than 30 universities for content development (Voss, 2013). The number of students enrolled in

Figure 4. Distribution of MOOCs by content providers
(Shah, 2014)

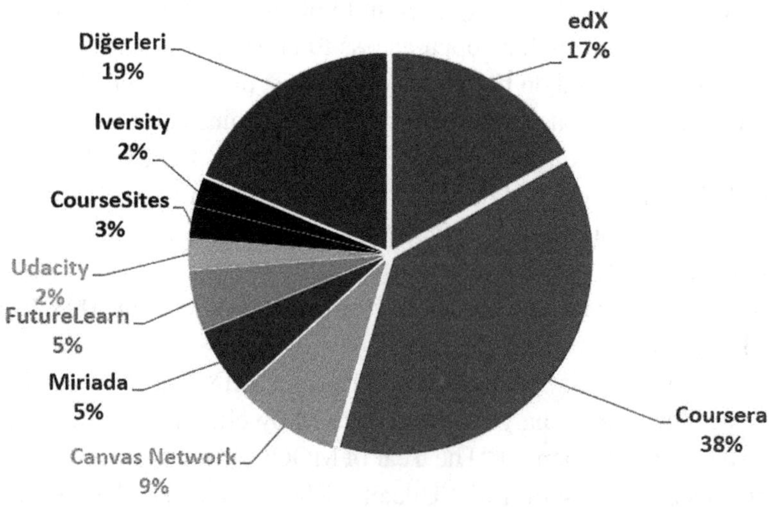

approximately 100 courses, prepared by 118 institutions, most of which are universities is 11,573,416 (Coursera, 2015). In this study, Coursera is being used as an example because of the widespread usage of its mobile interface.

The mobile app for Coursera was analyzed using the iPhone 6 mobile device and this application was evaluated using Khan's eight-dimensional e-Learning framework.

Results obtained from this evaluation are as follows for each dimension:

- **Pedagogical:** Some educational experts suggest that MOOCs are weak in terms of quality and pedagogy. This situation results from the fact that most of the students who enroll and start a MOOC do not complete their courses. For example, only 7% of those who started the course "Software Engineering" in Coursera at California University completed the course (Yuan &Powell, 2013). Since such online systems have a flexible structure, learners appear to feel relaxed and this leads to difficulties in following the course. Particularly when students do not have the self-discipline to set their own study schedule, unfortunately efficient learning may not be possible. Besides, digitization of courses whose content is not suitable or has been redesigned to be taught online leads to a failure in learning. In addition, teaching methods and strategies used for each course may not be suitable since each student has a unique learning style. This is another problematic issue in pedagogic terms. On the other hand, the Coursera system offers blended learning and a mastery learning environment to the users. Most of the institutions working in cooperation with Coursera provide an online platform for their students who already enrolled in formal training in order to improve their learning experiences. Studies reveal that students take a more active role in the course and obtain higher performance in this combined education model (Coursera, 2015).
- **Technological:** Hardware limitations and software problems in mobile devices lead to problems in mobile learning environments. Today, many mobile content developers design their courses with consideration of these limitations. In the Coursera system, a mobile learning environment was developed by thoughtfully considering the limitations inherent in small mobile devices. Videos, documents and other resources in the Coursera system were added to the system based on the perspective that argues that these resources can be downloaded to a mobile device. In addition, Coursera is presented through both a mobile web interface and as a native application. The native application was developed for mobile devices using either iOS or Android operating systems.
- **Interface Design:** Web design in the Coursera system interface is simple and plain. It is well organized; can be easily used by every user. Prior information about the courses in the system enable users to investigate the courses before taking them. Subtitle options for some courses are also a positive feature. The week duration of the course and the length of educational videos in minutes are specified in the course outline. In addition, watching faster and slower options are available for course videos. Presence of areas such as discussion forums, comments and announcements about the course ensures communication and interaction between students and instructors.

Tree structure, segmentation, and getting around menus in the system are satisfactory. Division of the course into categories, as presented in Figure 5, brings order to the contents. As presented in Figures 6 and 7, these menus bring simplicity to the user as one click on the course shows the content under each section and another click on each section gives a small explanation and shows sub-sections. In addition, being able to go directly to the searched course through the search function at the top of the screen is a significant feature for navigation.

Figure 5. Coursera interface

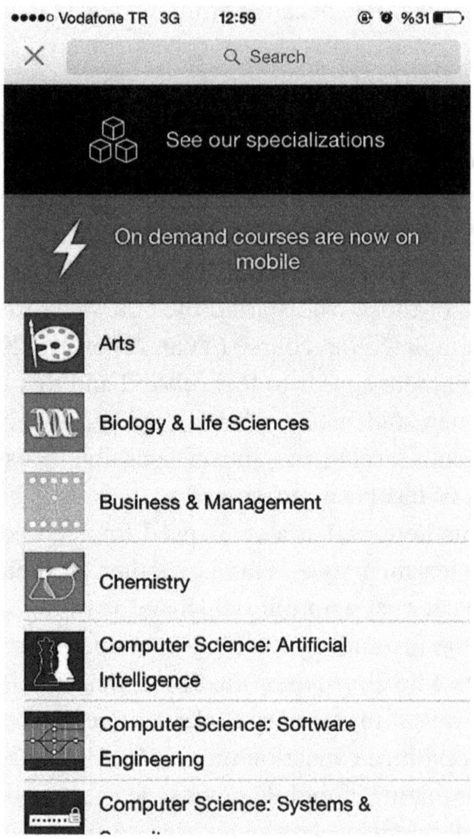

Figure 6. Coursera interface

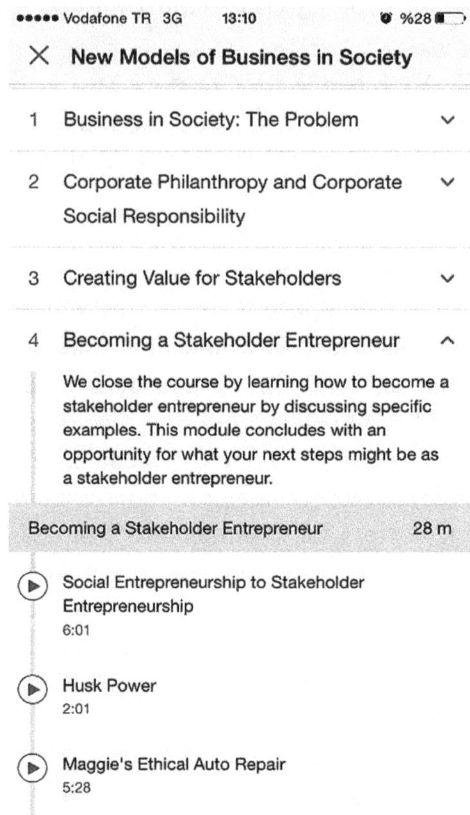

In interface design, a flexible and always accessible learning environment is important. Users should be able to access to course contents at any time from any place. The Coursera platform also gives students the opportunity to download course content to their mobile devices. Users can download a part of the course or the whole course onto their devices so they can access the course content when they do not have Internet access. Figures 8, 9, and 10 show screen shots of the process of downloading course content from Coursera.

- **Evaluation:** The Coursera platform includes evaluation areas such as system quizzes, final exams, exercises, general discussions, a 'meet and greet' area etc. In this way, students have the opportunity for self-assessment. Users can convey their feedback and views about the learning environment to authorities via "Send Feedback".
- **Management:** The system has a discussion section; its interface is shown in Figure 11. By means of these discussion areas, students can create a discussion forum about the course and can stay in interaction and communication with both other students and the instructor. In addition, the system includes evaluation systems such as system quizzes, assignments, exams etc. For any problems about the course, announcement e-mails are sent to students to inform them as presented in Figure 12.

Figure 7. Coursera interface

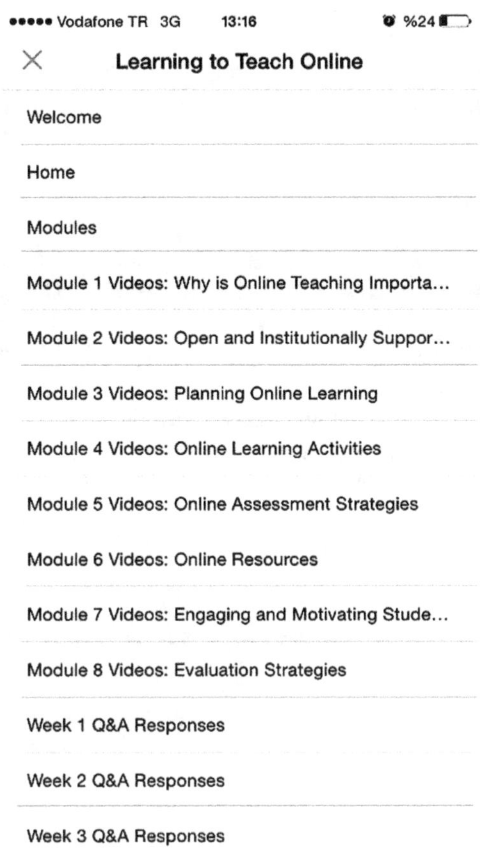

Figure 8. Coursera interface

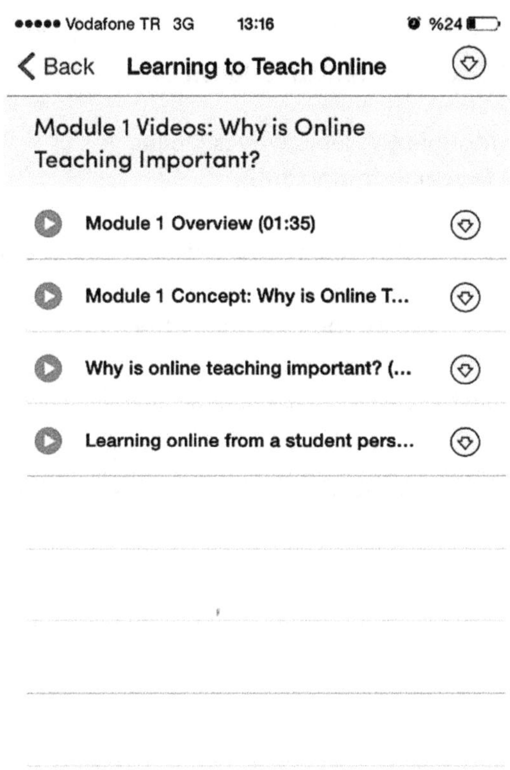

- **Resource Support:** The Coursera system gives online support as presented in Figure 13. Users can use the "Help" menu whenever they need support (see Figure 13). In addition, they can convey their feedback about the learning environment to authorities via "Send Feedback". They can reach many resources concerning the course through the 'Course Resources Library'. Figure 14 shows the library for the course used in these examples. Resources in this library are ordered as 'Module Resources', 'OER Examples', 'Useful Tools' etc. The categorization of resources in this way makes it easier to reach the resource that students are searching for. However, the interface in this section is not arranged in accordance with the size of mobile device. Therefore, user needs to slide the page from left to right and up and down while reading the text on the screen and this makes it harder for the user to read.

- **Ethical:** The Coursera platform demonstrates (Figure 15) sensitivity about ethical issues. It respects their students' privacy and also pays particular attention to security. The copyright for catalog data belongs to university partners. The system published courses in more than 30 languages demonstration a consideration for geographical diversity. Another ethical issue to which Coursera pays special attention is plagiarism, as academic integrity is important for both Coursera and its institutional partners.

Figure 9. Coursera interface

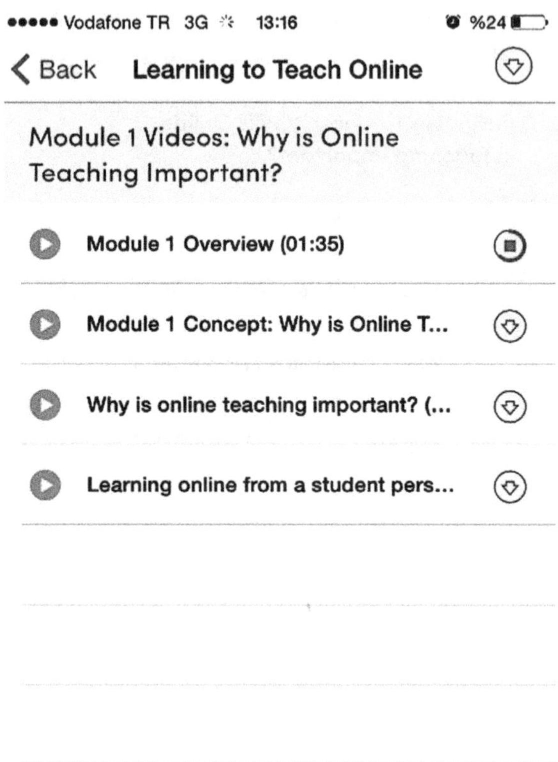

Figure 10. Coursera interface

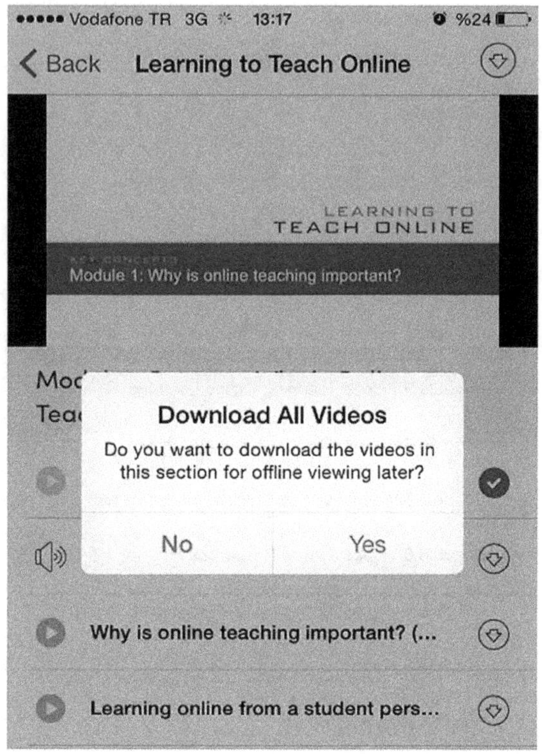

- **Institutional**: The Coursera system also demonstrates sensitivity in academic, administrative and student services. In administrative affairs, it supports students and partners in following issues; assessment, partnerships with other institutions, program and course information catalogs, marketing and recruitment, admissions, financial aid, academic calendar and course schedules, tuition and fees, registration and payment, information technology services, instructional design, grades etc. It also provides academic services by developing appropriate policies, monitoring instructional quality, providing instructor support etc. The system is also sensitive about student services apart from administrative and academic support. Advising, counseling, online library support, tutorial services, social support network and other services are among the services offered by Coursera and its partner institutions.

FURTHER RESEARCH

MOOCs are still at an early stage of development and further research is needed to learn more about them. In order to support this idea and proliferate this extensive framework in different learning platforms, not only MOOCs, but also LMS and e-Learning contents that have a mobile interface can be evaluated in further research in a more detailed way. Moreover, quantitative studies can be conducted by collecting numerical data to generalize concepts more widely and investigate causal relationships more easily. In

Figure 11. Coursera interface

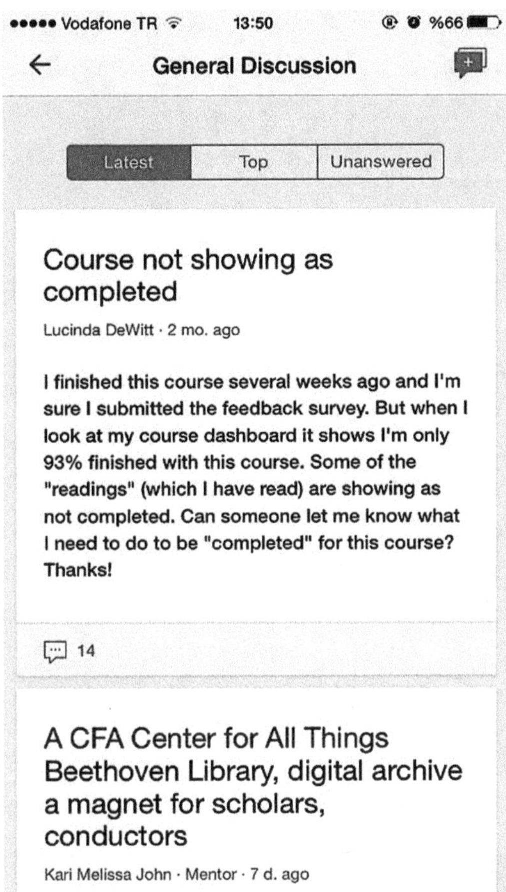

Figure 12. Coursera interface

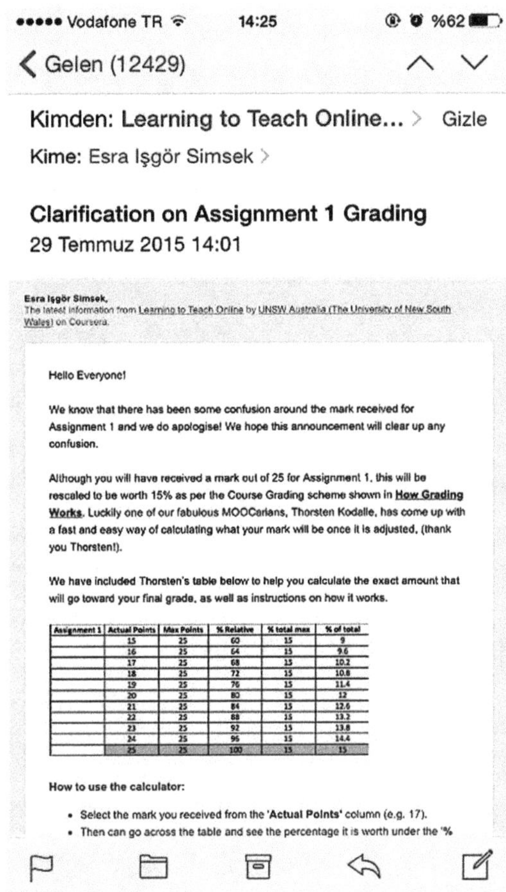

addition to this, innovative business models can be created by content providers or companies. For example, learners sign up to enroll in the courses in massive numbers, but after completing a few units, they do not follow the courses due to the lack of promotion policy. In spite of high enrollment rates, course completion rates are low for many reasons including poor or confusing course organization, inadequate support, technical problems, lack of flexibility, and students having met their own learning goals before completing the course etc. Therefore, development of a promotion policy can be one of the further research areas to improve MOOCs. Another research area is the adaptation of the curriculum to the MOOC platforms. Actually, most of the courses are not redesigned specifically for presentation in MOOCs. So the type of materials that are put into the course by instructors, the course timing, the courses' division into units or modules etc. may become a problem for these MOOC platforms. Therefore, a conceptual study could be done to solve the adaptation problem of curriculum in terms of MOOC platforms.

Figure 13. Coursera interface

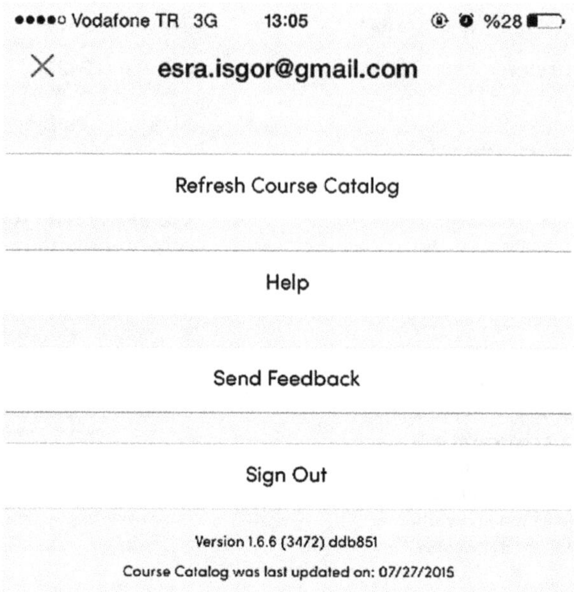

Figure 14. Coursera interface

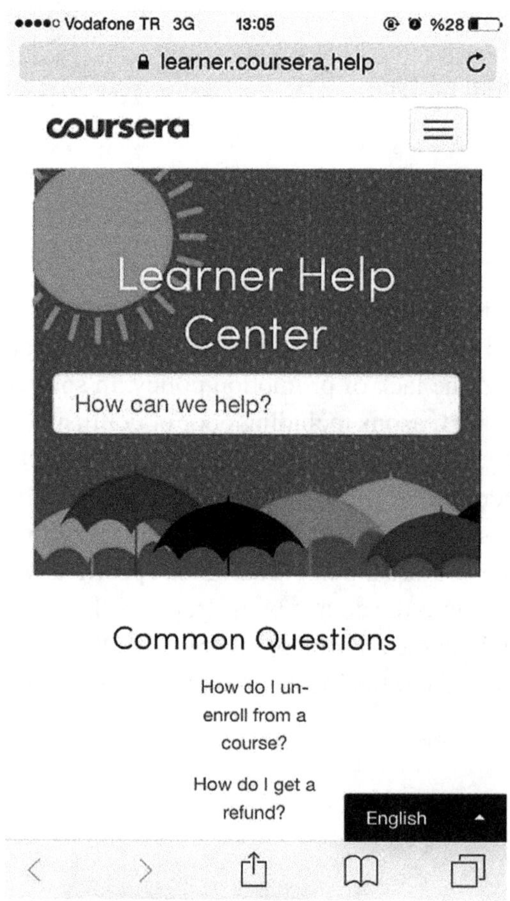

CONCLUSION

Mobile devices such as phones, smart phones, palmtop computers, tablets, and portable media players are frequently used in our daily life and they facilitate many facets of our lives. Making many transactions through devices without any time and place limitations such as reading e-mails, banking transactions, playing games, having fun, socializing, reading news, surfing websites, and shopping provides convenience to users. Education is another field where mobile devices are used extensively for study and learning, besides these daily transactions.

Developing new technologies, like MOOCs, offers new opportunities to people who want to reach new information, especially for restructuring learning processes. People can access Internet resources without being affiliated to any institution and without any time and space limitations and thus they can bring some dynamism to their learning processes (Kop, 2011). In recent years, the proliferation opportunities for receiving education through mobile devices has brought into being the concept 'mobile learning'. In the mobile learning process, people use bourgeoning new technologies and have the chance to access to new information and educational content everywhere (Mishra, 2013). Mobile learning has been used alone sometimes, thanks to its many advantages, and it has also been used to support intra-class education. It will be useful to analyze this learning method using small, ubiquitous mobile devices that have become an irrevocable part of life in different dimensions.

In the social change process that has emerged as a result of new technologies, one of the approaches adopted to meet the varying educational needs of people is open and distance education. As a result of the development of opportunities that allow people to access their increasing and varying learning needs from anywhere and in any period of time, new perspectives have emerged in open and distance education. After the proliferation of the use of open course materials, we can see massive open online courses (MOOC) as the newest phenomenon, the popularity of which has increased over time. MOOCs are characterized as a large-scaled learning environment that brings learners who would like to steer their own learning process together. MOOCs and e-Learning opportunities offer significant chances to students, adults, employees, and indeed those people who want to improve themselves in the life-long learning process (Stracke, 2014). In this scope, MOOCs give the opportunity to access larger-scaled, high quality open courses and provide education services at lower costs. The structuring and offering of MOOCs by institutional and reputable higher education institutions and giving education service through these courses have enabled decision makers and researchers in international global higher education field to focus on MOOC courses more than before. (Baker et al., 2014). In addition, MOOCs have been included in mobile learning through the development mobile applications (apps) to directly access the MOOC platform rather than going through an Internet browser.

In this chapter, mobile learning has been analyzed after it was adapted to the Khan's eight-dimensional e-Learning framework. In order to demonstrate this analysis, the Coursera mobile application - being a sample of an application to directly access MOOC delivery system and one used widely in online learning - was selected as an example. Each of Khan's dimension was evaluated after it was matched with the content in the interface of the Coursera mobile application. Considering *the pedagogic dimension*, it was observed that the obligation to follow up the attendance of students and to ensure course completion is an important problem in online learning in general and was experienced in mobile learning as well. Similarly, the unsuitability of methods and strategies used in online platforms where students have varying learning styles, languages, and cultures are another problem encountered in mobile learning. In terms of *technology,* much work has been done to ameliorate the limitations in small, mobile devices.

Interface design, being a significant dimension in online learning, was transferred into the mobile environment by considering the related limitations and these limitations were mostly eliminated by means of frequent updates in accordance with the feedbacks given by the users. In the *evaluation* section, it was observed that students could easily convey their feedback. In terms of *management*, it was determined that a simple and plain interface ensures interaction between students and their instructor. *Resource support* is provided extensively by means of an online library being open for students to access. When concerning *ethics,* it was observed that students are extensively informed through menus. *Institutionally,* the variety of services offered by this application that was examined as a platform consisting of reputable institutions around the world is very high.

Finally, it can be concluded that Khan's eight-dimensional e-Learning framework can be successfully applied in mobile learning when considering all these evaluations.

REFERENCES

Alican, Ö. (2011). *Mobil Medyada Grafik Tasarımcının Galaksi Rehberi*. Ankara: Pusula Yayıncılık.

Ally, M. (2014). *Increasing Access to Education for All Through Mobile Learning*. Retrieved May 26, 2015, from http://asianvu.com/bk/framework/wp-content/uploads/2014/11/MobileLearning-Increasing-Access-to-Education.pdf

Ally, M., & Samaka, M. (2013). Open education resources and mobile technology to narrow the learning divide. *The International Review of Research in Open and Distributed Learning*, *14*(2), 14–27.

Attewell, J. (2005). Mobile technologies and learning. Learning and Skills Development Agency, 2(4).

Baker, R., Evans, B., Greenberg, E., & Dee, T. (2014). Understanding persistence in moocs (massive open online courses): Descriptive & experimental evidence. *EMOOCs*, 5-10.

Bannan, B., & Milheim, W. D. (1997). Existing Web-based courses and their design. In B. H. Khan (Ed.), *Web-based instruction* (pp. 381–388). Englewood Cliffs, NJ: Educational Technology Publications.

Barnhart, F. D., & Pierce, J. E. (2011). Becoming mobile: Reference in the ubiquitous library. *Journal of Library Administration*, *51*(3), 279–290. doi:10.1080/01930826.2011.556942

Baykul, Y. (2000). *Eğitimde ve Psikolojide Ölçme: Klasik Test Teorisi ve Uygulaması*. Ankara: ÖSYM Yayınları.

Boettcher, J. V., & Kumar, M. S. (2000). The Other Infrastructure: Distance Education's Digital Plant. *Syllabus, 13*(10).

Castle, R. (2013). Mobile Learning: Is your content fit for purpose? *Training & Development*, *40*(2), 22–23.

Coursera. (2015). *Coursera.* Retrieved May 26, 2015, from www.coursera.org

Daniel, J. (2012). Making sense of MOOCs: Musings in a maze of myth, paradox and possibility. *Journal of Interactive Media in Education*, *2012*(3), 18. doi:10.5334/2012-18 de Waard, I. (2014). Using BYOD, Apps, Sensors, Mobile Social Media for Meaningful Learning. In M. Aly & A. Tsakos (Eds.), *Mobile learning development for flexible learning*. Edmonton, Canada: Athabasca University Press.

Downes, S. (2013). *Quality of Massive Open Online Courses by Stephen Downes*. Retrieved June 2, 2015, from http://mooc.efquel.org/week-2-the-quality-of-massive-open-online-courses-by-stephen-downes/#sthash.YOitClcH.dpuf

Elias, T. (2011). Universal instructional design principles for mobile learning. *The International Review of Research in Open and Distributed Learning*, *12*(2), 143–156.

Esposito, A. (2012). Research Ethics in Emerging Forms of Online Learning: Issues Arising from a Hypothetical Study on a MOOC. *Electronic Journal of e-Learning, 10*(3), 315-325.

Glance, D. G., Forsey, M., & Riley, M. (2013). The pedagogical foundations of massive open online courses. *First Monday*, *18*(5). doi:10.5210/fm.v18i5.4350

Godwin-Jones, R. (2011). Emerging technologies: Mobile apps for language learning. *Language Learning & Technology*, *15*(2), 2–11.

Griggs, K., Bridges, L. M., & Rempel, H. G. (2009). Library/mobile: tips on designing and developing mobile web sites. *Code4lib Journal, 8*.

Gülbahar, Y. (2012). *E-öğrenme*. Ankara: Pegem Akademi.

Harding, N. (2012). *Online Course Revolution*. Retrieved June 1, 2015, from http://thepositive.com/mooc-massive-open-online-courses-uk/

Hartnell-Young, E. A. (2008). Mobile phones for learning in mainstream schooling: resistance and change. *Proc. World Conf. Mobile and Contextual Learning 'The Bridge from Text to Context' (mLearn '08).*

Hedberg, J. G. (2014). Extending the pedagogy of mobility. *Educational Media International*, *51*(3), 237–253. doi:10.1080/09523987.2014.968447

Hill, P. (2012). *Four Barriers That MOOCs Must Overcome To Build a Sustainable Model*. Retrieved June 1, 2015, from http://mfeldstein.com/four-barriers-that-moocs-must-overcome-to-become-sustainable-model/

Hollands, F. M., & Tirthali, D. (2014). *MOOCs: Expectations and reality. Center for Benefit-Cost Studies of Education*. Teachers College, Columbia University.

Howell, M., Love, S., & Turner, M. (2008). User characteristics and performance with automated mobile phone systems. *International Journal of Mobile Communications*, *6*(1), 1–15. doi:10.1504/IJMC.2008.015994

Hudson, A. (2010). Measuring the impact of cultural diversity on desired mobile reference services. *RSR. Reference Services Review*, *38*(2), 299–308. doi:10.1108/00907321011045052

Jones, V., & Jo, J. H. (2004, December). Ubiquitous learning environment: An adaptive teaching system using ubiquitous technology. In *Beyond the comfort zone:Proceedings of the 21st ASCILITE Conference* (*Vol. 468*, p. 474).

Kambourakis, G. (2013). Security and Privacy in m-Learning and Beyond: Challenges and State-of-the-art. *International Journal of u-and e-Service Science and Technology*, *6*(3), 67–84.

Khan, B. H. (1997). Web-based instruction: What is it and why is it? In B. H. Khan (Ed.), *Web-based instruction* (pp. 5–18). Englewood Cliffs, NJ: Educational Technology Publications.

Khan, B.H. (2000). A Framework for E-Learning. *Distance Education Report*, *4*(24).

Khan, B. H. (2001). Web-based Training. Academic Press.

Khan, B. H. (2005). *Managing E-Learning Strategies: Design, Delivery, Implementation and Evaluation*. Idea Group Publishing. doi:10.4018/978-1-59140-634-1

Khan, B. H. (2007). Flexible learning in an open and distributed environment. In B. H. Khan (Ed.), *Flexible learning in an information society*. Hershey, PA: Information Science Publishing. doi:10.4018/978-1-59904-325-8.ch001

Khan, B. H. (2012). *User Interface Design for Virtual Environments: Challenges and Advances*. Information Science Reference. doi:10.4018/978-1-61350-516-8

Khan, B. H. (2014). *Continuum in E-Learning: People, Process and Product (P3)*. Retrieved from http://elearningindustry.com/continuum-in-e-Learning-people-process-and-product-p3

Kop, R. (2011). The Challenges to Connectivist Learning on Open Online Networks: Learning Experiences during a Massive Open Online Course. *International Review of Research in Open and Distance Learning*, *12*(3).

Kukulska-Hulme, & Traxler. (2004). Mobile teaching and learning. In *Mobile learning-a handbook for educators and trainers*. Academic Press.

Kukulska-Hulme, A., & Traxler, J. (2007). Designing for mobile and wireless learning. In H. Beetham & R. Sharpe (Eds.), *Rethinking Pedagogy for a Digital Age: Designing and Delivering E-Learning* (pp. 180–192). London: Routledge.

Laouris, Y., & Eteokleous, N. (2005, October). We need an educationally relevant definition of mobile learning. In *Proceedings of the 4th World Conference on Mobile Learning* (pp. 290-294). Academic Press.

Laurillard, D. (2007). Pedagogical forms of mobile learning: framing research questions. In Mobile learning: towards a research agenda. London: WLE Centre, IoE.

Liu, Y. (1997). Queuning Network Modeling of Human Performance and Concurrent Spatial and verbal tasks. *IEEE Transactions on Systems Man and Cybernetics Part a-Systems and Humans*, *27*, 195–207.

Low, L., & O'Connell, M. (2006, September). Learner-centric design of digital mobile learning. In *Proceedings of the OLT Conference* (pp. 71-82). Academic Press.

Madeira, R. N., Sousa, J. L., Pires, V. F., Esteves, L., & Dias, O. P. (2009). A mobile and web-based student learning system. *Procedia: Social and Behavioral Sciences*, *1*(1), 2441–2448. doi:10.1016/j.sbspro.2009.01.430

Mangelsdorf, M. (2012). *Massive Open Online Courses (MOOCs): An Assessment Based on Personal Experience.* Retrieved June 2, 2015, from http://www.iedp.com/Pages/DocumentManager/Massive%20Open%20Online%20Courses%20_%20Full%20Article.pdf

Mcconatha, D., Praul, M., & Lynch, M. J. (2008). Mobile Learning in Higher Education: An Empirical Assessment of a New Educational Tool. *Online Submission, 7*(3).

Mishra, S. K. (2013). Quality education for children, youth and adults through mobile learning. In J. Keengwe (Ed.), Pedagogical applications and social effects of mobile technology integration içinde (pp. 225-237). Hershey, PA: Information Science Reference.

Nielsen, J. (1993). *Usability Engineering*. Boston: Academic Press.

Nielsen, J. (1997). *Be Succinct! (Writing for the Web)*. Retrieved May 24, 2015, fromhttp://www.nngroup.com/articles/be-succinct-writing-for-the-web/

Pappano, L. (2012). *The Year of the MOOC*. Retrieved June 6, 2015, from http://www.nytimes.com/2012/11/04/education/edlife/massive-open-online-courses-are-multiplying-at-a-rapid-pace.html?pagewanted=1&_r=0

Passey, D. (2010). Mobile learning in school contexts: Can teachers alone make it happen? *Learning Technologies. IEEE Transactions on*, *3*(1), 68–81.

Peng, H., Su, Y. J., Chou, C., & Tsai, C. C. (2009). Ubiquitous knowledge construction: Mobile learning re-defined and a conceptual framework. *Innovations in Education and Teaching International*, *46*(2), 171–183. doi:10.1080/14703290902843828

Quinn, C. (2000). mLearning: Mobile, wireless, in-your-pocket learning. *LiNE Zine, 2006*.

Riva, G., & Villani, D. (2005). CyberEurope. *Cyberpsychology & Behavior*, *8*(1), 89–95. doi:10.1089/cpb.2005.8.101 PMID:15738696

Rogers, K. D. (2011). *Mobile learning devices*. Solution Tree Press.

J. L. Schnase, & E. L. Cunnius (Eds.). (1995). Learning in the 21st century and beyond. In *Proceedings of the First International Conference on Computer Support for Collaborative Learning (CSCL '95)*. Mahwah, NJ: Erlbaum.

Schwabe, G., & Göth, C. (2005). Mobile learning with a mobile game: Design and motivational effects. *Journal of Computer Assisted Learning*, *21*(3), 204–216. doi:10.1111/j.1365-2729.2005.00128.x

Shah, D. (2014). *Online Courses Raise Their Game: A Review of MOOC Stats and Trends in 2014.* Retrieved June 2, 2015, from https://www.class-central.com/report/moocs-stats-and-trends-2014/

Sharples, M. (2000). The design of personal mobile technologies for lifelong learning. *Computers & Education*, *34*(3), 177–193. doi:10.1016/S0360-1315(99)00044-5

Shonola, S. A., & Joy, M. S. (2014, July). Mobile learning security issues from lecturers' perspectives (Nigerian Universities Case Study). In *6th International Conference on Education and New Learning Technologies.*

Siemens, G. (2013). Massive Open Online Courses: Innovation In Education? In Open Educational Resources: Innovation, Research and Practice (pp. 5-16). Athabasca University, Commonwealth of Learning.

Skaalid, B. (1999). *Human computer interface design*. University of Saskatchewan, Faculty of Education. Retrieved from http://www.usask.ca/education/coursework/skaalid/theory/interface.htm

Stracke, C. M. (2014). How can e-Learning and MOOCs reveal and exploit the hidden treasures of open research and open education? In *From education to employment and meaningful work with ICTs. Proceedings of EDEN Annual Conference*.

Traxler, J. (2007). Defining, Discussing and Evaluating Mobile Learning: The moving finger writes and having writ..... *The International Review of Research in Open and Distributed Learning*, *8*(2).

Traxler, J. (2010). Distance education and mobile learning: Catching up, taking stock. *Distance Education*, *31*(2), 129–138. doi:10.1080/01587919.2010.503362

Traxler, J., & Bridges, N. (2005). Mobile learning–the ethical and legal challenges. *Mobilelearning anytimeeverywhere*, 203.

Voss, B. D. (2013). *Massive open online courses (MOOCs): A primer for university and college board members*. Retrived from http://agb.org/sites/agb.org/files/report_2013_MOOCs.pdf

Waldrop, M. (2013). Campus 2.0. *Nature*, *495*(7440), 160–163. doi:10.1038/495160a PMID:23486040

Woodill, G. (2011). *The mobile learning edge*. The McGraw Hill Companies.

Yuan, L., Powell, S., & Cetis, J. (2013). *MOOCs and open education: Implications for higher education*. Academic Press.

Zhou, X., & Xia, X. (2010). Design and research for Mobile web learning platform accessibility. In *2010 International Conference on Artificial Intelligence and Education (ICAIE)* (pp. 478-481). doi:10.1109/ICAIE.2010.5640970

Chapter 6
Massive Open Program Evaluation:
Crowdsourcing's Potential to Improve E-Learning Quality

Tonya B. Amankwatia
Regent University, USA

ABSTRACT

Given the complexity of developing programs, services, policies, and support for e-learning, leaders may find it challenging to regularly evaluate programs to improve quality. Are there new opportunities to expand user and stakeholder input, or involve others in e-learning program evaluation? This chapter asks researchers and practitioners to rethink existing paradigms and methods for program evaluation. Crowdsourced input may help leaders and stakeholders address persistent evaluation challenges and improve e-learning quality, especially in Massive Open Online Courses (MOOCs). After reviewing selected evaluation paradigms, models, and methods, this chapter offers a possible role for crowdsourced input. This chapter examines the topics of crowd definition, affordances, and problems, to begin a taxonomical framework with possible applications for e-learning. The goal is to provide a reference for advancing the discussion and examination of crowdsourced input.

INTRODUCTION

E-learning programs vary. Many can be described as accelerated, flexible, global, and open (Crawford, 2012; Moore, 2013; Trekles & Sims, 2013). E-learning can also be characterized by its different pedagogical strategies—such as student-centered, socially-negotiated, or authentic learning—that sometimes involve gaming, personal profiles, and e-portfolios (Casey, 2008; Ke & Kwak, 2013). The extent to which e-learning programs implement these strategies effectively, or to which they align to complementary materials, support, and learner outcomes, is partly a question of program quality. When e-learning programs include repackaged massive open online courses (MOOCs), additional questions arise about intellectual property, credentials, and elements of learning (Haber, 2014). Put simply, people want answers about quality.

DOI: 10.4018/978-1-5225-0466-5.ch006

Some education stakeholders are dubious about the quality of e-learning programs and their impact on learning (Allen & Seaman, 2013; Garrison, 2011; Millirion, 2010). Taxpayers, parents, policymakers, employers, educators, and—in some cases—even learners want answers. Does e-learning make a difference in teaching and learning? Is the technology worth the effort and cost?

The purpose of program evaluation is to provide answers for decision-makers and stakeholders. Evaluation studies should show that administrators, educators, and designers have examined e-learning's various forms, grappled with its complex issues, and utilized representative data to undergird their decisions and designs (Barksdale & Lund, 2001; Preskill & Russ-Eft, 2005). Moreover, program evaluation experts have contended that evaluation can be a viable means for educational change and improvement when integrated as an ongoing activity, rather than as an isolated event (Patton, 2008, 2001; Shelton, 2011). Nonetheless, given the complexity of developing programs, services, policies, and support for e-learning, leaders might find it challenging to evaluate programs, make decisions, and solve problems to improve quality.

Furthermore, some historical challenges remain for e-learning program evaluation and qualitative research. For example, the time and resources required to collect, analyze, and apply evaluation data can be problematic. Also, it can be challenging to implement qualitative research paradigms and methods that aspire to extend localized findings to contexts beyond that of the evaluation, to involve stakeholders early in program design, or to use negotiation and collaboration strategies to reach consensus about evaluation methods (Denzin & Lincoln, 2003; Reeves & Hedberg, 2008). Finally, defining *quality* programs is a challenge, especially when several models exist for partial and holistic e-learning evaluation (Shelton & Saltsman, 2005). However, some key technological advances potentially address the complexities and challenges of e-learning program evaluation.

Buoyed by diverse networked communities, anti-cheating mechanisms, information retrieval systems (IR), and big data analytics, crowdsourcing might hold promise for program evaluation beyond market research and bug fixes (Amir & Haider, 2014; Vuurens & de Vries, 2012). Crowdsourced input could potentially make the e-learning evaluation process more open, integrated, and innovative, and thereby provide timely and useful data to answer questions about e-learning programs. To frame the discussion of the potential of crowdsourced input, this chapter identifies and reviews well-established evaluation paradigms and models suitable to crowdsourcing. Next it defines crowdsourcing and reports its affordances and limitations. Finally, this chapter proposes a taxonomy and then models its potential application to program evaluation using Khan's Eight Dimensions of E-learning Framework (2001). The chapter concludes by emphasizing opportunities to rethink stakeholders' and others' participation in e-learning program evaluation.

PROMISES AND CHALLENGES OF PROGRAM EVALUATION

Reeves and Hedberg (2008) maintained that e-learning has promise but lacks results, mostly due to inadequate evaluation from design to implementation. However, a similar critique might be launched at program evaluation. To move closer to the goal of this chapter, this section will review program evaluation literature, highlighting salient definitions, paradigms, and models noted for involving stakeholders in ongoing and meaningful ways to inform program quality, impact, or design. This review thus focuses on qualitative research, along with *interpretivist* and *postmodernist* paradigms and models, delineating their promises and challenges.

Program evaluation (also referred to as evaluation research) is applied qualitative research, and exists to provide useful findings to decision-makers and stakeholders:

- **Stakeholders:** Are the individuals, organizations, and groups that have a major interest in the success and function of a program (Rossi, et al., 1999; Russ-Eft & Preskill, 2001). Program evaluation has its beginnings in social science research involving educational and social programs (Rossi, 2011; Preskill & Russ-Eft, 2005).
- **Program:** Can be defined as "an ongoing planned intervention that seeks to achieve some particular outcomes in response to some perceived educational, social, or commercial problem" (Fitzpatrick, et al., 2011, p.8).
- **Program Evaluation:** Then, is the systematic collection of information about activities, characteristics, and outcomes in order to determine quality, make improvements, and inform decision-making (Patton, 2008).

The early 2000s showed increased interest in participatory, collaborative, and learning-focused evaluations, and thus, more qualitative designs (Davidson, 2002; Preskill & Russ-Eft, 2005). With growing evaluation interests across so many fields, it is not surprising that that there would be several paradigms and models representing the work of e-learning evaluators (Shelton, 2011).

- **Paradigm:** Describes the approach or design for conducting scientific inquiry. Evaluators' paradigms will be congruent with their methods and approaches to e-learning evaluation.
- **Models:** Account for the activities, methods, and strategies in the evaluation process. According to Bishop (2000), models serve as a frame of reference for "generating, organizing, examining, and evaluating multiple sources of data and assumptions" (p. 12). The evaluation models discussed below are largely congruent with an interpretivist-constructivist or critical paradigm, as described by Denzin and Lincoln (2003).

Qualitative program evaluation is essentially interpretive and ethnographic, using a socio-anthropological research paradigm. The qualitative approach relies on detailed observations and self-report data. Atieno (2009) has explained that, rather than seeking definition, this approach pursues validity by seeking to observe the whole context, its specificities and generalities, and all its complexities. A qualitative research paradigm does not seek to understand people apart from their natural settings.

A postmodern paradigm contests traditional forms of qualitative evaluation research. Although postmodern and critical theories cannot be simply encapsulated by one definition or theory, they share some assumptions and characteristics. First, because there are always multiple interpretations of phenomena, everything—truth, right, effectiveness, and quality—is open to question and should be deconstructed and contested. Evaluation contexts involve issues of power occurring in socio-political spheres. Justice, empowerment, action, transformation, diversity, and pluralism therefore help characterize a postmodern-critical paradigm (Kincheloe & McLaren, 2003; Smith, 1999). Also, many provisional stories by individuals in their own voices and settings help explain the world (Merriam, 2002).

Fourth Generation Evaluation (Guba & Lincoln, 1989) is an example of an interpretivist-constructivist paradigm. Guba and Lincoln have insisted that evaluations meet two conditions: that the evaluation is organized by the claims, concerns, and issues of stakeholders, and that its methodology uses the constructivist paradigm. Constructivism instantiates facts in a value framework to derive meaning, and regards truth as a socially-negotiated construct. Phenomena are thus understood only within their context and cannot be generalized.

The Fourth Generation Evaluation Model heavily utilizes observation methodology as a strategy for collecting evaluation data. As observed above, Guba and Lincoln have made stakeholders the focus for data collection, and thereby embrace an emergent research design. One of the strengths of this model is its focus on empowering both individuals and groups, with the potential for creating greater self-awareness and understanding of others. Again, evaluation strategies value local understanding over generalizability of findings to other contexts. One obvious challenge is the great deal of energy and time evaluators must expend "simply to identify the several stakeholders and to interact with them sufficiently to understand what their claims, concerns, and issues are" (Guba & Lincoln, 1989, p. 55).

Utilization-focused evaluation and developmental evaluation exemplify a model and approach that aim to involve stakeholders in program evaluation in ongoing and meaningful ways. As such, these may be good candidates for the reassessment of crowdsourced input. For e-learning program evaluation, they promise empowerment and increased use due to greater stakeholder participation (Brisolara, 1998; Patton, 2008).

Utilization-focused evaluation (Patton, 1994; 2008) concentrates on the intended program users' need for evaluation data to make decisions. Responsive evaluation (Abma & Stake, 2001; Stake, 1975) and practical participatory evaluation (Brisolara, 1998) share similar stakeholder and facilitation ideals. Patton (1994) has maintained that utilization-focused evaluation must inherently lend itself to any evaluation purpose, design, or methodology to accommodate the needs of the users. Even so, those who thrive in such evaluation contexts most likely hold to interpretivist-constructivist or critical-postmodernist paradigms. This approach appreciates values, negotiations, multiple alternatives, and localized contexts for making program improvements. Thus, these evaluators may employ quantitative research methodology, focus groups, Delphi group techniques, surveys, market research, and software usability checklists to provide e-learning stakeholders with useful information.

Additionally, utilization-focused evaluators may move into developmental evaluation roles, where they collaborate as members of design teams and contribute evaluation strategies, findings, and experiences to the decision-making process (Patton, 1994). Evaluators facilitate discussions about how to apply findings and what to pursue next, which may include options to deconstruct the old and create the new. Developmental evaluation is not ongoing formative evaluation (that would be continuous product improvement); instead, developmental evaluation should make the e-learning program different for various settings, populations, technologies, and the like. In short, utilization-focused evaluation, especially with a developmental evaluation purpose, is emergent, real-time, adaptive, and sometimes innovative or transformative. The challenge here seems to be repeated stakeholder access and consultations, preferably in their natural settings, over an indefinite amount of time. In addition, decision-making challenges arise for evaluators to provide various types of information and evaluation guidance within an emergent framework.

Some have claimed that social research is stymied by the difficulty in finding the resources, time, and tools necessary for engaging in multiple rigorous evaluations capable of producing usable findings on a regular basis (Rossi et al., 2004). Others have contended that evaluation research is undertaken too infrequently, with no real dialogue, reflection, or consensus about the effectiveness of paradigms or methods (Reeves & Hedberg, 2003). These research design challenges notwithstanding, the fact is that additional challenges exist defining or framing what constitutes quality in e-learning programs.

QUALITY IN E-LEARNING PROGRAMS

Many discussions regarding e-learning quality start with statements about the complexity, vagueness, or difficulty involved in determining quality, and end with imperatives to figure it out (Casey, 2008; Cavanaugh, 2002; Shelton & Saltsman, 2004).

Shelton (2011), in a review of literature between 2000 and 2009, has documented 13 "paradigms" (designs or models) for evaluating quality for entire e-learning programs, not stand-alone courses. Upon closer inspection, one finds that Shelton identified models and commissioned reports with categories and indicators of success. (See, for example Western Cooperative for Educational Telecommunications (1997) and Institute for Higher Education Policy (1998).). Shelton accurately identified which models actually provided a means to measure entire program quality in a comprehensive manner, instead of merely characterizing instructional technology quality, or dimensions of quality online learning. Shelton's review grouped the most-cited indicators of quality in the 13 paradigms by theme. Institutional commitment, support, and leadership were cited as the primary indicators of quality, followed by teaching and learning. Shelton also introduced yet another evaluative model: the research-based Quality Scorecard. Now called the Online Learning ™ Consortium Quality Scorecard (n.d.), the OLC is part of a members-only training program for helping leaders quantify indicators of quality against eight categories. (It should be noted that the OLC was formerly known as Sloan Consortium; however, Sloan was represented in Shelton's literature review by its Five Pillars of Quality.)

Since Shelton's review was limited to the United States, international and transnational conceptions of quality and their corresponding models were not included, but should be considered. One of the earliest models addressing quality assurance standards was introduced in 1994 by the International Organization for Standardization, or ISO (Rovai, 2009). These standards were generally applicable to almost any industry. The application to e-learning was mainly for information technology used for learning, education, and training, to primarily address customer satisfaction and applicable regulatory requirements. The latest revision of the ISO 9001 quality standard was done in 2008, and the ISO still focus on customer satisfaction and regulations (ISO, 2015).

In 2015, the International Council for Open and Distance Education (ICDE) published a global overview of quality models and found that building, sharing and coordination of knowledge among stakeholders was a greater need over creating new quality models (ICDE, 2015). The report addresses MOOCs and the need to make quality evaluation a mainstream activity. Only two of the models referenced in Shelton (2011) were included: Khan's Eight Dimensions of E-Learning Framework, and the OLC Quality Scorecard. Thus, limited scope, information dissemination, multiple quality models, and stakeholder coordination, seem to sum-up the international challenges to define quality in e-learning programs.

Issues of quality in online education will continue to be shaped by various societal and technological changes and, thus, impact evaluation approaches (Rossi, et al., 2004). As a result, some powerful changes for e-learning program evaluation should be expected on the horizon. One opportunity may be found in crowdsourced input for open enrollment courses and MOOCs. In 2012, programs like Coursera, edX, and Udacity seemingly renewed expectations for e-learning to fundamentally transform education, as the *New York Times* declared 2012 the year of the MOOC (Pappano, 2012).

Rovai and Baker (2014) have recognized that MOOC evaluation should be different from traditional or even online course evaluation, especially since MOOCs change the relationship between the learner and educational provider. They have posited that diverse strategies, pluralistic perspectives, multiple sources, and large numbers of student evaluations of teaching raters can help provide reliable and valid evaluation data. Rovai and Baker have also documented the high attrition rates of MOOCs. There is an opportunity cost with attrition. Evaluators may regularly need to gather and analyze large amounts of qualitative information from learners to help stakeholders understand why people leave. Stakeholders may not get a full, rich description of the reasons without crowdsourced input.

Potential of Crowdsourcing to Improve Program Evaluation

The intent of the evaluation research approaches discussed above is to empower users and to represent all stakeholders. Involving the 'crowd' in e-learning program evaluation can empower it to play a role in innovation through distributed knowledge gathering (Brabham, 2008). The crowd can offer fresh insights or new solutions to both the evaluation process and e-learning. In effect, each user contributes a nugget of gold to the decision-making process. If this were real money, MOOC providers, for example, could be crowdfunding high quality e-learning program support, resources, and design. To improve the quality of student support, stakeholders might benefit therefore from the information they get from an open evaluation process that potentially provides common themes from thousands of micro-histories, observations, and focus group interviews.

Developmental evaluation efforts may benefit from a crowd of experts collaborating and negotiating among each other from their experiences and "evaluation logic," as Patton (1994) calls it. The high speed and low cost of information retrieval systems (IR) using a crowdsourcing paradigm may benefit evaluators by making document analysis tasks faster and more efficient. Massive, open, diverse groups of instructors and learners might provide valuable information about resource support, or provide international and transnational understandings of quality learning, feedback, and interface design. The goal of this chapter is to provide information that serves as a reference for more discussion and examination about the potential for crowdsourced input to improve program evaluation using existing models and paradigms. The next section defines crowdsourcing, and delineates some of its affordances and problems for e-learning evaluation.

CrowdSourcing

Estelles-Arolas and González-Ladrón-de-Guevara (2012) have conducted an extensive literature review of the term "crowdsourcing" from mostly computer science sources dated between 2006 and 2011. SAGE and Emerald were the only non-computer science databases included. They have examined 209 unique documents in the literature, scrutinizing 40 definitions of crowdsourcing, with the goal of finding a common definition. Most of the documents were conference papers (n=127) and journal articles (n=68). However, the authors found that definitions varied: activities characterized as crowdsourcing by one source were not so classified by another. This does not seem surprising, given the relative novelty of the concept of crowdsourcing, a term coined by Howe (2006) in a *Wired* magazine article.

Estelles-Arolas and González-Ladrón-de-Guevara (2012) filtered results to only those citations that had an original definition, and looked for common elements distinguishing the activities that could be considered crowdsourcing. They emulated the approach *differentia specifica* used by Polish philosopher Tatarkiewtz to develop a global definition of art. After analyzing and testing the definition on 11 Internet cases, they found that some cases were crowdsourcing (such as Amazon Mechanical Turk), and some cases were not (such as Wikipedia). Crowdsourcing is not necessarily open source; product design and problem-solving occur with willing crowd labor, and someone who owns the solution or design benefits substantively (Brabham, 2008). The Estelles-Arolas and González-Ladrón-de-Guevara definition is as follows:

Crowdsourcing is a type of participative online activity in which an individual, an institution, a non-profit organization, or company proposes to a group of individuals of varying knowledge, heterogeneity, and number, via a flexible open call, the voluntary undertaking of a task. The undertaking of the task, of variable complexity and modularity, and in which the crowd should participate bringing their work, money, knowledge and/or experience, always entails mutual benefit. The user will receive the satisfaction of a given type of need, be it economic, social recognition, self-esteem, or the development of individual skills, while the crowdsourcer will obtain and utilize to their advantage that what the user has brought to the venture, whose form will depend on the type of activity undertaken. (Estelles-Arolas & González-Ladrón-de-Guevara, 2012, p. 9-10).

A valuable contribution of the research cited above, besides the integrated definition, is the compilation of the specific conditions and characteristics that define crowdsourcing, relative to the crowd, the initiator, and the process. These can serve as a heuristic for program evaluators contemplating the inclusion of crowdsourced input, and can help evaluators make connections to their evaluation purposes, data collections, and analysis processes. Of the 40 unique definitions, 10 referred to problem-solving

Table 1. Definitions with problem-solving dimensions

Document	Page	Definition: Crowdsourcing is...
Brabham [9]	75	...an online, distributed problem solving and production model already in use by for profit organizations such as Threadless, iStock...
Brabham [4]	79	...a strategic model to attract an interested, motivated crowd of individuals capable of providing solutions superior in quality and quantity to those that even traditional forms of business can.
DiPalantino and Vojnovic [28]	1	...[a set of] methods of soliciting solutions to tasks via open calls to large-scale communities.
Doan et al. [8]	2	...a general-purpose problem-solving method.
La Vecchia and Cisternino [34]	425	...a tool for addressing problems in organizations and business.
Liu & Porter [36]		...the outsourcing of a task or a job, such as a new approach to packaging that extends the life of a product, to a large group of potential innovators and inviting a solution. It is essentially open in nature and invites collaboration within a community.
Mazzola and Distefano [37]	3	...an intentional mobilization, through web 2.0, of creative and innovative ideas or stimuli, to solve a problem, where voluntary users are included by a firm within the internal problem solving process, not necessarily aimed to increase profit or to create product or market innovations, but in generally, to solve a specific problem.
Oliveira et al. [38]	413	...a way of outsourcing to the crowd tasks of intellectual assets creation, often collaboratively, with the aim of having easier access to a wide variety of skills and experience.
Ribiere & Tuggle [42]		...consists of making an open online call for a creative idea, or problem solving, or evaluation or any other type of business issues, and to let anyone (in the crowd) submit solutions.
Vukovic [6]	1	...new online distributed problem solving and production model in which networked people collaborate to complete a task.

in some way. The problem-solving nature of crowdsourcing seems to complement the decision-making purpose of program evaluation. Table 1 excerpts those 10 definitions from the table provided on pages 3-5 of Estelles-Arolas & González-Ladrón-de-Guevara's literature review.

The information gleaned from the literature review about how others, including Howe (2006), define the crowd, initiator, and process, should help guide considerations for program evaluation design (Estelles-Arolas & González-Ladrón-de-Guevara, 2012; Brabham, 2012).

- **Crowd**
    - Composition
        - Heterogeneity, number, and skills are determined by crowdsourcing initiative.
        - Crowds can vary: Internet public, individuals, users, organized and online communities.
        - Crowds should be well-trained; many are found to be already quite educated.
    - Tasks
        - Tasks need to have clear objectives and specifications about the difficulty or size.
        - Tasks need to be highly divisible at all levels (small human intelligence tasks or HITs) (Vuurens & de Vries, 2012).
        - Non-trivial problems of variable complexity benefit from crowdsourcing.
    - Motivation
        - Target non-material reward; passion about activity or participation for fun.
        - Relate to motivations consistent with Maslow's hierarch of needs such as social recognition, develop a skill, and self-esteem, economic reward (Maslow, 1987).
        - Specify any micro-payments or prizes per task; most volunteer.
- **Initiator**
    - Referred to as a crowdsourcer; can be a company, institution, non-profit organization, or individual.
    - Must have the means to fully support the crowdsourcing initiative.
    - Seeks to obtain from crowd external knowledge, talent, skills, and experience.
- **Process**
    - Characterized as business model for outsourcing, a problem-solving process, or production model.
    - Online, participatory, and distributed.
    - Other distinctions drawn from the crowdsourcing initiative.

Finally, the eight characteristics summarized by Estelles-Arolas and González-Ladrón-de-Guevara (2012 p. 9-10) are as follows:

1. There is a clearly-defined crowd.
2. The task has a clear goal.
3. The crowd's compensation is clear.
4. The crowdsourcer is clearly identified.
5. The compensation to be received by the crowdsourcer is clearly defined.
6. It is an online and participatory-assigned process.
7. It uses an open call of variable extent.
8. It uses the Internet.

Affordances

The applications and approaches for crowdsourcing depicted by Brabham (2008), Howe (2006), and Nakatsu et al. (2014) seem diverse. They indicate the adaptable quality of crowdsourcing. Thus, leaders can ponder how it may be used in e-learning program evaluation. In particular, crowdsourcing may offer evaluators new opportunities because it leverages networked individuals or communities, the Internet, and technologies for massive data collection and analytics.

Crowdsourcing involves networking people with diverse backgrounds and experiences to solve problems. Terms often associated with these crowds are *collective intelligence* and *crowd wisdom* (Gregg, 2010). Brabham (2008) has explained that the terms are not new to crowdsourcing, and that access to collective or distributed intelligence, and to crowd wisdom for problem-solving or creative purposes, can be beneficial. Brabham has also proposed using a crowdsourced model for problem-solving, with non-profit and social justice applications. The premise is that, under certain circumstances, groups can be more intelligent than any single member in said group, since no single member knows everything. For example, Gregg (2010) has reported on a collective intelligence application that used the Web to simplify the data collection and analysis activities of special education practitioners, allowing them to make what they deemed to be more informed decisions about the students.

E-learning program evaluation is essentially about decision-making and uses a socio-anthropological paradigm. It shows increased interest in collaborative and participatory qualitative designs (Davidson, 2002; Preskill & Russ-Eft, 2005). MOOCs, for example, involve large numbers of people with diverse backgrounds and face challenges, such as attrition, that crowdsourced input may help address. Aggregating millions of disparate and independent ideas can bring, in real-time, great diversity of thought to e-learning program problem-solving and help decision-makers avoid "group thinking, information effects and other suboptimal decision-making" (Nakatsu et al., 2014, p. 825).

Moreover, crowdsourcing most commonly uses the Internet—a medium which e-learning shares. Crowdsourcing activities have some commonalities with e-learning pedagogical tools and strategies (Salter, 2013). Some examples are the use of social media, collaboration, and gaming. With various communications and digital technologies, the Web facilitates interactions of the crowd as with e-learners. Also, qualitative research is naturalistic and situated. Potential crowd participation in e-learning program evaluations can occur via the Internet, where e-learning happens, using Web applications for observations, focus groups, and a variety of self-reported data collection.

Crowdsourcing involves gathering and processing large volumes of high velocity, structured (spreadsheets, databases) and unstructured (videos, images, audio) information (Gandomi & Haider, 2014). Data management and analytic processes help aggregate these millions of independent ideas and aid complex problem-solving. The techniques to acquire, clean, aggregate, represent, and analyze data are many, and beyond the scope of this chapter. Some helpful applications for possible qualitative research and e-learning program include "big data" techniques for information retrieval (IR), audio analytics, and video analytics (Gandomi & Haider, 2014).

To illustrate, Vuurens and de Vries (2012) have created an algorithm to test the performance of an IR system using crowdsourcing to make relevance judgments about the appropriateness of documents to answer specific questions. They were able to match the quality of crowd judgments with those of experts. Given all of this, crowdsourcing might provide evaluators with a resource for coding or cleaning large data sets. Moreover, the techniques crowdsourcers use for collecting and analyzing crowd data might be employed for collecting and analyzing large amounts of interview or observational data. Examples include information retrieval and relevance judgments (Alonso, et al., 2008), as well as video, audio, and social media analytics (Gandomi & Haider, 2014).

Problems

Despite its possible affordances to e-learning program evaluation, crowdsourcing has also presented problems typically associated with the crowd and the Internet. Crowd demographics are not very heterogeneous; members are usually young educated males (Brabham, 2008; 2012). In addition, Brabham (2008) has claimed that diverse opinions may be silenced by the crowd since one cannot assume a democratic process to finding a solution, ensuring difference or dissent is not muzzled. Also, some complain that crowdsourcing exploits a skilled labor pool because businesses profit from paying little or nothing for human intelligence tasks (HITs). Besides, some fear crowds may not be knowledgeable, skilled, or work with integrity (Alonso et al., 2008; Brabham, 2012; Fuchs et al., 2013; Lloret et al., 2013).

Malicious behavior is prevalent on the Internet, particularly with worms, bots, and spam (King, 2015; Zhang, et al., 2006). Worms are malicious software that spread via the Internet and replicate themselves on computers. Bad bots masquerade as legitimate human users, responding to Web advertisements and bypassing anti-bot measures like CAPTCHA at nearly 90% accuracy (King, 2015). Since email is instrumental to crowdsourcing, spam is of special concern. Spam reportedly accounts for approximately 85% of all email, even during the early part of this decade, and has become harder to block with bots and compromised machines propagating spam messages (Yeh, et al., 2011). Vuurens and de Vries (2012) have reported that studies found as much as 50% spam from crowdsourcing results.

Some of these problems may be resolved because of the application to the education field. Education and evaluation research typically require an institutional review board (IRB) to approve designs and monitor ethical research behavior, so it is unlikely that crowd exploitation and homogeneity will be issues. In fact, e-learning program evaluators should have a real advantage over commercial uses of crowdsourced input, thanks to the non-profit status of most e-learning programs and the research paradigms. It is difficult to imagine that someone operating from a postmodernist paradigm, or employing the Fourth Generation Evaluation Model, would allow the voices of diverse students or stakeholders to be silenced. The hope is that crowdsourced input allows for "differing worldviews [that] might produce differing solutions to a problem, some of which might be superior solutions." (Brabham, 2008, p. 86).

Regarding the crowd's knowledge, skill, and work ethic, program evaluators will have decided which human subjects to engage in their IRB-approved designs. Also, concerns over stakeholder data accuracy are not relegated to evaluation designs with potential crowdsourced input (Posavac, 1999). If program evaluations involve MOOCs, evaluators may engage the general Internet public. For example, identity verification and anti-cheating mechanisms (including qualification tests and measuring time on tasks) are common (Brabham, 2008; Vuurens & de Vries, 2012). Plus, there are companies that help manage the process. Table 2 provides company overviews, and a sample of five such companies (Crowdsourced Testing Companies, 2012).

Detecting and combatting malicious network attacks to verify identity and safeguard data continues to be the work of the computer science field and network administrators (Sawyer & Tapia, 2005). It is beyond the scope of this chapter to detail the names and workings of the various applications and protocols, but privacy management systems, machine learning, and network behavioral analytics that block and limit traffic from certain addresses will help mitigate security problems from humans and bots alike (Yumerefendi, et al., 2007; King, 2015).

Table 2. Crowdsourcing company examples

	UTest	Mob4Hire	Feedback Army	Pay4Bugs	99tests
Year Founded	**2008**	**2007**	**2008**	**2009**	**2010**
Country of Origin	USA – Southborough, Massachusetts	Canada – Calgary, Alberta	USA – Washington, DC	China – Peral River Delta in South China	India – Bangalore
Website	www.utest.com	www.mob4hire.com	www. feedbackarmy.com	www.pay4bugs.com	99tests.com
Number of Testers	47,000+ worldwide (181 countries)	55,000+ worldwide (155 countries) 32,000+ handsets on 430 operators Testers are called 'Mobsters'	?? – very large pool of people; testing service build to use Amazon's Mechanical Turk (crowdsourcing service pool provided by Amazon)	?? – appears to be somewhat small/ limited	1,600
Types of Test Offerings	• Functional • Security • Usability • Load •Localization	•MOBEXPERIENCE Mobile User Experience Usability Research • MOBTEST Real World App Testing • MOBSIMTEST How Well Do Your SIMs Roams? • MOBSMSTEST Do Your SMS Messages Get There?	• Website Usability	• Functional • Localization	• Functional
Types of Applications	• Web • Mobile • Games	• Mobile	• Web	• Web • Mobile	• Web
Some Major Clients	• Microsoft • Google • BBC • Groupon • UPromise	• Shazam • VeriSign • Teja Soft • Whompster.com	• Mozilla Firefox • Taxact	• CISCO • myplanet • Reborn	•Flipkart.com • NxtGenTV • Ennovent • Practo.com

Crowdsourced Data and E-Learning Quality

Shelton and Salstman (2004) defined quality as the combination of retention rate, academic outcomes, and success in online student and faculty support. This definition, like the research approaches above, seems to focus the decision-making on the users with perhaps the most at stake: learners.

Educators have already started to experiment with crowdsourcing in some limited, learner-focused ways. For example, a Canadian university professor used crowdsourcing to empower student decision-making in an introductory globalization course (2013). Another experimenter used crowdsourcing with a participatory action research approach to create a framework for students as producers and content-creators (Hills, 2015). These examples have made little or no mention of evaluation, which should accompany any new classroom innovation or technique to empower students to determine what constitutes a meaningful, high-quality learning experience.

With the various research approaches giving stakeholders a central role in providing input, negotiating meaning, and using evaluation data, it seems that evaluators could provide all stakeholders and users with regular learner-support data. Involving learners and others in evaluation not only empowers them, but also gives them responsibility for providing information to e-learning designers about the meaningfulness of certain resources and support to learner persistence and academic success. Again, learner and stakeholder involvement in the evaluation process should lead to increased use of e-learning services, support, and instruction (Patton, 2008). Learners and stakeholders should also play a role in determining the value of crowdsourced input to improving e-learning quality. To determine what some of those roles may be, the next section presents a taxonomy of crowdsourcing, and some possible applications for evaluators and e-learning leaders to consider.

Taxonomical Framework and Possible Applications

Nakatsu, et al. (2014) have endeavored to fill a gap in the crowdsourcing literature by creating a taxonomy of crowdsourcing, which includes the multidimensional nature of task complexity with empirically-validated categories. They conducted a literature review of 162 examples of crowdsourcing, and checked them against the crowdsourcing and new trends web portal crowdsourcing.org to confirm the comprehensiveness of their sample. Some of the 162 examples included taxonomies. The researchers also reviewed literature on task complexity and virtual teams. Using an iterative approach to taxonomy development, and exhibiting 88% inter-rater reliability, they offered a taxonomy based on three task characteristics: structure, interdependence, and commitment.

According to Nakatsu, et al. (2014):

- **Task Structure:** This differs between well-structured, clearly-defined crowd solutions or contributions, and unstructured, undefined tasks requiring development of solutions and contribution of ideas.
- **Task Interdependence:** The level of interaction between crowd members needed for the activities. Some tasks require people to work separately, with little or no interaction with others. Other tasks require aggregated solutions, collaborative products, or team problem-solving.
- **Task Commitment:** The effort and resources needed to complete a task or solve a problem. For example, low-commitment tasks are straightforward and less intense, such as tagging images. High-commitment tasks require more time and resources. Given the complexities of e-learning and the variety of program evaluation paradigms and approaches, it seemed useful to begin considerations with a multidimensional taxonomy such as this in Table 3.

Table 3. A modified version of the Nakatsu taxonomy

	Independent Tasks (Individuals)	Interdependent Tasks (Virtual Communities)
Well-Structured Tasks	I. Contractual Hiring • Low Commitment • High Commitment	II.Distributed Problem-solving • Low Commitment • High Commitment
Unstructured Tasks	III. New Idea Generation – Solo • Low Commitment • High Commitment	IV. Collaboration • Low Commitment • High Commitment

Nakatsu et al. (2014)

The most important modification to the taxonomy is the inclusion of high-commitment tasks in Quadrant II. Nakatsu et al. (2014) have argued that distributed problem-solving counts as low commitment because crowdsourcers know what they want, they get it from the crowd, and they simply aggregate information distributed among individuals in some meaningful way. This is problematic for two reasons. First, this aggregation may not be representative of some evaluation data collection and analysis methods. One such example is the Delphi technique. Second, because of the heterogeneous composition of the crowd, classifying evaluation tasks in terms of commitment should also account for the level of cognitive commitment as explained by theories such as cognitive load (Sweller, 1988), which may be the most helpful theory.

As discussed earlier, crowdsourced evaluation tasks must be divisible and must indicate the level of difficulty. Sweller has maintained that the formation of schemas is an important factor in problem-solving activities, distinguishing novices from experts, and often requiring unrelated cognitive processes. Cognitive load theory explains that the effects, number, and size of "chunks" in problem-solving strategies have been found to differ for novices and experts (Sweller, 1988). Hence, the addition of high-commitment should help account for the variety of program evaluation methods, and also raises the issue of characterizing commitment in terms of cognitive load when structuring crowd tasks.

Another modification to the taxonomy is the elimination of all of the bulleted low/high commitment examples supplied in each quadrant, since they may not apply to rigorous e-learning evaluation. Some examples are as follows: crowdsourcing marketplaces eliminated from quadrant I (low commitment), crowdfunding from quadrant II (low commitment), and open source design of hardware from quadrant IV (high commitment). Overall, the intent is to give leaders and researchers the opportunity to provide other relevant examples applicable to e-learning program evaluation.

Finally, the parenthetical descriptions for quadrants II and IV, and row headings, were deleted as well, since the terms "distributed problem-solving" and "collaboration" have recognizable educational meanings, and their taxonomical application can be taken at face value. These modifications should provide a beginning framework for considering a possible role for crowdsourced input adapted from a literature review of existing implementations.

Application Examples

An established e-learning quality model seems helpful for possible crowdsourcing applications. Khan's Eight Dimensions of E-learning Framework (Khan, 2005), which was cited in both of the e-learning research studies above (Ossiannilsson et al., 2015; Shelton, 2011), has been selected for this purpose. More specifically, Khan's Eight Dimensions of E-learning Framework (2005) includes all quality dimensions, accounts for stakeholders' values, recognizes international and transnational dimensions, and accommodates interpretivist and postmodernist paradigms.

Khan (2001; 2005) has maintained that effective e-learning programs employ ongoing evaluation and are meaningful for learners and all stakeholders. Leaders, stakeholders, and program evaluators can use Khan's Eight Dimensions of E-learning Framework to systematically make decisions and guide high-quality program implementations. Table 4, shown on page 15 of Khan's (2005) book on managing e-learning, identifies and describes each of the dimensions. Following that are three possible crowdsourced input applications implemented by fictitious program evaluators, with two crafted specially for MOOCs.

The institutional dimension above includes a marketing and recruitment sub-category that addresses attrition and dropout rates, which can be problematic with MOOCs.

Table 4. Khan's Eight Dimensions of E-learning Framework

Dimensions of E-Learning	Descriptions
Institutional	The institutional dimension is concerned with issues of administrative affairs, academic affairs, and student services related to e-learning.
Management	The management of e-learning refers to the maintenance of learning environment and distribution of information.
Technological	The technological dimension of e-learning examines issues of technology infrastructure in e-learning environments. This includes infrastructure planning, hardware, and software.
Pedagogical	The pedagogical dimension of e-learning refers to teaching and learning. This dimension addresses issues concerning content analysis, audience analysis, goal analysis, media analysis, design approach, organization, and learning strategies.
Ethical	The ethical considerations of e-learning relate to social and political influence, cultural diversity, bias, geographical diversity, learner diversity, digital divide, etiquette, and the legal issues.
Interface design	The interface design refers to the overall look and feel of e-learning programs. Interface design dimension encompasses page and site design, content design, navigation, accessibility, and usability testing.
Resource support	The resource support dimension of the e-learning examines the online support and resources required to foster meaningful learning.
Evaluation	The evaluation for e-learning includes both assessment of learners and evaluation of the instruction and learning environment.

Example: Dr. Greenleaf

A MOOC provider might hire Dr. Greenleaf, an e-learning program evaluator with a postmodernist-critical paradigm, to provide users with timely information to select resources that increase users' self-efficacy. These users also provide stakeholders with diverse perspectives that inform the selection and marketing of these student support resources. Dr. Greenleaf uses a utilization-focused evaluation model and solicits crowdsourced input through an open Internet call. After consulting with stakeholders, Greenleaf designs data collection tasks in quadrant II of the taxonomy and employs video analytics. This crowdsourced input could be characterized as follows:

- **Crowd**
  - Individuals, Internet public
  - Number and skill open, and heterogeneous
  - Task objective: Identify and deconstruct known barriers to persistence in MOOCs to better address diverse learner expectations via effective marketing of support resources
    - Quadrant II
    - Low Commitment
- **Initiator**
  - MOOC stakeholders
  - Academic Affairs leader

- **Process**
    - Online, distributed global problem-solving
    - Geographically-situated user video narratives
    - Compensation
        - Crowdsourcer—organizational learning to better allocate resources
        - Crowd-Self-Actualization and a badge

Example: Dr Raul

Khan's Interface Design dimension includes checklists to help leaders make decisions about the overall look and feel of the MOOC. Dr. Raul approaches the evaluation from an interpretivist-constructivist paradigm employing the Fourth Generation Evaluation model. Dr. Raul solicits crowdsourced input through an open call to instructional designers via the Online Learning Consortium. These designers undertake a collaborative design task categorized in quadrant IV. The crowdsourced input could be further characterized in the following way:

- **Crowd**
    - Organized community of professionals
    - Number 330, skilled, and heterogeneous
    - Task objective: Answer the question: Is the program attractive and appealing to the eye and ear? (Different colors and fonts appeal to different people) (Khan, 2005, p. 159)
        - Quadrant IV
        - High Commitment
- **Initiator**
    - E-learning stakeholders
    - Instructional design leader
- **Process**
    - Online, open and collaborative interface design
    - Proprietary learning management system test environment
    - Compensation
        - Crowdsourcer-Interface redesign to aid navigation and persistence
        - Crowd-Social recognition

Example: Dr. Donkor

Khan's Resource Support dimension includes checklists to help leaders make decisions about online support, online resources, and offline resources. Dr. Donkor, from an interpretivist paradigm, employs a developmental evaluation approach. As a member of the evaluation team, Donkor perceives that the organization can benefit from the evaluation logic of the crowd. Donkor solicits crowdsourced input from several e-learning evaluators. This is done through an open call to experienced program evaluators via the American Evaluation Association Website to tap crowd wisdom, encourage innovation, and solve attrition and dropout problems through tasks in quadrant III, which can be characterized as follows:

- **Crowd**
  - Organized community of professionals
  - Number 10, skilled and retired, and heterogeneous
  - Task objective: Identify new ideas to assist instructors to provide meaningful assistance to students "who encounter problems completing their assignments" (Khan, 2005, p. 178)
    - Quadrant III
    - High commitment
- **Initiator**
  - E-learning stakeholders
  - Student support administrator
- **Process**
  - Online, emergent, open-ended, participatory
  - Compensation
    - Crowdsourcer-Innovative strategies and program support
    - Crowd-Self-Actualization

These examples are offered to encourage other possibilities situated in program evaluation approaches and methods.

FUTURE RESEARCH DIRECTIONS

Meeker (2015) has reported that the Internet has indeed changed the way people work, with a growing percentage (up 34%) of freelance and on-demand workers. Crowdsourcing can change the way evaluators work, giving them access to just-in-time assistance in performing evaluation tasks. Researchers and practitioners will need more information to help determine if existing paradigms, approaches, and methods should be reassessed to accommodate crowdsourcing.

Additional questions remain and need more examination. Does e-learning program evaluation need to develop its own definition of crowdsourcing, or merely validate Estelles-Arolas and González-Ladrón-de-Guevara's (2012) definition? Moreover, members of the American Evaluation Association task force may want to consider conducting a needs-assessment for whether crowdsourced input will impact its guiding principles for evaluators (American Evaluation Association, 1995). Evaluators should also think carefully about what tasks might be appropriate for various program evaluation approaches, given some of the problems with crowdsourcing. How might researchers and practitioners advance a taxonomical framework based on task characteristics? What are relevant examples for each quadrant? What other methodological affordances or unintended consequences does crowdsourcing have, especially for learners in MOOCs?

CONCLUSION

Program evaluation should provide people with answers, and regularly undergird e-learning activities and decisions. More recent program evaluation models and approaches emphasize utilization, collaboration, empowerment, and stakeholder participation. This chapter is an open call to leaders and evaluators to find ways to revolutionize e-learning evaluation with crowdsourced input. The definitions, taxonomy, and potential applications serve as a reference to advance the use of large amounts of structured and unstructured crowd data in meaningful ways. Crowd intelligence can potentially move e-learning stakeholders closer to realizing more innovative designs and learner support. As educators strive to make e-learning more global, inclusive, and learner-centered, program evaluators should do the same with e-learning evaluation.

REFERENCES

Abma, T. A., & Stake, R. E. (2001). Stake's responsive evaluation: Core ideas and evolution. In Responsive Evaluation. San Francisco, CA: Jossey-Bass.

Allen, E., & Seaman, J. (2013). *Changing course: Ten years of tracking online education in the United States* [PDF document]. Retrieved from http://www.onlinelearningsurvey.com/reports/changingcourse.pdf

Alonso, O., Rose, D., & Stewart, B. (2008). Crowdsourcing for relevance evaluation. *ACM SIGIR Forum*, 9-9.

American Evaluation Association, Task Force on Guiding Principles for Evaluators. (1995). Guiding principles for evaluators. In W. R. Shadish, D. L. Newman, M. A. Scheirer, & C. Wye (Eds.), Guiding principles for evaluators. San Francisco, CA: Jossey-Bass.

Atieno, O. P. (2009). An analysis of the strengths and limitation of qualitative and quantitative research paradigms. *Problems of Education in the 21st Century, 13*, 13-18.

Barksdale, S., & Lund, T. (2001). *Rapid evaluation: Tools, worksheets, and job aids to help you develop an evaluation strategy, use the right evaluation approach, understand and analyze evaluation data.* Alexandria, VA: American Society for Training & Development.

Benchmark Quality Assurance. (2012, May 1). *Crowdsourced testing companies* [PDF document]. Retrieved May 24, 2015 from http://www.benchmarkqa.com/wp-content/uploads/2012/04/Crowdsourced-Testing-Companies.pdf

Bishop, M. J. (2000). The systematic use of sound in multimedia instruction to enhance learning. *Dissertation Abstracts International*, *61*(07), 2669.

Brabham, D. C. (2008). Crowdsourcing as a model for problem solving. *Journal of Research into New Media*, *14*(1), 75–90.

Brabham, D. C. (2012). The myth of amateur crowds. *Information Communication and Society*, *15*(3), 394–410. doi:10.1080/1369118X.2011.641991

Brisolara, S. (1998). The history of participatory evaluation and current debates in the field. *New Directions for Evaluation*, *1998*(80), 25–41. doi:10.1002/ev.1115

Casey, D. M. (2008). A journey to legitimacy: The historical development of distance education through technology. *TechTrends: Linking Research & Practice to Improve Learning*, *52*(2), 45–51. doi:10.1007/s11528-008-0135-z

Cavanaugh, C. (2002). Distance education quality: Success factors for resources, practices, and results. In R. Discenza, C. D. Howard, & K. Shenck (Eds.), *The design & management of effective distance learning programs* (pp. 171–189). Hershey, PA: Idea Group. doi:10.4018/978-1-930708-20-4.ch011

Crawford, C. M. (2012). Knowledge and freedom: Massive open online courses as anywhere and anytime community of practice efforts. *Ubiquitous Learning: An International Journal*, *5*(2), 29–39.

Davidson, E. J. (2002). The discipline of evaluation: A helicopter tour for I-O psychologists. *The Industrial-Organizational psychologist*, *40*(2), 31–35.

Denzin, N. K., & Lincoln, Y. S. (2003). *The landscape of qualitative research: Theories and issues* (2nd ed.). Thousand Oaks, CA: SAGE Publications.

Estelles Arolas, E., & González-Ladrón-de-Guevara, F. (2012). Towards an integrated crowdsourcing definition. *Journal of Information Science*, *38*(2), 189–200. doi:10.1177/0165551512437638

Fitzpatrick, J., Sanders, J., & Worthen, B. (2011). *Program evaluation: Alternative approaches and practical guidelines* (4th ed.). Boston, MA: Pearson.

Fuchs, C., Prandelli, E., Schreier, M., & Dahl, D. W. (2013). All that is users might not be gold: How labeling products as user designed backfires in the context of luxury fashion brands. *Journal of Marketing*, *77*(5), 75–91. doi:10.1509/jm.11.0330

Gandomi, A., & Haider, M. (2014). Beyond the hype: Big data concepts, methods, and analytics. *International Journal of Information Management*, 137–144.

Garrison, D. R. (2011). *E-learning in the 21st century: a framework for research and practice*. New York, NY: Routledge.

Greene, J. C., & Abma, T. A. (2001). *Responsive evaluation*. San Francisco, CA: Jossey-Bass.

Gregg, D. (2010). Designing for collective intelligence. *Communications of the ACM*, *53*(4), 134. doi:10.1145/1721654.1721691

Guba, E., & Lincoln, Y. (1989). *Fourth generation evaluation*. Newbury Park, CA: SAGE Publications.

Haber, J. (2014). *MOOCs*. Cambridge, MA: The MIT Press.

Hegarty, B. (n.d.). Evaluation of eLearning for effective practice guidebook. In *WikiEducator*. Retrieved December 11, 2013 from http://wikieducator.org/Evaluation_of_eLearning_for_Effective_Practice_Guidebook

Hills, T. (2015). Crowdsourcing content creation in the classroom. *Journal of Computing in Higher Education*, *27*(1), 47–67. doi:10.1007/s12528-015-9089-2

Junho, S. (in press). Roadmap for e-commerce standardization in Korea. *International Journal of IT Standards and Standardization Research*.

Ke, F., & Kwak, D. (2013). Online learning across ethnicity and age: A study on learning interaction participation, perception, and learning satisfaction. *Computers & Education, 61*, 43-51. EBSCOhost (accessed March 4, 2015).

Khan, B. H. (2001). A framework for web-based learning. In Web-based Training, (pp. 75-98). Englewood Cliffs, NJ: Educational Technology.

Khan, B. H. (2004). The people-process-product continuum in E-learning: The E-learning P3 Model. *Educational Technology*, *44*(5), 33.

Khan, B. H. (2005). *Managing e-learning: Design, delivery, implementation and evaluation*. Hershey, PA: Information Science Publishing. doi:10.4018/978-1-59140-634-1

Kincheloe, J., & McLaren, P. (2003). Rethinking critical theory and qualitative research. In *The landscape of qualitative research: Theories and issues* (pp. 433–488). Thousand Oaks, CA: SAGE Publications.

King, S. (2015, May 25). *Who is really reading your ads?* [Web log post]. Retrieved fromhttps://www.linkedin.com/pulse/who-really-reading-your-ads-steve-king

Lanktree, C., & Briere, J. (1991, January). *Early data on the trauma symptom checklist for children (TSC-C)*. Paper presented at the meeting of the American Professional Society on the Abuse of Children, San Diego, CA.

Lloret, E., Plaza, L., & Aker, A. (2013). Analyzing the capabilities of crowdsourcing services for text summarization. *Lang Resources & Evaluation Language Resources and Evaluation, 47*(2), 337-369. Retrieved June 11, 2015, from http://www.jstor.org/stable/42636372

Marshall, S. (n.d.). *E-Learning Maturity Model*. Retrieved May 26, 2015, from http://www.utdc.vuw.ac.nz/research/emm/

Meeker, M. (2015). *Internet trends 2015: Code conference*. Retrieved June 1, 2015, fromhttp://www.kpcb.com/internet-trends

Merriam, S. B. (2002). *Qualitative research in practice: Examples for discussion and analysis*. San Francisco, CA: Jossey-Bass.

Milliron, M. D. (2010, October31). Online education vs. traditional learning: Time to end the family feud. *The Chronicle of Higher Education*, B30–B32.

Moore, M. (Ed.). (2013). *Handbook of distance education* (3rd ed.). New York, NY: Routledge.

Nakatsu, R. T., Grossman, E. B., & Iacovou, C. L. (2014). A taxonomy of crowdsourcing based on task complexity. *Journal of Information Science*, *40*(6), 823–834. doi:10.1177/0165551514550140

OLC Quality Scorecard. (n.d.). Retrieved June 19, 2015, fromhttp://onlinelearningconsortium.org/consult/quality-scorecard/

Omar, A., Rose, D. E., & Stewart, B. (2008). *Crowdsourcing for relevance evaluation*. SIGIR.

Ossiannilsson, E., Williams, K., Camilleri, A., & Brown, M. (2015). Quality models in online and open education around the globe: State of the art and recommendations. *The ICDE Reports Series*. Retrieved May 26, 2015, from http://icde.org

Pappano, L. (2012, November 3). *The Year of the MOOC*. Retrieved June 15, 2015, from http://www.nytimes.com/2012/11/04/education/edlife/massive-open-online-courses-are-multiplying-at-a-rapid-pace.html?_r=0

Patton, M. Q. (1994). Developmental Evaluation. *Evaluation Practice*, *15*(3), 311–319. doi:10.1016/0886-1633(94)90026-4

Patton, M. Q. (2001). *Qualitative research & evaluation methods* (3rd ed.). Thousand Oaks, CA: SAGE Publications.

Patton, M. Q. (2008). *Utilization-focused evaluation*. Thousand Oaks, CA: SAGE Publications.

Posavac, E. J. (1999). Ethical challenges: Commentary: Can we help Gee-Gaws stay a family? *The American Journal of Evaluation*. doi:10.1016/S1098-2140(99)00045-4

Preskill, H., & Russ-Eft, D. (2005). *Building evaluation capacity: 72 activities for teaching and training*. Thousand Oaks, CA: SAGE Publications. doi:10.4135/9781412983549

Reeves, T. C., & Hedberg, J. G. (2003). *Interactive learning systems evaluation*. Englewood Cliffs, NJ: Educational Technology Publications.

Rossi, P. H., Lipsey, M. W., & Freeman, H. E. (1999). *Evaluation: A systematic approach* (6th ed.). Thousand Oaks, CA: SAGE Publications.

Rossi, P. H., Lipsey, M. W., & Freeman, H. E. (2004). *Evaluation: A systematic approach* (7th ed.). Thousand Oaks, CA: SAGE Publications.

Rovai, A. P., & Baker, J. D. (2014). *Massive online learning: A topical record of the MOOC pansophy*. Chesapeake, VA: Watertree Press LLC.

Russ-Eft, D., & Preskill, H. (2001). *Evaluation in organizations. A systematic approach to enhancing learning, performance, and change*. Cambridge, MA: Perseus Publishing.

Salter, M. (n.d.). Crowdsourcing: Student-driven learning using web 2.0 technologies in an introduction to globalization. *Journal of Political Science Education*, 362-365.

Sawyer, S., & Tapia, A. (2005). The sociotechnical nature of mobile computing work: Evidence from a study of policing in the United States. *International Journal of Technology and Human Interaction*, *1*(3), 1–14. doi:10.4018/jthi.2005070101

Shelton, K. (2010). A quality scorecard for the administration of online education programs: A Delphi study. *Journal of Asynchronous Learning Networks*, *14*(4), 36–62.

Shelton, K. (2011). A review of paradigms for evaluating the quality of online education programs. *Online Journal of Distance Learning Administration*, *4*(1). Retrieved from http://westga.edu

Shelton, K., & Saltsman, G. (2005). *An administrator's guide to online education*. Greenwich, CT: Information Age Publishing.

Smith, N. L. (1999). A framework for characterizing the practice of evaluation, with application to empowerment evaluation. *Canadian Journal of Program Evaluation/La Revue Canadienne D'evaluation De Programme*, 39-68.

Stake, R. E. (1975). *Evaluating the arts in education: A responsive approach*. Columbus, OH: Merrill.

Sweller, J. (1988). Cognitive load during problem solving: Effects on learning. *Cognitive Science*, *12*(2), 257–285. doi:10.1207/s15516709cog1202_4

Trekles, A. M., & Sims, R. (2013). Designing instruction for speed: Qualitative insights into instructional design for accelerated online graduate coursework. *Online Journal of Distance Learning Administration*, *16*(3).

UPCEA Hallmarks of Excellence in Online Leadership. (n.d.). Retrieved May 26, 2015, fromhttp://www.upcea.edu/hallmarks

VandenBos, G., Knapp, S., & Doe, J. (2001). *Role of reference elements in the selection of resources by psychology undergraduates*. Retrieved October 13, 2001, from http://jbr.org/articles.html

Vuurens, J. B., & de Vries, A. P. (2012). Obtaining high-quality relevance judgments using crowdsourcing. *IEEE Internet Computing*, *16*(5), 20–27. doi:10.1109/MIC.2012.71

Wilson, K., & Doz, Y. L. (2012). 10 rules for managing global innovation. *Harvard Business Review*, *90*(10), 84–90, 130. PMID:23074868

Yumerefendi, A., Mickle, B., & Cox, L. (2007). Tightlip: Keeping applications from spilling the beans. *Proceedings of the 4th USENIX Conference on Networked Systems Design*, *38*, 12.

Zhang, Y., Cooke, E., & Mao, Z. (2006). Internet-scale malware mitigation: Combining intelligence of the control and data plane.*Proceedings of the 4th ACM Workshop on Recurring Malcode*, 33-40. doi:10.1145/1179542.1179549

Zhao, F. (Ed.). (2006). *Maximize business profits through e-partnerships*. Hershey, PA: IRM Press. doi:10.4018/978-1-59140-788-1

KEY TERMS AND DEFINITIONS

Massive Open Online Course (MOOC): A course available to large groups of people, typically for free online.

Online Program Quality: The combination of various factors in regards to the success of an e-learning program, including retention rate, learning outcomes, and support for students and faculty.

Paradigm: A system of thought within a certain field that underlies actions and guides future developments or inquiries.

Practical Participatory Evaluation: A system of evaluation in which stakeholders and other important program contributors assist in forming its evaluation process (Brisolara, 1998).

Qualitative Research: A research method that involves observing and collecting self-report data through interviews, life stories, case studies, and other documents (Denzin & Lincoln, 2003).

Responsive Evaluation: A system of evaluation in which the evaluator facilitates problem-solving that arises from stakeholder questions or issues found within a program (Stake, 1975).

Stakeholders: A person or group that has reason to take interest in a program because of its potential impact.

Taxonomy: A branch of science dealing with how things are classified.

Utilization-Focused Evaluation: A method of evaluation that judges a program based on its usefulness to its users (Patton, 1994).

Chapter 7
To MOOC or Not to MOOC, That Is the Problem: A Learner's Perspective

Dilrukshi Gamage
University of Moratuwa, Sri Lanka

Shantha Fernando
University of Moratuwa, Sri Lanka

Indika Perera
University of Moratuwa, Sri Lanka

ABSTRACT

MOOCs are found to be next disruption for online education. It provides many avenues to students to who could not be access to world class education. xMOOCs have been experiencing by students since 2012 and courses keep adding every day in many MOOC platforms. However, it was found that not all the courses in MOOC platforms provide student satisfactions and quality. In other words, effectiveness of the courses in MOOCs varies significantly. Many MOOCs fail to meet the user goals. This concerns the MOOC consumers that there is no quality standard followed by the MOOC producers. In this chapter, authors evaluate 20 courses in MOOC platforms by actively participating and experiencing the behaviors. Evaluation is processed using 8 dimensional eLearning framework to explore the quality and readiness on the technology for future. Results expressed that MOOCs need thorough attention in designing so that it meets user goals and be effective to continue keeping the users interest.

INTRODUCTION

The concept of "openness" is changing the world of education in many ways. For some people access to education has been a dream, but with the aid of MOOCs (Massive Open Online Courses), this is becoming a reality. MOOCs are giving opportunities to massive crowds to access first class education from elite universities free of charge or at a very low cost. MOOCs are also providing access to areas

DOI: 10.4018/978-1-5225-0466-5.ch007

of education that an ordinary person could not participate in without prior qualifications, such as to medicine-related courses where prerequisite knowledge of biology and related areas are required. The free and open nature of MOOCs unlocks many educational barriers for many learners. At the same time MOOCs bring a new perspective to online education and distance education. With the development of tools, technology, and networks, the number of students participating in MOOCs increases while the number of platforms and institutions that offer them also increases. Many researchers and educators state that MOOCs provide educational gains for students, or they are very effective and are based on a sound pedagogy (Glance, Forsey, & Riley, 2013). However, some researchers are still skeptical (Bali, 2014). Although it is too soon to predict all the pitfalls, concerns are arising and lead to heated discussion, as many xMOOCs tend to transfer traditional didactic pedagogy into the online learning environment. At the same time, there are serious concerns whether MOOCs can provide students with the necessary skills to meet the challenges of the 21st century, such as creative thinking, and collaborative problem solving. Many xMOOCs consist of small selections of videos, peer-graded or self-graded assignments, quizzes and forums to support peer and instructor communications. xMOOCs are offered in many platforms such as Coursera, FutureLearn, edX, open2study, and NovoEd. Numerous courses are added every day; Coursera, for instance, has more than 1000 courses running at any given time. Nevertheless, the course completion rates of xMOOCs remain in the range on 7-13%, which means many participants leave without completing any of the courses they started. Researchers argue it is merely up to the participant's interest and personal goals to finish any course, yet others argue it is mainly the lack of quality standards in a course; and that courses also failed to attract and keep the attention of their participants (Liyanagunawardena, Parslow, & Williams, 2014). At the same time, educators and learning enthusiasts are concerned that xMOOCs are practicing a behavioral approach to learning. For many students who participate in MOOCs, the question is of concern as not all MOOCs are equally effective. Even in the same MOOC platform, some courses are highly satisfying and some are disappointing. In other words, it is evident from the low completion rates and the significant number of dropouts in courses that there is a quality variation in MOOCs. Though the New York Times pronounced 2012 as "The Year of MOOC" (Pappano, 2012), it can now be argued that the hype about MOOCs is fading. According to the Babson Survey Research Group's annual survey in 2012, 28 percent of respondents believed MOOCs were sustainable, while 26 percent thought they were not. However in 2014 Babson's survey, 16 percent believe MOOCs are sustainable, while 51 percent think they are not (Allen & Seaman, 2014).

Since the MOOC concept is fairly young and is still evolving, quality standards and controls for them are also still evolving. There are many quality frameworks that have been used for previous online learning technologies, and researchers are working to implement and optimize similar frameworks for MOOCs. Researchers have discovered that many platforms that are offering MOOCs have a wide deviation in their quality and their effectiveness. Because MOOCs have such widely varied quality levels, it is a daunting task for students to select courses that will meet their goals. When students select a course, it typically takes 4-7 weeks to complete a course and, unless they enroll in the course and experience it for 1 or 2 weeks, they cannot determine how effective it will be in helping them meet their goals. Sometimes students will tend to pick the trending MOOCs described by various organizations and in reviews such as those found at CourseTalk but those student reviews are not available for all courses. Having that concern in mind, the objective of this chapter is to investigate the quality issues while evaluating the educational technology and MOOC's readiness and opportunities for growth. The authors' hypothesis is "if the MOOC provider or the course is fulfilling the goals of the learner and their learning outcomes, the technology is ready and has many opportunities in future". In order to identify the quality gaps in MOOCs, the authors participated in 20 different MOOCs over the course of two years.

In this chapter, the authors will use Khan's eight-dimensional e-learning framework (Khan, 2005) to evaluate their experiences while participating in 20 MOOCs over two years. Firstly, as background, the authors will describe and discuss two main types of MOOCs. Next they will describe the MOOC evaluation frameworks to give a background to the quality or effectiveness of frameworks found in online learning. The next section will focus on systematically evaluating the MOOCs completed by the authors using Khan's eight-dimensional framework. The results of this evaluation are discussed in the following section and finally the chapter describes its conclusions drawn after examining MOOCs. The empathy developed by the authors towards the MOOC learners from experiencing each MOOC course leads to identifying future research directions.

BACKGROUND

MOOCs are the latest trend in a long history of online learning technologies. Before MOOCs, there were many online learning technologies used by users at different levels. Even the term *online learning* is described in many ways: Distance Learning, Web base learning, eLearning, Web Based Instruction (WBI), Distributed Learning (DL), etc. In the early days, the primary users of online learning resonated with the difficulty of attending full-time school, limited time to spend on traveling to school/college and students' desire to work at their own pace. However, since 2012, when New York Times announces it was *The Year of MOOCs* (Pappano, 2012), there has been tremendous global attention given to MOOCs. Although there are 2 types of MOOCs commonly identified as xMOOCs and cMOOCs (connectivist MOOCs), it the xMOOC that has received the most attention. xMOOCs are designed to accommodate very large numbers of students, are open to anyone who is interested in learning the subject and are primarily concerned with the transmission of information, with little opportunity for interaction.

cMOOCs

cMOOCs or Connectivist MOOCs practice an approach different to xMOOCs. They are heavily focused on content creation and networking among the co-creators. As identified by researchers, it features several key design principles: Autonomy, Diversity, Interactivity and Openness.

- **Autonomy:** Is explained as learners choosing what content or skills they wish to learn as it embraces a culture of having no set curriculum.
- **Diversity:** Is explained in terms of the range of tools used by participants with their different knowledge levels contributing varied contents.
- **Interactions:** Are mainly focused on co-operating with each other and communicating with other participants via various channels (social media, blogs, etc.), resulting in emergent knowledge among the communicators.
- **Openness:** Is explained in terms of the freely available content and no clear guidelines or structure to access the content and assessments.

It is clear that cMOOCs are creating a culture and structure of sharing knowledge between participating scholars while xMOOCs concentrate to transmission of information (Yeager, Hurley-Dasgupta, & Bliss, 2013) cMOOCs appeared to have significantly less structure and a more evolving set of practices than xMOOCs. As it is now, there are many cMOOC 'experts' or rather cMOOCs have created some experts in its organization and in the promotion of cMOOC, who provide nodes of content around which discussion tends to revolve (Bates, 2014). cMOOCs can be described by their use of communication via social media, its content, and its communication patterns.

Communication via Social Media

cMOOCs are loosely coupled with many forms of software platforms. It uses many social networking platforms such as Facebook, LinkedIn, Twitter and Canvas and commonly uses a predefined hash tag to keep track of information.

Content Driven by Participants

Commonly, organizers using the cMOOC design decide on the topics to discuss and the media to be used with it. Yet the content to be covered is decided upon and contributed by the participants themselves; in this sense they are very much like any other community of practice. In practice though, cMOOC organizers (who themselves tend to have some expertise in the topic of the cMOOC) are likely to invite potential participants, who have expertise, or are known already to have a well-articulated approach to a topic, to make contributions around which participants can discuss and debate. Other participants choose their own ways to contribute or communicate, the most common being through blog posts, tweets, or comments on other participants' blog posts, although some cMOOCs use wikis or open source online discussion forums. The key design practice with regard to content is that all participants contribute to and share content. Since there is no assessment or a necessity to measure the contributions as in xMOOCs, cMOOCs could be participated at students' own time and pace and to the extent that they choose to.

Communication Is Distributed

Communication is the most complex part of cMOOCs for those who have experience in cMOOCs. Communication is often replied to on the channel of the user who posts the subject matter that is of interest. With participants numbering in the hundreds or even thousands, each contributing individually through a variety of social media, there are myriad different inter-connections between participants that are impossible to track (in total) for any single participant. This results in many sub-conversations, more commonly at a binary level of two people communicating with each other than as an integrated group discussion, although all conversations are 'open' and all other participants are able to contribute to a conversation if they know it exists. The key design practice then with regard to communication is that it is a self-organizing network with many sub-components.

xMOOCs

xMOOCs are more common than cMOOCs and provide a more structured organization of the learning experience. Design features that are common to many MOOCs are: they are conducted via a specially designed software platform and feature short video lectures, computer assessments, peer graded assessments, certification after completion, less moderated or interactive forums and provide learning analytics for instructors (Rodriguez, 2013).

Short Video Lectures

xMOOCs are often designed with short videos, produced by the instructor and created by a production team, or individually screened from a tape. Some courses had recorded on-campus lecture-style videos and some videos were just recorded in front of a desktop computer or on a smartphone. Early on, the video time span started as recording 50 minutes average per video, but now, due to student retention requirements, the time span is reduced to an average of 10-20 minutes. Mostly the instructors follow a lecture-style in presenting; however, some courses contain attractive panel discussion type videos, drama types and many with interactions embedded in videos where students can be to ask quiz questions while watching. When the authors started taking MOOCs, there were courses that were 12 to 14 weeks long, however, the trend moved more to 4-5 weeks duration, due to the demand of other commitments on students.

Computer Graded Assessment

Many of the xMOOCs contain multiple choice questions used for formative and summative assessment of the student and to determine if they have earned the certificate. Many times students were allowed to have several attempts at the multiple choices questions. Occasionally there were courses with questions that expected one or two word answers and also some had with interactive activities such as drawing lines to make connections, or dragging the correct answer into a box.

Peer Assessment

One of the key features of xMOOCs is the system-supported design for peer assessment. Most of the answers in the formats described above were evaluated via peer assessment and it was found that peer assessment has often proved problematic, because of wide variations in expertise between the different members of a group, and because of the differing levels of involvement in the course by different participants. Peer assessment is conducted by assigning 3-5 participants to provide critical feedback to each other on their assignments, and then to grade them, using a rubric provided by the instructor. The peer assessment process takes a minimum of 1 week and could expand to 2 weeks.

Forum Discussions

The extent to which the discussion or comments are moderated or responded to by faculty varies probably more than any other feature in xMOOCs, but at its most, moderation comments are directed to all participants, rather than to individuals. Because of the very large numbers participating and commenting, responding to individual comments by the instructor(s) offering the MOOC is impossible. Some instructors offer no moderation or response whatsoever, so participants rely on other participants to respond to questions or comments. Some instructors 'sample' comments and questions, and post comments in response to these. Other instructors use teaching assistants to comb for or identify common areas of concern shared by a number of participants, then the instructor or teaching assistants will respond. However, in most cases, participants just respond to each other's comments or questions. The average time for a forum posting to be answered by someone depends on the interests and the attention given to the forums. On some occasions, or in some courses, it takes only minutes to get a reply and sometimes it takes as long as weeks or months.

Specially Design Platform

Unlike cMOOCs, xMOOCs are run on software platforms such as Coursera, Canvas, edX and many more. It is a specially designed platform software that allows for the registration of very large numbers of participants, provides facilities for the storing and streaming on demand of digital materials, and automates assessment procedures and student performance tracking.

Learning Analytics

Learning Analytics are not usually available to participants, but have many features to help course instructors to make a critical analysis. At the same time, some of the platforms support *big data* about participants and their performance, enabling, at least in theory, immediate feedback to instructors about areas where the content or design needs improving and possibly directing automated cues or hints to individuals. However, a few of the analytics, such as how many members viewed the forum messages or how many replied in the forum are visible to the learners as well. It creates a trend among the participants to choose the conversations that they like to follow. In some platforms, students are provided with poll information, up votes and down votes to make decisions on the concepts.

Quality Frameworks for MOOCs

Since MOOC concepts are growing at an exponential speed, researchers and educators express concerns in maintaining the quality of each course. Examining the efforts made in that direction, it has been found that effectiveness or quality indicators for online learning are widely available, backed with empirical evidence. However, those indicators will not be suitable for MOOCs due to their unique features. Hence, the critical success factors or factors affecting effectiveness of a MOOC requires research to be conducted among the MOOC participants (Yousef, Chatti, Schroeder, & Wosnitza, 2014). The authors discovered that, in the existing literature, there were many proposed quality aspects suggested for use in MOOCs. At the same time, the authors observed some literature proposals to use quality metrics that had already been explored in other technologies, before the emergence of MOOCs. Yet there is a strong argument by Yousef et al., (2014), which claims that any quality metric in online learning should not be used for assessing MOOCs because MOOCs have unique pedagogical features and those pre-existing metrics were had not been discovered and validated using MOOC participants.

A 10-dimensional proposal to evaluate quality in MOOCs was found in a publication edited by Sir John Daniel and Stamenka Uvalic-Trumbiæas "A guide to online learning" (2014). It was produced to address the rapidly growing quality issues from an international perspective. This brings together best practices and practical tools from around the world, organized around 16 key questions. Some of these questions are as follows:

- What constitutes quality in online learning?
- How can institutions assure quality?
- How can students judge quality of online courses?
- How can instructional design, learning materials, and course presentation contribute to quality online learning?
- How can the structure of the virtual environment facilitate quality online learning?

The authors of the publication produced 10 quality benchmarks based on an extensive review of previous literature (Butcher & Wilson-Strydom, 2014):

- Institutional support (vision, planning, & infrastructure),
- Course development,
- Teaching and learning (instruction),
- Course structure,
- Student support,
- Faculty support,
- Technology,
- Evaluation,
- Student assessment,
- Examination security.

The framework provided by the "Quality Matters" program proposes to use its metrics rubric in assessing MOOCs. This program consists of the latest quality dimensions for online learning (Shattuck, 2014). The rubric contains eight dimensions: Course Overview and Introduction, Learning objectives, Assessment and measurement, Instructional materials, Learner interaction and engagement, Course technology, Learner support and Accessibility. The program has analyzed 21 peer-reviewed journals and other academic databases such as ERIC, ProQuest and Google Scholar in order to produce the elements in the rubric. Although the eight dimensions appear to provide a reasonable argument for online learning, it does not specifically address the context of MOOCs. The primary focus of this literature review is focus on MOOC literature and studies based on examining MOOC participants in particular.

However, the MOOC Quality Project, which is an initiative of the European Foundation for Quality eLearning attempted to identify quality issues specifically focusing on MOOCs. In this project, a series of blog post by experts relating to the quality of MOOCs were taken into consideration to produce a quality report of MOOCs (Ehlers, Ossiannilsson, & Creelman, 2014). The report of this project highlight some factors related to the perception of MOOC quality: the notion of choice, what pre-course information is provided, the pedagogical approaches supported in a course, the level of student commitment required, if a course was scheduled or not, technical requirements, the role of the teaching team, availability and level of interaction, whether certification is available. An expert in the project, Downes (2013) argues that the success of a MOOC will not depend on the number of drop outs, counting test scores, or adding up students' satisfaction. Downes states four success factors: Autonomy, Diversity, Openness and Interactivity. Another expert (Conole, 2013) in her research argues that xMOOCs that are simply based on the interactions among students and between students and content are following the behaviorists' learning approach. Her research introduced the 7Cs approach to bring enhancements in leaner experience and quality assurances. In order to achieve effective learning, she argues it is essential to meet the characteristics of good learning:

- Encourages reflection,
- Enables dialogue,
- Fosters collaboration,
- Applies theory learnt to practice,
- Creates a community of peers,

- Enables creativity,
- Motivates the learners.

Further, her argument is to incorporate the 7Cs to create an effective learning experience in MOOCs. The 7Cs are Conceptualize (what is the vision for the course?), Capture (a resource audit), Communicate (mechanisms to foster communication), Collaborate (mechanisms to foster collaboration), Consider (assessment strategies), Combine (overarching views of the design), and Consolidate (implementing and evaluating the design in a real learning context).

The importance of determining success factors for Open Education Initiatives (OEI) was researched by Nagashima, (2014). The research found six factors: Brand/Reputation, Funding, Focus of Subjects, Interactivity, Social view of open education, and Localization. These factors were defined under three categories: Organizational, Pedagogical and Social factors. Although this research does not reveal any empirical exploration behind selecting the factors, it was evident that these factors were based on an analysis of previous literature. The research evaluated MIT OCW, OpenLearn OER Africa, Coursera, OpenLearn, and Udacity using the 6 factor model. Among all the results, authors emphasize the factor *Interactivity* was found low in MIT OCW and OER Africa but higher in other 3 platforms.

The research carried by Margaryan, Bianco, and Littlejohn, (2015) proposes 10 dimensional instructional design criteria to evaluate MOOCs quality. The research is highly focused in a pedagogical perspective of MOOCs by arguing that the instructional design quality of a course is a critical indicator and prerequisite of the potential of the course for effective learning. It states that a learner or participants' opinions of their experience may not reflect the effective result of MOOC quality because learners typically do not have the expertise to assess instructional design. Their research concludes it is critical to evaluate the quality of MOOC design by drawing on the knowledge of expert instructional designers. The 10 evaluation criteria were drawn from First Principles Instructions - interrelated prescriptive criteria for effective instruction abstracted from key instructional design theories and models (Merrill, 2002). Those are:

1. Problem Centered,
2. Activation,
3. Demonstration,
4. Application,
5. Integration,
6. Collective Knowledge,
7. Collaboration,
8. Differentiation,
9. Authentic resources, and
10. Feedback.

Although this dimensions do not provide empirical evidence to be applied to MOOCs, the researchers evaluated 76 MOOC courses using these dimensions, by focusing on the pedagogical opportunities for quality in instructional design in learning. Their results reflected that the instructional design quality of MOOCs is essentially low, by arguing that out of 72 possible total points that each course could score, according to the Course Scan instrument, none of these MOOCs scored above 28 points.

A framework named *mesoMOOC* proposed by Schoenak, (2013), addresses several challenges that hinder current effective delivery of MOOCs. The framework utilizes proven strategies in online learning to better implement MOOCs by addressing the orientation process, embedding a connectivist, synchronous component to the classroom, providing online formative and summative assessment, and develop subsections within classes. Although the criteria for the framework were explained in narrative literature, yet there was no evidence that the framework had been tested and validated using MOOC participants.

The literature search resulted in a limited number of research reports with empirical evidence in MOOC quality-related research. Empirical research is a way of gaining knowledge by means of direct and indirect observation or experience. In the research reported in this chapter, the empirical evidence (the record of one's direct observations or experiences that can be analyzed quantitatively or qualitatively) came straight from MOOC participants and/or MOOC courses.

Researchers taking this direction, Lyndon and Loch, (2014), explored academics' perception of the quality of a MOOC. In their research they distributed a survey, using the snowball sampling technique, to academics who are taking part in MOOC courses via twitter, e-mails, and personal networks. Although the research focused on the pedagogical aspects of the MOOC, it was evident from the results that the participants were empathizing that the technological aspects also to be considered as a factor in the delivery of a quality experience in a MOOC. However, their research does not directly quote quality metrics in MOOCs, yet their survey turned up some concerns with video quality, assessments, workload, and social interactions.

The research conducted by Yousef, Chatti, Schroeder, and Wosnitza, (2014) sorted MOOC quality criteria into 2 dimensions and 6 categories. Their model is depicted in Figure 1.

Figure 1. Classification of MOOC criteria according to Yousef, Chatti, Schroeder, & Wosnitza
Yousef, Chatti, Schroeder, & Wosnitza, (2014)

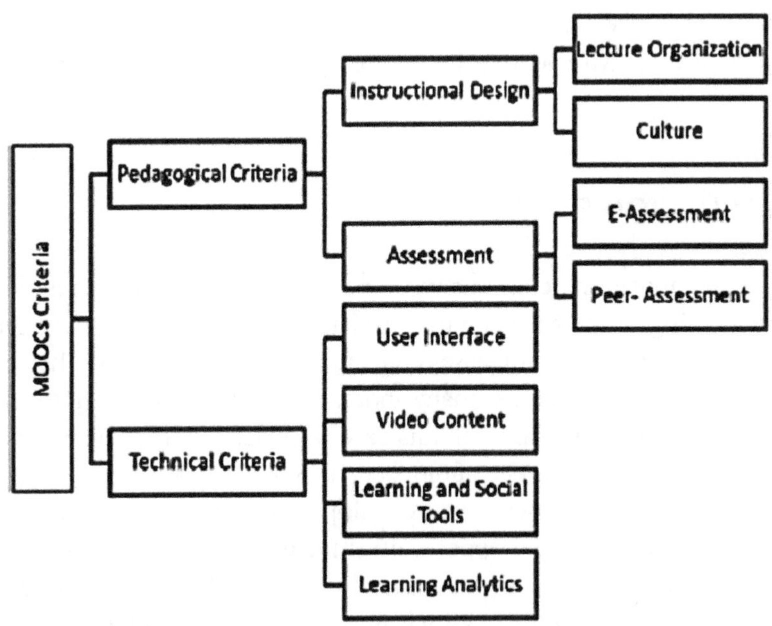

Their research surveyed 107 students and 98 professors who took part in MOOCs. Since they did not find a significant difference in 2 of the categories, they have merged those categories and found scaffolding, collaboration & self-organizing as the three categories that they should consider. The final results from analysis of the instrument used found 74 criteria for effective MOOC environments classified into 2 categories. The statistical results of the survey showed that learning analytics and assessment have obtained the highest average mean scores. Although there was wide agreement that usability, content, collaboration, and instructional design play a major role in achieving effective MOOCs, in this research these categories were identified as less important when compared to the learning analytics and assessment categories.

The research conducted by Gamage, Perera, and Fernando (2014) used the grounded theory methodology in order to analyze their observations of MOOC participants and to explore the quality dimensions in a MOOC. In their research, participants from 5 MOOC platforms within a period of 2 years (2012-2014) were observed. Their results revealed a 10 dimension model to evaluate MOOC quality:

1. Interaction,
2. Collaboration,
3. Motivation,
4. Network of Opportunities / Future directions,
5. Pedagogy,
6. Content,
7. Assessment,
8. Usability,
9. Technology, and
10. Support for Learners.

Their research argues that attention must be paid to the dimensions mentioned and doing so will increase the users' sustainability in MOOCs. There is evidence that this study will be a benchmark and a guide to any MOOC user or MOOC developer attempting to produce or participate in an effective e-learning experience.

THE MOOC EVALUATION STUDY

Besides those mentioned above, there are many frameworks and instruments aiding the evaluation of the quality of online learning, such as the eLearning Maturity Model, California eLearning Framework, Quality Matters Program framework for assessing eLearning and Badrul Khan's eight-dimensional e-learning framework (see Chapter 1) and many more. In this chapter, the authors aim is to evaluate the readiness of the education technology – in this case MOOCs – not from an organizational perspective, but from the perspective of users. The authors chose Khan's (2005) eight dimensional framework. Although the eight-dimensional framework was developed for institutions to organize their evaluation of educational technology readiness and opportunities for growth, the authors argue that evaluation is the same from the users perspective, as they are one of the key stakeholders. By analyzing the MOOCs participated in by the authors against the quality criteria, they have developed a way users can identify whether the MOOC is effective or not. In other words, since many MOOCs consume a lot of learning time, it is important to determine whether a particular MOOC is worth spending time on.

Table 1. MOOC platform and the name of the course completed by authors

#	Course	Platform
1	Foundations of Virtual Instructions	Coursera
2	Human Computer Interactions	Coursera
3	Advance Instructional strategies in Virtual classroom	Coursera
4	University Teaching 101	Coursera
5	Understanding research methods	Coursera
6	What future of education?	Coursera
7	Creative Problem Solving	Coursera
8	Assessment and Teaching 21st Century skills	Coursera
9	Open Knowledge:Changing the global Course of Learning	OpenLearn
10	11.132x Design and Development of Educational Technology	edX
11	15.390x Entrepreneurship 101	edX
12	GSE2x, Leaders of Learning	edX
13	Technology Entrepreneurship 1	NovoEd
14	Technology Entrepreneurship 2	NovoEd
15	Storytelling for a change	NovoEd
16	Design Thinking	Iversity
17	User Experience for Web	Open2study
18	Teaching adult learners	Open2study
19	Developing your research project	futureLearn
20	Elearning ecology	Coursera

Methodology

In order to evaluate the MOOCs, the authors participated and completed 20 randomly selected MOOCs from 7 different platforms. They particularly selected courses with some subject interest to them. Therefore the sampling technique is both random sampling and purposive sampling. When participating in the MOOCs, the authors were keen to interact with other participants to examine their perspective of the same course, as it was crucial to make unbiased evaluations. The MOOCs examined by the authors are listed in Table 1.

Courses listed in Table 1 were examined against the 8 dimensional framework (Khan, 2003) explained in Table 2. The sub-dimensions described in the framework were converted to questions where the answers could be quantified on a Likert scale from 1 to 5. This aided in understanding the aspects of each course that represent a quality value. This process of identifying issues in existing e-learning technology by converting the framework ideas into question form was highly encouraged in the 8 dimensional framework. However, open-ended questions answered with detailed descriptions were also taken into consideration, as it is important to understand the value of the courses in qualitative terms. The questions are shown in Table 3 and scored using a 5 point scale – least agreeable to most agreeable. Responses indicated a total of 34 points would indicate the lowest possible score and (34*5)=170 for highest possible value for technology readiness. By quantifying the measurement the evaluation of the MOOCs effectiveness made it more efficient in understanding the variance levels of MOOCs.

Table 2. Evaluation questions generated by the Eight Dimensions of Khan's framework

Dimensions in the Framework	Questions Reworded to Frame the Answers for a Likert Scale Assessment
Institutional	• Administrative Affairs maintained in the course? • Academic Affairs and relationships built into the course? • Student Services provided in the course?
Ethical Considerations	• Social and Cultural Diversity maintained in the course? • Political Issues handled well? • Embrace Geographical Diversity? • There is significant learner diversity? • How is Digital Divide handled in the course? • Etiquette is handled and embraced in the course? • Legal Issues are handled properly?
Management	• People, Process and Product (P3) Continuum managed well? • Management Team is promising and provide opportunities? • Managing E-Learning Content is easy? • Development of the course taken by Management? • Managing E-Learning Environment is less hassle?
Technological	• Not necessary to bring own Hardware? • Not necessary to update machines with new Software?
Pedagogical	• Content Analysis: Content in the course adequate? • Audience Analysis: Audience met their requirement? • Design Approach: Course design approach is fun to continue? • Instructional Strategies are well placed?
Evaluation	• Content Development Process is evaluated? • E-Learning Environment is Evaluated? • Evaluation of E-Leaning at the Program is done? • Evaluation of ELearning at the Institutional Levels is done?? • Assessment of Learners carried out?
Interface design	• Page and Site Design is effective? • Content Design is effective? • Navigation is easy? • Easy Accessibility is provided? • Usability testing being done? • The system is usable?
Resource Support	• Online Support is provided? • Necessary resources provided?

Results and Discussion

Each MOOC participated in by the authors was closely examined against the questions derived from the Khan's framework, as shown in Table 2. The scores were ranged from the lowest score of 42 to a highest of 161. Characteristics of the lowest scored course indicated many pitfalls detracting from an effective, satisfying delivery. Students who invest time on a MOOC expect to meet its learning goals in return. If the course could not meet its goals and requirements, it often triggers dropouts.

Figure 2 depicts the variation of the scores received after analyzing the MOOCs against the Khan's eight-dimensional framework. The highest score was achieved for course number 2 in the Table 2 (Human Computer Interactions) and the lowest score was received by course number 1 (Foundations of Virtual Instructions) in the same MOOC platform.

Figure 2. Distribution of scores determined using Khan's framework on MOOCs listed in Table 2
Khan (2003)

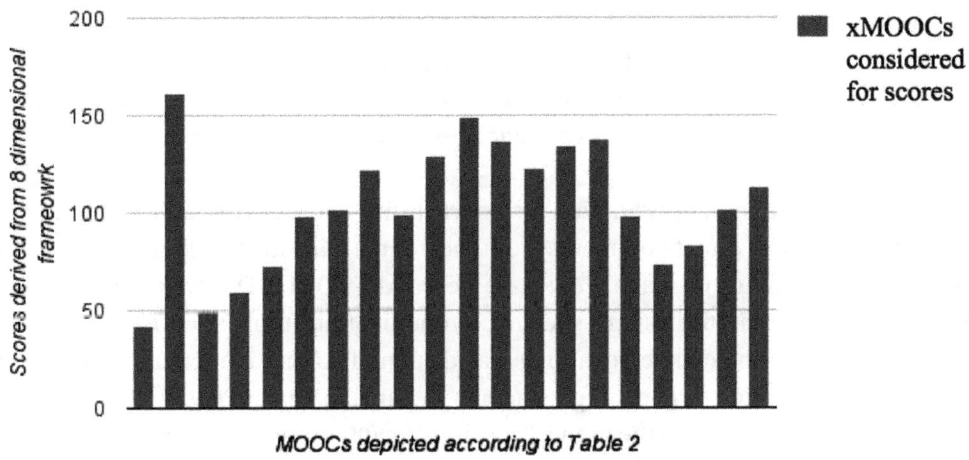

After analyzing the score distribution among various MOOCs listed in Table 2 from seven platforms, it is evident from Figure 2 that there is a significant variation among MOOCs. The first eight courses in Table 2 represented one MOOC platform and such variation gaps in the scores among them reflects that the MOOC platforms are not being carefully evaluated on their courses. Unless otherwise evaluated in a public course review channel, it is difficult to identify the quality of the MOOC in order to make the decision to enroll or not. Many students invest their time and effort in MOOCs, with no way of measuring the quality of the course before they enroll. The majority of enrollment decisions are based on the title and the content description and a topic that interests the individuals.

Resonating the Low Scores

The reason behind the lowest score was that the course had many pitfalls in effectiveness. For a course to be interesting, it is important give some evidence of instructional development. The content was not presented in a manner that attracted and retained the user. This particular course failed to maintain quality in the Pedagogical dimension and the Evaluation dimension. Many researchers state that the success of an e-learning event rests a significant weight on the design of the e-learning course, e-learning course quality, perceived usefulness, perceived ease of use, and diversity in assessments. In the lowest scored course, the short videos appear amateurish as the video was recorded by the lecturer, without any concern for the backgrounds, and the delivery of the instruction and the assessment quizzes were poorly organized (Sun, Tsai, Finger, Chen, & Yeh, 2008). In many low quality e-learning courses it was common to focus on the assessment of cognitive behavior, rather than evaluating to enhance the critical skills of a learner.

As stated by Glance, Forsey, and Riley (2013), MOOCs that contain sound pedagogy will have short videos of recorded lectures. However, many of the low score courses in Figure 2 had long videos that brought with them difficulties in keeping the students' attention. At the same time, the presenter in the video merely read or repeated the text on the instructor's slides rather than presenting the information in an attractive manner that would retain the student interest.

Resonating High Score MOOCs

The highest scoring MOOC on the list contained many features that increased the quality of the course. As an example, the MOOC that scored highest in pedagogy was designed such that it was very active and engaging to the users. The course contained short video lectures introducing to the concepts, and had many lessons that shared the instructor's experience, explained in a manner that attracted and retained the students' attention.

The course presented many opportunities for interactivity and networking among students and instructors and the feedback or direct comments from the course staff increased the students' motivation, leading to effective e-learning (Gamage, Perera, & Fernando, 2014). The course featured face-to-face synchronous meeting opportunities using a special communications tool called *Talkabout* that increased the learning effectiveness. The course pedagogy was designed so that it encouraged the creation of artifacts and leading gamification to encourage students to participate actively.

The evaluation techniques within the highest scoring MOOC were well organized so that it reflected formative and summative assessment. This MOOC provided and cultivated a culture of providing critical feedback to all students so they could learn from each other's creations and artifacts. The feedback mechanism was very fast and had several volunteer teaching assistants supporting and providing feedback; this increased the motivation of students to continue, while they providing valuable, insightful feedback.

Future Research Directions

Massive open online courses (MOOCs) have generated enthusiasm, excitement, and hype worldwide and recently, increasing skepticism. According to Macleod, Haywood, Woodgate, & Alkhatnai, (2015), an emerging pattern in MOOCs is that although there is participation from worldwide learners, the highest level of participation is among students from the USA. MOOCs are being used for career advancement and to increase learning opportunities for those who could not otherwise continue their education. At the same time, it appears that *serial MOOCers* are emerging. Serial MOOCers are tparticipants who have already participated in one or more MOOCs, before their current MOOC. These are participants who have experience in several platforms and other, perhaps more sophisticated course designs in other platforms. Keeping their interest level high is really important to any MOOC designer or provider and that can be done, in part, by maintaining a high level of quality in the MOOCs. As stated by Siemens, (2015), the promised transformation of higher education has failed to arrive. MOOCs have ended up raising as many questions as they have provided answers. Once some data from early MOOCs was published, it became clear that systemic change had not occurred. The flaws of these early MOOCs were eagerly dissected: high dropout rates, limited social interactions, heavy reliance on instrumented teaching, under-representation of many students' populations and so on. As skeptics like Daniels, (2012) pointed out, MOOCs are needed to provide meaningful educational experiences that can be usable to the participants, rather than just building behavioral aspects. The necessity of an innovative pedagogy that leads to active knowledge generation that could be useful in individual lives was highly demanded and expected. Transferring traditional face-to-face teaching and learning methods to the MOOCs new model has generated some common sense technological approaches like automated quizzes and marking. New pedagogical approaches have to be proposed for MOOCs to increase quality in design and effective adaptive learning. This situation indicates that MOOCs are still in their initial stages of experimentation and need some more course iterations to generate new approaches. The digitization efforts that are occurring in many fields will lead to the collection of data that can be useful to identify the learning patterns of millennial users. As of now, a significant amount of research is lacking that could enhance the user experience in learning rather than allow many MOOCs to continue to focus on transformative didactic learning practices. According to researchers it is really important to make quality design and deliverables for MOOCs (Ehlers, Ossiannilsson, & Creelman, 2014) that empower the learner. This idea of learner empowerment is directly associated with adaptive learning as Clark (2013) noted that adaptive learning is a possible approach to reduce the high dropout rates that MOOCs are experiencing.

Another aspect that MOOCs designers should be considering is the creation of powerful social networking cultures in the learners' lives. It appears that in many MOOCs the only or the major concern is the delivery of IT information rather than being designed to cultivate social interactions among the learners. MOOCs present a fascinating opportunity for diverse cultures to learn together, while learning from each other. However, most of the platforms have only very little space to facilitate rich social interactions among students. Social networking should be aimed to boost collaborative learning and build communities of practice to create learning opportunities so students can participate in a collective intelligence that is able to share knowledge in each peer-to-peer interaction, such as online forums and video discussions (Glance, Forsey, & Riley, 2013). Some researchers claim that MOOCs are neither social nor individual, but both, therefore some students will prefer to work alone and others will take full advantage of team learning (Blom, Verma, Li, Skevi, & Dillenbourg, 2013). Social qualities are the source of group forming and the establishment of durable peer cooperation. Therefore, guidance is needed to help learners create their own personal learning environment that can keep them in a permanent connection with the network (Sangrà, Guàrdia, & Maina, 2013).

CONCLUSION

In conclusion, there are increasing numbers of MOOC platforms and courses in the online learning field, that are promising new learning experiences and catering to the high demand for inexpensive and accessible education. However, many courses in MOOCs do not meet the learners' goals. Many courses lacked student-to-student and student-to-instructor interactions, collaborative opportunities, and networking culture. Learning is merely based on transformative learning or the behavioral aspect of pedagogies. When MOOCs emerged in 2012, they promised to change higher education, but those promised changes in higher education never arrived. According to Siemens (2015), as MOOCs provide answers to some questions, they have created more questions and debates and evidence of an incomplete system change in education. Along the way, the flaws of MOOCs were eagerly discussed as higher dropout rates, limited social interactions, heavy reliance on instructivist teaching, poor results for under-represented student populations and many more. MOOCs became *trendy* rather than supporting a range of knowledge and meeting the learning needs of individuals in a society that craves new models of learning experiences.

In this chapter, the authors have noted the flaws in different MOOC platforms. The authors used Khan's (2003) framework to identify the quality gaps. As the chapter provides the results of participation in and evaluation of 20 MOOCs, it is evident that even within the same platform courses have high variation in quality levels. Students who invest the time to attend these courses have concerns as they enroll to the courses: not all MOOCs include great learning experiences nor do they meet the users' goals. It is time that MOOC creators, designers, and developers consider providing regulated or moderated courses using MOOC quality frameworks.

REFERENCES

Allen, I. E., & Seaman, I. (2014). *Grade Change: Tracking online education in United States.* New York: Babson Survey Research Group and Quahog Research group.

Bali, M. (2014). MOOC Pedagogy: Gleaning Good Practice from Existing MOOCs. *Journal of Online Teaching and Learning*, *10*(1), 44–57.

Bates, T. (2014). MOOCs: Getting to know you better. *Distance Education*, *35*(2), 145–148. doi:10.1080/01587919.2014.926803

Blom, J., Verma, H., Li, N., Skevi, A., & Dillenbourg, P. (2013). MOOCs are More Social than You Believe. *eLearning Papers, 33*, 1-3. Retrieved from http://www.elearningpapers.eu/en/article/MOOCs-are-More-Social-than-You-Believe?paper=124335

Butcher, N., & Wilson-Strydom, M. (2014). *A Guide to Quality in Online Learning*. Dallas, TX: Acedemic Partnerships.

Cambre, J., Kulkarni, C., Bernstein, M. S., & Klemmer, S. R. (2014). Talkabout: small-group discussions in massive global classes.*First ACM conference on Learning@scale conference* (pp. 161-162). ACM. doi:10.1145/2556325.2567859

Conole, G. (2013). MOOCs as disruptive technologies: Strategies for enhancing the learner experience and quality of MOOCs. *Revista de Educación a Distancia*, *39*, 1–17.

CourseTalk Reviews. (n.d.). Retrieved from CourseTalk: https://www.coursetalk.com

Creelman, A., Ehlers, U., & Ossinnilsson, E. (2014). Perspectives on MOOC quality - An account of the EFQUEL MOOC Quality Project. *International Journal for Innovation and Quality in Learning, 2*(3), 78-87.

Daniel, J. (2012). Making sense of MOOCs: Musings in a maze of myth, paradox and possibility. *Journal of Interactive Media in Education*, (3). doi:10.5334/2012-18

Downes, S. (2013). *Week 2: The Quality of Massive Open Online Courses*. Retrieved from http://mooc.efquel.org/week-2-the-quality-of-massive-open-online-courses-by-stephen-downes

Gamage, D., Perera, I., & Fernando, S. (2014). Effectiveness of eLearning through MOOC: lessons learnt in selecting a MOOC. *The 22nd International Conference on Computers in Education (ICCE 2014).* Nara. Japan: Academic Press.

Gamage, D., & Perera, I. F. (2015). Quality of MOOCs: A review of literature on effectiveness and quality aspects.*8th International Conference on Ubi-Media Computing (UMEDIA)* (pp. 224 - 229). IEEE. doi:10.1109/UMEDIA.2015.7297459

Glance, D. G., Forsey, M., & Riley, M. (2013). The pedagogical foundations of massive open online courses. *First Monday*, *18*(5). doi:10.5210/fm.v18i5.4350

Khan, B. (2003, February). A framework for open, flexible and distributed e-learning. *eLearn Magazine*. Retrieved from http://elearnmag.acm.org/featured.cfm?aid=640561

Khan, B. H. (2005). *Managing e-learning: Design, delivery, implementation, and evaluation*. Hershey, PA: Information Science Publishing. doi:10.4018/978-1-59140-634-1

Liyanagunawardena, T. R., Parslow, P., & Williams, S. (2014). Dropout: MOOC participants' perspective. EMOOCs 2014, the Second MOOC European Stakeholders Summit, (pp. 95-100). Lausanne, Switzerland: Academic Press.

Lyndon, W., & Loch, B. (2014). Academics' Perceptions on the Quality of MOOCs: An Empirical Study. *International Journal for Innovation and Quality in Learning, 2*(3), 53-63.

Macleod, H., Haywood, J., Woodgate, A., & Alkhatnai, M. (2015). Emerging patterns in MOOCs: Learners, course designs and directions. *TechTrends*, *59*(1), 56–63. doi:10.1007/s11528-014-0821-y

Margaryan, A., Bianco, M., & Littlejohn, A. (2015). Instructional quality of Massive Open Online Courses (MOOCs). *Computers & Education*, *80*, 77–83. doi:10.1016/j.compedu.2014.08.005

Merrill, M. D. (2002). First principles of instruction. *Educational Technology Research and Development*, *50*(3), 43–59. doi:10.1007/BF02505024

Nagashima, T. (2014). What Makes Open Education Thrive? Examination of Factors Contributing to the Success of Open Education Initiatives. *International Journal for Innovation and Quality in Learning, 2*(3), 10-21.

Pappano, L. (2012, Nov 14). The Year of the MOOC. The *New York Times*. Retrieved from http://www.nytimes.com/2012/11/04/education/edlife/massive-open-online-courses-are-multiplying-at-a-rapid-pace.html

Rodriguez, O. (2013). The concept of openness behind c and x-MOOCs (Massive Open Online Courses). *Open Praxis*, *5*(1), 67–73. doi:10.5944/openpraxis.5.1.42

Sangrà, A., Guàrdia, L., & Maina, B. (2013). MOOC Design Principles. A Pedagogical Approach from the Learner's Perspective. *eLearning Papers, 33*. Retrieved from https://www.academia.edu/5819373/MOOC_Design_Principles._A_Pedagogical_Approach_from_the_Learners_Perspective

Schoenak, L. (2013). A New Framework for Massive Open Online Courses (MOOCs). *Journal of Adult Education*, *42*(2), 98–103.

Shattuck, K. (2014). *Quality Matters Higher Education Rubric* (5th ed.). Retrieved from Quality Matters Program: https://www.qualitymatters.org/rubric

Siemens, G. T. (2015). The Role of MOOCs in the Future of Education. In C. Bonk, M. Lee, T. C. Reeves, & T. H. Reyolds (Eds.), *MOOCs and Open Education Around the World*. New York: Routledge.

Sun, P. C., Tsai, R. J., Finger, G., Chen, Y. Y., & Yeh, D. (2008). What drives a successful e-Learning? An empirical investigation of the critical factors influencing learner satisfaction. *Computers & Education*, *50*(4), 1183–1202. doi:10.1016/j.compedu.2006.11.007

Uvalic-Trumbic, S., & Daniel, J. S. (Eds.). (2013). *A Guide to Quality in Online Learning*. Retrieved from http://www.contactnorth.ca/tips-tools/guide-quality-online-learning

Yeager, C., Hurley-Dasgupta, B., & Bliss, C. A. (2013). cMOOCs and Global Learning: An Authentic Alternative. *Journal of Asynchronous Learning Networks*, *17*(2), 133–147.

Yousef, A. F., Chatti, M. A., Schroeder, U., & Wosnitza, M. (2014). What Drives a Successful MOOC? An Empirical Examination of Criteria to Assure Design Quality of MOOCs. *Advanced Learning Technologies (ICALT) IEEE14th International Conference*, (pp. 44-48). IEEE.

Chapter 8
Hispanic LEP, MOOCs, and Meetups

Ramón Talavera-Franco
Northeastern University, USA

ABSTRACT

The 21st Century demands the transformation of education into a more collaborative system. School stakeholders should strengthen the sharing of educational resources to make them more attainable for students. Hispanic LEP Meetups as MOOC communities of practice hubs explores the challenges of one of the minority groups living in the United States that has been affected by school segregation practices: the Hispanic Limited English Proficient (HLEP) community—and proposes an alternative for them to continue their education by using Massive Open Online Courses (MOOCs) and by taking advantage of meetups to develop local communities of practice.

INTRODUCTION

This chapter explores how Massive Open Online Courses (MOOCs) might be implemented as an educational alternative for the Hispanic Limited English Proficient (HLEP) community, and how *meetup.com* can promote communities of practice where HLEP students can learn from each other, receive support from Spanish-speaking tutors, and reduce the sense of isolation that characterizes online learning.

BACKGROUND

According to LEP.gov (n.d.), Limited English Proficient refers to "individuals who do not speak English as their primary language and who have a limited ability to read, speak, write, or understand English." With regard to this population, the Migration Policy Institute (2013) reports:

In 2011, there were 25.3 million Limited English Proficient (LEP) invividuals, both foreign-born and U.S.-born, residing in the United States. Over the past 20 years, the LEP share of the total U.S. population has grown from close to 6 percent in 1990 to about 9 percent in 2011. The total number of LEP individuals

DOI: 10.4018/978-1-5225-0466-5.ch008

has grown by 81 percent since 1990, and has established a relatively large presence in California, Texas, and New York [...] Of the total immigrant population in 2011, about half were LEP. Although most LEP individuals are foreign born, a sizable share (about 19 percent, or 4.8 million) of this population is native born. (Wathely & Batalova, 2013)

About 63 percent of the LEP population is considered Hispanic; 12.7 million are foreign-born and 16.4 million (63%) speak Spanish (Wathely, & Batalova, 2013); followed by Chinese (6.4%), Vietnamese (3.4%) and Korean (2.5%). According to this report, the LEP population whose first language is Spanish outnumbers any other group of language speakers in the United States. Moreover, it is expected that by 2050 the Hispanic population will grow to 132.8 million (30% of the total U.S. population) (Beaudrier, & Ducar, 2012), and the Hispanic school age population is projected, by that same year, to be 28 million (Fry, & Gonzalez, 2008). Hence the U.S. education system, at all levels, needs to be prepared to provide the Hispanic population in general, and the Hispanic LEP (HLEP) population in particular, the necessary tools—in English and in Spanish—to be competitive in the workforce and in life.

HLEPs and Education

About 63 percent of the LEP population is considered Hispanic (Wathely, & Batalova, 2013); and the Hispanic population growth expectation is almost 133 million by 2050 (Beaudrier, & Ducar, 2012). However, the current public school system has not implemented robust systems to help them achieve their educational goals. At a high school level, the Hispanic dropout rate is the largest in the country (44 percent) (NCES, 2010). At the university level, the yearly-average college tuition is $30,000 (Selingo, 2013), which, along with the high cost of student loans, makes college attendance challenging for Hispanic students in general and for Hispanic Limited English Proficiency students in particular.

Wathely, & Batalova (2013) argue:

As a group, the LEP population in the United States is less educated and more likely to live below the federal poverty line than the overall U.S. population. LEP individuals are slightly more concentrated in the working ages and are comprised of a relatively small share of children. Employed LEP men in 2011 were more likely to work in construction, extraction, and transportation occupation than English-proficient men, while employed LEP women were more likely to work in service and personal care occupations than English-proficient women (np.)

Closing the job achievement gap for the LEP community would represent a change in a paradigm that has affected their lives for years. In order to help the LEP community fulfill the American dream, the nation needs to invest in social capital and educational programs designed to retain or bring back minority groups to school. For example, creating a robust K-16 schooling infrastructure and policies, fostering the collaboration of non-profit and for-profit organizations in the development of educational programs, and adapting post-secondary, innovative initiatives such as Massive Open Online Courses (MOOCs) are critical and necessary steps. These and other K-16 programs will allow LEP groups to gain access to better educational services, and the possibility to scale in the social and economical ladder.

Massive Open Online Courses (MOOCs)

MOOCs are high quality, college-like online courses. Top universities such as Harvard, MIT, and Duke offer these courses to thousands of students around the world for free—or for a very low fee. By 2015, 534 universities around the world offered over four thousand MOOCs worldwide (Class Central, n.d.). The number of universities interested in participating in this educational approach continues to increase. Hence, the opportunity to learn almost any subject, without the necessity of attending a brick and mortar college, is becoming a reality. Thousands of students who want to improve their academic and professional skills are benefiting from MOOCs.

Online Learning for the Hispanic Community

Khan's e-Learning framework (2009) claims that a successful online learning system has to encompass the requirements of students, instructors, support services staff, and institutions. The author explains that e-learning accessibility, flexibility, affordability, and learner-centric approaches can fulfill students' requirements, whereas increased students' participation and the achievement of course goals can be significant for instructors. Moreover, the Ethical Dimension in Khan's (2009) e-Learning Framework suggests the importance of taking into consideration the different cultural, social, and political environments—especially when designing an online course that is intended to reach students from different countries and cultures.

Instructors in online environments should be sensitive to the diversity of students that they teach. Instructors who teach their online course globally, and in the English language, must be aware that they might be teaching students who speak languages other than English, and that some of them are probably not proficient in English. Hence, instructors must implement strategies such as discussion forums, Google hangouts, Skype calls, chats, etc., that motivate the dialogue between teacher-students and students-students. Kahn (2005) argues that:

When it comes to online synchronous and asynchronous discussions, a non-native speaker of the discussion forum may encounter difficulty in expressing clearly in his/her writing which may present him/her as different to other participants. The instructor or discussion moderator should be sensitive in situations like this (p. 299).

On the other hand, Ally (2004) argues that the behaviorist, cognitivist, and constructivist schools of thought might connect in the designing of an online course:

According to Etmer and Newby (1993), the three schools of thought can, in fact, be used as a taxonomy for learning: Behaviorists' strategies can be used to teach the what (facts); cognitive strategies can be used to teach the how (processes and principles); and constructivist strategies can be used to teach the why (higher-level thinking that promotes personal meaning, and situated and contextual learning) (p. 20).

The active participation of students is of vital importance in the construction of knowledge. Most of the time, the construction of knowledge does not come isolated from the environment but is enriched by it. When attending school, students have the possibility to interact with that environment and be nurtured by it. Additionally, they nurture their learning process from the constant interaction with their peers. If a core concept is not clear, students often turn to each other in search for an answer. It is easier and less stressful for students to learn, while building relationships and connections.

In an online environment, students do not get the interactions, relationships, and connections that they can build in a brick-and-mortar facility. Hence, online students need to find ways to develop an online community that supports them along the course. The use of social media such as Facebook, Twitter, or LinkedIn, and the constant participation in course discussion forums, Google hangouts or webinars can foster communication and create online communities that reduce the isolation that the online environment entails.

In the particular case of the LEP community, or the English as a Second Language (ESL) students, online communities can benefit their learning process so that they feel that—despite the language barrier—they belong to a community where everybody has the same language learning skills. Hence, the process of communication among LEP or ESL students is more fluid despite their possibility of making grammar or vocabulary mistakes when communicating using discussion forums or chat rooms. Moreover, an online LEP or ESL community can motivate students to express their feelings and fears regarding the course content, but—most importantly—to support each other by sharing their learning strategies, English language resources, and promoting emotional support to be successful along the course.

The next section explores how Hispanic LEP individuals can receive support from Massive Open Online Courses (MOOCs) to get the academic knowledge that has been accessible in the past only to those who can afford to attend college. Also, we will explore how school stakeholders and other non-profit leaders might join efforts to help Hispanic LEP MOOC students move their online communities to a physical space where they can meet face to face, discuss the subject-matter and start to build a community of practice that might produce ideas that benefit the participants and the society they live in.

LEP Communities and Job Opportunities

The Bureau of Labor Statistics (BLS) reports that "one-third of all job openings and nearly half of all new jobs created between 2008 and 2018 will require a postsecondary degree or credential" (Pandya, 2012). In this respect, the Information Technology (IT) sector is demanding highly qualified people to fill over half a million jobs, making it the largest job offering industry in 2015 (THI, n.d.).

The TechHire Initiative and MOOCs

To support the IT industry, President Obama launched the TechHire Initiative in 2015 to help citizens—including minorities—get well-paid jobs in the IT sector. The initiative is designed to provide necessary IT training in partnership with tech industries, universities, colleges and high-quality online courses providers (THI, n.d.) such as those offering Massive Open Online Courses (MOOCs).

Currently, MOOC providers such as edX, Coursera, and Udacity are affiliated with the TechHire initiative and offer their Computer Science and Programming courses to any student who wants to benefit from them. Certifications vary according to the MOOC provider and its partnerships with the IT industry. For example, Udacity, has designed a new kind of certification called a "nanodegree" (Nanodegrees, n.d.). Nanodegrees are granted after students successfully complete an average of four MOOCs related to an IT specialization, such as web design or data analysis, that are in high demand by the IT industry. AT&T, Google, and Facebook have partnered with Udacity to offer nanodegrees. For those participants that successfully finish these MOOCs, the partners offer internships and the possibility of landing a job.

Although this initiative will benefit a large number of students, the major drawback for LEP students is that all these MOOCs are offered in English. Despite the fact that MOOC providers such as Coursera or edX have started to include Spanish translations in their video lectures, the reading material, as well as the assignments and assessments, must be submitted in English. This means that for the Spanish-speaking LEP community, Obama's TechHire program is still out of reach to help advance their careers.

How can Spanish-speaking LEPs benefit from Obama's TechHire initiative? How can MOOCs implement a Spanish-speaking strategy to reach a higher percentage of the 16 million Spanish-speaking LEPs living in the United States? In order to do that, MOOC providers need to include partnerships with Hispanic non-profit organizations, Hispanic governmental affairs offices, and other Hispanic public and private organizations and foundations. Also, it is necessary to design public, academic spaces where Spanish-speaking LEPs can develop communities of practices to learn from each other.

Plan for Change

Hispanic LEP MOOC Coding Meetups as Communities of Practice

One way to integrate the Spanish-speaking LEP community in Obama's TechHire initiative is by including Spanish curricula as ancillary material in IT MOOCs and by promoting the opening of communities of practice meetups to local Hispanic LEPs. According to Wenger (1998) "[c]ommunities of practice are groups of people who share a concern or a passion for something they do and learn how to do it better as they interact regularly" (p. 1). According to Wenger, three characteristics are crucial for a group to be considered as a community of practice: 1) a common interest (domain), 2) people who meet to explore such interest (community) and 3) the knowledge and expertise shared from such interest (practice).

Communities of Practice

Community of practice theory is based on Bourdieu's theory of practice (1977). For Bourdieu the dynamic of a group is based on what the members of that group do (Borzillo et al., 2010). Bourdieu's theory comprises of three elements: a) field, b) capital (economic, cultural and social) and 3) habitus (Walther, 2014). As we can see, Bourdieu's theory of practice elements are embedded and adjusted into Wenger's (1998) community of practice theory.

On the other hand, Jeon et al. (2011) highlights the social constructivism perspective that a community of practice applies to its learning process. According to these authors, knowledge is linked to the active participation and collaboration of the agents as well as their expertise and passion (Jeon et al., 2011). Therefore, the sharing of thoughts and the dissemination of information can lead to innovative solutions to old problems (Li, & Jhang-Li, 2010).

MOOCs + MeetUps

There are different ways to develop a community of practice. In the recent years *Meetup.com* has contributed to the establishment of a large variety of communities of practice within the United States. *Meetup.com* is a for-profit online company that enables people who share common interests to meet online and organize monthly face-to-face group meetings (meetups) in a relaxed environment (About, n.d.). Sander (2005) claims that meetups allow people to expand their social networks. Also, that meetups "increase [participants] political power by aggregating their interests" (Sanders, 2005, p.6) and by motivating others to participate. Hence, this author argues that meetups are important in the development of social capital and in building communities.

Over 9,000 face-to-face meetups get together daily around the world (About, n.d.). In 2014, a young entrepreneur living in Düsseldorf Germany started a MOOC meetup to connect MOOC students that were taking an entrepreneurial MOOC (Goldberg, 2015). During these meetups attendees watched videos, discussed topics related to the entrepreneurial MOOC and local experts visited who helped to expand the information about the topic, and facilitate understanding and brainstorming sessions among the participants. As a result, participants developed a 'pitch' clinic for local entrepreneurs with a specific goal: to explore solutions that benefited their own community. By exploring their own reality and needs, they transformed the entrepreneurial MOOC curriculum and made it useful for their community.

Many meetups are conceived as informal study groups. *IDCourserians* (Firmansyah, 2015*)* is a group founded in 2013 by Coursera students in Indonesia. The objective is to provide a physical space were MOOC students can meet face-to-face, exchange experiences, promote networking, and cultivate communities of practice. *IDCourserians* concentrate on the individual's learning process based on an active interaction in a group. Attendees benefit by including their own culture in the understanding of a subject matter. As they relate their learning to their culture, they provide a fresh view on the subject matter and contribute to the development of a richer dialogue.

IDCourserians is an example of how meetups could be used in conjunction with IT MOOCs for Spanish-speaking LEPs. This kind of MOOC meetup can be adjusted to meet the needs of the LEP community. Spanish-speaking IT teachers and specialists can meet and help Spanish-speaking LEPs participate and benefit from Obama's TechHire initiative.

THE HISPANIC LEP CODING MOOCs MEETUP PLAN

The *Hispanic LEP Coding MOOCs MeetUp* (HLEPCMM) is a MOOC curricular plan of change that includes the participation of different public and private sectors and the inclusion of Spanish IT resources that can be incorporated as ancillary material during the *Hispanic LEP Coding MOOCs Hubs.*

Plan Proposal

"Aristotle [...] points out that human beings tend to have a natural inclination toward civil interaction with each other" (Sen, 2004, p.40). The lack of MOOC face-to-face interaction between teachers and students limits the process of learning by engaging in direct discussions and leads to a sense of isolation among students. MOOCs' online synchronous and asynchronous communication, supported by the implementation of discussion forums or chats, is a way to supplement the lack of direct communication that students get in brick-and-mortar facilities. Despite the creation of study groups for MOOC students within the online environment, and that many Spanish speakers create their own, few students actively participate. Those LEPs or ESL students who might like to participate in the English language forums frequently restrain their participation due to their consciousness of their own English writing limitations.

Hispanic LEP Coding MOOCs MeetUps (HLEPCMM) could be a solution to promote active participation among Spanish-speaking LEPs. By focusing on the student's needs, the meetup will be designed from a Hispanic perspective, taking into consideration the following:

1. Relevant MOOCs teaching IT subjects including computer coding,
2. Culturally relevant educational curricula,
3. Inviting environment,
4. Spanish tutoring,
5. Participation of local stakeholders, and
6. Participation of foundations.

The participation of these actors would be as follows:

1. **Hispanic or Pro-Hispanic Organization:** *Hispanic LEP Coding MOOCs* MeetUps might work better under the wing of a Hispanic organization. The Mexican American Legal Defense and Educational Fund (MALDEF) or the League of United Latin American citizens—just to mention two organizations— might take ownership of the program, or can help locate an organization that wants to be responsible of these meetups.
2. **Relevant Computer Programming and Coding MOOCs:** MOOCs platforms in partnership with the TechHire Initiative have computer and programming courses whose students would benefit from having access to meetups. It is recommended that the organization who takes ownership of the meetups, analyze which MOOC best suits the computer and programming job market in their cities, and what IT companies are participating in the TechHire Initiative when planning the curriculum.
3. **Culturally Relevant Educational Curricula:** Computer coding MOOCs could be supported with ancillary Spanish coding literature (links, books, e-books, etc.). There are significant collections of Spanish Programming and Coding Open Education Resources (OER) available from Hispanic universities such as the "Toda la UNAM en Línea" from the National Autonomus University of Mexico (TLUEL, n.d.), and other online resources offered by different Latin American higher education institutions.
4. **Inviting Environment:** The setting must include free Internet connection so students can connect to MOOC platforms during the meetups. The meetups should encourage BYOD (Bring Your Own Device). It would be helpful if the setting provided additional computers for those attendees who cannot comply with this policy. The setting could be furnished with Hispanic ornaments and include refreshments or food sponsored by Hispanic snack brands and local restaurants. A relaxing environment that reflects the culture of the students might encourage more participation, and motivate students to come back.
5. **Spanish Tutoring:** Meetup organizers can find partnerships with universities and community colleges interested in supporting tutoring as this will aid in finding Hispanic-origin Computer Science students and teachers who are interested in volunteering for the length of a course (typically 8 weeks). Spanish tutors are a key element for the success of the program since computer programming and coding are seen as a "new language" that LEPs have to learn on top of the English language. Hence, students need the help of a Spanish speaker who can culturally translate concepts that literal translation cannot. Tutors who volunteer in this program should understand the Hispanic culture and language to be able to connect with the students.
6. **Participation of Local Stakeholders:** State congressmen of Hispanic districts, local government offices for Hispanic affairs, local departments of education, Hispanic non-profit organizations, Hispanic media, and Hispanic Consulates should be invited to participate in this endeavor to create consciousness among the Hispanic community about the importance of Obama's TechHire initia-

tive. In the particular case of the Latin American consulates, they could promote the *Hispanic LEP Coding MOOCs Meetup* (HLEPCMM) in their facilities during office hours. According to the size and location of the consulate, they receive hundreds of people daily looking for passports and other official documents. Therefore, Latin American consulates might generate the interest in the Spanish LEP community to participate in this program, as well as to provide them with information about other MOOCs that might be of their interest.

7. **Participation of Foundations:** Foundations such as *Carlos Slim Foundation*, *Fundación Azteca América*, *Televisa Foundation* or any other foundation interested in Hispanic affairs could contribute with grants to pay for tutoring, Spanish ancillary material, and publicity. For example, Univision is always interested in facilitating information about education opportunities to the Hispanic community. In partnership with them, HEPCMM might reach and serve thousands of Spanish speakers. Moreover, Univision might be a promoter to establish *Hispanic LEP Coding MOOCs Meetups* (HLEPCMM) in different cities.

How Could This Project Be Carried Out?

Latin American consulates alliances with Hispanic organizations could help to launch the Hispanic *LEP Coding MOOCs Meetups* (HLEPCMH). The most active consulates in developing educational programs for the Hispanic population are the Mexican consulates through their *Plaza Comunitaria* initiative. *Plaza Comunitaria* is an effort to provide online elementary and high school education in Spanish (Medina, 2013, March 19). The Mexican consulates do not administer *Plazas Comunitarias*. They locate organizations that will be responsible of the *Plaza Comunitaria* and coordinate efforts with the different educational stakeholders involved. Since Mexican consulates have included *Plazas Comunitarias* as part of their services, and the Hispanic community already recognizes them as part of the educational services provided for their benefit, HLEPCMM could be easily incorporated as part of a *Plaza Comunitaria* service.

Implementation Steps

Consulates of Latin American Countries could Provide Support in:

- Locating the organization responsible in hosting the HLEPCMM.
- Finding Spanish tutors.
- Finding programming and computer science literature in Spanish from Latin American universities and Open Educational Resources (OERs).
- Promoting the LEPCMM at their consulates.

Organization hosting LEPCMM:

- Connects with Obama's TechHire initiative to get the necessary information to participate.
- Organizes and administers the HLEPCMM.
- Finds and invites possible Hispanic LEPs interested in participating in *Hispanic LEP Coding MOOCs Meetups.*
- Schedules a weekly HLEPCMM.
- Takes care of the setting of the HLEPCMM.

- Works with tutors to include Spanish ancillary material in the MOOCs curricula.

Local Spanish Media:

- Informs the local community where and how to participate in the HLEPCMM.
- Follows up with success stories.

Foundations and Local Stakeholders:

- Provide grants to maintain the optimal operations of HLEPCMM.
- Provide support according to their own mission for the Hispanic community.

By offering a place with the appropriate learning resources where people can meet and discuss the subject matter, it is expected that Hispanic LEPs learn IT skills to participate in Obama's TechHire initiative, benefit from it, improve their professional lives, and participate in the social and economic health of this country.

FUTURE RESEARCH DIRECTIONS

Topics such as how to develop pedagogical, psychological, linguistic, and sociological strategies to help the adult Hispanic LEP community to get the knowledge, abilities, and skills from MOOCs still needs to be studied. Moreover, how meetups can influence their learning process is also a topic for further research. The expectation with this Plan Proposal is to invite Hispanic organizations to put together the TechHire Initiative + MOOCs to motivate the HLEP community to continue their education to advance in their careers.

CONCLUSION

The Hispanic *LEP Coding MOOCs MeetUps* (HLEPCMM) could give students the opportunity to participate in the construction of curriculum from an Hispanic and LEP perspective. For example, HLEPCMM could explore multicultural diversity of opinions and creativity and help participants separate themselves from close systems and pre-setting goals. The HLEPCMM could also help participants to build social capital and expand social networks with people that share their own interest. Furthermore, they could be part of Obama's TechHire initiative and improve their lives both professionally and economically.

Hispanic LEPs are an important sector of the United States population and should receive the support needed in order to better contribute to their academic development and professional improvement. It is necessary to remember the following:

In 2000, American adults aged 25 and older who dropped out of high school were nearly twice as likely to be unemployed as high school graduates (6.4% vs. 3.5%; National Center for Educational Statistics 2002). Moreover, the median income of those who did not complete high school was substantially less *than the median income of high school graduates with no college education ($25,095 vs. $34,303 for men and $17,919 vs. $24,970 for women; National Center for Educational Statistics 2002) (Perreira et al. 2006, p. 511).*

MOOCs and the TechHire Initiative might reduce the numbers of the Hispanic LEP community from these statistics. Moreover, the development of Massive Open Online Courses to foster academic opportunities for minority groups in the United States supports the progressivism ideas of:

1. Promoting democracy,
2. Advocating for active learning, and
3. Exploring humanistic education that leads to growth and development (Ornstein et al., 2011).

They also build upon the reconstructionist ideas of education as a way to achieve social reform, from its precepts of "[e]quality of education; cultural pluralism; [and] international education" (Ornstein et al., 2011, p. 6). Hence, the development of *Hispanic LEP Coding MOOCs MeetUps* might be the answer to match solutions with the governmental rhetoric and make education attainable for all the Hispanic and other minority sectors of the nation.

REFERENCES

About Meetup. (n.d.). Retrieved from http://www.meetup.com/about/

Ally, M. (2004). Foundations of educational theory for online learning. In T. Anderson & F. Elloumi (Eds.), *Theory and practice of online learning* (pp. 3–31). Athabasca, AB: Athabasca University.

Beaudrier, S., & Ducar, C. (2012). Language Placement and Beyond: Guidelines for the Design and Implementation of a Computerized Spanish Heritage Language Exam. *Heritage Language Journal*, *9*(1), 77–99.

Borzillo, S., Aznar, S., & Schmitt, A. (2011). A journey through communities of practice: How and why members move from the periphery to the core. *European Management Journal*, *29*(1), 25–42. doi:10.1016/j.emj.2010.08.004

Bourdieu, P. (1977). *Outline of Theory of Practice*. Cambridge, UK: Cambridge University Press. doi:10.1017/CBO9780511812507

Class Central. (n.d). Retrieved from: https://www.class-central.com/universities

Firmansyah, M. (2015). Idcourserians, a MOOCs learning community in Indonesia. Teaching & Education Conference, Florence, Italy.

Fry, R., & Gonzalez, F. (2008). *One-in-five and growing fast: A profile of Hispanic public school students*. Pew Research Center. Retrieved from http://pewhispanic.org/files/reports/92.pdf

Goldberg, M. (2015). *MOOCs and Meetups together make for better learning*. Retrieved from: http://www.huffingtonpost.com/michaelgoldberg/moocs-and-meetups-togethe_b_6538414.html

Jeon, S. H., Kim, Y. G., & Koh, J. (2011). Individual, social, and organizational contexts for active knowledge sharing in communities of practice. Elsevier, 38, 12423-12431.

Khan, B. H. (2005). *Managing e-learning: Design, delivery implementation and evaluation.* Hershey, PA: Information Science Publishing.

Khan, B. H. (2009). The global E-learning framework. *Stride*, 42-51.

LEP.gov. (n.d.). *Limited English Proficiency (LEP). A federal interagency website*. Retrieved from: ww.lep.gov/faqs/faqs.html

Li, Y. M., & Jhang-Li, J. H. (2010). Knowledge sharing in communities of practice. *European Journal of Operational Research*, *207*(2), 1052–1064. doi:10.1016/j.ejor.2010.05.033

Medina, Y. (2013, March 19). *Plaza Comunitaria, Literacy programming @ the library*. Retrieved from: http://publiclibrariesonline.org/2013/03/plaza-comunitaria-literacy-programming-the-library/

Nanodegrees. (n.d.). Retrieved from: https://www.udacity.com/nanodegree

Ornstein, A., Pajak, E., & Ornstein, S. (2011). *Contemporary Issues in Curriculum*. Boston, MA: Allyn & Bacon.

Pandya, Ch. (2012). *Limited English Proficient workers and the workforce investment act: Challenges and opportunities*. Retrieve from: http://www.migrationpolicy.org/article/limited-english-proficient-workers-and-workforce-investment-act-challenges-and-opportunities

Perreira, K. M., Mullan Harris, K., & Lee, D. (2006). Making it in America: High school completion by immigrant and native youth. *Demography*, *43*(3), 511–536. doi:10.1353/dem.2006.0026 PMID:17051825

Sander, T. (2005). *E-association? Using technology to connect citizens: The case of Meetup.com.Annual meeting of the American Political Science Association*, Washington, DC.

Selingo, J. J. (2013). *College (Un)Bound: The future of Higher Education and what it means for students*. New York, NY: Houghton Mifflin.

Sen, A. (2004). How does culture matter? In Culture and public action (pp. 37-58). Stanford, CA: Stanford University Press.

TechHire Initiative. (n.d.). Retrieved from: https://www.whitehouse.gov/issues/technology/techhire

Toda la UNAM en Línea. (n.d.). Retrieved from: http://www.unamenlinea.unam.mx

U.S. Department of Education, Institute of Education Sciences, National Center for Education Statistics (NCES). (2010). *Tabla 130. Percentage of high school dropouts among persons 16 through 24 years old (status dropout rate) and number of status dropouts, by noninstitutionalized or institutionalized status, birth in or outside of the United States, and selected characteristics*. Retrieved from: http://nces.ed.gov/programs/digest/d12/tables/dt12_130.asp

Walter, M. (2014). *Repatriation to France and Germany. A Comparative Study Based on Bourdieu's Theory of Practice*. Wiesbaden: Springer Fachmedien. doi:10.1007/978-3-658-05700-8

Wathely, M., & Batalova, J. (2013). *Limited English proficient population of the United States*. Migration Policy Institute. Retrieve from: http://www.migrationpolicy.org/article/limited-english-proficient-population-united-states

Wenger, E. (1998). *Communities of Practice: learning, meaning, and identity*. Cambridge, UK: Cambridge University Press. doi:10.1017/CBO9780511803932

Chapter 9
Guidelines for Design and Implementation of Mobile Learning

Mohamed Ally
Athabasca University, Canada

Mohammed Samaka
Qatar University, Qatar

ABSTRACT

As technology evolves, there is a shift towards the use of mobile technology to deliver education both on-campus in a blended format and online delivery. This shift is moving at a very fast pace which is a major challenge for educational organizations which has to train staff and build the infrastructure for mobile delivery. Educators have to be trained on how to develop quality mobile learning materials, how to use the technology for the delivery, and how to provide quality support to students so that they are successful when using mobile technology to learn. This chapter provides guidelines for designing and implementing mobile learning.

INTRODUCTION

As more people around the world use mobile technology there will be an increasing need for designing and delivering education on mobile technology. There is a sense of urgency to develop learning materials for mobile learning because of the rapid increase in the use of mobile devices such as cell phones, smart phones, tablet PCs, web pads, and palmtop computers by learners and individuals for everyday tasks. By the end of 2016 there will be over four and a half billion mobile phones worldwide and mobile connection will bypass landline connections. As a result, there will be more access to information and learning materials from anywhere and at anytime, using these mobile devices (Ally et al., 2014). The trend in society today is learning and working "on the go" rather than having to be at a specific location to learn and work. Also, there is a trend towards ubiquitous computing, where computing devices will be invisible to the users because of the wireless connectivity of mobile devices. As a result, we are seeing

DOI: 10.4018/978-1-5225-0466-5.ch009

more use of mobile learning in education and training that will require development of quality mobile learning materials (Jalil et al., 2015). A good model for designing mobile learning materials is essential if there is to be quality mobile learning. Badrul Khan (2005) proposed a framework for developing learning materials that can be used for developing high quality mobile learning materials This chapter will describe how Badrul Khan Framework can be used to develop high quality mobile learning materials to meet the needs of a variety of learners.

BACKGROUND

There are many definitions of mobile learning. According to Ally (2004), mobile learning is the use of electronic learning materials with built-in learning strategies for delivery on mobile computing devices to allow access from anywhere and at anytime. O'Malley et al (2003) defined mobile learning as any sort of learning that happens when the learner is not at a fixed, predetermined location, or learning that happens when the learner takes advantage of the learning opportunities offered by mobile technologies. Traxler (2005) defined mobile learning as any educational provision where the sole or dominant technologies are handheld or palmtop devices. The definition of mobile learning we will be using in the chapter is "the delivery of learning materials and providing learning support on mobile devices to provide flexibility to the learner so that the learner can learn while they are mobile".

Because of the proliferation in the use of mobile technologies around the world, there is a significant interest in mobile learning to provide flexibility in learning. The design of the mobile learning interface from a pedagogical viewport is critical to promote success in learning (Subramanya & Yi, 2006). A systematic framework must be used for the design of mobile learning so that developers can produce high quality learning materials that meet the needs of learners. This chapter will describe how to design, develop, and deliver mobile learning materials using Badrul Khan's (2005) Framework (see Figure 1). However, it is important to discuss why mobile learning should be implemented in education and the benefits of mobile learning.

Benefits of Mobile Learning

Mobile learning contributes to global education since learners can access mobile learning materials from anywhere at their convenience regardless of time zones. Mobile devices are small enough to be portable, which allows learners to use the device from any location to interact with other learners from anywhere, and at anytime to share information and expertise, complete a task, or work collaboratively on a project. Learners can use the wireless capability of their mobile devices to access up-to-date and relevant learning materials from the web and to communicate with experts in the field that they are studying. Situated learning, which is the application of knowledge and skills in specific contexts, is facilitated, since learners can complete courses while working on the job or in their own space, and apply what they learn at the same time.

Mobile devices have many benefits because they allow for mobility while learning and working; however, there are some limitations to mobile devices that designers must be aware of when designing learning materials for delivery on mobile devices. Some of the limitations of mobile devices in delivering learning materials include the small screen size for the output of information, small or restricted input devices, low bandwidth, and challenges when navigating through the information. As a result, it is

Figure 1. Badrul Khan's framework for mobile learning
(Adapted by permission)

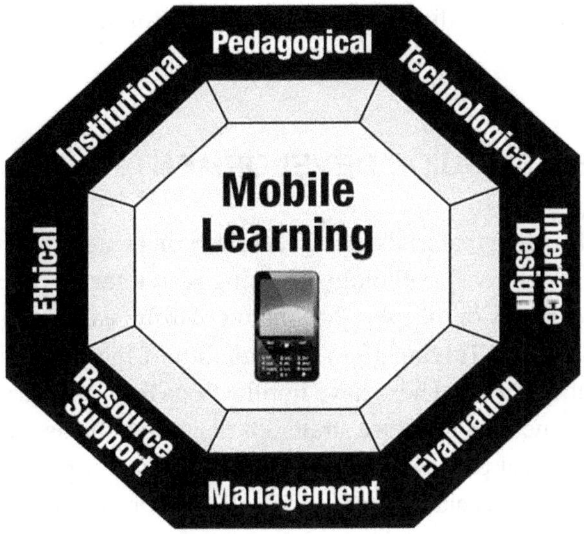

critical that the learning materials be designed properly for easy access and must include quality learner interaction (Ally, 2009). Khan's (2005) framework (see Figure 1) can be used to develop high quality mobile learning materials.

PEDAGOGICAL PRINCIPLES FOR DESIGNING MOBILE LEARNING

The first component of Badrul Khan (2005) Model (see Figure 1) is *pedagogical* which includes analysis and the use of proper methods and strategies for designing mobile learning materials. To maximize learning using mobile devices, proper pedagogical principles must be followed to take advantage of the capabilities of the mobile device and to compensate for the current limitations of the technology. The challenge for educators is to develop learning materials for access and display on mobile devices and to develop user interaction strategies on these devices. Also, designers of learning materials for mobile devices must use strategies to reduce the user's mental workload when using the devices to leave enough mental capacity to maximize deep processing of the learning materials. According to O'Malley et al. (2003), effective methods for presenting information on mobile devices and the pedagogy of mobile learning have yet to be developed.

Designers of information and learning materials have to aware of the limitations of screen size and input devices when designing for usability. Navigation techniques must allow users of mobile devices to go directly to the information and move back and forth with ease. Information should be targeted to the user needs when they need it and should be presented efficiently to maximize the display on the mobile device. To compensate for the small screen size of mobile devices, learning materials must use rich media to convey the message to the user. For example, rather than present information in text, graphics and pictures can be used to convey the message using the least amount of text. Graphic organizers can be used as the interface to allow users to get the big picture of the lesson and at the same time navigate to any part of the lesson. To present procedures and real life situations, video clips can be used to present real life simulations to the user. Also, the interface must be appropriate for individual users and the software system should have the intelligence to be able to customize the interface based on individual user's preferences.

LEARNING THEORIES TO GUIDE DEVELOPMENT

To prepare quality mobile learning materials, designers must of aware of learning theories that can guide development. According to cognitive psychology, learning is an internal process and the amount learned depends on the processing capacity of the user, the amount of effort expended during the learning process (Craik & Lockhart 1972; Craik & Tulving 1975), the quality of the processing, and the user's existing knowledge structure (Ausubel, 1974). These have implications for how learning materials should be designed for mobile devices. Educators must use strategies that allow the user to activate existing cognitive structures and conduct high level processing of the materials. Memory is enhanced when information is represented both in verbal and visual forms (Paivio, 1986). Presenting materials in both textual and visual forms will involve more cognitive processing, resulting in better storage and integration into long term memory (Mayer et al., 2004).

According to constructivism, learners are active during the learning process and they use their existing knowledge to process and personalize the information. Learners interpret information and the world according to their personal reality, and they learn by observation, processing, and interpretation, and then personalize the information into their existing knowledge base (Cooper, 1993). As a result, learning strategies for mobile learning must include strategies to allow learners to actively process and internalize the information. Learning is facilitated when learners can contextualize what they learn for immediate application and thus acquire personal meaning. According to Sharples (2000), mobile learning devices allow learners to learn where they are located and in their personal context. Also, mobile learning facilitates personalized learning since learners can learn in their own context from anywhere and anytime.

Design Principles for Mobile Learning Based on Learning Theories

Based on learning theories, the following guidelines are presented for the development of mobile learning materials to maximize the amount learned and to meet the needs of the user:

- Learning materials must be sequenced appropriately to promote learning. Proper sequencing will allow learners to have smooth transition between learning sequence and experience success as they complete the segments of the lesson. Common methods of sequencing include simple to complex, known to unknown, and knowledge to application.
- Learners should be informed of the learning outcomes so that they can plan for their learning sessions, set expectations, and search for resources to achieve the learning outcomes. Mobile learning allows learners to explore and discover additional learning resources because of the connectivity of mobile devices.

- Information should be chunked to prevent overload during processing in working memory for both humans and devices. This is based on Miller's (1956) observation that because of the limited processing capacity in human working memory, materials should be organized in seven plus or minus two chunks. To facilitate efficient processing in working memory, mobile learning materials should present between five and nine items on a screen.
- Learning strategies should be presented in different modes to make use of different parts of the brain to maximize processing for quality learning. Where possible, textual, verbal, and visual information should be presented to encourage encoding. Presenting information in different modes also accommodates individual differences in processing.
- Learning strategies that motivate learners should be included in lessons so that learners can be motivated to learn especially when using mobile technology in distributed learning. According to Keller (1983), instruction should capture and maintain the learners' attention, should be relevant to the learner, should build the learner's confidence, and learners should be satisfied with their achievements.
- A major advantage of using mobile technology in education is that learners can use the communication capabilities of the technology to communicate with each other and with the teacher or tutor. Collaborative and cooperative learning strategies should be implemented to facilitate coaching and mentoring during learning.
- Learning should be interactive to promote higher-level learning and to establish social presence and to help develop personal meaning. According to Heinich et al. (2002), learning is the development of new knowledge, skills, and attitudes as the learner interacts with information and the environment. Hirumi (2002) proposes a framework of interaction in online learning that consists of three levels. Level one is learner-self interaction, which occurs within learners to help monitor and regulate their own learning. Level two is learner-human and learner-non-human interactions, where the learner interacts with human and non-human resources. Level three is learner-instruction interaction, which consists of activities to achieve a learning outcome. In mobile learning, different types of interaction can be used to facilitate learning. At the lowest level of interaction, there must be learner-interface interaction to allow the learner to access and sense the information. The interface is where learners use their senses to register the information in sensory storage. In mobile learning, the interface is with the mobile device, to access the content and to interact with others. Once learners access the learning materials, there must be learner-content interaction to process the information. Learners navigate through the content to access the components of the lesson, which could take the form of pre-learning, learning, and post-learning activities. Learners should be given the ability to choose their own sequence of learning, or should be given one or more suggested sequences. As learners interact with the content, they should be encouraged to problem solve, apply, assess, analyze, synthesize, evaluate, and reflect on what they learn. During the learner-content interaction, learners process the information to transform it from short-term to long-term memory. The higher the level of processing, the more associations are made in the learners' long-term memory, which results in higher-level learning.
- Mobile technologies allow learners to be connected to the outside world and to other learners during the learning process. Hence, learning is taking place in a networked environment (Siemens, 2004). Because of the information explosion, learners should be allowed to explore and research current information. Learners of the future need to be autonomous and independent learners so that they can acquire current information to build a valid and accurate knowledge base.

- Because of globalization, information is not location-specific, and, with the increasing use of telecommunication technologies, experts and learners from around the world can share and review information. Learning and knowledge rests in a diversity of opinions. As a result, learners must be allowed to connect with others around the world to examine others' opinions and to share their thinking with the world. Mobile learning promises to help learners to function in a networked world where they can learn at any time and from anywhere (Ally & Avgoustos, 2014; Avgoustos & Ally, 2013; Ally, 2005;).
- Because of the information explosion, learners of the future must be willing to acquire new knowledge on an ongoing basis. Mobile learning strategies must give learners the opportunity to research and locate new information in a discipline so that they can keep up-to-date in the field. The Internet is expanding education into a global classroom, with learners, teachers, and experts from around the world. As a result, learners must network with other learners and experts to make sure that they are continually learning and updating their knowledge.

TECHNOLOGICAL CONSIDERATIONS FOR MOBILE LEARNING

In order for mobile learning to be successful, the infrastructure must be in place for learners to access the learning materials and for the teacher to provide support in mobile learning. There are two strategies that are being used for the mobile hardware when implementing mobile learning. One option is for the organization to provide the mobile technologies to learners. This is efficient for the organization since the technology can be standardized across the organization and will require support for a limited number of mobile technologies. A second option that is being adopted by some organizations is Bring Your Own Device (BYOD). In this approach, learners bring their own mobile device to school to use for learning. This provides flexibility since learners can also take the device with them anywhere and anytime to learn. This approach is cost effective since the educational organization does not have to provide the mobile technology; however, the organization must make sure that the learning materials can be accessed on a variety of mobile devices. Responsive design must be used that will allow for delivery on any mobile device. Also, the mobile learning system must have the intelligence to detect which mobile devices the learners are using and format the learning materials for different devices.

Educational organizations must also make sure that learning materials that are web-based can be downloaded efficiently on learners' mobile devices. For users in remote locations with low bandwidth or with limited wireless access, information that takes a long time to download should be re-designed to facilitate efficient download. For example, low resolution graphics should be used or a description of the graphic should be provided. Another option is to develop applications (apps) and ask learners to download the apps on their mobile devices; this will require occasional connection to the Internet to download the apps.

To provide support to learners in mobile learning, the teacher must track learner progress and provide appropriate feedback. Learning Management Systems (LMS) are available for mobile learning to deliver learning materials to learners, to track performance, and to allow learners to interact with each other and with the teacher using forums and chats. However, the use of LMS on mobile devices requires that learners have reasonable connectivity to the server to access the learning materials.

INTERFACE DESIGN FOR MOBILE LEARNING

Designers of learning materials for delivery on mobile devices must use effective interface design techniques to make the learning process sufficiently efficient and flexible to meet the needs of learners. The mobile device interface should cater for users' individual needs since the interface must coordinate the interaction between the user and the information (Chong et al., 2004). To compensate for the small screen size of the display of the mobile device, the interface of the mobile device must be designed properly. The interface can be graphical and should present limited information on the screen to prevent information overload in short-term memory. The system should contain intelligent software agents to determine what the user did in the past and adapt the interface for future interaction with the information. The software system must be proactive by anticipating what the user will do next and provide the most appropriate interface for the interaction to enhance learning. Users must be able to jump to related information without too much effort. The interface must allow the user to access the information with minimal effort and move back to previous information with ease. For sessions that are information intense, the system must adjust the interface to prevent information overload.

Some ways to prevent information overload include presenting less concepts on one screen or organizing the information in the form of concept maps to give the overall structure of the information and then presenting the details by linking to other screens with the details. The interface must also use good navigational strategies to allow users to move back and forth between displays. Navigation can also be automatic, based on the intelligence gathered on the user's current progress and needs. Below are key strategies to build the interface and learning materials for mobile learning:

- Because of the small size of current input devices, learning materials must be designed to require minimum input from users. Input can use pointing or voice input devices to minimize typing and writing. Because mobile devices allow information to be accessed from anywhere at anytime, the device must have input and output options to prevent distractions when using the mobile devices. For example, if someone is using a mobile device in a remote location, it may be difficult to type on a keyboard or use a pointing device. The mobile technology must allow the user to input data using voice input or touch screen.
- Intelligent software systems can be built to develop an initial profile of the user and then present materials that will benefit the specific user, based on the user profile. As the intelligent agent interacts with the user, it "learns" about the user and adapts the format of the information, the interface and navigation pattern according to the user's style and needs. Knowing the user needs and style will allow the intelligent software system to access additional materials from the Internet and other networks to meet the user's needs.
- Information and learning materials can be presented to the user in a personalized style or a formal style. In a learning situation, information should be presented in a personalized style since the user of the mobile device may be in a remote location and will find this style more connected and personal. Mayer et al. (2004) found that learners who received a personalized version of a narrated animation performed significantly better on a transfer test when compared to learners who received a non-personalized, formal version of the narrated animation. They claimed that the results from the study are consistent with the cognitive theory of learning where personalization results in learners processing the information in an active way, resulting in higher level learning and transfer to other situations.

- Strategies should be used to allow learners to perceive and attend to the information so that it can be transferred to working memory. Learners use their sensory systems to register the information in the form of sensations so that the information can be process efficiently for transfer. Strategies to facilitate maximum sensation should be used. Examples include the proper location of the information on the screen, the use of colors for highlighting, the pacing of the information, and the mode of delivery (audio, visuals, animations, or video). Learners must receive the information in the form of sensations before perception and processing can occur; however, the learner must not be overloaded with sensations, which could be counterproductive to the learning process.
- Information critical for learning should be highlighted to focus learners' attention. For example, headings should be used to organize the details, and formatted to allow learners to attend to and process the details under the headings.
- Learners should be told why they should take the lesson, so that they can attend to the information throughout the lesson. This is critical for motivation and to focus on the learning especially for learners on the move and those who reside in remote locations.
- The difficulty level of the material must match the cognitive level of the learner, so that the learner can both attend to and relate to the material. Links to both simpler and more complicated materials can be used to accommodate learners at different knowledge levels.
- Interface and learning strategies must match the learning style of learners. Learners' learning styles can be determined by a learning style analysis tool such as the Kolb Learning Style Inventory (Kolb, 1984). Mobile learning materials should include activities for different learning styles, so that learners can select appropriate activities based on their preferred learning style.
    - Concrete-experience learners prefer specific examples in which they can be involved, and they relate to peers more than to people in authority. They like group work and peer feedback, and they see the instructor as a coach or helper. These learners prefer support methods that allow them to interact with peers and obtain coaching from the tutor.
    - Reflective-observation learners like to observe carefully before taking any action. They prefer all the information be available for learning, and they see the tutor as the expert.
    - Abstract-conceptualization learners like to work more with things and symbols and less with people. They like to work with theory and to conduct systematic analyses.
    - Active-experimentation learners prefer to learn by doing practical projects and participating in group discussions. They prefer active learning methods and interact with peers for feedback and information. They tend to establish their own criteria for evaluating situations.
    - Adequate supports should be provided for learners with different learning styles.
- Because of the limited processing capability of humans, information should be organized or chunked in segments of appropriate and meaningful size to facilitate processing in working memory. A learning session on a mobile device can be seen as consisting of a number of segments sequenced in a pre-determined way or sequenced based on the user needs. Information and learning materials for mobile devices should take the form of information and learning objects that are in an electronic format, reusable, and stored in a repository for access anytime and from anywhere. Information objects and learning objects allow for instant assembly of learning materials by users and intelligent software agents to facilitate just-in-time learning and information access. Giving learners the ability to access learning materials from electronic repositories will empower the learners to select resources to meet their needs.

- High level concept maps should be used to show the important concepts in the information and the relationship between the concepts, rather than presenting information in a textual format. High level concept maps and networks can be used to represent information spatially so that learners can see the main ideas and their relationships (Novak, Gowin, & Johanse 1983). Use of graphics in mobile learning materials will minimize the amount of textual materials learners have to read on the small device screen (Tarasewich, 2008).

EVALUATION IN MOBILE LEARNING

After the mobile learning materials are developed with the appropriate interface and the technologies are selected and implemented, it is important to evaluate the effectiveness of the learning materials and the delivery system. Also, the learners' performance must be evaluated to determine whether the mobile learning lessons facilitate learning and improve performance. The effectiveness of the delivery system must also be evaluated so that it can be improved to meet learners' needs. Survey questionnaires can be used to get feedback on the delivery system from learners.

Mobile learning lesson must use evaluation techniques to allow learners to evaluate themselves to determine whether or not they have achieved the learning outcome. This becomes even more important when mobile learning is implemented in a distance education format. Also, feedback should be provided to learners so that they can monitor how they are doing and take corrective action if required. Feedback can be provided immediately with the mobile device and can take different forms such as text, audio, or video because of the multimedia capability of the mobile technology.

MANAGING THE DEVELOPMENT AND DELIVERY OF MOBILE LEARNING

For efficiency in design, development, and delivery and for the development of high quality learning materials, proper procedures and standards must be followed and proper project management techniques must be implemented especially if many organizations are involved in the mobile learning development projects. Below is a list of common reasons why mobile learning development projects fail; this shows the need for proper project management techniques.

- *The instructors/tutors who will deliver the mobile learning course are not involved during the development.* It is critical to involve the person who is instructing or tutoring the course. The instructors or tutors could be part of the development team or they could be reviewers of the developed product.
- *The quality of the mobile learning material is not up to standard.* Good process management must be used throughout the project to make sure the standard identified in the analysis stage of the project and set by the project sponsors are maintained throughout the project.
- *The learning materials have too many errors.* Throughout the project, good quality assurance and quality control techniques must be used to prevent error in the learning materials. Quality assurance should be used to ensure techniques are in place to prevent errors from occurring in the learning materials. These include hiring staff with the right skills to work on the projects, division of the course content into manageable pieces, and using the right software to develop the materials.

Quality control techniques must be used to detect errors in the learning materials. Some quality control techniques include expert review and pilot testing with the target audience.

- *The scope of the project changes during the development of the products.* It is acceptable for the users and the sponsors of the project to make minor changes to the scope of the projects; however, if there are too many changes or the changes are major, the project may get out of hand and may fail. When this happens, the project manager must ask for an official revision of the project scope and must request the additional resources that are required to successfully complete the project.
- *Not enough resources were allocated to complete the project.* Before a mobile learning project is started, there must be a detailed work plan, which specifies the resources required to complete the tasks for the project. Each partner in the project is expected to contribute resources to complete the project. The project manager must get commitment for the resources from the project sponsor before the project is started.
- *The budget for the project is too low.* Proper costing techniques must be used to get an accurate cost for the project. If the money available is less than the cost for completing the project, the project manager should request additional funding; otherwise, the project should be delayed until additional funding is acquired or the project should be cancelled.
- *Not enough communication between project team members.* Interaction between team members is critical, especially for collaborative projects. The project managers must involve all team members in the project. Communication technology must be in place to allow team members to communicate with each other.
- *Lack of commitment from upper management.* For collaborative mobile learning projects, upper management from all participating institutions must be sponsors for the project and must commit to the successful completion of the project. If upper management from a collaborative institution is not committed to complete the project, then other partners should be approached to join the project.
- *Team members not trained properly to complete their assigned tasks.* This is critical since mobile technologies are still emerging and are changing at a very fast rate. If team members do not have the right skills, the quality of the learning materials could be affected. Upon hiring, team members' knowledge and skills should be assessed to determine if they have the expertise to work on the project. If there is a gap, then appropriate training should be provided to fill the gap.

The duration and complexity of mobile learning projects vary considerably. These projects are difficult to manage because of the number of team members involved and the multidisciplinary background of the team. Projects normally involve several team members performing interrelated activities, coordinated by a project manager to make sure there is effective use of resources to complete the project in an efficient and timely manner. A typical mobile learning development team could include a project manager, instructional designer, content experts, editor, technical experts and a steering committee. In some projects, members of the development team could be in different locations and time zones. The challenge for the mobile learning project manager is how to manage a project that uses a virtual team with team members in different location and in different time zones.

Most of problems that result in failed mobile learning projects is the result of poor project management. Below is a list of principles that project managers must follow when managing projects to develop mobile learning materials.

1. Involve the project sponsors and users. The sponsors are the ones who fund the project and could cancel the project at any time; hence, it is critical to inform the sponsor on the progress of the project and any changes required to complete the project. If there are changes, especially to the scope, the sponsor must be informed and the appropriate approval obtained. The users of the product or system are the instructors or tutors and learners. They should be involved in the development of the project or involved in the review of the materials.
2. Divide the project into phases and specify activities for each phase. Projects with phases are easy to manage and the output from one phase feeds into the next phase. Standard phases for developing mobile learning course materials are analysis, design, development, and implementation.
3. Prepare standards for the mobile learning materials. The standards should be set and communicated to the team members so that they can complete their tasks according to the standards. The will ensure quality learning materials are produced.
4. Convince stakeholders that the project is a good investment. Mobile learning development projects could be expensive and take a long time to complete. The project manager must justify the cost of the project by specifying the benefits of the project.
5. Divide the end product into small segments and complete one segment at a time. If the outcome of the project is to develop a course, the project team should divide the course into modules and develop one module at a time. The process for the first module can then be refined for subsequent modules.
6. Design for the future so that the materials can be used for a long time. When developing materials for mobile learning, the project team should think about future application and target audience so that the materials can be used for a long time without many changes.

Feasibility Analysis

After the analysis and design phases, feasibility analysis must be completed to determine whether the mobile learning project is worthwhile to continue. Feasibility is a measure of how beneficial the project will be to the learners and to the institutions. There are four types of feasibility:

- **Operational Feasibility:** Does the mobile learning material suit the learners and will they use the materials to improve their knowledge and skills? Will the developed materials help learners achieve the learning outcomes for the course or lesson? If the learning materials will not meet learners' needs, then it will not be feasible to continue with the project.
- **Technical Feasibility:** Do learners have the technical expertise to use the mobile technology while learning the materials and do they have the necessary hardware and software to access and interact with the materials and the instructor? If the institution does not have the technical infrastructure to deliver the mobile learning materials, they will not be used.
- **Schedule Feasibility:** Will the project be completed in a reasonable time? If the project will not be completed on time to meet the institution needs, it may not be worthwhile to complete the project.
- **Cost Feasibility:** What cost benefits will be realized from the mobile learning project? Is it worth the investment? After the analysis and design phases, cost benefit analysis should be conducted to determine whether it is worthwhile to invest in the development of the learning materials.

PROVIDING SUPPORT TO LEARNERS IN MOBILE LEARNING

There must be support for learners in mobile learning for the learning to be effective. The role of the teacher is as a facilitator of learning rather than a deliverer of instruction. The use of ICT as a support tool is important in mobile learning. Depending on the geographic distribution of learners, the teacher can use synchronous or asynchronous communication tools to communicate and interact with learners. The support for using the technology could be synchronous where the teacher and learners interact in real time or asynchronous where the interaction is done at different times. In synchronous learning, support is provided in real time using two-way text, two-way audio, or two-way video. The student and the teacher are able to interact with each other in real time. In the asynchronous mode, there is a delay in the communication between the teacher and learners. For example, in computer conferencing, learners post their comments and other learners and the teacher respond at a later time. Hence, as teachers start using emerging technology, their roles will change drastically to function effectively in the new learning environment (Ally, 2002). The teacher role will shift from a dominant person in front of the classroom to being a facilitator of learning by managing the learning process, providing one-to-one coaching to learners, and supporting and advising learners. As a result, teachers will have to be trained to use ICT effectively in education.

Teachers must be trained on how to be good facilitators for mobile learning. The teacher has to facilitate learning by role modeling behavior and attitudes that promote learning, encourage dialogues, and use of appropriate interpersonal skills. The teacher must be trained on how to recognize different learning styles and how to cater for the different styles. An effective teacher must recognize that learners have different styles when learning and some learners prefer certain strategies than others. The teacher should use techniques that will satisfy and develop different learning styles and should include activities for the different styles to allow learners to experience all of the learning activities. Also, appropriate learning support should be provided depending on the learning style of the learner (Ally & Fahy, 2002).

The teacher should be trained on the importance of feedback and how to provide effective and constructive feedback to learners. Timely feedback is important in learning to maintain presence in the learning process. Teachers should make learners feel comfortable and should show enthusiasm about the course materials to keep learners motivated. As a result, appropriate training on when and how to provide feedback to learning is critical in facilitating learning. The teacher has to adapt to learners' needs and provide timely feedback to learners. Motivating learners can be done by letting them know what they are learning is beneficial and then challenging learners by suggesting additional learning activities.

The teacher must be a good problem solver to interpret learners' problems and provide solutions to the problems. This implies that the teacher must have the content expertise to solve content problems. The teacher solves content problems by keeping up to date in the field, interpreting learners' questions, communicating at the level of the learner, providing remedial activities, and conducting follow up on help provided. Interaction with learners requires good oral and written communication skills. Also, the teacher is required to develop and revise courses on an on-going basis. As part of the problem solving process, the teacher needs good listening skills to understand what the learner is saying in order to respond to the learner.

The teacher must be trained on how to use the technology effectively to promote learning. This is critical in education since the teacher must model proper use of the technology. The teacher should be patient, project a positive image, enjoy working with learners, and be a good role model.

ETHICAL CONSIDERATIONS IN MOBILE LEARNING

The use of mobile learning in education improves access to education since learners can learn anywhere and at anytime. However, the learning materials must be appropriate for different cultures since different cultures have different values and needs. Also, there should be no biases because of cultural, geographical, and economic differences. One of the variables that designers tend to ignore when they develop learning materials for mobile devices is the user of the devices. Different users have different learning styles and some users may be more visual while others may be verbal (Mayer & Massa, 2003). Preferences and strategies must be included and information presented in different ways to cater for different learning styles and preferences (Ally & Fahy, 2002). Graphic overviews can be used to cater to users who prefer to get the big picture before they go into the details of the information. For the active learners, information can be presented on the mobile device and then the device will give the user the opportunity to apply the information. For the creative users, there must be opportunities to apply the information in real life applications so that they go beyond what was presented. The learning materials and information have to be designed with the user in mind to facilitate access, learning, and comprehension. Also, the user should have control over what they want to access so that they can go through the learning materials based on their preferred learning styles and other preferences.

INSTITUTIONAL ROLE IN MOBILE LEARNING

Educational organizations must have policies that promote the implementation of mobile learning and service standards for successful delivery of mobile learning. For example, there should be policies on hardware and software to be used for mobile learning. Also, there must be policies on the ethical use of mobile technologies to prevent malicious use of mobile technology. It is important to have policies on how to authenticate learners when they access learning materials and policies on keeping learners' information private and confidential,

In mobile learning, as in other delivery methods, support services must be available for learners using information and communicate technologies. Examples of necessary services include academic advising, counseling, service specials needs learners, and technical support.

CONCLUSION

The proliferation of mobile devices and globalization is determining what learners learn, from where and when they learn and how they learn. Mobile devices can be used to deliver information and learning materials to users, but the materials must be designed properly to compensate for the small screen of the devices and the limited processing and storage capacity of users' working memory. Learning materials for delivery on mobile devices must be designed to meet the needs of individual learners and provide flexibility to learn from anywhere and at anytime. Following the framework (see Figure 1) developed by Badrul Khan will ensure quality development of mobile learning materials.

The challenge for designers of learning materials for mobile devices is how to standardize the design for use on different types of devices. Intelligent software agents should be built into mobile devices so that most of the work is done behind the scenes, minimizing input from users and the amount of information presented on the display of the mobile devices. Also, intelligent agents should be built to detect the mobile device the learner is using and format and present the information for the specific device (Chen & Hsu, 2008). This will allow users to use their existing devices, rather than having to purchase new devices.

In the past, the development of learning materials for mobile devices concentrated on the technology rather than the user. Future development of learning materials for mobile devices should concentrate on the user to drive the development and delivery of mobile learning materials. Learning materials need to use multimedia strategies that are information rich rather than being mostly text and should follow sound learning and interface design theories.

While mobile devices, like smartphones, have small screens, with the advent of the iPad and similar larger format mobile devices, the limitations are lifting on the amount of information that can be presented comfortably on screen. As mobile technologies advanced there will be significant changes in how users interface with such devices. Sensors within the human body will communicate with the device and there will be increasing use of biometrics (Hook, 2008). Human emotions could determine when learning takes place and there could be direct communication between the human brain and the device. Also, in the future, devices could be embedded in the human body. The challenge to educators is how to design for the rapid changes in technology.

ACKNOWLEDGMENT

This publication was made possible by NPRP Grant # 4 - 125 - 5 – 016 from the Qatar National Research Fund (a member of Qatar Foundation). The statements made herein are solely the responsibility of the authors.

REFERENCES

Ally, M. (2004). *Using learning theories to design instruction for mobile learning devices.* Paper presented in the Mobile Learning 2004 International Conference Proceedings, Rome, Italy.

Ally, M. (2009). Mobile Learning: Transforming the delivery of education and training. Athabasca University Press.

Ally, M., & Fahy, P. (2002). Using learners' learning styles to provide support in distance education. In *Proceedings of the Eighteenth Annual Conference on Distance Teaching and Learning*.

Ally, M., Grimus, M., & Ebner, M. (2014, March). Preparing Teachers for a Mobile World to Improve Access to Education. Prospects. *Quarterly Review of Comparative Education*, *44*(1), 43–59. http://www.doi.org/10.1007/s11125-014-9293-2

Ally, M., & Lin, O. (2005). An intelligent agent for adapting and delivering electronic course materials to mobile learners.*Proceedings of the International Mobile Learning Conference*.

Ally, M., & Tsinakos, A. (2014). Increasing access through mobile learning. Commonwealth of Learning, Vancouver, Canada.

Ausubel, D. P. (1974). *Educational psychology: A cognitive view*. New York: Holt, Rinehart and Winston.

Chen, C. M., & Hsu, S. H. (2008). Personalized intelligent mobile learning system for supporting effective English learning. *Journal of Educational Technology & Society*, *11*(3), 153–180.

Chong, P. H. J., So, P. L., Shum, P., Li, X. J., & Goyal, D. (2004, November). Design and implementation of user interface for mobile devices. *IEEE Transactions on Consumer Electronics*, *50*(4), 1156–1161. doi:10.1109/TCE.2004.1362513

Cooper, P. A. (1993). Paradigm shifts in designing instruction: From behaviorism to cognitivism to constructivism. *Educational Technology*, *33*(5), 12–19.

Heinich, R., Molenda, M., Russell, J. D., & Smaldino, S. E. (2002). *Instructional media and technologies for learning*. Pearson Education.

Hirumi, A. (2002). A framework for analyzing, designing, and sequencing planned e-learning interactions. *The Quarterly Review of Distance Education*, *3*(2), 141–160.

Hook, K. (2008). Knowing, communicating, and experiencing through body and emotion. *IEEE Transactions on Learning Technologies*, *1*(4).

Jalil, A., Beer, M., & Crowther, P. (2015). Pedagogical Requirements for Mobile Learning: A Review on MOBIlearn Task Model. *Journal of Interactive Media in Education*, *12*(1), 1–17.

Khan, B. H. (2005). *Managing e-learning: Design, delivery, implementation and evaluation*. Hershey, PA: Information Science Publishing. doi:10.4018/978-1-59140-634-1

Khan, B. H. (Ed.). (2007). *Flexible learning in an information society*. Hershey, PA: Information Science Publishing. doi:10.4018/978-1-59904-325-8

Kolb, D. A. (1984). *Experiential learning: Experience as the source of learning and development*. Englewood Cliffs, NJ: Prentice-Hall.

Mayer, R. E., Fennell, S., Farmer, L., & Campbell, J. (2004). A personalization effect in multimedia learning: Learners learn better when words are in conversational style rather than formal style. *Journal of Educational Psychology*, *96*(2), 389–395. doi:10.1037/0022-0663.96.2.389

Mayer, R. E., & Massa, L. J. (2003). Three facets of visual and verbal learners: Cognitive ability, cognitive style, and learning preference. *Journal of Educational Psychology*, *95*(4), 833–846. doi:10.1037/0022-0663.95.4.833

Miller, G. A. (1956). The magical number seven, plus or minus two: Some limits on our capacity for processing information. *Psychological Review*, *63*(2), 81–97. doi:10.1037/h0043158 PMID:13310704

Novak, J. D., Gowin, D. B., & Johanse, G. T. (1983). The use of concept mapping and knowledge Vee mapping with junior high school science learners. *Science Education*, *67*(5), 625–645. doi:10.1002/sce.3730670511

O'Malley, C., Vavoula, G., Glew, J. P., Taylor, J., Sharples, M., & Lefrere, P. (2003). Guidelines For learning/teaching/tutoring in a mobile environment. *MOBIlearn Project Report*. Retrieved from http://www.mobilearn.org/results/results.htm

Paivio, A. (1986). *Mental representations: A dual coding approach*. Oxford, UK: Oxford University Press.

Sharples, M. (2000). The design of personal mobile technologies for lifelong learning. *Computers & Education*, *34*(3-4), 177–193. doi:10.1016/S0360-1315(99)00044-5

Siemens, G. (2004). *A learning theory for the digital age*. Retrieved from http://www.elearnspace.org/Articles/connectivism.htm

Subramanya, S. R., & Yi, B. K. (2006). User interfaces for mobile content. *Computer*, *39*(April), 85–87. doi:10.1109/MC.2006.144

Tarasewich, P., Gong, J., Nah, F.F., & DeWester, D. (2008). Mobile interaction design: Integrating individual and organizational perspectives. *Information Knowledge Systems Management, 7*, 121–144.

Traxler, J. (2005). Defining mobile learning.*Proceedings of the 2005 IADIS International Conference*.

Tsinakos, A., & Ally, M. (2013). *Global Mobile Learning Implementations and Trends*. Beijing, China: CCRTVU Press.

Chapter 10
Learning without Boundaries MOOCs in Malaysia:
Design and Implementation

Rachel Thomas Tharmabalan
University Science Malaysia, Malaysia

ABSTRACT

Massive Open Online Courses (MOOCs) have been the focus of mainstream media which promises to change the entire world education and create a meaningful impact for all. This book chapter reports on the design and implementation of Malaysian MOOC. Malaysia is the first country in the world to implement the MOOCs initiative for public universities. This new platform of learning is also in line with the National Higher Education Strategic Plan that includes life-long learning, e-Learning, internationalization, and knowledge transfer.

INTRODUCTION

The use of ICT in the Malaysian education system is relatively modest. Many plans to introduce ICT at the school-level were announced at the onset of the establishment of Multimedia Super Corridor1 (MSC) in 1996, such as the "Smart School" project – an effort to encourage ICT integration in school-based learning; the "SchoolNet" initiative – a project to provide broadband Internet to Malaysian schools; and "EduWebTV" – a YouTube-based portal for educational videos for consumption by school teachers and students (see MSC, 2011).

At the higher education level, Siti Rafidah et al. (2009) found that ICT resources were modest in both public and private higher education institutions, although usage of ICT, either for communication or information retrieval, was common amongst faculty members and students. The level of ICT proficiency amongst faculty members was good, although those in public universities tended to be more cautious and resistant to use ICT in their teaching activities. These observations demonstrate that to a notable extent, technology has played a relatively limited role in teaching and learning, both at the primary and secondary school and higher education levels. The initial interest in MOOCs within the last two years

DOI: 10.4018/978-1-5225-0466-5.ch010

suggests that Malaysia is open to exploring the use of MOOCs in higher education, although currently there is no indication if Malaysian MOOCs will take the form of currently prominent platforms such as Coursera, edX and Udacity. This is not necessarily a negative observation, as the adoption of MOOCs in Malaysia may have very different connotations than those of the North American-based providers. The pervasiveness of ICT, which has had its own tremendous impact in higher education, is a disruptive force that cannot be ignored. Higher education institutions must learn to adapt and innovate to ICT, or run the risk of being rendered obsolete or irrelevant. We view MOOCs as one such positive disruption that can hopefully lead to a modernised, effective, and compatible higher education model in Malaysia, although it must be acknowledged that the greatest contention at this point is whether or not Malaysian academia can deal with the threat of such an innovation that is represented by MOOCs.

BACKGROUND

The landscape of the open education movement is changing every day and is gaining momentum throughout the world. Terms such as Web 2.0, social media, OCW, OER, and the latest one, MOOCs, have been the focus of mainstream media stories on education, including those posted on educational websites and blogs. The emergence of MOOCs—or Massive Open Online Courses—is a phenomenon that has the potential to disrupt the education world and to significantly impact achievement of the 'Education for All' movement of the United Nations.

MOOCs are simply online courses aimed at large-scale participation that are available by open and free access via the Internet. They are similar to university courses but currently do not tend to offer academic credit unless explicitly stated. The whole idea of MOOCs is to empower interested learners from around the globe who lack access to higher education.

The first MOOC was offered by the University of Manitoba in 2008 (Fini, 2009), and since then MOOCs have been gaining momentum as two trends converge, namely the inability of physical campuses to cater to the higher education needs of the growing world population and the maturity of the technology that makes broadband internet more accessible and reliable.

A number of leading world universities are offering a growing number of courses to a worldwide audience, and many others are seriously considering joining the movement. MOOCs are delivered over a number of platforms; some of them are widely available, such as Coursera, Udacity, Canvas, OpenLearning, and Course-Builder (by Google), whereas others are institution-specific platforms, such as Edx (jointly developed by Harvard and MIT) and Class2Go (developed by Stanford) (Pappano, 2012). Although the MOOC approach is currently not as common as that of traditionally offered courses, it is being heralded as the beginning of a revolution in the education industry. As Seth Godin (2012), an American entrepreneur, noted, the future of education is flexibility and mobility. The traditional approach to education appears to be no longer viable for the future in which we will be living. With that being said, there is still no clear and sustainable model of MOOCs in terms of education and technology. Hence, universities worldwide seem to be riding the wave of change without proper direction.

Malaysia currently is ranked seventh in Asia with regards to Internet penetration, with an estimated figure of 67% of the citizens who use the Internet (Zainol- Abidin et al., 2014). This puts Malaysia in a good position to harness the power of online learning to widen access to good quality content, enhance the quality of teaching and learning, lower the cost of delivery, and bring Malaysian expertise to the global community. Generally speaking, Malaysia has sufficient places at its institutions of higher learning for its citizens. The country has a healthy combination of 20 public and 45 private universities as well as foreign university campuses, including those of the University of Nottingham, Monash University, Curtin University, Swinburne University of Technology, Newcastle University, and Herriot Watts University. The Malaysian Government plans to attract more international students to Malaysia to make it a regional educational hub. Careful implementation of MOOCs can be a useful tool for achieving this goal, as it can play a role in internationally branding Malaysian universities and in providing risk-free trials to interested international students who can attend MOOCs at the universities (or programmes) of their choice before registering. We postulate here that it would be useful for Malaysian universities to offer an array of high-quality MOOCs that reflect the standards of the higher education in the country.

In Malaysia, the development of online material is slowly improving with the implementation of the National e-Learning Policy (DePAN). Universiti Putra Malaysia (UPM) became the first university in Malaysia to launch an online platform for its academic staff to impart knowledge to anyone interested. Universiti Teknologi Malaysia (UTM) and Universiti Malaya (UM) also became members of the Open Educational Resources (Consortium, and more Malaysian universities are expected to join the bandwagon.

Rani Wenel (Yunus, 2014), a chief operating officer for MyMobileUniversity, stated that Malaysia has the infrastructure to implement MOOCs and, in fact, it has already been outlined in the National Education Blueprint. It is only a matter of setting an effective timeline and not delaying its implementation. This scenario provides another reason to start up global Malaysian MOOCs that focus on providing an education and learning environment that is advanced, up-to-date with worldwide trending, and aimed at enhancing people's achievement in their lives.

PutraMOOC, which uses the OpenLearning platform, is UPM's latest public service to the community and the world at large. It offers courses on various areas of knowledge that are made available through video lectures, interactive forums, chats, quizzes, and other forms of assessment.

Dato' Seri Idris Jusoh (Kuah, 2015), Malaysia's Education Minister, said he had first broached the subject of MOOCs with representatives of public universities in Malaysia on 11 March 2014 and that these universities registered themselves as part of the OpenCourseWare (OCW) Consortium first before migrating to MOOCs. He also said that Malaysia is the first country in the world to implement a MOOCs initiative for public universities. The initiative was meant to ensure that online learning was implemented by institutions of higher learning (IPTAs) and that class time was reduced. His ministry, he said, would consider allocating RM500 million under the 11th Malaysia Plan for all public universities to implement MOOCs. The minister said he also saw the potential of expanding the programme to a stage that would allow working people to opt to study part-time to fulfill their desire to earn a university degree if they did not have one. This new platform of learning is also in line with the Malaysia's National Higher Education Strategic Plan that includes life-long learning, e-learning, internationalization, and knowledge transfer.

As of 2015, 13 selected Malaysian public universities will work together with MIMOS, a research centre for Information Communication Technology under the purview of the Ministry of Science, Technology, and Innovation to upload the e-content of their courses to a local MOOC platform (Juhary, 2014). What this means is that the government is adamant about the use of not only digital technologies but also the concept of resource sharing and content development.

PRESENT SCENARIO AND POLICIES

The National e-Learning Policy was introduced by the Ministry of Education (MOE) of Malaysia as an innovative approach to improving human capital development, and it is in line with the implementation of MOOCs, which were launched on 16 April 2011 (The National Higher Education Strategic Plan Beyond 2020, 2007). It focuses mainly on Malaysian higher education institutions (HEIs) and on a better developed nation, which would lead to Malaysia being recognised both nationally and internationally. These efforts will lay a solid foundation for producing graduates who are smart, responsible, independent, self-reliant, and who can compete globally. In addition, it will provide an equitable higher education system for all in accordance with the concept of life-long learning. Dato' Seri Mohamed Khaled Nordin, the Minister of Higher Education of Malaysia, developed the National e-Learning Policy, which was designed to provide a framework and direction for implementation of e-Learning in HEIs for a period of 5 years (2011 to 2015). Through this policy, HEIs was able to progress into better aspects of e-learning. This new movement must be utilised to the maximum level to improve the quality of teaching and learning. The policy was executed in three phases: Beginning Phase (2011–2012), Filling Phase (2013–2014), and Optimal Phase (2015). This policy has an e-learning framework that encompasses five main pillars: infrastructure, organisational structure, professional development, curriculum and e-content, and enculturation (see Figure 1). These pillars are key drivers for implementing e-learning education for all by teaching and learning using online learning pedagogy or online and distance learning, supported by information and communication technology.

The pillars and scope of Key Performance Index (KPIs) outlined in DePAN are shown in Table 1.

Apart from that, the current blended learning approach, which is being practiced in Malaysia, supports or replaces the face-to-face learning mode. The requirement is that a threshold of a minimum of 30–80% of the learning content should be conveyed online.

Figure 1. National e-learning policy
(Ministry of Education Malaysia 2004)

Table 1. Pillar and key performance index (KPIs)

Pillar	Key Performance Index (KPIs)
Infrastructure	• Broadband • Help Desk • ICT Equipment
Organisation	• Mission • Plan • Team Leadership • Policy • e-Learning Unit
Curriculum and e-Content	• Curriculum • e-Content Development • e-Assessment • e-Learning Skills
Professional Development	• Skills • Knowledge • Attitude
Enculturation	• Readiness to Use • Incentive and Motivation

CURRENT STATUS OF E-LEARNING IN TERTIARY EDUCATION INSTITUTIONS

On the other hand, an interesting question begs to be asked – what is the state of e-learning in Malaysian tertiary education institutions at this present moment in time?

In the tertiary sector across the globe, Robertson (2003), Guri-Rosenblit (2005), and Njenga and Fourie (2010) found many difficulties and problems faced by national governments and education providers in the tertiary sector. For instance, although e-learning, as a novel idea, is being embraced in many parts of the world, the actual deployment of e-learning infrastructures and implementation of e-learning based instructional methodologies are still patchy even in more developed regions.

In Malaysia, several empirical studies were carried out by Embi (2010; 2011) and Embi & Adun (2010) to collect actual data on e-learning in Malaysian higher education institutions. The studies were endorsed and fully funded by the Malaysian Ministry of Higher Education. The following are three salient findings by Embi and Adun based on data gathered from public tertiary institutions (several private institutions failed to provide any form of data to the researchers):

- **Staffing:** First and foremost, the biggest challenge to e-learning deployment seems to be the lack of highly trained staff members and low incentives given to staff members who are directly responsible for e-learning deployment. In other words, the IT departments in Malaysian higher education institutions are not fully staffed with e-learning experts.
- **Web 2.0 Use:** Another finding is that only one third of public higher education institutions in Malaysia allow their academic staff members and students to use Web 2.0 applications for teaching and learning in a formal manner.
- **Faculty Commitment:** The third finding is that nearly two third of all academic staff members in local public universities report low motivation to incorporate e-learning tools and materials in their day-to-day teaching. In addition, nearly half of the teaching staff also report that they lack commitment towards using e- learning as part of their teaching portfolio. These academic staff

members find it hard to balance between using and developing e-learning tools and materials with classroom teaching and academic research activities. Time constraint and lack of personal expertise are clearly debilitating factors for e-learning deployment at this moment in time in Malaysian higher education.

PREVIOUS OUTCOMES AND RESULTS

The MOOC Implementation Committee conducted a study of every university's achievements based on the DePAN implementation plan. The findings of this study are crucial for assessing the readiness of universities to accept and implement DePAN at the university level. Some of the important findings from the study are listed as below:

1. Twelve universities have prepared 1MB broadband facilities at the university level with a wifi coverage area exceeding 60% of the campus.
2. Six universities have prepared 100% online materials for the students' convenience.
3. Students from seven universities have fully utilised e-learning (100%).
4. All universities have a platform for e-learning that was developed either by the university or with open source software.

Objectives of the "Big Idea"

"Big Idea" is a team of people grouped together by the Ministry of Education to draft out the *Malaysian Education Blueprint for Higher Education: Transforming Higher Education for Excellence* which was launched in September 2014. This Blueprint is supposed to guide Higher Education for 10 years. The working committee consists of both local and international stakeholders. A total of 10 big ideas were set in place together with key strategies to achieve it. Big Idea #3 was tailored specifically for MOOCs.

The objectives of the implementation of MOOCs are as follows:

1. To increase the quality of teaching and learning (T&L) through the use of OER/OCW/MOOCs of world-recognised universities, and flipped classroom/blended learning in T&L.
2. To optimize the sharing of expertise and resources through learning without borders.
3. To bring the country's HEIs niche area to global arena.
4. To increase the visibility, positioning, and branding of Malaysia as the disseminator of knowledge at international level.
5. To increase public access to high quality content through creative and interactive learning experiences.
6. To save costs, all university courses/IPTA equivalents will be managed by one university and adapted by the other IPTAs.

Some of the key strategies include:

1. To start up a National e-content development team.
2. Create new niche areas in e-content.
3. Implement innovative Learning and Teaching strategy (flipped and blended).

4. Personalized learning environments.
5. New engagement and collaboration with reputable institutions.
6. Ensure Malaysian HEI presence in International MOOC consortium.
7. DevelopMyMOOC platform.

Through the implementation of MOOCs, student learning time will be retained, independent learning will be increased, and lecturers' efforts in T&L can be optmised. This will allow:

1. IPTAs' niche areas, such as Sustainability Study, Tropical Diseases, Islamic Finance & Business, Halal Industry, and Tropical Biodiversity to be brought to global standards
2. Malaysia's name to be recognised at the global level through international consortia and widened education access to society in an effort to encourage life-long learning

Blue Ocean Strategy: Eliminate, Reduce, Increase, Create

MOOCs will indirectly eliminate pedagogical methods that only utilise conventional methods of T&L. Lecturers should ignore the negative reception to innovation in T&L and support the effort to create an environment conducive to learning.

The application of MOOCs can also reduce costs, as the development of courses will be handled by a university and the course will be shared among other IPTAs in Malaysia. Additionally, the number of lecturers in the same field can be reduced, allowing focus on fields that are more in need of manpower. Through increased virtual learning, time spent on teaching can be reduced, which would allow more focus on discussion and debate of ideas in the classroom.

The increase of MOOC usage in pedagogy will refine the quality of T&L so that it moves in a more interactive and creative direction. The community's access to higher learning can also be increased with the implementation of the MOOC concept in IPTAs.

A meaningful learning environment can also be created through the interaction between local and foreign students via the MOOC concept. The idea of borderless learning can be achieved by involving students from various higher learning institutions across the globe.

Implementation of the Big Idea (Activities and Programmes)

The MOOC Implementation Plan consists of two implementation phases. The first phase involves development of four general subjects: Islamic Civilization and Asian Civilization TITAS, Ethnic Relations, Internet Technology literacy, and Entrepreneurship as shown in Figure 2. These subjects will be uploaded to a platform that will be developed further. At the same time, 13 IPTAs will have to identify at least 20 videos to be uploaded to the platform. All universities will be required to register for the OCW Consortium as an early step before migrating to MOOCs. Universities are also encouraged to register on the mooc.org platform.

The second phase will involve the development and uploading of other general subjects into the same platform.

Figure 2. Malaysian MOOCs

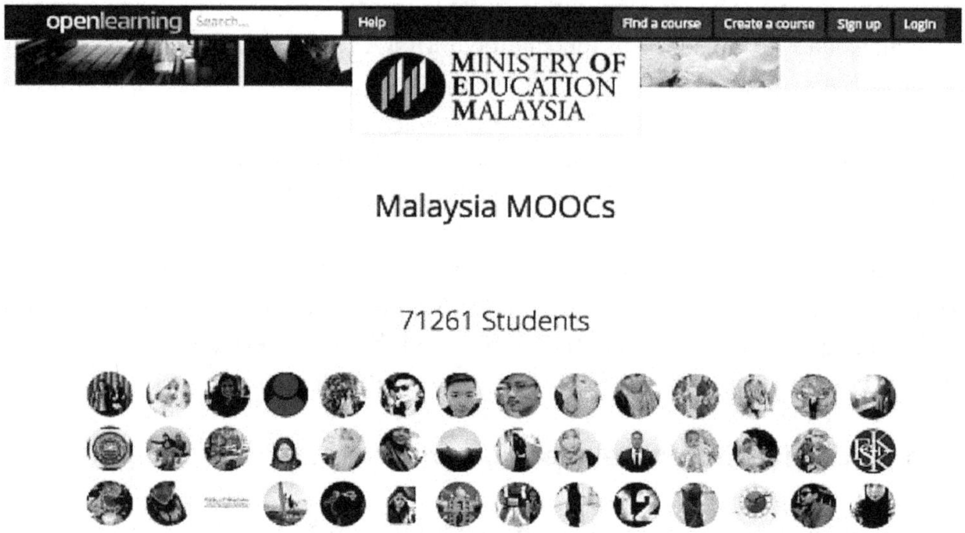

In addition, The Higher Education Leadership Academy (AKEPT) has taken on a major role in promoting awareness of the importance of MOOCs as shown in Figure 3. MOOC training for trainers (TOT) workshops have been conducted at Malaysian universities to introduce MOOCs as a part of the tertiary education offered in our country. Top-notch professionals were hired to develop the TOT programme. The aims of this programme are to allow:

- Development of modules for design and the delivery of MOOCS.
- Design training for courseware developers.
- Design training for technical personnel.

Figure 3. The road to MOOC@Malaysia

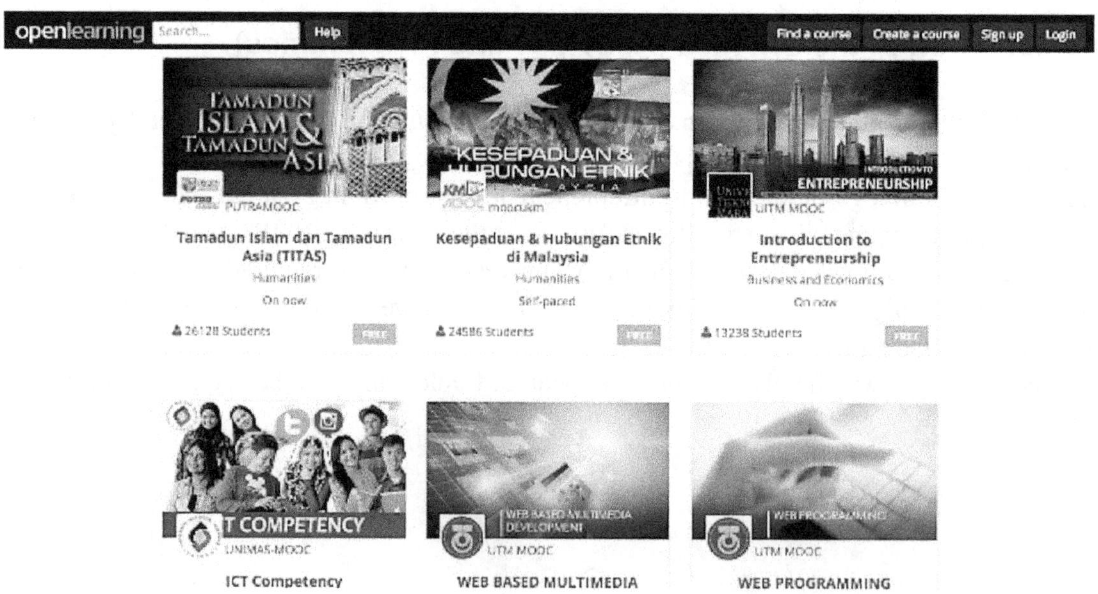

Some of the topics included in the training are:

- Overview, instructional design, content development, copyright issues, online facilitation and collaboration, and online assessment.
- MOOC specific design.
- MOOC implementation strategies for active and engaging learning.
- Flipped classrooms, blended learning, best practices, case studies, challenges, and opportunities.

Budget for Implementation of the Big Idea

Long-term costs of implementing MOOCs involve the costs required to upgrade infrastructures, equipment, and platforms; development of e-content, and providing training. The required allocation for expenditures for 5 years is still in discussion with the University and the government.

CURRENT STATUS

Taylor's University College offered the first MOOC course in Malaysia on 13 March 2014. The topic was entrepreneurship, and it was offered using the OpenLearning.com platform. In addition to 60 on-campus students, this MOOC attracted 2581 online students from 115 countries (Al-Atabi & DeBoer, 2014). This course was followed by the launch of PutraMOOC, Malaysia's public university, in April 2014. A major trial run was conducted on 17 July 2014, and it involved three different platforms (Open4Learning, OpenLearning, and Coursite).

OpenLearning was chosen as the main platform because it provides many social media-like features, such as forums to enable students to comment and receive comments that encourage interaction while learning. Currently there are 11 different MOOCs available on OpenLearning, with a total enrolment of 72,554 students. OpenLearning has other interesting features, including karma points that are gained through positive comments from peers and badges that can be issued either automatically or when a certain learning goal is achieved. These features, together with a live progress bar, encourage learning and collaboration throughout the course. The number of enrollees is expected to grow by leaps and bounds, as the Malaysian MOE has made it mandatory that 30% of courses offered at public HEIs be online as of 2015.

E-LEARNING SUSTAINABILITY

Having invested heavily on the infrastructure and training of lecturers in e-learning, the Ministry of Higher Education realized the urgency to optimise the use of e-learning and to make it sustainable. Therefore, several mechanisms to drive e-learning are being put in place by Ministry of Higher Education, and these will be described in the following sections.

Mechanisms to Drive E-Learning for the MOHE's Caps

For E-Learning under the MOHE's First Phase of the National Higher Education Strategic Plan (2007–2010), the foremost target set for e-learning Critical Agenda Projects (CAPs) required public institutions to make an e-learning platform available by 2010. The plan was perceived as a directive to every HEI to focus on e-learning, and it seems to have succeeded. In April 2011, the MOHE launched the National e-Learning Policy, which was based on five pillars: infrastructure, organisational structure, curriculum and e-content, professional development, and enculturation. All 13 Key Performance Indicators (KPIs) were set to be achieved in phases, which will end in 2015, the targeted year when e-learning is supposed to be fully optimised in Malaysia. Some of the other things included in the KPIs are having good Internet connectivity, incorporation of Web 2.0 tools, training staff in e-learning, a proper governance structure, and a reward system. With the inclusion of the new KPIs, all HEIs have no choice but to chart their e-learning implementation according to the timeline given, although some of them are still trying to determine their e-learning infrastructure and choice of Learning Management System.

The University of Malaya, the oldest university in Malaysia, made it compulsory for all lecturers to use e-learning for at least one of their undergraduate courses. As time progressed, the success of e-learning KPIs became more critical, and HEIs decided to consolidate their efforts and learn from each other. This led to the formation of the Council of Malaysian Public HEIs e-Learning Coordinators (MEIPTA), which was formed in 2007. MEIPTA acts as a platform for cooperation in the field of e-learning among Malaysian public universities (see Figure 4). The portal is hosted by the University of Malaya. The council meets at least three times a year at various HEIs to discuss issues such as the latest development in e-learning and best practices, such as incentive and reward systems, used by the respective member institutions. This collaboration is expected to push Malaysia further to the front in terms of E-Learning and MOOCs.

Figure 4. MOOC@Malaysia: mobilising people

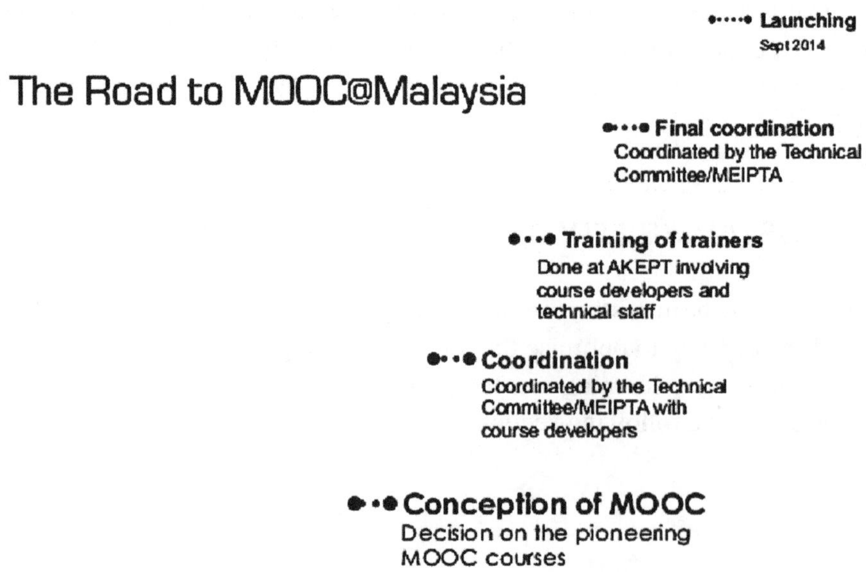

SOLUTIONS AND RECOMMENDATIONS

Suggested Models

The strategies in making MOOCs a reality are related to accessibility, support services, assessment, and certification. In order to ensure constant availability, learning materials should be stored in multiple physical servers as well as on cloud hosting services. To ensure easy accessibility, the software, hardware, and network used must be suitable for the needs of online courses and learners. As MOOCs involve high numbers of learners and users, excellent support services are crucial. Two models can be used to serve this purpose.

Khan's E-Learning Framework

The first model involves Badrul H. Khan's e-Learning framework (Khan, 2009), which is one of the best and most comprehensive theoretical e-learning models. E-Learning can be defined now as Khan (2009) stated:

A innovative approach for delivering well designed, learner-centred, interactive, and facilitated learning environment to anyone, anyplace, anytime, by utilising the attributes and resources of various digital technologies along with other forms of learning materials suited for open and distributed learning environment. (p. 42)

This framework can be divided into three major domains:

1. The educational sector contains pedagogical, ethical, and evaluation dimensions.
2. The technological sector contains technology and interface design dimensions.
3. The managerial sector contains institutional, resource support, and management dimensions.

The emergence of this framework had a great impact on the evolution of e-learning that has taken place in all learning sectors over the last 13 years. It provided a logical basis for e-learning instructional designers to design and implement an effective learning environment using the interactions afforded by computers and the Internet. The Khan framework is widely utilised today.

From our point of view, the Khan framework is a complete educational planning and evaluation system that can be defined as an e-education framework for technology-enhanced education. Redefining the framework as e-education shows that the Khan framework could be used for other educational technologies. However, slight modifications could improve the framework.

In the other model, the main academic instructor is aided by a number of tutors and facilitators. Through this model, MOOCs are managed through artificial intelligence, which can play an instructive or assisting role. Other aspects that need to be considered when developing successful MOOCs are assessment and certification. Because many of the learners who sign up for particular courses are committed to MOOCs, is it a good idea to provide them with certificates.

Although MOOCs are only in the early stages of development, they are expected to transform and evolve over time to create new approaches to online learning. The collaborative spirit of MOOCs that encourages an interactive, user-led perspective in higher education should be appreciated by all HEIs.

In addition, proper planning should take place when developing MOOCs. Since the council's formation, council members felt that there was a need to develop a generic e-learning policy that could be used as a guideline for all institutions, especially those without a policy in place. The experience of policy formulation has put the council in a significant position to contribute to the development of the national e-learning policy.

FUTURE RESEARCH DIRECTIONS

The potentially significant role MOOCs can play should be acknowledged in the larger context of lifelong learning. This is crucial not only to determine the best move forward where MOOCs are concerned, but also to leverage on MOOCs as an innovation that can boost the lifelong learning cause in this country. Malaysia has declared lifelong learning as the third pillar in human capital development: an educational agenda equally important to the school and higher education systems and one that emphasises the creation of learning opportunities for the entire population, whether for formal, non-formal, or informal learning interests. We believe that MOOCs may hold the key to intensifying lifelong learning efforts and we hope to see that future developments will go beyond the needs of higher education and university students. Future research could also be carried out to integrate life-long learning concepts and practices in the current e-learning policies. Future collaborations between Asia and Europe could be further enhanced in terms of publications, research, and content development.

CONCLUSION

The implementation of e-learning has been an uphill battle for HEIs in Malaysia. For more than 10 years HEIs in Malaysia have been engaged in providing new learning experiences to students through the use of e-learning. Initial efforts were made by individual HEIs to equip themselves with e-learning infrastructure and know-how. However, many HEIs have fallen into the trap of regarding e-learning as a fad, and e-learning was seen as an effort to provide technology as tools but very little attention was paid to the use of technology to achieve the learning outcomes needed by 21st century graduates. Realizing the need to put in place a mechanism for successful implementation of e-learning, the MOHE established CAPs for e-learning, approved development of a council of e-learning coordinators in public HEIs, and launched the national e-learning policy. The goal is to drive change and transform teaching and learning through the use of e-learning in public universities. With the introduction of the CAPs and the policy for e-learning, the hope is that HEIs will be guided to implement e-learning to achieve the vision of effective T&L. The challenge for HEIs in Malaysia is to keep researching the best ways to support learning, especially through the use of technology by students, lecturers, and staff. The challenge is also to develop a curriculum that takes into consideration the rate of change in digital technology and to manage the transformation.

Malaysia also needs to move away from a mass production delivery model to one in which technology-enabled innovations are harnessed to democratise access to education and offer more personalised learning experiences to all students. Blended learning models will become a staple pedagogical approach in all HEIs. Students will benefit from a robust cyber infrastructure that can support the use of technologies such as videoconferencing, live streaming, and MOOCs. Malaysian HLIs should and will develop

MOOCs in their niche areas of expertise while also participating in international MOOC consortiums and building the Malaysia education brand globally. To achieve these outcomes, the Ministry will work together with HLIs to build the capabilities of the academic community and to explore the establishment of a national e-learning platform to co-ordinate and spearhead content development.

Key initiatives include:

1. Launching MOOCs in subjects of distinctiveness for Malaysia, such as Islamic banking and finance, in partnership with high profile international MOOC consortiums such as EdX and Coursera, so as to build Malaysia's global brand.
2. Making online learning an integral component of higher education and life long learning, starting with the conversion of common undergraduate courses into MOOCs and requiring up to 70% of programmes to use blended learning models.
3. Establishing the required cyber infrastructure (physical network infrastructure, information structure, platform, devices, and equipment) and strengthening the capabilities of the academic community to deliver online learning at scale.

REFERENCES

Al-Atabi, M., & DeBoer, J. (2014). (2014). Teaching entrepreneurship using Massive Open Online Course (MOOC). *Technovation*, *34*(4), 261–264. doi:10.1016/j.technovation.2014.01.006

Embi, M. A. (Ed.). (2010). Amalan, Keberkesanan & Cabaran Pelaksanaan e-Pembelajaran di IPT Malaysia. WP Putrajaya: Kementerian Pengajian Tinggi Malaysia.

Embi, M. A. (Ed.). (2011). *E-Learning in Malaysian Higher Education Institutions: Status, Trends, & Challenges*. Putrajaya: Department of Higher Education, Ministry of Higher Education.

Embi, M. A., & Adun, M. N. (Eds.). (2010). e-Pembelajaran di IPTA Malaysia. Bangi & WP Putrjaya: Universiti Kebangsaan Malaysia &Kementerian Pengajian Tinggi Malaysia.

Fini, A. (2009). The Technological Dimension of a Massive Open Online Course: The Case of the CCK08 Course Tools. *The International Review of Research in Open and Distance Learning*, *10*(5). Retrieved from http://www.irrodl.org/index.php/irrodl/article/view/643/1402

Grodin, S. (2012). *Stop stealing dreams: On the future of education and what we can do about it.* Seth Grodin at TEDxYouth@BFS. Retrieved from https://www.youtube.com/watch?v=sXpbONjV1Jc&feature=share

Guri-Rosenblit, S. (2005). Eight paradoxes in the implementation process of eLearning in higher education. *Higher Education Policy*, *18*(1), 5–29. doi:10.1057/palgrave.hep.8300069

Juhary, J. (2014). Perceived Usefulness and Ease of Use of the Learning Management System as a Learning Tool. *International Education Studies.*, *7*(8), 23–34. doi:10.5539/ies.v7n8p23

Khan, B. H. (2009). E-learning - The Global e-Learning Framework. In STRIDE Handbook 8 (pp. 42-52). New Delhi: The Indira Gandhi National Open University (IGNOU).

Kuah, G. O. (2015). *UPM Blazes Trail in Online Platform to Impart Knowledge to All.* Retrieved from http://www.upm.edu.my/berita/details/putramoocbi?LANG=en

Multimedia Super Corridor. (2011). *Policy on ICT in Education Malaysia - 2010.* Retrieved from http://www.mscmalaysia.my/sites/default/files/pdf/publications_references/Policy%20on%20ICT%20in%20Education%20Malaysia%202010.pdf

Njenga, J. K., & Fourie, L. C. H. (2010). The myths about e-learning in higher education. *British Journal of Educational Technology*, *41*(2), 199–212. doi:10.1111/j.1467-8535.2008.00910.x

Pappano, L. (2012, Nov 14). The Year of the MOOC. The *New York Times*. Retrieved from http://www.nytimes.com/2012/11/04/education/edlife/massive-open-online-courses-are-multiplying-at-a-rapid-pace.html

Robertson, H. J. (2003). Toward a theory of negativity teacher education and information and communications technology. *Journal of Teacher Education*, *54*(4), 280–296. doi:10.1177/0022487103255499

Siti Rafidah, M. D. (2009). The Use of ICT in Public and Private Institutions of Higher Learning, Malaysia. *Computer and Information Science*, *2*(4), 122–128.

The National Higher Education Strategic Plan Beyond 2020. (2007). Putrajaya: Ministry of Higher Education Malaysia.

World Internet Usage and Population Statistics. (2013). Retrieved from www.internetworldstats.com

Yunus, A. (2014). *Learning Without Boundaries Through Online Courses*. Retrieved from http://www.thestar.com.my/news/nation/2014/09/19/learning-without-boundaries-through-online-courses/

Zainol-Abidin, M.J., Pourmohammadi, M., Varasingam, N., & Lean, O.C. (2014). The Online Reading Habits of Malaysian Students. *The Reading Matrix*, *14*(2), 164–172.

Chapter 11
Semantic Modelling for E-Learning Coordination

Atilla Elçi
Aksaray University, Turkey

Duygu Çelik Ertuğrul
Istanbul Aydin University, Turkey

Alev Elçi
Aksaray University, Turkey

ABSTRACT

This chapter reports a metadata model for e-learning coordination based on content semantics grounded on Semantic Web concepts. To start with, e-learning models are surveyed identifying process content, such as phases, activities, data schema, rules and relations, so on, as relevant for a coordination model. The study looks into the mechanism of e-learning environment and how e-learning processes can be classified for purposes of activity coordination. A metadata model for coordination of e-learning is being sought as expressed in Semantic Web concepts and transcribed using the related languages like OWL, RDF, SPARQL and others. A learner centric proposal is advanced which augments the IEEE Learning Technology Standards Committee's industry leader Learning Technology System Architecture. Examples are worked out and future research directions are identified. This is a continuing research project on application of Semantic Web initiative in e-learning; i.e., design and development of markup and annotation tools, relevant ontologies and intelligent agents in meeting learner needs.

INTRODUCTION

Open, flexible and distributed learning activities are named variously, including:

- e-Learning,
- Web-Based Learning (WBL),
- Web-Based Instruction (WBI),

DOI: 10.4018/978-1-5225-0466-5.ch011

- Web-Based Training (WBT),
- Internet-Based Training (IBT),
- Distributed Learning (DL),
- Advanced Distributed Learning (ADL),
- Distance Education (DE),
- Distance Learning (DL),
- dlearning,
- D-Learning,
- Online Learning (OL),
- Mobile Learning (or m-Learning) or Nomadic Learning,
- Remote Learning,
- Off-site Learning,
- a-Learning (anytime, anyplace, anywhere learning),
- Virtual learning.

Also, of late, terms such as:

- Instructional Technology,
- Learning Technologies,
- Learning Management System,
- Massive open online courses (MOOCs) precise definitions of such terms can be found in the literature (see, for example: ACM eLearn; CDLP; CMC, 2008; Imperial; LTSC, 1996; Moore, 1996; Tsai & Machado, 2002; and Wiki, 2014).

While we concede to that there is considerable difference among some of these in one or more of the issues involving pedagogy, learner purpose, computerized application, stake-holder parties involved, tools used, technology required, and timing and scheduling, we tend to regard e-learning as an all-encompassing generic term. This is quite in line with our predisposition in this chapter for we wish to consider e-learning in its generic form equally akin to any flavor of it. We will dig into e-learning deeper.

A decade ago, an e-learning system was considered as a learning content manager as asserted in the Multidimensional Dynamic Learning (MDL) Model (Lytras, Pouloudi & Poulymenakou, 2002; see Figure 3). Visions of e-learning have changed considerably. In outlining its 2020 initiative in digital agenda, European Commission (2014) strives for member states to mainstream e-learning in national policies for modernizing education and training. It is stated that "Today eLearning is not sufficiently present in Member States' education and training policies. However, the benefits of eLearning are enormous: it enables people to acquire skills anywhere, anytime; it empowers teachers to adopt new practices, to tailor interventions on the basis of personal learning needs and to individualize assessment. It also caters for self-regulated and informal learning, accommodates different learning styles, innovative collaborative learning practices, and supports more efficient workforce training, at a global scale, improving delivery, reducing training costs and time-to-competencies." This statement succinctly lists the virtues of e-learning, and in the process, provides hints to what it should cater for. Yet, "how" is missing? What would it take to achieve e-learning as expected? If not succeeding full virtues, why one is failing? Clearly, information and communication technologies (ICT) on the one hand is decisively influential at the delivery end of the e-learning spectrum, while instructional technology at the service heart.

Figure 3. IEEE1484.12.1 learning object Metadata LOM base schema
Retrieved from (http://upload.wikimedia.org/wikipedia/meta/a/ae/LOM.PNG)

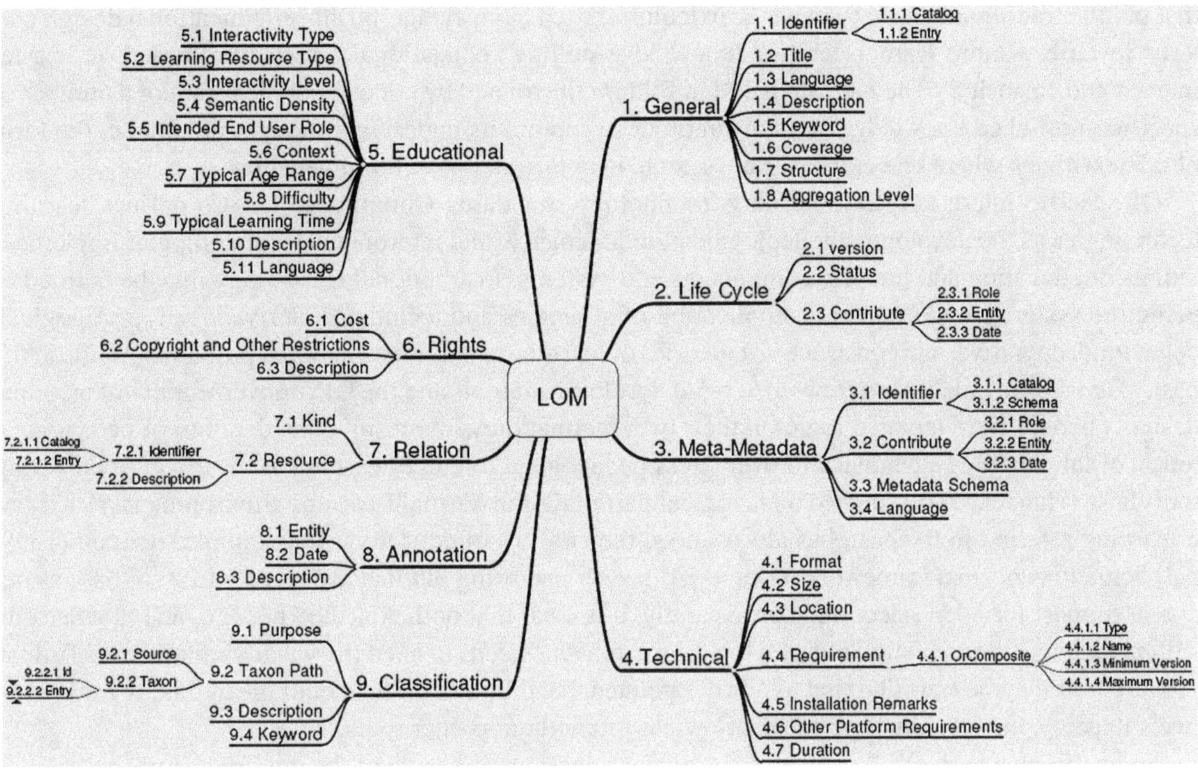

Information technology (IT) has always attracted attention from all quarters of interest. The learning and teaching front, be it for education or training, is no exception where IT and communication blended in with pedagogy even gets to be called the 'learning technology', and eventually leading to technology-enhanced learning (TEL). The famous learning technologist Chris Dede, in a keynote address during a recent inaugural conference on the emergence of Massive Open Online Courses (MOOCs), considers virtual worlds and augmented realities as complementary to digitized classroom instruction by providing "simulated apprenticeships, embedded support for learning everywhere, and transformed social interactions... To reach massive with universal access and powerful outcomes, we must creatively expand our visions of platforms, pedagogy, and financing" (Dede, 2014). We highly sympathize with such utilization of IT gadgetry towards the individual learner's benefit, and our interest too lies in 'creatively expanding our vision of platforms', the softer side of it, that is, typically in affecting e-content and rendering it accessible through instructional design. For example, Sun, Joy and Griffiths (2005, 2007) report a case where learning objects (LOs) and learning style are used in an agent-based learning system in order to enhance adaptivity. They achieved personalization and adaptivity by using learning style schemes in tailoring the presentation of LOs to individual students. Schemes were implemented by a set of intelligent software agents that use learning styles and LOs appropriate for individual students based on prebuilt and gathered knowledge. A similar research was also reported by Pena, Marzo and de la Rosa (2005). In addressing the individual's personalized learning needs, a relatively recent project work headed by Ambjörn Naeve has been carried out to develop an interactive learning environment based on Semantic

Web technology, open source software and open international ICT standards. When used in the context of education, the so-called Knowledge Manifold-architecture represents a paradigm shift, away from that of "the traditional teacher-centric, curriculum-based "knowledge-pushing" educational design patterns towards a more learner-centric, "knowledge-pulling" educational architecture based on learner interest and curiosity". The Knowledge Manifold is constructed by conceptual modeling of a number of specific interlinked knowledge domains in order to capture its underlying thought patterns in the form of context-maps where one can navigate, search, annotate and present information.

Of specific interest, IEEE Learning Technology Standards Committee (LTSC) defines learning technologies as the development, deployment, maintenance, and interoperation of computer implementations of education and training components and systems. Instructional technology may be defined as being the systemic and systematic application of strategies and techniques derived from pedagogical, behavioral, cognitive, and constructivist theories of learning to solve instructional problems. While in the past, "Given the availability of low-cost, rapid development tools and the DIY movement in instructional design", people were tempted to go on their own inclination without full consideration of pedagogical tones, of late, there is a tendency to over stress pedagogical role in e-learning to the effect of demoting tools base (Handel, 2014). Indeed pedagogical part played in Virtual Learning Environments (VLE), as e-learning referred in the past, has always been the concern of educators; for example, Brittain (1999, p.3) actually evolved a framework to review, discover and bring out that aspect of VLE tool base as decision support for VLE selection. Consequently, it is clear that both educated pedagogical practice and suitable computer application must go hand-in-hand. One needs to heed the wisdom minted in a Turkish proverb that may be transliterated as "Tool operates, hand boasts". This could mean that, regardless of one's mastery, one could not perform a flawless job without proper tools.

So, in this chapter we will inquire into tools for e-learning in search of the missing feature base. What features are covered by prominent e-learning frameworks, de facto practices and standards? What opponents are indicating as missing crucial features? How can such features be inserted into the existing standards and related tools base? And, would such remedial action be feasible? These questions will be taken up in the succeeding sections. Next section puts forward the need for control, coordination and semantics in e-learning tools. Then in the following section a proposal is advanced addressing the three crucial lacking. Examples are then worked out showing the power of the proposed features. Conclusions and suggestions for further work conclude this chapter.

THE MISSING CRUCIAL FEATURES AND REMEDIAL ACTION

Many e-learning models exist, some heuristic, others well-grounded on pedagogy and specific instructional design approaches. Some draw benefit from the support of a dedicated framework. We will mention a few prominent ones here with a point of interest on semantics, control and coordination (SCC) aspects by which we allude to 'actionable meaning' in the context of e-learning regardless of the specific pedagogical approach, the framework, or the tools base.

The well-known creativity researcher Mihaly Csikszentmihalyi coined the term "flow" to mean a creative activity process that is both enjoyable and challenging that engulfs one to the extent of losing track of time while doing it (Csikszentmihalyi, 1990). Likening the instructional design process to the flow concept and striving to create a flow-like environment for instructional design, Ceraulo (2003a) identifies seven characteristics for carrying it out highly effectively:

1. Focus goals,
2. Eliminate distractions,
3. Match student skills and course level,
4. Create a supportive environment,
5. Create order through rules,
6. Let students express themselves,
7. Provide timely and consistent feedback.

According to Ceraulo (2003b), similar characteristics apply in the case of online teaching. Of those, with respect to SCC, we would be reasonably interested in activities relating to 3 through 7. These may be further scrutinized in detail by analyzing each with respect to SCC Layers for all semantic, control and coordination.

Salmon (2001) argues that the role of online teacher is evolving from that of conveying known information to one of facilitating exploration and generating new knowledge. Primarily this shift in the part played, but also the complexity of the technology employed, necessitates a highly elevated designation such as "e-moderator". It is understood that the elevated role of e-moderator is mostly due to SCC it exercises.

On the other hand, the Learning Federation hints on the future shape of education based on crucial observations, such as that "The process of learning will dramatically extend from "teacher push" to "learner pull" and that "A combination of automated monitoring tools, tutors and other specialists will make it possible to continuously adjust the pace, nature and style of the learning process to ensure a learning experience optimized for each learner" (TLF, 2001). By the year 2020, it conjectures that the next generation learning systems will draw from a "robust array of software tools" and that software will provide intelligent and context sensitive support on all aspects of learning and teaching. Such eventuality can only be possible through e-learning integrating with an SCC base among others. It may be noted here that the Knowledge Manifold architecture project mentioned above appears to be a stone thrown in the right direction.

The well-known and respected speaker, author, educator and consultant in matters relating to e-learning and educational technology, Badrul H. Khan, puts forward a framework (Khan, 2003; Khan, 2014). Khan's "Framework for e-Learning" (Figure 1) encompasses the following eight essential dimensions of the interest area:

- **Institutional Dimension:** Concerns the issues in relation to administrative and academic affairs, and student services with respect to e-learning.
- **Pedagogical Dimension:** For e-learning is of teaching and learning; this dimension takes stock of the issues relating to analysis of content, audience, goals, media, design approach, organization and methods and evolving strategies for e-learning environments towards services delivery.
- **Technological Dimension:** Refers to issues involving infrastructure planning, hardware and software for proper setting up of technology infrastructure towards development of e-learning environments and delivery of e-learning.
- **Interface Design Dimension:** Relates to the design of content, page and Web site, navigation support, and usability testing of the overall look and feel of e-learning services platform.

Figure 1. A framework for e-learning

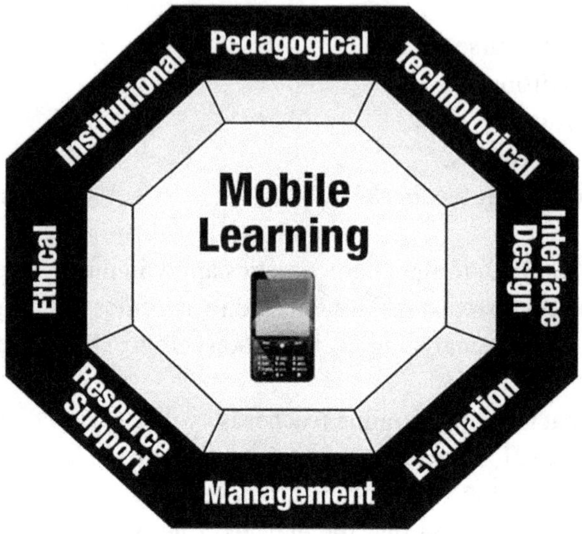

- **Evaluation Dimension:** Of an e-learning platform includes both assessment of learner's topic-specific achievement and overall development, and evaluation of the instruction and learning environment.
- **Management Dimension:** Of e-learning refers to the maintenance of learning environment and distribution of information.
- **Resource Support Dimension:** Relates to the study of the recommended online support and resources in order to maintain meaningful learning environments; and,
- **Ethical Dimension:** Takes into consideration all issues relating to legal, social, cultural, etiquette and netiquette, plagiarism and privacy of learner's personal data as well as social and political influence, cultural diversity, bias, geographical diversity, learner diversity and information accessibility concerns.

Each dimension of Khan's Framework for e-Learning involves several indicative and detailed sub-issues of focus. The purpose of the framework is to assist during steps of institutional e-learning design process. The framework with its concomitant checklist (http://BooksToRead.com/checklist) can be used to ensure that all relevant factors are taken into consideration during the design and development of e-learning. It is clearly a welcome contribution, as the scope and extent of e-learning expands rapidly, consequently projects will require complex team efforts. Existence of a mature framework and an extensive checklists stemming from it, help greatly to control and coordinate activities of parties involved. The complete list of dimensions and sub-dimensions may be accessed at (Khan, 2014a).

Khan's framework presents a model of "dimensions", that is to say, interest areas in e-learning life cycle, visually from planning to design, development, deployment, operations, and up to maintenance. The so-called "E-Learning P3 Model" spells out a people-process-product specification embodying a process standpoint. It provides a comprehensive picture of the e-learning process helping in identifying roles and responsibilities for stages of planning, design, development, implementation, evaluation, delivery, instruction, marketing and maintenance of all e-learning and blended learning materials and systems (Khan, 2004). Considering the people–process–product continuum in e-learning, it contributes greatly towards this study. Altogether 35 distinct roles and their responsibility are meticulously identified in Table 1. Just to mention a few of the roles here, one can recount Director, Project Manager, Consultant / Advisor, Research and Design Coordinator, Content or Subject Matter Expert, Instructional Designer, and so on. It is judged that almost all of these roles involve control-cum-coordination and better carried out considering semantic relations inherent in the processes and related data as well. That observation would justify our concern with SCC aspects in e-learning systems and solutions.

The examples mentioned above have been early projects each with their particular empirical foundation aimed at the resolution of pragmatic e-learning matters. Findings of them have triggered and eventually enriched important studies of e-learning models by prominent research organizations in subsequent years. The major bodies involved have been the IEEE LTSC, Aviation Industry CBT Committee (AICC), Instructional Management Project and Global E-Learning Consortium (IMS), ISO Subcommittee on Information Technology for Learning Education and Training, the Alliance of Remote Instructional Authoring and Distribution Networks for Europe (European Union ARIADNE) project, Advanced Distributed Learning (ADL) Initiative of the US Department of Defense- SCORM (Sharable Courseware

Table 1. Labels of class, subclass, and class assertion in material ontology (in OWL2.0)

1	<?xml version="1.0"?>
2	Ontology xmlns=http://www.w3.org/2002/07/owl#
3	xml:base=http://.../OKB/2012/Material.owl
4	<Declaration><Class IRI="#Assess_Performance"/></Declaration>
5	<Declaration><Class IRI="#Intellectual_Skills"/></Declaration>
6	<Declaration><Class IRI="#Cognitive_Strategies"/></Declaration>
7	<Declaration><Class IRI="#EducationDegree"/></Declaration>
8	<SubClassOf><Class IRI="#Intellectual_Skills"/><Class IRI="#Learning_Levels"/></SubClassOf>
9	<SubClassOf><Class IRI="#Motor_Skills"/><Class IRI="#Learning_Levels"/></SubClassOf>
10	<SubClassOf><Class IRI="#Present_Stimulus"/><Class IRI="#Methodology"/></SubClassOf>
11	<SubClassOf><Class IRI="#Presentation"/><Class IRI="#Material"/></SubClassOf>
12	<SubClassOf><Class IRI="#Problem_Solving"/><Class IRI="#Intellectual_Skills"/></SubClassOf>
13	<SubClassOf><Class IRI="#Procedure_Following"/><Class IRI="#Intellectual_Skills"/></SubClassOf>
14	<SubClassOf><Class IRI="#Provide_Feedback"/><Class IRI="#Methodology"/></SubClassOf>
15	<SubClassOf><Class IRI="#Recall_Prior_Learning"/><Class IRI="#Methodology"/></SubClassOf>
16	<SubClassOf><Class IRI="#Student"/><Class IRI="#Person"/></SubClassOf>
17	<SubClassOf><Class IRI="#Test"/><Class IRI="#Material"/></SubClassOf>
18	<SubClassOf><Class IRI="#Use_Of_Terminology"/><Class IRI="#Intellectual_Skills"/></SubClassOf>
19	<SubClassOf><Class IRI="#Video"/><Class IRI="#Material"/></SubClassOf>
20	<ClassAssertion><Class IRI="#MaterialType"/><NamedIndividual IRI="#Book"/></ClassAssertion>
21	<ClassAssertion><Class IRI="#Math"/><NamedIndividual IRI="#Triangles"/></ClassAssertion>
22	...

Object Reference Model) developments, and Microsoft Learning Resource Interchange (LRI) specification. Works of these bodies have been far reaching both in content and of influence; in the end, especially the IEEE LTSC's contribution has been profound, lasting, and culminated in standards.

The SCORM (Dodds, 2003) collection of standards and specifications of the ADL (http://www.adlnet.org) Initiative was based on the AICC and LTSC Learning Object Metadata (LOM) standards. It aimed for portability of learning content among compliant Learning Management Systems (LMS) as well as among compliant WBT applications. SCORM facilitated reusability and portability of learning objects through file transfer via standardized interfaces; it became the most successful interoperability model for learning technology. The best side of it was that it incorporated the LOM standard metadata model useable for retrieval of learning objects, the atomic units called the Sharable Content Object (SCO). An SCO was the SCORM's content of lowest granularity designed as independent of learning context for reusability. In principle several SCOs could be lined up to compose learning and exercise units but each that gets executed under the control of the LMS as an SCO must not launch other SCOs. This version was SCORM 1.2 which is still being served by ADL although SCORM 2004 Edit 4 dated March 2009 and subsequent evolution of service orientation addressing the most of the criticism is also available.

The LTSC, a chartered body of the IEEE Computer Society Standards Activity Board, has been developing widely recognized technical standards and guides for learning technology. Its activities encompass several eLearning areas we are concerned in this chapter, namely, Computer Managed Instruction, Learning Object Metadata, and Resource Aggregation Models for Learning, Education and Training. The LTSC has been developing definitions of all aspects of learning technology (LTSC, n.d.). It introduced the broad definition of 'learning objects' (LOs) concept together with its concomitant models. Likewise it has been producing relevant standards, for example, the Learning Technology System Architecture (LTSA, 2002). The LTSA is meant by specification to cover a wide range of learning systems, such as learning technology, intelligent tutoring, computer-based training, computer assisted instruction, education and training technology, metadata, and to not favor any particular pedagogical approach, content, culture, and platform. It is meant to provide a future-proof framework which would be adaptable to new technologies and learning technology systems for understanding existing and future systems, promoting interoperability and portability among learning systems by identifying critical system interfaces, thus aiming to incorporate a technical applicability of 10 to 15 years.

The LTSA standard has been widely accepted by others. ADL adopted LTSA as bases for further improvement of the Content Aggregation Model (CAM) of the SCORM. However, one year after adoption and into subsequent development it was realized that "there's something missing": "the process of creating complex behaviors, such as remediation branching, wasn't supported well (or at all) in the current CAM specifications". It was understood that the LTSA model as it stood did not provide for SCC. So ADL had to build a "Navigation and Sequencing" part in cooperation with IMS and grafted it to SCORM. Indeed, other critical views on SCORM were raised early on issues concerning "the market value of SCOs, the process of producing WBTs on the basis of different SCO providers, maintenance of SCOs and WBTs (consisting of several SCOs), and the quality of WBTs based on SCOs of different providers" (Bohl, Schellhase, Sengler & Winand, 2002). There was also the fundamental concern: "it is not pedagogically sound to cut content up, and expect learning to be effective" (Welsch, 2002). In other words, there is a potential for the interactions between the content to be significantly diminished with this approach. How will the content be sequenced to provide pedagogically sound learning? A second problem relates to current online pedagogical approaches that highlight the concept of learning as a result of interaction between learners (i.e. online collaborative learning environments). SCORM is currently viewed as a model for e-learning that is focused on a single self-paced learner interacting with the instruction." (Hartshorne, 2003).

E-Learning standards development-wise, LTSC/LTSA initiative benefitted from the output of all the major players such as AICC, IMS Project, ANSI IISP, ARIADNE Project of European Union, OMG CORBAMED, and ISO (LTSA, 1998). Although the most advanced of them all, it is not immune to criticism, either; limits of the original LTSA model was considered by a few research. To start with, the term "learning object" (LO) sounded too technical due to very specific technological paradigm and precise connotations of the concept "object" in computer sciences on the one hand. Yet on the other hand, the term LO is rather vague due to the extreme vagueness, generality and broadly non-technical nature of the term "learning". Consequently, LO defies proper definition, meaning different things at different quarters. E-Learning standards and concomitant specifications claim to support multiple forms and practices of learning thus being frequently described as "pedagogically neutral" or "pedagogically agnostic". However there are claims that such specs have a limited pedagogical model that may be unsuitable for some environments, and essentially for a self-paced and self-directed single-learner. It may be concluded that such problems arise due to "the juxtaposition of narrow technical and specialized concepts with the general and varied dimensions and contexts of learning". "Perhaps most importantly for e-Learning content and standardization, it is important to recognize that objects and infrastructures for learning cannot simultaneously be both pedagogically neutral and pedagogically valuable. Developers and designers will have to recognize and choose relevant (and probably differing) pedagogical positions, or risk pedagogical irrelevance" (Friesen, 2004a). On the other hand, developers of LMS Software find LTSA model constricting: student evaluation records are stored but their utilization is not specified; student counseling is not included in the LTSA architecture; students take courses generally just by the name often overlooking the prerequisites; the LTSA layer II algorithm enters an infinite iterative cycle if the feedback system fails to notice that a distance mode learner possess some fundamental wrong/ incomplete idea; "It has been observed that LTSA is too abstract to be adapted in a uniform way by LMS developers" (Sengupta, Chaki & Dasgupta, 2008). Corbière and Choquet (2004) assert that the LTSA model does not cater for the learning object designer as an integral stakeholder in the learning process. They propose a new stakeholder perspective, consequently, recommends incorporating a new high-level architecture for information technology through modifications in the layers 1, 3 and 5 of the LTSA model. Recently LTSC was reconsidering LOM striving to identify the course of remedial action in the cases of issues raised (LTSC LOM WG, n.d.). Researchers are striving to circumvent shortcomings of LOM by devising schemes to enlist the services of content semantics in addressing the issues. One such issue pertains to behavioral aspects which concerns reuse of assets as in the cases of personal learning requirements; more on this line under the Future Research Directions section.

The E-Learning Framework (ELF), a joint initiative of the U.K's Joint Information Services Committee (JISC) and Australia's Department of Education, Science and Training (DEST), following a vision in the right direction, strived to build a common framework for e-learning utilizing service-oriented architectures (www.elframework.org/). The ELF relied on the assumption that the learning content exposed as simple networked services offers all stake-holders more flexibility and room for pedagogic innovation. However, this initiative was more concerned with the approach to the description and discovery of services for e-learning in the same sort as for Web services. Its extensively populated "e-learning framework" lacks real semantics and learner as well as it is more concerned with evolving the software application base for a wider scope rather than e-learning. This initiative has long been folded.

The Centre for Educational Technology, Interoperability and Standards (Cetis, http://www.cetis.ac.uk/), based at the University of Bolton in partnership with Heriot-Watt University, UK, appears to have inherited the work of the ELF. Specialized in technology innovation and interoperability standards in learning, education and training, it provides strategic, technical and pedagogical advice to funding bodies, standards agencies, government, institutions and commercial parties on educational technology and standards. Cetis has been executing several relevant projects, some alone some in association with parties such as JISC, European Commission, Creative Commons and Learning Resource Metadata Initiative (LRMI, http://www.lrmi.net/). Some of the projects of relevant interest for the purposes of this chapter would be on learning analytics (LA) and educational data mining (EDM) (http://www.laceproject.eu/), support for educational resource movement (http://wiki.cetis.ac.uk/Oer), virtual and personal learning environments (http://wiki.cetis.ac.uk/DVLE_Support), futuristic trends in technology enhanced learning (http://www.telmap.org/), and the Learning Metadata Resource Initiative (LMRI) project (Barker & Campbell, 2014). The latter project is to ease the discovery of educational resources by search engines to refine their search services using embedded metadata. LRMI is extending the schema.org metadata vocabulary with terms of specific relevancy to learning resources. Clearly, Cetis work is on metadata, resource sharing and related standards not touching topic related semantics of extended learning resource content, or control and coordination issues empowering individual learner.

There are some other frameworks that are suggested based on pedagogical grounds (Khan, 2014b) but are not considered further in this chapter.

Stephen Downes (2005) in his seminal article explains how trends in Web affect the eLearning community and education at large. "In the future it will be more widely recognized that the learning comes not from the design of learning content but in how it is used. Most e-learning theorists are already there, and are exploring how learning content-whether professionally authored or created by students--- can be used as the basis for learning activities rather than the conduit for learning content." In the same line of thought, whereas other studies have been preoccupied with modeling learning objects, and in that, especially static metadata, this chapter recounts on attempts aiming at eventually developing a metadata model for e-learning coordination and expressing it using semantic web technologies. The objective of this inclination is to empower the learner to act upon own progression through training and learning so to proceed along the especially self-imposed targets. Control over prescribed advancement of learner through courseware is a basic delivery requirement. Backtracking (for remedial purpose), reiterating (for coverage of further detail), synchronizing several learners at stages (say, before testing), temporary digression (say for deficiency training or info look up) with or without freezing the current state, etc. are also required. Learner's control over and prerogative to explore and choose alternatives should be supported. We summarize the above exposition by stating that, in order to affect learner-oriented selective learning, e-learning requires a model and associated tools catering for a heavy dose of semantics, control and coordination at all layers. The next section introduces the proposal where the findings of this study can be put to good use; and, examples are provided thereafter.

THE PROPOSAL

Sorel Reisman (2014) observes that "Today's LMSs are simply online content presenters and test administrators that don't tailor the presentation to the learner's "performance." They're essentially CMI (computer-managed instruction) systems without diagnostic tools for monitoring a learner's progress and prescribing remedial or other instructional materials following diagnosis."

Figure 2. The IEEE 1484 Learning Technology Systems Architecture, LTSA: components and interactions (Shoikova, 2002; LTSA, 2001; LTSA 1998)

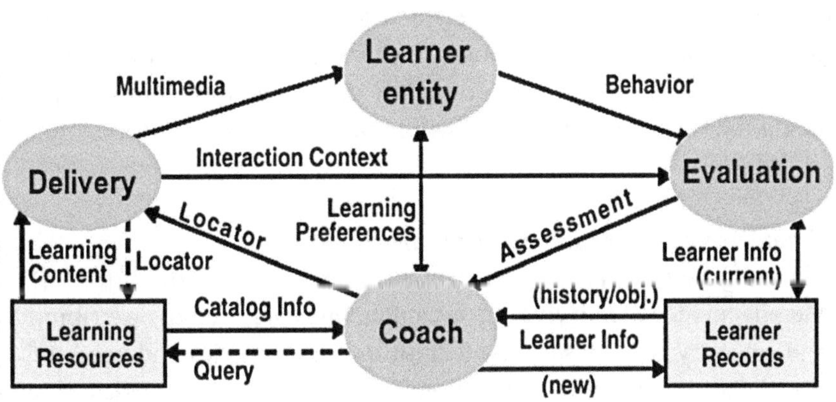

Current e-learning models, related standards and associated virtual learning environments do not seem to fully support the learners' wish to learn selectively. Learner's options are nonexistent, or at best severely limited in selecting LOs from among the discovered ones based on content semantics. This outcome is essentially a model-theoretic problem and exactly due to lacking of what we have been pointing out as a must flow of semantics, control and coordination through the learning environment integrating all stake holders and resources.

To consider the most up to date and advanced one, the origin of such lacking is actually stemming from the LTSA model. LTSA originally was described in terms of its four components, two data stores and 13 interactions among them as depicted in the following figure (Figure 2). To briefly review this graphics, in terms of operation, the Learner and the Coach negotiate learning styles, strategies, methods, and so on which then are noted as learning preferences. The Learner's interaction and behavior are observed and evaluated as the interactions for Delivery of learning object (multimedia) take place. The Evaluation component produces assessment and learner information which are then stored in the Learner Records for (future) reference by the Coach. The Coach, after reviewing the Learner's performance, preferences and objectives, may search the Learning Resources for proper material to serve. Then the locators of such material are passed to the Delivery component as a lesson plan. The Delivery extracts the material from the Learning Resources and administers it to the Learner as an interactive multimedia presentation. Although over simplified, the above mentioned highlights of operation serve to indicate the lack of learner's control over learning progression for proper environment integration.

It should be noted that the Coach's querying of the Learning Resources repository and selecting the 'appropriate' LO are both through using whatever metadata indication was available on the LOs in the repository. LTSA is bounded by the LOM data model specification in this case. The (IEEE1484.12.1 – 2002 Learning Object Metadata) LOM standard is essentially a Dublin Core (http://dublincore.org/) metadata element set level specification. As such, whatever semantic annotation exists, it deals with the 'media item description' based on a very limited vocabulary not necessarily reflecting content semantics. The LOM data model indicates the aspects of a learning object that would be specified and the concept terms to use for that purpose; it would also allow extensions and restrictions limited to the stated relations. In order to visually depict the vocabulary, various descriptive graphics exists displaying the LOM metadata items; for example, a precise UML diagram of LOM base schema is available for the

UML-savvy ones here: http://en.wikipedia.org/wiki/File:LOM_base_schema.png; Original size: http://upload.wikimedia.org/wikipedia/commons/1/14/LOM_base_schema.png. We will prefer the following mind map image (Figure 3) as it is easy to understand for all without intimate knowledge of UML. As seen on the image, LOM consists of nine primary hierarchy categories of metadata, visually, General, Life Cycle, Meta-Metadata, Technical, Educational, Rights, Relation, Annotation, and Classification. In briefly introducing these categories the following may be noted with respect to a LOM description of a learning object:

- The General category is for overall description of the LO;
- The Lifecycle category is for production history and version control of the LO;
- The Meta-Metadata is for identifying the metadata instance used in describing the LO;
- The Technical category is for describing technical characteristics and needs of the LO;
- The Educational category is for the educational and pedagogic properties of the LO;
- The Rights category is for stating the intellectual property rights and conditions of use;
- The Relation category is for defining the relationship between this and another LO;
- The Annotation category is used to leave comments on the LO;
- The Classification category is for classifying the LO.

In turn, each of these categories has further lower levels of hierarchy terms altogether making up the LOM Base Schema. The lowest levels (the leaves) would be filled in with data qualifying the element; the collection of such descriptions would make up the LOM record of the LO.

LTSA architecture description has five hierarchical layers representing the different aspects of the learning process as follows:

Layer 1: Defines the interaction between the learner and its environment regarding information acquisition, transfer, exchange and discovery;
Layer 2: Defines the learner's interaction with the environment;
Layer 3: Defines the organization of the learning process in terms of data and control flow among the stake holders; this is the components and interactions system as depicted in Figure 2;
Layer 4: Allows the identification of the system's activities, especially exploitation of Layer 3 component system, in order to formalize technological design constraints;
Layer 5: Defines the software development cycle from requirements to functionality design, to conceptual model and to semantics.

Figure 4 displays the hierarchical layers of LTSA where Layer 1 (user side) is at the top and Layer 5 (base system side) at the bottom. From Layer 1 down to Layer 5 there exists an interface between any two neighboring layers performing the "filtration" function between the "abstraction" state from the layer above down to the "implementation" state at the lower layer. A lot of SCC issues need be inserted at the interfaces; the way it is, with the most going into the layer. The rest that is not suitable for handling or not feasible for inclusion in that layer's logic would either going to be pushed down the interface or left unnoticed/unhandled. Instead, LTSA should have a dedicated SCC layer separate from the others. It is conjectured that, due to lasting relations with each of the LTSA layers, the SCC layer should actually be positioned in close connection (perpendicular) to all others, that is, in full contact with all the interfaces and layers of LTSA at all times. This we depict graphically in Figure 4.

Figure 4. The IEEE LTSA layers. The SCC (S&C&C) layers column sketched on the right hand side of this drawing is not part of the LTSA but being proposed by this treatise.
(Shoikova, 2002; LTSA 1998).

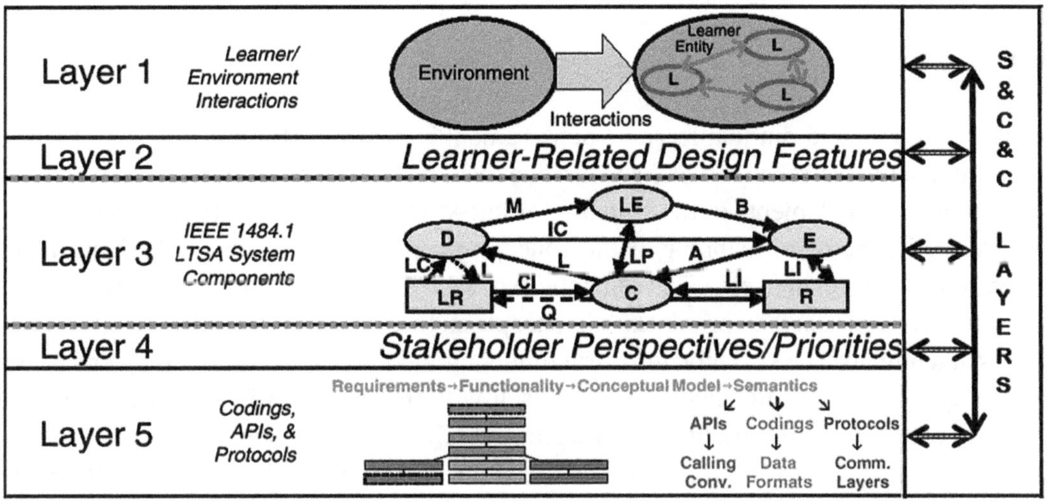

In our proposal, each LTSA layer communicates with the SCC Layer for all semantic, control and coordination issues. LTSA layers become processing plateaus for their designated specific functions also catering for SCC connections. Layer interfaces similarly implement pass-through function calls to down-up layers where filtering is based on that specified by the SCC Layer. Consequently, LTSA becomes a generic architecture model, that is, not involving inclinations towards any pedagogical or LMS scheme or kind of e-learning approach.

SCC can allow on the spot change of course based on the learner's discretion at any moment which is conveyable through SCC Layers to all layers of the LTSA. At this scheme, due to flexible sequencing of LOs, none of which would include embedded sequence indication, will allow shareable free standing LOs at the pick-and-choose decision of the learner. The learner can be empowered to pursue its own way when and how the learner wishes to. So, at this juncture, there is an opportunity not to be missed: incorporation of Semantic Web based approach to LO design and hooking of SCC layers (column) to LTSA standard. This process may start with infusion of Semantic Web approach into the design of the SCC Layer and into LTSA for which an extensive set of metadata will be required to be gathered on SCC issues. However, at this time LTSC appears to be content with LOM at the moment; little if any activity is going on for updating the standard creating something of the sort of an SCC column or allowing link ups into the framework from/to VLE with respect to implementing learner discretionary action (LTSC, 2013). However, LTSC has recently embarked on an ambitious new project that can revolutionize the modality of learning material and maybe even more (Richards & Robson, 2014); more on this initiative under the Additional Reading section.

Although there is the IEEE Standard for Learning Object Metadata (IEEE Standard 1484.12.1-2002 (R2009) and IEEE Standard 1484.12.1-2002/Cor 1-2011), its content is far short of the SCC issues needed. Currently, the LTSC has quite a few approved standards and further current new or revision projects (LTSC, 2013). It appears that none on the existing or current work seems to satisfy the learner need for discretion.

In the following section, we will introduce which SCC issues need be catered for empowering the discerning learner and how this may be done.

SCC LAYERS

Mih and Mih (2011) found out that learning achievement is enhanced by self-regulated training. Self-regulated training emphasizes the role of a technique that "makes concepts, and propositions composed of concepts, the central elements in the structure of knowledge and construction of meaning" (Novak, 1996, p.7), visually, the mind mapping or the concept mapping. This is why and where the semantic Web technology would get in to play. The semantic Web technology marks the content with well-defined ontological annotations based on pre-declared concepts so that it renders the content equally accessible by machines and human. The semantic infrastructure integrated with concept mapping can be embodied in the SCC Layers column. This innovative approach will provide essentially semantics-rich searches but as well as catering for the traditional syntactic search queries. Semantic queries will enable the learning environment to make meaningful inference thus coming up with more relevant results for users in human-computer interaction and in educational data mining. Semantic approach complete with proper annotation and use of appropriate ontologies can then be applied equally well in the cases of LOs, processes, learner performance monitoring, and control and coordination for activity in favor of the learner. For example, in line with the concept proposed here, but not implemented the same, Çelik, Elçi and Elverici (2011) reports a semantic system architecture, which also employs intelligent software agents, for use in planning learner-centered choice of teaching materials automatically as a result of student's performance in the course of a semester. The individual learner's overall particular needs in individualized learning processes may be resolved through personal and professional learning portfolios (Sherry, Havelock & Gibson, 2005). The learning portfolio would include a base framework providing guidance, an informational framework providing personalized information with semantic structure, and an operational framework for self-assessment. The LOs of a portfolio reside in the VLE, specifically, in an industry-standards-compliant LMS. Specific SCC features of LOs will have already been gathered in the ontologies in the repository of the SCC Layers semantic infrastructure. The infrastructure would house the full info on the learning activities, interactions, outcomes, and learner integration. The local or virtual ontologies on learning methods, models, and techniques would also be accessible as needed (Railean, Elçi, Çelik & Elçi, 2015).

The SCC Layers Semantic Infrastructure consists of descriptive protocols and functional capabilities organized in a hierarchy. The Figure 5 depicts the hierarchy while also identifying the layer contents. LOs are found in the first layer at the bottom, local but also possibly accessed virtually through the distributed Internet of Things network. This is an interface access layer to VLE. Semantic description of each LO and related concepts are saved in the repository based on the upper ontology. Inference through a rule-based scheme is done on its contents in (re-)generating a study plan. The application program interface (API) provides the internal functions for semantic inference and interfacing the infrastructure to VLE as well as to the (user-) learner's environment. API affects the functions for concept matching, inference and execution engines, planner and monitoring while also accessing the repository and user rule base.

Figure 5. SCC layers semantic infrastructure: layers and functions

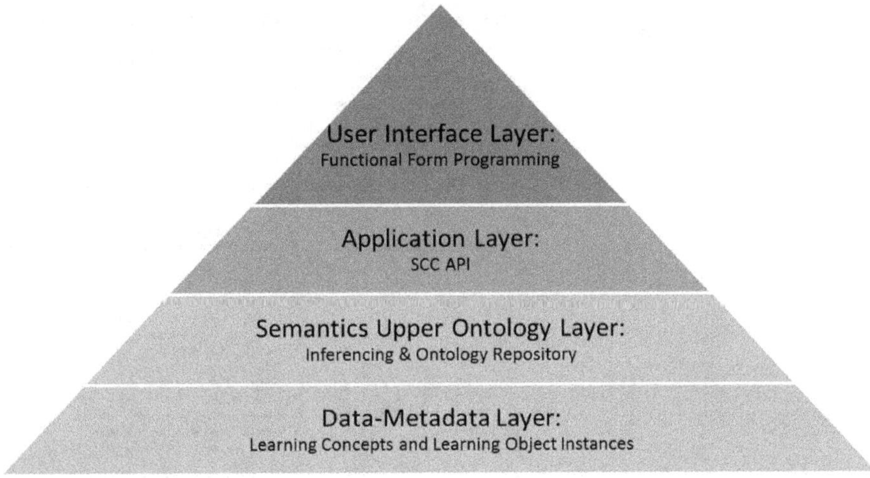

The SCC Layers Semantic Infrastructure combines semantics and learning processes activity (C&C). The framework building up a semantic base for learning interactions can then be used for both in building new LOs and in utilizing existing ones. It is a generic tool with ease of integration to any LTSA-compliant VLE and standards-compliant LMS for both uses. As long as the relevant domain ontologies are available, it would be usable in any area of study.

In the following final section, we will take up several examples showing how the SCC Layers Semantic Infrastructure may be used for learner empowerment.

EXAMPLES

The SCC Layers Semantic Infrastructure includes an ontology repository of methods, concepts, inference rules, study units and a study plan generator among others. The Materials upper Ontology (MO, for short) includes semantic descriptions of all LOs contained in the LMS totally covering their concepts, properties and relationships. In order to give an example, the initial portion of this ontology containing declarations of commonly used concepts and properties of LOs is being depicted. Figure 6 displays the initial portion of the MO on the Protégé editor; Figure 7 shows the same as graphics, and the text (OWL2 in XML) is shown in Table 1. Incidentally, in working with ontologies, the Protégé editor (http://protege.stanford.edu) is used. Protégé is a free, open-source ontology editor and framework for building knowledge-based intelligent systems.

The MO upper ontology is modeled on Gagné's Conditions of Learning Theory (Kearsley, 1994) which focuses on mental processes. Gagné's Theory is prescriptive and contains five categories of human performance established by learning that are identified as following outcomes (Kearsley 1994):

- Verbal information,
- Intellectual skills,
- Cognitive strategies,
- Motor skills,
- Attitudes.

Figure 6. Initial portion of Material Upper Ontology (MO) on the Protégé editor

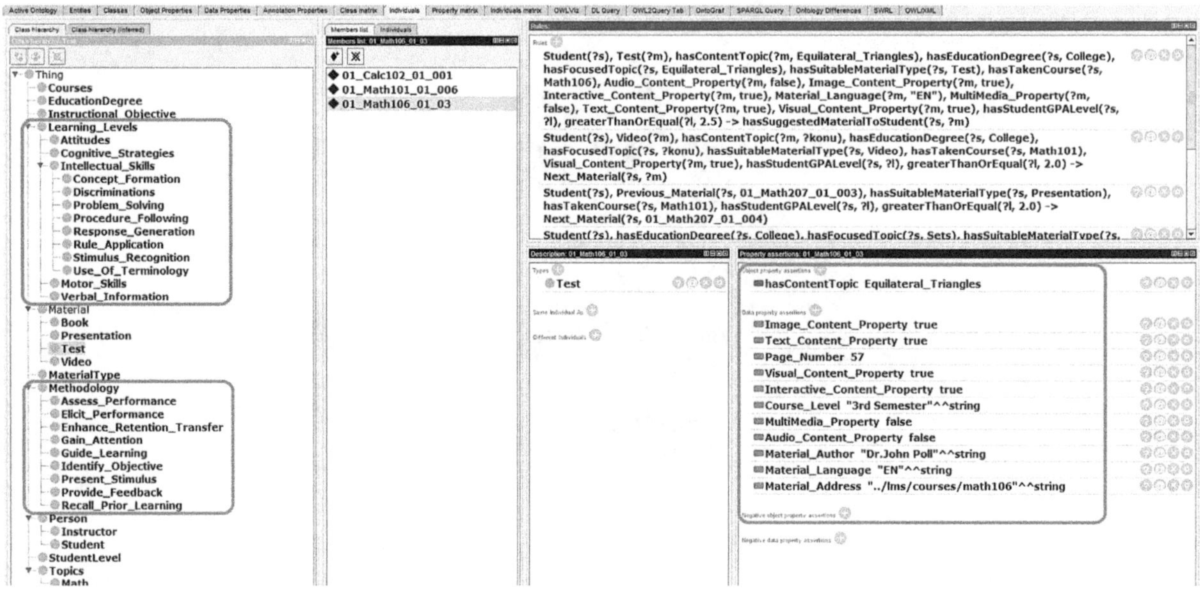

Figure 7. A part of Material Upper Ontology (MO) on OntoGraf in the Protégé framework

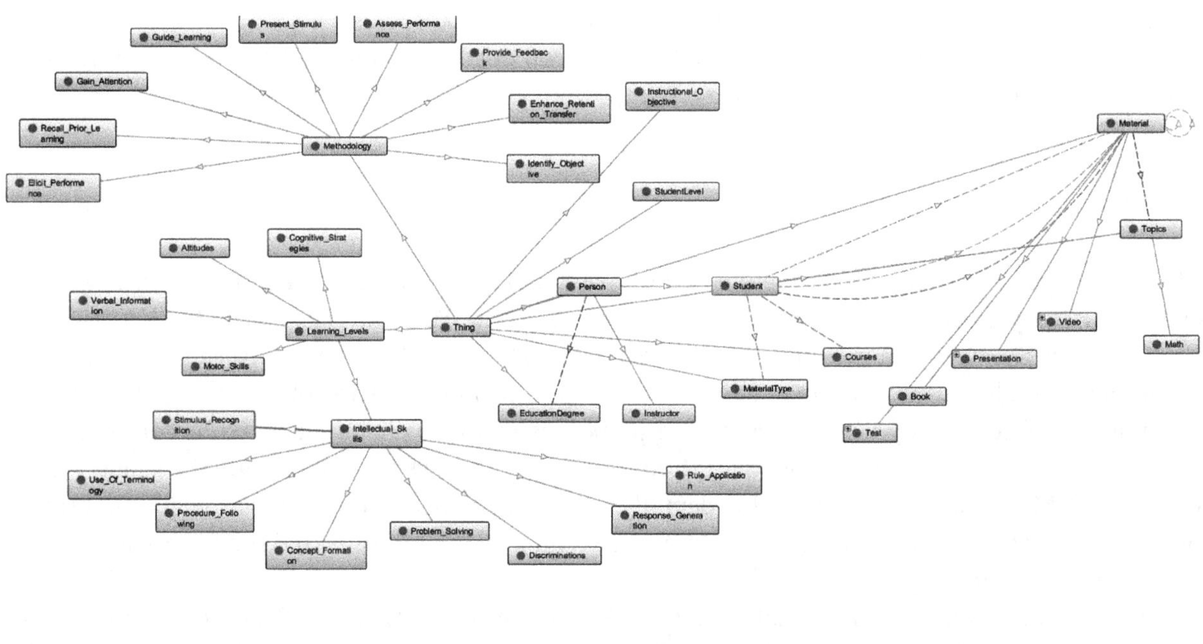

The importance of the learning outcomes classification is that each learning level requires "different internal and external conditions", i.e., each learning level requires different types of instruction. Gagné mentioned the following example: 'for cognitive strategies to be learned, there must be a chance to practice developing new solutions to problems; to learn attitudes, the learner must be exposed to a credible role model or persuasive arguments' (http://www.patsula.com/usefo/webbasedlearning/tutorial1/learning_theories_full_version.htm).

In addition, Gagné recommends organizing the learning tasks for intellectual skills in a hierarchy according to task complexity as follows:

- Stimulus recognition,
- Response generation,
- Procedure following,
- Use of terminology,
- Discriminations,
- Concept formation,
- Rule application,
- Problem solving.

The learning tasks in the hierarchy are inserted into MO as subclasses of intellectual skills concept. For instance, 'Problem Solving' learning task is marked as a subclass of 'Intellectual_Skills' as shown in the line 12 of Table 1.

Similarly, partial content for the creation and definitions of a course and its existing units are given in Table 2 from a lower level ontology. Table 2 depicts 01 (first) year Math 106 material for 01 (first) chapter 003 numbered: "#01_Math106 01_003" with the object and data type properties such as

```
"#Next_Material", "#Covered_by", "#Covers", "#Audio_Content_Property",
"#Course_Level", "#Image_Content_Property", "#Interactive_Content_Property",
"#Material_Address", "#Material_Author", "#Material_Language", "#MultiMedia_
Property", "#Page_Number" and so on.
```

For instance, the lines 7-9 depict a relationship that the material "#01_Math106_01_03" "#hasContentTopic" object type property "#Equilateral_Triangles" unit, such as:

```
Material: "#01_Math106_01_03" → ObjectType Property: "#hasContentTopic"→ Top-
ic: "#Equilateral_Triangles"
```

Ontologies are utilized as bases for drawing conclusions, that is to say, generating implications of the existing instance data under the guidance of inference rules. Inference rules are semantically defined by using the Semantic Web Rule Language (SWRL, http://www.w3.org/Submission/SWRL/). Very briefly, a SWRL rule is an IF-THEN conditional statement. IF part states the conditions that must be satisfied in order for the THEN part to become true. The IF part, i.e. the antecedent or the body of the rule, consists of atoms computed using the instance data in the ontology as well as performing basic computations. The atoms in the body are data queries into the repository. The THEN part, that is the head or the consequent of the rule, contains atoms showing assertions. Incidentally, the assertions of the consequent may be inserted in to the repository as new facts.

The SWRL rules apply the stated search criteria to find a suitable LO satisfying a particular requirement. Let's work out a few cases.

Table 2. Creation and definitions of the material of course and its existing units (partial content)

1	<ObjectPropertyAssertion>
2	<ObjectProperty IRI="#Covered_by"/><NamedIndividual IRI="#01_Math106_01_03"/>
3	<NamedIndividual IRI="#01_Math207_01_004"/></ObjectPropertyAssertion>
4	<ObjectPropertyAssertion>
5	<ObjectProperty IRI="#Covers"/><NamedIndividual IRI="#01_Math106_01_03"/>
6	<NamedIndividual IRI="#01_Math101_04_001"/></ObjectPropertyAssertion>
7	<ObjectPropertyAssertion>
8	<ObjectProperty IRI="#hasContentTopic"/><NamedIndividual IRI="#01_Math106_01_03"/>
9	<NamedIndividual IRI="#Equilateral_Triangles"/></ObjectPropertyAssertion>
10	<DataPropertyAssertion>
11	<DataProperty IRI="#Audio_Content_Property"/><NamedIndividual IRI="#01_Math106_01_03"/>
12	<Literal datatypeIRI="&xsd;boolean">false</Literal></DataPropertyAssertion>
13	<DataPropertyAssertion>
14	<DataProperty IRI="#Course_Level"/><NamedIndividual IRI="#01_Math106_01_03"/>
15	<Literal datatypeIRI="&xsd;string">3rd Semester</Literal></DataPropertyAssertion>
16	<DataPropertyAssertion>
17	<DataProperty IRI="#Image_Content_Property"/><NamedIndividual IRI="#01_Math106_01_03"/>
18	<Literal datatypeIRI="&xsd;boolean">true</Literal></DataPropertyAssertion>
19	<DataPropertyAssertion>
20	<DataProperty IRI="#Interactive_Content_Property"/><NamedIndividual IRI="#01_Math106_01_03"/>
21	<Literal datatypeIRI="&xsd;boolean">true</Literal></DataPropertyAssertion>
22	<DataPropertyAssertion>
23	<DataProperty IRI="#Material_Address"/><NamedIndividual IRI="#01_Math106_01_03"/>
24	<Literal datatypeIRI="&xsd;string">../lms/courses/math106</Liter al></DataPropertyAssertion>
25	<DataPropertyAssertion>
26	<DataProperty IRI="#Material_Author"/><NamedIndividual IRI="#01_Math106_01_03"/>
27	<Literal datatypeIRI="&xsd;string">Dr.John Poll</Literal></DataPropertyAssertion>
28	<DataPropertyAssertion>
29	<DataProperty IRI="#Material_Language"/><NamedIndividual IRI="#01_Math106_01_03"/>
30	<Literal datatypeIRI="&xsd;string">EN</Literal></DataPropertyAssertion>
31	<DataPropertyAssertion>
32	<DataProperty IRI="#MultiMedia_Property"/><NamedIndividual IRI="#01_Math106_01_03"/>
33	<Literal datatypeIRI="&xsd;boolean">false</Literal></DataPropertyAssertion>
34	<DataPropertyAssertion>
35	<DataProperty IRI="#Page_Number"/><NamedIndividual IRI="#01_Math106_01_03"/>
36	<Literal datatypeIRI="&xsd;integer">57</Literal></DataPropertyAssertion>
37	<DataPropertyAssertion>
38	<DataProperty IRI="#Text_Content_Property"/><NamedIndividual IRI="#01_Math106_01_03"/>
39	<Literal datatypeIRI="&xsd;boolean">true</Literal></DataPropertyAssertion>
40	<DataPropertyAssertion>
41	<DataProperty IRI="#Visual_Content_Property"/><NamedIndividual IRI="#01_Math106_01_03"/>
42	<Literal datatypeIRI="&xsd;boolean">true</Literal></DataPropertyAssertion>
43	…

Case 1

Let's take the case of a learner with *College* degree, taking *Math 106* but wishing to study *Equilateral_Triangles* using *Tests*, and GPA standing at *level l* between *2.50* and *4.00*, then what to recommend for the learner to take next? So, the corresponding SWRL rule is shown circled red at the top of the rightmost column on Figure 8. SWRL syntax is so that the '?' mark denotes that the symbol following it is a variable whose value is being sought. Following the '→' symbol, the *'hasSuggestedMaterialToStudent'* object type property is considered which has two parameters, *s* and *m*. The first parameter stands for any student in the student individual lists (in the middle window). The second parameter indicates any suitable material in the material individual lists. This object type property is asserted for any and all pairs of *s* and *m* for which the antecedent of the rule is satisfied.

The SWRL rule for Case 1 at the top of the rightmost column on Figure 8 is repeated below:

```
Student(?s), Test(?m), hasContentTopic(?m, Equilateral_Triangles),
hasEducationDegree(?s, College), hasFocusedTopic(?s, Equilateral_Triangles),
hasSuitableMaterialType(?s, Test), hasTakenCourse(?s, Math106), Audio_Con-
tent_Property(?m, false), Image_Content_Property(?m, true), Interactive_Con-
tent_Property(?m, true), Material_Language(?m, "EN"), MultiMedia_Property(?m,
false), Text_Content_Property(?m, true), Visual_Content_Property(?m, true),
hasStudentGPALevel(?s, ?l), greaterThanOrEqual(?l, 2.5) → hasSuggestedMaterial
ToStudent(?s, ?m)
```

Figure 8. Rule syntax from SWRL Tab of Protégé for Case 1 and the asserted data for the student id '00004'.

Figure 9. Rule syntax from SWRL Tab of Protégé for Case 2 and the asserted data for the student id '00004'.

Figure 8 displays the outcome of the above SWRL rule in the Property Assertions window at the right bottom where the execution result is shown circled in red. The *hasSuggestedMaterialToStudent* property suggests the *Test* type material *01_Math106_01_03* for the student id *'00004'*.

Case 2

For this casework, the system will try to obtain a study plan for a college student having id *'00004'*, whose suitable learning material type being *Test*, concerning Equilateral Triangles in *Math106* course, according to the grade level being *3.0* and also the *Previous_Material* taken being *01_Math106_01_003*, then, the reasoner prefers the outcome *01_Math106_01_004* as the *Next_Material* for the student to use. This result is being displayed in the Property Assertions window at the right bottom corner. In fact, it should be noted that before the inferencing task got executed, there was no value suggested for the *Next_Material* property. As inferencing takes place, the system infers a new truth according to the 4th rule. Figure 9 displays the outcome which the reasoner recommends to take, that is, *01_Math106_01_004* as the next material. Incidentally, inferencing is affected using the Pellet Reasoner plugin by Clark & Parsia (http://clarkparsia.com/pellet/protege/) for Protégé 4 in these examples.

```
The 4th Rule: Student (?s), Previous_Material (?s, 01_Math106_01_003), hasEducationDegree (?s, College), hasFocusedTopic (?s, Equilateral_Triangles), hasSuitableMaterialType (?s, Test), hasTakenCourse (?s, Math106), hasStudentLevel (?s, ?l), greaterThanOrEqual (?l, 2.0) → Next_Material (?s, 01_Math106_01_004)
```

Gagné's hierarchy of learning offers guidance for instructors to *"identify prerequisites that should be completed to facilitate learning at each level"* (Kearsley, 1994). This learning hierarchy also delivers a base for sequencing instruction. Gagné sequences the following nine events of instruction from the first to the last and their corresponding cognitive processes (Kearsley, 1994):

1. Gaining attention (reception),
2. Informing learners of the objective (expectancy),
3. Stimulating recall of prior learning (retrieval),
4. Presenting the stimulus (selective perception),
5. Providing learning guidance (semantic encoding),
6. Eliciting performance (responding),
7. Providing feedback (reinforcement),
8. Assessing performance (retrieval),
9. Enhancing retention and transfer (generalization).

These nine instructional actions are inserted into the MO being the steps of the instructor methodology as marked by a red oval on the Protégé left column in the Figure 10. They are utilized by the reasoner while generating a suitable learning plan to help students achieve instructional objectives. Next, let's take a teaching strategy scenario involving the learning hierarchy of Gagné.

Case 3

Instructor may define the nine sequencing instructions to demonstrate '*equilateral triangle*' for the students according to their learning preferences, focused topic, grade levels, interests or learning abilities, so on.

Instructional Objective

Recognize an equilateral triangle (example from Kearsley, 1994).

Methodology

1. **Gain_Attention:** Show a variety of computer generated triangles (to do that find a list of all *Animation* type materials suitable and relevant for the *Gain Attention* stage)
2. **Identify_Objective:** Pose question: "What is an equilateral triangle?" (to do that list interactive type *Test* materials related to the *Identify_Objective* stage)
3. **Recall_Prior_Learning:** Review definitions of triangles (find a list of all related *Books*, *Presentations* etc. for this stage)
4. **Present_Stimulus:** Give definition of equilateral triangle (find/list all related *Books*, *Presentations* etc.)
5. **Guide_Learning:** Show example of how to create equilateral triangle (find/list all related *Animations*, *Videos* etc. for this stage)
6. **Elicit_Performance:** Ask students to create 5 different examples (find/list all related interactive type *Tests*, interactive type *Animations*, etc. for this stage)
7. **Provide_Feedback:** Check all examples as correct/incorrect (instructor marks *Test* results)

8. **Assess_Performance:** Provide scores and remediation (instructor evaluates scores – success or fail)
9. **Enhance_Retention_Transfer:** Show pictures of objects and ask students to identify equilateral triangles (find/list all related interactive type *Tests* for this stage).

All seven of the stages (*Gain_Attention, Identify_Objective, Recall_Prior_Learning, Present_Stimulus, Guide_Learning, Elicit_Performance* and *Enhance_Retention_Transfer*) are inserted into the ontology as shown on the Class Hierarchy window on the left column in Figure 10. They are expressed through SWRL rules in the system to find suitable LOs from the learning materials pool according to the objectives of these stages. Namely, the aim of these stages is to provide the set of materials that are of suitable type and content for the students to finish each stage successfully. By the way, it does not make sense to try express *Provide_Feedback* and *Assess_Performance* stages in SWRL rules as they are carried out by the instructor.

Initially when an LO material is uploaded to the system the instructor links it with one of the methodology stages. For instance, Figure 6 and Table 2 represent the material "#01_Math106_01_003" of the Math 106 with the object and data type properties such as "#Audio_Content_Property" is false, "#Image_Content_Property" is true, "#Interactive_Content_Property" is true, "#Material_Language" is English, "#MultiMedia_Property" is false, etc. The asserted data "#01_Math106 01_003" of the Math 106 is assigned by the instructor.

Figure 10 depicts the inference results for Case 3. The system tries to obtain a learning plan for the student id *'00004',* whose suitable learning material type being *Test*, concerning *Math106* course, having GPA level *3.4.* These are displayed in the Property Assertions window at the right bottom corner (in bold, outside of the red rectangle. Then, the reasoner tries to find suitable *Next_Material* (s) by taking into account only *Gain_Attention_StageandIdentify_Objective_Stage* properties while generating his/

Figure 10. Rule syntax from SWRL Tab of Protégé for the fourth and sixth rules and the asserted data for the student id '00004'. The rule base suggests a set of suitable next materials for the Gain Attention and Identify Objective stages of the Gagné learning hierarchy.

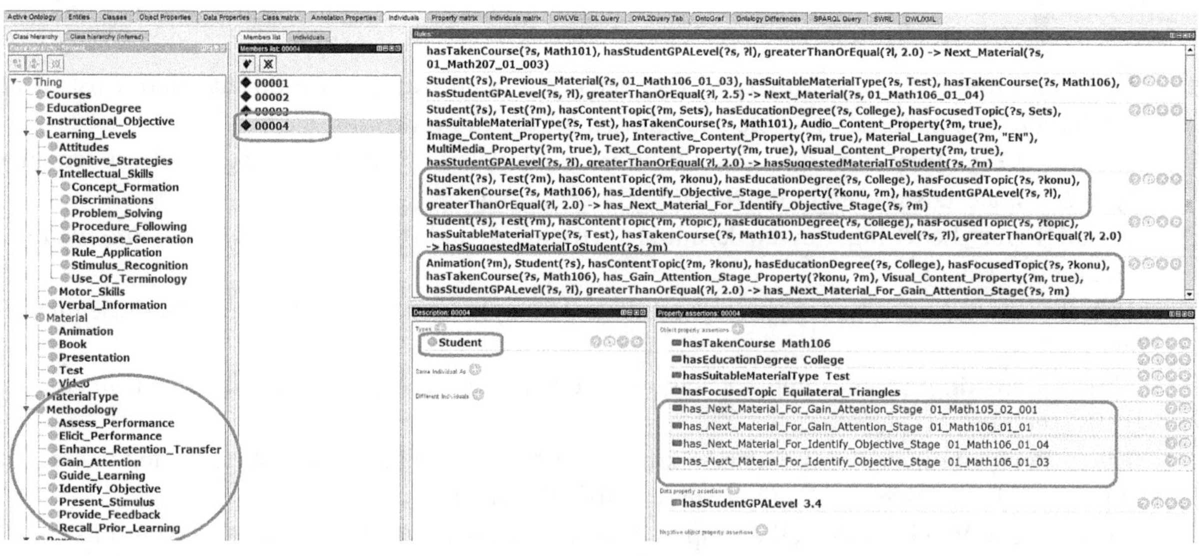

her study plan.). In fact, before the inferencing task, there is no values suggested for *has_Next_Material_For_Gain_Attention_Stage* and none for *has_Next_Material_For_Identify_Objective_Stage* properties. As the inferencing takes place, the system infers new truths according to Rules 4 and 6 as follows:

```
Student: 0004 ->for the property: has_Next_Material_For_Gain_Attention_Stage
->Inferred Next Material: 01_Math105_02_001
Student: 0004 ->for the property: has_Next_Material_For_Gain_Attention_Stage
->Inferred Next Material: 01_Math106_01_01
Student: 0004 ->for the property: has_Next_Material_For_Identify_Objective_
Stage
->Inferred Next Material: 01_Math106_01_04
Student: 0004 -> for the property: has_Next_Material_For_Identify_Objective_
Stage
->Inferred Next Material: 01_Math106_01_03
```

As shown above, the reasoning system is able use the asserted data for each LO to classify it as appropriate for one or more of the nine stages of instruction. Then, this feature forms the groundwork for the system in suggesting a set of materials for each stage for a student through evaluating that individual's background and standing through the SWRL rule base.

Along the same lines, teaching strategy can be expressed using SWRL rules in an intelligent tutoring system. For example, Wang, Kashani and Kim (2005) investigates a generic framework for determining a sequence of actions on the fly based on the circumstances and conditioned by prevailing rule base of the intelligent tutoring systems. The ontological base for representing generic teaching strategies as well as their explicit expression in terms of SWRL rules is studied. Teaching goals are modeled through a generic hierarchical representation where each teaching goal may have subgoals and strategies. Due to hierarchical organization, subgoals to any depth can be represented. Each teaching strategy is actually encoded as a SWRL rule. Protégé SWRL Tab is used to enter and edit rules and Jess (Friedmann-Hill, 2003) reasoner plugin is employed as the inference engine. As an example, "Practice If Low Confidence" teaching strategy computing an eligible set of suitable LOs is implemented and explained in detail. The study, actually aiming to explore the suitability of SWRL and the set of tools for this application, concludes that organizing the development of teaching strategy rules in SWRL programming language makes sense. (PS: Currently, the SWRLJessTab is available as a plug-in to the SWRLTab in Protege-OWL and it supports SWRL rules automatic conversion and execution using the Jess inference engine. http://protege.cim3.net/cgi-bin/wiki.pl?SWRLJessTab). It should be noted that in all the examples worked out above we used the Pellet reasoner.

Semantic technologies have been also applied in education to a much larger problem space such as degree-program design. Gluga, Kay, and Lever (2013) report on a design, development and extensive successful testing of a semantic approach ensuring that constraints of the degree program are satisfied by the sequence of learning activities, topics, and assessments.

FUTURE RESEARCH DIRECTIONS

The need for a metadata model based on semantic web technologies in order to help coordinate e-learning, especially remedial action, was expressed a decade ago (Elçi, 2004; Elçi, 2005). The study looked into the mechanisms of e-learning environment and the question concerning how e-learning could become more effective. The objective was to eventually build e-learning environment displaying capability to semantically integrate and selectively retrieve e-content. It was noted that LTSC LTSA needed augmenting with respect to control and coordination of processes and expressing semantics of LO contents. Subsequently, various theoretical and operational aspects of the issue, but especially on searching (Çelik & Elçi, 2012) and finding LOs based on semantic keys (Çelik et al., 2011; Çelik, Elçi, İnan, Elverici & Elçi, 2014), sequencing them to satisfy learner criteria (Çelik, & Elçi, 2014; Çelik & Elçi, 2012), serving LOs to the learner and monitoring progress with remedial action and employing agent systems in such research were done. Of late, the research was focused on VLE design based on metasystems learning design approach for teaching and learning of Science, Technology, Engineering, and Mathematics (STEM) topics. The approach emphasizes the role of educational data mining, semantic technology, participatory design, personalized curricula, and learning processes (Railean et al, 2015).

Semantic description and presentation-wise standardized LOs have better chance of being re-used as learning materials. Increased use of content specific metadata and expression in XML to incorporate tags or labels within e-learning content help improve the structure of LOs that software systems can interpret. Encoding the tags in a particular way, say, using the Resource Description Framework (RDF, http://www.w3.org/RDF/) allows dynamically building learning plans consisting of a network of related LOs. Combining with the use of ontology concepts in further defining relations among objects and the use of specific ontology expression transcription languages will likely lead to the "Semantic e-Learning" (after Berners-Lee, Hendler & Lassila, 2001).

The true power of the Semantic e-Learning will likely be realized by employing intelligent software agents (ISA) in seeking out LOs, helping learner to decide on appropriate material, monitoring development of the learner through learning plan and possibly charting a new course when needed. ISA, software programs that can search the repositories in the VLE as well as in the open sources on the public cloud and the Web to find LOs based on the semantically specified search criteria. This could herald a new era of collaborative developments, enhancing tutors' abilities to work within e-learning environments and providing learners with what they want, when they want it. This would be quite in line with the findings of a think-tank workshop organized by Computing Research Association on determining the "Grand Research Challenges in Information System" (CRA, 2003, p.16). One of the five grand challenges is "Providing a teacher for every learner", that is, tutoring each individual in a tailored, learner-centered approach and content in order to enable people to more fully realize their potential. Five research areas required to overcome the challenge are listed as follows:

- Cognitive tutors (and knowledge representations).
- Simulation-based (clip) models.
- Massive multiplayer online games.
- Collaborative authoring.
- Learning in context/just-in-time learning.

The Semantic E-Learning initiative is likely address the areas of Cognitive tutors and knowledge representation, Collaborative authoring, and Learning in context/just-in-time learning. More work along these lines is highly recommended.

Utilization of multi-agent modality in implementing e-learning environments should be looked into with a keen interest rather than as a passing hobby. Intelligent agent paradigm has a solid base in theory and practice, hence can contribute to educational technology as it did to other research areas. There have been approaches employing intelligent agents in connection with SCORM and LTSA models as already mentioned. In an interesting and novel research, Wilges, Mateus, Silveira and Nassar (2007) chooses to build 'intelligent LOs' on a whole new semantics and agent oriented e-learning framework based on the Foundation for Intelligent Physical Agents (FIPA-OS) framework (FIPA, 2014). This framework uses an ontology represented in the FIPA Semantic Language (FIPA-SL) and in connection with the FIPA Agent Communication Language (FIPA-ACL). As opposed to the API-based static communication between SCORM package and the VLE being necessarily fixed at design time, ILOs built using this new framework communicate by messages through the ACL and a content language. The use of the ACL affords a 'wider dynamic to the process' by 'giving more semantics to the communication.' ILOs, responsible for animation within the environment in communication with the Animated Pedagogical Agent (APA), help adaptation, flexibility and increasing interoperability among the components in the VLE. Sun et al. (2007) combines metadata, learner profile and multi-agent technology in using learning style to address personalization of learning.

In addressing personal learning needs of individuals repurposing of LOs will be required for which semantics technology will likely help greatly. Recognizing this pressing need, researchers have inquired into organizing LOs so that they could be searched, discovered, refitted and may be even inserted into learning plans easily on the go. Altun and Askar (2008) propose a model for designing granules of LOs based on concept and skill ontologies developed from K-12 curricula. By using a 'learning space metaphor', LOs built by separating expectations as skills and concepts, can eventually be used to provide adaptive and personalized learning resources. Repurposing of small size LOs with clear semantic connection is inherently easier. Noor, Yusof and Hashim (2011) recognizing that as the LO size decreases its potential for reuse increases, proposes a prototype of learning objects repository to contain granular LOs to show the process of granularizing an LO. The process extracts an existing LO into granular elements with the associated metadata a-la-LTSC LOM. Ontological classification of LOs and LO repositories is extremely important towards achieving interoperability of resources. Lee, Tsai, Hsieh, Chiu and Wang (2007) evolves a semantics-aware classification algorithm automatically mapping sharable learning objects from heterogeneous repositories into a local e-learning ontology knowledge base through the semantic inference rules. Should learning resources get built in unison with an e-learning ontological model it would be all the more easy to repurpose them by retrofitting them to the needs of individual learners. Su, Ma, Li, Cheng and Huang (2008) work out an exemplary model and the associated resource management environment. Titled the 'semantic-oriented ubiquitous learning object model', the SULOM can be used to describe ubiquitous learning resources, to construct semantic relationship between LOs thus forming the foundation for resource enquiry, reorganization and collaborative knowledge building. It would be highly desirable that during creation of their content LOs are annotated with links to e-learning ontologies so that their content semantics could be marked up explicitly as opposed to item description only which is the case for LOM. In any case, early research had shown that relying on LOM only for classification is not the way to go (Friesen, 2004b). Actually, the LOM model caters for the inclusion of custom elements not in the specification in order to describe resource characteristics. This feature is useful to indicate, say, version compatibility or specific purpose metadata links for example to an e-learning ontology for the time being. However, it should be noted that this is a stop-gap measure until LOM gets a full overhaul fitting to serve fully e-learning ontology purposes. A rich set of content related semantics through ontologies will help broaden and enhance the impact of personalization as well (Zhuhadar & Nasraoui, 2008). In any case, mature e-learning ontologies would be highly useful any time. Personalization of learning would also call for sequencing of LOs into a learning program on demand, possibly and preferably by the learner. To be able to wholly achieve that end, LOs must support semantics beyond what LOM provides so researchers are looking for ways to realize that. Considering competences of the learner and LO metadata, de-Marcos, Martinez and Guiterrez (2007) developed an approach to personalize courseware. Similarly, Chen (2008) compares learner ability against courseware difficulty level to determine curriculum sequencing. Tugsgerel, Anane and Theodoropoulos (2010) proposes a framework to reconcile learner profile and LO metadata to enable learners to construct learning paths (LP). The paper assumes that LOs are advertised as Web services; discovered and used as such. However, description of Web services through the Web Services Description Language (WSDL) is syntactic and LOM metadata provides resource description not content semantics.

For obtaining any meaningful result, researchers find it necessary either to extend LOM with custom terms or enhance its reach to additional learning resources. For example, Menolli, Reinehr and Malucelli (2012) recognize that the LOM standard has limitations in terms of expressiveness needed for representing hierarchical taxonomies, relations, properties, as well as semantic constraints between LOs, properties and categories. They developed OOLO Ontology based on LOM standard and FOAF Ontology in order to represent organizational learning objects taking into account educational and organizational properties. OOLO ontology is for adding organizational properties in order to allow companies to organize information at the same time facilitating content reuse thus helping to improve organizational learning. OOLO together with an ontology or educational concept map (Adorni, Coccoli & Vivanet, 2011) can be used to create a generic context of learning environments. Extending the search for and harvesting of LOs based on Dublin Core ontology, which is essentially LOM, to semantic repositories of the Linked Open Data cloud, such as Wikipedia, is another complimentary paradigm (Bizer, Heath & Berners-Lee, 2009). Approaches to annotate automatically the subject of an LO with instances of the DBPedia ontology are being offered as well (Lama, Vidal, Otero-Garcia, Bugarin & Barro, 2011; Bizer, Lehmann, Auer, Becker, Cyganiak & Hellmann, 2009).

On the pragmatics side, several organizations besides IEEE LTSC have been playing rather influential roles in e-learning arena thus developments at their fronts must be followed with distinctive attention to detail. The IMS Global Learning Consortium (IMS GLC; http://www.imsglobal.org/) is a global, nonprofit, member organization addressing education and corporate learning sectors towards enabling the growth and impact of learning technology. IMS GLC is concerned with interoperability in learning systems and content towards enterprise capability integration. The Advanced Distributed Learning (ADL, http://www.adlnet.gov, http://www.adlnet.org) Initiative, being a part of the USA Federal Government, is charged with "to provide flexible training opportunities to employees and to explore how federal training programs, initiatives, and policies can better support lifelong learning through the use of learning technology." The originator of the SCORM compendium of standards and specifications recently has been researching on "The Personal Assistant for Learning (PAL)." This research likely to span two decades is aiming to create a capability that "anticipates learner needs, seamlessly integrates yet-to-be available information, and provides ubiquitous access to effective, personalized learning content and/or job performance aids that can be accessed from multiple non-invasive devices and platforms"

(Poltrack, Branon & Nelson, 2011 August). Last, but not least, the Aviation Industry CBT Committee (AICC, http://www.aicc.org) has been a pace setter all along. The AICC, a nonprofit, membership-driven consortium, is dedicated "to helping the training community get the most out of training technology" by bringing together all interested stakeholders such as trainers, courseware developers, software vendors, simulator designers and plain manufacturers to develop standards, technology recommendations and analysis of best practices.

Security and privacy of learner data in e-learning environments have not attracted much interest. Security would be concerned with ways and means of implementing data integrity and protection policies. Privacy on the other hand can be described as a learner's ability to maintain personal boundaries within which the use of personal information is controlled by the learner. Security and privacy were of little concern if any for early standards developers such as IMS, ADL, AICC, ARIADNE, so on; most of them focused on content management, meta-data specification and process monitoring with little reference, if any, to security and privacy. LTSC on the other hand identified security features in LTSA but without a fully elaborated model and practically leaving privacy to be protected as the consequence of information security (El-Khatib, Korba, Xu & Yee, 2003). Very recently another important development happened that is likely to exacerbate the security and privacy situation: ADL Initiative developed the successor to SCORM runtime which became the Experience API (http://www.adlnet.gov/tla/experience-api/). The xAPI for short is bigdata and cloud data compatible technology so all of a sudden the personal learning data became ubiquitous and mobile. In exploiting this new found capability, the tool is augmented with the Learning Record Store (LRS, http://www.adlnet.gov/tla/lrs/), a repository for learner activity data, such as, test scores, training session completions and participation in any learning event, anywhere. The LRS learning technology renders data and the analysis of learning events available in a snap. Combined facts that user tracking becoming a legal requirement almost universally (May & George, 2011), social learning is expanding and turning ubiquitous, more learners resorting to open source Internet resources for training material, are casting a fresh spell on security and privacy, but especially the latter, of personal learning data. Furthermore, the trend to migrate even the traditionally in house application systems such as VLE and LMS to cloud servers is creating big data repositories already. Doubtless the cloud-based data resources are well guarded but mishaps do happen and when they do data leak is at catastrophic scale. With security and privacy concerns trust erodes; soon there will be a dire need for trust and privacy-preserving e-learning environments (Anwar & Greer, 2012).

As quoted already, Sorel Reisman (2014) considers today's LMSs as mere online content presenters without being able to custom fit the content to the learner's needs. In winding up this section let's recall the continuation of that quote: "The real solution to this situation is something called "adaptive learning"—a model of instruction that we tried to implement in the 1950s, but without the kind of success that we can begin to realize today with technologies that were absent in those days."

CONCLUSION

A metadata model based on content semantics was explored in this chapter aiming for e-learning coordination in order to meet learner needs. E-learning models were reviewed noting the lacking features to affect learner-centric on demand action. In this respect, the study inquired into e-learning environments considering the question of how processes may be controlled and coordinated. Semantic Web concepts and related languages were employed in the learner centric proposal involving semantics, control and coordination of e-learning and which coexists with the IEEE Learning Technology Standards Committee's industry leader Learning Technology System Architecture. Examples were worked out and future research directions were identified.

There is need to involve Semantic Web approach throughout all stages of e-learning. The Semantic Web renders web resources equally intelligible for both human and software. By incorporating the meaning and context (semantics) of information, it brings structure to the Web through capability to interpret its constituent resource. The concept of Web services, where online transactional services are loosely coupled through common directories and exchange protocols, has also gained solid ground in e-content therefore in e-learning as well. Eventually, e-content will be rendered easier and friendlier to consume and a better tool to serve all information needs. E-learning activities doubtless will draw benefit from being able to generate semantic metadata, to structure, filter, retrieve and maintain it in semantically so as to turn data into shareable and repurposed knowledge. Thus, in the near future, e-learning systems will use Semantic Web-based knowledge systems as key parts of everyday learning cycles. It appears that the future as envisioned a decade ago is likely to materialize with major involvement of the semantic, agent and linguistic technologies in learning sciences perhaps to some extent due to cognitive sciences backdrop of both sides: "Our vision of teachers and learners immersed in a network of rich learning objects that are continually enriched and enhanced by the participants is achievable through anticipated advances in information technology and learning sciences" (CRA, 2003, p.16).

April 2014 issue of the Computing Now's theme is 'Semantics in Education' in which the recent trends in the research field are reviewed. It is showcased among others how to simplify and improve access to LOs in VLEs across institutions and networks. This is through support of interoperable knowledge repositories and employing semantics of content and context in effectively seeking contents meeting queries of students and teachers. To conclude with the conclusion of that review, "The opportunities for semantic technologies in education are enormous. They offer a mechanism to address technical, organizational, linguistic, and other constraints that can hinder the seamless sharing, processing, and adaptation of heterogeneous learning resources. We invite you to dig into the wealth of possibilities, starting with the topics in this month's theme" (Lamberti, Gatteschi, Demartini, Sanna & Montuschi, 2014).

REFERENCES

ACM eLearn Magazine. (n.d.). Retrieved from http://elearnmag.acm.org/

ADL. (n.d.). *Advanced Distributed Learning Initiative of the US Government, Department of Defense*. Retrieved October 1, 2014. Retrieved from http://www.adlnet.org

Adorni, G., Coccoli, M., & Vivanet, G. (2011). Educational concept maps: a knowledge based aid for Instructional Design. *Proceedings of the 17th International Conference on Distributed Multimedia Systems, DMS 2011*, (pp. 234-237). Retrieved from http://www.ksi.edu/seke/Proceedings/dms11/DET/6_Giuliano_Vivanet.pdf

AICC (Aviation Industry CBT Committee). (n.d.). *Computer Managed Instruction (CMI)*. Retrieved from http://www.aicc.org/

Altun, A., & Askar, P. (2008). *From Blocks to Granules: An Alternative Approach to Designing Learning Objects*. Paper presented at the Eighth IEEE International Conference on Advanced Learning Technologies ICALT '08. doi:doi:10.1109/ICALT.2008.68 doi:10.1109/ICALT.2008.68

Anwar, M., & Greer, J. (2012). Facilitating trust in privacy-preserving E-Learning environments. *IEEE Transactions on Learning Technologies*, *5*(1), 62–73. doi:10.1109/TLT.2011.23

Barker, P., & Campbell, L. M. (2014). *Learning Resource Metadata Initiative: using schema.org to describe open educational resources*. Presented in OCW (Open Course Ware) Consortium Global Conference, Ljubljana, Slovenia. Retrieved from http://conference.ocwconsortium.org/2014/wp-content/uploads/2014/02/Paper_34-LMRI1.pdf

Belfanti, P., & Gylling, M. (2014). *What is EDUPUB?* Presented in EDUPUB 2 Workshop, Salt Lake City, UT. Retrieved from http://www.imsglobal.org/edupub/WhatisEdupubBelfantiGylling.pdf

Berners-Lee, T., Hendler, J., & Lassila, O. (2001). The Semantic Web. *Scientific American*. Retrieved from http://www.scientificamerican.com/article.cfm?articleID=00048144-10D2-1C70-84A9809EC588EF21&catID=2

Bizer, C., Heath, T., & Berners-Lee, T. (2009). Linked data: The story so far. *International Journal on Semantic Web and Information Systems*, *5*, 1–22.

Bizer, C., Lehmann, J., & Auer, G. K. A. (2009). DBpedia: A crystallization point for the Web of Data. *Journal of Web Semantics*, *7*(3), 154–165. doi:10.1016/j.websem.2009.07.002

Bohl, O., Schellhase, J., Sengler, R., & Winand, U. (2002). The Sharable Content Object Reference Model (SCORM) - A Critical Review.*Proceedings of the International Conference on Computers in Education (ICCE'02)*. doi:10.1109/CIE.2002.1186122

Bray, B., & McClaskey, K. (n.d.). *Personalized Learning Chart* [Online]. Retrieved from https://sites.google.com/site/personalizedlearningtoolkits/

Brittain, S. (1999). *A framework for pedagogical evaluation of Virtual Learning Environments*. The Joint Information Systems Committee (JISC) Framework (JISC) Technology Applications Programme, Report no: 41. Retrieved from http://www.jisc.ac.uk/jtap/htm/jtap-041.html

CDLP. (n.d.). *California Distance Learning Project: What is Distance Learning?* Retrieved March 21, 2014, Retrieved from http://www.cdlponline.org/index.cfm?fuseaction=whatis

Çelik, D., & Elçi, A. (2011). Towards a semantic-based workflow model to composition of OWL-S based atomic processes through process similarity matching and inferencing techniques. *Journal of Internet Technology*, *12*(1), 153–170.

Çelik, D. & Elçi, A. (2012). A broker-based semantic agent for discovering Semantic Web services through process similarity matching and equivalence considering quality of service. *Science China Information Sciences, 56*(1), 012102:1–012102:24.

Çelik, D., & Elçi, A. (2014). Semantic composition of business processes using Armstrong's Axioms. *The Knowledge Engineering Review*, *29*(2), 248–264. doi:10.1017/S0269888914000083

Çelik, D., Elçi, A., & Elverici, E. (2011). Finding suitable course material through a semantic search agent for Learning Management Systems of distance education. *Proceedings of 6th IEEE International Workshop on Engineering Semantic Agent Systems(ESAS 2011) in conjunction with the 35th Computer Software and Applications Conference (COMPSAC 2011)* (pp. 386-391).

Çelik, D., Elçi, A., İnan, N., Elverici, E., & Elçi, A. (2014). Educational Activity Discovery System for Individuals with Pervasive Developmental Disorders through Web Ontology Language (OWL). *Education and Science*, *39*(171), 52–73.

Ceraulo, S. C. (2003). Instructional design for flow in online learning. *ACM eLearn Magazine*. Retrieved, from http://www.elearnmag.org/subpage/sub_page.cfm?section=4&list_item=10&page=1

Chen C. M. (2008). Intelligent web-based learning system with personalized learning path guidance. *Computers & Education, 51*(2) 2008, 787-814.

CMC. (2008). *eLearning glossary*. Retrieved from http://www.cybermediacreations.com/elearning/glossary.html

Corbière, A., & Choquet, C. (2004). Designer Integration in Training Cycle. *Proceedings of International Conference on Computer Aided Learning in Engineering Education (CALIE 2004)*. Retrieved from http://telearn.archives-ouvertes.fr/docs/00/19/03/08/PDF/Alain-Corbiere-2004.pdf

CRA. (2003). *Grand research challenges in Information Systems*. Final report of CRA Conference on "Grand Research Challenges" in Computer Science and Engineering, Warrenton, VA. Retrieved from http://archive.cra.org/reports/gc.systems.pdf

Csikszentmihalyi, M. (1990). *The Psychology of Optimal Experience*. New York, NY: Harper Collins.

de-Marcos, L., Pages, C., Martinez, J., & Gutierrez, J. (2007). Competency-Based Learning Object Sequencing Using Particle Swarms.*19th IEEE International Conference on Tools with Artificial Intelligence*, *2*, 111-116. doi:10.1109/ICTAI.2007.14

Dede, C. (2014). *New wine in no bottles: immersive, personalized, ubiquitous learning*. Keynote talk at Learning @ Scale, Atlanta, GA. Retrieved from http://learningatscale.acm.org/talks/keynote_chris_dede.pdf

Dodds, P. (Ed.). (2003). Sharable Courseware Object Reference Model (SCORM) Version 1.0. Alexandria, VA: Institute for Defense Analysis. Retrieved from http://www.adlnet.gov/wp-content/uploads/2011/07/SCORM_1_2_pdf.zip

Downes, S. (2005). E-learning 2.0. *ACM eLearn Magazine*. Retrieved from http://elearnmag.acm.org/archive.cfm?aid=1104968

El-Khatib, K., Korba, L., Xu, Y., & Yee, G. (2003). Privacy and security in E-Learning. *International Journal of Distance Education*, *1*(4), 1–19. doi:10.4018/jdet.2003100101

Elçi, A. (2004): A Metadata for E-Learning Coordination through Semantic Web Languages. In A. İşman, & F. Dabaj (Eds.), *Proceedings of The IETC 2004, IV. International Symposium on Educational Technology* (pp. 27-32).

Elçi, A. (2005). A metadata for E-Learning coordination through semantic web languages. *The Turkish Online Journal of Educational Technology, 4*(3), 27-32. Retrieved from http://www.tojet.net/articles/433.pdf

European Commission. (2014). *Digital Agenda for Europe: A Europe 2020 Initiative*. Retrieved from Action 68: Member States to mainstream eLearning in national policies of Pillar VI: Enhancing digital literacy, skills and inclusion at http://ec.europa.eu/digital-agenda/en/pillar-vi-enhancing-digital-literacy-skills-and-inclusion/action-68-member-states-mainstream

FIPA (Foundation For Intelligent Physical Agents). (n.d.). *FIPA-OS publicly available agent platform implementation*. Retrieved from http://fipa.org/resources/livesystems.html#os

Friedmann-Hill, E. (2003). *Jess in Action*. Greenwich, CT: Manning.

Friesen, N. (2004a). Three objections to Learning Objects and E-learning standards. In R. McGreal (Ed.), Online Education Using Learning Objects (pp. 59-70). London, UK: Routledge.

Friesen, N. (2004b). The International Learning Object Metadata Survey. *International Review of Research in Open and Distance Learning*, *5*(3). Retrieved from http://www.irrodl.org/index.php/irrodl/article/view/195/277

Gluga, R., Kay, J., & Lever, T. (2013). Foundations for modeling university curricula in terms of multiple learning goal sets. *IEEE Transactions on Learning Technologies*, *6*(1), 25–37. doi:10.1109/TLT.2012.17

Handel, S. (2014). *The evolving role of Instructional Design in a 70:20:10 World*. [K16 online Jan 23, 2014]. Retrieved from http://www.k16online.com/blog/bid/371326/The-Evolving-Role-of-Instructional-Design-in-a-70-20-10-World?goback=%2Egde_72496_member_5832573999493705730

Hartshorne, R. (2003). Thoughtful creation of online course content: implications of SCORM for educators. *The Free Library*. Retrieved from http://www.thefreelibrary.com/Thoughtfulcreationofonlinecourse content:implicationsofSCORM...-a0101943714

Imperial College. (n.d.). *An E-Learning Glossary*. Retrieved from http://www3.imperial.ac.uk/ict/services/e-learning/old site/aboutelearning/elearningglossary

Kearsley, G. (1994). *Conditions of Learning (R. Gagne)*. [Online]. Retrieved from http://www.instructionaldesign.org/theories/conditions-learning.html

Khan, B. H. (2003). A Framework for Open, Flexible and Distributed E-Learning, in *ACM eLearn Magazine*. Retrieved, from http://www.elearnmag.org/subpage/sub_page.cfm?section=3&list_item=12&page=1

Khan, B. H. (2004). People, process and product continuum in e-learning: The e-learning P3 model. *Educational Technology*, *44*(5), 33–40. http://asianvu.com/bookstoread/etp/elearning-p3model.pdf

Khan, B. H. (2014a). *E-Learning Framework*. Retrieved from http://asianvu.com/bk/framework/ and http://www.asianvu.com/bookstoread/framework/scroller.htm

Khan, B. H. (2014b). *Other Frameworks on E-Learning*. Retrieved from http://asianvu.com/bk/framework/?page_id=2396

Lama, M., Vidal, J. C., Otero-Garcia, E., Bugarin, A., & Barro, S. (2011). Semantic Linking of a Learning Object Repository to DBpedia. *11th IEEE International Conference on Advanced Learning Technologies (ICALT)* (pp.460-464). doi:10.1109/ICALT.2011.143

Lamberti, F., Gatteschi, V., Demartini, C., Sanna, A., & Montuschi, P. (2014). Semantics in Education. *Computing Now, 7*(4). Retrieved from http://www.computer.org/portal/web/computingnow/archive/april2014

Lee, M. C., Tsai, K. H., Hsieh, T. C., Chiu, T. K., & Wang, T. I. (2007). An ontological approach for semantic learning objects interoperability. *Proceeding of Seventh IEEE International Conference on Advanced Learning Technologies ICALT 2007* (pp. 222-226). doi:10.1109/ICALT.2007.63

LTSA. (1998). *Learning Technology Systems Architecture (LTSA).* Retrieved from http://ltsc.ieee.org/wg1/files/ltsa-400.doc

LTSA. (n.d.). *IEEE Learning Technology System Architecture (LTSA).* Retrieved from http://www.informatik.uni-bremen.de/uniform/gdpa/gdpa06.htm

LTSC. (2013). *IEEE Standards Activities in the eLearning Space*. Retrieved from http://standards.ieee.org/develop/msp/elearning.pdf

LTSC. (n.d.). *The IEEE LTSC home page.* Retrieved from http://ieeeltsc.org/

LTSC LOM WG. (n.d.). *LOM: What next?* Retrieved from http://ariadne.cs.kuleuven.be/mediawiki2/index.php/lomwhatnext/issues

Lytras, M. D., Pouloudi, N., & Poulymenakou, A. (2002). Knowledge management convergence: Expanding learning frontiers. *Journal of Knowledge Management*, *6*(1), 40–51. doi:10.1108/13673270210417682

May, M., & George, S. (2011). Privacy concerns in E-learning: Is using tracking system a threat? *International Journal of Information and Education Technology*, *1*(1), 1–8. doi:10.7763/IJIET.2011.V1.1

Menolli, A. L. A., Reinehr, S., & Malucelli, A. (2012). Ontology for organizational learning objects based on LOM standard. *XXXVIII Conferencia Latinoamericana En Informatica*, *2012*, 1–10.

Mih, C., & Mih, V. (2011). Conceptual maps as mediators of self-regulated learning. *Social and Behavioral Sciences*, *29*, 390–395.

Noor, S. F. M., Yusof, N., & Hashim, S. Z. M. (2011). Creating granular learning object towards reusability of Learning Object in e-learning context. *International Conference on Electrical Engineering and Informatics (ICEEI)* (pp. 1-5). doi:10.1109/ICEEI.2011.6021645

Novak, J., & Gowin, D. (1996). *Learning How To Learn*. New York, NY: Cambridge University Press.

Pena, C. I., Marzo, J. L., & de la Rosa J. L. (2005). Intelligent agents to improve adaptivity in a web-based learning environment. *Knowledge-Based Virtual Education - Studies in Fuzziness and Soft Computing, 178*, 141-170.

Poltrack, J., Branon, R., & Nelson, J. (2011 August). *SCORM Update*. Presented in iFest 2011, Orlando, FL. Retrieved from http://www.adlnet.gov/wp-content/uploads/2011/08/poltrack_branon_nelson_SCORM_update_iFest2011.pdf

Railean, E., Elçi, A., Çelik, D., & Elçi, A. (2015). Metasystems learning design approach for STEM teaching and learning. In E. C. Ostler (Ed.), An Overview of Contemporary Research, Trends, and Perspectives (pp. 54-83). Elkhorn, Nebraska: Cycloid Publications. ISBN 978-0-9966741-1-9.

Reisman, S. (2014). The Future of Online Instruction, Part 1. *Computer*, *47*(4), 92–93. doi:10.1109/MC.2014.106

Richards, T. (2014). *IEEE Actionable Data Book - IEEE LTSC*. [Presentation]. Retrieved from http://www.gtn-quebec.org/wp-content/uploads/2014/03/Tyde-Richards-IEEE-ADB-Montreal.pdf

Richards, T., & Robson, R. (2014). *The next disruption in digital learning*. Retrieved from http://www.computer.org/portal/web/Musings-from-the-Ivory-Tower/content?g=7512968&type=article&urlTitle=the-next-disruption-in-digital-learning

Salmon, G. (2001). Masters or slaves to the technology? The role of the e-moderator in e-learning. *ACM eLearn Magazine,* (6), 2. Retrieved from http://elearnmag.acm.org/archive.cfm?aid=566946

SCORM. (n.d.). *SCORM2004* (4th ed.). Retrieved from http://www.adlnet.org/scorm/scorm-2004-4th/

Sengupta, S., Chaki, N., & Dasgupta, R. (2008). Design of a Learning Management System on LTSA framework. *Proceedings of the 7th WSEAS International Conference on Education and Educational Technology* (pp. 65-70). Retrieved from http://www.wseas.us/elibrary/conferences/2008/venice/edu/edu11.pdf

Sherry, L., Havelock, B., & Gibson, D. (2005). The personal and professional learning portfolio: an online environment for mentoring, collaboration, and publication. In T. Roberts (Ed.), Computer Supported Collaborative Learning in Higher Education (pp. 201-217). Hershey, PA: Idea Group Publishing.

Shoikova, E. (2002). E-Learning Standards Overview.*The Vienna International Working Conference - eLearning and eCulture, VIEWDET 2002*.

Su, L., Ma, J., Li, Y., Cheng, M. X., & Huang, R. (2008). Semantic-oriented ubiquitous Learning Object model.*Proceedings of the 7th IEEE International Conference on Cybernetic Intelligent Systems CIS 2008*.

Sun, S., Joy, M., & Griffiths, N. (2005). To support adaptivity in agent-based learning systems - the use of learning objects and learning style.*Fifth IEEE International Conference on Advanced Learning Technologies ICALT 2005* (pp.846-847).

Sun, S., Joy, M., & Griffiths, N. (2007). The Use of Learning Objects and Learning Styles in a Multi-Agent Education System. *Journal of Interactive Learning Research, 18*(3), 381–398.

TLF (The Learning Federation). (2001). Next generation learning systems and the role of teachers. In *2020 Visions: Transforming Education and Training through Advanced Technologies* (pp: 46-51). Washington DC: Technology Administration, U.S. Department of Commerce. Retrieved from http://usa.usembassy.de/etexts/tech/2020Visions.pdf

Tsai, S., & Machado, P. (2002). *E-learning, online Learning, web-based learning, or distance learning: unveiling the ambiguity in current terminology*. Retrieved from http://www.elearnmag.org/subpage/sub_page.cfm?section=3&list_item=6&page=1

Tugsgerel, B., Anane, R., & Theodoropoulos, G. (2010). An Integrated Approach to Learning Object Sequencing. *IEEE 10th International Conference on Advanced Learning Technologies (ICALT).*

Wang, E., Kashani, L., & Kim, Y. S. (2005). Teaching strategies ontology using SWRL Rules.C. Looi, D. Jonassen, & M. Ikeda (Eds.). *Proceedings of the 2005 conference on Towards Sustainable and Scalable Educational Innovations Informed by the Learning Sciences: Sharing Good Practices of Research, Experimentation and Innovation* (pp. 532-539). Amsterdam, The Netherlands: IOS Press.

Welsch, E. (2002, Summer). SCORM: Clarity of calamity. *Online Learning*, 14-18.

Wilges, B., Mateus, G. P., Silveira, R. A., & Nassar, S. M. (2007). An animated pedagogical agent as a Learning Management System manipulating Intelligent Learning Objects.J. M. Spector, D. G. Sampson, T. Okamoto, S. A. Cerri, M. Ueno, & A. Kashihara (Eds.). *Proceedings of the 7th IEEE International Conference on Advanced Learning Technologies ICALT 2007* (pp. 186-188). doi:10.1109/ICALT.2007.53

Yli-Luoma, P., & Naeve, A. (2006). Towards a semantic E-learning theory by using a modeling approach. *British Journal of Educational Technology, 37*(3), 445-459. Retrieved from http://kmr.nada.kth.se/papers/TEL/Semantic-eLearning-theory.pdf

Zhuhadar, L., & Nasraoui, O. (2008). Semantic information retrieval for personalized E-Learning.*International Conference on Tools and Artificial Intelligence* (pp. 364-368).

KEY TERMS AND DEFINITIONS

Advanced Distributed Learning (ADL): This is an initiative of The U.S. Department of Defense with the goal to afford access to the highest quality learning according to individual needs and delivered anytime and anywhere with low cost. ADL Initiative has produced the SCORM model and the ExperienceAPI infrastructure.

Concept Map: A concept map is a diagram aiming to organize and structure knowledge by illustrating the relationships known to exist between some concepts. Concept map can be an abstraction of a system or set of concepts. Compare with mind mapping.

Educational Modeling Language (EML): Educational modeling language is the semantic information model binding instructional design and pedagogical theories with the aim of addressing the shortcomings of e-learning systems.

E-Learning (or eLearning): It is teaching and learning conducted via electronic media and information and communication technologies (ICT). E-learning uses various forms of educational technology to create a virtual learning environment (VLE) by providing equivalent technology enhanced access to classes, content, homework, tests, assessments and grades.

Framework for e-Learning: It is a foundation of technology enhanced teaching and learning systems including various dimensions that guide design, development and implementation of e-learning curriculum.

IEEE Learning Technology Standards Committee (LTSC): LTSC is established by the IEEE Computer Society Standards Activity Board. It coordinates with other organizations to develop accredited technical standards for learning technologies, recommends practices, and acts as a facilitator for learning technologies in an international basis.

IEEE Learning Technology System Architecture (LTSA): Produced by IEEE LTSC, this architecture describes the high-level system design which covers a broad range of systems such as educational technology, computer-based training, electronic performance support systems, computer assisted instruction, intelligent tutoring, learning technology and metadata.

Intelligent Agents: In reference to e-learning, intelligent agents are the software systems for improving teaching and learning performances by providing adaptivity through individualized instruction in virtual learning environments. Intelligent agents relate to Learning Objects in delivering education. See ILO.

Intelligent Learning Objects (ILO): An ILO is a learning object that extends the concept, possibly by use of software agent technology, thus combining the technologies for learning objects and for multi-agent systems. An ILO is to be reusable, interoperable, discoverable and modular.

Learning Management System (LMS): LMS is a software system used for storing, delivering, tracking and managing learning objects and full courses globally; it offers the opportunity of online learning, communication, collaboration and content sharing.

Learning Object Metadata (LOM): LOM is a multipart standard where for each learning object the IEEE 1484.12.1-2002 LOM standard specifies a conceptual data schema outlining the structure of its metadata instance. LOM consists of nine primary hierarchy categories of metadata, visually, General, Life Cycle, Meta-Metadata, Technical, Educational, Rights, Relation, Annotation, and Classification.

Massive Open Online Course (MOOC): An MOOC is a model for creating global virtual learning environments by delivering learning content online to any person who is interested to take the course, without cost and limit on attendance.

Mind Mapping: A knowledge discovery and representation technique used to draw a diagram to identify a *single* major concept by showing the associated ideas with items, words, tasks or concepts with the aim of organizing information visually. This can reflect individual or group brainstorming and maybe useful in taxonomy and ontology construction.

Sharable Content Object (SCO): An SCO is a learning object that communicates with the run-time environment (learner's web browser or in a frame in an HTML) that launched it. SCO launched for a learner will communicate with the LMS so that LMS can store/track information about learner's experiences.

Sharable Content Object Reference Model (SCORM): SCORM is the most accepted packaging standard for online learning developed by the U.S. Department of Defense, Advanced Distributed Learning Laboratories to improve the combat readiness of U.S. Military as a result improving U.S. national security. It is a set of related technical standards, specifications, and guidelines stated to improve accessibility, interoperability, durability, and reusability of content and systems.

Chapter 12
E-Learning and Faculty Development in Higher Education: A Comprehensive Project

Susan Gallagher-Lepak
University of Wisconsin, USA

Christine Vandenhouten
University of Wisconsin, USA

ABSTRACT

Growth of online higher education and advances in technology justify and encourage new models of faculty development related to e-learning. This chapter describes a multi-campus faculty development program using distance technology, a Community Of Practice (COP) model, and an e-learning framework. The Flexible Framework for E-Learning by Khan (2005) guided planning and implementation of the faculty development program. A variety of strategies were used to deliver the faculty development program including use of campus-based site leaders, participating scholars, monthly videoconferences, a faculty development handbook, hands-on use of new e-learning technologies, and a year-end conference. The program also included an evaluation of the interface design of courses used in a collaborative online nursing program with findings reported to faculty. Along with strategies used, barriers and evaluation of the multi-campus faculty development model are presented so that the faculty development model can be replicated across other universities and disciplines.

INTRODUCTION

With the growth of personal computers in the 1980s and the worldwide web in 1990s, then called the "information super highway", online learning became a new possibility. 'Online learning' typically refers to the use of an electronically supported environment which offers a structure for knowledge acquisition by the learner. Online education continues to evolve and numerous new technologies (and new versions)

DOI: 10.4018/978-1-5225-0466-5.ch012

have come to market in the past decade to improve online learning. New technologies include course management systems (e.g., Moodle, Blackboard, Desire 2 Learn), Twitter, Massive Open Online Courses (MOOCs), Local Open Online Courses (LOOCs), WIKIs, lecture capture, and mobile technology to name just a few. According to the Sloan Foundation 2013 survey, over 7.1 million higher education students in the U.S. were enrolled in at least one online course (OLC, 2013). Growth in online enrollments far exceeds growth rates in the overall population of higher education students. The evolution of distance education technologies has created conditions that require faculty to adapt to a new way of teaching and communicating with their students.

As one of the largest systems of public higher education in the country, the University of Wisconsin (UW) System serves approximately 180,000 students and employs statewide more than 39,000 faculty and staff (UW System, 2015). The UW System consists of 13 four-year universities, 13 two-year Colleges campuses, and a statewide UW-Extension. The UW system has been a major supporter of faculty development in e-learning for many years. With over a hundred years of experience in educational innovation, UW-Madison, the system's flagship university, began offering correspondence courses in 1891. In 1993, the university launched a distance education certificate program for educators at the K-12 through post-secondary systems to help educators launch courses in the World Wide Web (UW-Madison, 2013). Additionally, for over 30 years, UW-Madison has offered a popular, annual conference on distance teaching and learning which brings experts in the field of e-learning to enhance practitioners' knowledge, skill, and credibility in the delivery of online teaching.

Nursing programs in the UW System have been leaders in distance education. A 2002 survey of the National League for Nursing Accrediting Commission (NLNAC) found the greatest enrollment in online nursing programs was by far in RN-to-BSN programs (91%), a whole 35 times greater than other nursing programs with enrollment in online Masters of Science in Nursing (MSN) at only four percent (Hodson-Carlton, Siktberg, Flowers, & Scheibel, 2003). An early adopter of online education, the BSN@Home collaborative RN-to-BSN program in the University of Wisconsin System, began in 1995 using the course management system Blackboard. The BSN@Home program involves each of the nursing campuses in the UW System.

As one of the comprehensive institutions making up the UW System, the University of Wisconsin-Green Bay had a dramatic increase (316%) in the number of students enrolling in distance education courses between 2007 and 2012. This represents a 393% increase in the overall percentage of credits taken online. University leaders recognized the need to have a structure in place to ensure the same quality standards for teaching and learning are in place for the online classroom as well as in the face-to-face classroom. To accomplish this, the university initiated a faculty-centered, continuous improvement model for assuring quality of online courses through peer review using the Quality Matters system (QM, 2014). During the QM peer-review process, faculty apply a rubric to ensure online courses meet the national standards of best practice (QM, 2014). With a goal initiated in 2013 to obtain QM certification for 100 online courses within four years, UW-Green Bay committed to enhance the learning experience for students regardless of the delivery method.

A Multi-Campus Project

This project involved the nursing programs at the UW campuses of Eau Claire, Green Bay, Madison, Milwaukee, and Oshkosh. These nursing campuses collaborate to deliver an innovative distance education program, the BSN@Home program, which enables associate degree prepared Registered Nurses to complete baccalaureate level nursing education while remaining in their communities thus overcoming the barrier of distance and varied work schedules. This type of program is often referred to as RN-to-BSN Completion. The nursing curriculum and teaching responsibilities for this online program are shared among the nursing campuses involved, with each campus taking the lead for one of the five required core courses in the collaborative program. Elective courses are shared among the campuses. UW-Extension, a non-degree granting partner, provides liaison services and resources to the program. A division of UW-Extension provides course management and technical support for the BSN@Home collaborative program.

Each of the UW nursing campuses has its own administrative structure (e.g., School of Nursing) and array of other nursing programs (e.g., traditional BSN, MSN, DNP). The campuses, however, collaborate to deliver the BSN@Home online collaborative program. Established relationships between these campuses were the impetus to pursue grant funding for a collaborative faculty development project aimed at addressing a critical need to educate nursing faculty on current technologies related to online education and healthcare technologies. This chapter discusses the background, development, process, and evaluation of the collaborative faculty development project and will present suggestions to enable the replication of this program in other institutional settings.

BACKGROUND

The five UW Schools of Nursing have offered an online, collaborative RN to BSN program called BSN@ Home since 1995. The nursing programs are the University of Wisconsin at Eau Claire, Green Bay, Madison, Milwaukee, Oshkosh. These five schools were involved in a Wisconsin Technology Enhanced Collaborative Nursing Education (WITECNE) five-year grant (2006-2011) from the Department of Health & Human Services, Health Resources & Services Administration [HRSA] (Project #U1KHP07714) designed to infuse technology into nursing education (WI-TECNE, 2010).

With growth in the number of e-learning courses and programs at all levels and greater digital literacy among college students, it was clear there was a growing need for qualified faculty to teach online courses. Faculty are often uncomfortable moving from traditional face-to-face classroom formats to online environments and may feel ill prepared to adopt instructional and pedagogical strategies necessary for online teaching and learning. Students' skill and technology adoption level overall often exceed that of the instructor. This was particularly relevant for nursing programs since the average age of nursing faculty is much older than found in most disciplines. The mean age of Wisconsin nursing faculty, for example, is 58 years (Wisconsin Center for Nursing, 2013). Most nursing faculty are educationally prepared through traditional, face-to-face graduate programs. These factors reinforce the need for e-learning faculty development programs.

What Do Instructors Need to Teach Online?

Ryan, Hodson-Carlton, & Ali (2004) identified "conditions" conducive for faculty teaching online through focus groups with nursing faculty from schools of nursing offering an online master's degree. Using dimensional analysis, the authors identified four dimensions of the *Model for Faculty Teaching Online* which included antecedent conditions, context, strategies, and consequences (Ryan, Hodson-Carlton, & Ali, 2004); Ryan, Hodson-Carlton, & Ali, 2005). Antecedent conditions included support systems (administrative support, technology partnerships, online resources, and faculty teams), use of technology to teach online (hardware and software, course management system, and technical skills), and policies for distance learning (ownership, compensation, workload) to successfully launch online courses (Ryan et al., 2005). The dimension, Context, included online curriculum, online environment, and adjusting timeframes. The fact that online courses, for example, are highly accessible to students often results in an expectation of immediate faculty availability, or "24/7". What is timely for faculty in a traditional face to face classroom environment may not be perceived by students to be so in the online environment (Ryan et al., 2005). The third dimension, strategies for teaching online, addressed ways faculty redesigned their teaching for the online environment. Participants noted the need for course redesign (using outside experts, test security, trial and error), collaborative planning strategies (faculty development, mentoring, and faculty team development), and the importance of using new forms of communication to engage learners (engaging web pages, motivating media, reflective writing by students). In this study, faculty recognized the need to prepare the online course far in advance of the semester in which it was taught (Ryan et al., 2005). The last dimension of the model addressed the consequences of moving to the online environment, both positive (flexibility, thoughtful responses from students) and negative (asynchronous responses where spontaneity is lost, increased faculty workloads) consequences of teaching online. Ultimately, despite there being negative consequences, participants felt that online teaching resulted in greater levels of collaborative learning and a shift in the faculty role from one of expert to one of facilitator.

How Do Instructors Learn to Teach Online and Use New Technologies?

The primary methods of faculty development for online learning are attendance at conferences and webinars, and review of journal articles. Increasingly online methods have been employed (Niebuhr, Niebuhr, Trumble, & Urbani, 2014). Faculty development has typically been an individual endeavor involving instructors identifying areas that need strengthening and patching together resources and learning opportunities to build knowledge and skills in needed areas. Elkind and Smith (2008) conducted a national study in which they examined institutions' practices in nursing faculty development programs for teaching online, and faculty satisfaction with their online instruction preparedness (Elkind & Smith, 2008). Of the nursing programs responding, 62% (n=829) offered online nursing courses with an additional 19% (n=255) in the planning stages. The majority of faculty respondents (66%, n=350) had taught online courses from one to four years. The most frequently reported training format was "as-needed" support from their own IT or faculty. Other formats for faculty development in online teaching (in order of frequency- high to low) included workshops, one-on-one tutoring, in-service, outside continuing education, and finally training via faculty development online courses. Only 27% of participating nursing programs required faculty training before teaching an online course with about half (48%) indicating the training was provided by the information technology (IT) department at their institution. When asked about their confidence in teaching online before and after training, not surprisingly, faculty reported that their confidence increased after training. The authors suggested the findings provided a clear need for faculty development programs in online teaching as online nursing education continues to expand.

Collaborative approaches to faculty development, although rarely used, can be highly efficient, cost effective, and foster deeper learning among faculty. One collaborative approach to faculty development is the development and use of learning communities. A *community of practice* (COP) is a group of people who share an interest in a domain of study and engage in a process of collective learning that creates bonds between them (Shearer, Shea, & Kristensen, 2003). Main characteristics of a COP include:

1. Domain (shared knowledge and competence in the focus area),
2. Community (interactive members learning together),
3. Practice (repertoire of resources, tools and experiences).

A COP can occur within a single institution (the most common type), a multi-institution scenario, or on a global scale; anywhere a group of practitioners can come together for mutual education and support.

FACULTY DEVELOPMENT FOR E-LEARNING

Faculty Development Structure

Each UW School of Nursing was charged to develop a yearlong faculty development program as part of the Wisconsin Technology Enhanced Collaborative Nursing Education (WITECNE) five-year grant. A specific topic for each year of the grant was identified in the grant: telehealth (year 1), virtual worlds [Second Life®] (year 2), simulation learning (year 3), problem-based learning (year 4), and e-learning (year 5). A total of 150 unduplicated scholars, including nursing and non-nursing faculty (e.g., instructional designers) from each of the 5 UW nursing schools and the Wisconsin Technical College system, tribal and private colleges participated over the five-year grant period. Scholars participated in the yearlong program of those topics that were of high interest to them. A number of scholars participated in more than one faculty development year.

A structure for the yearly faculty development programs was developed by the grant's principal investigators and included monthly synchronous videoconferences across the five campus sites and the bridge, or call center, which coordinated the videoconference broadcasts, an asynchronous Desire to Learn (D2L) course, and an annual face-to face conference. Each UW campus had a site leader who maintained regular communication with their campus scholars about the schedule of videoconferences and available resources, handled the campus grant budget, and attended monthly leader meetings. Some campuses had the same site leader for all five years of the grant while the site leader's role rotated on other campuses. Compensation to site leaders varied (e.g., course release, monetary) and was determined by individual campuses.

E-Learning Faculty Development Program

E-Learning was the topic of faculty development for the fifth, and final, year of the grant and was hosted by the UW-Green Bay campus. A multi-disciplinary planning group of nine members (e.g., nursing educators, instructional technologists, outreach specialist) was formed almost two years before the yearlong faculty development program was delivered. Various approaches, models, and topics were considered in planning the yearlong e-learning faculty development program. The focus of e-learning at the institutional level often becomes the technologies and competency with the available delivery technologies is often a major emphasis in faculty development. The planning group wanted the e-learning year to be about more than simply using specific technologies in nursing education. The group recognized that a comprehensive view of E-Learning, as reflected in the Flexible E-Learning Framework, could be used to structure monthly topics and help scholars in understanding roles, functions, and scope of activities involved in E-Learning.

Significant time was required of the planning team and necessitated the full support of the nursing department and university. Major areas requiring time by the UW-Green Bay site leader and planning team included:

- Initial group meetings to consider how to approach faculty development about e-learning including review of various e-learning frameworks.
- Narrowing topics for each monthly videoconference session from broad e-learning dimensions (e.g., Management) and identifying experts to present content.
- Identifying survey items reflective of each e-learning dimension for a monthly surveys of scholars.

The Khan Flexible E-Learning Framework, used to guide the faculty development program, provides a comprehensive view of e-learning. The model is composed of eight e-learning dimensions including: pedagogical, technological, interface design, evaluation, management, resource support, ethical and institutional (see Figure 1) (Khan, 2005). The model is further described in the introductory chapter of this text. Five dimensions (one each month) were explored in videoconferences with scholars and included the dimensions of Pedagogical, Technological, Management, Ethical, and Institutional. The remaining three dimensions of the framework (i.e., Resource Support, Interface Design, and Evaluation) were woven throughout the year and/or covered during the culminating face to face conference at the end of e-learning faculty development year. Surveys corresponding to seven of the eight dimensions were developed and used to explore faculty scholar's understanding of e-learning issues (the dimension of Interface Design was addressed differently).

Figure 1. The e-learning framework

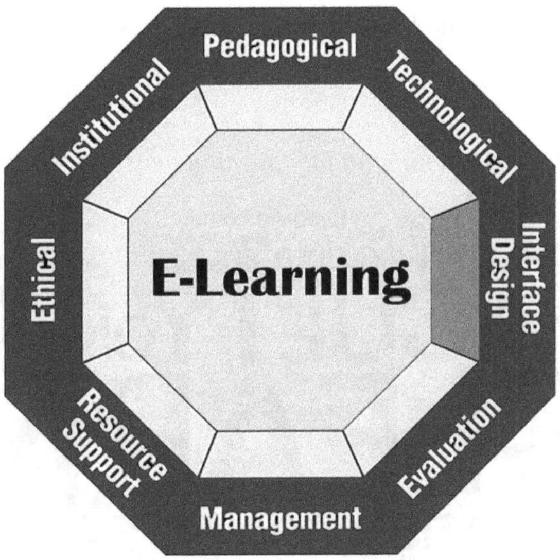

Components of the Faculty Development Program

An extensive faculty development program focused on e-learning was developed with the following major components:

- Campus site leaders,
- Scholars,
- Scholar handbook,
- Synchronous videoconferences,
- Use of new educational technologies,
- Monthly surveys on e-learning dimensions completed by scholars,
- Evaluation of interface design of core courses in a collaborative online RN to BSN program,
- A year-end conference,
- An overall program evaluation.

The extensive nature of this project is depicted using Wordle software to show major elements of the year's activities (see Figure 2). Description of each component of the faculty development program below will allow others to replicate the program or select components of the faculty development program applicable to their setting.

Campus Site Leaders

Each campus had a site leader who served as a point of contact for their campus scholars. The roles of the site leader included cheerleader and coach to maintain energy, enthusiasm, and engagement in the yearlong faculty development program. Site leaders served as the main source of communication on each campus, keeping scholars apprised of the videoconference schedule, answering questions and directing scholars to available resources. All site leaders met monthly to share issues and accomplishments.

Figure 2. Major elements of the e-learning faculty development program

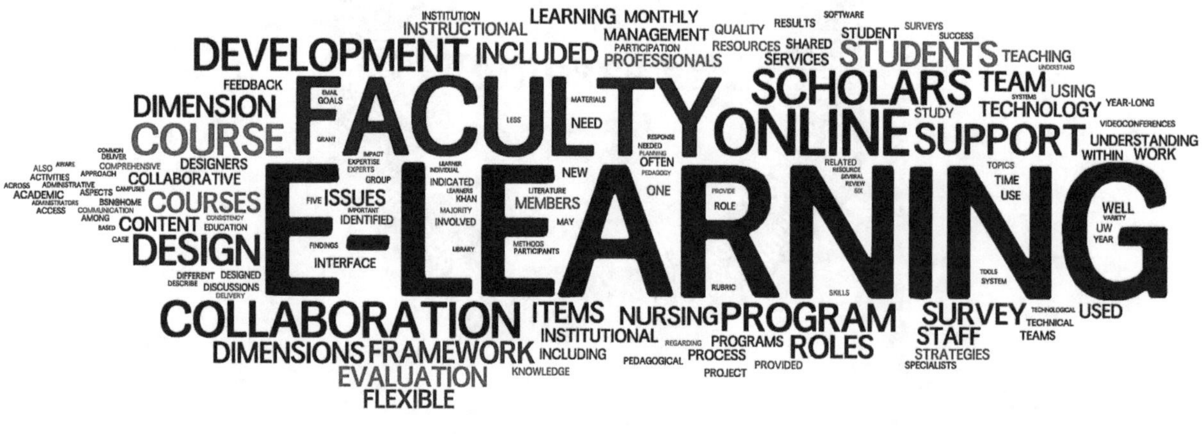

The UW-Green Bay campus site leader took on the major responsibility for leading the host campus planning team and communicating in monthly meetings with site leaders from other campuses about upcoming sessions and plans. The host campus site leader also dealt with the budget and details related to the monthly videoconference schedule and year-end conference, but did not handle all aspects of the e-learning faculty development program. A faculty member with expertise in assessment handled monthly surveys of scholars. A faculty member with expertise in informatics handled the interface design review process involving consultants. Each monthly videoconference topic was coordinated by a UW-Green Bay faculty or staff with expertise and/or interest in the topic.

Scholars and Scholar Handbook

The term "scholar" was consistently used for those individuals selected from each campus to participate in the e-learning faculty development year. The term reflected the additional study in a particular area that participants did over a sustained period of time. A total of 54 scholars participated in the e-learning faculty development year. Scholars represented nursing and non-nursing faculty from the UW nursing schools and also from the Wisconsin Technical College System and Tribal Colleges. Most scholars had a high degree of interest in e-learning and some experience teaching online. Over sixty percent of the scholars taught a fully online or hybrid (face to face with an online component) course. Even those who had never taught online recognized the need to develop skill in teaching online.

A handbook was distributed to all scholars at the start of the e-learning faculty development year. A calendar of the monthly topics, videoconference dates, and information about the final faculty development e-learning conference were given. Other information in the handbook included information about the Khan Flexible E-Learning Framework, learning objectives for the year, scholar expectations (e.g., complete monthly surveys), and information about new technologies that were introduced during the year. Scholars were encouraged to add to and personalize the contents of the handbook to serve them as an ongoing e-learning resource beyond the completion of the year.

Synchronous Videoconferences

To overcome the distance between the five UW campuses, scholars were connected through monthly videoconferences offered synchronously during the academic year. Videoconference sessions were one hour in duration and scheduled on a consistent day and time. While this served to provide consistency in scheduling, faculty whose teaching schedule conflicted were unable to participate in the live monthly sessions, but did have subsequent access to the archive in a D2L course.

The Flexible Framework for E-Learning was introduced and explained to scholars during the first videoconference by its author, Dr. Badrul Khan using Adobe Connect. Topics for subsequent monthly sessions were (in chronological order) Pedagogical, Technological, Ethical, Management, and Institutional. Pedagogical, for example, focused on online discussions and rubrics. The topic of Management focused on the structure and roles of collaborative work teams and maximizing available resources to deliver e-learning. During each session, content experts presented relevant content and engaged scholars in discussion using similar web conferencing technology (Adobe Connect) to connect the five campuses from either remote locations or directly from the UW-Green Bay campus. Following the videoconferences, session materials (e.g., recordings of videoconferences, PowerPoint presentations, etc.) were archived in a D2L course.

Use of Educational Technologies

A D2L course was used to store and share information and resources, and allow for asynchronous interaction among scholars. Resources such as journal articles and assignments were posted for scholars to access prior to videoconference sessions. Resources and webliographies were uploaded to the course for each of the dimensions of the Flexible E-Learning Framework. Online discussion boards in the D2L course were also used to continue dialogue and encourage questions between sessions. Scholars, however, engaged with the content to a larger extent in the monthly videoconference sessions than in the D2L course discussion.

Several other instructional technology methods were integrated into the faculty development program to permit scholars to gain experience with new technologies as e-learners. New technologies such as Twitter, Skype, and Polleverywhere.com were introduced and practiced. Handouts and tutorial video links with instructions were given to scholars in the e-learning handbook, the D2L course and through email to help scholars be successful with these new technologies. Some technologies were practiced during videoconference sessions and integrated with the content of the videoconference topic. It was hoped that through exposure to a variety of new technologies, scholars would increase their confidence, and perceived self-efficacy with technologies and that this would translate to a greater use of technologies in their future in nursing education.

Monthly Surveys Related to E-Learning Dimensions

Evaluation was a planned, intentional aspect of the yearlong e-learning faculty development program. An evaluation instrument, based on seven of the eight dimensions of the Khan Flexible E-learning framework was developed to better understand scholars' knowledge and practice in e-learning. Khan's book, *Managing E-Learning Strategies: Design, Delivery, Implementation, and Evaluation (2005)*, provides over 600 items to assist those involved in the e-learning process to reflect on aspects of e-Learning in a comprehensive way (Khan, 2005).

Members of the planning team reviewed the 600 items from the e-learning text by Khan (2005), selected items, and adapted these to design the six online surveys corresponding to the dimension(s) featured in the monthly e-learning sessions. Items were selected with particular emphasis on their relevance to online teaching and the scope of faculty involvement in e-learning. Items were reviewed by outside experts with expertise in online course design, education program evaluation, and e-learning to ensure that dimensions were sufficiently represented.

The resulting monthly surveys contained from 9 to 36 items including a few demographic questions for an aggregate total of 98 items (3 demographic items and 95 items covering seven e-learning dimensions). To review sample items used in the monthly surveys, a website was created for online instructors and instructional designers to explore e-learning issues based on the Flexible Framework for E-Learning. Sample questions can be accessed at http://www.uwgb.edu/witecne/.

Qualtrics© survey software was used to distribute the electronic surveys and monitor scholar participation with planned email reminders sent to non-responders at weekly intervals post videoconference. Recognizing the busy nature of the faculty role and importance of evaluation data to the overall faculty development program, an opportunity to win an incentive prize was offered to scholars that completed all of the monthly surveys. Significant findings from the monthly surveys are noted in Table 1.

Table 1. Select findings from e-learning surveys

Dimensions of E-Learning: Select Findings
Pedagogy: Over half of the scholars described their learning activities as both program- and learner-centered; Learner-centered methods: students were able to guide content via choice of project topics, flexible due dates, and help determine discussion questions. The predominant role of the instructor was that of facilitator (82%). Scholars employed a variety of strategies to reduce information overload including use of rubrics, limiting the number of posts, and rotating the responsibility of summarizing peer posts among students.
Technology: Half of the scholars indicated that minimum internet capabilities were specified and an orientation program including technical training was provided to students. Over half (57%) of scholars did not feel cost was a deterrent to student enrollment in online courses, however one-third were unsure. Seven out of ten respondents indicated students received special pricing on software and a third noted they provide links to required software in their course.
Evaluation: A wide array of evaluation of student learning methods were used by scholars including individual and group assignments, case studies, journals, online presentations, and online tests/quizzes. Almost all (94%) scholars used the dropbox and/or electronic gradebook to share feedback on student assignments. Regarding reducing instances of academic misconduct, the most common methods used were time limits on exams/quizzes, scrambling test items, and plagiarism detection software built into the online course.
Management: Scholars recognized a wide array of roles including instructional designers, media production specialists, and course developers; about half of the scholars felt there was not enough budgetary support for e-learning; many scholars did not have a course backup plan should there be a technological failure and those who did used email.
Resource Support: Faculty were often sought out by students for technical assistance due to a lack of university-provided 24/7 technical support and to meet the needs of older, less tech savvy students. Specific examples of requested student support with e-learning include uploading and downloading files, opening files in e-mail, attaching pictures, installing required software, and creating online presentations. Phone and email were the primary means of communication for requests for support.
Ethics: Over half the scholars identified cheating, socioeconomic, and political issues as influencing e-learning. Other issues noted include the need to be sensitive to the varied work schedules of the RN to BSN student and differences in the geographic location/time zones in which students lived. Strategies to address these issues included use of asynchronous discussions, keeping exams open for 48 hours, and the need to clearly identify the time zone when establishing assignment deadlines.
Institution: Results were mixed with some scholars noting institutional support in the areas of instructional design, software, and technology while others had little support for e-learning from their institution beyond IT support. Some specifically identified a lack of release time to develop skill in the use of e-learning technologies. Scholars compared online and face-to-face instruction and noted differences in class size (30 vs. 80) with most faculty indicating their institution did not differentiate teaching load based on the delivery method. In terms of preparation for teaching online, scholars participated in a variety of methods including an online orientation course, virtual practice, a one hour workshop and for some, no identified process. The majority of scholars (80%) were unsure of the budget for e-learning.

Evaluation of Interface Design

Interface Design is one of the dimensions in the Flexible E-Learning Framework and refers to the overall look and feel of an e-learning program from the user's perspective. This is a very familiar concept to instructional designers and less so to nursing faculty. This dimension was handled differently than other e-learning dimensions for this reason and one other; the planning group recognized that course interface design of the core nursing courses in the BSN@Home program had not been a priority in course development. Instead, most courses had been modeled after their own campus course design style and format. This resulted in the present situation of low interface design consistency across courses.

To conduct an evaluation of the interface design of the BSN@Home online core nursing courses, two experts in educational design and curriculum and instruction were commissioned (Tyczkowski, Bauman, Gallagher-Lepak, Vandenhouten, & Reilly, 2012). An evaluation rubric was developed based on Khan's E-Learning Framework, reviewer knowledge of educational technology, and other contemporary learning theories (Khan, 2005). The consultants reviewed the core nursing courses in the BSN@Home program using a six point scale (0 to 5 rating) to identify strengths and weaknesses of each course relative to other courses using the Interface Design rubric. The rubric consisted of four categories:

1. Consistency and Coherence,
2. Content Management,
3. Engagement,
4. Curriculum and Design.

This process of course review served as a method of continuous quality improvement with the aim of strengthening the BSN@Home program, especially in the four areas identified.

Consistency and coherence refers to the standardization within and between courses (e.g., use of a course template, similar tools used throughout program). Content management covers areas such as user access to content and overall scope of content (e.g., content volume and flow). Engagement involves the level of interaction with the content by the user (e.g., individual versus group activities). The final category in the rubric, curriculum design, refers to the degree of curricular coherence across courses (clarity of objectives, suitability of content for online delivery).

Concerns and recommendations identified in the interface design review fell into two types:

1. "Quick fix" changes (involve one or two of the courses and/or small and easy changes) and,
2. Changes requiring significant time and/or resources.

For example, a recommended "quick fix" was the need for greater consistency with the location of course materials (e.g., textbook readings, other readings, videos, web sites) in a course. A more involved fix, for example, was the recommendation to improve group assignments from simple discussions to a greater level of collaboration and consensus-building. Faculty were made aware of the findings of the interface design review at the year-end conference. Instructional designers who worked with the BSN@ Home program developed a plan to incorporate the findings of the interface design review into courses to improve student learning and course satisfaction.

Evaluation of the Project

Evaluation of both the year-end conference and the year-long e-learning program are described below. The year-end conference involved participation by e-learning scholars as well as an audience of professionals interested in e-learning. The evaluation of the year-long e-learning program involved only the e-learning scholars.

End of Year Conference

A 2-day E-learning conference entitled, *E-Learning in Nursing: Design, Innovation, Delivery and Evaluation* brought both nationally recognized nurse educators known for their knowledge of e-learning technologies and a showcase of innovations that resulted from the grant from each of the five campuses. Faculty scholars shared success stories of incorporating new technologies into their courses such as use of WIKIs, lessons learned in the use of Second Life simulations, and incorporation of case scenario builder software. Day two of the conference featured a variety of sessions including the results of the interface design evaluation of the core courses in the collaborative BSN@HOME nursing program. Other breakout sessions included topics such as E-learning and the Americans with Disabilities Act (ADA), instructional gaming, and a closing session on the topic of international and cultural perspectives in e-learning.

One session shared the overall findings from the monthly surveys of scholars on e-learning dimensions. The presenter provided not only a summary of the overall survey results for all participating scholars, but also a campus specific summary to each site leader. Site leaders were encouraged to discuss these results and any implications for future faculty development needs related to E-learning at their home institutions.

Conference attendees were asked to identify the degree to which the conference enhanced their knowledge, understanding, and ability to design, deliver, and evaluate e-learning in their course/program. Overwhelmingly participants (92%) felt their participation in the conference enhanced their understanding of e-learning much or very much (5 point Likert-type scale with 1= not at all and 5= very much; mean = 4.57). In response to whether their participation enhanced their ability to evaluate the design and delivery of e-learning in online courses, almost all (95%) indicated participation enhanced their ability much (25%) or very much (70%) (mean = 4.66). Conference attendees specifically noted the value of networking with colleagues, understanding student perspectives in e-learning, considerations of culture (i.e., First Nation and African American) in e-learning, and learning new technologies and/or innovative ways to incorporate technologies used in the past as benefits of their participation. They further noted the content of the conference gave them much to think about and motivated them to continue to learn about e-learning and new technologies.

Evaluation of the E-Learning Faculty Development Program

In addition to evaluating the content of the e-learning conference, scholars were also asked to evaluate the impact of their participation in the activities of the entire e-learning year on their understanding of e-learning issues. Ninety-five percent of scholars indicated their participation had a moderate to substantial impact (5 point Likert-type scale with 1= no impact and 5 = substantial impact) on their understanding of e-learning issues (mean = 4.40). When asked about specific examples of how they applied new knowledge of e-learning to their teaching, research, or outreach, participants provided a wide array of examples including use of a self-directed readiness tool for students, tools for engaging learners with learning content such as use of student cafes and case builder software, and e-portfolios. One scholar described recruiting other faculty to increase involvement in e-learning in his/her institution.

In addition to identifying ways they applied e-learning in their teaching, scholars were asked ways they planned to apply new e-learning knowledge, attitudes or skills to teaching, research or outreach in the future. Many scholars noted they planned to adopt a new electronic health record (EHR) in their courses to enhance student understanding of the use of technology in healthcare settings. Other plans for applying e-learning included additional use of e-technology including incorporation of plagiarism detection software, Wikis, twitter, gaming, podcasts, and case scenario builder.

CURRENT CHALLENGES FACING THE ORGANIZATION

A number of challenges became evident during the faculty development program. Description of challenges is limited to those encountered during the e-learning faculty development year.

Challenges of Faculty Time and Engagement

Difficulties in finding available time to prepare and participate in videoconference sessions for the duration of the year-long faculty development program were realities of this endeavor. Overall, scholars were highly interested in e-learning content but had difficulty on some occasions preparing for and attending videoconferences due to their teaching and other responsibilities. Additionally, time limited the extent to which scholars took advantage of the program resources available. An effort to capture the content of the synchronous videoconference sessions was made throughout the e-learning year for this reason and this video was archived and made available in a D2L course.

Faculty took on the role of "learners" in the faculty development program. Similar to the experiences of online students, some faculty experienced feelings of uncertainty, frustration, and inadequacy in dealing with new educational technologies and social media used during the year. Not all scholars were early (or comfortable) adopters of new e-learning technologies. Learning curves were steep for some technologies during the faculty development year, even though there was a community of learners to communicate with in dealing with technology challenges. Also, supports were given to scholars (e.g., tutorials, links, online discussion forums, verbal instructions) to foster successful use of the technologies. Practice time was given with some technologies. For example, many scholars had not used Twitter before and needed to set up an account before practicing with this technology during the monthly session.

A variety of methods were used to overcome faculty challenges. Site leaders were creative and persistent in fostering a culture of excitement and engagement about the e-learning faculty development program for scholars. Content experts too used creativity to generate interest in monthly topics. For example, an engaging audio message was e-mailed to scholars prior to the videoconference on pedagogical issues. Case scenarios related to ethical issues in e-learning were posted in the D2L course for scholars to review prior to the videoconference on this topic. Scholars voluntarily chose to participate in the e-learning faculty development program and their interest in e-learning helped to sustain engagement of most scholars.

Cost Considerations

Implementation of a multi-campus faculty development program required both monetary and human resources. Consideration of both direct costs and in-kind support are provided. Direct costs are listed in Table 2. Monthly videoconference costs were very reasonable, totaling approximately $50 total for the hub to coordinate per session. However, additional charges for campus media staff time in trouble shooting during the pilot tests or addressing problems could exceed this amount. Honoraria for expert presenters for monthly videoconferences averaged about $350 a month. Experts ranged from on-campus individuals to experts from across the country. A costly item was the interface design review of core courses by experts, but the positive changes to the collaborative BSN@Home program resulting from this expert review were significant. The year-end conference cost was also significant because a number of national speakers presented. Due to the nature of the grant used to fund the year-end conference, a conference fee and meals were not charged to participants.

In-kind support from the university (nursing program) included time for planning committee members to design the evaluation tool, attend pilot tests of technology, and assist with numerous details during the faculty development program, monthly videoconferences, and the two-day final conference. Qualtrics® software was used for monthly scholar surveys and the D2L course platform was used to host

Table 2. Select costs for the e-learning faculty development program

Item	Estimated Cost
Videoconference costs	$50 ($10 for each campus) per month
Honoraria for expert videoconference presenters	Average of $350 per month
Scholar Handbook copies	$907.00 (60 copies)
Campus site leaders	UW-Green Bay site leader was given a 3 credit course release
Interface Design Consultants	$3000
Year-end Conference	Site fee: $1,020 Speaker fees: $11, 795 Technology services: $1,402 Conference hand-outs and supplies $815.00
Assistance from a campus department experienced in conference planning	$10,200

the online e-learning faculty development course. An academic support person was used to assist with many details during the faculty development year (e.g., collate scholar handbooks, process agreements with consultants).

The cost benefit of a multi-campus faculty development program needs to be mentioned. Although the costs in Table 2 may appear high for a one-year e-learning faculty development program (including a large conference), bear in mind that each campus benefitted from five years of faculty development activities but each campus only handled the planning and costs for one year of the program.

Technology Challenges

Videoconferencing, usually considered a relatively easy way to connect the campuses each month, presented a challenge in the first videoconference. Adobe Connect® was used to connect an expert presenter located in another state however, variations in bandwidth speed between the expert's campus, the UW system campus sites, and the hosting UW-Green Bay campus resulted in a delay of the start time of the monthly videoconference session and difficulty receiving audio from the expert presenter during the first session for some campus sites. A quick "work around" used was to have sites access the presenter's PowerPoint slides that were previously uploaded to the D2L course. This was a discouraging way to start the e-learning faculty development year hosted by UW-Green Bay and resulted in a planned pilot of the technology with technical support prior to the next few sessions to be sure that technology was fully operational.

Additionally, the type of technology used and campus technology support available varied among campuses as well as at the hub site that coordinated the videoconference signals. Some campuses had permanent videoconference rooms with stationary equipment, while other campuses used a variety of classroom settings and portable equipment that involved advanced set up and greater technology support. This created some challenges for trouble-shooting and problem solving. For example, telephone lines and/or Internet access was not available in the videoconference room for some campuses. This limited options when trouble-shooting technology issues during synchronous videoconferences. Personal cell phones were used in some cases to problem-solve technology challenges and/or questions. Lack of Internet access in some of the videoconference rooms also hindered scholars from Tweeting, adding opinions to a web-based poll, or accessing the D2L e-learning course during monthly videoconference sessions.

REFLECTIONS AND RECOMMENDATIONS

This detailed description of the faculty development program is intended to give the reader new ideas and strategies for e-learning faculty development, including collaborative approaches.

- **Institutional Support:** Administrative support was essential to the success of this year-long faculty development program. Persistence, flexibility, and a clear commitment by UW nursing programs were key to the success of this project. Such commitment was enacted through a leadership structure composed of site leaders from each campus. Site leaders qualified to serve as role models and project coordinators were selected. Site leaders used a "can do" attitude to work through challenges and foster engagement and enthusiasm. The following Question can be used to encourage new ways to evaluate existing resources and move forward with a faculty development project:
    - What is your institution's priority with e-learning faculty development and how is this supported at your institution?
    - What are existing resources on your campus and how can these be employed to engage faculty in ongoing faculty development in e-learning.
    - What methods used in the described project are potentially useful and could be incorporated into the existing faculty development program at your institution (e.g., monthly videoconferences on e-learning, yearly conference on e-learning, interface design evaluation of an online program)?
    - How could grant funding be pursued to access resources to develop e-learning faculty development opportunities or expand existing faculty development programs?
- **Collaboration:** The authors highly recommend that readers consider collaborating on faculty development (e.g., multi-campus, multi-department). There are many reasons for this, including the development of peer relationships as well as cost savings. In implementing a faculty development program, funding can be a major challenge. Sharing of costs among all institutions or departments involved in a collaborative model may reduce the scope of this challenge. Questions to consider related to a collaborative program include:
    - How could collaborating on e-learning faculty development with another institution, program, or department on your campus be useful to explore?
    - How would development of an e-learning scholars group (community of practice) within your institution or with colleagues from outside your institution be useful to share e-learning knowledge and experiences?
    - How would joining an existing e-learning scholars group (community of practice) be useful to you as an e-learning faculty or staff (e.g., Sloan-C, Educause)?
- **Framework to Guide Faculty Development:** The authors recommend that a broad e-learning framework be used to guide planning of an integrated faculty development program. E-learning faculty development is often approached from a narrow perspective, such as considering solely technology or pedagogy dimensions. Questions to consider related to use of an e-learning framework include:
    - How could the Khan E-Learning Framework be used to guide e-learning and institutional assessment at your institution?

- What dimensions of the Khan E-Learning Framework are commonly addressed in faculty development programs at your institution? What dimensions of the Framework are rarely or never addressed at your institution?
- Is there another e-learning or faculty development framework to consider using to guide e-learning faculty development?

Use of Khan's framework helped those implementing this project to consider other professionals required to deliver quality e-learning. Teamwork among all professionals in an e-learning program is needed to address all dimensions of the Khan E-learning Framework.

The faculty program was viewed as a success. The formal faculty development program ended with grant completion but residual benefits have continued. Most notable, although somewhat intangible, is the continuing spirit of innovation with e-learning and use of new technologies among faculty at UW nursing campuses. Nursing faculty continue to experiment with new technologies in online teaching and course development, and value the search for new knowledge of best practices in e-learning and use of technologies. A new, required course on Information Management and Healthcare Technologies is now offered in the BSN@Home curriculum, partially as a result of the grant and its focus on infusing technology into nursing education. New technologies have been incorporated into assignments throughout the BSN@Home curriculum (e.g., a leadership WIKI, simulation videos). Faculty have enhanced their use of new technologies and several faculty have incorporated online learning or new technologies into their research agendas.

CONCLUSION

This multi-campus faculty development program was grounded in an e-learning framework that integrated teaching-learning technologies and involved scholars in self-assessment of e-learning practices. Faculty development is often organized by topical content or types of technologies. In contrast, the Flexible Framework for E-Learning by Khan (2005) was the foundation for the faculty development program, and each e-learning dimension was addressed in the year-long program. A wide range of strategies were used in the faculty development program such as use of campus site leaders, selected scholars (participating faculty and staff), monthly videoconferences, and a year-end conference. The chapter includes a description of the program as well as outcomes of the faculty development program.

This type of program design provided opportunities for faculty to engage in a learning community or COP, bridging distant faculty and campuses and responsibly utilizing limited resources. Program success required administrative support from each participating campus, as well as dedicated faculty willing to invest time and energy to improve their understanding and comfort with e-learning, and use of educational technologies. The benefits of the programs were well worth the investment of time and energy.

REFERENCES

Elkind, E., & Smith, K. (2008). *Online teaching preparedness: What about faculty?* Paper presented at Jefferson School of Nursing Faculty Papers & Presentations. Abstract retrieved from http://jdc.jefferson.edu/nursfp/57/

Hodson-Carlton, K., Siktberg, L., Flowers, J., & Scheibel, P. (2003). Overview of distance education in nursing: Where are we now and where are we going? In M. Oermann & K. Heinrich (Eds.), *Annual review of nursing education* (Vol. 1, pp. 165–189). New York: Springer.

Khan, B. (2005). *Managing E-Learning strategies: Design, Delivery, Implementation and Evaluation.* Hershey, PA: Information Science Publishing. doi:10.4018/978-1-59140-634-1

Niebuhr, V., Niebuhr, B., Trumble, J., & Urbani, M. J. (2014). Online faculty development for creating e-learning materials. *Education for Health, 27*(3), 255–261. doi:10.4103/1357-6283.152186 PMID:25758389

Online Learning Consortium (OLC). (2013). *2013 Survey of Online Learning Report.* Retrieved from http://sloanconsortium.org/publications/survey/grade-change-2013

Quality Matters (QM). (2014). Retrieved fromhttps://www.qualitymatters.org/

Ryan, M., Hodson-Carlton, K., & Ali, N. S. (2004). Reflections on the role of faculty in distance learning and changing pedagogies. *Nursing Education Perspectives, 25*(2), 73–80. PMID:15124511

Ryan, M., Hodson-Carlton, K., & Ali, N. S. (2005). A model for faculty teaching online: Confirmation of a dimensional matrix. *The Journal of Nursing Education, 44*(8), 357–365. PMID:16130342

Shearer, P. D., Shea, T. P., & Kristensen, E. (2003). Online communities of practice: A catalyst for faculty development. *Innovative Higher Education, 27*(3), 183–194. doi:10.1023/A:1022355226924

Tyczkowski, B., Bauman, E., Gallagher-Lepak, S., Vandenhouten, C., & Reilly, J. (2012). An interface design evaluation of courses in a nursing program using an e-learning framework: a case study. In B. Khan (Ed.), *User interface design for virtual environments* (pp. 285–304). Hershey, PA: IGI Global. doi:10.4018/978-1-61350-516-8.ch018

University of Wisconsin System (UW System) Board of Regents. (2015). *What is the UW System?* Retrieved from https://www.wisconsin.edu/about-the-uw-system/

UW-Madison Continuing Studies. (2013). *Distance education professional development.* Retrieved from http://continuingstudies.wisc.edu/distance-education/index.html

Wisconsin Center for Nursing. (2013). *The Wisconsin Nursing Workforce: Status and Recommendations.* Retrieved from http://www.wisconsincenterfornursing.org/workforce_report.html

Wisconsin Technology Enhanced Collaborative Nursing Education (WI-TECNE). (2010). Retrieved from: http://research.son.wisc.edu/tecne/

ADDITIONAL READING

Aleckson, J., & Ralston-Berg, P. (2011). *MindMeld: Micro-Collaboration between eLearning Designers and Instructor Experts.* Madison, WI: Atwood Publishing.

Baran, E., Correia, A., & Thompson, A. (2011). Transforming online teaching practice: Critical analysis of the literature on the roles and competencies of online teachers. *Distance Education*, *32*(3), 421–439. doi:10.1080/01587919.2011.610293

Berquist, W., & Phillips, S. (1975). Components of an effective faculty development program. *The Journal of Higher Education*, *46*(2), 177–211. doi:10.2307/1980880

Birman, B. F., Desimone, L., Porter, A. C., & Garet, M. S. (2000). Designing professional development that works. *Educational Leadership*, *57*(8), 28–33.

Bristol, T. J., & Zerwekh, J. (2011). *Essentials of e-learning for nurse educators*. Philadelphia: F.A. Davis.

Kidney, G. (2004). When the cows come home: A proven path of professional development for faculty pursuing e-learning. *The Journal*, *31*(11), 12–15.

Meyer, J. D., & Barefield, A. C. (2010). Infrastructure and administrative support for online programs. *Online Journal of Distance Learning Administration*, *13*(3). Retrieved from http://www.westga.edu/~distance/ojdla/fall133/meyer_barfield133.html

Milheim, W. (2001). Faculty and administrative strategies for the effective implementation of distance education. *British Journal of Educational Technology*, *32*(5), 535–542. doi:10.1111/1467-8535.00223

Owusu-Ansah, A., Neill, P., & Haralson, M. K. (2011). Distance education technology: Higher education barriers during the first decade of the twenty-first century. *Online Journal of Distance Learning Administration, 14*(2). Downloaded from: http://www.westga.edu/~distance/ojdla/summer142/ansah_142.html

Pruett, C. D., & Pollard, T. (2013). Virtual space (e-learning) faculty development. *New Directions for Teaching and Learning*, *2013*(133), 61–69. doi:10.1002/tl.20046

Rovai, A. P. (2003). A practical framework for evaluating online distance education programs. *The Internet and Higher Education*, *6*(2), 109–124. doi:10.1016/S1096-7516(03)00019-8

Shearer, P. D., Shea, T. P., & Kristensen, E. (2003). Online communities of practice: A catalyst for faculty development. *Innovative Higher Education*, *27*(3), 183–194. doi:10.1023/A:1022355226924

Signer, B. (2008). Online professional development: Combining best practices from teacher, technology, and distance education. *Journal of In-service Education*, *34*(2), 205–218. doi:10.1080/13674580801951079

Sutton, M., White, L., Mbizo, J., & Stewart, G. (2010). Assessment in online programs: Use in strategic planning for faculty/adjunct development and course instruction to improve faculty and student engagement. *International Journal on E-Learning*, *9*(1), 129–145.

Svinicki, M., & McKeachie, W. J. (2011). McKeachie's Teaching Tips: Strategies, Research, and Theory for College and University Teachers (13th ed.). Belmont, CA: Wadsworth Cengage learning.

Taylor, A., & McQuiggan, C. (2008). Faculty development programming: If we build it, will they come? *EDUCAUSE Quarterly*, *31*(3). Retrieved from http://www.educause.edu/EDUCAUSE+Quarterly/EDUCAUSEQuarterlyMagazineVolu m/FacultyDevelopmentProgrammingI/163099

Tyczkowski, B., Bauman, E., Gallagher-Lepak, S., Vandenhouten, C., & Reilly, J. (2012). An interface design evaluation of courses in a nursing program using an e-learning framework: a case study. In B. Khan (Ed.), *User interface design for virtual environments* (pp. 285–304). Hershey, PA: IGI Global.

Weaver, D., Robbie, D., & Borland, R. (2008). The practitioner's model: Designing a professional development program for online teaching. *International Journal on E-Learning*, *7*(4), 759–775.

KEY TERMS AND DEFINITIONS

Community of Practice: A group of individuals with a shared interest in a specific domain of study and collective processes for learning and interaction.

E-learning Instructional Designer: An individual who develops effective instruction (e.g., courses, modules) using online delivery formats. The individual has knowledge of software tools, content management systems, curriculum & instruction, and project management.

E-Learning: The use of network technologies to create, foster, deliver and facilitate learning any time, and anywhere.

Evaluation: One of the themes in the Flexible E-learning Framework which refers to the assessment of learners and evaluation of the teaching.

Faculty Development: Professional learning opportunities for educators. This can also be referred to as professional development.

Flexible E-Learning Framework: A model of e-learning composed of eight e-learning themes including: pedagogical, technological, interface design, evaluation, management, resource support, ethical and institutional.

Interface Design: One of the themes in the Flexible E-learning Framework which refers to the overall look and feel of an e-learning program from the user's perspective.

Online Teaching: Instructing via distance education through online courses using a learning management content system. Courses can be set up as either synchronous or asynchronous learning experiences.

Pedagogical: One of the themes in the Flexible E-learning Framework which refers to teaching and learning processes.

Scholars: Individuals that participated in the Wisconsin Technology Enhanced Collaborative Nursing Education (WITECNE) grant activities. These include nursing and non-nursing faculty from the five University of Wisconsin Schools of Nursing, Wisconsin Technical College System (WTCS), and Wisconsin Tribal Colleges.

Chapter 13
E-Learning Readiness in Public Institutions

Fayiz Munsher Aldhaferri
Kuwait University, Kuwait

ABSTRACT

This chapter reports on an e-Learning readiness study that was supported by Kuwait Foundation for Advancement of Sciences (KFAS) under project number (2013-11109-05) and carried out to assess the organizational and individual factors of the two major stakeholder groups (teachers and students) in the secondary education institutions to provide significant information to the policy makers and regulatory bodies for the development of successful e-Learning strategies. The chapter looks specifically at some factors at the initial stage of an e-Learning introduction that can have tremendous impact on the later stages of the process. Later on this chapter, discussion and suggestions are presented to be instrumental in implementing successful eLearning strategies for many countries, specifically Kuwait, and will also benefit e-Learning initiatives in similar institutions in other Gulf Cooperation Council (GCC) and beyond.

INTRODUCTION

This chapter reports on a study of e-Learning readiness in Kuwait that was supported by the Kuwait Foundation for Advancement of Sciences (KFAS) under project number (2013-11109-05). It was carried out to assess the organizational and individual preparedness and readiness for e-Learning of the two major stakeholder groups (teachers and students) in Kuwaiti secondary education institutions. This study provided significant information to the policy makers and regulatory bodies for the development of successful e-learning strategies. The chapter looks specifically at some factors at the initial stage of an e-learning introduction that can have tremendous impact on the later stages of the process. Discussion and suggestions are presented to be instrumental in implementing successful e-learning strategies specifically in Kuwait, but applicable in many countries, and will also benefit e-learning initiatives in similar institutions in other Gulf Cooperation Council (GCC) countries and beyond.

e-learning "readiness" means different things to different writers, but one commonly used approach is to assess the organizational and individual factors that should be addressed if organizations are to be

DOI: 10.4018/978-1-5225-0466-5.ch013

successful with the introduction of e-learning strategies (Chapnick 2000; Redmon and Salopek 2000; Hall 2001:2; Rosenberg 2001). This assessment is part of the organization's initial needs analysis, which is defined by DeSimone and Harris (1998: 101) as "a process used to better understand the characteristics of the organization to determine where training and HRD efforts are needed and the conditions within which they will be conducted."

BACKGROUND

Learning is an ongoing process that takes place as knowledge is utilized, regardless of the place and time. Thus, 'learning' does not have to refer to taking formal instructional courses; many can learn without attending courses. Many learners prefer to share experiences and not constantly sit in classrooms. British Prime Minister Winston Churchill once said, "I am always ready to learn, although I do not always like being taught" (Waller, 2005).

In a globalized and knowledge-based information society, every community is trying to transform itself into an information society. Advancements in information technology have great potential for enhancing education and training. Academic institutions, corporations, and government agencies worldwide are increasing their use of the Internet and digital technologies to deliver instruction and training. At all levels in these institutions, individuals are being encouraged to participate in online learning activities that focus on real change in pedagogy and the promotion of life-long learning. New educational policies are being formulated in various communities worldwide to enable educational institutions to come to terms with new learning technologies and their implications.

Online open and distributed learning, commonly known as e-learning, increasingly enhanced by the availability of newer emerging information and communication technologies (ICTs), is growing globally. There is no doubt that the impact of technology use is dramatically changing traditional learning and teaching practices. However, it is necessary to define eLearning with a focus on learning, as does Khan (2005):

...e-learning can be viewed as an innovative approach for delivering well-designed, learner-centered, interactive, and facilitated learning environments to anyone, anyplace, anytime by utilizing the attributes and resources of various digital technologies along with other forms of learning materials suited for the open and distributed learning environment (p.9).

Learning-focused educational and training systems are those where "the learner is the key entity and occupies the nucleus of the system's complex of education" (Banathy, 1991, p. 96). For Banathy (1991), "when learning is in focus, arrangements are made in the environment of the learner that communicate the learning task, and learning resources are made available to learners so that they can explore and master learning tasks" (p. 101). A distributed learning environment that can effectively support learning-on-demand must be designed by placing the learners at the center of the focus. In support of the learner-centered approach, Moore (1998) states:

Our aim as faculty should be to focus our attention on making courses and other learning experiences that will best empower our students to learn, to learn fully, effectively, efficiently, and with rewarding satisfaction. It is the responsibility of our profession to study ways of maximizing the potential of our environments to support their learning and to minimize those elements in their environments that may impede it (p. 4).

An e-learning system involves a systematic process of planning, designing, evaluating, and implementing online learning environments where learning is actively fostered and supported. To implement such a learning-focused system, all stakeholder groups including teachers, support services staff, and the institution should be prepared to provide learners with the most meaningful learning environment supported by well-designed learning materials. For successful e-learning, a comprehensive understanding of the issues related to all the various dimensions of e-learning and the needs, capabilities, interests, and willingness of all major stakeholder groups including instructors and students is sorely needed (Chapnick, 2005; Morrison & Khan, 2003). Like any other major innovation, e-learning strategies require considerable up-front analysis, development time, money, technological infrastructure, and leadership support to be successful; that is why experts such as Tubaishat and Lansari (2011), Bean (2003), Chapnick (2000), and Clark and Mayer (2003) recommend that organizations assess all stakeholders' readiness for e-learning before adopting this innovation. According to these experts, adopting e-learning without careful planning will most likely meet with stakeholder resistance, and end with cost overruns, unappealing training products, and failure. Therefore, one of the most critical front-end tasks of any e-learning initiative is to conduct a comprehensive assessment of organizational and individual readiness factors.

E-LEARNING READINESS FRAMEWORK

Rosenberg (2001) emphasizes that e-learning readiness must be determined before initiating any steps in the design and development process; however, readiness factors should be assessed continually throughout the stages to ensure overall success. Engholm and McLean (2001) emphasize that e-learning "readiness" is the assessment of certain organizational and individual factors that should be considered if organizations are to be successful with the introduction of an e-learning strategy. DeSimone and Harris (1998) supported readiness assessment as "a process used to better understand the characteristics of the organization to determine where training and human resources development efforts are needed and the conditions within which they will be conducted" (p. 27). Therefore, a comprehensive assessment of organizational and individual readiness factors should include critical perspectives from major stakeholders groups, including students and teachers. E-readiness assessment allows one to design comprehensive e-learning implementation strategies and effectively implement ICT goals (Abas, Kaur, & Harun, 2004). E-learning readiness assessment provides key information to organizations so they can design and supply solutions that can cater to the specific preparedness needs of each learning group (McConnell International, 2000). Masoumi (2006) states that in terms of e-learning, critical success factors can be viewed as those activities and constituents that must be addressed in order to ensure its successful implementation. For the development of the readiness assessment survey (see Appendix A) used in the project described in this chapter, various e-learning issues and critical success factors were sought out and an extensive literature review was conducted.

Readiness Model Components

Chapnick (2000) grouped a wide variety of factors into eight categories, which practitioners could use to assess the vastly different stakeholders in the system: psychological, sociological, environmental, human resources, financial readiness, technological skill (aptitude), equipment, and content readiness. Tubaishat and Lansari (2011) looked into five critical success factors to help companies make sound e-learning decisions: culture, content, capability, cost, and clients. Tham and Werner (2005) present a framework for addressing the institutional, technological, and student issues that should be addressed simultaneously in order for online courses to be effective. Volery (2000), using an empirical study among college students, proposed a framework for the critical success factors in online education with emphasis on three aspects: technology (ease of access and navigation, interface design and level of interaction); instructor (attitudes towards students, technical competence, and classroom interaction); and previous use of technology from a student's perspective, or students' pervious computer knowledge.

Abas, Kaur, and Harun (2004) developed a readiness instrument for Malaysia with items asking for views of readiness in eight areas: learner, management and personnel, content, technical, environmental, cultural, and financial. Borotis and Poulymenakou (2004) proposed a model with seven components: business, technology, content, training process, culture, human resources and financial. Haney (2002) classified seven categories of organizational readiness: human resources, learning management system, learners, content, information technology, finance, and vendor. Psycharis (2005) proposed a new model built from five e-learning models developed by Rosenberg (2000), Chapnick (2000), Broadbent (2001), and Borotis and Poulymenakou (2004) that groups eight e-learning readiness factors into three categories: resources (technological readiness, economic readiness and human resources readiness), education (content readiness and educational readiness), and environment (entrepreneurial readiness, leadership readiness and cultural readiness).

Figure 1. Khan's e-learning readiness framework

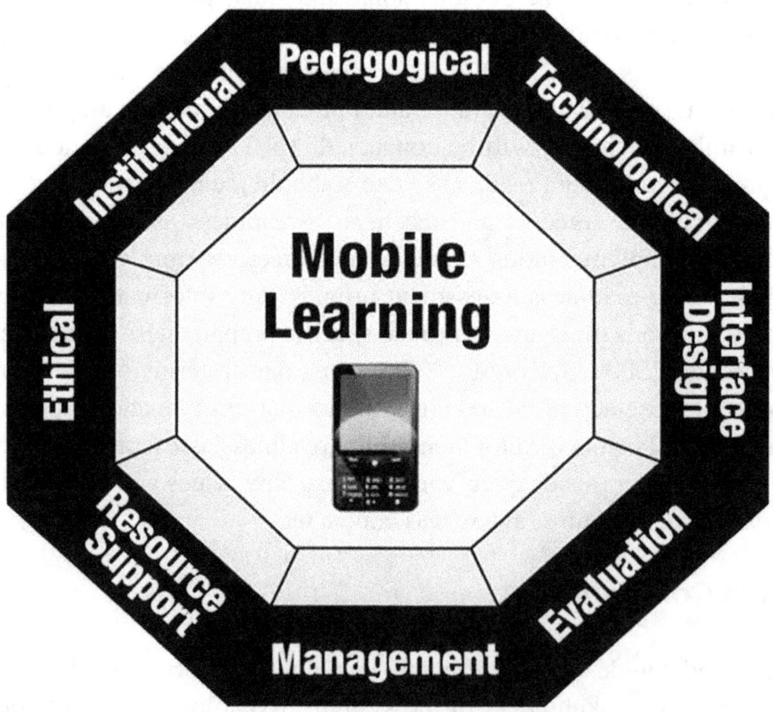

Khan (2001, 2005a, 2007, 2012) developed a comprehensive framework for e-learning by clustering various e-learning issues and factors into eight critical dimensions of the e-learning environment: pedagogical, institutional, technological, interface design, evaluation, management, resource support, and ethical considerations (see Figure 1). Each dimension has several sub-dimensions, and each sub-dimension consists of issues related to a specific aspect of an e-learning environment that must be considered to assess readiness (Morrison, 2003). Khan's octagonal e-learning framework was chosen because it encompasses most of the e-learning readiness categories mentioned by the researchers and practitioners cited above.

ISSUES OF E-LEARNING READINESS

Previous studies that have been conducted in the area of e-learning readiness used various methodologies and adopted different theoretical frameworks. The vigilant assessment of e-learning readiness prolongs the attainment of e-learning. Yet, one of the difficulties of adopting e-learning is the absence of appropriate considerations of the individual and organizational factors of e-learning readiness (Kong, Chan, Huang & Cheah, 2014). E-Learning readiness, indeed, satisfies the needs of the implementers to trust technology through assuring effective learning interactions. Though assessing e-learning readiness has been shown to be a suitable process for technology based learning as demonstrated by Demir and Yurdugül (2015), many educational institutions failed because they have initiated their e-learning solutions without considerations for institutional readiness or, for that matter, any other issues of e-learning readiness. Consequently, the accurate assessment of e-learning readiness is a vital step before implementing supplemented, online, or blended classroom instruction, as the use of technology alone does not grant successful employment of e-learning systems. Prior e-learning readiness literature was reviewed and the two leading categories of e-learning readiness where issues were identified: individual and organizational readiness.

Issues Related to Individual Readiness

Being E-learning ready supports individual needs to accept learning tailored with adequate instructional approaches. Similar to face-to-face learners, online learners are responsible for their own learning; individual accountability is a major characteristic of successful e-Learners, as they are able to undertake and implement their own learning and development strategies. Regrettably, e-learning designers have a tendency to carry out predefined instructional strategies in their designs. Course design rarely begins with investigations of the unambiguous characteristics and requirements of the learners, in spite of the fact that knowing the e-learning readiness of prospective students can deliver the designers with flexible systems to confirm that learners receive authentic teaching and instruction.

Schweighofer and Ebner (2015) encouraged the usage of e-learning readiness assessment to make learning more innovative and pleasurable, while still being adaptable. They nevertheless caution educational institutions against eliminating the adjustment of self-directed instruction to match individual specific needs. There are no explicit strategies that can be used to choose an effective e-learning individual readiness model that is totally suitable for all learners. However, there are general guidelines that specialists can follow to ensure successful implementation. When students' have a high level of e-learning readiness, this enables a collaborative learning environment and enables learners to realize strategies of self-directed learning to support learning online (Panuwatwanich & Stewart, 2014). Another study shows that both self-directed learning and learner control of the learning process during an online course by college students in Taiwan was found to be important dimensions of courses that were e-learning ready (Hung, Chou, Chen, & Own, 2010).

In Japan, a study explored the relationships between teaching strategies and individual eLearning readiness, which was found to be strong (Nakata, 2011). This was also advocated by Schreurs and Al-Huneidi (2013), who stress that school curriculum and teaching strategies ought to be varied in order for students to be ready for successful e-learning. They also encouraged continuous professional development for teachers, both technologically and pedagogically, in order for them to be ready for teaching in an e-learning environment. Al-Furaydi (2013) outlines two issues influencing technological readiness, which are lack of software reliability and lack of time. He additionally criticizes the existing gap between governmental policies and those of local school districts, which are found to be an obstacle for e-learning implementation.

Besides enhancing the superiority of individualized e-learning instruction, the presentation of online content can be varied from one person to another, making teaching and learning materials more personalized and adapted. Moreover, teachers and students are encouraged toward paced-based teaching and learning because it is more expedient (Farid, 2014). In online courses, students can seek out instruction at a time that is most suitable to them. This feature can be effortlessly adapted to the e-learning readiness approach, which makes the learning process pertinent to the desires of the learners (Rahim & Rashidah, 2013; Schweighofer & Ebner, 2015).

Demir and Yurdugül (2015) conclude that being e-learning ready can support individual learning in several ways, as it responds to stakeholders' various needs. Analysis of the proposed e-learning system, prior to its implementation, allows both teachers and students to participate enthusiastically in the design and development process (Awidi & Cooper, 2015). Lin, Huang, and Chuang (2015) suggested that enhancing e-learning readiness should be used as a solution to accommodate the different technological abilities of all parties involved and to create a flexible e-learning environment with different ethical, cultural, and pedagogical experiences. According to Henniing and Westhuizen (2004) two factors might affect the adoption of e-learning: acceptance of the technology and readiness to use it.

Other studies have shown that culture and ethics play significant roles in embracing e-learning. The reaction of individuals to receiving innovation varies from one place to another in this world; some parts of the world would rather avoid innovation and change while others embrace it. In Kenya for example, Ouma, Awuor, and Kyambo (2013) found that both teachers and students are ready for e-learning implementation at the public schools. They have measured the level of preparedness of the public schools in ten government school districts. However, the model used in their study was limited to studying only four critical issues, technology, acceptance, training, and school management. In a neighboring country to Kuwait, Keramati, Afshari-Mofrad, and Kamrani (2011) surveyed 96 teachers in Iran and identified three main factors influencing e-learning readiness: technical, organizational and social. The study revealed that institutional readiness has the most effect when it accompanies teachers' motivation. Memene and Simmons (2015) studied Togolese Higher Education Intuitions (THEIs) readiness for eLearning implementation. The study assessed the integration, development, and enhancement of ICT in THEIs. The study furthermore recommended that educational institutions should consider the state of the physical infrastructure, such as maintained equipment, high bandwidth, and reliability as an important indicators of readiness.

Conducting an e-learning readiness assessment of computer security systems should allow both teachers and learners to be able to accomplish their purposes in the most protected and confidential way. Assessment of security and policy elements provides more control over the learning process, with greater consideration toward learning pace and topics (Memene & Simmons, 2015; Kong, Chan, Huang & Cheah, 2014). In their study of e-learning readiness and online learning environments, Lin, Huang, and Chuang (2015) compared two learning environments that were advanced, accompanied with different levels of security and privacy during an academic year at two public schools in the US. The purpose of the study was to examine students' readiness for e-learning in light of students' involvement and interaction in the learning process. The study found that a high level of e-learning readiness improved students' involvement during electronic based classroom time, however, it did not increase their involvement when e-learning was implemented without prior analysis of learners' and instructors' privacy and security needs.

Issues Related to Organizational Readiness

Effective e-learning readiness solutions allow educational institutions to improve performance and productivity by responding to the demands of the learners and by making learning readily available (Farid, 2014). This approach generates a high return on investment; in addition, positive attitudes toward e-learning increase. E-Learning readiness depends on the availability of organizational assessments including self-assessments in areas such as computer literacy, availability of e-services, and attitude towards the choice of the mode of e-learning (Vilkonis, Bakanoviene, & Turskiene, 2013; Schreurs & Al-Huneidi, 2012). A study in Finland revealed that beliefs play a big role in e-learning adoption (Valtonen, Kukkonen, Dillon, & Väisänen, 2009). This study differentiates between three types of belief: negative, neutral, and positive. The researchers conclude that negative and neutral beliefs towards online learning discourage the use of collaborative learning strategies by students.

One of the main characteristics of e-learning readiness is that it can lead to a nationally recognized implementation of e-learning. Conducting e-learning readiness studies allows for the integration of new technologies to improve communications and skills development through accessible learning, and actual practices (Lin, Huang, & Chuang, 2015). Indeed, e-learning readiness approaches combine the requirements of education with the specific needs of the organizations. Memene and Simmons (2015) conclude that e-learning readiness preparation, when conducted on the organizational level, effect school administrators' beliefs about matching teaching and learning strategies with existing methods of face-to-face instruction. He also advises institutions to involve a wide range of stakeholders when planning, developing, and facilitating a range of strategies to meets their needs. According to Hung, Chou, Chen, and Own (2010) considering cultural differences during the e-learning design and layout process prevents reluctance to participate among the learners.

Content and adequate institutional infrastructure are the two major components necessary for e-learning readiness (Parlakkılıc, 2015). Content varies from basic websites to completely interactive models to classroom meetings. Institutional infrastructure, on the other hand, is accountable for enabling access to this content through the creation, distribution, tracking, and administering the learning content. Lin, Huang, and Chuang (2015) outline three main elements of technology infrastructure readiness, which are management systems, facilities, and services. E-Learning systems deliver and support the content by providing the ability to track, manage, and report students' learning actions. Adequate infrastructure facilities help instructors and students to interact better with the learning process. In essence, facilities flatten the transition from traditional to online instruction (Awidi & Cooper, 2015). As far as the services element is concerned, Panuwatwanich and Stewart (2014) found that content development services supplement authoring and presentation of content, which helps the designers to choose optimal strategies for delivering content. Demir and Yurdugül (2015) suggest e-learning designers assess the institutions' internal consulting services, which provide guidelines and instructions for using and preparing learning strategies and their implementation.

When e-learning readiness is in an optimal state, the outcome of online learning significantly influences online teaching and learning (Ouma, Awuor, & Kyambo, 2013); this finding is also supported by Keramati, Afshari-Mofrad, & Kamrani (2011), who extend the effect of e-learning readiness to make instruction more motivating, relevant, and current. They conclude that learning can become more active, realistic, and constructive; as a result, it provides learners with rich experiences and allows for growing knowledge. Therefore, this type of learning is based on the philosophy that learning is the responsibility of all, not the teachers nor the learners alone.

Using a blend of diverse tools is an efficient methodology in the e-learning readiness approach. Schreurs and Al-Huneidi (2012) stated that the availability of different ways of analyzing and measuring organizational readiness before the implementation of e-learning increases the acceptance of presented e-learning models in schools. These ways and tools include communication, management, ethics, and services. Hung, Chou, Chen, and Own (2010) determined that e-learning readiness has a unique ability for discovering both areas of weaknesses and strengths that institutions should repeatedly watch for. In addition, teachers in schools can utilize the e-learning readiness tools and methods to support and prepare students for the online learning process. Schultz (2015) found that teachers favor an online curriculum to a traditional one; they reported that 83% of the public school teachers studied use online materials for their teaching. They also advised that five areas make e-learning more effective when studying its readiness: infrastructure, communication, content, culture, and pedagogy. When there is a likelihood of having a limited availability in any of these areas, then the choice of traditional instruction is more valuable.

Noticeably, most previous studies have encouraged the employment of e-learning readiness strategies to improve learning and engage learners. Most of the findings of the previous research studies devoted great attention toward the issues of e-learning readiness, which augment learning when carefully considered and used in schools. Several studies advocated the inclusion of individual and organizational factors during the process of studying and assessing e-learning readiness, such as cultural, institutional, and technological issues. The international literature revealed that many parts in the world pay attention to e-learning readiness on the part of institutions and individuals to ensure the return on investment.

KUWAITI VIEWS TOWARDS E-LEARNING

The following part of this chapter focuses on the findings of a study conducted in Kuwait to explore teachers' and students' view of the state of their e-learning readiness. The study aimed at:

1. Designing a valid and reliable instrument for assessing e-learning readiness in schools, particularly the public schools;
2. Identifying issues related to e-learning readiness for both teachers and students at the secondary schools;
3. Investigating teachers' and students' individual and organizational factors of e-learning readiness present in their schools; and

Figure 2. Views towards readiness issues

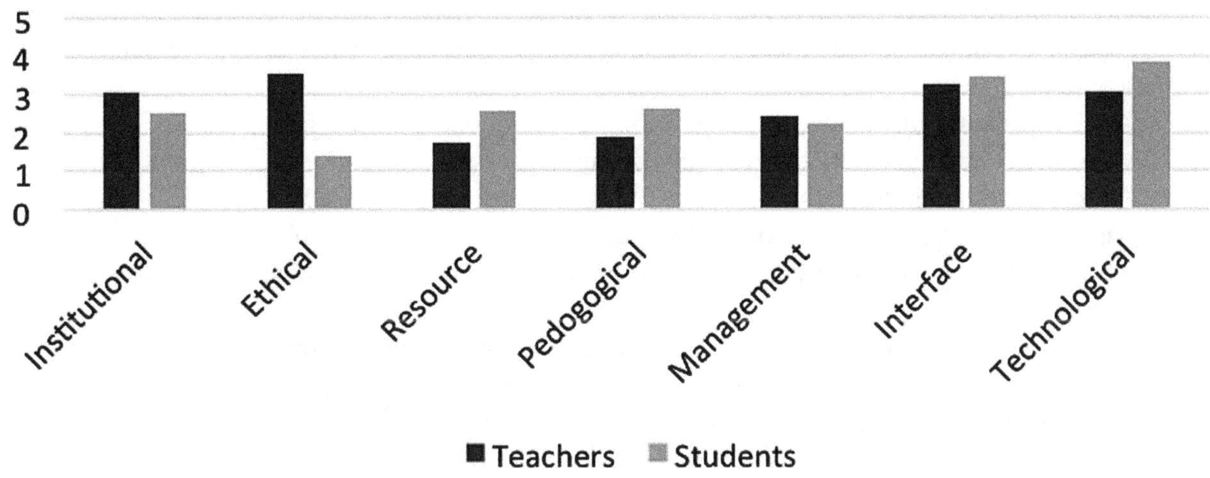

4. Assessing the e-learning readiness of Kuwaiti public secondary schools of both students and teachers, and their relative schools.

Appendix A and Appendix B report the surveys details for Kuwaiti teachers and students, respectively, with responses in percentages for the issues and their corresponding items. Figure 2 explains the mean scores for each group, teachers and students, towards eLearning readiness issues.

Figure 2 shows that teachers have higher agreement than students on readiness in the institutional, ethical, and management areas. While students have higher agreement towards readiness in the resource support, pedagogical, interface design, and technological areas.

Kuwait Readiness for eLearning

In their Kuwaiti case study, Ali and Magalhaes (2008) point out that in Kuwait there is a resistance to organizational, cultural, and personal change which must be addressed in the planning stages of any e-learning project. Schools may need to communicate their own story of readiness to the community. For example, what are they doing to make themselves ready? Are training and technology infrastructure being ramped up in anticipation? Are instructor support teams being created to teach effective teaching strategies, effective communication methods and tools? Further investigation of the disparity in gender responses may be needed to find out whether skill sets are the same by gender, or whether access to basic training is not as readily available to females because of home or other work obligations.

- **Technical Support:** Teachers' agreement that technical support does a good job of supporting students is abysmally low and needs to be carefully examined. Possible explanations include 1) a generalized lack of faith that technical support is available, 2) poor accessibility options and 3) too much "tech-speak" that is not understandable by lay instructors and students. A follow up survey that is entirely focused on support issues (methods used, quality of communications, time of operations, response times, appropriateness/correctness of responses, satisfaction-frustration levels) may be required.

- **Insufficient Assessment of Student Readiness:** The relatively low level of agreement with the amount of time and effort spent in studying the needs of students may be attributed to the perception that too little effort was spent in assessing student needs or to a low level of teacher involvement in the process.
- **Teacher Orientation:** The evidence in the prior literature tells us that an orientation program for instructors is important. Are they actually getting this orientation and is the orientation more like a "one-shot event" in the form of lectures? Or is it ongoing so that teachers can access it as their own needs arise? Another question is whether it includes "just-in-time" access because, as Ali and Megalhaes (2008) and Mercado (2008) point out, timeliness is critical to instructor success and morale.
- **Institutional Communication:** The view that the Ministry of Education in Kuwait supports that initiative for e-learning may reflect some skepticism about the official pronouncements. Perhaps there is a general lack of awareness of possible interest and support from the leading administration. It also seems that authority at the Ministry of Education does not make an effort to stay in contact with institutions and instructors, and seems that the communication always goes one way, downstream, as in broadcasting policy to the masses. Good working relationships require open and honest communications both up and down the hierarchy of power. Digging deeper into the evidence reveals more about what specific resources are thought to be scarce. Have instructors tried and failed to get certain goods and services that they consider very important, while the Ministry of Education considers them irrelevant? Is there a mentality of "scarcity" at the school or district level or from the Ministry of Education?
- **Teachers' Concerns:** Teachers do not feel free to be flexible in their working hours, as is usual with teaching online at a distance. It seems there is a real problem due to policies or social expectations, or perhaps this perceived lack of flexibility is due to self-imposed pressures, or to external pressures to complete all work in the office during designated "office hours." Policies mandate extensive office hours. Instructors feel that they must be in the office all day and still be responsive to students during the evenings and at night. Perhaps policy and personal issues need to be discussed in an open and forthright manner. Inadequate time allocated to prepare for new content could lead to stale course content. At this point instructors need to be assured that they will be given support from instructional designers, graphic artists, and other kinds of specialists in order to create original materials, as they need them. This low of agreement level is troubling because it shows that teachers believe they are not being supported. Further examination of this response may reveal possible problems with scheduling or lack of qualified supervisors.
- **Need for Technical Support:** technology access is probably not sufficient when teachers are expected to create their own videos in a timely manner. Slow access to equipment may impede teachers' workflow and reduce morale. Inadequate staff support, especially combined with limited access to equipment, may also contribute to lower quality video lectures, as well as lowered student and teacher morale. This perceived shortage of time for lesson preparation may come from policy mandates from above or simply from poor management of personal time. These findings reflect a lack of experience in essential skills needed in e-learning. Teachers' comfort when working with technological equipment, like scanners coupled with access to hardware and support using the hardware, is cause for concern. Does this lack of use reflect a lack of self-confidence? Or a lack of time or access to training and equipment? Perhaps some change in management strategies

would help to create a shift in the instructors' views of the value of technology. It is essential that they understand how and why new technology can be used to their advantage in the classroom (Chapnick, 2000; Mercado, 2008). Teachers' assert that e-learning provides increased flexibility in their teaching, which indicate a high level of optimism in the value of e-learning in providing flexibility. They seem to believe that soft skills in leadership and management are essential in e-learning. This evidence signals a lack of self-perceived skill levels and/or signal emotional insecurity with their communication skills. There may be a need to implement training to boost self-efficacy (self-confidence) in this particular area. Implementing partnerships for training, collaborative work groups, etc. may be particularly useful. Another option, suggested by McInnerney and Roberts, (2004), would be to start with incremental phasing in of courses in order to reduce the stress load. Therefore, special effort must be placed on developing appropriate teacher training methods. Mercado (2008) and others point out that these efforts must be integrated into the course development process rather than in the form of one-shot lectures.

- **Teacher-Student Online Communication:** There is a special need for discussion about the quality of teacher-student relationships in an online classroom. Clarity in requirements and possibly even extra training may be needed in order to assure teachers that they can deal with this issue. These results show a strong need for support or seminars on the issue of fairness and openness with students. It may be necessary to teach a section on how to better enable personal communications, including how to provide more scaffolding for students, who typically get left out of discussions (shy, introverted, students with disabilities). It may also be necessary to introduce emotional intelligence into the training. Overall, both teachers and students seem to be confident of their ability to use technology tools and the related skills but less confident in their communication skills or ability to handle problems related to dealing with communication issues online.
- **Teachers' Sense of Personal Preparedness:** Moreover, the findings presented in this chapter revealed that teachers perceive a low level of actual readiness or a lack of confidence in their readiness. This is another reason to provide integrated advanced training sessions that allow teachers to build skills and self-confidence. However, teachers may be overly optimistic about their knowledge of the subject and the amount of time that may be needed to adapt to the new ways of teaching. This is why teachers showed additional indications that they are optimistic about the value of e-learning as a method of motivation as emphasized by Bean (2003), Chapnick (2000), and Clark and Mayer (2003). In addition, Tubaishat and Lansari (2011), support this finding probably because teachers perceive e-learning as a good supplemental tool. This supports the existing debate on the need for practicing the use of technological devices (such as mobile phone, tablet PCs, etc.) in the classroom.
- **Students' Sense of Personal Readiness:** As far as the students' sense of e-learning readiness is concerned, results showed that secondary stage students at Kuwaiti governmental schools view that their schools are ready for e-learning introduction. Obviously, students showed higher level of optimism than teachers towards e-learning readiness. This finding was also supported by Tubaishat & Lansari (2011) and Gülbahar (2012). However, Ilgaz and Gülbahar (2015) justifies students' optimistic views toward e-learning readiness due to their focus is on an individual level such as technological, resource and economic support, but not on the organizational level such as management and institutional dimensions. Both teachers and student feel that they are technologically ready to use e-learning.

- **Library Staff:** Since trained library staff is essential for the success of e-learning programs, the question to be addressed for the Ministry of Education in Kuwait is whether these expressed values match up with the proposed or current budgets. Of interest here is whether or not their budgeting for libraries can take care of these specific training and hiring needs and priorities? Unlike teachers, students perceive that library staff are not technically ready. Perhaps students have experienced limited assistance from library staff when using school services (Broadbent, 2001). These results contrast sharply with those from the teachers.
- **Students with Special Needs:** This study found that accommodation for students with special needs and disabilities is generally perceived as a very low priority. This indicates a need to clarify the issue concerning learners with disabilities and if necessary, investigate and document the reasons for the low level of institutional and teacher perceptions of the value of accommodation. Apparently students are not as certain as are the teachers about the motivational value of eLearning. Surprisingly, students' view that eLearning courses should be accessible by those with any kind of disability is an interesting finding. Probably open learning environment caused by modern ICTs such social media has increased the level of awareness of students with special needs among students in Kuwait
- **Lack of Technology Support:** Like their teachers, students report that they can get the equipment for recording and editing materials for their courses, but do not believe that they can get the help they need with the equipment. Possibly their higher enthusiasm than that of the teachers because they may have more experience with doing this for entertainment purposes and in the use of social media. Apparently students feel a lack of preparation to use all the technologies necessary for e-learning. However, a policy to allow a "Bring Your Own Device" policy for technology, like smart phones, laptops, notepads and personal digital assistants, into the classroom for use by students and teachers can enhance e-learning activities, which was advocated by Mercado (2008).

SUGGESTIONS FOR GOVERNMENT AND SCHOOL ADMINISTRATORS

The following suggestions will help governments and public schools administrators prepare their constituencies for eLearning. They are:

1. Teachers should receive training in online pedagogy (i.e., instructional design training for developing online learning materials) as part of their professional development training. Such training can be accomplished in a number of ways: teachers receive onsite training by instructional design experts; teachers attend e-learning workshops and conferences; and teachers take specific e-learning design course(s) or earn certificates at the university. In many respects teachers and students are optimistic about being successful in their respective roles. However, these assessment results show either a lack of knowledge of existing institutional resources, or a lack of trust in the ability of the institution to support them with what it already has in place.
2. Teachers should have enough information about their institution's capability and the institutional leadership's buy-in that is needed for an e-learning initiative. There is some indication that teachers and students know the value of support, but feel that it is not available in the quantity or quality or at the time that they need.

3. In their Kuwaiti case study, Ali and Magalhaes (2008) point out that organizational, cultural, and personal resistance to change must be addressed in the planning stages of any e-learning project. Schools may need to communicate their own story of readiness to the community while also making more effort to listen to the concerns of teachers and students. There may be a lack of awareness of the need for team collaboration in order to implement this e-learning venture. For example, what is the institution doing to make things ready for teachers and students to effectively communicate with each other? Are social and instructional values of sharing and mutual support being communicated both up and down the institutional hierarchy? Are goals for better training and cooperation being modeled from the top down in a visible manner that teachers and students can emulate in the learning arena?
4. Training and technology infrastructure, especially Internet connectivity, should be ramped up in anticipation. Support staff must be encouraged to model positive attitudes toward change in the highly ambiguous situations in which they will find themselves operating. Compassionate concern for students' well-being and for empowering teachers and students to explore learning options, above and beyond the basic curricular needs, will go a long way toward reducing stress and anxiety levels throughout the year. Training should be monitored and provided early on, with appropriate scaffolding designed to first support and then enhance the learning of new technology itself, while also encouraging empowerment that will then allow use of the technology in creative and transformative ways (Chou, et al. 2013).
5. Instructor support teams should be created to implement effective teaching strategies, and model effective communication methods and tools. Teachers have a tendency to teach in the manner in which they were taught, but this venture will require changes in thinking and the willingness to challenge old models of teaching, as well as the social expectations of what goes on in the new learning environment. Those who are training teachers must model different ways of teaching and leading.
6. Teachers, and to a lesser extent students, have confidence in their own technical skills, but much less confidence in gaining support from those in support positions. Improvement in this area needs to be a priority in the venture.
7. In a nutshell, both teachers and students are somewhat confident in their own technical skills, but less confident of their non-technical skills such as communication and management. However, they had the least expectation of gaining support from the institution or the support staff.

CONCLUSION

This chapter has reported on the results of a "Readiness for e-learning" survey of teachers and students in secondary schools in Kuwait. The study was conducted to provide information to policy makers and regulatory bodies to assist in the successful implementation of e-learning at the secondary school level.

Results suggest that intensive orientation training should be offered initially to both instructors and students. This initial training should be followed by a flow of instruction and support so that their IT knowledge and skills are upgraded continually over time. In addition, results indicate that pedagogical innovations are required to develop and implement an effectiveness e-learning program. These pedagogical innovations can come about only after the technological hurdles have been removed and instructors and students are comfortable with making cognitive shifts in their thinking and behavior. The fact that teachers and students alike feel alone in learning is an indicator that a shift in culture must take place. Schwartz (1996) points out that society is changing in ways that resemble the thinking, intelligent being. In his perspective, isolation is no longer possible and the needs of all the components of a system must be addressed and dealt with in a systematic manner, much as the human body addresses its own needs for overall well-being by supplying nutrients to all its extremities. This process can take place only where open, caring, and trusting relationships are built through honest discussions that simultaneously address the needs of students, teachers, and administrators.

REFERENCES

Abas, Z. W., Kaur, K., & Harun, H. (2004). *ELearning readiness in Malaysia: A national report submitted to the Ministry of Energy, Water and Communications*. Retrieved from http://asiapacific-odl2.oum.edu.my/C33/F70.pdf

Al-Furaydi, A. A. (2013). Measuring e-learning readiness among EFL teachers in intermediate public schools in Saudi Arabia. *English Language Teaching*, *6*(7), 110–121.

Ali, G., & Megalhaes, R. (2008). Barriers to implementing eLearning: A Kuwaiti case study. *International Journal of Training and Development*, *12*(1), 36–53. doi:10.1111/j.1468-2419.2007.00294.x

Atallah, F., & Moussa-Inaty, J. (2012). Exploring faculty and student readiness for e-Learning in a UAE Public University. In T. Bastiaens & G. Marks (Eds.), *Proceedings of E-Learn: World Conference on E-Learning in Corporate, Government, Healthcare, and Higher Education 2012* (pp. 1747-1754). Chesapeake, VA: Association for the Advancement of Computing in Education (AACE). Retrieved from http://www.editlib.org/p/41862

Awidi, I. T., & Cooper, M. (2015). Using management procedure gaps to enhance e-learning implementation in Africa. *Computers & Education*, *90*(1), 64–79. doi:10.1016/j.compedu.2015.08.003

Aydin, C. H., & Tasci, D. (2005). Measuring readiness for eLearning: Reflections from an emerging country. *Journal of Educational Technology & Society*, *8*(4), 244–257.

Azimi, H. M. (2013). Readiness for implementation of eLearning in colleges of education. *Journal of Novel Applied Sciences*, *2*(12), 769–775.

Banathy, B. H. (1991). *Systems designs of education: A journey to create the future*. Englewood Cliffs, NJ: Educational Technology Publications.

Banathy, B. H. (1992). *A systems view of education: Concepts and principles for effective practice*. Englewood Cliffs, NJ: Educational Technology Publications.

Barotis, S., & Poulymenakou, A. (2004). *ELearning readiness components: Key issues to consider before adopting elearning interventions*. Retrieved from https://www.academia.edu/954823/Critical_Success_Factors_for_ELearning_Adoption

Bean, M. (2003). *Are you ready for eLearning? Assessing eLearning readiness: Tips and tricks of the trade*. Retrieved from http://www.mediapro.com/html/resources/news1-vol5-01.htm

Broadbent, B. (2001). *Tips to help decide if your organization ready for e-Learning*. Retrieved from http://icde.net/en/arshive/articles/012.htm

Chapnick, S. (2000). *Needs assessment for eLearning: Info-line, American Society for Training and Development (ASTD)*. Retrieved from http://store.astd.org/Default.aspx?tabid=167&ProductId=8034

Chapnick, S. (2005). Are you ready for eLearning? *Learning Circuits: ASTD's Online Magazine All about eLearning*. Retrieved from http://blog.uny.ac.id/nurhadi/files/2010/08/are_you_ready_for_eLearning.pdf

Chen, M. P. (2009). An evaluation of the ELNP eLearning quality assurance program: Perspectives of gap analysis and innovation diffusion. *Journal of Educational Technology & Society*, *12*(1), 18–33.

Chou, C., Block, L., & Jesness, R. (2012). A case study of mobile learning pilot project in K-12 schools. *Journal of Educational Technology Development and Exchange*, *5*(2), 11–26.

Clark, R. C., & Mayer, R. E. (2003). *ELearning and the science of instruction: Proven guidelines for customers and designers of multimedia learning*. San Francisco, CA: Pfeiffer.

Demir, Ö., & Yurdugül, H. (2015). The Exploration of models regarding e-learning readiness: Reference model suggestions. *International Journal of Progressive Education*, *11*(1).

DeSimone, R. L., & Harris, D. M. (1998). *Human resource development*. Fort Worth, TX: Harcourt Brace College Publishers.

Engholm, P., & McLean, J. (2001). *What determines an organization's readiness for eLearning?* Retrieved from http://www2/sbbs.se/hp/erson/academia/Thesis%20FINAL.htm

Farid, A. (2014). Student online readiness assessment tools: A systematic review approach. *Electronic Journal of e-Learning*, *12*(4), 375-382.

Gülbahar, Y. (2012). Study of developing scales for assessment of the levels of readiness and satisfaction of participants in e-learning environments. *Ankara University Journal of Faculty of Educational Sciences*, *45*(2), 119–137.

Haney, D. (2002). Assessing organizational readiness for eLearning: 70 questions to ask. *Performance Improvement*, *41*(4), 8–13. doi:10.1002/pfi.4140410404

Hopson, M. H., Simms, R. L., & Knezek, G. A. (2002). Using a technology-enriched environment to improve higher-order thinking skills. *Journal of Research on Technology in Education*, *34*(2), 109–119. doi:10.1080/15391523.2001.10782338

Hung, M. L., Chou, C., Chen, C. H., & Own, Z. Y. (2010). Learner readiness for online learning: Scale development and student perceptions. *Computers & Education*, *55*(3), 1080–1090. doi:10.1016/j.compedu.2010.05.004

Ilgaz, H., & Gülbahar, Y. (2015). A snapshot of online learners: E-readiness, e-satisfaction and expectations. *International Review of Research in Open and Distributed Learning*, *16*(2).

Keramati, A., Afshari-Mofrad, M., & Kamrani, A. (2011). The role of readiness factors in E-learning outcomes: An empirical study. *Computers & Education*, *57*(3), 1919–1929. doi:10.1016/j.compedu.2011.04.005

Khan, B. H. (Ed.). (2001). *Web-based training*. Englewood Cliffs, NJ: Educational Technology Publications.

Khan, B. H. (2005a). *ELearning quick checklist*. Hershey, PA: Information Science Publishing. doi:10.4018/978-1-59140-812-3

Khan, B. H. (2005b). *Managing eLearning: Design, delivery, implementation and evaluation*. Hershey, PA: Information Science Publishing. doi:10.4018/978-1-59140-634-1

Khan, B. H. (Ed.). (2007). *Flexible learning in an information society*. Hershey, PA: IGI Global. doi:10.4018/978-1-59904-325-8

Khan, B. H. (Ed.). (2012). *User interface design for virtual environments: Challenges and advances*. Hershey, PA: IGI Global Publishing. doi:10.4018/978-1-61350-516-8

Khan, B. H., & Ally, M. (Eds.). (2015). International handbook of eLearning:Vol. 1. *Theoretical perspectives and research*. London: Routledge.

Kong, S. C., Chan, T. W., Huang, R., & Cheah, H. M. (2014). A review of e-Learning policy in school education in Singapore, Hong Kong, Taiwan, and Beijing: Implications to future policy planning. *Journal of Computers in Education*, *1*(2-3), 187–212. doi:10.1007/s40692-014-0011-0

Lin, J. W., Huang, H. H., & Chuang, Y. S. (2015). The impacts of network centrality and self-regulation on an e-learning environment with the support of social network awareness. *British Journal of Educational Technology*, *46*(1), 32–44. doi:10.1111/bjet.12120

Masoumi, D. (n.d.). *Critical factors for effective eLearning*. Retrieved from http://asianvu.com/digitalibrary/eLearning/Critical_factors_for_effective_eLearning_by_DMasoumi%5B1%5D.pdf

McConnell International LLC. (2000). *Risk e-Business: Seizing the opportunity of global e-readiness*. Retrieved from http://www.witsa.org/papers/e-readiness.pdf

McInnerney, J. M., & Roberts, T. S. (2004). Online learning: Social interaction and the creation of a sense of community. *Journal of Educational Technology & Society*, *7*(3), 73–81.

Memene, D., & Simmons, P. (2015). A Study of eLearning implementation readiness in Togolese Higher Education Institutes. *International Journal of Scientific & Technology Research*, *4*(2), 24–28.

Mercado, C. A. (2008). *Readiness assessment tool for an eLearning environment implementation*. Paper presented at the Fifth International Conference on eLearning for Knowledge-Based Society, Bangkok, Thailand. Retrieved from http://www.eLearningap.com/eLAP2008/Proceedings/18_fullpaper_cecilia%20 Mercado_Revised.pdf

Ministry of Education. (2013). *Statistics of public school system in Kuwait*. Retrieved from http://www.moe.edu.kw/News/69327

Morrison, J. L. (2003). The global eLearning framework: An interview with Badrul Khan. *The Technology Source*. Michigan Virtual University. Retrieved from http://technologysource.org/article/336/

Nakata, Y. (2011). Teachers' readiness for promoting learner autonomy: A study of Japanese EFL high school teachers. *Teaching and Teacher Education*, *27*(5), 900–910. doi:10.1016/j.tate.2011.03.001

National Education Association. (2000). *Quality on the line: Benchmarks for success in internet-based distance education*. Retrieved from http://www.ihep.org/sites/default/files/uploads/docs/pubs/quality-ontheline.pdf

National Education Association. (2006). *Guide to teaching online courses*. Retrieved from http://www.nea.org/assets/docs/onlineteachguide.pdf

O'Malley, M. (2012). *Learning house instructor readiness questionnaire*. Retrieved from http://sloan-consortium.org/conference/2012/aln/assessing-instructor-readiness-teach-online-courses

Ouma, G. O., Awuor, F. M., & Kyambo, B. (2013). E-Learning readiness in public secondary schools in Kenya. *European Journal of Open, Distance and e-Learning*. Retrieved from http://www.eurodl.org/?p=archives&year=2013&halfyear=2&article=592

Panuwatwanich, K., & Stewart, R. A. (2014). Understanding students' use of online learning tools through online learning readiness assessment. *Using Technology Tools to Innovate Assessment, Reporting, and Teaching Practices in Engineering Education*, 227-240. doi:10.4018/978-1-4666-5011-4.ch017

Parlakkılıc, A. (2015). E-Learning Readiness in Medicine: Turkish Family Medicine (FM) Physicians Case. *Turkish Online Journal of Educational Technology*, *14*(2), 59.

Peslak, A. R. (2003). Teaching computer information systems via distance education: A researched and personal perspective. *Information Systems Education Journal*, *1*(12), 1–18.

Phillips, K. A., Terras, K. L., Swinney, L., & Schneweis, C. (2012). Online disability accommodations: Faculty experiences at one public university. *Journal of Postsecondary Education and Disability*, *25*(4), 331–344.

Psycharis, S. (2005). Presumptions and action affecting an eLearning adoption by the educational system: Implementation using virtual private networks. *European Journal of Open and Distance Learning*, *2*, 1–10.

Rahim, B. A., & Rashidah, S. (2013, October). Teachers' attitudes towards a learning management system, MC Online: An exploratory study in a Singapore secondary school. In *Educational Media (ICEM), 2013 IEEE 63rd Annual Conference International Council for IEEE* (pp. 1-18).

Red, E. R., Borlongan, H. G. S., Briagas, T. T., & Mendoza, M. J. M. (2013). *An assessment of the eLearning readiness state of faculty members and students at Malayan Colleges Laguna*. Retrieved from http://www.ijcim.th.org/past_editions/2013V21N3/3.Page_20-26.pdf

Rosenberg, M. (2000). *The eLearning readiness survey*. Retrieved from http://books.mcgraw-hill.com/training/eLearning/eLearning_survey.pdf

Rosenberg, M. J. (2001). *ELearning: Strategies for delivering knowledge in the digital age*. New York: McGraw-Hill.

Schreurs, J., & Al-Huneidi, A. (2012). E-learning readiness in organisations: Case KBC bank. *International Journal of Advanced Corporate Learning*, *5*(1), 4–7.

Schultz, S. (2015). *Comparison of online student vs. public student performance on the ACT* (Master Thesis, Dordt College, Iowa). Retrieved from http://digitalcollections.dordt.edu/med_theses/88

Schwartz, P. (1996). *The art of the long view: Paths to strategic insight for yourself and your company*. New York: Broadway Business.

Schweighofer, P., & Ebner, M. (2015). Aspects to be considered when implementing technology-enhanced learning approaches: A literature review. *Future Internet*, *7*(1), 26–49. doi:10.3390/fi7010026

So, K. T., & Swatman, P. M. C. (2006). *eLearning Readiness of Hong Kong Teachers*. Paper presented at the Hong Kong International IT in Education Conference 2006, Hong Kong.

So, K. T., & Swatman, P. M. C. (2012). *ELearning readiness in the classroom: A study of Hong Kong primary and secondary teachers*. Retrieved from https://nurhadiw.files.wordpress.com/2010/08/swatman-hongkong.pdf

Soong, B. M., Chan, H., Chua, B. C., & Loh, K. F. (2001). Critical success factors for on-line course resources. *Computers & Education*, *36*(2), 101–120. doi:10.1016/S0360-1315(00)00044-0

SREB. (2009). *Guidelines for professional development of online teachers*. Retrieved from http://publications.sreb.org/2009/09T01_Guide_profdev_online_teach.pdf

Tham, C. M., & Werner, J. M. (2005). Designing and evaluating eLearning in higher education: A review and recommendations. *Journal of Leadership & Organizational Studies*, *11*(2), 15–25. doi:10.1177/107179190501100203

Tubaishat, A., & Lansari, A. (2011). Are students ready to adopt e-learning? A preliminary e-readiness study of a university in the Gulf region. *International Journal of Information and Communication Technology Research*, *5*(1).

Turskienė, S., Bakanovienė, T., & Vilkonis, R. (2013). Readiness of adults to learn using e-learning, m-learning and t-learning technologies. *Informatics in Education: An International Journal*, *12*(2), 181–190.

Valtonen, T., Kukkonen, J., Dillon, P., & Väisänen, P. (2009). Finnish high school students' readiness to adopt online learning: Questioning the assumptions. *Computers & Education*, *53*(3), 742–748. doi:10.1016/j.compedu.2009.04.014

Volery, T., & Lord, D. (2000). Critical success factors in online education. *International Journal of Educational Management*, *14*(5), 216–223. doi:10.1108/09513540010344731

Waller, V. (2005). *Is learning for everyone achievable?* Retrieved Nov. 1, 2005 from http://www.learningtechnologies.co.uk/magazine

APPENDIX A

Table 1. E-learning readiness survey items for teachers including distribution of response options in percentages

Items	Issues	SD	D	N	A	SA	NA
1. My school is ready to venture into eLearning.	Institutional	5.3	9.2	15.3	44.0	16.8	9.3
2. Copyright issues are important in creating eLearning materials.	Ethical	3.2	7.0	14.0	50.2	21.4	4.2
3. Accommodation to students with special needs and disabilities is a very low priority.	Ethical	3.7	12.6	14.1	36.9	24.5	8.1
4. Online advising for students is very important to student motivation.	Institutional	2.1	3.4	7.8	49.8	35.8	1.1
5. Trained library staff is essential for the success of our eLearning program.	Institutional	1.4	3.2	4.7	37.9	51.5	1.3
6. The people in technical support do a great job of supporting students.	Resource Support	10.4	26.3	20.9	26.9	8.2	7.3
7. We have spent adequate time and effort in studying the needs of our students.	Institutional	4.0	11.3	14.2	47.4	21.0	2.2
8. Instructor orientation to eLearning is a high priority.	Institutional	2.1	2.2	7.5	44.8	.42.6	0.8
9. The eLearning initiative has direct support from the Ministry of Education.	Institutional	10.1	23.5	20.7	30.1	8.8	6.7
10. My school has adequate funding for eLearning.	Institutional	21.6	29.5	17.2	17.9	6.3	7.5
11. My school will allow me to work on a flexible schedule to teach online (e.g. working from home).	Pedagogical	27.3	29.4	13.6	13.4	4.4	8.9
12. ELearning provides a great return on investment.	Institutional	3.0	7.5	19.9	42.5	17.6	9.6
13. ELearning is a very efficient way to learn.	Pedagogical	3.6	4.8	10.4	46.9	33.6	0.8
14. We are given adequate planning time to create materials for our courses without plagiarizing from others.	Institutional Management	9.4	21.7	17.0	35.2	13.1	3.7
15. ELearning courses should be accessible by those with any kind of disability.	Ethical Interface Design	1.8	2.9	8.0	40.8	44.0	2.5
16. Curriculum supervisors are very supportive of my student's instructional needs.	Institutional Pedagogical	10.7	21.9	21.2	31.4	8.5	6.3
17. If I need additional resources (for example: simulations, virtual labs, etc.) for my classes, my school will provide them.	Institutional Pedagogical	19.9	29.5	17.5	21.2	6.5	5.5
18. I can get access to video recording and editing equipment as I need it.	Technological	5.0	13.7	15.2	47.3	13.6	5.3
19. School staff is available to teach me how to record and edit video files.	Technological	12.8	22.7	19.8	31.0	7.2	6.6
20. Instructors are given adequate time to prepare lessons for each class.	Institutional Pedagogical	8.2	16.8	15.7	43.7	12.2	3.4
21. At home I have access to a computer with Internet connection.	Technological	2.8	3.9	5.7	44.4	41.8	1.4
22. If eLearning is implemented for my class, I will upgrade my personal computer.	Technological	2.4	4.3	8.2	47.7	35.0	2.4
23. I can easily upload video and audio files for students.	Technological	4.9	9.7	10.7	45.7	25.1	3.9
24. Maintaining a grade book online is easy.	Technological	4.6	11.3	13.9	40.3	25.6	4.3
25. I am comfortable working with the hardware used for scanning.	Technological	3.5	9.7	16.8	39.7	20.8	9.4
26. I have used the latest emerging technology in my classroom.	Technological	5.0	12.0	18.7	38.4	19.6	6.4

continued on following page

Table 1. Continued

Items	Issues	SD	D	N	A	SA	NA
27. I enjoy learning to use new technologies such as smartphones and tablets for teaching.	Technological	3.0	5.7	10.4	41.1	37.6	2.2
28. ELearning provides increased flexibility in my teaching.	Pedagogical	2.3	4.0	9.8	45.1	36.2	2.6
29. I can master the skills necessary to lead/manage students in an eLearning course.	Technological Management	2.9	5.1	11.6	46.0	31.1	3.4
30. My online communication skills are not quite ready for teaching an eLearning course.	Pedagogical	8.4	25.6	18.6	30.3	11.1	6.1
31. I can easily master the skills I need to teach an eLearning course.	Pedagogical Technological Management	3.5	7.3	14.7	47.0	24.1	3.4
32. Teaching online makes it more difficult to be fair and open-minded with students.	Pedagogical Ethical	7.2	25.8	24.3	25.3	10.1	7.3
33. Online learning opens up a world of opportunities for students to learn.	Pedagogical	2.4	4.5	12.0	47.5	30.7	2.9
34. ELearning offers many opportunities for me to teach more effectively.	Pedagogical	2.3	4.6	12.1	46.4	31.4	3.4
35. I am not prepared for online teaching.	Pedagogical Technological	15.8	35.1	15.3	19.6	9.2	5.0
36. I am very capable of selecting teaching strategies for eLearning.	Pedagogical Technological	2.4	9.2	25.9	48.2	19.5	4.8
37. Using eLearning in my courses will give my students more incentive to study than does traditional lecturing.	Pedagogical Ethical	3.5	5.9	12.6	44.8	29.5	3.7
38. Using eLearning along with my face-to-face class will improve student learning.	Pedagogical	3.0	4.4	11.3	43.9	33.9	3.4
39. A policy to allow "Bring Your Own Device" (BYOD) such as smart phones, laptops, and personal digital assistants, into the classroom for use by students and teachers can enhance eLearning activities.	Institutional Pedagogical Technological	8.1	11.3	15.0	38.6	23.4	2.6
40. The "flipped" classroom approach (in which students view lectures and materials such as videos before class) makes the face- to-face classroom environment more interactive and meaningful.	Pedagogical Technological	2.7	5.2	12.6	48.0	28.4	3.2

APPENDIX B

Table 2. E-learning readiness survey items for students and distribution of response options in percentages

Items	Issues	SD	D	N	A	SA	NA
1. ELearning provides increased flexibility in my learning.	Pedagogical	9.0	11.0	16.1	41.2	20.0	2.9
2. I prefer to use new technologies such as smartphones and tablets for learning.	Pedagogical Technological Ethical	10.2	13.3	13.9	36.5	25.5	0.6
3. I can master the skills necessary to participate in an eLearning course.	Technological	2.3	3.3	4.8	42.6	45.9	1.1
4. Trained library staff is essential for our eLearning program.	Institutional Resource Support	5.2	6.4	14.8	41.3	24.9	7.4
5. Technical support personnel do a great job of supporting students.	Institutional Resource Support	6.5	13.3	21.7	35.5	12.2	10.8
6. I believe eLearning is a valuable supplement to traditional classroom instruction.	Pedagogical Ethical	6.3	9.8	18.1	38.4	20.6	6.9
7. ELearning courses should be accessible by those with any kind of disability.	Ethical Interface Design	2.9	4.4	7.8	40.7	39.9	4.2
8. I can get access to video recording and editing equipment as I need it.	Technological Resource Support	4.4	8.4	11.0	46.1	25.4	4.3
9. School staff is available to assist me when I need help with recording and editing video files.	Institutional Resource Support	12.0	21.1	13.9	34.8	12.5	5.6
10. At home I have access to a computer with an Internet connection.	Technological	3.4	6.2	4.4	44.5	39.6	1.8
11. If eLearning is implemented for my class, I will upgrade my personal computer.	Technological Pedagogical	4.7	7.6	9.9	43.2	32.1	2.4
12. I can easily upload video and audio files.	Technological	4.7	7.0	8.9	45.1	32.4	2.0
13. I am comfortable working with the hardware used for scanning.	Technological	6.0	13.2	20.4	35.3	17.2	8.0
14. My online communication skills are not quite ready for success in an eLearning course.	Pedagogical Technological Management	13.5	22.8	23.2	22.2	14.9	3.4
15. I am not prepared for online learning.	Ethical Pedagogical Technological	21.3	31.2	15.1	19.1	10.8	2.5
16. Using eLearning provides more incentives for me to study than does traditional lecturing.	Pedagogical Technological	9.6	13.9	16.1	35.7	21.6	3.0
17. A policy to allow "Bring Your Own Device" (BYOD) such as smart phones, laptops, and personal digital assistants, into the classroom for use by students and teachers can enhance eLearning activities.	Institutional Pedagogical Technological	7.5	11.4	10.0	37.5	31.6	2.0
18. The "flipped" classroom approach (in which students view lectures and materials such as videos before class) makes the face to face classroom environment more interactive and meaningful.	Pedagogical Technological	4.3	5.8	10.5	41.6	36.1	1.7

Chapter 14
Building Sustainable Capacity in Health Research through e-Learning in Resource Constrained Countries

Manu Gupta
IIHMR University, India

ABSTRACT

Social determinants like income level, nutrition, education, occupation, gender, and poverty influence the health status of individual, resulting in wide disparities in the health status of different socio-economic groups. Efforts to reduce health inequities can be strengthened by incorporating a Social Determinants of Health approach in creating Health Care policy. This will require an increase in the number of scientists in low and middle-income countries, with the necessary skills. This chapter focuses on a novel capacity building approach, adopted by a European Union funded project, entitled "Asian Regional Capacity Development for Research on Social Determinants of Health". The project uses innovative educational technologies to deliver education and training that would be helpful in building new research training capacity on social determinants of health, in low and middle-income countries. The capacity building approach adopted by the project, will reduce brain drain, is more climate friendly and also encourage gender equity within low and middle-income country-based training.

INTRODUCTION

The increased use of e-Learning, has become a common feature globally, providing cost effective solutions to bridge the gap between the supply and demand crisis faced by health systems research. Health inequities exists within and between countries and are prevalent in low and middle income countries (LMICs). Health equity can be improved by incorporating social determinants of health approach into policy. This requires an increased number of scientists with the necessary interdisciplinary skills. Currently there is a lack of national capacity in low and middle income countries of people with the neces-

DOI: 10.4018/978-1-5225-0466-5.ch014

sary interdisciplinary skills. This is a barrier to revitalize primary health care and attain the Millennium Development Goals (MDGs), which are time bound targets, adopted at the Millenium Summit in 2000, to reduce extreme poverty by the year 2015 (Millenium Project, 2006). It is thus critical to strengthen the health research capacity in resource constrained countries (Sithi & Somrongthong, 2010).

The development of innovative educational technologies (van de Wende, 2003) has led to the implementation of an increasing number of multimedia-based e-Learning approaches to curriculum delivery around the world (Tinio, 2003). The increasing use of educational technologies in supporting teaching and learning, the increased accessibility of the Internet, has led researchers to suggest that e-Learning can be used to give a larger audience access to flexible and high quality teaching at a greatly reduced cost (Bates,1995). The aim of this chapter is to present a region wide approach, developed by the Asian Regional Capacity Development for Research on Social Determinants of Health (ARCADE RSDH) project, which by the integration of e-Learning, has developed an innovative education model to strengthen the research capacity in resource constrained countries.

BACKGROUND

Importance of Health Research

The social determinants of health (SDH) are the conditions into which people are born, live, work, and age, including the area of health system. These conditions play a critical role in maintaining the health status of the people. They are risk factors found in one's living and working conditions (like distribution of income, wealth, influence, and power), rather than individual factors (like behavioural risk factors or genetics) which influence the risk of disease or increases vulnerability to disease or injury. The social determinants of health are shaped by the distribution of money, power, and resources at global, national, and local levels and are mostly responsible for health inequities – the unavoidable differences in health status seen within and between countries. (WHO, Social Determinants of Health, 2012)

Health inequities are a major concern and are a key focus for policy makers in low and middle income countries. Reducing health inequities can improve outcomes for public health programmes, while also promoting social justice and human right to health. (Whitehead, 1992; Lee, 2005).

According to the World Health Organization's Commission on Social Determinants of Health, health inequities are the result of policy failures (WHO, 2012). An effective policy to tackle health inequity must address the underlying social conditions that make disadvantaged people more vulnerable (Marmot, 2005). Without an effective action on the social determinants of health, many countries will neither meet the Millennium Development Goals (Millennium Project,2006), nor can they attain the global targets for reducing chronic diseases, such as cardiovascular diseases, cancer, and diabetes (Strong, Mathers, Leeder, & Beaglehode, 2005). Efforts to improve health equity can be reduced by incorporating a SDH approach with the exiting approaches (Satcher, 2010).

Adopting this approach will require a substantial increase in number of scientists with the necessary skills. This local capacity (enough people to do the job) is required for research on SDH, promotion of multidisciplinary research, and dissemination of research findings to guide policymaking (WHO, 2004).

Capacity Building in Health Research

Health research capacity is the ability to define problems, set objectives, priorities, build sustainable institutions and organizations, identify solutions to health problems, and evaluate interventions and actions (COHRED, 2008). Capacity building for health research, in low and middle income countries (LMICs) was brought to global attention in 1990 by the Report of the Commission on Health Research for Development (Commission on Health Research for Development, 1990). The 10/90 Report on Health Research (2001–2002), also highlighted the importance of strengthening research capacity (Global Forum for Health Research, 2002).

But research capacity is very weak in many LMICs and as a result LMICs are often unable to participate effectively in national and international health policy development. It is therefore important to strengthen health research capacity in LMICs, so that greater health equity can be achieved (Sitthi & Somrongthong, 2000).

Approaches to Strengthen Research Capacity

The report on "Changing mindsets: Research Capacity Strengthening in LMICs" (COHRED, 2008), proposed strategies to strengthen research capacity. It recommended that research capacity must be strengthened both at individual and institutional levels. The report recommended actions for the retention of skilled researchers. It also laid emphasis on collaboration between higher educational institutes within low and middle income countries. Another study published by the U.S. Centers for Disease Control and Prevention also laid emphasis on collaborative partnership for population health and health equity (Fawcett, Schultz, Watson, Fox, & Bremby, 2010). Various initiatives have been launched for capacity strengthening, but evidence on the strengths and weakness of such projects is small and the quality of the data present is poor (Mayhew et al., 2008; Lutumba, 2010)

E-Learing has been recognized as an innovative education tool by various international organizations like WHO, UNESCO, UNICEF, and the World Bank (WHO, 2015). Advances in educational technologies have redefined boundaries of education. "E- learning is an educational approach, which by the integration of information and communication technology, facilitates new ways of learning by increasing access to training, communication and interaction" (Sangra, Vlachopoulos, & Cabrera, 2012). The World Health Organization has also recognized e-Learning as an important tool for partnership and an effective strategy to overcome shortages in the healthcare workforce (WHO, 2015). However, e-Learning is not utilized to its full potential in health care. Therefore, in this context, the author present an innovative administrative model adopted by project ARCADE RSDH. The project, by the use of e-Learning, aims to build sustainable training capacity in low and middle income countries (LMICs), to expand and strengthen research on health and the social determinants of health.

ISSUES, CONTROVERSIES AND PROBLEMS IN HEALTH RESEARCH

Social Determinants of Health is becoming a key focus for policy makers in many LMICs, but despite the evidence, there is relatively little understanding as how these complex issues can be addressed by public policy (Exworthy, 2008). Decision makers urgently need detailed guidance on how they might both assess SDH and tackle health inequities.

CSDH proposed a framework, to explain the relationship between health inequities and SDH. The framework pointed out that health equities cannot be achieved by the health sector alone, but rather requires commitment and partnerships across a wide range of actors (Solar & Irwin, 2007).

In order to achieve this substantial increase in the number of scientists, with sufficient multidisciplinary skills is required. But the field of Health policy and system research (HPSR), faces many health workforce related challenges, which act as a hindering factor to achieve global health objectives and these factors are listed below (Global Forum for Health Research, 2004; Bennett, et al, 2011):

1. There is a shortage in the number of skilled researchers with necessary multi-disciplinary skills:
2. There are few organizations with required expertise in the discipline.
3. Research funding in low and middle income countries is low for research, with grants typically in the range of $20,000 to 30,000, which is less than needed to conduct a good quality of research.
4. Several conditions in host countries, (for example: a better standard of living and quality of life; access to advanced technology; and more stable political conditions), have given rise to a 'brain drain' of these highly trained or skilled scientists. They decide not to work in their own countries and migrate to, or simply stay after graduation, in developed countries, working for institutions outside their homelands (Castanos, 1998; Kupfer et al., 2004).
5. Salaries of health system researchers are low, giving little incentive for them to work in universities or in other public settings. This situation gradually leads to the brain drain problems in countries, and the ill-paid researchers migrate abroad or look for alternatives in the private sector.
6. Training models are outdated, and need to be updated.
7. There is an over-reliance for curative services in secondary and tertiary care settings.

Besides the factors mentioned above, research capacity building in health research takes a longer time period. It also requires institution building, along with the individual strengthening for a sustained capacity (Rispela & Doherty, 2011).

Considering the extent of health system research challenges, the field requires both the increased investment and an efficient and effective use of available resources. Therefore, in this context, it becomes important to explore the potential of new educational technologies to produce a new generation of research scientists. The increased accessibility of the Internet has led researchers to suggest that e-Learning can be used to give a larger audience access to flexible and high quality teaching and learning at a greatly reduced cost (Bates, 1995). However, e-Learning has been not used to its full potential to support health workforce capacity building (WHO, 2015). Recently a European Union funded project ARCADE RSDH, is promoting and enhancing progress towards health equity, by the use of educational technologies. The project model is described in the section below.

SOLUTIONS AND RECOMMENDATIONS

The ARCADE RSDH is a consortium project of leading research institutes spread across three continents Europe (Finland, Sweden, United Kingdom), Asia (China, India, Oman, Vietnam) and Africa (South Africa). There are 12 partner institutes in the project. This is a four-year project (2011-2015), funded by the European Commission's 7th Framework Programme.

Table 1. Work packages (WP) in the project

WP	Type of Activity
WP1	Project Management
WP2	Research capacity needs assessment
WP3	Learning module development
WP4	Blended learning platform and courses in hub institutions
WP5	Design and operation of networked group mentoring research projects
WP6	Institutional capacity for joint training and research management
WP7	Institutional capacity development of dissemination activities

The project would add new research training capacity, in low and middle-income countries (LMICs) in Asia, in the area of social determinants of health (RSDH). This capacity building approach would reduce brain drain, promote gender equity and is more climate friendly.

The project uses innovative education technologies to strengthen health research on social determinants on health in Asia. This region-wide capacity building approach is possible due to the rapidly evolving Internet connectivity in the targeted regions. Internet connectivity in the entire region is already in place (World Bank, 2015). According to the International Telecommunication Union, there are 2.7 billion people using the Internet, which is 39% of the world's population. In developing countries only 31% of the population is online, in comparison to 77% of developed countries (ICT, 2013). Therefore, by harnessing the power of information and communication technologies, the project has developed a cost–effective education model, to provide students with rapid access of high quality course materials from prestigious universities.

The project has three components:

1. Producing high quality training resources.
2. Institutional capacity development at two high level regional training hubs.
3. South-south a network in low and middle income countries, to be developed for training and research.

Education Model

The educational model is intended to provide a common framework within which all the partners operate and the integration of e-Learning is at the heart of the model. The model is divided into 7 different work packages (WP) and each one is lead by a different partner university. Table 1 presents different work packages. The project works at two levels:

1. Individual Level, and
2. Institutional Level.

At the Individual Level

The project focuses on post-graduate, doctoral, and post-doctoral level students by using innovative "education technologies" to strengthen health research across Asia. The students are trained and mentored on different areas of social determinants of health. Innovative sandwich model for trainings are used, where the students receive trainings in hub institutions, but take part in mentored research programmes at their home health system to design and conduct research to support health policy makers at their home country.

Joint training programmes between European partners and Asian partners and between Asian partners, have been developed. Senior scientists collaborate across institutions on the design of these programmes of research mentoring, and undertake cross-institutional mobility to improve inter-institutional networking and collaboration.

The courses cover social, health, and evaluative research methodologies, needed to support evidence-based responsive decision making in health equity and SDH. These courses are taught by web-based educational technologies in both synchronous and asynchronous learning environment. Several activities like research clinics (i.e. online seminars) mentorship programme for scientific writing, grant writing, provide support, and mentorship to young researchers are used to increase sustainability.

These courses are shared centrally through Moodle-based platforms. The platforms are developed to host ARCADE courses and train researchers through decentralized learning in an effective virtual learning environment. In order to ensure maximum accessibility, sustainability, and efficiency the courses are implemented in China and India.

The Moodle-based platforms contain web mounted, downloadable training courses for RSDH training, which allow for both self-directed and face-to-face learning. These modules are a significant innovation in distance education for social determinants of health. The courses are developed by subject area specialists from the partner institutes or are invited external contributors where appropriate and these modules are regularly updated.

These Moodle-based sites are user friendly, and students can easily access the uploaded modules and can download them, read and complete them at their own pace and time. Students can register themselves for free, using the registration system in Moodle, enrol for the courses, and complete assessments. In addition, the system provides a platform for interaction among students, tutors, and lecturers.

The courses are shared through an open course repository, which can be accessed at http://www.arcade-project.org/about/open-course-repository/. The course materials are released under Creative Commons Attribution Non-Commercial-ShareAlike 3.0 license. The ARCADE OCR is not password protected and allows anyone interested to access the training materials including course outlines, reading materials, full-text open-access articles, practical examples. and exercises and use them for teaching or learning.

A blended learning approach is also used for mentoring, which is a mix of face-to-face and web based education. The approach is useful for real time interaction with the students, and they are able to receive individual feedback and contact with their supervisors, irrespective of their geographical spread. By an integration of technologies, the project has increased the potential world of possibilities for the students, where they are mentored by senior scientists at prestigious universities. This is especially important for the students who don't have access to the materials and who have not been able to travel; they can do so now by touch of a button.

Institutional Strengthening

The organizational innovation inherent in this project is to form an Asian network for social determinants of health and health equity. There are two sub-regional training centres, one each in India and China. The ARCADE RSDH project works at an institutional level to strengthen education services, financial and administrative research management, research uptake capacity, and network building in low and middle income countries (LMICs).

The training centres located in India and China are equipped with substantial infrastructure and institutional capacity, acting as a hub for training doctoral and post-doctoral students, from their own countries or other Asian or European partners. This is also open to international students. These hub institutes each have their own Moodle platform and institutions in the network support each other through the exchange of course materials, experience, skills, and staff. Partner institutes are trained by staff and policy exchange among Asian partners, and with EU partner institutes.

Institutional capacity is also enhanced by conducting regular workshops for the staff for delivering courses, both in synchronous and asynchronous environment. The partners also attend distance learning discussions and forums at their home countries to remain updated about the innovations in course delivery.

Grant office capacity has been strengthened at Asian hubs. This is useful in identifying grant opportunities, grant writing – including budgeting and funding of institutional overheads – grant financial management, monitoring, disbursement, and reporting to funders. This new capacity has been useful for acquiring competitive research grants and salary awards from external funders for doctoral and post-doctoral level students. Assisting in grant capture creates an effective retention system for junior staff, and encourages their continued research activity, thus building the next generation of university faculty.

In order to ensure that the research gets into the right hands, an effective, innovative, and impactful communication strategy is in place, which is an integral part of the research process. The project consortium is continuously involved in active dissemination of courses and project promotion. An active dissemination team has been formed in each partner institute, and works as a network of partners in Asia and Europe and are actively engaged in disseminating ARCADE project outputs.

Their communication strategy targets two main groups: end-users and stakeholders. The end-users are teachers, students, researchers, and education administrators. Stakeholders are the funding agencies and other related national and international organizations. YouTube and informal discussion groups are formed for PhD students and researchers and ARCADE RSDH partners have developed their own websites and profiles to engage with both global and local communities of learners and teachers. A mobile application has also been launched (see Table 2).

The ARCADE YouTube channel is another tool that helps in sharing ARCADE materials, and hosts approximately 101 videos of lectures and seminars, most of which are open access for wide public, and can be viewed at: https://www.youtube.com/user/ARCADEproject2015

Impact of the Project

Getting doctoral level training away from their home country distances the researcher from national development and networks and they have less access to influential decision makers. With successful local mentoring of doctoral and post-doctoral fellows, these graduates will be highly eligible for new faculty positions in partner institutions. These faculty positions will create a development path for the graduates of the teaching, mentoring, and research activities of ARCADE, and, in turn, will ensure that

Table 2. Features of mobile application

A mobile phone application, iECHO, was designed for sharing the latest information about health research and promoting education opportunities in postgraduate training with health care professionals in low and middle-income countries in Asia. Current features of the application include sharing information about: • ARCADE activities, including online, blended courses and workshops • Other online courses offered by premium organisations like World Bank Institute, Coursera, etc. • New publications, conferences, workshops and funding opportunities worldwide. The application is free of cost, readily installable from Google Play and available on all android phones version 3.0, windows and Iphone versions.

Source: ARCADE Report, 2014.

these graduates contribute to a sustainable broad base of capacity building for teaching and research within the Asian network. Since the start of the project, more than 300 young researchers have benefited from the ARCADE courses and workshops; more than 50 Ph.D students/post-docs are participating in mentored proposal writing and are receiving mentors' support for writing manuscripts for publication; 14 young researchers are employed via ARCADE-related grants.(ARCADE Report, 2014)

This novel capacity building approach will reduce the 'brain-drain' problem in low and middle income countries, improve gender equity by improving female student access through LMIC-based training, and strengthen the local research capacity. The approach used is more climate friendly, as inter-continental travel is replacing by national and regional travel, thereby reducing economic cost.

Doctoral and post-doctoral level training requires long absences from families, especially if students have to undertake training in a European or American institution. These absences are difficult to sustain, both financially and socially. For female students, who carry major responsibilities in families, travel is a major barrier for attaining high level training. Through the "sandwich" approach to training, a student, after getting training from a foreign institute, can come back and conduct research in their home country.

FUTURE RESEARCH DIRECTIONS

Technology is used widely to achieve better learning outcomes, in a cost effective manner. The emergence of various pedagogical models like open/flexible learning, distributed learning, knowledge building communities, and asynchronous learning has now facilitated improved access to global resources (Dabbagh, 2005). E-Learning does have the potential to deliver educational materials to far more people than can be achieved by traditional teaching methods that require teachers and students to come together within a brick and mortar building (Hvorecký, 2005).

Successful implementation of e-Learning systems requires careful planning. Technology in itself doesn't enhance learning; it depends on the design and implementation strategy for the technology, and how the users (both teachers and students) are supported to use it and how outcomes are measured (TEL, 2015).

Language is a problem in hosting online courses. In Asian countries, the local language is used for courses, which then cannot be transferred to some other country. There are a number of research projects that involve more than one partner that may also grow into training networks in the future, but due to the relatively young nature of collaboration, partner institutes lack information about the strength and expertise of other partner institutions.

Technical issues range from acquiring initial hardware and software and its regular maintenance. The project developed its Moodle-based platform in bigger partner institutes having sufficient infrastructure and expertise to manage the same. Internet connectivity still remains an issue while conducting online courses. Sometimes, these courses are technically and logistically somewhat difficult to implement. One reason is the time difference between countries and sometimes there are technological issues like limited bandwidth, leading to poor internet connectivity. Therefore, future research could be conducted to explore effective solutions for bandwidth management.

CONCLUSION

In this chapter we discussed a capacity building approach adopted by the world's leading universities, the collaboration used to innovative education technologies, and developed a cost effective education model, to deliver high quality courses for the students, especially from resource constrained countries.

The functionality of the technological infrastructure, support services for students and staff, institutional support, and policies to facilitate e-Learning are critical to the success of the e-Learning implementation and adoption process. By adopting a holistic approach and considering all stakeholders, a successful educational model can be implemented to overcome the challenges of increasing the health sector workforce.

REFERENCES

Bates, A. W. (1995). *Technology Open Learning and Distance Education*. London, UK: Routledge.

Bennett, S., Agyepong, I. A., Sheikh, K., Hanson, K., Ssengooba, F., & Gilson, L. (2011). Building the Field of Health Policy and Systems Research: An Agenda for Action. *PLoS Medicine*, *8*(8). doi:10.1371/journal.pmed.1001081

COHRED. (2008). *Changing mindsets: Research capacity strengthening in low- and middle-income countries*. Retrieved from http://www.cohred.org/downloads/cohred_publications/Changing_Mindsets.pdf

Commission on Health Research for Development. (1990). Oxford, UK: Health Research.

Dabbagh, N. (2005). Pedagogical Models for E-Learning: A Theory-Based Design Framework. *International Journal of Technology in Teaching and Learning*, *1*(1), 25–44.

Exworthy, M. (2008). Policy to tackle the social determinants of health: Using conceptual models to understand the policy process. *Health Policy and Planning*, *23*(5), 318–327. doi:10.1093/heapol/czn022

Fawcett, S., Schultz, J., Watson, T. J., Fox, M., & Bremby, R. (2010). Building multisectoral partnerships for population health and health equity. *Preventing Chronic Disease*, *7*(6), A118.

Global Forum for Health Research. (2002). *10/90 Report on Health Research*. Author.

Global Forum for Health Research. (2004). *Strengthening health systems: the role and promise of policy and systems research*. Geneva: Alliance for Health Policy and Systems Research.

Hvorecký, J. (2005). Can E-learning break the Digital Divide? *European Journal of Open, Distance and E-Learning*. Retrieved from www.eurodl.org/?p=archives&year=2004&&article=143

ICT. (2013). Geneva: International Telecommunication Union.

Lee, J. W. (2005). Public Health is a social issue. *Lancet*, *365*(9694), 1005–1006.

Lutumba, S. H. (2010). Research capacity strengthening in the DRC. *Lancet*, *375*(1080).

Marmot, M. (2005). Social determinants of health inequalities. *Lancet*, *365*(9464), 1099–1104. doi:10.1016/S0140-6736(05)74234-3

Mayhew, S. H., Doherty, J., & Pitayarangsarit, S. (2008). Developing health systems research capacities through north-south partnership: An evaluation of collaboration in South Africa and Thailand. 6:8-19. *Health Research Policy and Systems*, *6*(1), 8–19. doi:10.1186/1478-4505-6-8

Millenium Project. (2006). *Millenium Project*. Retrieved from http://www.unmillenniumproject.org/goals/

Rispela, L. C., & Doherty, J. (2011). Research in support of health systems transformation in South Africa: The experience of the Centre for Health Policy. *Journal of Public Health Policy*, *32*, S10–S29. doi:10.1057/jphp.2011.33

Sangra, A., Vlachopoulos, D., & Cabrera, N. (2012). Building an inclusive definition of e-learning: An approach to the conceptual framework. *International Review of Research in Open and Distance Learning*, *13*(2), 145–159.

Satcher, D. (2010). Include a social determinants of health approach to reduce health inequities. *Public Health Reports (Washington, D.C.)*, *125*(4), 6–7.

Sitthi, A. C., & Somrongthong, R. (2000). Strengthening health research capacity in developing countries: A critical element for achieving health equity. *BMJ (Clinical Research Ed.)*, *321*(7264), 813–817. doi:10.1136/bmj.321.7264.813

Solar, O., & Irwin, A. (2007). A conceptual framework for action on the social determinants of health. Social Determinants of Health. *Discussion Paper 2 (Policy and Practice).*

Strong, K., Mathers, S., Leeder, S., & Beaglehode, R. (2005). Preventing chronic diseases: How many lives can we save? *Lancet*, *366*(9496), 1578–1582. doi:10.1016/S0140-6736(05)67341-2

TEL. (c2015). *Technology Enhanced Learning*. Retrieved from http://tel.ioe.ac.uk/

Tinio, V. L. (2003). *ICT in education.* Paper presented at the World Summit on the Information Society.

van der Wende, M. C. (2003). Globalisation and Access to Higher Education. *Journal of Studies in International Education*, *7*(2), 193–206. doi:10.1177/1028315303007002006

Whitehead, M. (1992). The concpets and principles of equity and health. *International Journal of Health Services*, *22*(3), 429–445. doi:10.2190/986L-LHQ6-2VTE-YRRN

WHO. (2004). *World report on knowledge for better health: strengthening health systems.* Retrieved on April 2, 2015 Retrieved from http://www.who.int/rpc/meetings/en/world_report_on_knowledge_for_better_health2.pdf

WHO. (2012). *Social Determinants of Health.* Retrieved on April 12, 2015. Available from: http://www.who.int/social_determinants/sdh_definition/en/

WHO. (2015). e-Learning for undergraduate health professional education: a systematic review informing a radical transformation of health. Geneva: WHO.

World Bank. (2015). *Information Communications Technology for Development.* Retrieved from http://live.worldbank.org/information-communications-technology-development

KEYWORDS AND DEFINITIONS

Arcade RSDH: Asian Regional Capacity Development for Research on Social Determinants of Health, is a European Union funded project. The project uses innovative educational technologies, to strengthen research on social determinants of heath for low and middle income countries in Asia.

Brain Drain: The emigration of highly educated or skilled professional from their home location to another that will provide them better wages or quality of life.

E-Learning: Use of information and communication technologies, for teaching and learning.

Health Research Capacity: An institution's ability to define health-related problems, set objectives, priorities, build sustainable institutions and organizations, identify solutions to health problems, and evaluate interventions and actions.

Heath Equity: Health equity means all people have equal access to the resources, required to improve and maintain a positive health status.

Institutional Capacity: The ability and resources of an institution needed to perform functions, solve problems, set and achieve objectives.

Millennium Development Goals: The international development plan, and time bound targets, adopted at the United Nations Millennium Summit in 2000, held in New York during September 2000, for reducing extreme poverty.

MOODLE: A free and open-source program for an internet-accessible learning management system that can be used to host courses and classes and to distribute documents.

Resource Constrained Countries: In this chapter, resource constrained countries refer to low and middle income countries, as per World Bank classification.

SDH: The Social Determinants of Health are the social and cultural conditions into which people are born, live, work, and age, including the area of health system and play a critical role in maintaining the health status of the people.

Chapter 15
Exploiting 3D Medical Equipment Simulations to Support Biomedical Engineering Academic Courses:
Design Methodology and Implementation in a Small Scale National Project

Adam Damianakis
Conceptum S.A., Greece

George Loudos
TEI of Athens, Greece

Pavlos Kallonis
Conceptum S.A., Greece

Dimitris Tsatsos
Conceptum S.A., Greece

Antonios Tsoukalis
TEI of Athens, Greece

ABSTRACT

Biomedical Imaging is a rapidly evolving area, where new versions of advanced medical equipment/new methodologies based on complex physical phenomena are developed. The cost for the effective training of both academic students/company employees in real training environments is high and in many cases impossible. Most of the times, it is not possible to effectively transfer knowledge due to the limitations of these environments, which has a strong effect both on the theoretical understanding and the practical skills of students. On the other hand, the exploitation of 3D simulations enables for better knowledge acquisition by learners, although not efficiently explored yet. Several studies support that this can be achieved by maximizing the interaction with simulations. To this end, interactive 3D Medical Equipment Simulations have been developed, by exploiting open source software and delivering them through the Web and eLearning Environments. The proposed chapter aims to present the need for such Environments, the development tools, challenges, solutions and possible applications.

DOI: 10.4018/978-1-5225-0466-5.ch015

INTRODUCTION

Biomedical Imaging is a rapidly evolving area, where new advanced medical equipment and new methodologies based on complex physical phenomena are continuously being developed. A growing number of academic students or trainees in corporate environments require continuous inservice training. The authors' experience from Greece shows that there is a wide variety of both undergraduate and postgraduate academic programmes in this domain and new programs are being designed. The learners/trainees should understand concepts and acquire skills by interacting with complex phenomena and processes on which the function of medical equipment is based (Shyam et al., 2011); however, this cannot be easily covered using conventional educational means and as a consequence, the exploitation of advanced equipment in clinical practice is not optimal. By achieving this type of interaction with state-of-the-art equipment in a hands-on setting, the gap between the general theoretical concepts and the efficient usage of medical equipment can be bridged. In this way it would be possible to educate a new generation of learners/trainees, who can acquire competences (knowledge, skills and values/beliefs) regarding the latest and innovative technologies and subject matters (Hofer et al., 2013; Holzinger et al., 2009).

Student/trainee access to actual, state-of-the-art systems is often difficult due to practical restrictions. The daily workload of medical staff, safety issues and other complications apply limitations to the learning/training experience. Usually, training is limited to a small number of visits, demonstration without hands-on practice and only, in a few cases, interaction with the external parts of the medical equipment. Furthermore, a most of the latest and innovative medical equipment is only available to a selected number of hospitals, making them inaccessible to most of the learners/trainees. These problems are acknowledged in the international literature and existing studies define the basic reasons that make the design, development, and implementation of Integrated Virtual Labs e-Training Environments a necessity (Bedia et al., 2011). Other studies support the argument that the exploitation of 3D Technologies is flourishing and presents advantages (Boulos et al., 2007), including the use of simulations for other similar areas, such as medicine, nursing, physics, chemistry and others (Wiecha et al., 2011).

Specific studies (Dieckmann, 2009) (Table 1) acknowledge that the need for the design, development and implementation of Integrated Virtual Labs eLearning Environments due to:

1. The high cost of acquiring the most recent and innovative medical equipment along with the cost of the educators, which cannot be omitted, as this area is growing and changing rapidly

Table 1. Needs and objectives

Need	Type of Need	General Objectives
Reduce the high cost of buying equipment for training purposes	Economic	Cost effective eLearning Environment platform using open and widely available tools and services
Reduced need for large space to interact with medical equipment	Spatial	Design, Develop and Implement 3D Simulations of Medical Equipment providing high interaction
Provide multidisciplinary training	Training/ Education	Provide Integrated 3D Simulations of Medical Equipment and Phenomena along with training material
Relate Medical Equipment with physical phenomena	Training/ Education	Design and implement by combining the Medical Equipment with the corresponding physical phenomena

2. The lack of space, because many medical equipment units are as large as a whole room and usually are operated continuously
3. The lack of multidisciplinary experiments, because most of the times learners/trainees interact only with diagrams and results from a specific machine, and
4. The need to integrate study of the medical equipment with the phenomena that occur while it is being used.

To this end, the authors proposed the design and development of highly interactive 3D Medical Equipment Simulations, which have been implemented and partially tested in real environments. To build these simulations, available open source tools were used. The final achievement of this work is an integrated eLearning Environment that can be used by for both Health Industry and Academic Technological Institutions and which is unique on international level.

The general objective of this research is to present and describe the design, development and implementation of highly interactive 3D Medical Equipment Simulations to support the Biomedical Engineering Academic Course of TEI Athens, as part of a small scale National Project. This main objective can be split into five sub-objectives

Objective 1 - Literature Review and Analysis: Initially,

1. Determine the different types of needs and difficulties related to Biomedical Engineering learning/training,
2. Describe ways to fulfil those needs and bypass those difficulties and
3. Discuss the possible exploitation of 3D Simulations as a means to provide high quality interactive learning/training activities.

Objective 2 - Create Robust General Design Specifications: In order to develop and implement suitable 3D Simulations of medical equipment, it is first necessary to analyse the needs of the trainees/learners and teachers/trainers. The objective of this analysis is to present the design specifications that were used as a guide for the implementation. See below for a list of the design specifications.

Objective 3 - Select the Most Appropriate Medical Equipment: In order to provide the most appropriate 3D Simulations of the medical systems it was necessary to visit several sites and interact with the equipment. In our first implementation 10 different systems along with 10 different physical phenomena which are related to them were chosen. See below for these choices and their selection criteria.

Objective 4 - Develop 3D Medical Equipment Simulations for Learning/Training: To develop the 10 different systems and their corresponding physical phenomena, we will:

1. Described the open source technology used,
2. Implement 10 selected Medical Simulations and 10 selected corresponding physical phenomena and
3. Assess the interactivity provided within those 3D Medical Simulations.

Objective 5 - Provide a Solid E-Learning Environment on Medical Equipment: Finally, the authors presented the implementation of the 3D Medical Equipment Simulations in Learning Management System they had developed and it is currently being used in TEI Athens. The authors conducted a pilot test study with the cooperation of students and tutors.

BACKGROUND

Introduction in Medical Imaging

Biomedical Engineering is a rapidly evolving area, where new versions of advanced medical equipment and new methodologies based on complex physical phenomena are continuously developed (Figure 1). The development of diagnostic technologies, based on medical imaging, is a multidisciplinary field where expertise from engineering, physics, medicine and computer science meet. *Medical imaging* is based on technologies that mainly use energy and, through interaction with matter, it is possible to non-invasively obtain information of the interior of the patient, either on anatomical or functional levels (Figure 2). The main anatomical imaging technologies are Computerized Tomography (CT), Magnetic Resonance Imaging (MRI), and Ultrasound (US), while the major functional imaging methods are Single Photon Emission Computed Tomography (SPECT) and Positron Emission Tomography (PET). Recently, combined modalities can simultaneously offer both anatomical and functional information i.e PET/CT, SPECT/CT and PET/MRI. Those technologies are considered mature and cover a large share of the diagnostic market. A large number of such clinical systems are installed worldwide with millions of diagnostic exams taking place every day. Apart from the diagnostic value, these systems are used to guide therapy and/or assess therapeutic effects; thus their optimal use by the technologists is necessary, in order to provide to the physicians with the most accurate information. However, this optimal level of use requires extensive training and, in most cases, deep understanding of the physical phenomena on which their function is based.

- **The Need:** A continuously growing number of students and trainees in academic and corporate environments request training in the field of medical imaging, both at undergraduate and post-graduate levels. In every case, the learners should understand concepts and acquire skills by interacting with the complex phenomena and processes (Figure 3) on which the function of this medi-

Figure 1. Representation of brain based on different imaging techniques

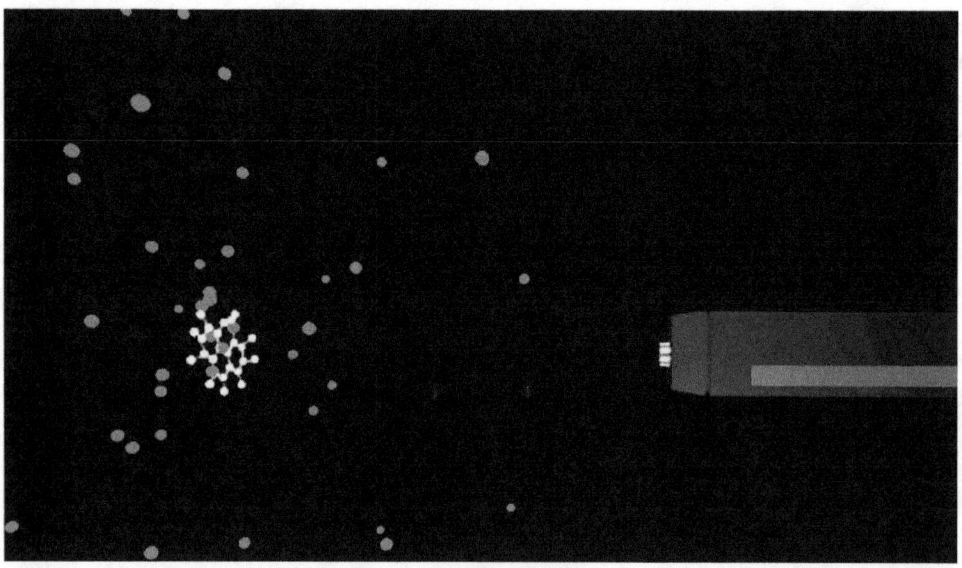

Figure 2. Interior of a clinical CT system; its complexity demonstrates the need for the development of advanced educational tools

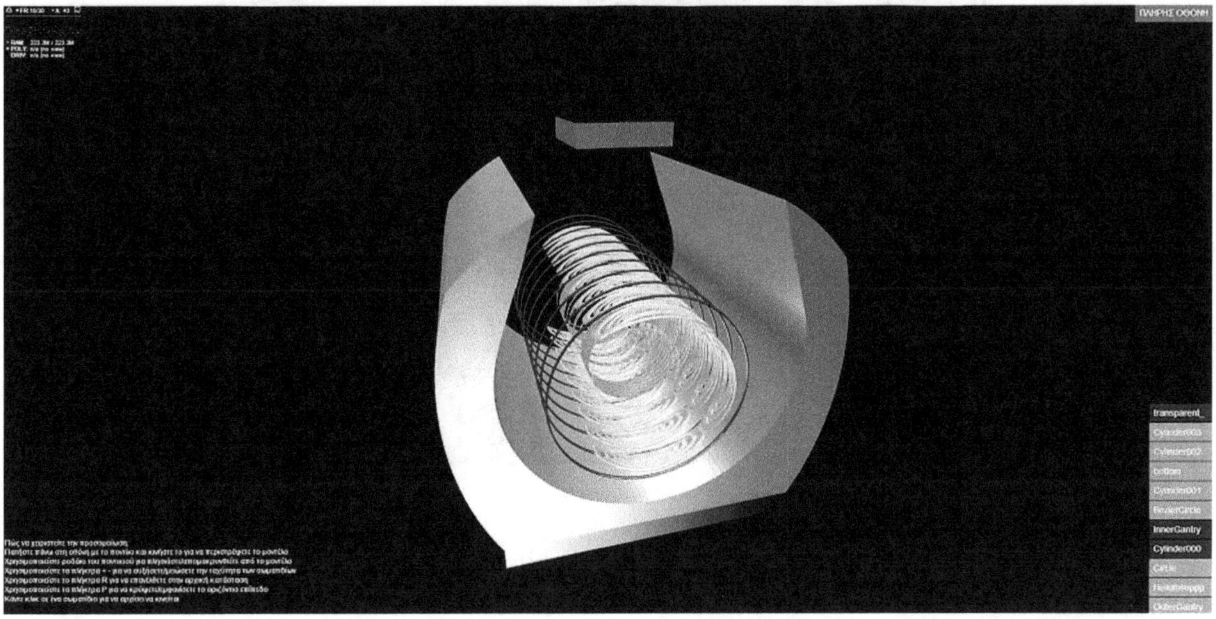

cal equipment is based (Shyam et al., 2011). This cannot be easily achieved using conventional educational means and the exploitation of advanced equipment in clinical practice has not reached optimal levels. By achieving this type of interaction for learners/trainees, it would be possible to bridge the gap between general theoretical concepts and the efficient usage of medical equipment. In this way it would be possible to educate a new generation of learners/trainees, who should be able to acquire competences (knowledge, skills and values/beliefs) regarding the latest/innovative technologies and subject matter (Hofer et al., 2013; Holzinger et al., 2009).

- **The Current Limitations:** The access to actual, state of art systems is frequently difficult due to practical restrictions. Most of the time, the daily workload of medical staff, safety concerns and other reasons apply limitations to the opportunities for students' learning/training experience. Training is limited to a small number of visits, demonstration without hands-on experience and only, in a few cases, interaction with the external parts of the medical imaging systems. Furthermore, most of the latest and most innovative medical equipment is only available to a selected number of hospitals, making the equipment inaccessible to most of the learners/trainees. Moreover, learners/trainees with disabilities face additional difficulties as most training programs do not take into account the specific learning needs that this category of learners has. Furthermore, although it is generally acknowledged that more women are needed in the fields of science and engineering (Hunt, 2010), the actual number of women participating in these fields is low. Vetri et al. (2010) state that the reasons that may have led to this can be grouped into three main categories: differences in aptitude, discrimination, and personal choice (Rosenbloom, Ash, Dupont, & Coder, 2008). Impaired access to formal, technical, and vocational education and training, stereotyping, cultural barriers and gender imbalance in research (European Commission *She Figures 2012)* all contribute to the underrepresentation of women in science and technology. This project will therefore have a special focus on ensuring equal access and opportunity.

Figure 3. Phenomena in γ-camera collimator

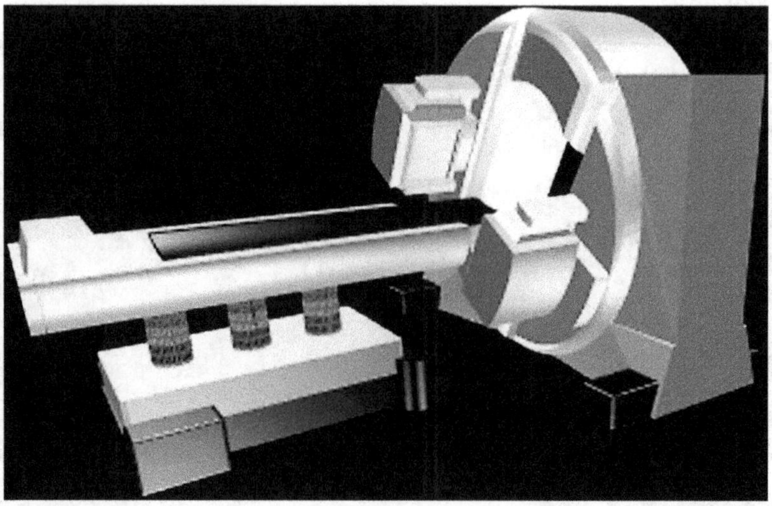

While the need for such Learning Environments is obvious, following a detailed search very few existing solutions were found. Those that were found wererather incomplete and passive, compared with the project objectives. More specifically:

- *Dosch Design* (Dosch Design, 2015) provides some 3D models of medical tools, that are limited to either simple instruments, more advanced equipment or patient rooms and hospital facilities and are passive. The completely textured 3D-models are provided in multiple file formats: 3DS, 3dsmax, Lightwave, Maya, OBJ, VRML and Cinema 4D, but the user cannot explore the equipment's functionality.
- *ARCreative* (ARCreative, 2015) offers models of some medical systems, mainly for visualization purposes. The emphasis of these implementations is on accuracy from an aesthetic point of view.
- An Initiative of the *Ministry of Human Resource Development* (MHRD) from India (MHRD, 2015) includes some labs related to Medical Instrumentation, but with no interactive and visualization tools and simple technologies are used.
- *Epic Systems* is a company that is creating 3D Virtual Reality representations of medical facilities for training (EPIC, 2015), without providing any instrumentation simulation or functional visualization.
- *Virtlab: A Virtual Laboratory* (Virtlab, 2015) is a series of hands-on experiments using a simulated chemistry laboratory, which has low skill requirements compared to the use of complex medical systems.
- Some implementations (i.e. a Scanner) are available in Archive 3D (Archive3D, 2015) but, with no additional medical systems (e.g., MRI, PET).

Those and many more examples show that there is *no existing integrated product/solution*, that is designed specifically for educational purposes and includes both the visualization of medical systems and the physical phenomena on which their function is based. For this reason, in terms of a small national project the authors implemented a Biomedical Engineering Virtual Lab, using limited resources.

The lab describes on a *basic level,* 10 basic Medical Systems and 10 major Physical Phenomena, with advanced visualization tools and accompanying exercises. At the moment this lab is restricted to Greek students (the program language is Greek) and the prototype will need to be upgraded in order to include additional simulations of systems components and phenomena details.

Building on the experience acquired during this prototype implementation, the authors understand the need for *re-design* and to build it on a global platform to be internationally accessible and transformed into a unique product that meets users' needs. Using the existing development as a starting point, it is necessary to further exploit existing software tools, carry out original research to combine them with novel teaching and training methodsin order to derive a software platform, which can be used to provide efficient training in the field of medical imaging systems and can be further extended to other scientific domains, not limited to medical imaging.

DESIGN, DEVELOPMENT AND IMPLEMENTATION OF 3D MEDICAL SIMULATIONS

Design Specifications

As noted above, the authors have identified the most important design specifications for the design and development of the 3D Medical Simulations. The following list describes each one of them:

Design Specification 1: Each one of the 3D Medical Equipment Simulations (3DMES) should be related with its corresponding physical phenomena.

Design Specification 2: The 3DMES should provide extensive features for customizing the phenomena/equipment and functions for creating exercises, with parameterization for specific users.

Design Specification 3: The 3DMES should include modification features of the phenomena/equipment and functions, to further upgrade/improve the exercises or for their scientific update.

Design Specification 4: The 3DMES should allow the implementation of new phenomena/equipment and functions in the virtual environment for the future expansion of the lab.

Design Specification 5: The 3DMES should implement an interactive user interface with mouse enabled navigation.

Design Specification 6: The 3DMES should implement authoring tools for the design and development of educational activities/exercises.

Design Specification 7: The 3DMES should be accessible through the web and be compatible with web-based learning management systems.

Design Specification 8: The 3DMES should be multilingual.

Selected Systems and Corresponding Physical Phenomena

In the first version of this virtual lab the authors have selected the most common full medical imaging systems, plus two cardiac monitoring devices. The authors have also selected some basic physical phenomena, which are characteristic for the presented imaging systems.

The selected devices can be grouped in two categories:

Imaging Systems

- **X-Ray:** Which is the standard system that provides anatomical images using radiation, with very good resolution and tissue to bone contrast.
- **Computerized Tomography (CT):** Which is based on the X-ray and, by using rotation, provides anatomical tomographic images of patients' internal structures with very high spatial resolution.
- **Magnetic Resonance Imaging (MRI):** Which also provides tomographic images with high spatial resolution and good soft tissue contrast, without the use of radiation.
- **Ultrasound:** Which provides high resolution anatomical images of human tissue and has the advantage of no radiation use.
- **γ-Camera:** Which provides functional information of a radiotracer distribution and can monitor the existence of tumors and/or the function of several organs including heart, kidneys, and thyroid.
- **Single Photon Emission Computed Tomography (SPECT):** Which is based on the rotation of one or more γ-cameras and can provide similar tomographic information.
- **Positron Emission Tomography (PET):** Which is based on a similar principle as SPECT, but offers higher sensitivity and resolution and is mainly used for whole body cancer screening.
- **Optical Imaging:** Which is mainly used as a research tool for imaging cells, small animals and/or thin human tissues.

Cardiac Monitoring Devices

- **Electrocardiograph:** Which is used to monitor cardiac signals and can identify different heart malfunctions.
- **Phonocardiograph:** Which is based on recording heart sounds and is a simple way to detect cardiac rate and arrhythmias.

The selected basic physical phenomena are:

- **Production of X-Rays from a Source:** Which is a typical phenomenon in X-ray and CT imaging.
- **Matter and X-Ray Interaction:** Which is the main principle on which the formulation of images in X-ray and CT imaging is based.
- **Magnetic Nuclear Resonance:** Which is the basic phenomenon on which MRI imaging is based.
- **Interaction between Matter and Ultrasound:** Which highlights how ultrasound imaging works.
- **Positron Annihilation and Pair Production:** On which PET imaging is based.
- **Biofluorescence:** on which optical imaging is based.
- **Collimator in γ-Camera:** Which shows the role of the main module of γ-camera and SPECT system.
- **Absorption of Photons in a Scintillator:** Which is one of the most important phenomena in γ-camera, SPECT and PET.
- **Photoelectric Phenomenon:** Which is present in X-ray, CT, γ-camera, SPECT and PET.
- **Principle of Operation of a Conventional and a Position Sensitive Photomultipler:** Which are present in γ-camera, SPECT and PET.

The last 4 phenomena are connected and they can be incorporated in the corresponding imaging systems, in order to add more detail for their functionality. This list was a proof of concept effort to test the level of detail for the description of imaging systems. More levels of detail can be added by including other phenomena.

Development Methodology

Based on the above Design specifications, the authors have devised a development methodology that consisted of multiple steps and the incorporation of different programming tools andplatforms. The main criteria for the selection of the programming tools/platforms was that they were to be open source and their exports compatible with the web and web based learning management systems. The following list describes the steps of the authors' development methodology:

Step 1: The creation of a detailed description and design of every equipment based on available material or on site visits to hospitals and definition of the most relevant to the equipment physical phenomena
Step 2: The description of each phenomena in the form of an algorithm, based on the relevant physics theory
Step 3: The development of the 3D model simulating the equipment and the physical phenomena with appropriate 3D Programming tool/platform.
Step 4: The processing of the 3D representation models so that they were able to be imported in a variety of programming tools.
Step 5: The import of the 3D representation models into a selected programming tool/platform in order to develop the algorithm
Step 6: The development of all the configurable variables based on the designed algorithm. This step enables the different scenarios of the 3DMES behavior.
Step 7: The export of the final 3DMES and integration with the developed corresponding physical phenomena.
Step 8: The integration of the 3DMES within existing e-classes offered by TEI ATHENS.

To support the above-mentioned steps, the authors selected and exploited a mix of open source programming tools and platforms that provided the necessary features. The following list describes each one of the tools/platforms used and the steps supported with them (see Table 2).

- **Blender 2.69 (Blender, 2015):** Blender is a designing/programming platform that enables 3D Graphics design/development. It is a free program and is distributed under the GNU General Public License v3. It is mainly used for modeling, rigging, simulations, animation, rendering and the development of interactive 3D Applications, such as videogames. It is available to be used with most of the current Operating Systems, such as Windows, Linux and MAC OS. Blender enables the user to save the 3D data (models) in .blend format (this file format is only supported by Blender) and in other formats such as .3ds which is compatible with other programming tools/platforms. Blender has been used in our application for steps 3 and 4.
- **PreFab 2.1 (Prefab, 2015):** PreFab is a programming platform based on the Flash (Actionscript 3) programming language and it utilizes the Adobe Air technology. This enables the user to design and develop applications that can be compatible with Windows and Mac OS systems, using an in-

Table 2. Exploitation of open source tools to support the development methodology

Tool/Platform	Supported Steps	How They Were Supported
Blender 2.68	3 and 4	Blender has been used to support the development of 3D Models of both the systems and their corresponding physical phenomena. The models were extracted in .3ds format in order to be imported to other programming tools (PreFab)
PreFab 2.1	4 and 5	Prefab has been used to edit the 3D Models and export them in a format suitable for adding high interaction with FlashDevelop. The exported format that the authors have used is the awd format, utilizing the Away 3D library.
FlashDevelop 4.6.1	6,7 and 8	FlashDevelop has been used in order to import the .awd format of the 3D Models, develop their available interactions and configurable variables. Then, the authors have exploited Blender in order to integrate the 3D Models with their corresponding physical phenomena and finally they have exported the 3DMES in suitable format for TEI Athens e-class (SCORM format).

tegrated user friendly programming environment. The main aspect that made PreFab usable is this initiative is its ability to import and interact with the most known types of 3D files, such as Collada (.dae), Wavefront (.obj) and 3D Studio MAX (.3ds). Once the model is imported, the user can edit every aspect of it. The tools provided by PreFab are less than the tools provided by Blender, but PreFab enables the user to export the 3D models in .awd and Actionstript 3 formats, so that they can be imported into Flash based tools. The import of those files to Flash-based tools is done with the Away 3D library. PreFab has been used in our application for steps 4 and 5.

- **FlashDevelop 4.6.1 (FlashDevelop, 2015):** FlashDevelop is an open source programming platform distributed under the open source MIT License. Its development was started in 2005 and is still an on-going project with frequent updates. Its main purpose is to provide an open source programming environment for Flash based programming languages, such as Actionscript 3. As Flash became more and more flexible in developing web applications, the Flash Develop programming platform evolved into a tool for developing applications for multiple platforms and operating systems. The main aspect of FlashDevelop, that made the authors exploit it in this initiative, is its ability to develop highly interactive applications available through the Web. Flash Develop has been used in our application for steps 6, 7 and 8

Presentation of 3D Medical Simulations

Collimator of γ-Camera

The γ-camera (see Figure 3) is one of the most common medical systems, which is used for scintigraphic studies of the heart, thyroid, bones etc. The person to be examined receives a radiopharmaceutical, which is concentrated in the organ/tissue to be imaged and emits photons isotropically, which are detected by the γ-camera. The collimator is its most important component and its role is to allow only the photons that travel perpendicular to the γ-camera to be detected. There are four basic phenomena that take place in a collimator. The first is when a photon travels parallel to the collimator hole and is correctly detected by the system. The second is when the photon is absorbed by the collimator walls and is never detected. The third is when the photon is scattered on the collimator walls and finally is detected, which means that the position is not accurately recorded. Finally, if a photon has high energy, it can pass through the collimator walls and be detected at a completely wrong position, thus adding to image noise.

For this reason those four scenarios are visualized and four photons have been simulated, which follow predefined orbits to demonstrate the abovementioned phenomena In Figure 1 a square hole collimator and four photons are drawn. Each photon simulates one of these phenomena and the student can see them through different viewing points, in order to fully understand them. There is provision to develop different exercises, based on this geometry and the student will have to guess what will happen when the geometric parameters of the collimator or photons energy change.

Absorption of γ-Rays in Scintillator

The second, basic phenomenon on which the operation of a γ-camera is based is the radiation detection in the scintillator, which is placed right after the collimator (see Figure 4). The photons which reach the scintillator are absorbed and emit other photons of lower energy. The main phenomenon that takes place is the photoelectric effect. Here a γ-photon interacts with an electron of an atom, transfers its energy to it and, as a result, the γ-photon disappears, while the electron starts moving freely with kinetic energy described asEK=hv-Eβ, where h is Plank constant, ν is the frequency of the γ-photon and EB is the ionizing energy of the electron. This means that part of the photon energy is used for moving the electron from its normal state and the rest is transferred as kinetic energy to the electron.

To make the procedure clear, the interaction between a γ-photon and an electron, as well as electron release are simulated. In Figure 4 the first implementation of the photoelectric effect is shown. The photon kinetic energy can be parameterized, in order to allow the implementation of different exercises for the students. In addition, it is possible to include other physical phenomena, such as Compton scattering, where there is no photon absorption.

Figure 4. Absorption of γ-radiation in a scintillator

Photomultipler Tube (PMT)

The PMT is the main detector component of a gamma camera, SPECT and PET. The object that is imaged i.e. patient, is absorbed by the scintillator and converted to optical photons. These optical photons enter the entrance window of the PMT (brown left part) and they produce a photo-electron at the photocathode (gray part in the middle). This electron is attracted by a high voltage what? and enters a dynode stage (brown components in the middle). When an electron hits a dynode, more electrons are produced, which are attracted by the next dynode, until a large electron cloud reaches the anode (gray part on the right in the figure) and are converted to current. The implementation shows the entire procedure from the moment that an electron enters the PMT, until the electrons are absorbed by the anode. The user can navigate inside the PMT and see the procedure of electrons multiplication (see Figure 5).

Biofluorescence

The fourth phenomenon, on which optical imaging is based, is biofluorescence. Optical imaging methods depict the distribution of a tracer in a target area and is based on tracers that emit optical photons, which are detected usually by a CCD system. In biofluorescnce, the optical signal comes from a fluorescent molecule that can be either endogenous (collagen, hemoglobin) or injected (green fluorescent protein and other optical contrast agents). An external light source is used to excite the fluorophore and a CCD detects the lower energy emission light. In Figure 6 a screenshot of this process is shown, when a light sources triggers a chromophore (marked as white) and optical photons are emitted (marked as red). In the implementation the user can see how the light source on the right triggers the chromophore, which absorbs this energy, starts to rotate and emits the optical photons. When the extra energy is released the procedure stops (See Figure 6).

Figure 5. Photomultiplier principle of operation

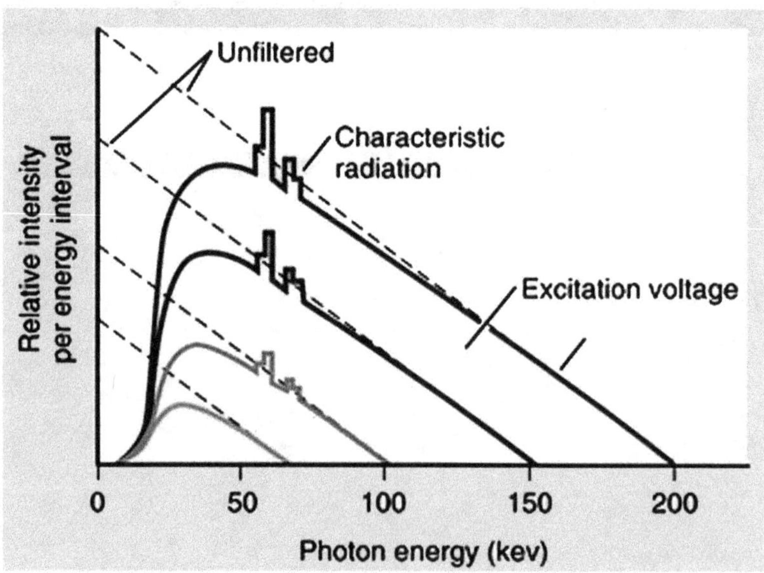

Figure 6. Biofluorescence

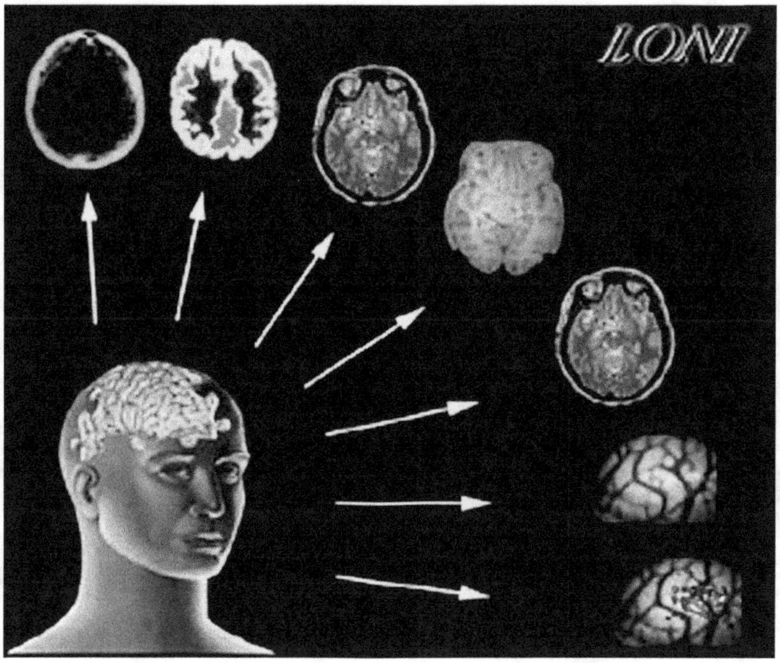

Figure 7. MRI scanner (internal)

Figure 8. SPECT

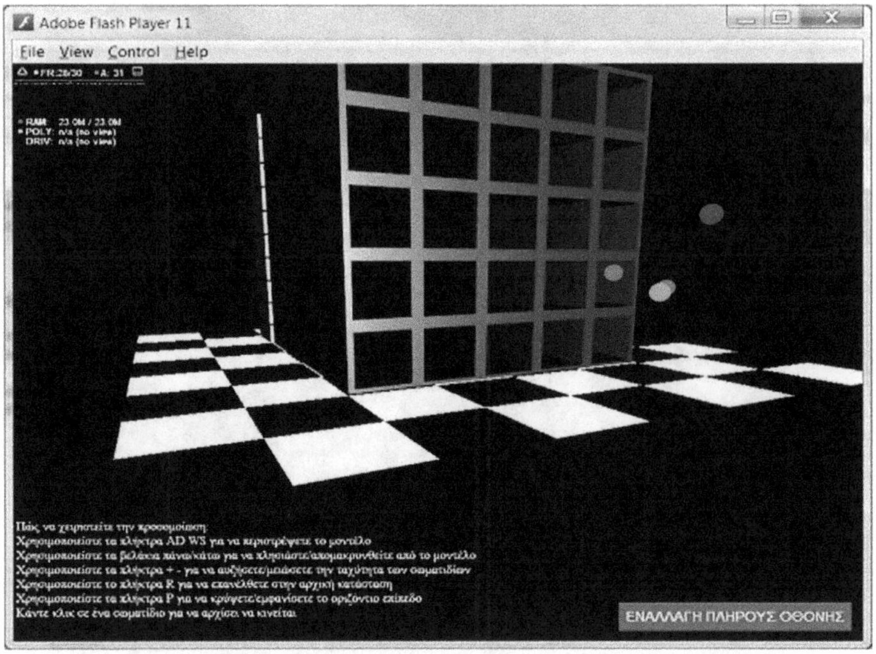

Figure 9. Screenshot of the virtual laboratory at the Department of Biomedical Engineering at Technological Educational Institute of Athens (1/2)

Figure 10. Screenshot of the virtual laboratory at the Department of Biomedical Engineering at Technological Educational Institute of Athens (2/2)

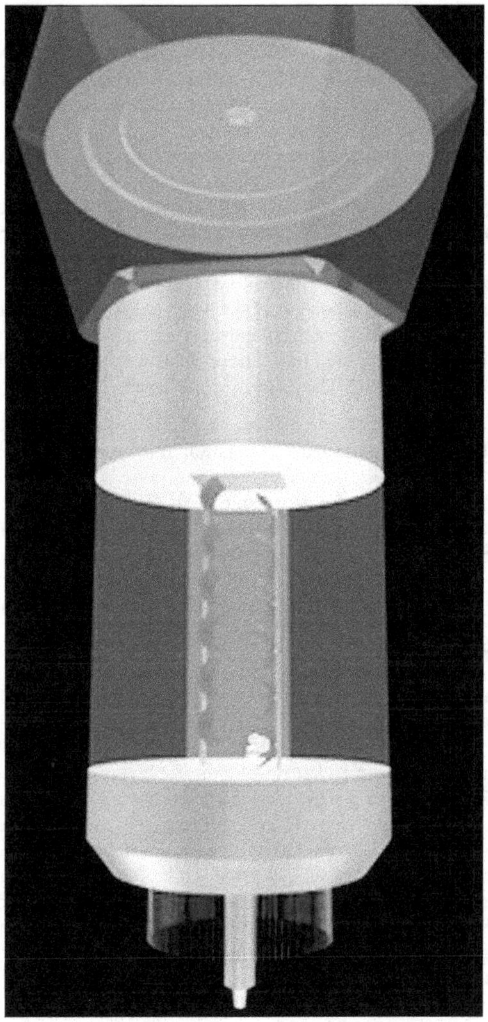

MRI and SPECT

In Figure 5 the internal part of an MRI scanner is shown. In this implementation the user has the option to make different components of the MRI scanner transparent, so the learner/trainee could understand its structure in detail. It is possible to add text on these components and/or the tutor can add exercises in order to educate the trainees, as well as set up exams, which can assess their level of understanding. Although linking with the relative physical phenomena has not been implemented yet, it is possible to link the different components of the MRI with the phenomena that they exploit (See Figure 7).

In Figure 8 a realistic representation of a SPECT camera is shown. The system includes the patient bed and the two camera heads that rotate around it. By initiating the simulation, the user can see a typical scenario of an exam, with the bed moving inside the field of view and the 2 camera heads rotating around it. Each head consists of a γ-camera, thus it is possible to link the implementation of a γ-camera

Table 3. Issues and related research directions

Issue	Research Directions (RD)
Limited/no access to train on real systems for students, engineers, health practitioners, and sales representatives	**RD1:** The description of the major medical imaging systems (e.g CT, MRI, SPECT, PET, Ultrasounds etc). The user will be able to navigate outside and inside the systems (as he could do if he were in front of the real system); view and interact with their components and see examples of their principles of operation; set up test scenarios of standard calibration procedures, quality assurance tests and common problems **RD2:** Link with open source simulation tools (GATE toolkit, 2015), which would allow the user to not only visualize the physical phenomena, but also to run realistic simulations and produce original data by exploiting existing and well validated physics libraries. At least one such implementation (clinical g-camera) will be part of the initial product, with detailed description of the procedures to add similar implementations for all imaging systems. **RD3:** Additional tools, which allow for continuous scale up, including the design and implementation of more detailed components of the medical systems or descriptions of physical phenomena. In the architecture provided, each component of a medical system will be an independent item, initially static, which can be split in smaller compartments, which will be linked with the corresponding physical phenomena. The platforms that have been used for the initial implementation follow this philosophy.
Limited educational materials to efficiently describe the physical phenomena on which medical imaging systems are based	**RD4:** The description and visualization of the major physical phenomena (magnetic resonance, photoelectric effect, radiation absorption, etc). The user will be able to visualize those complex phenomena, and change their parameters, in order to fully understand them and overcome the limitations that are present in conventional educational materials. **RD5:** Test examples with answers and self-evaluation questions, which will be combined with the provided material, in order to evaluate the learner/trainee. Additional tools will be provided, in order to allow tutors/trainers to create new questions and/or examples.
Limited and/or hidden common reference points •Lack of a common competences framework •Hidden methodologies within existing educational/ training practices •Lack of a valid Certification	**RD6:** Proposed common framework describing the knowledge (what do I need to know?), the skills (how can I perform this action?) and the values/belief (are there ethical or other dilemmas related to my actions?), for three levels of expertise (basic, advanced and expert). Such a framework is not available at the moment and it could be most useful for situations such as the design of a job description by industry, the selection of appropriate educational/training programs by the learners/ trainees and the design and development of appropriate educational activities by the teachers/trainers. **RD7:** Provision of generic teaching/training templates that could be exploited by teachers/trainers along with the provided educational material (which, in our case, are the 3D models of Medical Imaging Systems) in order to design and develop their own lessons. This type of tools is available for other specific subjects such as physics (COSMOS project) or as generic design tools such as LAMS, but such a tool is not available as an integrated solution for medical equipment education/training. **RD8:** The existence of an acknowledged service, which provides learners/trainees with a valid certification, is not available in the market. The proposed accreditation service would give a) the learners/trainees a way to certify on new technologies (e.g. the latest models of Medical Imaging Systems) as part of their continuing education/training (lifelong learning), b) the industry a reference to evaluate its potential and current employees and c) the vocational training providers a new and innovative mechanism of certification provision.

with the SPECT system. As the four different phenomena, on which the function of a γ-camera is based have already been simulated, it is possible to also link them, thus the description of the SPECT system can start from the level of full system, then to γ-camera and finally to the corresponding phenomena. This is the ultimate goal of the entire Virtual Laboratory, although the authors recognize the need to attract additional resources for such an implementation.

Implementation TEI of ATHENS Case

Currently this Virtual Laboratory is hosted at the e-class of the Department of Biomedical Engineering at Technological Educational Institute of Athens (TEI ATHENS, 2015). At the moment, it is accessible only upon request, but the last stage of the project includes its open release to the public. Currently the platform is available only in the Greek language and a screenshot of the exercises that are available are shown in Figure 9 and Figure 10.

Taking advantage of the e-class tools, the tutor can add more exercises, set up questionnaires and evaluate the students on line. It is also possible to also add educational material to the existing virtual representations of the systems and the phenomena, and to upgrade the existing models, by adding new simulations.

FUTURE RESEARCH DIRECTIONS

Based on the authors' work, we have devised a table with current issues and proposed solutions as future research directions of this initiative. Table 3 presents each indentified issue with a proposed research directions (see Table 3).

CONCLUSION

This chapter has discussed the design and development of interactive 3D medical equipment simulations using open source software and delivering them through the web and e-learning environments. The presentation included the identification of the need for such environments, a proposal for their development tools, the description of the challenges, the solutions and their possible applications.

The authors believe that, although this effort could be the first step for providing integrated and meaningful technology supported learning/training to both academic students and industrial trainees, there are a lot of aspects that should be considered for future research. Some of those aspects are the design/development of educational methodologies and the provision of specifically tailored tools that will enable teachers and trainers to utilize the provided 3D Medical Simulations in their own educational/training practices.

REFERENCES

Archive3D. (2015). Retrieved June 3, 2015, from http://archive3d.net/?a=download&id=a3cfcbf4

ARCreative. (2015). Retrieved June 3, 2015, from http://www.arcreativemedical.com/

Bedia, A., Zohra, F. B., & Benyoucef, B. (2011). 2D Device Modeling and Simulation / FET for Biomedical Applications. *Physics Procedia*, *21*, 35–41. doi:10.1016/j.phpro.2011.10.006

Blender. (2015). Retrieved June 3, 2015, from https://www.blender.org/

Boulos, M., Kamel, N., Hetherington, L., & Wheeler, S. (2007). Second Life: An overview of the potential of 3-D virtual worlds in medical and health education. *Health Information and Libraries Journal*, *24*(4), 233–245. doi:10.1111/j.1471-1842.2007.00733.x PMID:18005298

Dieckmann, P. (Ed.). (2009). *Using Simulations for Education, Training and Research*. Lengerich, Germany: Pabst.

Dosh Design. (2015). Retrieved June 3, 2015, from http://www.doschdesign.com/productlist2.php?line=4&subrubrik=41

EPIC. (2015). Retrieved June 3, 2015, from https://www.youtube.com/watch?v=zzhTlCO3JS8

FlashDevelop. (2015). Retrieved June 3, 2015, from http://www.flashdevelop.org/

GATE Toolkit. (2015). Retrieved June 3, 2015, from http://www.opengatecollaboration.org/

Hofer, E., Wiener, T., Arnold, R., & Ahammer, H. (2013). Evaluation of Computer Simulation and Computer Animation used as eLearning Tools in Biophysics Lectures and in the self-learning Process of Medical Students In *Proceedings of in the proc. of the WCMPBE*. doi:doi:10.1007/978-3-642-29305-4_450 doi:10.1007/978-3-642-29305-4_450

Holzinger, A., Kickmeier-Rust, M. D., Wassertheurer, S., & Hessinger, M. (2009). Learning performance with interactive simulations in medical education: Lessons learned from results of learning complex physiological models with the HAEMOdynamics SIMulator. *Computers & Education*, *52*(2), 292–301. doi:10.1016/j.compedu.2008.08.008

Hunt, J. (2010). *Why Do Women Leave Science and Engineering?* NBER Working Paper No. 15853.

MHRD. (2015). Retrieved June 3, 2015, from http://www.vlab.co.in/ba_labs_all.php?id=6

Prefab. (2015). Retrieved June 3, 2015, from http://www.closier.nl/prefab/

Rosenbloom, J. L., Ash, R. A., Dupont, B., & Coder, L. A. (2008). Why are there so few women in information technology? Assessing the role of personality in career choices. *Journal of Economic Psychology*, *29*(4), 543–554. doi:10.1016/j.joep.2007.09.005

She Figures. (2012). Retrieved June 3, 2015, from http://ec.europa.eu/research/science-society/document_library/pdf_06/she-figures-2012_en.pdf

Shyam, D., Krishnashree, A., Prema, N., & Bipin, N. (2011). Enhanced Facilitation of Biotechnology Education in Developing Nations via Virtual Labs: Analysis, Implementation and Case-studies. *International Journal of Computer Theory and Engineering*, *3*(1), 1793–8201.

TEI ATHENS eclass. (2015). Retrieved June 3, 2015, from http://medisp.bme.teiath.gr/eclass/modules/exercice/exercice.php?course=TIO222

Veltri, N. F., Webb, H. W., & Papp, R. (2010). GETSMART: An Academic-Industry Partnership to Encourage Female Participation in Science, Technology, Engineering and Math Careers. In A. Cater-Steel & E. Cater (Eds.), *Women in Engineering, Science and Technology: Education and Career Challenges* (pp. 56–77). doi:10.4018/978-1-61520-657-5.ch003

Virtlab. (2015). Retrieved June 3, 2015, from http://www.virtlab.com

Wiecha, J., Heyden, R., Sternthal, E., & Merialdi, M. (2011). Learning in a virtual world: Experience with using second life for medical education. *Journal of Medical Internet Research*, *12*(1). PMID:20097652

KEY TERMS AND DEFINITIONS

Blender: Blender is a design/programming platform that enables 3d graphics design/development.

Competence: A competence describes the knowledge, skills and values/beliefs, which characterize a person. It could be used as a measure to identify a person's ability to do something and how well and efficiently he/she can do it.

Computerized Tomography (CT): CT is based on the X-ray and, by using rotation, provides anatomical tomographic images of patients' interior structures with very high spatial resolution.

FlashDevelop: FlashDevelop is an open source programming platform distributed under the open source MIT License.

Magnetic Resonance Imaging (MRI): Provides tomographic images with high spatial resolution and good soft tissue contrast, without use of radiation.

PreFab: PreFab is a programming platform based on the Flash (Actionscript 3) programming language and it utilizes the Adobe Air technology.

STEM: It is the field of education that includes Science, Technology, Engineering and Mathematics.

Ultrasound: Provides high resolution anatomical images of human and has the advantage of no radiation use.

X-Ray: The standard system that provides anatomical images using radiation, with very good resolution and tissue to bone contrast.

Compilation of References

Abas, Z. W., Kaur, K., & Harun, H. (2004). *ELearning readiness in Malaysia: A national report submitted to the Ministry of Energy, Water and Communications*. Retrieved from http://asiapacific-odl2.oum.edu.my/C33/F70.pdf

Abma, T. A., & Stake, R. E. (2001). Stake's responsive evaluation: Core ideas and evolution. In Responsive Evaluation. San Francisco, CA: Jossey-Bass.

About Meetup. (n.d.). Retrieved from http://www.meetup.com/about/

Ackerman, R., & Lauterman, T. (2012). Taking reading comprehension exams on screen or on paper? A metacognitive analysis of learning texts under pressure. *Computers in Human Behavior*, *28*(5), 1816–1828. doi:10.1016/j.chb.2012.04.023

ACM eLearn Magazine. (n.d.). Retrieved from http://elearnmag.acm.org/

ADL. (n.d.). *Advanced Distributed Learning Initiative of the US Government, Department of Defense*. Retrieved October 1, 2014. Retrieved from http://www.adlnet.org

Adorni, G., Coccoli, M., & Vivanet, G. (2011). Educational concept maps: a knowledge based aid for Instructional Design. *Proceedings of the 17th International Conference on Distributed Multimedia Systems, DMS 2011*, (pp. 234-237). Retrieved from http://www.ksi.edu/seke/Proceedings/dms11/DET/6_Giuliano_Vivanet.pdf

AICC (Aviation Industry CBT Committee). (n.d.). *Computer Managed Instruction (CMI)*. Retrieved from http://www.aicc.org/

Alario-Hoyos, C., Pérez-Sanagustín, M., Delgado-Kloos, C., Muñoz-Organero, M., & Rodríguez-de-las-Heras, A. (2013). Analyzing the impact of built-in and external social tools in a MOOC on educational technologies. In D. Hernández-Leo, T. Ley, R. Klamma, & A. Harrer (Eds.), *Scaling up learning for sustained impact* (pp. 5–18). Berlin: Springer. doi:10.1007/978-3-642-40814-4_2

Al-Atabi, M., & DeBoer, J. (2014). (2014). Teaching entrepreneurship using Massive Open Online Course (MOOC). *Technovation*, *34*(4), 261–264. doi:10.1016/j.technovation.2014.01.006

Al-Furaydi, A. A. (2013). Measuring e-learning readiness among EFL teachers in intermediate public schools in Saudi Arabia. *English Language Teaching*, *6*(7), 110–121.

Alican, Ö. (2011). *Mobil Medyada Grafik Tasarımcının Galaksi Rehberi*. Ankara: Pusula Yayıncılık.

Ali, G., & Megalhaes, R. (2008). Barriers to implementing eLearning: A Kuwaiti case study. *International Journal of Training and Development*, *12*(1), 36–53. doi:10.1111/j.1468-2419.2007.00294.x

Allen, E., & Seaman, J. (2013). *Changing course: Ten years of tracking online education in the United States* [PDF document]. Retrieved from http://www.onlinelearningsurvey.com/reports/changingcourse.pdf

Allen, I. E., & Seaman, I. (2014). *Grade Change: Tracking online education in United States.* New York: Babson Survey Research Group and Quahog Research group.

Ally, M. (2004). *Using learning theories to design instruction for mobile learning devices.* Paper presented in the Mobile Learning 2004 International Conference Proceedings, Rome, Italy.

Ally, M. (2009). Mobile Learning: Transforming the delivery of education and training. Athabasca University Press.

Ally, M. (2014). *Increasing Access to Education for All Through Mobile Learning.* Retrieved May 26, 2015, from http://asianvu.com/bk/framework/wp-content/uploads/2014/11/MobileLearning-Increasing-Access-to-Education.pdf

Ally, M., & Tsinakos, A. (2014). Increasing access through mobile learning. Commonwealth of Learning, Vancouver, Canada.

Ally, M. (2004). Foundations of educational theory for online learning. In T. Anderson & F. Elloumi (Eds.), *Theory and practice of online learning* (pp. 3–31). Athabasca, AB: Athabasca University.

Ally, M., & Fahy, P. (2002). Using learners' learning styles to provide support in distance education. In *Proceedings of the Eighteenth Annual Conference on Distance Teaching and Learning.*

Ally, M., Grimus, M., & Ebner, M. (2014, March). Preparing Teachers for a Mobile World to Improve Access to Education. Prospects. *Quarterly Review of Comparative Education, 44*(1), 43–59. http://www.doi.org/10.1007/s11125-014-9293-2

Ally, M., & Lin, O. (2005). An intelligent agent for adapting and delivering electronic course materials to mobile learners.*Proceedings of the International Mobile Learning Conference.*

Ally, M., & Samaka, M. (2013). Open education resources and mobile technology to narrow the learning divide. *The International Review of Research in Open and Distributed Learning, 14*(2), 14–27.

Alonso, O., Rose, D., & Stewart, B. (2008). Crowdsourcing for relevance evaluation. *ACM SIGIR Forum*, 9-9.

Altun, A., & Askar, P. (2008). *From Blocks to Granules: An Alternative Approach to Designing Learning Objects.* Paper presented at the Eighth IEEE International Conference on Advanced Learning Technologies ICALT '08. doi:doi:10.1109/ICALT.2008.68 doi:10.1109/ICALT.2008.68

American Evaluation Association, Task Force on Guiding Principles for Evaluators. (1995). Guiding principles for evaluators. In W. R. Shadish, D. L. Newman, M. A. Scheirer, & C. Wye (Eds.), Guiding principles for evaluators. San Francisco, CA: Jossey-Bass.

Amrein-Beardsley, A., Foulger, T. S., & Toth, M. (2007). Examining the Development of a Hybrid Degree Program: Using Student and Instructor Data to Inform Decision-Making. *Journal of Research on Technology in Education, 39*(4), 27.

Anderson, T., & Dron, J. (2010). Three generations of distance education pedagogy. *The International Review Of Research In Open And Distributed Learning, 12*(3), 80-97. Retrieved from http://www.irrodl.org/index.php/irrodl/article/view/890/1663

Anwar, M., & Greer, J. (2012). Facilitating trust in privacy-preserving E-Learning environments. *IEEE Transactions on Learning Technologies, 5*(1), 62–73. doi:10.1109/TLT.2011.23

Archive3D. (2015). Retrieved June 3, 2015, from http://archive3d.net/?a=download&id=a3cfcbf4

ARCreative. (2015). Retrieved June 3, 2015, from http://www.arcreativemedical.com/

Arnseht, H. C. (2006). Learning to play or playing to learn. A critical account of the models of communication informing educational research in computer gameplay. *The International Journal of Computer Game Research*, *6*(1). Retrieved from http://gamestudies.org/0601/articles/arnseth

Aspden, L., & Helm, P. (2004). Making the Connection in a Blended Learning Environment. *Educational Media International*, *41*(3), 245–252. http://www.doi.org/10.1080/0952398041000l680851

Atallah, F., & Moussa-Inaty, J. (2012). Exploring faculty and student readiness for e-Learning in a UAE Public University. In T. Bastiaens & G. Marks (Eds.), *Proceedings of E-Learn: World Conference on E-Learning in Corporate, Government, Healthcare, and Higher Education 2012* (pp. 1747-1754). Chesapeake, VA: Association for the Advancement of Computing in Education (AACE). Retrieved from http://www.editlib.org/p/41862

Atieno, O. P. (2009). An analysis of the strengths and limitation of qualitative and quantitative research paradigms. *Problems of Education in the 21st Century, 13*, 13-18.

Attewell, J. (2005). Mobile technologies and learning. Learning and Skills Development Agency, 2(4).

Australia Parliament House of Representatives Standing Committee on Education and Vocational Training, & Hartsuyker, L. (2007). *Top of the class: Report on the inquiry into teacher education.* Canberra: House of Representatives Publishing Unit.

Australian Government. (2015). *Study in Australia.* Retrieved from https://http://www.studyinaustralia.gov.au/global/australian-education/universities-and-higher-education

Australian Institute for Teaching and School Leadership (AITSL). (2011). *Accreditation of initial teacher education programs in Australia: Standards and procedures*. Retrieved from: www.aitsl.edu.au/docs/default-source/default-document-library/accreditation-of-initial-teacher-education

Ausubel, D. P. (1974). *Educational psychology: A cognitive view*. New York: Holt, Rinehart and Winston.

Awidi, I. T., & Cooper, M. (2015). Using management procedure gaps to enhance e-learning implementation in Africa. *Computers & Education*, *90*(1), 64–79. doi:10.1016/j.compedu.2015.08.003

Aycock, A., Garnham, C., & Kaleta, R. (2002). Lessons learned from the hybrid course project. *Teaching with Technology Today, 8*(6), 9-21.

Aydin, C. H., & Tasci, D. (2005). Measuring readiness for eLearning: Reflections from an emerging country. *Journal of Educational Technology & Society*, *8*(4), 244–257.

Azimi, H. M. (2013). Readiness for implementation of eLearning in colleges of education. *Journal of Novel Applied Sciences*, *2*(12), 769–775.

Baggaley, J. (2013). MOOC rampant. *Distance Education*, *34*(3), 368–378. doi:10.1080/01587919.2013.835768

Bailey, B. P., & Iqbal, S. T. (2007). Understanding changes in mental workload during execution of goal-directed tasks and its application for interruption management. *ACM Transactions on Computer-Human Interaction*, *14*(21), 1-21.

Baker, R., Evans, B., Greenberg, E., & Dee, T. (2014). Understanding persistence in moocs (massive open online courses): Descriptive & experimental evidence. *EMOOCs*, 5-10.

Bali, M. (2014). MOOC pedagogy: Gleaning good practice from existing MOOCs. *MERLOT. Journal of Online Learning and Teaching*, *10*(1), 44–56.

Bali, M. (2014). MOOC Pedagogy: Gleaning Good Practice from Existing MOOCs. *Journal of Online Teaching and Learning*, *10*(1), 44–57.

Balsamo, A., Boyer, P., Cole, C. L., Fernandes, M., Gajjala, R., Irish, S., ...Wexler, L. (2013). *Transforming higher education with distributed open collaborative courses (DOCCs): Feminist pedagogies and networked learning*. FemTechNet Whitepaper. Retrieved from: http://femtechnet.org/wp-content/uploads/2014/10/FemTechNetWhitePaperSept30_2013.pdf

Banathy, B. H. (1991). *Systems designs of education: A journey to create the future*. Englewood Cliffs, NJ: Educational Technology Publications.

Banathy, B. H. (1992). *A systems view of education: Concepts and principles for effective practice*. Englewood Cliffs, NJ: Educational Technology Publications.

Bandura, A. (1978). The self-system in reciprocal determinism. *The American Psychologist*, *33*(4), 344–358. doi:10.1037/0003-066X.33.4.344

Bangert, A. W. (2008). The influence of social presence and teaching presence on the quality of online critical inquiry. *Journal of Computing in Higher Education*, *20*(1), 34–61. doi:10.1007/BF03033431

Bannan, B., & Milheim, W. D. (1997). Existing Web-based courses and their design. In B. H. Khan (Ed.), *Web-based instruction* (pp. 381–388). Englewood Cliffs, NJ: Educational Technology Publications.

Barker, P., & Campbell, L. M. (2014). *Learning Resource Metadata Initiative: using schema.org to describe open educational resources*. Presented in OCW (Open Course Ware) Consortium Global Conference, Ljubljana, Slovenia. Retrieved from http://conference.ocwconsortium.org/2014/wp-content/uploads/2014/02/Paper_34-LMRI1.pdf

Barksdale, S., & Lund, T. (2001). *Rapid evaluation: Tools, worksheets, and job aids to help you develop an evaluation strategy, use the right evaluation approach, understand and analyze evaluation data*. Alexandria, VA: American Society for Training & Development.

Barnhart, F. D., & Pierce, J. E. (2011). Becoming mobile: Reference in the ubiquitous library. *Journal of Library Administration*, *51*(3), 279–290. doi:10.1080/01930826.2011.556942

Barotis, S., & Poulymenakou, A. (2004). *ELearning readiness components: Key issues to consider before adopting elearning interventions*. Retrieved from https://www.academia.edu/954823/Critical_Success_Factors_for_ELearning_Adoption

Baruch, Y., & Nicholson, N. (1997). Home, sweet work: Requirements for effective home-working. *Journal of General Management*, *23*(2), 15–30.

Bates, A. W. (1995). *Technology Open Learning and Distance Education*. London, UK: Routledge.

Bates, T. (2014). MOOCs: Getting to know you better. *Distance Education*, *35*(2), 145–148. doi:10.1080/01587919.2014.926803

Baykul, Y. (2000). *Eğitimde ve Psikolojide Ölçme: Klasik Test Teorisi ve Uygulaması*. Ankara: ÖSYM Yayınları.

Bean, M. (2003). *Are you ready for eLearning? Assessing eLearning readiness: Tips and tricks of the trade*. Retrieved from http://www.mediapro.com/html/resources/news1-vol5-01.htm

Beaudrier, S., & Ducar, C. (2012). Language Placement and Beyond: Guidelines for the Design and Implementation of a Computerized Spanish Heritage Language Exam. *Heritage Language Journal*, *9*(1), 77–99.

Bedia, A., Zohra, F. B., & Benyoucef, B. (2011). 2D Device Modeling and Simulation / FET for Biomedical Applications. *Physics Procedia*, *21*, 35–41. doi:10.1016/j.phpro.2011.10.006

Belfanti, P., & Gylling, M. (2014). *What is EDUPUB?* Presented in EDUPUB 2 Workshop, Salt Lake City, UT. Retrieved from http://www.imsglobal.org/edupub/WhatisEdupubBelfantiGylling.pdf

Benchmark Quality Assurance. (2012, May 1). *Crowdsourced testing companies* [PDF document]. Retrieved May 24, 2015 from http://www.benchmarkqa.com/wp-content/uploads/2012/04/Crowdsourced-Testing-Companies.pdf

Bennett, S., Agyepong, I. A., Sheikh, K., Hanson, K., Ssengooba, F., & Gilson, L. (2011). Building the Field of Health Policy and Systems Research: An Agenda for Action. *PLoS Medicine*, *8*(8). doi:10.1371/journal.pmed.1001081

Bernard, R. M., Abrami, P. C., Borokhovski, E., Wade, C. A., Tamim, R. M., Surkes, M. A., & Bethel, E. C. (2009). A meta-analysis of three types of interaction treatments in distance education. *Review of Educational Research*, *79*(3), 1243–1289. doi:10.3102/0034654309333844

Berners-Lee, T., Hendler, J., & Lassila, O. (2001). The Semantic Web. *Scientific American.* Retrieved from http://www.scientificamerican.com/article.cfm?articleID=00048144-10D2-1C70-84A9809EC588EF21&catID=2

Billett, S. (2011). *Vocational education: Purposes, traditions and prospects*. Dordrecht, Netherlands: Springer. doi:10.1007/978-94-007-1954-5

Bishop, M. J. (2000). The systematic use of sound in multimedia instruction to enhance learning. *Dissertation Abstracts International*, *61*(07), 2669.

Bizer, C., Heath, T., & Berners-Lee, T. (2009). Linked data: The story so far. *International Journal on Semantic Web and Information Systems*, *5*, 1–22.

Bizer, C., Lehmann, J., & Auer, G. K. A. (2009). DBpedia: A crystallization point for the Web of Data. *Journal of Web Semantics*, *7*(3), 154–165. doi:10.1016/j.websem.2009.07.002

Blender. (2015). Retrieved June 3, 2015, from https://www.blender.org/

Bliuc, A.-M., Goodyear, P., & Ellis, R. A. (2007). Research focus and methodological choices in studies into students' experiences of blended learning in higher education. *The Internet and Higher Education*, *10*(4), 231–244. Retrieved from http://www.doi.org/10.1016/j.iheduc.2007.08.001

Blom, J., Verma, H., Li, N., Skevi, A., & Dillenbourg, P. (2013). MOOCs are More Social than You Believe. *eLearning Papers, 33*, 1-3. Retrieved from http://www.elearningpapers.eu/en/article/MOOCs-are-More-Social-than-You-Believe?paper=124335

Boettcher, J. V., & Kumar, M. S. (2000). The Other Infrastructure: Distance Education's Digital Plant. *Syllabus, 13*(10).

Bohl, O., Schellhase, J., Sengler, R., & Winand, U. (2002). The Sharable Content Object Reference Model (SCORM) - A Critical Review.*Proceedings of the International Conference on Computers in Education (ICCE'02)*. doi:10.1109/CIE.2002.1186122

Borzillo, S., Aznar, S., & Schmitt, A. (2011). A journey through communities of practice: How and why members move from the periphery to the core. *European Management Journal*, *29*(1), 25–42. doi:10.1016/j.emj.2010.08.004

Bouhnik, D., & Marcus, T. (2006). Interaction in distance,Äêlearning courses. *Journal of the American Society for Information Science and Technology*, *57*(3), 299–305. http://www.doi.org/10.1002/asi.20277

Boulos, M., Kamel, N., Hetherington, L., & Wheeler, S. (2007). Second Life: An overview of the potential of 3-D virtual worlds in medical and health education. *Health Information and Libraries Journal*, *24*(4), 233–245. doi:10.1111/j.1471-1842.2007.00733.x PMID:18005298

Bourdieu, P. (1977). *Outline of Theory of Practice*. Cambridge, UK: Cambridge University Press. doi:10.1017/CBO9780511812507

Brabazon, T. (2002). *Digital hemlock: Internet education and the poisoning of teaching*. Sydney: UNSW Press.

Brabham, D. C. (2008). Crowdsourcing as a model for problem solving. *Journal of Research into New Media, 14*(1), 75–90.

Brabham, D. C. (2012). The myth of amateur crowds. *Information Communication and Society, 15*(3), 394–410. doi:10.1080/1369118X.2011.641991

Brandl, K. (2002). Integrating internet-based reading materials into the foreign language curriculum: From teacher-to student-centered approaches. *Language Learning & Technology, 6*(3), 87–107.

Bray, B., & McClaskey, K. (n.d.). *Personalized Learning Chart* [Online]. Retrieved from https://sites.google.com/site/personalizedlearningtoolkits/

Bredl, K., & Bösche, W. (Eds.). (2013). *Serious games and virtual worlds in education, Professional development, and healthcare*. Hershey, PA: IGI Global. doi:10.4018/978-1-4666-3673-6

Breslow, L., Pritchard, D. E., DeBoer, J., Stump, G. S., Ho, A. D., & Seaton, D. T. (2013). Studying learning in the worldwide classroom: Research into edX's first MOOC. *Research & Practice in Assessment, 8*(1), 13–25.

Brimble, M., & Freudenberg, B. (2010). Will WIL'ing work? *B-Hert News, 28*, 2–4.

Brisolara, S. (1998). The history of participatory evaluation and current debates in the field. *New Directions for Evaluation, 1998*(80), 25–41. doi:10.1002/ev.1115

Brittain, S. (1999). *A framework for pedagogical evaluation of Virtual Learning Environments*. The Joint Information Systems Committee (JISC) Framework (JISC) Technology Applications Programme, Report no: 41. Retrieved from http://www.jisc.ac.uk/jtap/htm/jtap-041.html

Broadbent, B. (2001). *Tips to help decide if your organization ready for e-Learning*. Retrieved from http://icde.net/en/arshive/articles/012.htm

Bruce, C. (1997). *The Seven Faces of Information Literacy*. Adelaide: Auslib Press.

Bryman, A., & Teevan, J. J. (2004). *Social research methods* (Vol. 2). Oxford University Press.

Bufe, W., & Giessen, H. W. (2011). Videokonferenz als medium der grenzdidaktik. In Wider den einheitsunterricht. Deutschlernen an der grenze (pp 23-35). Liberec: Technical University of Liberec Press.

Bufe, W., & Giessen, H. W. (Eds.). (2005). Videoconferencing grenzübergreifend - La visioconference transfrontaliere. Paris: L'Harmattan.

Butcher, N., & Wilson-Strydom, M. (2014). *A Guide to Quality in Online Learning*. Dallas, TX: Acedemic Partnerships.

Cambre, J., Kulkarni, C., Bernstein, M. S., & Klemmer, S. R. (2014). Talkabout: small-group discussions in massive global classes. *First ACM conference on Learning@scale conference* (pp. 161-162). ACM. doi:10.1145/2556325.2567859

Casey, D. M. (2008). A journey to legitimacy: The historical development of distance education through technology. *TechTrends: Linking Research & Practice to Improve Learning, 52*(2), 45–51. doi:10.1007/s11528-008-0135-z

Castle, R. (2013). Mobile Learning: Is your content fit for purpose? *Training & Development, 40*(2), 22–23.

Cavanaugh, C. (2002). Distance education quality: Success factors for resources, practices, and results. In R. Discenza, C. D. Howard, & K. Shenck (Eds.), *The design & management of effective distance learning programs* (pp. 171–189). Hershey, PA: Idea Group. doi:10.4018/978-1-930708-20-4.ch011

CDLP. (n.d.). *California Distance Learning Project: What is Distance Learning?* Retrieved March 21, 2014, Retrieved from http://www.cdlponline.org/index.cfm?fuseaction=whatis

Çelik, D. & Elçi, A. (2012). A broker-based semantic agent for discovering Semantic Web services through process similarity matching and equivalence considering quality of service. *Science China Information Sciences, 56*(1), 012102:1–012102:24.

Çelik, D., Elçi, A., & Elverici, E. (2011). Finding suitable course material through a semantic search agent for Learning Management Systems of distance education. *Proceedings of 6th IEEE International Workshop on Engineering Semantic Agent Systems(ESAS 2011) in conjunction with the 35th Computer Software and Applications Conference (COMPSAC 2011)* (pp. 386-391).

Çelik, D., & Elçi, A. (2011). Towards a semantic-based workflow model to composition of OWL-S based atomic processes through process similarity matching and inferencing techniques. *Journal of Internet Technology*, *12*(1), 153–170.

Çelik, D., & Elçi, A. (2014). Semantic composition of business processes using Armstrong's Axioms. *The Knowledge Engineering Review*, *29*(2), 248–264. doi:10.1017/S0269888914000083

Çelik, D., Elçi, A., İnan, N., Elverici, E., & Elçi, A. (2014). Educational Activity Discovery System for Individuals with Pervasive Developmental Disorders through Web Ontology Language (OWL). *Education and Science*, *39*(171), 52–73.

Ceraulo, S. C. (2003). Instructional design for flow in online learning. *ACM eLearn Magazine*. Retrieved, from http://www.elearnmag.org/subpage/sub_page.cfm?section=4&list_item=10&page=1

Chamberlin, S., & Moon, S. (2005). Model-eliciting activities: An introduction to gifted education. *Journal of Secondary Gifted Education*, *17*(1), 37–47.

Chapnick, S. (2000). *Needs assessment for eLearning: Info-line, American Society for Training and Development (ASTD)*. Retrieved from http://store.astd.org/Default.aspx?tabid=167&ProductId=8034

Chapnick, S. (2005). Are you ready for eLearning? *Learning Circuits: ASTD's Online Magazine All about eLearning*. Retrieved from http://blog.uny.ac.id/nurhadi/files/2010/08/are_you_ready_for_eLearning.pdf

Chen C. M. (2008). Intelligent web-based learning system with personalized learning path guidance. *Computers & Education, 51*(2) 2008, 787-814.

Chen, C. M., & Hsu, S. H. (2008). Personalized intelligent mobile learning system for supporting effective English learning. *Journal of Educational Technology & Society*, *11*(3), 153–180.

Chen, M. P. (2009). An evaluation of the ELNP eLearning quality assurance program: Perspectives of gap analysis and innovation diffusion. *Journal of Educational Technology & Society*, *12*(1), 18–33.

Chen, W., & Looi, C.-K. (2007). Incorporating Online Discussion in Face to Face Classroom Learning: A New Blended Learning Approach. *Australasian Journal of Educational Technology*, *23*(3), 307–326.

Chong, P. H. J., So, P. L., Shum, P., Li, X. J., & Goyal, D. (2004, November). Design and implementation of user interface for mobile devices. *IEEE Transactions on Consumer Electronics*, *50*(4), 1156–1161. doi:10.1109/TCE.2004.1362513

Chou, C., Block, L., & Jesness, R. (2012). A case study of mobile learning pilot project in K-12 schools. *Journal of Educational Technology Development and Exchange*, *5*(2), 11–26.

Churcher, K. M. A., Downs, E., & Tewksbury, D. (2014). "Friending" Vygotsky: A social constructivist pedagogy of knowledge building through classroom social media use. *The Journal of Effective Teaching*, *14*(1), 33–50.

Clark, R. C., & Mayer, R. E. (2003). *ELearning and the science of instruction: Proven guidelines for customers and designers of multimedia learning*. San Francisco, CA: Pfeiffer.

Clark, R. E. (1983). Reconsidering research on learning from media. *Review of Educational Research*, *53*(4), 445–459. doi:10.3102/00346543053004445

Class Central. (n.d). Retrieved from: https://www.class-central.com/universities

CMC. (2008). *eLearning glossary*. Retrieved from http://www.cybermediacreations.com/elearning/glossary.html

COHRED. (2008). *Changing mindsets: Research capacity strengthening in low- and middle-income countries*. Retrieved from http://www.cohred.org/downloads/cohred_publications/Changing_Mindsets.pdf

Commission on Health Research for Development. (1990). Oxford, UK: Health Research.

Concannon, F., Flynn, A., & Campbell, M. (2005). What campus-based students think about the quality and benefits of e-learning. *British Journal of Educational Technology*, *36*(3), 501–512.

Conole, G. (2013). MOOCs as disruptive technologies: Strategies for enhancing the learner experience and quality of MOOCs. *Revista de Educación a Distancia*, *39*, 1–17.

Conrad, D. (2005). Building and maintaining community in cohort-based online learning. *Journal of Distance Education*, *20*(1), 1.

Cooper, P. A. (1993). Paradigm shifts in designing instruction: From behaviorism to cognitivism to constructivism. *Educational Technology*, *33*(5), 12–19.

Corbière, A., & Choquet, C. (2004). Designer Integration in Training Cycle. *Proceedings of International Conference on Computer Aided Learning in Engineering Education (CALIE 2004)*. Retrieved from http://telearn.archives-ouvertes.fr/docs/00/19/03/08/PDF/Alain-Corbiere-2004.pdf

Coursera. (2015). *Coursera*. Retrieved May 26, 2015, from www.coursera.org

CourseTalk Reviews. (n.d.). Retrieved from CourseTalk: https://www.coursetalk.com

CRA. (2003). *Grand research challenges in Information Systems*. Final report of CRA Conference on "Grand Research Challenges" in Computer Science and Engineering, Warrenton, VA. Retrieved from http://archive.cra.org/reports/gc.systems.pdf

Crawford, C. M. (2012). Knowledge and freedom: Massive open online courses as anywhere and anytime community of practice efforts. *Ubiquitous Learning: An International Journal*, *5*(2), 29–39.

Creelman, A., Ehlers, U., & Ossinnilsson, E. (2014). Perspectives on MOOC quality - An account of the EFQUEL MOOC Quality Project. *International Journal for Innovation and Quality in Learning*, *2*(3), 78-87.

Cronbach, L. J. (1975). Beyond the two disciplines of scientific psychology. *The American Psychologist*, *30*(2), 116–127.

Csikszentmihalyi, M. (1990). *The Psychology of Optimal Experience*. New York, NY: Harper Collins.

Dabbagh, N. (2005). Pedagogical Models for E-Learning: A Theory-Based Design Framework. *International Journal of Technology in Teaching and Learning*, *1*(1), 25–44.

Daft, R. L., & Lengel, R. H. (1984). Information richness: A new approach to managerial behavior and organizational design. In Research in organizational behavior (vol. 6, pp. 191-233). Homewood, IL: JAI Press.

Daniel, J. (2012). Making sense of MOOCs: Musings in a maze of myth, paradox and possibility. *Journal of Interactive Media in Education*, *3*(18), 1–20. doi:10.5334/2012-18

Darling-Hammond, L. (2010). Teacher education and the American future. *Journal of Teacher Education*, *61*(1-2), 35–47. doi:10.1177/0022487109348024

Davidson, E. J. (2002). The discipline of evaluation: A helicopter tour for I-O psychologists. *The Industrial-Organizational psychologist*, *40*(2), 31–35.

De Coutere, B. (2014). To MOOC, or not to MOOC. *Training Journal*, 18-22.

De Lange, P., Suwardy, T., & Mavondo, F. (2003). Integrating a virtual learning environment into an introductory accounting course: Determinants of student motivation. *Accounting Education*, *12*(1), 1–14.

de Waard, I. (2014). Using BYOD, Apps, Sensors, Mobile Social Media for Meaningful Learning. In M. Aly & A. Tsakos (Eds.), *Mobile learning development for flexible learning*. Edmonton, Canada: Athabasca University Press.

DeBoer, J., Ho, A. D., Stump, G. S., & Breslow, L. (2014). Changing ''course'': Reconceptualizing educational variables for massive open online courses. *Educational Researcher*, *43*(2), 74–84. doi:10.3102/0013189X14523038

Dede, C. (2014). *New wine in no bottles: immersive, personalized, ubiquitous learning*. Keynote talk at Learning @ Scale, Atlanta, GA. Retrieved from http://learningatscale.acm.org/talks/keynote_chris_dede.pdf

de-Marcos, L., Pages, C., Martinez, J., & Gutierrez, J. (2007). Competency-Based Learning Object Sequencing Using Particle Swarms.*19th IEEE International Conference on Tools with Artificial Intelligence*, *2*, 111-116. doi:10.1109/ICTAI.2007.14

Demetriadis, S., & Pombortsis, A. (2007). E-lectures for flexible learning: A study on their learning efficiency. *Journal of Educational Technology & Society*, *10*(2), 147.

Demir, Ö., & Yurdugül, H. (2015). The Exploration of models regarding e-learning readiness: Reference model suggestions. *International Journal of Progressive Education*, *11*(1).

Denzin, N. K., & Lincoln, Y. S. (2003). *The landscape of qualitative research: Theories and issues* (2nd ed.). Thousand Oaks, CA: SAGE Publications.

DeSimone, R. L., & Harris, D. M. (1998). *Human resource development*. Fort Worth, TX: Harcourt Brace College Publishers.

Dieckmann, P. (Ed.). (2009). *Using Simulations for Education, Training and Research*. Lengerich, Germany: Pabst.

Dosh Design. (2015). Retrieved June 3, 2015, from http://www.doschdesign.com/productlist2.php?line=4&subrubrik=41

Downes, S. (2005). E-learning 2.0. *ACM eLearn Magazine*. Retrieved from http://elearnmag.acm.org/archive.cfm?aid=1104968

Downes, S. (2013). *Quality of Massive Open Online Courses by Stephen Downes*. Retrieved June 2, 2015, from http://mooc.efquel.org/week-2-the-quality-of-massive-open-online-courses-by-stephen-downes/#sthash.YOitClcH.dpuf

Downes, S. (2013). *Week 2: The Quality of Massive Open Online Courses*. Retrieved from http://mooc.efquel.org/week-2-the-quality-of-massive-open-online-courses-by-stephen-downes

Dzakiria, H., Wahab, M. S. D. A., & Rahman, H. D. A. (2012). Blended Learning (BL) as Pedagogical Alternative to Teach Business Communication Course: Case Study of UUM Executive Diploma Program. *Turkish Online Journal of Distance Education, 13*(3).

Dziuban, C., & Moskal, P. (2001). Evaluating distributed learning at metropolitan universities. *EDUCAUSE Quarterly*, *24*(4), 60–61.

Edginton, A., & Holbrook, J. (2010). A blended learning approach to teaching basic pharmacokinetics and the significance of face-to-face interaction. *American Journal of Pharmaceutical Education*, *74*(5). PMID:20798797

Ehlers, U. (2004). *Qualität im e-learning aus lernersicht. Grandlagen, empirie and modellkonzeption subjektiver qualität.* Wiesbaden: VS-Verlag. doi:10.1007/978-3-663-11211-2

Elçi, A. (2005). A metadata for E-Learning coordination through semantic web languages. *The Turkish Online Journal of Educational Technology, 4*(3), 27-32. Retrieved from http://www.tojet.net/articles/433.pdf

Elçi, A. (2004): A Metadata for E-Learning Coordination through Semantic Web Languages. In A. İşman, & F. Dabaj (Eds.), *Proceedings of The IETC 2004, IV. International Symposium on Educational Technology* (pp. 27-32).

Elias, T. (2011). Universal instructional design principles for mobile learning. *The International Review of Research in Open and Distributed Learning*, *12*(2), 143–156.

El-Khatib, K., Korba, L., Xu, Y., & Yee, G. (2003). Privacy and security in E-Learning. *International Journal of Distance Education*, *1*(4), 1–19. doi:10.4018/jdet.2003100101

Elkind, E., & Smith, K. (2008). *Online teaching preparedness: What about faculty?* Paper presented at Jefferson School of Nursing Faculty Papers & Presentations. Abstract retrieved from http://jdc.jefferson.edu/nursfp/57/

Ellis, R. A., Goodyear, P., Prosser, M., & O'Hara, A. (2006). How and what university students learn through online and face-to-face discussion: Conceptions, intentions and approaches. *Journal of Computer Assisted Learning*, *22*(4), 244–256.

Ellis, R. A., Steed, A. F., & Applebee, A. C. (2006). Teacher conceptions of blended learning, blended teaching and associations with approaches to design. *Australasian Journal of Educational Technology*, *22*(3), 312.

Embi, M. A. (Ed.). (2010). Amalan, Keberkesanan & Cabaran Pelaksanaan e-Pembelajaran di IPT Malaysia. WP Putrajaya: Kementerian Pengajian Tinggi Malaysia.

Embi, M. A., & Adun, M. N. (Eds.). (2010). e-Pembelajaran di IPTA Malaysia. Bangi & WP Putrjaya: Universiti Kebangsaan Malaysia &Kementerian Pengajian Tinggi Malaysia.

Embi, M. A. (Ed.). (2011). *E-Learning in Malaysian Higher Education Institutions: Status, Trends, & Challenges.* Putrajaya: Department of Higher Education, Ministry of Higher Education.

Engholm, P., & McLean, J. (2001). *What determines an organization's readiness for eLearning?* Retrieved from http://www2/sbbs.se/hp/erson/academia/Thesis%20FINAL.htm

EPIC. (2015). Retrieved June 3, 2015, from https://www.youtube.com/watch?v=zzhTlCO3JS8

Esposito, A. (2012). Research Ethics in Emerging Forms of Online Learning: Issues Arising from a Hypothetical Study on a MOOC. *Electronic Journal of e-Learning, 10*(3), 315-325.

Estelles Arolas, E., & González-Ladrón-de-Guevara, F. (2012). Towards an integrated crowdsourcing definition. *Journal of Information Science*, *38*(2), 189–200. doi:10.1177/0165551512437638

European Commission. (2014). *Digital Agenda for Europe: A Europe 2020 Initiative*. Retrieved from Action 68: Member States to mainstream eLearning in national policies of Pillar VI: Enhancing digital literacy, skills and inclusion at http://ec.europa.eu/digital-agenda/en/pillar-vi-enhancing-digital-literacy-skills-and-inclusion/action-68-member-states-mainstream

Exworthy, M. (2008). Policy to tackle the social determinants of health: Using conceptual models to understand the policy process. *Health Policy and Planning*, *23*(5), 318–327. doi:10.1093/heapol/czn022

Farid, A. (2014). Student online readiness assessment tools: A systematic review approach. *Electronic Journal of e-Learning*, *12*(4), 375-382.

Fawcett, S., Schultz, J., Watson, T. J., Fox, M., & Bremby, R. (2010). Building multisectoral partnerships for population health and health equity. *Preventing Chronic Disease*, *7*(6), A118.

Ferrari, M., & Sternberg, R. J. (1998). *The development of mental abilities and styles*. In W. Damon, D. Kuhn, & R. S. Siegler (Eds.), Handbook of child psychology (Vol. 2, pp. 899–946). New York: Wiley.

Fini, A. (2009). The Technological Dimension of a Massive Open Online Course: The Case of the CCK08 Course Tools. *The International Review of Research in Open and Distance Learning*, *10*(5). Retrieved from http://www.irrodl.org/index.php/irrodl/article/view/643/1402

Fini, A. (2009). The technological dimension of a Massive Open Online Course: The case of the CCK08 course tools. *International Review of Research in Open and Distance Learning*, *10*(5). Retrieved from http://www.irrodl.org/index.php/irrodl/article/view/643/1402

FIPA (Foundation For Intelligent Physical Agents). (n.d.). *FIPA-OS publicly available agent platform implementation.* Retrieved from http://fipa.org/resources/livesystems.html#os

Firmansyah, M. (2015). Idcourserians, a MOOCs learning community in Indonesia. Teaching & Education Conference, Florence, Italy.

Fitzpatrick, J., Sanders, J., & Worthen, B. (2011). *Program evaluation: Alternative approaches and practical guidelines* (4th ed.). Boston, MA: Pearson.

FlashDevelop. (2015). Retrieved June 3, 2015, from http://www.flashdevelop.org/

Flavell, J. H. (1992). Cognitive development: Past, present, and future. *Developmental Psychology*, *28*(6), 998–1005. doi:10.1037/0012-1649.28.6.998

Friedmann-Hill, E. (2003). *Jess in Action*. Greenwich, CT: Manning.

Friesen, N. (2004a). Three objections to Learning Objects and E-learning standards. In R. McGreal (Ed.), Online Education Using Learning Objects (pp. 59-70). London, UK: Routledge.

Friesen, N. (2004b). The International Learning Object Metadata Survey. *International Review of Research in Open and Distance Learning*, *5*(3). Retrieved from http://www.irrodl.org/index.php/irrodl/article/view/195/277

Fromme, J., & Unger, A. (Eds.). (2012). *Computer games and new media cultures. A handbook of digital games studies*. Heidelberg, Germany: Springer. doi:10.1007/978-94-007-2777-9

Fry, R., & Gonzalez, F. (2008). *One-in-five and growing fast: A profile of Hispanic public school students*. Pew Research Center. Retrieved from http://pewhispanic.org/files/reports/92.pdf

Fuchs, C., Prandelli, E., Schreier, M., & Dahl, D. W. (2013). All that is users might not be gold: How labeling products as user designed backfires in the context of luxury fashion brands. *Journal of Marketing*, *77*(5), 75–91. doi:10.1509/jm.11.0330

Fussell, S. R., & Benimoff, N. I. (1995). Social and cognitive processes in interpersonal communication: Implications for advanced telecommunications technologies. *Human Factors*, *37*(2), 228–250. doi:10.1518/001872095779064546 PMID:7642182

Gamage, D., Perera, I., & Fernando, S. (2014). Effectiveness of eLearning through MOOC: lessons learnt in selecting a MOOC. *The 22nd International Conference on Computers in Education (ICCE 2014)*. Nara. Japan: Academic Press.

Gamage, D., & Perera, I. F. (2015). Quality of MOOCs: A review of literature on effectiveness and quality aspects.*8th International Conference on Ubi-Media Computing (UMEDIA)* (pp. 224 - 229). IEEE. doi:10.1109/UMEDIA.2015.7297459

Gandomi, A., & Haider, M. (2014). Beyond the hype: Big data concepts, methods, and analytics. *International Journal of Information Management*, 137–144.

Gardner, H. (2009). Fünf kompetenzen für die zukunft. In Medienpädagogik: Emotionale Intelligenz in der Schule. Unterrichten mit Geschichten (pp. 138-149). Weinheim: Beltz-Verlag.

Garrison, D. R., & Vaughan, N. (2008). *Blended learning in higher education; framework, principles, and guidelines* (Vol. 23). Academic Press.

Garrison, D. R. (2011). *E-learning in the 21st century: a framework for research and practice.* New York, NY: Routledge.

Garrison, D. R., & Anderson, T. (2003). *E-learning in the 21st century: A framework for research and practice.* New York: Routledge.

Garrison, D. R., & Arbaugh, J. B. (2007). Researching the community of inquiry framework: Review, issues, and future directions. *The Internet and Higher Education*, *10*(3), 157–172.

Garrison, D. R., & Kanuka, H. (2004). Blended learning: Uncovering its transformative potential in higher education. *The Internet and Higher Education*, *7*(2), 95–105. http://www.doi.org/10.1016/j.iheduc.2004.02.001

GATE Toolkit. (2015). Retrieved June 3, 2015, from http://www.opengatecollaboration.org/

Gedik, N., Kiraz, E., & Ozden, M. Y. (2013). Design of a blended learning environment: Considerations and implementation issues. *Australasian Journal of Educational Technology*, *29*(1).

Gerbic, P. (2011). Teaching using a blended approach - what does the literature tell us? *Educational Media International*, *48*(3), 221.

Giessen, H. W. (2006). *Videosegmente als authentische lehrmaterialien für den sprachunterricht in computergestützten multimedia-produktionen?* Retrieved from http://www.vep-landau.de/bzf/2006_45/07_Giessen_091-096.pdf

Giessen, H. W. (2014). Über den Einsatz medienadäquater Präsentationsformen im Fremdsprachenunterricht: Darstellung der Methode und Anmerkungen zum thematisierten Inhalt. In Fremdsprachenunterricht im Spannungsfeld zwischen Sprachwissen und Sprachkönnen. Saarbrücken: htw.

Giessen, H. W. (2004). *Sprachnetzwerke in grenzräumen*. Saarbrücken: LPM.

Giessen, H. W. (2013). Formale aspekte bei der videoproduktion für handys. *Journal of Serial Narration on Television*, *4*(Winter), 33–52. Retrieved from http://www.uni-saarland.de/fileadmin/user_upload/Professoren/fr41_ProfSolteGresser/serial-narration/PDFs/Journal_04-2013/033-052_a23dnd7.pdf

Giessen, H. W. (2015a). Serious games effects: An overview. *Procedia: Social and Behavioral Sciences*, *174*, 2240–2244. doi:10.1016/j.sbspro.2015.01.881

Giessen, H. W. (2015b). Media-based learning methodology: Stories, games, and emotions. In *The international handbook of e-learning* (Vol. 2, pp. 43–54). London: Routledge.

Glance, D. G., Forsey, M., & Riley, M. (2013). The pedagogical foundations of massive open online courses. *First Monday*, *18*(5). doi:10.5210/fm.v18i5.4350

Global Forum for Health Research. (2002). *10/90 Report on Health Research.* Author.

Global Forum for Health Research. (2004). *Strengthening health systems: the role and promise of policy and systems research.* Geneva: Alliance for Health Policy and Systems Research.

Gluga, R., Kay, J., & Lever, T. (2013). Foundations for modeling university curricula in terms of multiple learning goal sets. *IEEE Transactions on Learning Technologies*, *6*(1), 25–37. doi:10.1109/TLT.2012.17

Godwin-Jones, R. (2011). Emerging technologies: Mobile apps for language learning. *Language Learning & Technology*, *15*(2), 2–11.

Goldberg, M. (2015). *MOOCs and Meetups together make for better learning*. Retrieved from: http://www.huffingtonpost.com/michaelgoldberg/moocs-and-meetups-togethe_b_6538414.html

Gonzalez, C. (2009). Conceptions of, and approaches to, teaching online: A study of lecturers teaching postgraduate distance courses. *Higher Education*, *57*(3), 299–314.

Gonzalez, C. (2010). What do university teachers think eLearning is good for in their teaching? *Studies in Higher Education*, *35*(1), 61–78.

Graetz, K. A., & Goliber, M. J. (2002). Designing collaborative learning places: Psychological foundations and new frontiers. *New Directions for Teaching and Learning*, (92): 13–22. http://www.doi.org/10.1002/tl.75

Greene, J. C., & Abma, T. A. (2001). *Responsive evaluation.* San Francisco, CA: Jossey-Bass.

Gregg, D. (2010). Designing for collective intelligence. *Communications of the ACM*, *53*(4), 134. doi:10.1145/1721654.1721691

Griggs, K., Bridges, L. M., & Rempel, H. G. (2009). Library/mobile: tips on designing and developing mobile web sites. *Code4lib Journal, 8.*

Grigorenko, E. L., & Sternberg, R. J. (1995). Thinking styles. In International handbook of personality and intelligence (pp. 205-229). London: Plenum Press doi:doi:10.1007/978-1-4757-5571-8_11 doi:10.1007/978-1-4757-5571-8_11

Grodin, S. (2012). *Stop stealing dreams: On the future of education and what we can do about it.* Seth Grodin at TEDxYouth@BFS. Retrieved from https://www.youtube.com/watch?v=sXpbONjV1Jc&feature=share

Grossman, P., Hammerness, K., & McDonald, M. (2009). Redefining teacher: Re-imagining teacher education. *Teachers and teaching. Theory into Practice*, *15*(2), 273–290.

Guba, E., & Lincoln, Y. (1989). *Fourth generation evaluation.* Newbury Park, CA: SAGE Publications.

Gülbahar, Y. (2012). *E-öğrenme*. Ankara: Pegem Akademi.

Gülbahar, Y. (2012). Study of developing scales for assessment of the levels of readiness and satisfaction of participants in e-learning environments. *Ankara University Journal of Faculty of Educational Sciences*, *45*(2), 119–137.

Guri-Rosenblit, S. (2005). Eight paradoxes in the implementation process of eLearning in higher education. *Higher Education Policy*, *18*(1), 5–29. doi:10.1057/palgrave.hep.8300069

Haber, J. (2014). *MOOCs*. Cambridge, MA: The MIT Press.

Halpern, D., & Gibbs, J. (2013). Social media as a catalyst for online deliberation? Exploring the affordances of Facebook and YouTube for political expression. *Computers in Human Behavior*, *29*(3), 159–1168. doi:10.1016/j.chb.2012.10.008

Handel, S. (2014). *The evolving role of Instructional Design in a 70:20:10 World.* [K16 online Jan 23, 2014]. Retrieved from http://www.k16online.com/blog/bid/371326/The-Evolving-Role-of-Instructional-Design-in-a-70-20-10-World?goback=%2Egde_72496_member_5832573999493705730

Haney, D. (2002). Assessing organizational readiness for eLearning: 70 questions to ask. *Performance Improvement*, *41*(4), 8–13. doi:10.1002/pfi.4140410404

Harding, N. (2012). *Online Course Revolution*. Retrieved June 1, 2015, from http://thepositive.com/mooc-massive-open-online-courses-uk/

Hartnell-Young, E. A. (2008). Mobile phones for learning in mainstream schooling: resistance and change. *Proc. World Conf. Mobile and Contextual Learning'The Bridge from Text to Context' (mLearn '08).*

Hartshorne, R. (2003). Thoughtful creation of online course content: implications of SCORM for educators. *The Free Library*. Retrieved from http://www.thefreelibrary.com/Thoughtfulcreationofonlinecoursecontent:implicationsofSCORM...-a0101943714

Hayes, J., & Allinson, C. W. (1998). Cognitive style and the theory and practice of individual and collective learning in organizations. *Human Relations*, *51*(7), 847–871. doi:10.1177/001872679805100701

Hazeltine, E., Ruthruff, E., & Remington, R. W. (2006). The role of input and output modality pairings in dual-task performance: Evidence for content-dependent central interference. *Cognitive Psychology*, *52*(4), 291–345. doi:10.1016/j.cogpsych.2005.11.001 PMID:16581054

Hedberg, J. G. (2014). Extending the pedagogy of mobility. *Educational Media International*, *51*(3), 237–253. doi:10.1080/09523987.2014.968447

Heers, R. (2005). *Being there: Untersuchungen zum Wissenserwerb in virtuellen Umgebungen*. Tübingen: Eberhard-Karls-Universität, Diss. Informations-und Kognitionswissenschaften.

Hegarty, B. (n.d.). Evaluation of eLearning for effective practice guidebook. In *WikiEducator*. Retrieved December 11, 2013 from http://wikieducator.org/Evaluation_of_eLearning_for_Effective_Practice_Guidebook

Heinich, R., Molenda, M., Russell, J. D., & Smaldino, S. E. (2002). *Instructional media and technologies for learning*. Pearson Education.

Heinze, A., & Procter, C. (2004). *Reflections on the use of blended learning*. Academic Press.

Hill, P. (2012). *Four Barriers That MOOCs Must Overcome To Build a Sustainable Model*. Retrieved June 1, 2015, from http://mfeldstein.com/four-barriers-that-moocs-must-overcome-to-become-sustainable-model/

Hills, T. (2015). Crowdsourcing content creation in the classroom. *Journal of Computing in Higher Education*, *27*(1), 47–67. doi:10.1007/s12528-015-9089-2

Hirumi, A. (2002). A framework for analyzing, designing, and sequencing planned e-learning interactions. *The Quarterly Review of Distance Education*, *3*(2), 141–160.

Hiscott, R. (2013, Oct. 8). *The Beginner's Guide to the Hashtag* [Web log post]. Retrieved from http://mashable.com/2013/10/08/what-is-hashtag/

Ho, A., Lu, L., & Thurmaier, K. (2006). Testing the reluctant professor's hypothesis: evaluating a blended-learning approach to distance education. *Journal of Public Affairs Education*, 81-102.

Hodson-Carlton, K., Siktberg, L., Flowers, J., & Scheibel, P. (2003). Overview of distance education in nursing: Where are we now and where are we going? In M. Oermann & K. Heinrich (Eds.), *Annual review of nursing education* (Vol. 1, pp. 165–189). New York: Springer.

Hofer, E., Wiener, T., Arnold, R., & Ahammer, H. (2013). Evaluation of Computer Simulation and Computer Animation used as eLearning Tools in Biophysics Lectures and in the self-learning Process of Medical Students In *Proceedings of in the proc. of the WCMPBE*. doi:doi:10.1007/978-3-642-29305-4_450 doi:10.1007/978-3-642-29305-4_450

Hollands, F. M., & Tirthali, D. (2014). *MOOCs: Expectations and reality. Center for Benefit-Cost Studies of Education.* Teachers College, Columbia University.

Holzinger, A., Kickmeier-Rust, M. D., Wassertheurer, S., & Hessinger, M. (2009). Learning performance with interactive simulations in medical education: Lessons learned from results of learning complex physiological models with the HAEMOdynamics SIMulator. *Computers & Education*, *52*(2), 292–301. doi:10.1016/j.compedu.2008.08.008

Hook, K. (2008). Knowing, communicating, and experiencing through body and emotion. *IEEE Transactions on Learning Technologies*, *1*(4).

Hopson, M. H., Simms, R. L., & Knezek, G. A. (2002). Using a technology-enriched environment to improve higher-order thinking skills. *Journal of Research on Technology in Education*, *34*(2), 109–119. doi:10.1080/15391523.2001.10782338

Howell, M., Love, S., & Turner, M. (2008). User characteristics and performance with automated mobile phone systems. *International Journal of Mobile Communications*, *6*(1), 1–15. doi:10.1504/IJMC.2008.015994

Hudson, A. (2010). Measuring the impact of cultural diversity on desired mobile reference services. *RSR. Reference Services Review*, *38*(2), 299–308. doi:10.1108/00907321011045052

Hung, H., & Yuen, S. C. (2010). Educational use of social networking technology in higher education. *Teaching in Higher Education*, *15*(6), 703–714. doi:10.1080/13562517.2010.507307

Hung, M. L., Chou, C., Chen, C. H., & Own, Z. Y. (2010). Learner readiness for online learning: Scale development and student perceptions. *Computers & Education*, *55*(3), 1080–1090. doi:10.1016/j.compedu.2010.05.004

Hunt, J. (2010). *Why Do Women Leave Science and Engineering?* NBER Working Paper No. 15853.

Hvorecký, J. (2005). Can E-learning break the Digital Divide? *European Journal of Open, Distance and E-Learning.* Retrieved from www.eurodl.org/?p=archives&year=2004&&article=143

ICT. (2013). Geneva: International Telecommunication Union.

Ilgaz, H., & Gülbahar, Y. (2015). A snapshot of online learners: E-readiness, e-satisfaction and expectations. *International Review of Research in Open and Distributed Learning*, *16*(2).

Imperial College. (n.d.). *An E-Learning Glossary.* Retrieved from http://www3.imperial.ac.uk/ict/services/e-learning/old site/aboutelearning/elearningglossary

Jalil, A., Beer, M., & Crowther, P. (2015). Pedagogical Requirements for Mobile Learning: A Review on MOBIlearn Task Model. *Journal of Interactive Media in Education*, *12*(1), 1–17.

Jefferies, P., Grodzinsky, F., & Griffin, J. (2003). Advantages and problems in using information communication technologies to support the teaching of a multi-institutional computer ethics course. *Journal of Educational Media*, *28*(2-3), 191–202.

Jeon, S. H., Kim, Y. G., & Koh, J. (2011). Individual, social, and organizational contexts for active knowledge sharing in communities of practice. Elsevier, 38, 12423-12431.

Johnson, L., Adams Becker, S., Estrada, V., & Freeman, A. (2014). *NMC Horizon Report: 2014 Higher Education Edition.* Austin, Texas: The New Media Consortium.

Jokinen, P., & Mikkonen, I. (2013). Teachers' experiences of teaching in a blended learning environment. *Nurse Education in Practice*. PMID:23608218

Jones, & Lau, A. M. S. (2010). Blending learning: widening participation in higher education. *Innovations In Education And Teaching International, 47*(4), 405-416.

Jones, V., & Jo, J. H. (2004, December). Ubiquitous learning environment: An adaptive teaching system using ubiquitous technology. In *Beyond the comfort zone:Proceedings of the 21st ASCILITE Conference* (*Vol. 468*, p. 474).

Jones, S., Johnson-Yale, C., Millermaier, S., & Pérez, F. S. (2008). Academic work, the Internet and US college students. *The Internet and Higher Education, 11*(3-4), 165–177.

Juhary, J. (2014). Perceived Usefulness and Ease of Use of the Learning Management System as a Learning Tool. *International Education Studies.*, *7*(8), 23–34. doi:10.5539/ies.v7n8p23

Juhasz, A., & Balsamo, A. (2012). An idea whose time is here: FemTechNet – A distributed online collaborative course (DOCC). *Ada: A Journal of Gender, New Media, and Technology*, (1). doi:10.7264/N3MW2F2J

Junho, S. (in press). Roadmap for e-commerce standardization in Korea. *International Journal of IT Standards and Standardization Research.*

Kambourakis, G. (2013). Security and Privacy in m-Learning and Beyond: Challenges and State-of-the-art. *International Journal of u-and e-Service Science and Technology*, *6*(3), 67–84.

Kanuka, H., & Kelland, J. (2008). Has e-learning delivered on its promises? Expert opinion on the impact of e-learning in higher education. *Canadian Journal of Higher Education*, *38*(1), 45–65.

Kariya, S. (2003). Online education expands and evolves. *IEEE Spectrum*, *40*(5), 49–51. doi:10.1109/MSPEC.2003.1200179

Ke, F., & Kwak, D. (2013). Online learning across ethnicity and age: A study on learning interaction participation, perception, and learning satisfaction. *Computers & Education, 61*, 43-51. EBSCOhost (accessed March 4, 2015).

Kearsley, G. (1994). *Conditions of Learning (R. Gagne).* [Online]. Retrieved from http://www.instructionaldesign.org/theories/conditions-learning.html

Kearsley, G., & Blomeyer, R. (2004). Preparing K-12 teachers to teach online. *Educational Technology: The Magazine for Managers of Change in Education,* (1), 49-52.

Ke, F. (2009). A qualitative meta-analysis of computer games as learning tools. In R. E. Ferdig (Ed.), *Handbook of research on effective electronic gaming in education* (pp. 1–32). Hershey, PA: IGI-Global. doi:10.4018/978-1-59904-808-6.ch001

Kember, D., & Kwan, K.-P. (2000). Lecturers' approaches to teaching and their relationship to conceptions of good teaching. *Instructional Science*, *28*(5), 469–490.

Keramati, A., Afshari-Mofrad, M., & Kamrani, A. (2011). The role of readiness factors in E-learning outcomes: An empirical study. *Computers & Education*, *57*(3), 1919–1929. doi:10.1016/j.compedu.2011.04.005

Kerres, M., Bormann, M., & Vervenne, M. (2009). Didaktische konzeption von serious games: Zur verknüpfung von spiel- und lernangeboten. *Medienpädagogik* Retrieved from http://mediendidaktik.uni-due.de/sites/default/files/kerres0908_0.pdf

Khalil, H., & Ebner, M. (2013). "How satisfied are you with your MOOC?" - A Research Study on Interaction in Huge Online Courses. In J. Herrington et al. (Eds.), *Proceedings of World Conference on Educational Multimedia, Hypermedia and Telecommunications 2013* (pp. 830-839). Chesapeake, VA: Association for the Advancement of Computing in Education (AACE).

Khalil, H., & Ebner, M. (2013). How satisfied are you with your MOOC? - A Research study on interaction in huge online courses. In J. Herrington et al. (Eds.), *Proceedings of World Conference on Educational Media and Technology 2013* (pp.830–839). Victoria, British Columbia: Association for the Advancement of Computing in Education (AACE).

Khan, B. (2003, February). A framework for open, flexible and distributed e-learning. *eLearn Magazine*. Retrieved from http://elearnmag.acm.org/featured.cfm?aid=640561

Khan, B. H. (2001). A framework for web-based learning. In Web-based Training, (pp. 75-98). Englewood Cliffs, NJ: Educational Technology.

Khan, B. H. (2001). Web-based Training. Academic Press.

Khan, B. H. (2003). A Framework for Open, Flexible and Distributed E-Learning, in *ACM eLearn Magazine*. Retrieved, from http://www.elearnmag.org/subpage/sub_page.cfm?section=3&list_item=12&page=1

Khan, B. H. (2005). *Managing e-learning: Design, delivery implementation and evaluation.* Hershey, PA: Information Science Publishing.

Khan, B. H. (2009). E-learning - The Global e-Learning Framework. In STRIDE Handbook 8 (pp. 42-52). New Delhi: The Indira Gandhi National Open University (IGNOU).

Khan, B. H. (2009). The global e-Learning framework. In S. Mishra (Ed.), STRIDE handbook 8 (pp. 42-51). New Delhi, India: The Indira Gandhi National Open University (IGNOU).

Khan, B. H. (2009). The global E-learning framework. *Stride*, 42-51.

Khan, B. H. (2014). *Continuum in E-Learning: People, Process and Product (P3).* Retrieved from http://elearningindustry.com/continuum-in-e-Learning-people-process-and-product-p3

Khan, B. H. (2014a). *E-Learning Framework.* Retrieved from http://asianvu.com/bk/framework/ and http://www.asianvu.com/bookstoread/framework/scroller.htm

Khan, B. H. (2014b). *Other Frameworks on E-Learning.* Retrieved from http://asianvu.com/bk/framework/?page_id=2396

Khan, B. H., & Granato, L. A. (2008). *Program evaluation in e-learning*. Retrieved from http://asianvu.com/bk/elearning_evaluation_article.pdf

Khan, B. H., & Granato, L. A. (2008). *Program evaluation in e-learning*. Retrieved from http://citeseerx.ist.psu.edu/viewdoc/download?doi=10.1.1.456.3097&rep=rep1&type=pdf

Khan, B.H. (2000). A Framework for E-Learning. *Distance Education Report*, *4*(24).

Khan, B. H. (1997). Web-based instruction: What is it and why is it? In B. H. Khan (Ed.), *Web-based instruction* (pp. 5–18). Englewood Cliffs, NJ: Educational Technology Publications.

Khan, B. H. (2004). People, process and product continuum in e-learning: The e-learning P3 model. *Educational Technology*, *44*(5), 33–40. http://asianvu.com/bookstoread/etp/elearning-p3model.pdf

Khan, B. H. (2004). The people-process-product continuum in E-learning: The E-learning P3 Model. *Educational Technology*, *44*(5), 33.

Khan, B. H. (2005a). *ELearning quick checklist.* Hershey, PA: Information Science Publishing. doi:10.4018/978-1-59140-812-3

Khan, B. H. (2007). Flexible learning in an open and distributed environment. In B. H. Khan (Ed.), *Flexible learning in an information society*. Hershey, PA: Information Science Publishing. doi:10.4018/978-1-59904-325-8.ch001

Khan, B. H. (2012). *User Interface Design for Virtual Environments: Challenges and Advances*. Information Science Reference. doi:10.4018/978-1-61350-516-8

Khan, B. H. (Ed.). (2001). *Web-based training*. Englewood Cliffs, NJ: Educational Technology Publications.

Khan, B. H. (Ed.). (2005). *Managing e-learning: Design, delivery, implementation, and evaluation*. Hershey, PA: IGI Global. doi:10.4018/978-1-59140-634-1

Khan, B. H. (Ed.). (2007). *Flexible learning in an information society*. Hershey, PA: Information Science Publishing. doi:10.4018/978-1-59904-325-8

Khan, B. H., & Ally, M. (Eds.). (2015). International handbook of eLearning:Vol. 1. *Theoretical perspectives and research*. London: Routledge.

Kincheloe, J., & McLaren, P. (2003). Rethinking critical theory and qualitative research. In *The landscape of qualitative research: Theories and issues* (pp. 433–488). Thousand Oaks, CA: SAGE Publications.

King, S. (2015, May 25). *Who is really reading your ads?* [Web log post]. Retrieved fromhttps://www.linkedin.com/pulse/who-really-reading-your-ads-steve-king

King, S. E., & Arnold, K. C. (2012). Blended Learning Environments in Higher Education: A Case Study of How Professors Make It Happen. *Mid-Western Educational Researcher*, *25*(1), 44–59.

Kirriemuir, J., & McFarlane, A. (2004). *Literature review in games and learning*. Bristol: Futurelab. Retrieved from http://hal.archivesouvertes.fr/docs/00/19/04/53/PDF/kirriemuir-j-2004-r8.pdf

Kolb, D. A. (1984). *Experiential learning: Experience as the source of learning and development*. Englewood Cliffs, NJ: Prentice-Hall.

Kong, S. C., Chan, T. W., Huang, R., & Cheah, H. M. (2014). A review of e-Learning policy in school education in Singapore, Hong Kong, Taiwan, and Beijing: Implications to future policy planning. *Journal of Computers in Education*, *1*(2-3), 187–212. doi:10.1007/s40692-014-0011-0

Kop, R. (2011). The challenges to connectivist learning on open online networks: Learning experiences during a massive open online course. *International Review of Research in Open and Distance Learning*, *12*(3), 19–38.

Kop, R. (2011). The Challenges to Connectivist Learning on Open Online Networks: Learning Experiences during a Massive Open Online Course. *International Review of Research in Open and Distance Learning*, *12*(3).

Kop, R., Fournier, H., & Mak, J. (2011). A pedagogy of abundance or a pedagogy to support human beings? Participant support on massive open online courses. *International Review of Research in Open and Distance Learning*, *12*(7), 74–93. Retrieved from http://www.irrodl.org/index.php/irrodl/article/view/1041/2025

Kuah, G. O. (2015). *UPM Blazes Trail in Online Platform to Impart Knowledge to All*. Retrieved from http://www.upm.edu.my/berita/details/putramoocbi?LANG=en

Kukulska-Hulme, & Traxler. (2004). Mobile teaching and learning. In *Mobile learning-a handbook for educators and trainers*. Academic Press.

Kukulska-Hulme, A., & Traxler, J. (2007). Designing for mobile and wireless learning. In H. Beetham & R. Sharpe (Eds.), *Rethinking Pedagogy for a Digital Age: Designing and Delivering E-Learning* (pp. 180–192). London: Routledge.

Lama, M., Vidal, J. C., Otero-Garcia, E., Bugarin, A., & Barro, S. (2011). Semantic Linking of a Learning Object Repository to DBpedia.*11th IEEE International Conference on Advanced Learning Technologies (ICALT)* (pp.460-464). doi:10.1109/ICALT.2011.143

Lamberti, F., Gatteschi, V., Demartini, C., Sanna, A., & Montuschi, P. (2014). Semantics in Education. *Computing Now, 7*(4). Retrieved from http://www.computer.org/portal/web/computingnow/archive/april2014

Lameras, P., Paraskakis, I., & Levy, P. (2008). *Conceptions of teaching using virtual learning environments: preliminary findings from a phenomenographic inquiry.* Paper presented at the 6th International Conference on Networked Learning.

Lameras, P., Levy, P., Paraskakis, I., & Webber, S. (2012). Blended university teaching using virtual learning environments: Conceptions and approaches. *Instructional Science*, *40*(1), 141–157. http://www.doi.org/10.1007/s11251-011-9170-9

Lanktree, C., & Briere, J. (1991, January). *Early data on the trauma symptom checklist for children (TSC-C).* Paper presented at the meeting of the American Professional Society on the Abuse of Children, San Diego, CA.

Laouris, Y., & Eteokleous, N. (2005, October). We need an educationally relevant definition of mobile learning. In *Proceedings of the 4th World Conference on Mobile Learning* (pp. 290-294). Academic Press.

Laurillard, D. (2007). Pedagogical forms of mobile learning: framing research questions. In Mobile learning: towards a research agenda. London: WLE Centre, IoE.

Lee, J. W. (2005). Public Health is a social issue. *Lancet*, *365*(9694), 1005–1006.

Lee, M. C., Tsai, K. H., Hsieh, T. C., Chiu, T. K., & Wang, T. I. (2007). An ontological approach for semantic learning objects interoperability.*Proceeding of Seventh IEEE International Conference on Advanced Learning Technologies ICALT 2007* (pp. 222-226). doi:10.1109/ICALT.2007.63

LEP.gov. (n.d.). *Limited English Proficiency (LEP). A federal interagency website.* Retrieved from: ww.lep.gov/faqs/faqs.html

Levy, D. (2011). *Lessons learned from participating in a connectivist massive online open course (MOOC).* Paper presented at the Chais Conference on Instructional Technologies Research 2011: Learning in the technological era, Raanana, Israel.

Lewin, K. (1942). Field theory of learning. In Yearbook of the national society for the study of education (pp. 215-242). doi:doi:10.1037/11335-006 doi:10.1037/11335-006

Liaw, S.-S., Huang, H.-M., & Chen, G.-D. (2007). An activity-theoretical approach to investigate learners' factors toward e-learning systems. *Computers in Human Behavior*, *23*(4), 1906–1920. Retrieved from http://www.doi.org/10.1016/j.chb.2006.02.002

Lin, J. W., Huang, H. H., & Chuang, Y. S. (2015). The impacts of network centrality and self-regulation on an e-learning environment with the support of social network awareness. *British Journal of Educational Technology*, *46*(1), 32–44. doi:10.1111/bjet.12120

Lin, M. G., Hoffman, E. S., & Borengasser, C. (2013). Is social media too social for class? A case study of Twitter use. *TechTrends*, *57*(2), 39–45. doi:10.1007/s11528-013-0644-2

Liu, M., McKelroy, E., Kang, J., Harron, J., & Liu, S. (2016). Examining the use of Facebook and Twitter as an additional social space in a MOOC. American Journal of Distance Education, 30(1), 14-26.

Liu, Y. (1997). Queuning Network Modeling of Human Performance and Concurrent Spatial and verbal tasks. *IEEE Transactions on Systems Man and Cybernetics Part a-Systems and Humans*, *27*, 195–207.

Liu, M., Kang, J., Cao, M. W., Lim, M. H., Ko, Y. J., Myers, R., & Schmitz Weiss, A. S. (2014). Understanding MOOCs as an emerging online learning tool: Perspectives from the students. *American Journal of Distance Education*, *28*(3), 147–159. doi:10.1080/08923647.2014.926145

Liu, M., Kang, J., & McKelroy, E. (2015). Examining learners' perspective on taking a MOOC: Reasons, excitement, and perception of usefulness. *Educational Media International*, *52*(2), 129–146. doi:10.1080/09523987.2015.1053289

Li, Y. M., & Jhang-Li, J. H. (2010). Knowledge sharing in communities of practice. *European Journal of Operational Research*, *207*(2), 1052–1064. doi:10.1016/j.ejor.2010.05.033

Liyanagunawardena, T. R., Parslow, P., & Williams, S. (2014). Dropout: MOOC participants'perspective. EMOOCs 2014, the Second MOOC European Stakeholders Summit, (pp. 95-100). Lausanne, Switzerland: Academic Press.

Lloret, E., Plaza, L., & Aker, A. (2013). Analyzing the capabilities of crowdsourcing services for text summarization. *Lang Resources & Evaluation Language Resources and Evaluation, 47*(2), 337-369. Retrieved June 11, 2015, from http://www.jstor.org/stable/42636372

Lock, J. V. (2006). A new image: Online communities to facilitate teacher professional development. *Journal of Technology and Teacher Education*, *14*(4), 663–678.

Losh, E. (2014). *The war on learning: Gaining ground in the digital university*. Cambridge, MA: The MIT Press.

Low, L., & O'Connell, M. (2006, September). Learner-centric design of digital mobile learning. In *Proceedings of the OLT Conference* (pp. 71-82). Academic Press.

LTSA. (1998). *Learning Technology Systems Architecture (LTSA)*. Retrieved from http://ltsc.ieee.org/wg1/files/ltsa-400.doc

LTSA. (n.d.). *IEEE Learning Technology System Architecture (LTSA)*. Retrieved from http://www.informatik.uni-bremen.de/uniform/gdpa/gdpa06.htm

LTSC LOM WG. (n.d.). *LOM: What next?* Retrieved from http://ariadne.cs.kuleuven.be/mediawiki2/index.php/lom-whatnext/issues

LTSC. (2013). *IEEE Standards Activities in the eLearning Space*. Retrieved from http://standards.ieee.org/develop/msp/elearning.pdf

LTSC. (n.d.). *The IEEE LTSC home page*. Retrieved from http://ieeeltsc.org/

Lutumba, S. H. (2010). Research capacity strengthening in the DRC. *Lancet*, *375*(1080).

Lyndon, W., & Loch, B. (2014). Academics' Perceptions on the Quality of MOOCs: An Empirical Study. *International Journal for Innovation and Quality in Learning, 2*(3), 53-63.

Lytras, M. D., Pouloudi, N., & Poulymenakou, A. (2002). Knowledge management convergence: Expanding learning frontiers. *Journal of Knowledge Management*, *6*(1), 40–51. doi:10.1108/13673270210417682

Macleod, H., Haywood, J., Woodgate, A., & Alkhatnai, M. (2015). Emerging patterns in MOOCs: Learners, course designs and directions. *TechTrends*, *59*(1), 56–63. doi:10.1007/s11528-014-0821-y

Madeira, R. N., Sousa, J. L., Pires, V. F., Esteves, L., & Dias, O. P. (2009). A mobile and web-based student learning system. *Procedia: Social and Behavioral Sciences*, *1*(1), 2441–2448. doi:10.1016/j.sbspro.2009.01.430

Mak, S., Williams, R., & Mackness, J. (2010). *Blogs and forums as communication and learning tools in a MOOC*. Paper presented at the 7th International Conference on Networked Learning 2010, Lancaster.

Mangelsdorf, M. (2012). *Massive Open Online Courses (MOOCs): An Assessment Based on Personal Experience*. Retrieved June 2, 2015, from http://www.iedp.com/Pages/DocumentManager/Massive%20Open%20Online%20Courses%20_%20Full%20Article.pdf

Marcinkonienė, R., & Zdanytė, J. (2015). Conventional and digital media in language learning. *Proceedings ICoN, 2015*, 101–111.

Margaryan, A., Bianco, M., & Littlejohn, A. (2015). Instructional quality of Massive Open Online Courses (MOOCs). *Computers & Education, 80*, 77–83. doi:10.1016/j.compedu.2014.08.005

Marmot, M. (2005). Social determinants of health inequalities. *Lancet, 365*(9464), 1099–1104. doi:10.1016/S0140-6736(05)74234-3

Marshall, S. (n.d.). *E-Learning Maturity Model*. Retrieved May 26, 2015, from http://www.utdc.vuw.ac.nz/research/emm/

Marton, F. (1988). Phenomenography: A research approach to investigating different understandings of reality. *Qualitative Research in Education: Focus and Methods, 21*, 143-161.

Marton, F. (1994). Phenomenography. In T. Husen & T. N. Postlethwaite (Eds.), The International Encyclopedia of Education (2nd ed.; pp. 4424-4429). Pergamon.

Marton, F. (1986). Phenomenography - A research approach to investigating different understandings of reality. *Journal of Thought, 21*, 28–94.

Marton, F., & Booth, S. (1997). *Learning and awareness*. Mahwah, NJ: L. Erlbaum Associates.

Masalela, R. K. (2009). Potential benefits and complexities of blended learning in higher education: The case of the University of Botswana. *Turkish Online Journal of Distance Education, 10*(1), 66–82.

Mason, R. (2004). Online education using learning objects. *British Journal of Educational Technology, 35*(6), 752–754. doi:10.1111/j.1467-8535.2004.00432_9.x

Masoumi, D. (n.d.). *Critical factors for effective eLearning*. Retrieved from http://asianvu.com/digitalibrary/eLearning/Critical_factors_for_effective_eLearning_by_DMasoumi%5B1%5D.pdf

Mayer, R. E., Fennell, S., Farmer, L., & Campbell, J. (2004). A personalization effect in multimedia learning: Learners learn better when words are in conversational style rather than formal style. *Journal of Educational Psychology, 96*(2), 389–395. doi:10.1037/0022-0663.96.2.389

Mayer, R. E., & Massa, L. J. (2003). Three facets of visual and verbal learners: Cognitive ability, cognitive style, and learning preference. *Journal of Educational Psychology, 95*(4), 833–846. doi:10.1037/0022-0663.95.4.833

Mayhew, S. H., Doherty, J., & Pitayarangsarit, S. (2008). Developing health systems research capacities through north-south partnership: An evaluation of collaboration in South Africa and Thailand. 6:8-19. *Health Research Policy and Systems, 6*(1), 8–19. doi:10.1186/1478-4505-6-8

May, M., & George, S. (2011). Privacy concerns in E-learning: Is using tracking system a threat? *International Journal of Information and Education Technology, 1*(1), 1–8. doi:10.7763/IJIET.2011.V1.1

Mcconatha, D., Praul, M., & Lynch, M. J. (2008). Mobile Learning in Higher Education: An Empirical Assessment of a New Educational Tool. *Online Submission, 7*(3).

McConnell International LLC. (2000). *Risk e-Business: Seizing the opportunity of global e-readiness*. Retrieved from http://www.witsa.org/papers/e-readiness.pdf

McConnell, D., & Zhao, J. (2006). Chinese higher education teachers' conceptions of e-Learning: Preliminary outcomes. Paper presented at the 23rd Annual Ascilite Conference: Who's Learning? Whose technology?

McInnerney, J. M., & Roberts, T. S. (2004). Online learning: Social interaction and the creation of a sense of community. *Journal of Educational Technology & Society*, *7*(3), 73–81.

McLuhan, H. M. (1962). *The gutenberg galaxy: The making of typographic man*. Toronto: University of Toronto Press.

McShane, K. (2004). Integrating face-to-face and online teaching: Academics' role concept and teaching choices. *Teaching in Higher Education*, *9*(1), 3–16.

Medina, Y. (2013, March 19). *Plaza Comunitaria, Literacy programming @ the library*. Retrieved from: http://publiclibrariesonline.org/2013/03/plaza-comunitaria-literacy-programming-the-library/

Meeker, M. (2015). *Internet trends 2015: Code conference*. Retrieved June 1, 2015, fromhttp://www.kpcb.com/internet-trends

Memene, D., & Simmons, P. (2015). A Study of eLearning implementation readiness in Togolese Higher Education Institutes. *International Journal of Scientific & Technology Research*, *4*(2), 24–28.

Menolli, A. L. A., Reinehr, S., & Malucelli, A. (2012). Ontology for organizational learning objects based on LOM standard. *XXXVIII Conferencia Latinoamericana En Informatica*, *2012*, 1–10.

Mercado, C. A. (2008). *Readiness assessment tool for an eLearning environment implementation*. Paper presented at the Fifth International Conference on eLearning for Knowledge-Based Society, Bangkok, Thailand. Retrieved from http://www.eLearningap.com/eLAP2008/Proceedings/18_fullpaper_cecilia%20Mercado_Revised.pdf

Merriam, S. (1998). *Qualitative research and case study applications in education* (Rev. ed.). San Francisco, CA: Jossey-Bass.

Merriam, S. B. (1988). *Case study research in education: A qualitative approach*. Jossey-Bass.

Merriam, S. B. (2002). *Qualitative research in practice: Examples for discussion and analysis*. San Francisco, CA: Jossey-Bass.

Merrill, M. D. (2002). First principles of instruction. *Educational Technology Research and Development*, *50*(3), 43–59. doi:10.1007/BF02505024

MHRD. (2015). Retrieved June 3, 2015, from http://www.vlab.co.in/ba_labs_all.php?id=6

Mih, C., & Mih, V. (2011). Conceptual maps as mediators of self-regulated learning. *Social and Behavioral Sciences*, *29*, 390–395.

Miles, M. B., Huberman, A. M., & Saldaña, J. (2014). *Qualitative Data Analysis: A Methods Sourcebook*. SAGE Publications, Inc.

Millenium Project. (2006). *Millenium Project*. Retrieved from http://www.unmillenniumproject.org/goals/

Miller, G. A. (1956). The magical number seven, plus or minus two: Some limits on our capacity for processing information. *Psychological Review*, *63*(2), 81–97. doi:10.1037/h0043158 PMID:13310704

Milligan, C., Littlejohn, A., & Margaryan, A. (2013). Patterns of engagement in connectivist MOOCs. *MERLOT Journal of Online Learning and Teaching, 9*(2), 149-159. Retrieved from http://jolt.merlot.org/vol9no2/milligan_0613.pdf

Milliron, M. D. (2010, October31). Online education vs. traditional learning: Time to end the family feud. *The Chronicle of Higher Education*, B30–B32.

Ministry of Education. (2013). *Statistics of public school system in Kuwait*. Retrieved from http://www.moe.edu.kw/News/69327

Mishra, S. K. (2013). Quality education for children, youth and adults through mobile learning. In J. Keengwe (Ed.), Pedagogical applications and social effects of mobile technology integration içinde (pp. 225-237). Hershey, PA: Information Science Reference.

Miyazoe, T., & Anderson, T. (2013). Interaction equivalency in an OER, MOOCS and informal learning era. *Journal of Interactive Media in Education*, *2*, 1–15. doi:10.5334/2013-09

Montgomery, D. A. (1999). Human sensitivity to variability information in detection decisions. *Human Factors*, *41*(1), 90–105. doi:10.1518/001872099779577246

Moore, M. (Ed.). (2013). *Handbook of distance education* (3rd ed.). New York, NY: Routledge.

Moore, M. G. (1989). Editorial: Three types of interaction. *American Journal of Distance Education*, *3*(2), 1–7. doi:10.1080/08923648909526659

Morrison, J. L. (2003). The global eLearning framework: An interview with Badrul Khan. *The Technology Source*. Michigan Virtual University. Retrieved from http://technologysource.org/article/336/

Motteram, G. (2006). Blended education and the transformation of teachers: A long term case study in postgraduate UK Higher Education. *British Journal of Educational Technology*, *37*(1), 17–30. Retrieved from http://www.doi.org/10.1111/j.1467-8535.2005.00511.x

Mueller, P. A., & Oppenheimer, D. M. (2014, June). The pen is mightier than the keyboard: Advantages of longhand over laptop note taking. *Psychological Science*, *25*(6), 1–10. doi:10.1177/0956797614524581 PMID:24760141

Multimedia Super Corridor. (2011). *Policy on ICT in Education Malaysia - 2010.* Retrieved from http://www.mscmalaysia.my/sites/default/files/pdf/publications_references/Policy%20on%20ICT%20in%20Education%20Malaysia%202010.pdf

Nagashima, T. (2014). What Makes Open Education Thrive? Examination of Factors Contributing to the Success of Open Education Initiatives. *International Journal for Innovation and Quality in Learning, 2*(3), 10-21.

Nakata, Y. (2011). Teachers' readiness for promoting learner autonomy: A study of Japanese EFL high school teachers. *Teaching and Teacher Education*, *27*(5), 900–910. doi:10.1016/j.tate.2011.03.001

Nakatsu, R. T., Grossman, E. B., & Iacovou, C. L. (2014). A taxonomy of crowdsourcing based on task complexity. *Journal of Information Science*, *40*(6), 823–834. doi:10.1177/0165551514550140

Nanodegrees. (n.d.). Retrieved from: https://www.udacity.com/nanodegree

Napier, N. P., Dekhane, S., & Smith, S. (2011). Transitioning to Blended Learning: Understanding Student and Faculty Perceptions. *Journal of Asynchronous Learning Networks*, *15*(1), 20–32.

National Education Association. (2000). *Quality on the line: Benchmarks for success in internet-based distance education.* Retrieved from http://www.ihep.org/sites/default/files/uploads/docs/pubs/qualityontheline.pdf

National Education Association. (2006). *Guide to teaching online courses*. Retrieved from http://www.nea.org/assets/docs/onlineteachguide.pdf

Niebuhr, V., Niebuhr, B., Trumble, J., & Urbani, M. J. (2014). Online faculty development for creating e-learning materials. *Education for Health*, *27*(3), 255–261. doi:10.4103/1357-6283.152186 PMID:25758389

Nielsen, J. (1997). *Be Succinct! (Writing for the Web).* Retrieved May 24, 2015, fromhttp://www.nngroup.com/articles/be-succinct-writing-for-the-web/

Nielsen, J. (1993). *Usability Engineering*. Boston: Academic Press.

Njenga, J. K., & Fourie, L. C. H. (2010). The myths about e-learning in higher education. *British Journal of Educational Technology, 41*(2), 199–212. doi:10.1111/j.1467-8535.2008.00910.x

Noor, S. F. M., Yusof, N., & Hashim, S. Z. M. (2011). Creating granular learning object towards reusability of Learning Object in e-learning context.*International Conference on Electrical Engineering and Informatics (ICEEI)* (pp. 1-5). doi:10.1109/ICEEI.2011.6021645

Novak, J. D., Gowin, D. B., & Johanse, G. T. (1983). The use of concept mapping and knowledge Vee mapping with junior high school science learners. *Science Education, 67*(5), 625–645. doi:10.1002/sce.3730670511

Novak, J., & Gowin, D. (1996). *Learning How To Learn*. New York, NY: Cambridge University Press.

O'Malley, C., Vavoula, G., Glew, J. P., Taylor, J., Sharples, M., & Lefrere, P. (2003). Guidelines For learning/teaching/tutoring in a mobile environment. *MOBIlearn Project Report*. Retrieved from http://www.mobilearn.org/results/results.htm

O'Malley, M. (2012). *Learning house instructor readiness questionnaire*. Retrieved from http://sloanconsortium.org/conference/2012/aln/assessing-instructor-readiness-teach-online-courses

O'Neil, H. F., Wainess, R., & Baker, E. L. (2005). Classification of learning outcomes: Evidence from the computer games literature. *Curriculum Journal, 16*(4), 455–474. doi:10.1080/09585170500384529

Ocak, M. A. (2011). Why are faculty members not teaching blended courses? Insights from faculty members. *Computers & Education, 56*(3), 689–699. Retrieved from http://www.doi.org/10.1016/j.compedu.2010.10.011

Oh, E., & Park, S. (2009). How are universities involved in blended instruction? *Journal of Educational Technology & Society, 12*(3), 327–342.

OLC Quality Scorecard. (n.d.). Retrieved June 19, 2015, fromhttp://onlinelearningconsortium.org/consult/quality-scorecard/

Oliver, M., & Trigwell, K. (2005). Can'Blended Learning'Be Redeemed? *E-Learning and Digital Media, 2*(1), 17–26.

Omar, A., Rose, D. E., & Stewart, B. (2008). *Crowdsourcing for relevance evaluation*. SIGIR.

Onah, D. F., Sinclair, J., & Boyatt, R. (2014). Exploring the use of MOOC discussion forums. In *Proceedings of London International Conference on Education*. LICE.

Online Learning Consortium (OLC). (2013). *2013 Survey of Online Learning Report*. Retrieved from http://sloanconsortium.org/publications/survey/grade-change-2013

Ornstein, A., Pajak, E., & Ornstein, S. (2011). *Contemporary Issues in Curriculum*. Boston, MA: Allyn & Bacon.

Orrell, J. (2011). *ALTC good practice report: Work-integrated learning*. Sydney, Australia: Australian Learning and Teaching Council.

Ossiannilsson, E., Williams, K., Camilleri, A., & Brown, M. (2015). Quality models in online and open education around the globe: State of the art and recommendations. *The ICDE Reports Series*. Retrieved May 26, 2015, from http://icde.org

Ouma, G. O., Awuor, F. M., & Kyambo, B. (2013). E-Learning readiness in public secondary schools in Kenya. *European Journal of Open, Distance and e-Learning*. Retrieved from http://www.eurodl.org/?p=archives&year=2013&halfyear=2&article=592

Oxford Dictionary. (2011). Concise Oxford English Dictionary (A. Stevenson & M. Waite Eds.; 12th ed.). Oxford, UK: Oxford University Press.

Paivio, A. (1986). *Mental representations: A dual coding approach*. Oxford, UK: Oxford University Press.

Pandya, Ch. (2012). *Limited English Proficient workers and the workforce investment act: Challenges and opportunities.* Retrieve from: http://www.migrationpolicy.org/article/limited-english-proficient-workers-and-workforce-investment-act-challenges-and-opportunities

Panuwatwanich, K., & Stewart, R. A. (2014). Understanding students' use of online learning tools through online learning readiness assessment. *Using Technology Tools to Innovate Assessment, Reporting, and Teaching Practices in Engineering Education*, 227-240. doi:10.4018/978-1-4666-5011-4.ch017

Pappano, L. (2012, Nov 14). The Year of the MOOC. The *New York Times*. Retrieved from http://www.nytimes.com/2012/11/04/education/edlife/massive-open-online-courses-are-multiplying-at-a-rapid-pace.html

Pappano, L. (2012). *The Year of the MOOC.* Retrieved June 6, 2015, from http://www.nytimes.com/2012/11/04/education/edlife/massive-open-online-courses-are-multiplying-at-a-rapid-pace.html?pagewanted=1&_r=0

Pappano, L. (2012, November 3). *The Year of the MOOC.* Retrieved June 15, 2015, from http://www.nytimes.com/2012/11/04/education/edlife/massive-open-online-courses-are-multiplying-at-a-rapid-pace.html?_r=0

Park, J., Yang, J., & Hsieh, Y. C. (2014). University level second language readers' online reading and comprehension strategies. *Language Learning & Technology*, *18*(3), 148–172.

Parlakkılıc, A. (2015). E-Learning Readiness in Medicine: Turkish Family Medicine (FM) Physicians Case. *Turkish Online Journal of Educational Technology*, *14*(2), 59.

Passey, D. (2010). Mobile learning in school contexts: Can teachers alone make it happen? *Learning Technologies. IEEE Transactions on*, *3*(1), 68–81.

Patton, M. Q. (1994). Developmental Evaluation. *Evaluation Practice*, *15*(3), 311–319. doi:10.1016/0886-1633(94)90026-4

Patton, M. Q. (2001). *Qualitative research & evaluation methods* (3rd ed.). Thousand Oaks, CA: SAGE Publications.

Patton, M. Q. (2008). *Utilization-focused evaluation.* Thousand Oaks, CA: SAGE Publications.

Pena, C. I., Marzo, J. L., & de la Rosa J. L. (2005). Intelligent agents to improve adaptivity in a web-based learning environment. *Knowledge-Based Virtual Education - Studies in Fuzziness and Soft Computing, 178*, 141-170.

Peng, H., Su, Y. J., Chou, C., & Tsai, C. C. (2009). Ubiquitous knowledge construction: Mobile learning re-defined and a conceptual framework. *Innovations in Education and Teaching International*, *46*(2), 171–183. doi:10.1080/14703290902843828

Perreira, K. M., Mullan Harris, K., & Lee, D. (2006). Making it in America: High school completion by immigrant and native youth. *Demography*, *43*(3), 511–536. doi:10.1353/dem.2006.0026 PMID:17051825

Peslak, A. R. (2003). Teaching computer information systems via distance education: A researched and personal perspective. *Information Systems Education Journal*, *1*(12), 1–18.

Phillips, K. A., Terras, K. L., Swinney, L., & Schneweis, C. (2012). Online disability accommodations: Faculty experiences at one public university. *Journal of Postsecondary Education and Disability*, *25*(4), 331–344.

Piccoli, G., Ahmad, R., & Ives, B. (2001). Web-Based Virtual Learning Environments: A Research Framework and a Preliminary Assessment of Effectiveness in Basic IT Skills Training. *Management Information Systems Quarterly*, *25*(4), 401–426.

Pillay, H. (1998). An investigation of the effect of individual cognitive preferences on learning through computer-based instruction. *Educational Psychology*, *18*(2), 171–182. doi:10.1080/0144341980180203

Pitman, A. J., Gosper, M., & Rich, D. C. (1999). Internet-based teaching in geography at Macquarie University: An analysis of student use. *Australasian Journal of Educational Technology*, *15*(2), 167–187. doi:10.14742/ajet.1855

Poltrack, J., Branon, R., & Nelson, J. (2011 August). *SCORM Update*. Presented in iFest 2011, Orlando, FL. Retrieved from http://www.adlnet.gov/wp-content/uploads/2011/08/poltrack_branon_nelson_SCORM_update_iFest2011.pdf

Posavac, E. J. (1999). Ethical challenges: Commentary: Can we help Gee-Gaws stay a family? *The American Journal of Evaluation*. doi:10.1016/S1098-2140(99)00045-4

Prefab. (2015). Retrieved June 3, 2015, from http://www.closier.nl/prefab/

Prendergast, G. (2004). *Blended collaborative learning: online teaching of online educators*. Global Educator.

Prensky, M. (2010). *Teaching Digital Natives*. London: SAGE Ltd.

Preskill, H., & Russ-Eft, D. (2005). *Building evaluation capacity: 72 activities for teaching and training*. Thousand Oaks, CA: SAGE Publications. doi:10.4135/9781412983549

Psycharis, S. (2005). Presumptions and action affecting an eLearning adoption by the educational system: Implementation using virtual private networks. *European Journal of Open and Distance Learning*, *2*, 1–10.

Purser, E. R., Towndrow, A., & Aranguiz, A. (2013). Realizing the potential of peer-to-peer learning: Taming a MOOC with social media. *e-Learning Papers, 33*, 1-5.

Quality Matters (QM). (2014). Retrieved fromhttps://www.qualitymatters.org/

Quinn, C. (2000). mLearning: Mobile, wireless, in-your-pocket learning. *LiNE Zine, 2006*.

Rahim, B. A., & Rashidah, S. (2013, October). Teachers' attitudes towards a learning management system, MC Online: An exploratory study in a Singapore secondary school. In *Educational Media (ICEM), 2013 IEEE 63rd Annual Conference International Council for IEEE* (pp. 1-18).

Railean, E., Elçi, A., Çelik, D., & Elçi, A. (2015). Metasystems learning design approach for STEM teaching and learning. In E. C. Ostler (Ed.), An Overview of Contemporary Research, Trends, and Perspectives (pp. 54-83). Elkhorn, Nebraska: Cycloid Publications. ISBN 978-0-9966741-1-9.

Red, E. R., Borlongan, H. G. S., Briagas, T. T., & Mendoza, M. J. M. (2013). *An assessment of the eLearning readiness state of faculty members and students at Malayan Colleges Laguna*. Retrieved from http://www.ijcim.th.org/past_editions/2013V21N3/3.Page_20-26.pdf

Reeves, T. C., & Hedberg, J. G. (2003). *Interactive learning systems evaluation*. Englewood Cliffs, NJ: Educational Technology Publications.

Rehder, B., & Hoffman, A. B. (2005). Eye tracking and selective attention in category learning. *Cognitive Psychology*, *51*(1), 1–41. doi:10.1016/j.cogpsych.2004.11.001 PMID:16039934

Reilly, C. (2013). MOOCs deconstructed: Variables that affect MOOC success rates. In J. Herrington et al. (Eds.), *Proceedings of World Conference on Educational Media and Technology 2013* (pp. 1308–1338). Victoria, British Columbia: Association for the Advancement of Computing in Education (AACE).

Reisman, S. (2014). The Future of Online Instruction, Part 1. *Computer*, *47*(4), 92–93. doi:10.1109/MC.2014.106

Richards, T. (2014). *IEEE Actionable Data Book - IEEE LTSC*. [Presentation]. Retrieved from http://www.gtn-quebec.org/wp-content/uploads/2014/03/Tyde-Richards-IEEE-ADB-Montreal.pdf

Richards, T., & Robson, R. (2014). *The next disruption in digital learning*. Retrieved from http://www.computer.org/portal/web/Musings-from-the-Ivory-Tower/content?g=7512968&type=article&urlTitle=the-next-disruption-in-digital-learning

Rispela, L. C., & Doherty, J. (2011). Research in support of health systems transformation in South Africa: The experience of the Centre for Health Policy. *Journal of Public Health Policy*, *32*, S10–S29. doi:10.1057/jphp.2011.33

Ritterfeld, U. (2011). Beim spielen lernen? Ein differenzierter blick auf die möglichkeiten und grenzen von serious games. *Computer + Unterricht, 84*, 54-57.

Ritterfeld, U., Cody, M. J., & Vorderer, P. (2009). *Serious games: Mechanisms and effects*. New York: Routledge.

Riva, G., & Villani, D. (2005). CyberEurope. *Cyberpsychology & Behavior*, *8*(1), 89–95. doi:10.1089/cpb.2005.8.101 PMID:15738696

Roberts, G. (2003). Teaching using the web: Conceptions and approaches from a phenomenographic perspective. *Instructional Science*, *31*(1-2), 127–150.

Robertson, H. J. (2003). Toward a theory of negativity teacher education and information and communications technology. *Journal of Teacher Education*, *54*(4), 280–296. doi:10.1177/0022487103255499

Rodriguez, M. A., & Anicete, R. C. R. (2010). Students' Views of a Mixed Hybrid Ecology Course. *MERLOT Journal of Online Learning and Teaching*, *6*, 791–798.

Rodriguez, O. (2013). The concept of openness behind c and x-MOOCs (Massive Open Online Courses). *Open Praxis*, *5*(1), 67–73. doi:10.5944/openpraxis.5.1.42

Rogers, K. D. (2011). *Mobile learning devices*. Solution Tree Press.

Rosenberg, M. (2000). *The eLearning readiness survey*. Retrieved from http://books.mcgraw-hill.com/training/eLearning/eLearning_survey.pdf

Rosenberg, M. J. (2001). *ELearning: Strategies for delivering knowledge in the digital age*. New York: McGraw-Hill.

Rosenbloom, J. L., Ash, R. A., Dupont, B., & Coder, L. A. (2008). Why are there so few women in information technology? Assessing the role of personality in career choices. *Journal of Economic Psychology*, *29*(4), 543–554. doi:10.1016/j.joep.2007.09.005

Rossi, P. H., Lipsey, M. W., & Freeman, H. E. (1999). *Evaluation: A systematic approach* (6th ed.). Thousand Oaks, CA: SAGE Publications.

Rovai, A. P., & Baker, J. D. (2014). *Massive online learning: A topical record of the MOOC pansophy*. Chesapeake, VA: Watertree Press LLC.

Russ-Eft, D., & Preskill, H. (2001). *Evaluation in organizations. A systematic approach to enhancing learning, performance, and change*. Cambridge, MA: Perseus Publishing.

Ryan, M., Hodson-Carlton, K., & Ali, N. S. (2004). Reflections on the role of faculty in distance learning and changing pedagogies. *Nursing Education Perspectives*, *25*(2), 73–80. PMID:15124511

Ryan, M., Hodson-Carlton, K., & Ali, N. S. (2005). A model for faculty teaching online: Confirmation of a dimensional matrix. *The Journal of Nursing Education*, *44*(8), 357–365. PMID:16130342

Saadatmand, M., & Kumpulainen, K. (2014). Participants' perceptions of learning and networking in connectivist MOOCs. *MERLOT Journal of Online Learning and Teaching*, *10*(1), 16–30.

Salmon, G. (2001). Masters or slaves to the technology? The role of the e-moderator in e-learning. *ACM eLearn Magazine,* (6), 2. Retrieved from http://elearnmag.acm.org/archive.cfm?aid=566946

Salmon, G. (2005). Flying not flapping: A strategic framework for e-learning and pedagogical innovation in higher education institutions. *ALT-J, 13*(3), 201–218.

Salter, M. (n.d.). Crowdsourcing: Student-driven learning using web 2.0 technologies in an introduction to globalization. *Journal of Political Science Education*, 362-365.

Sander, T. (2005). *E-association? Using technology to connect citizens: The case of Meetup.com.Annual meeting of the American Political Science Association*, Washington, DC.

Sangrà, A., Guàrdia, L., & Maina, B. (2013). MOOC Design Principles. A Pedagogical Approach from the Learner's Perspective. *eLearning Papers, 33.* Retrieved from https://www.academia.edu/5819373/MOOC_Design_Principles._A_Pedagogical_Approach_from_the_Learners_Perspective

Sangra, A., Vlachopoulos, D., & Cabrera, N. (2012). Building an inclusive definition of e-learning: An approach to the conceptual framework. *International Review of Research in Open and Distance Learning, 13*(2), 145–159.

Satcher, D. (2010). Include a social determinants of health approach to reduce health inequities. *Public Health Reports (Washington, D.C.), 125*(4), 6–7.

Sawyer, S., & Tapia, A. (2005). The sociotechnical nature of mobile computing work: Evidence from a study of policing in the United States. *International Journal of Technology and Human Interaction, 1*(3), 1–14. doi:10.4018/jthi.2005070101

J. L. Schnase, & E. L. Cunnius (Eds.). (1995). Learning in the 21st century and beyond. In *Proceedings of the First International Conference on Computer Support for Collaborative Learning (CSCL '95).* Mahwah, NJ: Erlbaum.

Schoenak, L. (2013). A New Framework for Massive Open Online Courses (MOOCs). *Journal of Adult Education, 42*(2), 98–103.

Schreurs, J., & Al-Huneidi, A. (2012). E-learning readiness in organisations: Case KBC bank. *International Journal of Advanced Corporate Learning, 5*(1), 4–7.

Schulman, A. H., & Sims, R. L. (1999). Learning in an online format versus an in-class format: An experimental study. *T.H.E. Journal, 26*(11), 59–65.

Schultz, S. (2015). *Comparison of online student vs. public student performance on the ACT* (Master Thesis, Dordt College, Iowa). Retrieved from http://digitalcollections.dordt.edu/med_theses/88

Schwabe, G., & Göth, C. (2005). Mobile learning with a mobile game: Design and motivational effects. *Journal of Computer Assisted Learning, 21*(3), 204–216. doi:10.1111/j.1365-2729.2005.00128.x

Schwartz, P. (1996). *The art of the long view: Paths to strategic insight for yourself and your company.* New York: Broadway Business.

Schweighofer, P., & Ebner, M. (2015). Aspects to be considered when implementing technology-enhanced learning approaches: A literature review. *Future Internet, 7*(1), 26–49. doi:10.3390/fi7010026

SCORM. (n.d.). *SCORM2004* (4th ed.). Retrieved from http://www.adlnet.org/scorm/scorm-2004-4th/

Scott, D., Durnell Cramton, C., Gauvin, S., Steinke, G., & Patterson, K. (1997). Internet-based collaborative learning. An empirical evaluation. *Proceedings of the 3rd Ausweb Conference.* Retrieved from http://ausweb.scu.edu.au/proceedings/donscott/index.html

See, S., & Conry, J. M. (2014). Flip my class! A faculty development demonstration of a flipped-classroom. *Currents in Pharmacy Teaching and Learning*, *6*(4), 585–588. doi:10.1016/j.cptl.2014.03.003

Selingo, J. J. (2013). *College (Un)Bound: The future of Higher Education and what it means for students*. New York, NY: Houghton Mifflin.

Selingo, J. J. (2014). *MOOC U: Who is getting the most out of online education and why*. New York: Simon and Schuster.

Sen, A. (2004). How does culture matter? In Culture and public action (pp. 37-58). Stanford, CA: Stanford University Press.

Sengupta, S., Chaki, N., & Dasgupta, R. (2008). Design of a Learning Management System on LTSA framework. *Proceedings of the 7th WSEAS International Conference on Education and Educational Technology* (pp. 65-70). Retrieved from http://www.wseas.us/elibrary/conferences/2008/venice/edu/edu11.pdf

Shah, D. (2014). *Online Courses Raise Their Game: A Review of MOOC Stats and Trends in 2014*. Retrieved June 2, 2015, from https://www.class-central.com/report/moocs-stats-and-trends-2014/

Sharpe, R. (2006). *The undergraduate experience of blended e-learning: a review of UK literature and practice*. The Higher Education Academy York.

Sharples, M. (2000). The design of personal mobile technologies for lifelong learning. *Computers & Education*, *34*(3), 177–193. doi:10.1016/S0360-1315(99)00044-5

Shattuck, K. (2014). *Quality Matters Higher Education Rubric* (5th ed.). Retrieved from Quality Matters Program: https://www.qualitymatters.org/rubric

She Figures. (2012). Retrieved June 3, 2015, from http://ec.europa.eu/research/science-society/document_library/pdf_06/she-figures-2012_en.pdf

Shearer, P. D., Shea, T. P., & Kristensen, E. (2003). Online communities of practice: A catalyst for faculty development. *Innovative Higher Education*, *27*(3), 183–194. doi:10.1023/A:1022355226924

Shelton, K. (2010). A quality scorecard for the administration of online education programs: A Delphi study. *Journal of Asynchronous Learning Networks*, *14*(4), 36–62.

Shelton, K. (2011). A review of paradigms for evaluating the quality of online education programs. *Online Journal of Distance Learning Administration*, *4*(1). Retrieved from http://westga.edu

Shelton, K., & Saltsman, G. (2005). *An administrator's guide to online education*. Greenwich, CT: Information Age Publishing.

Shen, C. W., & Kuo, C. J. (in press). Learning in massive open online courses: Evidence from social media mining. *Computers in Human Behavior*. doi:10.1016/j.chb.2015.03.013

Sherry, L., Havelock, B., & Gibson, D. (2005). The personal and professional learning portfolio: an online environment for mentoring, collaboration, and publication. In T. Roberts (Ed.), Computer Supported Collaborative Learning in Higher Education (pp. 201-217). Hershey, PA: Idea Group Publishing.

Shoikova, E. (2002). E-Learning Standards Overview.*The Vienna International Working Conference - eLearning and eCulture, VIEWDET 2002*.

Shonola, S. A., & Joy, M. S. (2014, July). Mobile learning security issues from lecturers' perspectives (Nigerian Universities Case Study). In *6th International Conference on Education and New Learning Technologies*.

Shyam, D., Krishnashree, A., Prema, N., & Bipin, N. (2011). Enhanced Facilitation of Biotechnology Education in Developing Nations via Virtual Labs: Analysis, Implementation and Case-studies. *International Journal of Computer Theory and Engineering*, *3*(1), 1793–8201.

Siemens, G. (2004). *A learning theory for the digital age*. Retrieved from http://www.elearnspace.org/Articles/connectivism.htm

Siemens, G. (2013). Massive Open Online Courses: Innovation In Education? In Open Educational Resources: Innovation, Research and Practice (pp. 5-16). Athabasca University, Commonwealth of Learning.

Siemens, G., Gaševića, D., & Dawson, S. (2015). *Preparing for the digital university: A review of the history and current state of distance, blended, and online learning*: Athabasca University. Retrieved from http://linkresearchlab.org/PreparingDigitalUniversity.pdf

Siemens, G. T. (2015). The Role of MOOCs in the Future of Education. In C. Bonk, M. Lee, T. C. Reeves, & T. H. Reyolds (Eds.), *MOOCs and Open Education Around the World*. New York: Routledge.

Sinha, T. (2014). *Supporting MOOC instruction with social network analysis*. arXiv preprint arXiv:1401.5175

Siti Rafidah, M. D. (2009). The Use of ICT in Public and Private Institutions of Higher Learning, Malaysia. *Computer and Information Science*, *2*(4), 122–128.

Sitthi, A. C., & Somrongthong, R. (2000). Strengthening health research capacity in developing countries: A critical element for achieving health equity. *BMJ (Clinical Research Ed.)*, *321*(7264), 813–817. doi:10.1136/bmj.321.7264.813

Skaalid, B. (1999). *Human computer interface design*. University of Saskatchewan, Faculty of Education. Retrieved from http://www.usask.ca/education/coursework/skaalid/theory/interface.htm

Smith, N. L. (1999). A framework for characterizing the practice of evaluation, with application to empowerment evaluation. *Canadian Journal of Program Evaluation/La Revue Canadienne D'evaluation De Programme*, 39-68.

So, K. T., & Swatman, P. M. C. (2006). *eLearning Readiness of Hong Kong Teachers*. Paper presented at the Hong Kong International IT in Education Conference 2006, Hong Kong.

So, K. T., & Swatman, P. M. C. (2012). *ELearning readiness in the classroom: A study of Hong Kong primary and secondary teachers*. Retrieved from https://nurhadiw.files.wordpress.com/2010/08/swatman-hongkong.pdf

Solar, O., & Irwin, A. (2007). A conceptual framework for action on the social determinants of health. Social Determinants of Health. *Discussion Paper 2 (Policy and Practice).*

Soong, B. M., Chan, H., Chua, B. C., & Loh, K. F. (2001). Critical success factors for on-line course resources. *Computers & Education*, *36*(2), 101–120. doi:10.1016/S0360-1315(00)00044-0

Squire, K. D. (2003). Video games in education. *International Journal of Intelligent Simulations and Gaming*, *2*(1). Retrieved from http://website.education.wisc.edu/~kdsquire/tenure-files/39-squire-IJIS

SREB. (2009). *Guidelines for professional development of online teachers*. Retrieved from http://publications.sreb.org/2009/09T01_Guide_profdev_online_teach.pdf

Stacey, E., & Gerbic, P. (2008). *Success factors for blended learning*. Paper presented at the Australian Society for Computers in Learning in Tertiary Education 2008, Melbourne.

Stake, R. E. (1975). *Evaluating the arts in education: A responsive approach*. Columbus, OH: Merrill.

Stake, R. E. (1995). *The art of case study*. Thousand Oaks, CA: Sage Publications.

Steel, C. (2009). Reconciling university teacher beliefs to create learning designs for LMS environments. *Australasian Journal of Educational Technology*, *25*(3), 399–420.

Stepp-Greany, J. (2002). Student perceptions on language learning in a technological environment: Implications for the new millennium. *Language Learning & Technology*, *6*(1), 165–180.

Sternberg, R. J. (1997). *Thinking styles*. New York: Cambridge University Press. doi:10.1017/CBO9780511584152

Sternberg, R. J., & Grigorenko, E. L. (1997). Are cognitive styles still in style? *The American Psychologist*, *52*(7), 700–712. doi:10.1037/0003-066X.52.7.700

Stewart, B. (2013). Massiveness + openness = new literacies of participation? *MERLOT Journal of Online Learning and Teaching*, *9*(2), 228-238. Retrieved from http://jolt.merlot.org/vol9no2/stewart_bonnie_0613.htm

Stracke, C. M. (2014). How can e-Learning and MOOCs reveal and exploit the hidden treasures of open research and open education? In *From education to employment and meaningful work with ICTs.Proceedings of EDEN Annual Conference.*

Strong, K., Mathers, S., Leeder, S., & Beaglehode, R. (2005). Preventing chronic diseases: How many lives can we save? *Lancet*, *366*(9496), 1578–1582. doi:10.1016/S0140-6736(05)67341-2

Subramanya, S. R., & Yi, B. K. (2006). User interfaces for mobile content. *Computer*, *39*(April), 85–87. doi:10.1109/MC.2006.144

Su, L., Ma, J., Li, Y., Cheng, M. X., & Huang, R. (2008). Semantic-oriented ubiquitous Learning Object model.*Proceedings of the 7th IEEE International Conference on Cybernetic Intelligent Systems CIS 2008.*

Sun, P. C., Tsai, R. J., Finger, G., Chen, Y. Y., & Yeh, D. (2008). What drives a successful e-Learning? An empirical investigation of the critical factors influencing learner satisfaction. *Computers & Education*, *50*(4), 1183–1202. doi:10.1016/j.compedu.2006.11.007

Sun, S., Joy, M., & Griffiths, N. (2005). To support adaptivity in agent-based learning systems - the use of learning objects and learning style.*Fifth IEEE International Conference on Advanced Learning Technologies ICALT 2005* (pp.846-847).

Sun, S., Joy, M., & Griffiths, N. (2007). The Use of Learning Objects and Learning Styles in a Multi-Agent Education System. *Journal of Interactive Learning Research*, *18*(3), 381–398.

Swan, K. (2002). Building learning communities in online courses: The importance of interaction. *Education Communication and Information*, *2*(1), 23–49. doi:10.1080/1463631022000005016

Sweller, J. (1988). Cognitive load during problem solving: Effects on learning. *Cognitive Science*, *12*(2), 257–285. doi:10.1207/s15516709cog1202_4

Tamim, R. M., Bernard, R. M., Borokhovski, E., Abrami, P. C., & Schmid, R. F. (2011, March). What forty years of research says about the impact of technology on learning: A second-order meta-analysis and validation study. *Review of Educational Research*, *81*(1), 4–28. doi:10.3102/0034654310393361

Tarasewich, P., Gong, J., Nah, F.F., & DeWester, D. (2008). Mobile interaction design: Integrating individual and organizational perspectives. *Information Knowledge Systems Management*, *7*, 121–144.

Teacher Education Ministerial Advisory Group (TEMAG). (2014). *Action now: Classroom ready teachers*. Retrieved from: http://docs.education.gov.au/node/36783

TechHire Initiative. (n.d.). Retrieved from: https://www.whitehouse.gov/issues/technology/techhire

TEI ATHENS eclass. (2015). Retrieved June 3, 2015, from http://medisp.bme.teiath.gr/eclass/modules/exercice/exercice.php?course=TIO222

TEL. (c2015). *Technology Enhanced Learning*. Retrieved from http://tel.ioe.ac.uk/

Tham, C. M., & Werner, J. M. (2005). Designing and evaluating eLearning in higher education: A review and recommendations. *Journal of Leadership & Organizational Studies*, *11*(2), 15–25. doi:10.1177/107179190501100203

The National Higher Education Strategic Plan Beyond 2020. (2007). Putrajaya: Ministry of Higher Education Malaysia.

Tinio, V. L. (2003). *ICT in education*. Paper presented at the World Summit on the Information Society.

TLF (The Learning Federation). (2001). Next generation learning systems and the role of teachers. In *2020 Visions: Transforming Education and Training through Advanced Technologies* (pp: 46-51). Washington DC: Technology Administration, U.S. Department of Commerce. Retrieved from http://usa.usembassy.de/etexts/tech/2020Visions.pdf

Toda la UNAM en Línea. (n.d.). Retrieved from: http://www.unamenlinea.unam.mx

Tomkin, J. H., & Charlevoix, D. (2014). Do professors matter? Using an a/b test to evaluate the impact of instructor involvement on MOOC student outcomes. In *Proceedings of the first ACM conference on Learning@ Scale Conference* (pp. 71-78). ACM.

Traxler, J., & Bridges, N. (2005). Mobile learning–the ethical and legal challenges. *Mobilelearning anytimeeverywhere*, 203.

Traxler, J. (2005). Defining mobile learning.*Proceedings of the 2005 IADIS International Conference*.

Traxler, J. (2007). Defining, Discussing and Evaluating Mobile Learning: The moving finger writes and having writ..... *The International Review of Research in Open and Distributed Learning*, *8*(2).

Traxler, J. (2010). Distance education and mobile learning: Catching up, taking stock. *Distance Education*, *31*(2), 129–138. doi:10.1080/01587919.2010.503362

Trekles, A. M., & Sims, R. (2013). Designing instruction for speed: Qualitative insights into instructional design for accelerated online graduate coursework. *Online Journal of Distance Learning Administration*, *16*(3).

Trigwell, K., Prosser, M., & Waterhouse, F. (1999). Relations between teachers' approaches to teaching and students' approaches to learning. *Higher Education*, *37*(1), 57–70.

Tsai, S., & Machado, P. (2002). *E-learning, online Learning, web-based learning, or distance learning: unveiling the ambiguity in current terminology*. Retrieved from http://www.elearnmag.org/subpage/sub_page.cfm?section=3&list_item=6&page=1

Tsinakos, A., & Ally, M. (2013). *Global Mobile Learning Implementations and Trends*. Beijing, China: CCRTVU Press.

Tubaishat, A., & Lansari, A. (2011). Are students ready to adopt e-learning? A preliminary e-readiness study of a university in the Gulf region. *International Journal of Information and Communication Technology Research*, *5*(1).

Tugsgerel, B., Anane, R., & Theodoropoulos, G. (2010). An Integrated Approach to Learning Object Sequencing. *IEEE 10th International Conference on Advanced Learning Technologies (ICALT)*.

Turkle, S. (1984). *The second self: Computers and the human spirit*. Cambridge, MA: MIT Press.

Turskienė, S., Bakanovienė, T., & Vilkonis, R. (2013). Readiness of adults to learn using e-learning, m-learning and t-learning technologies. *Informatics in Education: An International Journal*, *12*(2), 181–190.

Tyczkowski, B., Bauman, E., Gallagher-Lepak, S., Vandenhouten, C., & Reilly, J. (2012). An interface design evaluation of courses in a nursing program using an e-learning framework: a case study. In B. Khan (Ed.), *User interface design for virtual environments* (pp. 285–304). Hershey, PA: IGI Global. doi:10.4018/978-1-61350-516-8.ch018

U.S. Department of Education, Institute of Education Sciences, National Center for Education Statistics (NCES). (2010). *Tabla 130. Percentage of high school dropouts among persons 16 through 24 years old (status dropout rate) and number of status dropouts, by noninstitutionalized or institutionalized status, birth in or outside of the United States, and selected characteristics.* Retrieved from: http://nces.ed.gov/programs/digest/d12/tables/dt12_130.asp

University of Wisconsin System (UW System) Board of Regents. (2015). *What is the UW System?* Retrieved from https://www.wisconsin.edu/about-the-uw-system/

UPCEA Hallmarks of Excellence in Online Leadership. (n.d.). Retrieved May 26, 2015, fromhttp://www.upcea.edu/hallmarks

Ure, C., Gough, N., & Newton, R. (2009). *Practicum partnerships: Exploring models of practicum organisation in teacher education for a standards-based profession (final report)*. Retrieved from: http://www.vit.vic.edu.au/SiteCollectionDocuments/PDF/practicum%20partnerships.pdf

Usip, E. E., & Bee, R. H. (1998). Economics: A discriminant analysis of students' perceptions of web-based learning. *Social Science Computer Review*, *16*(1), 16–29. doi:10.1177/089443939801600104

Uvalic-Trumbic, S., & Daniel, J. S. (Eds.). (2013). *A Guide to Quality in Online Learning*. Retrieved from http://www.contactnorth.ca/tips-tools/guide-quality-online-learning

UW-Madison Continuing Studies. (2013). *Distance education professional development*. Retrieved from http://continuingstudies.wisc.edu/distance-education/index.html

Valtonen, T., Kukkonen, J., Dillon, P., & Väisänen, P. (2009). Finnish high school students' readiness to adopt online learning: Questioning the assumptions. *Computers & Education*, *53*(3), 742–748. doi:10.1016/j.compedu.2009.04.014

van der Wende, M. C. (2003). Globalisation and Access to Higher Education. *Journal of Studies in International Education*, *7*(2), 193–206. doi:10.1177/1028315303007002006

VandenBos, G., Knapp, S., & Doe, J. (2001). *Role of reference elements in the selection of resources by psychology undergraduates*. Retrieved October 13, 2001, from http://jbr.org/articles.html

Veltri, N. F., Webb, H. W., & Papp, R. (2010). GETSMART: An Academic-Industry Partnership to Encourage Female Participation in Science, Technology, Engineering and Math Careers. In A. Cater-Steel & E. Cater (Eds.), *Women in Engineering, Science and Technology: Education and Career Challenges* (pp. 56–77). doi:10.4018/978-1-61520-657-5.ch003

Verkroost, M. J., Meijerink, L., Lintsen, H., & Veen, W. (2008). Finding a balance in dimensions of blended learning. *International Journal on E-Learning*, *7*(3), 499–522.

Virtlab. (2015). Retrieved June 3, 2015, from http://www.virtlab.com

Vogel, J. J., Vogel, D. S., Cannon-Bowers, J., Bowers, C. A., Muse, K., & Wright, M. (2006). Computer gaming and interactive simulations for learning: A meta analysis. *Journal of Educational Computing Research*, *34*(3), 229–243. doi:10.2190/FLHV-K4WA-WPVQ-H0YM

Volery, T., & Lord, D. (2000). Critical success factors in online education. *International Journal of Educational Management*, *14*(5), 216–223. doi:10.1108/09513540010344731

Voss, B. D. (2013). *Massive open online courses (MOOCs): A primer for university and college board members.* Retrived from http://agb.org/sites/agb.org/files/report_2013_MOOCs.pdf

Vuurens, J. B., & de Vries, A. P. (2012). Obtaining high-quality relevance judgments using crowdsourcing. *IEEE Internet Computing*, *16*(5), 20–27. doi:10.1109/MIC.2012.71

Waldrop, M. (2013). Campus 2.0. *Nature*, *495*(7440), 160–163. doi:10.1038/495160a PMID:23486040

Wallace, D. R., & Mutooni, P. (1997). A comparative evaluation of world wide web-based and classroom teaching. *The Journal of Engineering Education*, *86*(3), 211–219. doi:10.1002/j.2168-9830.1997.tb00287.x

Waller, V. (2005). *Is learning for everyone achievable?* Retrieved Nov. 1, 2005 from http://www.learningtechnologies.co.uk/magazine

Walter, M. (2014). *Repatriation to France and Germany. A Comparative Study Based on Bourdieu's Theory of Practice*. Wiesbaden: Springer Fachmedien. doi:10.1007/978-3-658-05700-8

Wang, E., Kashani, L., & Kim, Y. S. (2005). Teaching strategies ontology using SWRL Rules.C. Looi, D. Jonassen, & M. Ikeda (Eds.). *Proceedings of the 2005 conference on Towards Sustainable and Scalable Educational Innovations Informed by the Learning Sciences: Sharing Good Practices of Research, Experimentation and Innovation* (pp. 532-539). Amsterdam, The Netherlands: IOS Press.

Ward, M., & Newlands, D. (1998). Use of the web in undergraduate teaching. *Computers & Education*, *31*(2), 171–184. doi:10.1016/S0360-1315(98)00024-4

Wästlund, E., Reinikka, H., Norlander, T., & Archer, T. (2005). Effects of VDT and paper presentation on consumption and production of information: Psychological and physiological factors. *Computers in Human Behavior*, *21*(2), 377–394. doi:10.1016/j.chb.2004.02.007

Wathely, M., & Batalova, J. (2013). *Limited English proficient population of the United States*. Migration Policy Institute. Retrieve from: http://www.migrationpolicy.org/article/limited-english-proficient-population-united-states

Welsch, E. (2002, Summer). SCORM: Clarity of calamity. *Online Learning*, 14-18.

Wenger, E. (1998). *Communities of Practice: learning, meaning, and identity*. Cambridge, UK: Cambridge University Press. doi:10.1017/CBO9780511803932

Whitehead, M. (1992). The concpets and principles of equity and health. *International Journal of Health Services*, *22*(3), 429–445. doi:10.2190/986L-LHQ6-2VTE-YRRN

WHO. (2004). *World report on knowledge for better health: strengthening health systems.* Retrieved on April 2, 2015 Retrieved from http://www.who.int/rpc/meetings/en/world_report_on_knowledge_for_better_health2.pdf

WHO. (2012). *Social Determinants of Health.* Retrieved on April 12, 2015. Available from: http://www.who.int/social_determinants/sdh_definition/en/

WHO. (2015). e-Learning for undergraduate health professional education: a systematic review informing a radical transformation of health. Geneva: WHO.

Widäng, I., & Fridlund, B. (2003). Self-respect, dignity and confidence: Conceptions of integrity among male patients. *Journal of Advanced Nursing*, *42*(1), 47–56. PMID:12641811

Wiecha, J., Heyden, R., Sternthal, E., & Merialdi, M. (2011). Learning in a virtual world: Experience with using second life for medical education. *Journal of Medical Internet Research*, *12*(1). PMID:20097652

Wilges, B., Mateus, G. P., Silveira, R. A., & Nassar, S. M. (2007). An animated pedagogical agent as a Learning Management System manipulating Intelligent Learning Objects.J. M. Spector, D. G. Sampson, T. Okamoto, S. A. Cerri, M. Ueno, & A. Kashihara (Eds.). *Proceedings of the 7th IEEE International Conference on Advanced Learning Technologies ICALT 2007* (pp. 186-188). doi:10.1109/ICALT.2007.53

Wilson, K., & Doz, Y. L. (2012). 10 rules for managing global innovation. *Harvard Business Review*, *90*(10), 84–90, 130. PMID:23074868

Wisconsin Center for Nursing. (2013). *The Wisconsin Nursing Workforce: Status and Recommendations*. Retrieved from http://www.wisconsincenterfornursing.org/workforce_report.html

Wisconsin Technology Enhanced Collaborative Nursing Education (WI-TECNE). (2010). Retrieved from: http://research.son.wisc.edu/tecne/

Woodill, G. (2011). *The mobile learning edge*. The McGraw Hill Companies.

Workman, M. (2004). Performance in Computer-based and Computer-aided Education: Do Cognitive Styles Make a Difference? *Journal of Computers in Human Behavior*, *20*, 517–534. doi:10.1016/j.chb.2003.10.003

World Bank. (2015). *Information Communications Technology for Development*. Retrieved from http://live.worldbank.org/information-communications-technology-development

World Internet Usage and Population Statistics. (2013). Retrieved from www.internetworldstats.com

Wouters, P., van der Spek, E. D., & van Oostendorp, H. (2009). Current practices in serious game research: A review from a learning outcomes perspective. In T. Connolly, M. Stansfield, & L. Boyle (Eds.), *Games-based learning advancements for multi-sensory human computer interfaces: Techniques and effective practices* (pp. 232–250). Hershey, PA: IGI-Global. doi:10.4018/978-1-60566-360-9.ch014

Yeager, C., Hurley-Dasgupta, B., & Bliss, C. A. (2013). cMOOCs and Global Learning: An Authentic Alternative. *Journal of Asynchronous Learning Networks*, *17*(2), 133–147.

Yli-Luoma, P., & Naeve, A. (2006). Towards a semantic E-learning theory by using a modeling approach. *British Journal of Educational Technology, 37*(3), 445-459. Retrieved from http://kmr.nada.kth.se/papers/TEL/Semantic-eLearning-theory.pdf

Young, J. R. (2002). 'Hybrid' teaching seeks to end the divide between traditional and online instruction. *The Chronicle of Higher Education*, *48*(28), A33.

Yousef, A. F., Chatti, M. A., Schroeder, U., & Wosnitza, M. (2014). What Drives a Successful MOOC? An Empirical Examination of Criteria to Assure Design Quality of MOOCs. *Advanced Learning Technologies (ICALT) IEEE14th International Conference*, (pp. 44-48). IEEE.

Yuan, L., Powell, S., & Cetis, J. (2013). *MOOCs and open education: Implications for higher education*. Academic Press.

Yumerefendi, A., Mickle, B., & Cox, L. (2007). Tightlip: Keeping applications from spilling the beans.*Proceedings of the 4th USENIX Conference on Networked Systems Design*, *38*, 12.

Yunus, A. (2014). *Learning Without Boundaries Through Online Courses*. Retrieved from http://www.thestar.com.my/news/nation/2014/09/19/learning-without-boundaries-through-online-courses/

Zainol-Abidin, M.J., Pourmohammadi, M., Varasingam, N., & Lean, O.C. (2014). The Online Reading Habits of Malaysian Students. *The Reading Matrix*, *14*(2), 164–172.

Zhang, Y., Cooke, E., & Mao, Z. (2006). Internet-scale malware mitigation: Combining intelligence of the control and data plane.*Proceedings of the 4th ACM Workshop on Recurring Malcode*, 33-40. doi:10.1145/1179542.1179549

Zhao, F. (Ed.). (2006). *Maximize business profits through e-partnerships*. Hershey, PA: IRM Press. doi:10.4018/978-1-59140-788-1

Zhou, X., & Xia, X. (2010). Design and research for Mobile web learning platform accessibility. In *2010 International Conference on Artificial Intelligence and Education (ICAIE)* (pp. 478-481). doi:10.1109/ICAIE.2010.5640970

Zhuhadar, L., & Nasraoui, O. (2008). Semantic information retrieval for personalized E-Learning.*International Conference on Tools and Artificial Intelligence* (pp. 364-368).

About the Contributors

Badrul H. Khan, Ph.D., is a world-renowned speaker, author, educator and consultant in the field of e-learning and educational technology. Professor Khan has the credit of first coining the phrase Web based instruction and popularizing the concept through his 1997 best-selling Web-Based Instruction book which paved the way for the new field of e-learning. Known as a founder of modern e-learning, Dr. Khan has been honored with many awards and worldwide acclamation throughout his career. In recognition of his unique contribution to the field of e-learning coupled with his services to worldwide e-learning communities, Egyptian E-Learning University Council on August 13, 2012 appointed Dr. Badrul Khan as an honorary distinguished professor of e-learning. Professor Khan is a United States Distance Learning Association (USDLA) 2015 Hall of Fame Inductee.

* * *

Fayiz Munsher Aldhaferri is Professor of Online Learning and Computing Education. Associate Dean for Research, Training, and Consultations. Former Kuwaiti Cultural Attache in London. Keynote Speaker in many International, Regional, and Local Conferences.

Mohamed Ally is Professor in the Centre for Distance Education and a Researcher in the Technology Enhanced Knowledge Research Institute (TEKRI) at Athabasca University in Canada. He obtained his Ph.D. from the University of Alberta, Canada. His current areas of research include mobile learning, e-learning, distance education, and use of information and communication technology in training and education. Dr. Ally is Past-President of the International Federation of Training and Development Organizations (IFTDO) and is one of the Founding Directors of the International Association of Mobile Learning (IamLearn). He was also on the board of the Canadian Society for Training and Development. He recently edited four books on the use of mobile technology in education, training and libraries. His book "Mobile Learning: Transforming the Delivery of Education and Training" won the Charles A. Wedemeyer Award for significant contribution to distance education. Dr. Ally has published in peer-reviewed journals, chapters in books and encyclopedia and served on many journal boards and conference committees. He has presented keynote speeches, workshops, papers, and seminars in many countries.

Tonya B. Amankwatia is the director of the Center for Teaching and Learning at Regent University. She has been involved with e-learning since 1998. She has several years' experience planning, managing, and evaluating online programs and large-scale technology implementations. With a distance learning specialty, Dr. Amankwatia serves as a peer reviewer for Middle States Commission on Higher Education.

She has taught at the undergraduate and graduate levels in both Africa and the U.S. She has published and presented on program evaluation at the annual meetings of the American Educational Research Association (AERA), the Association for Educational Communications and Technology (AECT), and the Distance Teaching and Learning Conference. Dr. Amankwatia was recognized by AECT as a future leader in the field and has served in various leadership positions within the organization. Dr. Amankwatia earned her PhD from Lehigh University in learning sciences and technology with a specialization in instructional design.

Vicki Caravias is an information and communication technologies (ICT) professional with several years' experience in the education industry, having worked across a diverse range of courses from certificate level through to diploma and degree levels. She is teaching in Pathways and Foundation programs at Swinburne University of Techhnology. Her area of specialisation is teaching students to develop e-commerce websites using a range of programming languages and applications. Her research study is focussed around teachers' conceptions and approaches to integrating pedagogy and content knowledge using blended learning environments.

Adam Damianakis is the CEO of Conceptum S.A. and holds a PhD in Image Processing. Since 1995 he has participated and coordinated several National and European projects of Computer Science and eLearning including Leonardo Da Vinci, Socrates and Media. At a National Level he has established contracts with companies, such as Pearson and Academic Institutes, such as the Technological Institute of Athens and the Biomedical Research Foundation Academy of Athens, to provide integrated etraining/elearning solutions. He also has several published papers and he is responsible for the idea, the design and the development of the LMA Learning Management and Authoring Tool (www.lmatool.com).

Alev Elçi, Ph.D., is working as Assistant Professor in Aksaray University, Department of Management Information Systems. Her main research areas are faculty development, technology enhanced learning, educational technology, social networks, learning communities, animation and game based learning, internationalization, and narrative approaches. She has a book titled "Faculty Beliefs and Needs: Opening the Gate to ICT-based Professional Development in Teaching and Learning". She is currently teaching database management, management information systems, knowledge economy. In 2015 she had the position of visiting researcher in faculty development for technology-enhanced learning at Roger Williams University, Bristol, RI, USA with a grant of Scientific and Technological Research Council of Turkey (TÜBİTAK).

Atilla Elçi is full professor and the chairman of Department of Electrical-Electronics and Computer Engineering at Aksaray University since August 2012. His professional practice includes the Intl Telecom Union, Switzerland, as chief technical advisor for computerization field projects (UNDP/ITU,1985-97) and Info Tech & Telecoms Pvt Ltd as founder/managing director, Turkey (1997-2003). He has organized/served for committees of numerous international conferences. He has organized IEEE COMPSAC & ESAS since 2006, SinConfs since 2007; and, IJRCS Symposiums 2008-9. He has published over a hundred journal and conference papers; co-authored The Composition of OWL-S based Atomic Processes - Towards a Semantic-based Workflow Model (LAP Lambert Academic Publishing, 2011); edited the Semantic Agent Systems (Springer, 2011), Theory and Practice of Cryptography Solutions for Secure Information Systems (IGI Global, 2013), Handbook of Applied Learning Theory and Design in Modern

Education (IGI Global, 2016) and the proceedings of SIN Conferences 2007-16 (ACM), ESAS 2006-16 by IEEE CS. He has been the general/program chair for conferences, notably the SIN Confs, ESAS, 36th IEEE COMPSAC (2012), ICPCA/SWS, track chair for 2008-2013 and Standing Committee Member 2014 onwards for COMPSAC. He is an associate editor of Expert Systems: The Journal of Knowledge Engineering and editorial board member of JSCI, IJAS, IJISS, and guest editor for several other journals. BSEE METU, Ankara (1970), M.Sc. & Ph.D. in Computer Sciences, Purdue Univ, USA (1973, 1975).

Jen Elsden-Clifton is an experienced school teacher and university educator at RMIT University. Jen has a strong research interest in the areas of professional experience, professional issues in teaching and health education, and has received grants and published in these fields. Jen is currently involved in the field of placement or Work-Integrated Learning and has developed a number of site-based and alternative pedagogical models for professional experience that blur theory/practice, schools/university, expert/novice and teachers/students in teacher education.

Duygu Çelik Ertuğrul is an Assistant Professor in the Computer Engineering Department at the Istanbul Aydin University, Turkey. Her research topics are related to the Web and Semantics, Composition and Discovery of Semantic Web Services, Semantic Search Agents, and Semantic Web based Mobile Health Services. She is one of the organizers of two international workshops and one international symposium: "IEEE International Workshop on ESAS: E-Health Systems and Semantic Web", "Security of Information and Networks" and "IEEE COMPSAC Symposium on Web Technologies & Data Analytics (WEDA)". She also supervises a number of research and development projects supported by the university, government, and industrial companies. She has published numerous articles in several international/ national journals and conferences on the topic of Web Semantics and Mobile Medical Services. She is also the author of various books or book chapters about 'Composition or Discovery of Semantic Web Services' and 'Semantic Web based e-Health Services'.

Shantha Fernando is a Senior Lecturer at the Department of Computer Science and Engineering, University of Moratuwa, and the Director, Center for IT Services, University of Moratuwa. He also served as the Director, Engineering Research Unit, University of Moratuwa. He is one of the founders and the Chief Advisor of TechCERT, a division of LK-Domain Registry. He obtained BSc Engineering Honours from the University of Moratuwa in 1993. He obtained his Master of Philosophy from the same university in 2000. His PhD was obtained from the Delft University of Technology, The Netherlands in 2010. He became the first Chartered Engineer in Sri Lanka in the field of IT in the Institution of Engineers Sri Lanka (IESL). He also served in the Council of the Computer Society of Sri Lanka (CSSL). His expertise is in Computer and Information Security, Information Systems, and e-Learning. He has provided advisory services for many government and commercial organisations in the areas of his expertise since 1994. He pioneered e-learning at University of Moratuwa.

Susan Gallagher-Lepak is a professor of Nursing at the University of Wisconsin – Green Bay, USA. Her education includes a PhD in Rehabilitation Counseling Psychology from the University of Wisconsin – Madison, and Master of Science in Nursing (MSN) from the University of Wisconsin – Milwaukee. She has taught online since 2003. Areas of scholarship include e-learning and nursing diagnosis. She is a registered nurse and licensed psychologist.

Dilrukshi Gamage is a researcher in Crowdsource Startup Daemo, an initiative by Stanford University worldwide research collective. She is also a director/ IT consultant of her own consultancy company - ISaC.lk. Currently Dilrukshi is a MPhil/PhD candidate at University of Moratuwa, Sri Lanka with research interests eLearning technologies, MOOC, Human computer interaction (UX ,UI) and Design Based Research (DBR). Apart from that she is involving in many multinational projects - Envisioning future of taxis 2025 - London Taxi Company, MOOC lab Inspiration stories - MOOCLab UK, Teach2Learn - MIT IDEA Global challenge - modeling the future of learning. She is the first Sri Lankan and one of the few in the world to finish 50 MOOC courses from 7 different MOOC platforms. She is a course catalyst in Human Centered Design (HCD) online course by IDEO +Acumen in NovoEd platform. Her dream is to bring effective online education to everyone and create a culture of learn by doing.

Hans W. Giessen studied in Berlin and Saarbrücken, Germany, and in Metz, France. Professor at Saarland University, Saarbücken, Germany.

Manu Gupta did her bacherlors in Dental Surgery from University of Agra, India. Later, she received her Masters in Health Management from a pioneer institute of health management at India, which is Institute of Health Management and Research (IIHMR). She has worked with various agencies like Government of India, WHO, Eurpean Union, UNICEF, NIDI. Her research interest focuses on health systems research, management information systems, e learning, health financing and other areas of health care. Presently, she is working on quality of care and patient safety.

Jason Harron is a Ph.D. student at The University of Texas at Austin studying Learning Technology at the College of Education.

Kathy Jordan is Deputy Head Higher Education in the School of Education at RMIT University. Kathy Jordan is an experienced researcher in the areas of teacher use of ICT, the introduction of ICT to school settings, blended learning, sociology of ICT, the teaching of English, beginning teachers, and teacher networks.

Pavlos Kallonis holds a BSc in "Digital Systems: eServices and Digital Systems track" and a Master's Degree (M.Sc.) in "Technology Education and Digital Systems". Pavlos as part of Conceptum S.A. has already developed and implemented Learning Management Systems (LMS) for the public sector (Hellenic Cord Blood Bank) and for the private sector (MyCosmiclab.com (Pearson)). He has also experience with 3D Simulations both academic with 10 published papers and work experience related to the proposed project as part of Conceptum S.A. by designing and developing 3D medical equipment simulations for the Technological Institute of Athens.

Jina Kang is a doctoral student in the Learning Technologies Program at the University of Texas at Austin. Her research interest is in learning analytics mainly in serious games. She is currently working on examining in-game learning behavior patterns using data mining and visualization techniques and providing just-in-time feedback to help teachers facilitate diverse students' learning.

Özlem Efiloğlu Kurt received her BS degree in Computer Education from Gazi University in 2002 and MA degree in Informatics from Marmara University in 2006. In 2011 she obtained her PhD degree in Informatics from Marmara University with her cross-cultural study about educational technologies in the UK and Turkey. Her professional teaching experience started as a computer teacher in high schools in 2002, then she started to work at Yalova University as a lecturer in 2010. She works as an assistant professor at Yalova University since 2012. Her research interests focus on e-learning, mobile learning, distance education, cross-cultural studies in education and management information systems.

Min Liu, Ed.D., is Professor of Learning Technologies at the University of Texas at Austin. She is the Program Coordinator & Graduate Advisor. Her teaching and research interests center on educational uses of new media and other emerging technologies and their impact on teaching and learning for learners at all age levels. She has published over 64 research articles in leading peer-reviewed educational technology journals (e.g., Educational Technology Research and Development (EDR&D), Computers in Human Behavior (CHB), Journal of Research on Technology in Education (JRTE), Journal of Educational Computing Research (JECR), Interdisciplinary Journal of Problem-Based Learning, (IJPBL), The American Journal of Distance Education, (AJDE), Journal of Educational Technology & Society, Journal of Interactive Learning Research, The International Journal of Gaming and Computer-Mediated Simulations), nine peer-reviewed book chapters, 48 peer-reviewed conference proceeding papers, and presents regularly at national and international conferences. She has also served on numerous editorial boards for peer-reviewed research journals, including: Educational Technology Research and Development, Interdisciplinary Journal of Problem-based Learning, Computers in Human Behavior, Journal of Research on Technology in Education, Journal of Educational Computing Research, Journal of Computing in Childhood Education. Her current R&D projects include studying the design and effectiveness of immersive, rich media environments on learning and motivation; learning analytics and data visualizations; understanding MOOCs as an emerging online learning tool; examining the affordances and constraints of using mobile technologies in teaching and learning; and use of Web 2.0 tools to facilitate instruction.

Sa Liu is a doctoral student in Curriculum and Instruction specializing in Learning Technologies. She has a master's degree in Educational Technology and a B.S. in Computer Science. Her research interests include problem solving, game based learning, technology promoted teacher development, and technology supported language learning.

George Loudos (40 years old) is an Assistant Professor at TEI Athens and co-founder of BET Solutions. Currently, he coordinates 3 EU projects (including a COST network), as well as a National Excellence grant, he participates in 4 additional EU projects and several smaller projects. He has published 90 articles in international journals and has more than 190 publications in conference proceedings and ~650 citations. He has given 35 invited lectures and holds one patent. He has been organizer of many international conferences, workshops and training schools. His research interests are focused on Molecular Imaging using Nuclear Medicine Techniques, Medical Instrumentation and he strongly supports interdisciplinary cooperation and education in the field of nanomedicine and molecular imaging.

Emily McKelroy is a Doctoral student in the Curriculum and Instruction department, specializing in Learning Technologies in the College of Education at the University of Texas at Austin. Her research interests include the use of project-based instruction and Web 2.0 tools to create technology assisted differentiated instruction and to enhance instructional practices in the learning environment.

Indika Perera received his bachelors and master's degrees in computer science and engineering from University of Moratuwa, Sri Lanka. He obtained his Ph.D. from the School of Computer Science, University of St Andrews, UK. At present he works as a Senior Lecturer, at University of Moratuwa, Sri Lanka. His research interests include software engineering, software process management, human computer interaction, and technology enhanced learning.

Mohammed Samaka is an Associate Professor of Computer Science in the Department of Computer Science and Engineering (CSE), College of Engineering at Qatar University. He obtained his PhD and Master from Loughborough University in England and a Post Graduate Diploma in Computing from Dundee University in Scotland. He obtained his Bachelor of Mathematics from Baghdad University. His current areas of research include Wireless Software Architecture and Technology, Mobile Applications and Services, Networking, e-Learning, and Computing Curricula Development.

Esra İşgör Şimşek holds a B.S. degree in Computer Education and Educational Technology from Boğaziçi University in 2010, and M.S. degree in Computer Aided Art and Design from Mimar Sinan Fine Arts University in 2015. Now she is a PhD student in department of Computer Education and Instructional Technology at Middle East Technical University. She has been working for more than 5 years on educational technology and related areas such as e-learning, distance learning, mobile learning, and game-based learning. She is good at creating interactive storyboards and her research interests are educational computer games, virtual worlds, and multimedia learning and design.

Ramón Talavera-Franco's field of interest includes research and design solutions to increase academic opportunities for Latino students (K-16), through organizational leadership, curriculum, and online and blended education. While working at the University of Texas at Austin, he implemented an innovative credit recover systems to reduce the Hispanic drop out rate in Texas, which has benefitted thousands of students since the year 2005. Currently, Ramón is exploring how MOOCs can be tailored to meet the needs of the Latino community in the United States and how leveraging massive open online courses and modules help individuals build their own career paths. Ramón is working towards a Doctor in Education (Ed.D.) program in curriculum, teaching, learning and leadership at Northeastern University.

Rachel Thomas Tharmabalan holds a BSc in Food Technology and a Msc in Applied Science from Universiti Sains Malaysia. She is a Research Officer at the Centre for Development of Academic Excellence and Student Advisory and Development and has been working for more than 3 years in the education technology field. Rachel is now working towards a Doctorate in Social Science.

Dimitris Tsatsos holds a BSc in Computer Programming and on European Culture. Since 2001 he has participated as an educational content developer on several National and European projects of Computer Science and eLearning including Leonardo Da Vinci, Socrates and Media. Finally, he has work experience related to the proposed project as part of Conceptum S.A. by designing and developing 3D medical equipment simulations for the TEI Athens.

Antonios Tsoukalis received his Diploma from the Department of Biomedical Engineering, TEI Athens, Greece, in 2014. He is now following the Master course of Informatique: Synthese D'image et Conception Graphique. His main domain of expertise is the Design and Development of 3d Graphics through Blender, Creation and development of Web Software and last but not least Monte Carlo Simulations. He has also experience with 3D Graphic Simulations both academic and work experience as designer and developer of 3D medical equipment simulations for the TEI Athens through Blender.

Christine Vandenhouten is an associate professor of Nursing at the University of Wisconsin – Green Bay, USA. Her education includes a PhD in Nursing from Marquette University and Master of Science in Nursing (MSN) from the University of Wisconsin – Oshkosh. Areas of scholarship include policy, community health nursing, and e-learning.

Index

A

Academic Pathways Program 57, 79
Advanced Distributed Learning (ADL) 197, 224
Advertisement 41
ancillary material 153-154
Arcade RSDH 267-269, 272, 276
Aviation Industry 197, 217

B

Blended Learning 6, 57-74, 79, 180, 188, 196, 271
Blended Learning Environments 56-61, 63-70, 73-74, 79
Blender 295
Brain Drain 266, 270, 276
BSN@Home 227-228, 235-236, 238, 241

C

capacity building 266, 268-270, 273-274
CBT Committee 197, 217
Community of Practice 134, 152-153, 226, 229, 244
Competence 248, 295
Computerized Tomography (CT) 280, 295
Concept Map 216, 224
Content-Centered Approaches 79
corporate environments 278
cost effective 166, 229, 266, 273-274
course discussion 34, 37, 152, 234
Course Reminders 27, 36, 41
Coursera 2, 80, 95-103, 113, 132, 136, 138, 152-154, 178
Crowdsourced input 109-110, 112-115, 117-118, 120-125

D

Data Visualizations 27, 32, 41
Discussion Forum 18-23, 25-26, 31, 34-35, 37, 41, 151

E

Educational Modeling Language (EML) 224
E-Learning 2, 6, 16, 19-20, 34-36, 43, 45, 51, 57, 59-61, 65-66, 69-73, 80, 83-84, 88-91, 93-95, 97, 100, 103-104, 109-114, 117-125, 129, 133, 140-141, 143-144, 151, 177, 179-181, 185-189, 191-192, 194-197, 199-201, 203, 214-218, 224-228, 230-241, 244-253, 257, 266-270, 273-274, 276, 293
E-learning Framework 2, 6, 16, 19, 34-36, 57, 59-61, 65, 73, 80, 95, 97, 103-104, 110, 113, 121, 133, 140, 151, 180, 187, 199, 215, 226, 230-231, 233-235, 241, 244, 249
E-learning Instructional Designer 244
e-Learning Readiness 245, 247-252
English language 2, 151-152, 154
Evaluation 4, 6, 14, 16, 45, 56, 61, 66, 70, 74, 80, 83, 88-89, 97, 104, 109-112, 114-125, 129-131, 133, 138, 140-141, 143-145, 169, 187, 196, 199, 201, 226, 228, 231, 234-238, 244, 249

F

Facebook Group 13, 21-22, 26-27, 31, 33, 35-36, 41
Faculty Development 226-234, 237-241, 244
FlashDevelop 295
Flexible E-Learning Framework 230-231, 233-235, 244
Framework for e-Learning 195-196, 199, 224, 226, 233-234, 241, 249
Framework for mobile learning 83, 163

G

German Federal-Länder-Commission 42, 44

H

health equity 266-269, 271-272, 276
health research 266-271, 276
Health Research Capacity 267-268, 276
higher education 1-3, 16, 20, 56-58, 61, 73, 103, 113, 144-145, 177-182, 184-188, 226-227, 250
Hispanic 149-154, 156-158
human capital 180, 188

I

IEEE Learning Technology Standards Committee (LTSC) 194, 224
IEEE Learning Technology System Architecture (LTSA) 225
Individual Readiness 247, 249
Infographic 22, 25, 41
innovation 58, 60, 95, 114, 119, 123, 178-179, 183, 188, 199-200, 227, 236, 241, 247, 250, 271-272
Institutional Capacity 272, 276
Intelligent Agents 174, 191, 215, 225
Intelligent Learning Objects (ILO) 225
Interaction 2, 19-21, 32, 34-35, 37, 41, 48, 58, 64, 66, 71, 73, 80, 83, 104, 133, 137, 145, 152, 154, 163, 167, 172, 183, 185, 199, 201, 204, 234, 236, 244, 248, 251, 268, 271, 277-278, 280, 287
Interface Design 18-19, 34-35, 37, 61, 69, 74, 83, 86, 90, 98, 104, 114, 123, 167, 174, 226, 231, 233, 235-236, 238, 244, 248-249, 253
Internet connectivity 186, 270, 274

K

Khan's E-Learning Framework 6, 57, 60, 65, 95, 151, 187, 235
Kuwait 245, 250, 252-253, 257
Kuwait Foundation for Advancement of Sciences (KFAS) 245

L

Learned-Centered Approaches 73, 79
learner types 44-45, 48-50
Learning Management System (LMS) 1, 19, 41, 56-57, 59-61, 65-69, 71-74, 79, 166, 186, 198, 225, 248, 276, 285
Learning Object Metadata (LOM) 198, 225
Learning theories 164, 235
LEP 149-150, 152-154, 156-158
life-long learning 3, 80, 103, 177, 179-180, 188, 246

M

Magnetic Resonance Imaging (MRI) 280, 295
Malaysia 58, 177-181, 183-186, 188-189, 248
Management 1, 14, 16, 19, 41, 56-57, 59-61, 65-74, 79, 83, 89-90, 104, 117-118, 166, 169-170, 186, 197-198, 215, 217, 225, 227-229, 231, 233, 236, 241, 244, 248-253, 272, 274, 276, 285
markup 191
Massive Open Online Course (MOOC) 95, 129, 225
media tools 19-20, 22-23, 34, 36-37
Media-based Learning 42-45, 48-51
Medical Equipment 277-280, 293
Medical Simulations 283, 286, 293
Meetups 149, 153-154, 156-158
metadata model 191, 198, 200, 214, 217
middle income 266-268, 272-273, 276
Millennium Development Goals 267, 276
Mind Mapping 204, 224-225
mobile interface 80, 96-97, 100
MOODLE 22-23, 41, 60, 227, 271-272, 276

N

National E-Learning Policy 179-180, 186, 188

O

online learning 1-2, 6, 16, 19, 58-61, 66, 68-69, 79, 94-95, 103-104, 113, 123, 132-133, 136-137, 139-140, 145, 149, 151, 178-180, 187, 225-227, 229, 241, 246-247, 251-252
Online Program Quality 129
Online Teaching 20, 72, 195, 227-229, 234, 241, 244, 252
ontology 204-207, 212, 214-216, 225
Open and Distributed Learning 16, 187, 246
Open Source 114, 121, 134, 194, 217, 277, 279, 285, 293, 295
Organizational Readiness 248-249, 251-252
OWL 191, 205

P

Paradigm 112, 114, 117-118, 122-123, 129, 150, 194, 199, 215-216

Peer Interaction 37
Peer Learning 11, 13, 15, 26-27, 34-35, 37, 41
personal computers 226
Personal Feeling 41
Phenomenography 64-65, 79
physical phenomena 277-278, 280, 282-284, 287, 291
policy makers 81, 245, 257, 267-268, 271
Practical Participatory Evaluation 112, 129
PreFab 295

Q

Qualitative Research 79, 110-111, 117, 129

R

RDF 191, 214
regulatory bodies 245, 257
Resource Constrained Countries 266-267, 274, 276
Resource Support 14, 16, 19, 34, 36, 56, 61, 66, 71, 74, 83, 91, 104, 114, 123, 231, 244, 249, 253
Responsive Evaluation 112, 130
retrieval systems 110, 114

S

SCC Layers 195, 203-205
Scholars 5, 49, 133, 226, 230-234, 236-239, 241, 244
screen size 162-163, 167
Semantic Web 191, 193, 200, 203-204, 207, 214, 217-218
Sharable Content Object (SCO) 198, 225
Sharable Content Object Reference Model (SCORM) 225
social capital 150, 154, 157
Spanish 150, 153-154, 156-157
Stakeholder 109, 112-113, 118, 120, 124, 130, 199, 245, 247
STEM 214, 295
systematic approach 51

T

Taxonomy 70, 110, 120-122, 125, 130, 151, 225
Teacher Education 1-5, 7, 10, 16
Teachers' conceptions 56, 61-66, 69, 73-74
TEI Athens 279, 292
The National Higher Education Strategic Plan 177, 180, 186
Twitter 18-23, 29-32, 34, 36-37, 41, 134, 139, 152, 227, 234, 237-238

U

Ultrasound 280, 295
United States 22, 113, 149-150, 153, 157-158
University of Wisconsin 227-228, 244
Usage Data 23, 25-26, 29, 41
Utilization-Focused Evaluation 112, 122, 130

W

Work-Integrated Learning 1-2

X

XML 205, 214
X-Ray 295

www.ingramcontent.com/pod-product-compliance
Lightning Source LLC
LaVergne TN
LVHW062142200926
848484LV00007B/1847